Microsoft Office® 2010

Tom Bunzel

que®
800 East 96th Street
Indianapolis, Indiana 46240

CHAPTER 1
Introducing the New Features in Office 2010 .... Pg. 1

PART 1: Word 2010

CHAPTER 2
Beginning a New Word Project .... Pg. 13

CHAPTER 3
Adjusting the Structure of Your Document .... Pg. 27

CHAPTER 4
Changing Project Appearance .... Pg. 45

CHAPTER 5
Creating a Table for a Schedule .... Pg. 65

CHAPTER 6
Working with Graphics and Effects .... Pg. 77

CHAPTER 7
Reviewing Documents and Working Online .... Pg. 97

PART 2: Excel 2010

CHAPTER 8
Getting Started with Excel .... Pg. 111

CHAPTER 9
Working with Data, Functions, and Formulas .... Pg. 127

CHAPTER 10
Create Charts, Data Tables, and PivotTable .... Pg. 141

CHAPTER 11
Sharing Your Project Online with Microsoft Office Web Apps .... Pg. 161

PART 3: PowerPoint 2010

CHAPTER 12
Getting Started with PowerPoint 2010 .... Pg. 173

CHAPTER 13
Telling Your Story with Effective Slides .... Pg. 187

CHAPTER 14
Adding Transitions, Animation, and Video .... Pg. 199

CHAPTER 15
Completing the Presentation .... Pg. 211

Part 4: OneNote

CHAPTER 16
Organize Your Project with OneNote .... Pg. 225

PART 5: Outlook 2010

CHAPTER 17
Coordinating Your Activities with Outlook .... Pg. 247

CONTENTS

CHAPTER 1 INTRODUCING THE NEW FEATURES IN OFFICE 2010 1

Opening Backstage View 3

Creating a New Blank Document 5

Introducing the Navigation Pane 7

Saving in Different Formats 9

Printing in Backstage View 11

CHAPTER 2 BEGINNING A NEW WORD PROJECT 13

Creating a New Letter from a Template 15

Revising the Letter Template 17

Formatting Text in Your Document 19

Inserting Symbols and Changing the Date Style 21

Adding Bullets and Numbered Lists 23

Searching and Replacing in the Document 25

CHAPTER 3 ADJUSTING THE STRUCTURE OF YOUR DOCUMENT 27

Changing the Margins in Your Project 29

Changing Page Orientation 31

Inserting Page Numbers 33

Inserting Headers and Footers 35

Adding Footnotes and Endnotes 37

Using Copy and Paste Preview 39

Creating Columns in a Longer Document or Newsletter 43

CHAPTER 4 CHANGING PROJECT APPEARANCE 45
Applying a Quick Style 47
Creating a Quick Style 49
Modifying a Quick Style 51
Updating Headings to Match a Selection 53
Copying Styles and/or Formatting with Format Painter 55
Inserting a Cover Page 57
Creating a New Quick Parts Entry 59
Using the Building Blocks Organizer 61
Applying a Theme to a Document 63

CHAPTER 5 CREATING A TABLE FOR A SCHEDULE 65
Creating a Table 67
Selecting and Changing Text Alignment 68
Adding or Deleting Rows or Columns 69
Merging Cells 70
Modifying Borders 71
Using the Table Styles Gallery 73
Using Quick Tables 75

CHAPTER 6 WORKING WITH GRAPHICS AND EFFECTS 77
Inserting a Picture 79
Adding a Clip Art Image 81
Moving a Graphic 83
Resizing a Graphic 84
Cropping an Image 85
Applying Picture Styles and Effects 87
Inserting a SmartArt Diagram 89
Using OpenType Ligatures 93
Using Screenshots or Screen Clippings 95

CHAPTER 7 REVIEWING DOCUMENTS AND WORKING ONLINE 97
Tracking Changes with Reviewers 99
Accept and Reject Reviewers' Changes 101
Hiding and Showing Markup 102
Creating a Folder for Web Applications 103
Uploading a File to Your Folder 106
Creating a New Web Application File 109

CHAPTER 8 GETTING STARTED WITH EXCEL 111
Aligning and Formatting Text 113
Inputting and Formatting Numbers 115
Filling in Your Data 117
Inserting a New Column or Row 119
Hiding and Unhiding Columns 121
Adding and Renaming a Worksheet 123
Using Cell Styles 125

CHAPTER 9 WORKING WITH DATA, FUNCTIONS, AND FORMULAS ... 127
Finding Data 129
Filling a Series 131
Entering Dates and Times 133
Using Functions: AutoSum 135
Using Functions: Average 136
Using Formulas for Calculations 137
Formatting and Tracing Formula Results 139

CHAPTER 10 CREATE CHARTS, DATA TABLES, AND PIVOTTABLE 141
Creating a Chart Using the Ribbon 143
Changing the Chart Type 145
Formatting Chart Elements 147
Moving a Chart 149
Sorting Data in a Table 151
Adding Sparklines 153
Using a Pivot Table 155
Filtering a Pivot Table with the Slicer 157
Highlighting Data with Conditional Formats 159

CHAPTER 11 SHARING YOUR PROJECT ONLINE WITH MICROSOFT OFFICE WEB APPS 161

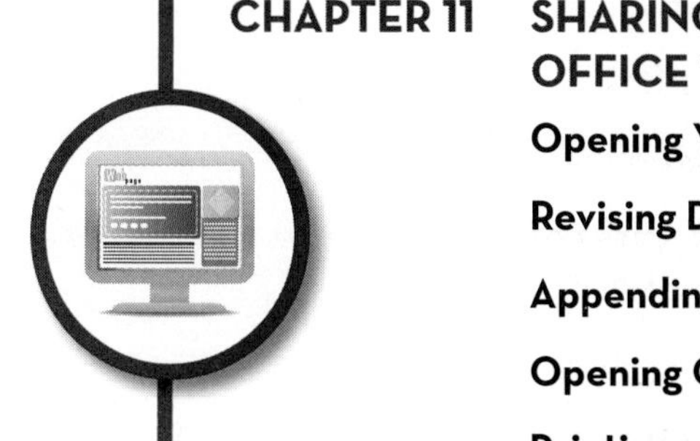

Opening Your Uploaded Project 163
Revising Data in the Web Application 165
Appending and Sorting a Data Table 167
Opening Online Files Locally 169
Printing an Excel Worksheet 171

CHAPTER 12 GETTING STARTED WITH POWERPOINT 2010 173

Adding and Editing Text 175
Adding a Slide with Bullets 177
Adding a New Section 179
Moving Slides (Slide Sorter View) 181
Applying a Theme from the Design Tab 183
Using Slide Masters 185

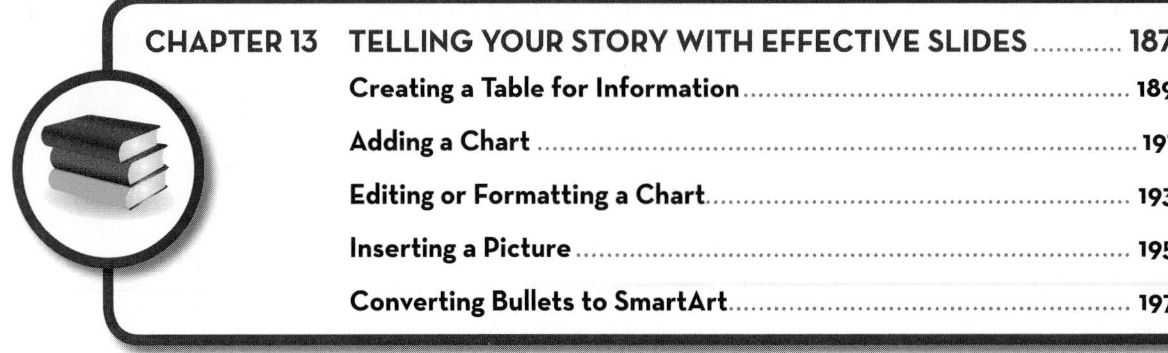

CHAPTER 13 TELLING YOUR STORY WITH EFFECTIVE SLIDES 187

Creating a Table for Information 189

Adding a Chart 191

Editing or Formatting a Chart 193

Inserting a Picture 195

Converting Bullets to SmartArt 197

CHAPTER 14 ADDING TRANSITIONS, ANIMATION, AND VIDEO 199

Adding Slide Transitions 201

Adding Animation to Content 203

Using the Animation Painter Tool 205

Inserting and Trimming Video 207

Using Online Video 209

CHAPTER 15 COMPLETING THE PRESENTATION 211

Previewing Slides in Reading View 213

Recording Your Presentation 215

Creating a Video of Your Show 217

Printing Notes and Handouts 219

Using Presenter View 221

Presenting from the PowerPoint Web App 223

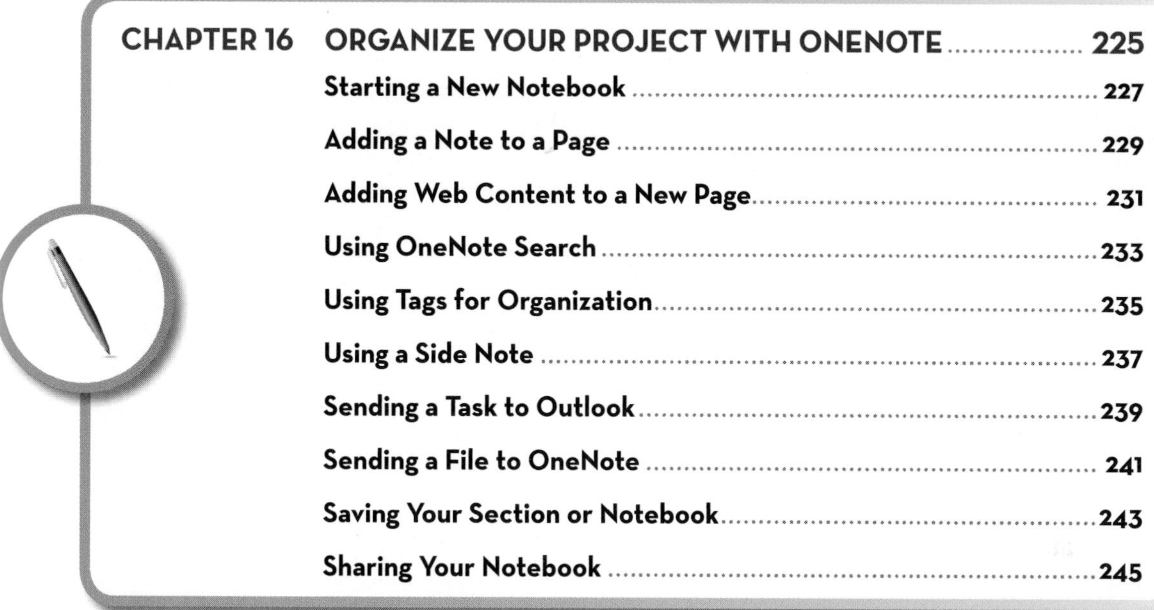

CHAPTER 16 ORGANIZE YOUR PROJECT WITH ONENOTE ... 225
Starting a New Notebook ... 227
Adding a Note to a Page ... 229
Adding Web Content to a New Page ... 231
Using OneNote Search ... 233
Using Tags for Organization ... 235
Using a Side Note ... 237
Sending a Task to Outlook ... 239
Sending a File to OneNote ... 241
Saving Your Section or Notebook ... 243
Sharing Your Notebook ... 245

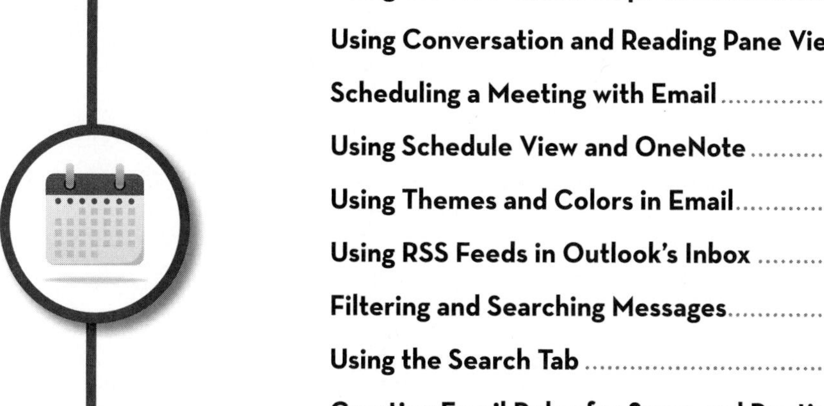

CHAPTER 17 COORDINATING YOUR ACTIVITIES WITH OUTLOOK ... 247
Sending an Email Message with an Attachment ... 249
Using the New Quick Steps ... 251
Using Conversation and Reading Pane Views ... 253
Scheduling a Meeting with Email ... 255
Using Schedule View and OneNote ... 257
Using Themes and Colors in Email ... 259
Using RSS Feeds in Outlook's Inbox ... 261
Filtering and Searching Messages ... 263
Using the Search Tab ... 265
Creating Email Rules for Spam and Routing ... 267
Managing Your Contacts ... 269
Creating a New Contact Group ... 271
Publishing or Sharing Your Calendar Online ... 273

EASY MICROSOFT OFFICE® 2010

ISBN-13: 978-0-7897-4328-2
ISBN-10: 0-7897-4328-0

U.K. ISBN-13: 978-0-7897-4373-2
U.K. ISBN-10: 0-7897-4373-6

Library of Congress Cataloging-in-Publication Data
Bunzel, Tom.
Easy Microsoft Office 2010 / Tom Bunzel.
p. cm.
Includes index.
ISBN-13: 978-0-7897-4328-2
ISBN-10: 0-7897-4328-0
1. Microsoft Office. 2. Business--Computer programs. I. Title.
HF5548.4.M525B847 2010
005.5--dc22
2010012723

Printed in the United States of America
First Printing: June 2010

TRADEMARKS

All terms mentioned in this book that are known to be trademarks or service marks have been appropriately capitalized. Que Publishing cannot attest to the accuracy of this information. Use of a term in this book should not be regarded as affecting the validity of any trademark or service mark.

WARNING AND DISCLAIMER

Every effort has been made to make this book as complete and as accurate as possible, but no warranty or fitness is implied. The information provided is on an "as is" basis. The author and the publisher shall have neither liability nor responsibility to any person or entity with respect to any loss or damages arising from the information contained in this book.

BULK SALES

Que Publishing offers excellent discounts on this book when ordered in quantity for bulk purchases or special sales. For more information, please contact

U.S. Corporate and Government Sales
1-800-382-3419
corpsales@pearsontechgroup.com

For sales outside of the U.S., please contact

International Sales
international@pearson.com

Associate Publisher
Greg Wiegand

Acquisitions Editor
Michelle Newcomb

Development Editor
Todd Brakke

Managing Editor
Sandra Schroeder

Project Editor
Mandie Frank

Copy Editor
Chuck Hutchinson

Indexer
Ken Johnson

Proofreader
Language Logistics, LLC

Technical Editor
Vince Averello

Publishing Coordinator
Cindy Teeters

Designer
Anne Jones

Compositor
Studio Galou, LLC

ABOUT THE AUTHOR

Tom Bunzel specializes in knowing what presenters need and how to make technology work. He has appeared on Tech TV's *Call for Help* as "Professor PowerPoint" and has been a featured speaker at InfoComm and PowerPoint LIVE. In addition, he has worked as a technology coach for corporations including Iomega, MTA Films, Nurses in Partnership, and the Neuroscience Education Institute. He has taught regularly at Learning Tree International, West LA College Extension, and privately around Southern California and does presentation and video consulting in Southern California.

He has written a number of books; the latest was *Master Visually Microsoft Office 2007*. He also has served as the Office Reference Guide for InformIT.com. In 2006, he published *Solving the PowerPoint Predicament: Using Digital Media for Effective Communication*, which is a detailed, project-oriented approach to creating effective multimedia presentations. His new eBook, *Do Your Own Ning Thing: A Step-By-Step Guide to Launching an Effective Social Network,* is available at http://www.professorppt.com/ning_how.htm.

Among Bunzel's other books are *Sams Teach Yourself PowerPoint 2003 in 24 Hours*, *Easy Digital Music*, *Easy Creating CDs and DVDs*, *How to Use Ulead DVD Workshop*, *Digital Video on the PC*, and the update to the PeachPit Press book *Visual QuickStart Guide to PowerPoint 2002/2001*. He can be reached through his website (www.professorppt.com) or his blog (tbunzel.blogspot.com).

DEDICATION

This book is dedicated to my mother and father.

ACKNOWLEDGMENTS

I want to convey my appreciation to my agent, Lynn Haller, and to Michelle Newcomb, Todd Brakke, and Mandie Frank at Que for making this book happen. I would also like to deeply thank Debra Swihart, Dr. Orli Peter, Freeman Michaels, and Terrence Gargiulo for their tremendous support during this process.

WE WANT TO HEAR FROM YOU!

As the reader of this book, *you* are our most important critic and commentator. We value your opinion and want to know what we're doing right, what we could do better, what areas you'd like to see us publish in, and any other words of wisdom you're willing to pass our way.

As an associate publisher for Que Publishing, I welcome your comments. You can email or write me directly to let me know what you did or didn't like about this book—as well as what we can do to make our books better.

Please note that I cannot help you with technical problems related to the topic of this book. We do have a User Services group, however, where I will forward specific technical questions related to the book.

When you write, please be sure to include this book's title and author as well as your name, email address, and phone number. I will carefully review your comments and share them with the author and editors who worked on the book.

Email: feedback@quepublishing.com

Mail: Greg Wiegand
Associate Publisher
Que Publishing
800 East 96th Street
Indianapolis, IN 46240 USA

READER SERVICES

Visit our website and register this book at www.informit.com/title/9780789743282 for convenient access to any updates, downloads, or errata that might be available for this book.

INTRODUCTION

Office 2010 is the latest version of Microsoft's famous productivity suite, which includes Word, Excel, and PowerPoint, along with Outlook for email and OneNote for information tracking.

Because so many users have already worked with one or more versions of Office, this book makes it easy to get up to speed on many of the newer features while reviewing and expanding on the most common and important tasks you need to perform at work or for leisure.

What sets this version of Office apart is that Word, Excel, PowerPoint, and OneNote have light versions that can work in your web browser and store files online. Although some users have this functionality as part of SharePoint services, we cover the web applications that are available on the Windows Live site. Because these programs are so new, the versions you see online may vary slightly from those covered here, but you will be able to get up to speed quickly.

To make things more realistic, wherever possible we have shown the features and tasks of the programs relative to an ongoing project; this is an imaginary incentive travel agency that has corporate clients. As we cover the various programs, as many of the samples as possible relate to real-world situations and work, representing several tasks and functions that a company might need to do in the various programs.

WHAT'S IN THIS BOOK

First, we cover Microsoft Word as the main example, introducing some of the newer features in Office 2010, including its Navigation pane and the Backstage view, which is present in Word, Excel, PowerPoint, and OneNote. Backstage view makes it easy to perform many of the most important tasks from one central location.

Then we continue with Word, creating some basic documents using its newer features, including Copy and Paste Preview, Ligatures, and Screenshots and Screen Clippings.

We conclude our discussion of Word with a chapter on sharing and reviewing your work with others. It is here that we introduce the first web application, the online version of Excel 2010, and how the online web storage, file system, and uploading works, all the while using the same project documents we created in the first few chapters.

We continue with Excel and its newer features for making calculations and working with data. Our project covers both, in terms of using formulas and functions and filtering and sorting in a data table.

In our chapters, we cover some of the newer Excel 2010 features, such as the Sparklines and Data Slicer, which help visualize and analyze data from the sample files.

At the end of the section on Excel, we dig into the Excel web application as we actually work with the different parts of a spreadsheet entirely online, download it to our desktop, and print a final version. We also cover how other users can access our files and collaborate with us, with permission to access the online workspace.

PowerPoint 2010 has quite a few new features that we cover, including recording your presentation (with narration), making a video of your slide show, adding sections to slides, and previewing your slide show in the new Reading view.

We also cover some of the tips and techniques for getting ready to present and then show you how to actually present from the PowerPoint 2010 web application directly online.

OneNote is a powerful organizational tool, and we show how our imaginary travel agency can use it to store and sort through important information and also integrate important tasks with Outlook 2010.

Outlook 2010 is the email client, calendar, and contact management tool with some new wrinkles. There are new Conversation view features, new Quick Steps to perform common tasks quickly, and ways to share your calendar online. (Outlook is not a web application yet, but some tasks such as publishing a calendar are available.)

After going through the visual steps of these chapters, whether you've used Office in the past or are new to the programs, you'll be able to perform many of the most important tasks and also become familiar with the newest features.

INTRODUCING THE NEW FEATURES IN OFFICE 2010

The new version of Microsoft Office focuses on making many of your daily tasks more accessible and easy to perform.

Office 2010 uses the Ribbon, with its new File tab, along with other tabs to provide quick ways to work with documents, presentations, and spreadsheets. You open or create new files, change their appearance and format, and view and revise the content by working between the various tabs.

In Office 2010, clicking File opens Backstage view. This new feature in Word, Excel, and PowerPoint gives you numerous options to open, close, or save files; access information about a file; print or share a file; or access help.

A Navigation pane in Office 2010 also lets you see and move through your files by headings, thumbnails, or with a search window.

The main window of Office 2010 is designed to give you quick access to all its features and let you view and move through any file quickly and easily.

THE OFFICE 2010 WINDOW (WORD)

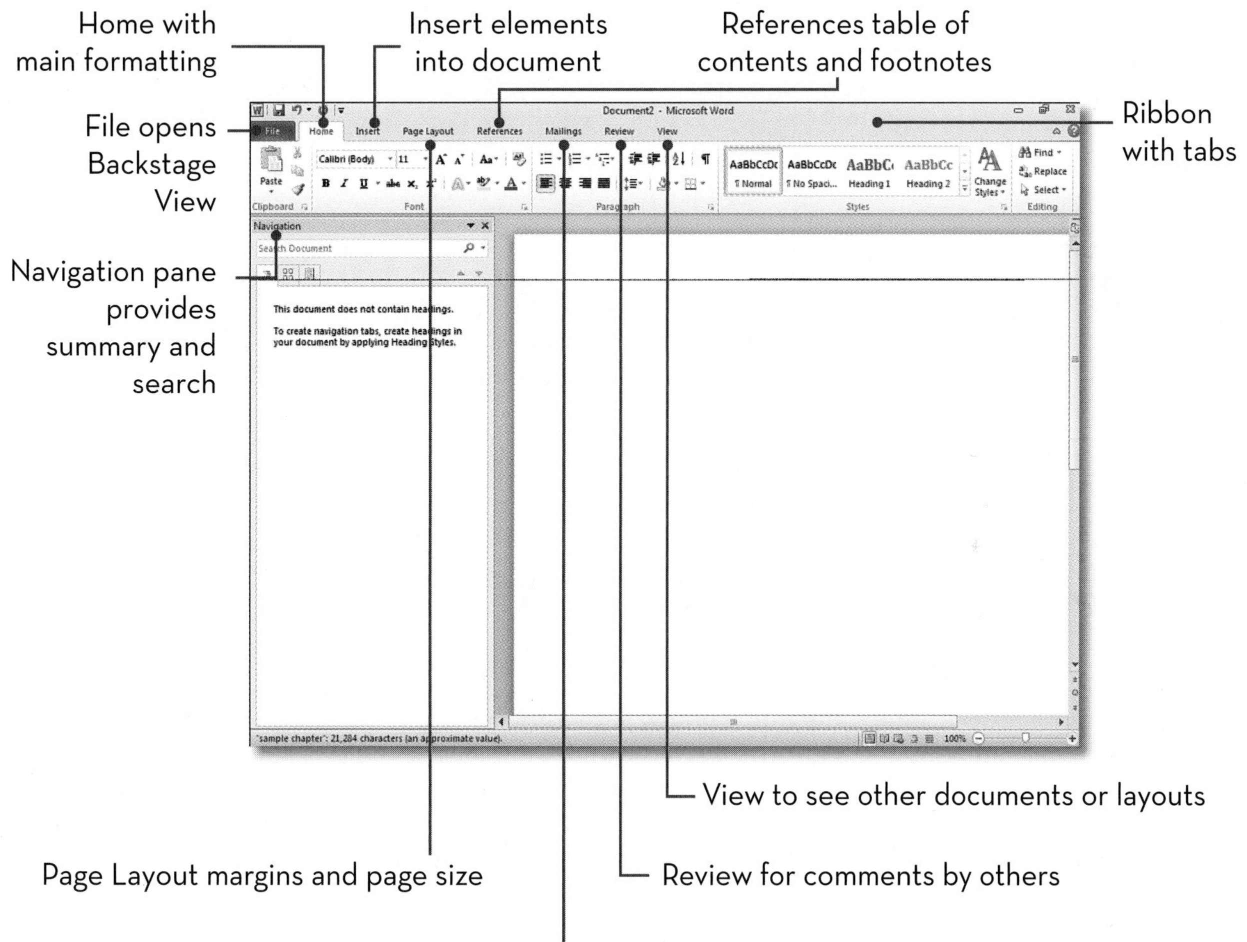

Home with main formatting
Insert elements into document
References table of contents and footnotes
File opens Backstage View
Ribbon with tabs
Navigation pane provides summary and search
View to see other documents or layouts
Page Layout margins and page size
Review for comments by others
Mailings for merges with address book

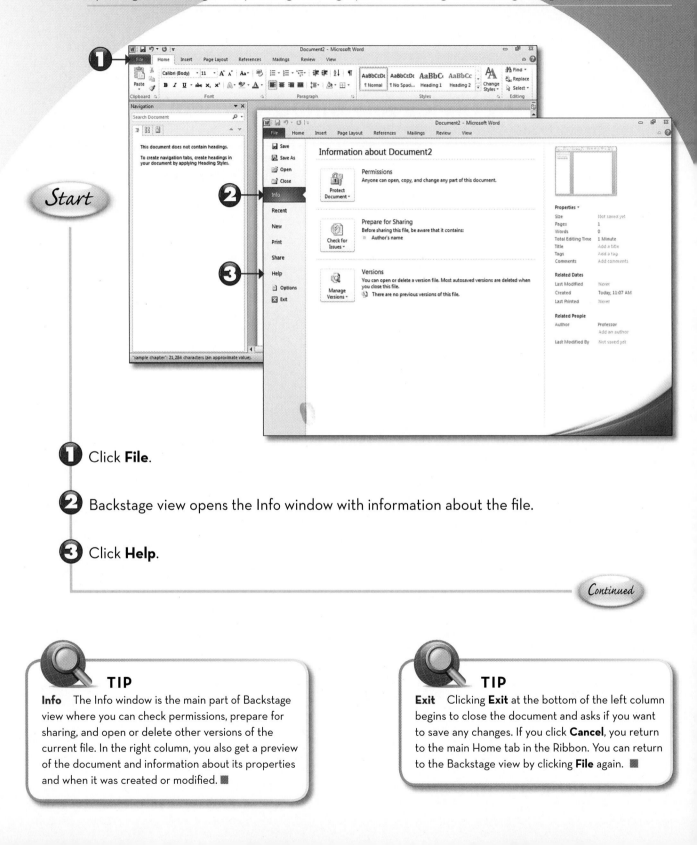

OPENING BACKSTAGE VIEW

Backstage view is a quick way to access many of your most common tasks, including opening and saving files, printing, setting options, sharing files, and getting help.

Start

1. Click **File**.
2. Backstage view opens the Info window with information about the file.
3. Click **Help**.

TIP

Info The Info window is the main part of Backstage view where you can check permissions, prepare for sharing, and open or delete other versions of the current file. In the right column, you also get a preview of the document and information about its properties and when it was created or modified. ■

TIP

Exit Clicking **Exit** at the bottom of the left column begins to close the document and asks if you want to save any changes. If you click **Cancel**, you return to the main Home tab in the Ribbon. You can return to the Backstage view by clicking **File** again. ■

4 You can click **Check for Updates** under Tools for Working With Office.

5 To use the other features of Backstage view, click the appropriate button in the left column.

End

TIP

Options The Options button in Backstage view gives you a way to make changes to various aspects of the program, including how it is displayed. Important options include the ability to customize the Ribbon and add and remove items from the Quick Access Toolbar. ■

NOTE

Recent The Recent button provides a list of the files previously created and/or modified by the program. This feature gives you a quick way to open and work with any of those files. At the bottom of the window is the option Recover Unsaved Documents, which opens a Drafts folder to recover unsaved files. ■

CREATING A NEW BLANK DOCUMENT

The New Document window in Backstage view lets you quickly create a new blank document, blog post, or file based on templates. You can also create a new document based on an existing file that was previously saved.

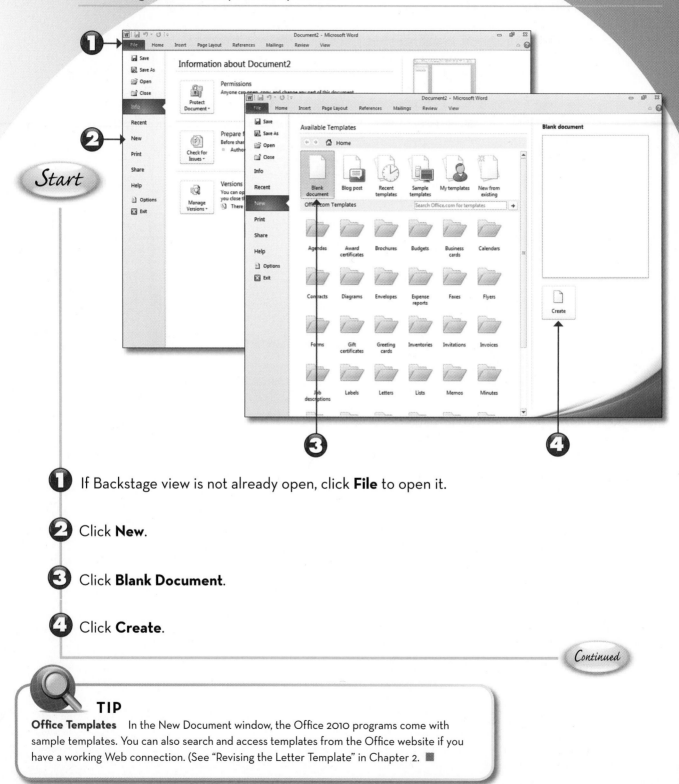

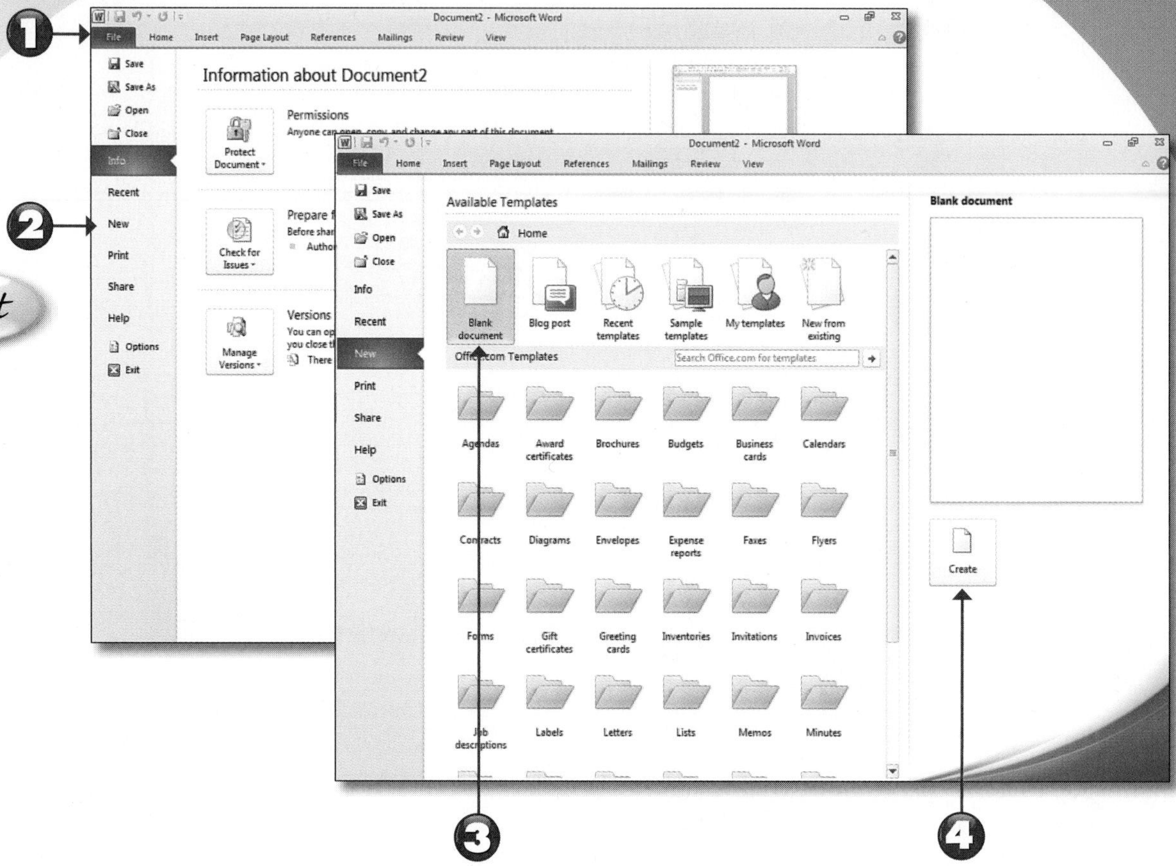

Start

1. If Backstage view is not already open, click **File** to open it.
2. Click **New**.
3. Click **Blank Document**.
4. Click **Create**.

Continued

TIP

Office Templates In the New Document window, the Office 2010 programs come with sample templates. You can also search and access templates from the Office website if you have a working Web connection. (See “Revising the Letter Template” in Chapter 2.

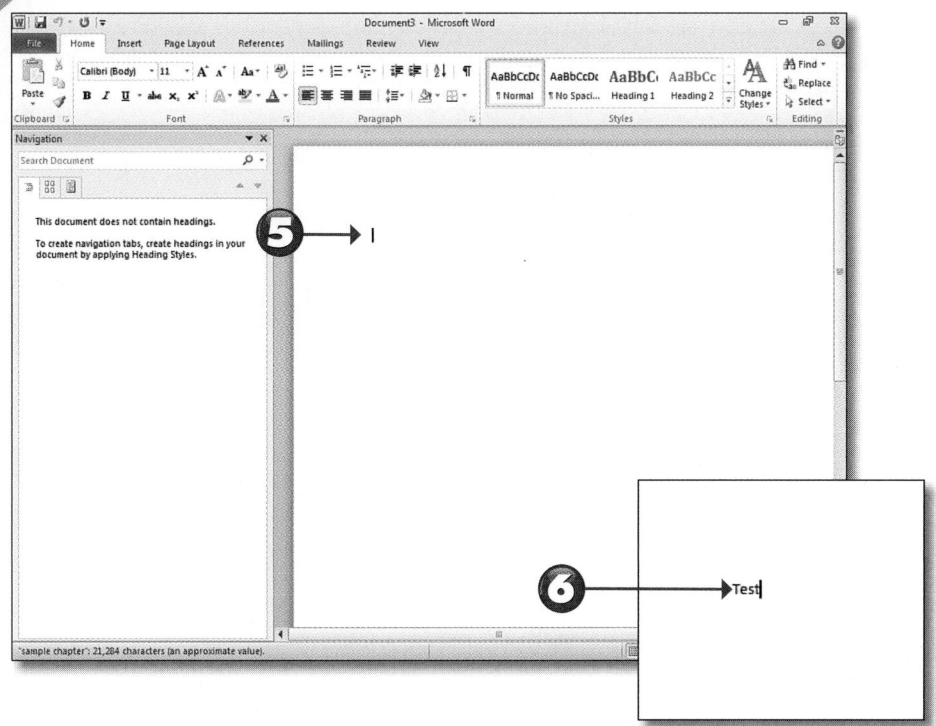

5 At the insertion point, you can begin typing.

6 The text you typed appears on the page.

End

TIP

Blog Post After you become a registered user of many online blogging programs, including Google Blogger, you can publish a blog post after creating one under Available Templates. Open the Blog post template, create the post, click **Publish**, and enter your blog's username and password.

TIP

Typed Text The text you type in the New Document window appears in the style (the default is Normal) highlighted in the Styles panel at the top of the Home tab on the Ribbon. (Styles are covered in more detail in Chapter 4). You can preview and apply an entirely different Style Set by clicking **Change Styles** on the Home tab.

INTRODUCING THE NAVIGATION PANE

The Navigation pane in Office 2010 lets you quickly move through a document by headings, browse thumbnails of pages, or search the document. You can close this pane any time to view the document in the full window and reopen the Navigation pane from the View tab of the Ribbon. (This replaces the Document Map view from previous versions of Word.)

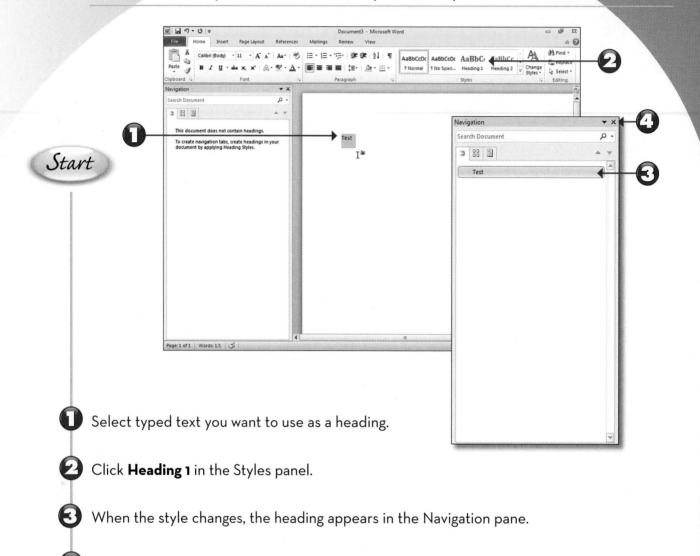

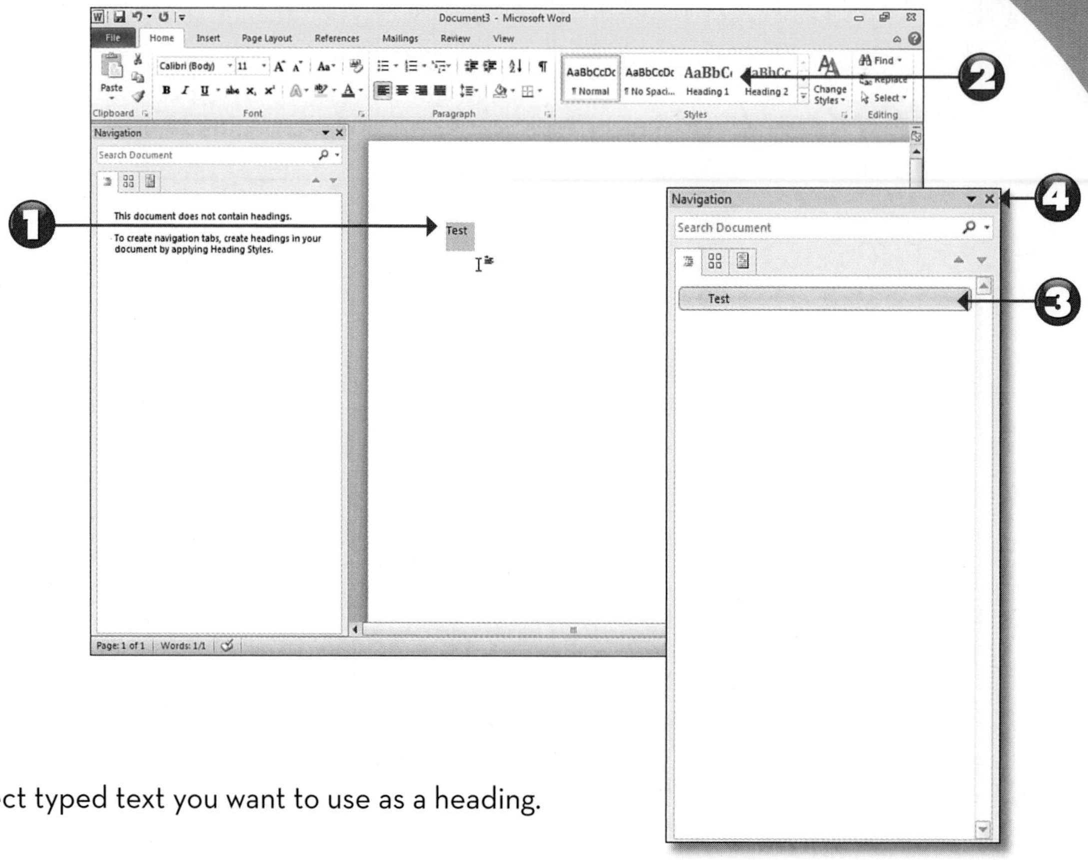

Start

1. Select typed text you want to use as a heading.
2. Click **Heading 1** in the Styles panel.
3. When the style changes, the heading appears in the Navigation pane.
4. Click **x** to close the Navigation pane.

Continued

NOTE

Understanding Headings To see headings and move to them directly in the Navigation pane, you must format them with a heading style from the Styles window. ■

TIP

Working with the Navigation Pane You can move, size, or close the Navigation pane by clicking the small down arrow to the left of the x (close) button at the top. You can also click the Thumbnail tab to see images of your pages or the Search tab to enter a search term. ■

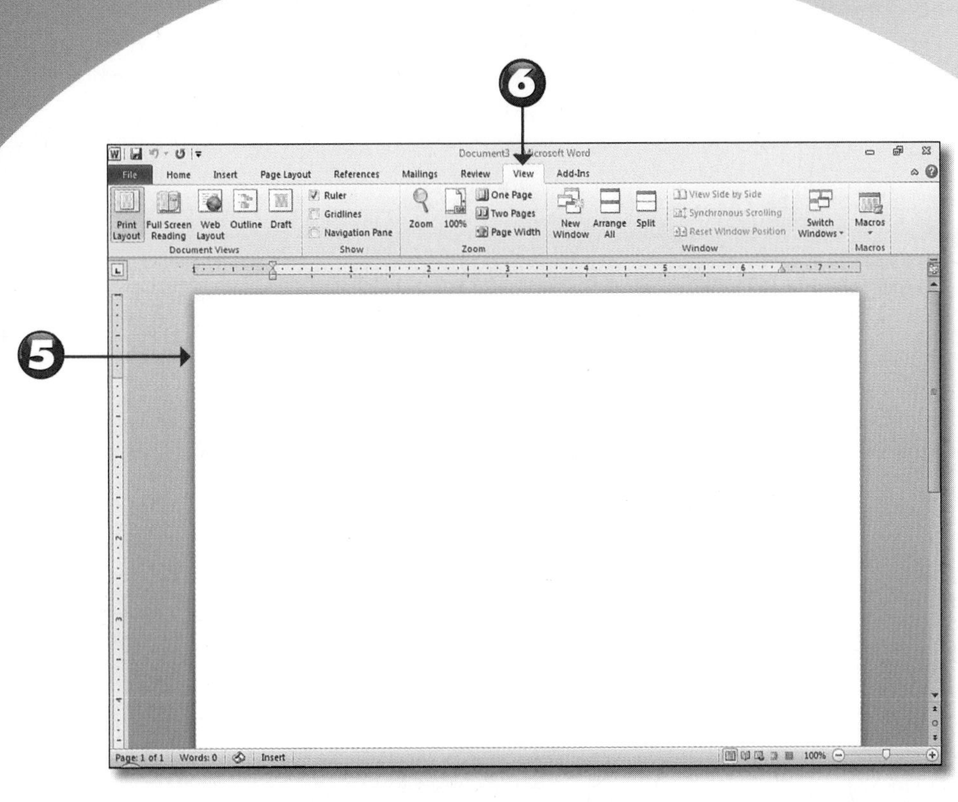

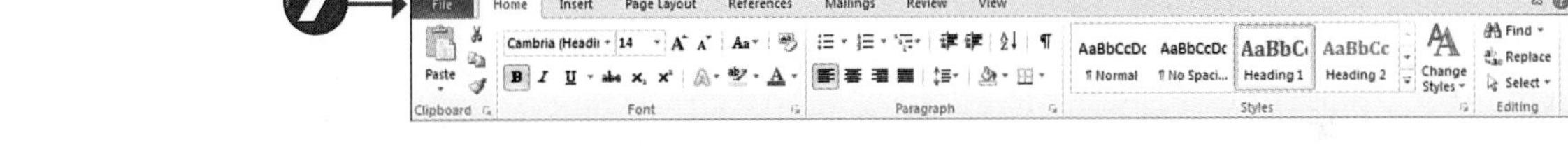

5 The Navigation pane is closed, and the document is viewed full screen.

6 Click the **View** tab on the Ribbon.

7 Click to check the box beside Navigation Pane. The Navigation pane reappears.

End

TIP

Using Search When your document has multiple headings and additional pages and content, entering a word or phrase in the Search panel and clicking the magnifying icon highlights all instances of the search in the document and moves to the first one. You can click any heading to move through the document or the up arrow to return to the top. ■

SAVING IN DIFFERENT FORMATS

After you complete a document, you can save it in any of many different formats. The default format is Word, Excel, or PowerPoint in Office 2010. However, you can save it as an earlier version (97-2003) for users who are not working in Office 2010, as a web page, as a PDF or XPS file, or in various other formats that provide compatibility with other applications. The Office 2010 format is also compatible with files from Office 2007.

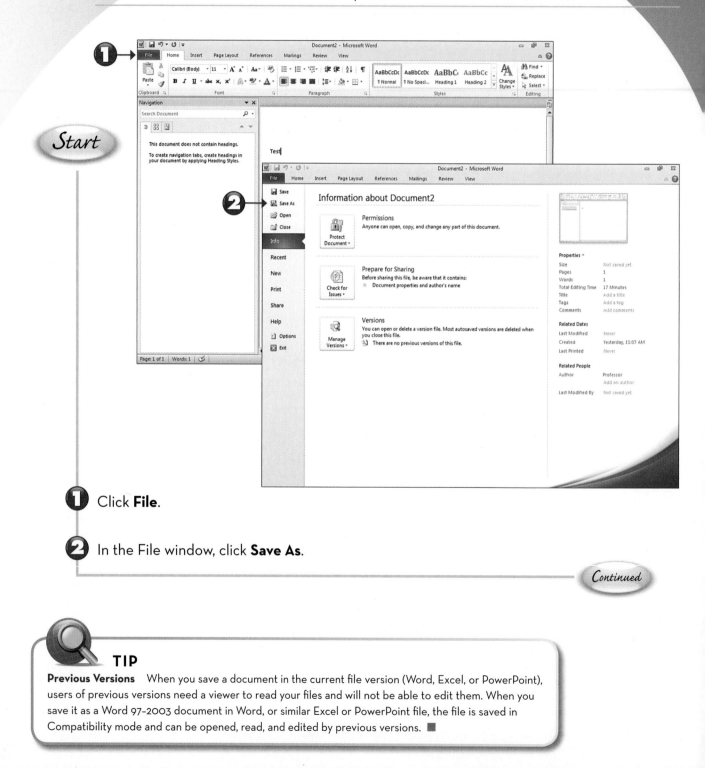

Start

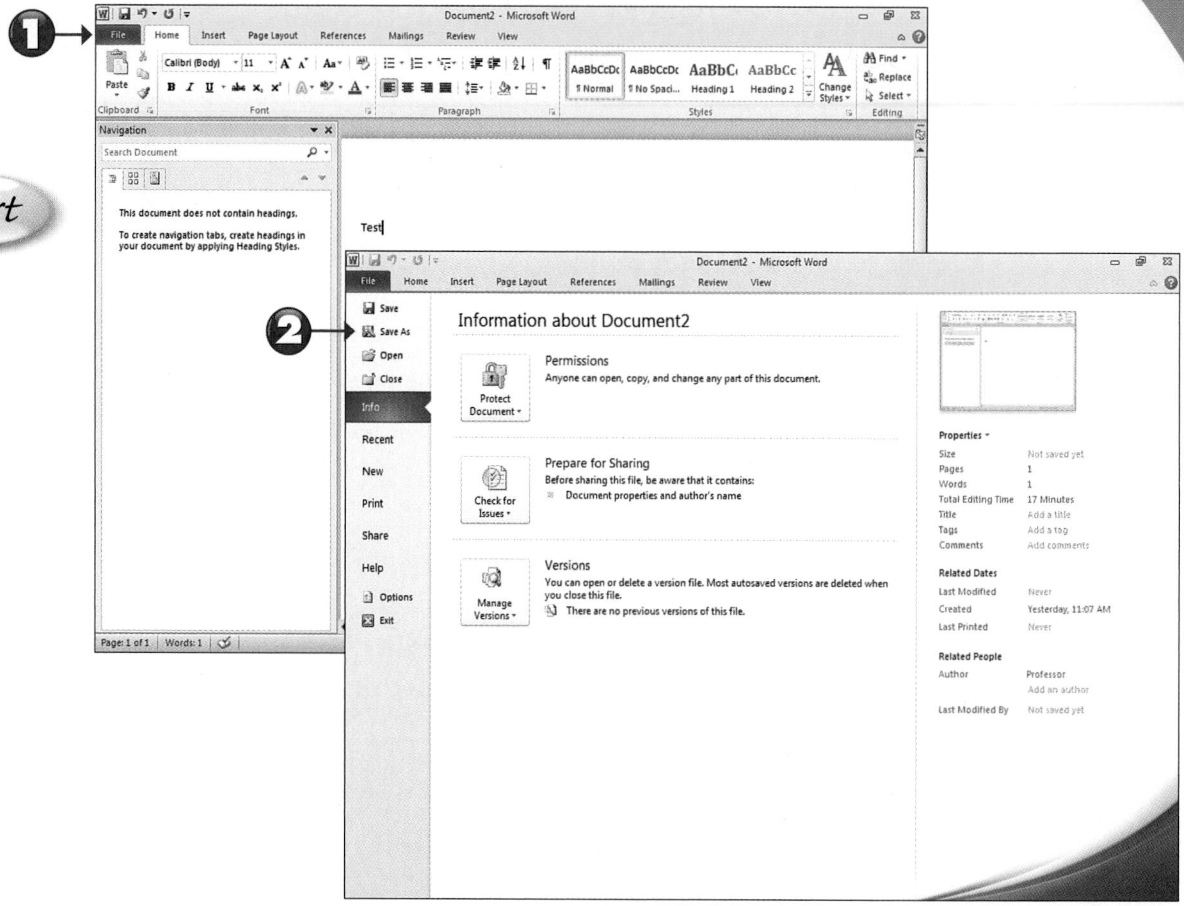

1. Click **File**.
2. In the File window, click **Save As**.

Continued

TIP

Previous Versions When you save a document in the current file version (Word, Excel, or PowerPoint), users of previous versions need a viewer to read your files and will not be able to edit them. When you save it as a Word 97-2003 document in Word, or similar Excel or PowerPoint file, the file is saved in Compatibility mode and can be opened, read, and edited by previous versions. ■

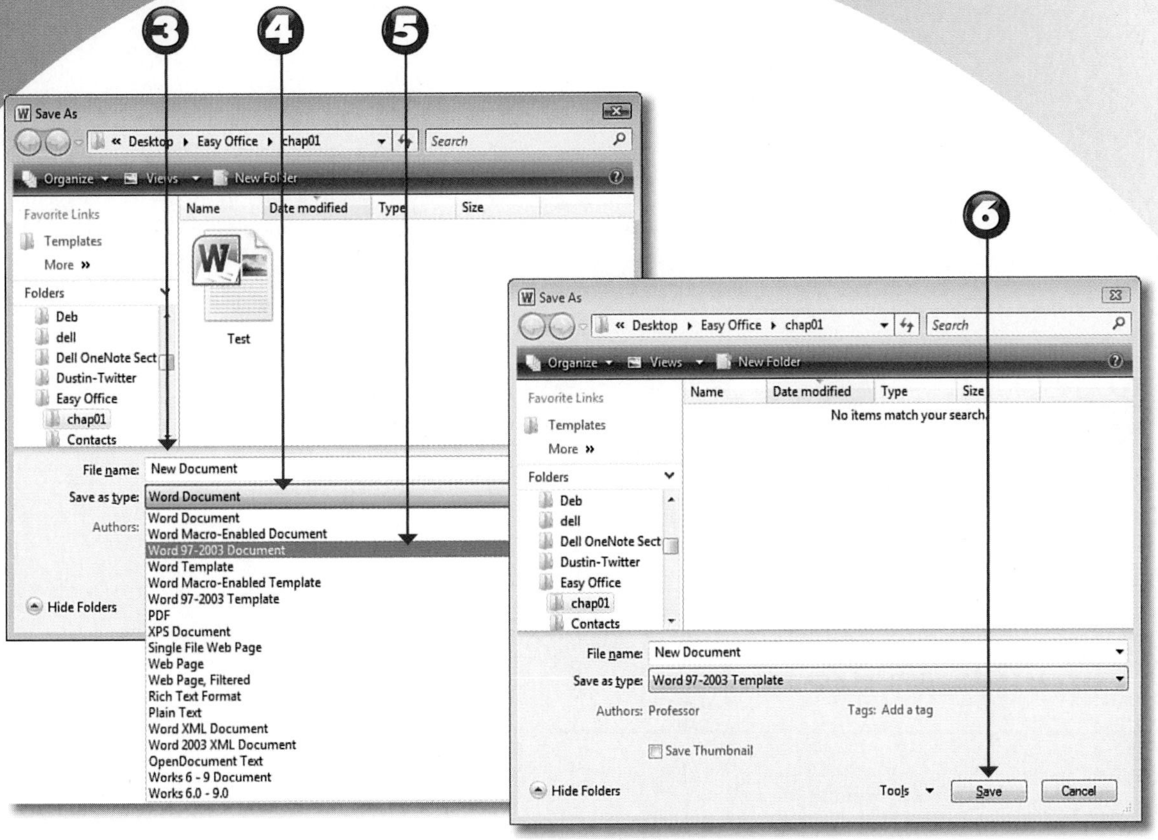

3 You can type in a new name for the document if desired.

4 Click the **Save as type** drop-down arrow.

5 Select the type of file to save as.

6 Click **Save**.

End

TIP

Converting Files If you open or save a document in 97-2003 format so that it is in Compatibility mode, a Convert option appears in the Info panel of Backstage view. It lets you convert the document to the current format to enable all the features of Office 2010.

TIP

Saving as Templates Saving in one of the various template formats makes the file available in your Recent Templates folder in Backstage view. You can also save a new template file directly to your My Templates folder to access it when you click to create a new document in Backstage view.

PRINTING IN BACKSTAGE VIEW

After completing and saving a new file, you might want to print the document. To print in Office 2010, you use Backstage view, where you get a full range of printing options all available in one page, including a preview of the document.

Start

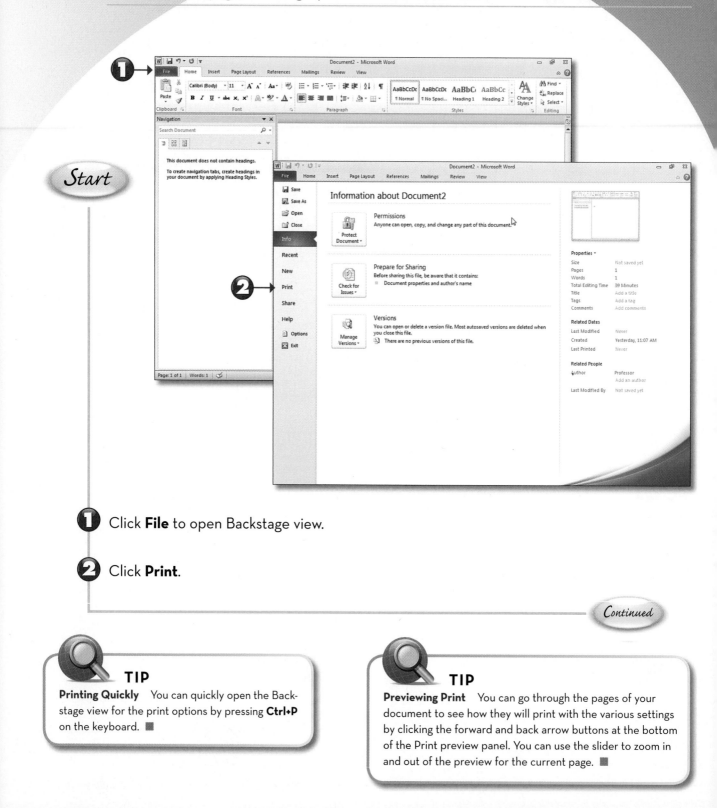

1. Click **File** to open Backstage view.
2. Click **Print**.

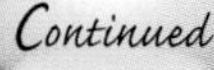

TIP

Printing Quickly You can quickly open the Backstage view for the print options by pressing **Ctrl+P** on the keyboard. ■

TIP

Previewing Print You can go through the pages of your document to see how they will print with the various settings by clicking the forward and back arrow buttons at the bottom of the Print preview panel. You can use the slider to zoom in and out of the preview for the current page. ■

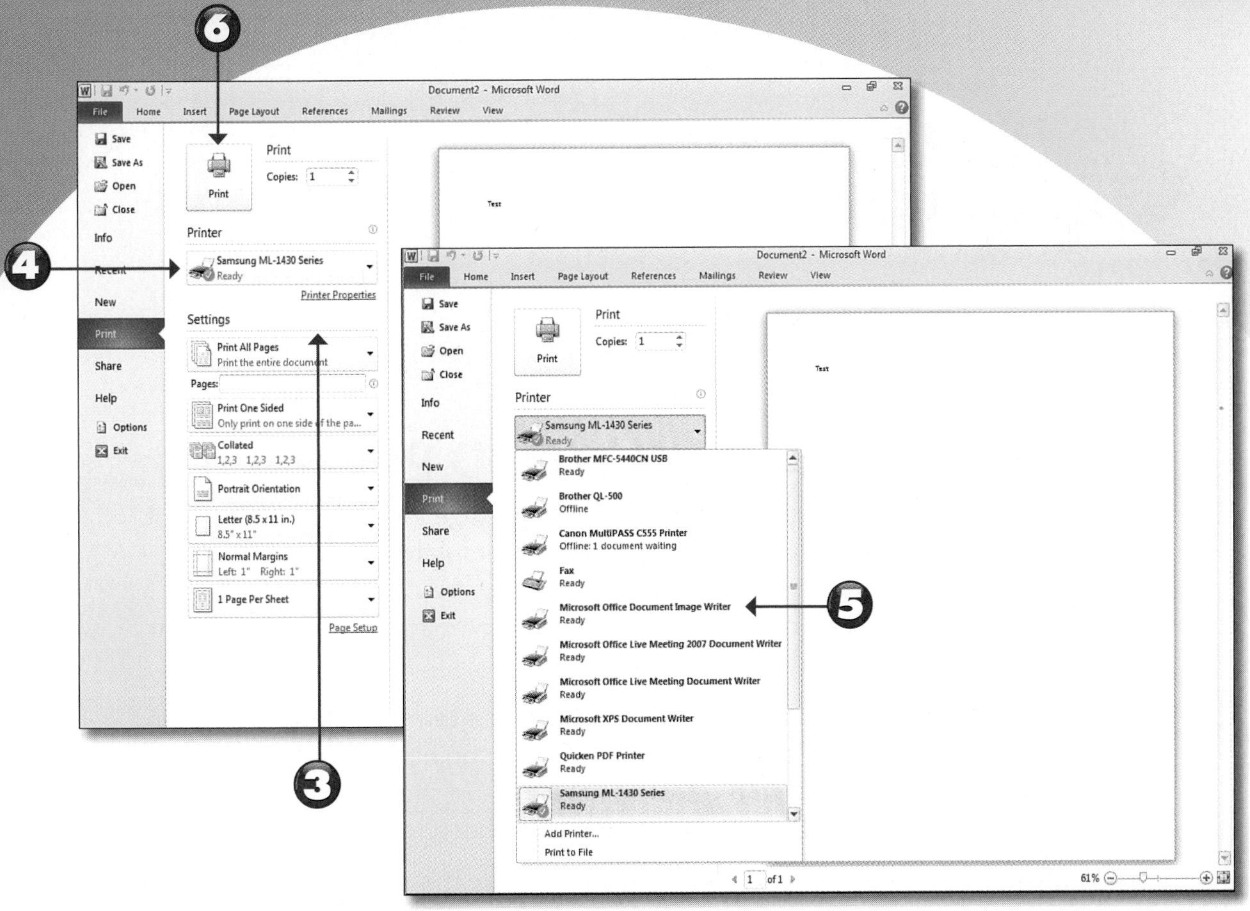

3. In Backstage view, change any settings for printing the document.

4. Click the down arrow to select another printer.

5. Choose the printer to which you want to print.

6. Click **Print**.

TIP

Changing Orientation You can change the orientation of a document by clicking **Printer Properties** in the Print window of Backstage view. Or you can click **Orientation** in the Page Setup panel of the Page Layout tab of the Ribbon. ■

BEGINNING A NEW WORD PROJECT

You can create a new Word document from Backstage view's New Document window, and Word provides a number of preset templates to make it easier to get started. By using a template, you can quickly create a particular kind of document, like an introductory letter for your company, and just fill in your information to complete the project.

Whether you begin with a new blank document or a template, you can immediately begin adding text by typing at the insertion point. You can move text by dragging your mouse through the text to select it and then dragging it to another location or copying or cutting and pasting it elsewhere.

To move through a document in Word, you can drag the slider on the right side of the window or use the down arrow on your keypad. With longer files, the Document Browser lets you go to specific parts of your document that you select; you can use the Find tool or browse to the next heading or browse to any of a number of elements in your file.

After selecting text, you can format it by changing the font, font size, or font color or making it bold, italic, or underline. You also can make further adjustments.

USING THE BACKSTAGE VIEW SAMPLE TEMPLATES

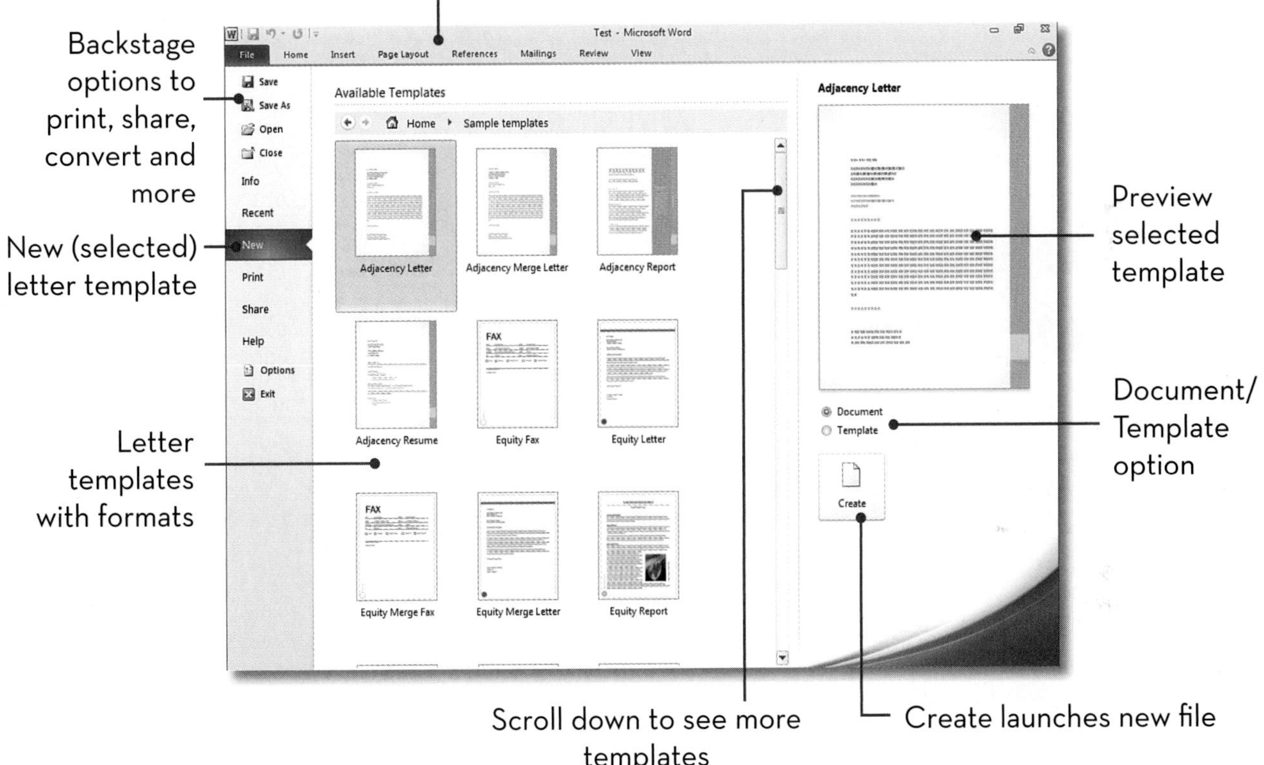

CREATING A NEW LETTER FROM A TEMPLATE

When you use a template to create a new document, it is already set up and formatted for you, so all you need to do is fill in your own information. Templates are available in the New Document window of Backstage view.

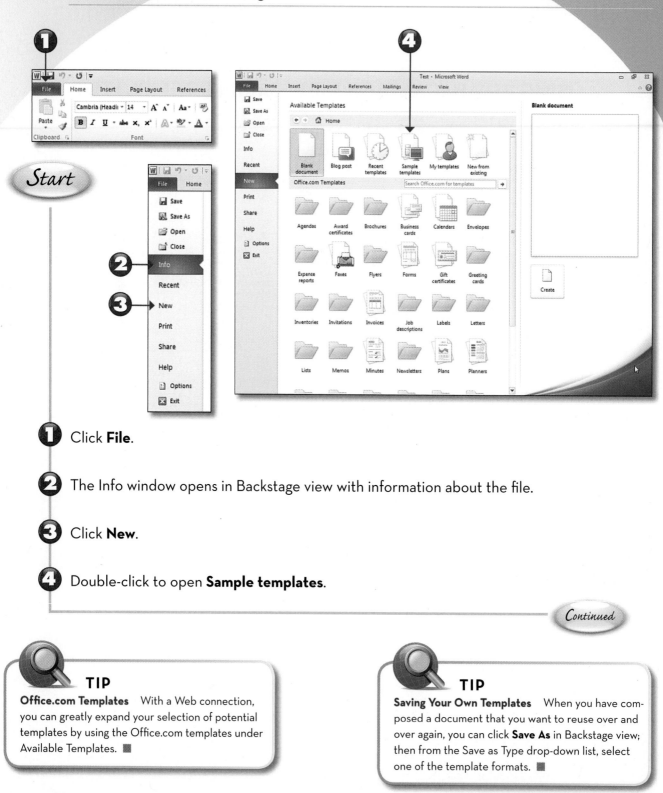

1. Click **File**.
2. The Info window opens in Backstage view with information about the file.
3. Click **New**.
4. Double-click to open **Sample templates**.

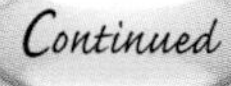

TIP

Office.com Templates With a Web connection, you can greatly expand your selection of potential templates by using the Office.com templates under Available Templates. ■

TIP

Saving Your Own Templates When you have composed a document that you want to reuse over and over again, you can click **Save As** in Backstage view; then from the Save as Type drop-down list, select one of the template formats. ■

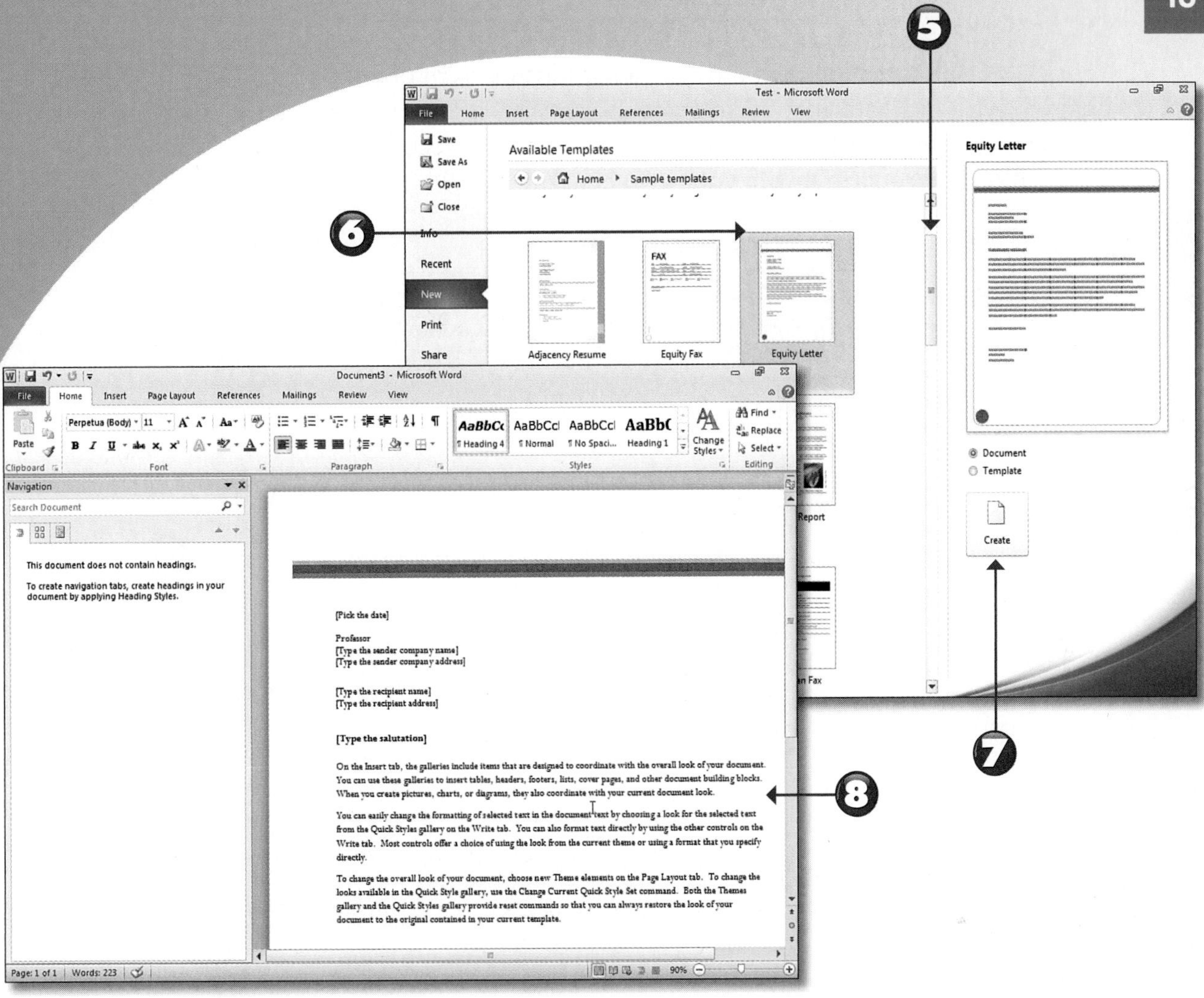

5 Scroll down through the Available Templates to select one.

6 Click one to select it.

7 Click **Create**.

8 A new document is created for you to revise.

End

TIP

Recent Templates The Recent Templates area shows you the various templates you've opened in the past. Using it is a good way to locate popular templates, particularly from Office.com, without searching through the various folders for them again. ■

REVISING THE LETTER TEMPLATE

Your new blank template contains Content Controls with preset formats where you can begin to type your information. In some cases, Word may have entered information from your registration page, like your first and last name or a username; you can delete that information and replace it with your own content.

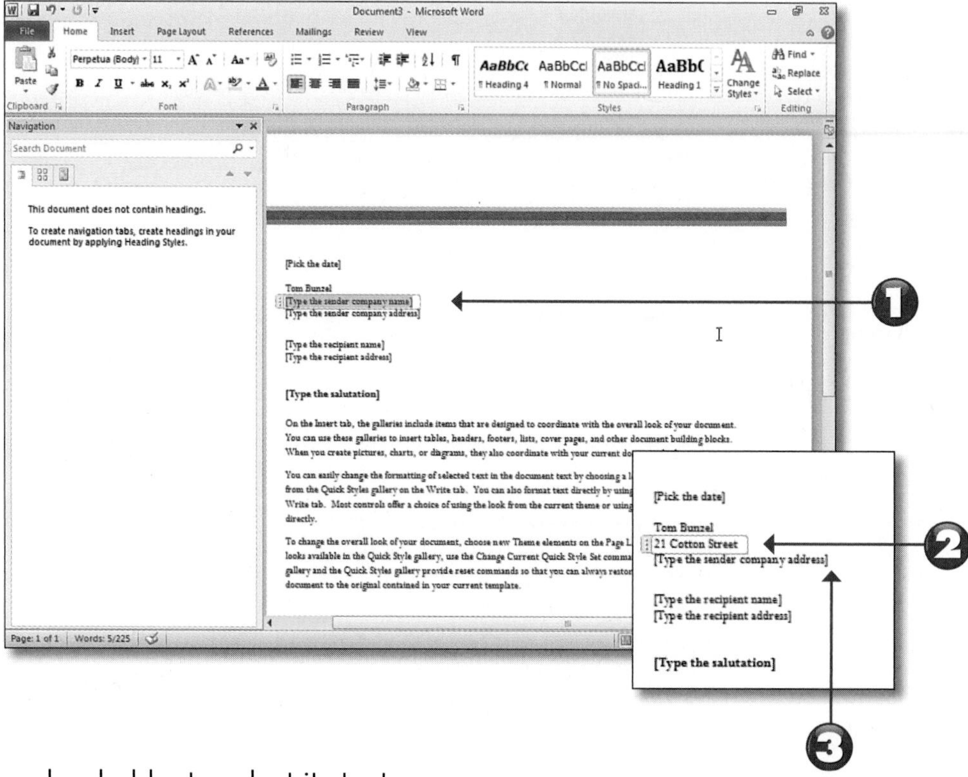

Start

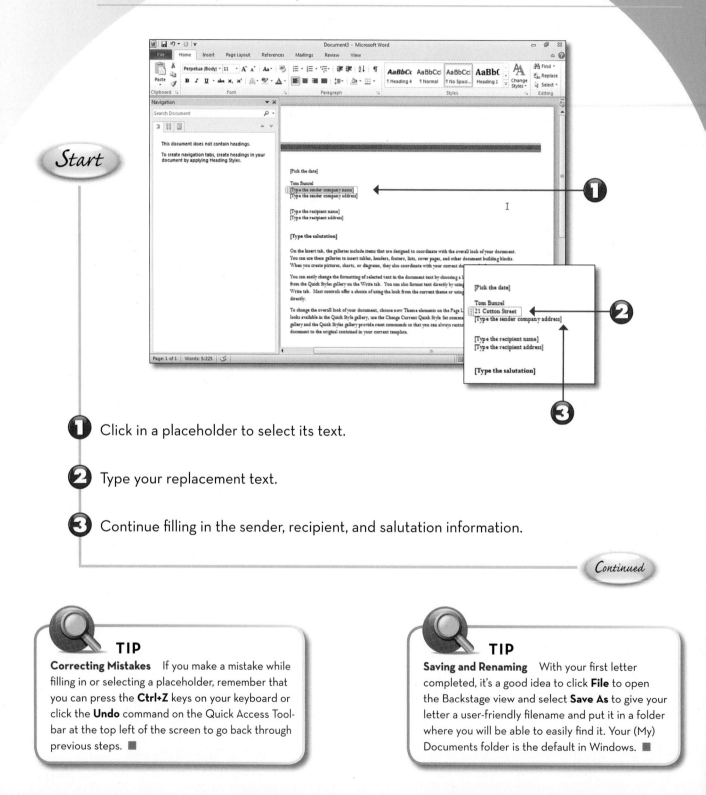

1. Click in a placeholder to select its text.
2. Type your replacement text.
3. Continue filling in the sender, recipient, and salutation information.

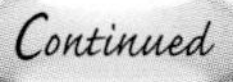

TIP

Correcting Mistakes If you make a mistake while filling in or selecting a placeholder, remember that you can press the **Ctrl+Z** keys on your keyboard or click the **Undo** command on the Quick Access Toolbar at the top left of the screen to go back through previous steps. ■

TIP

Saving and Renaming With your first letter completed, it's a good idea to click **File** to open the Backstage view and select **Save As** to give your letter a user-friendly filename and put it in a folder where you will be able to easily find it. Your (My) Documents folder is the default in Windows. ■

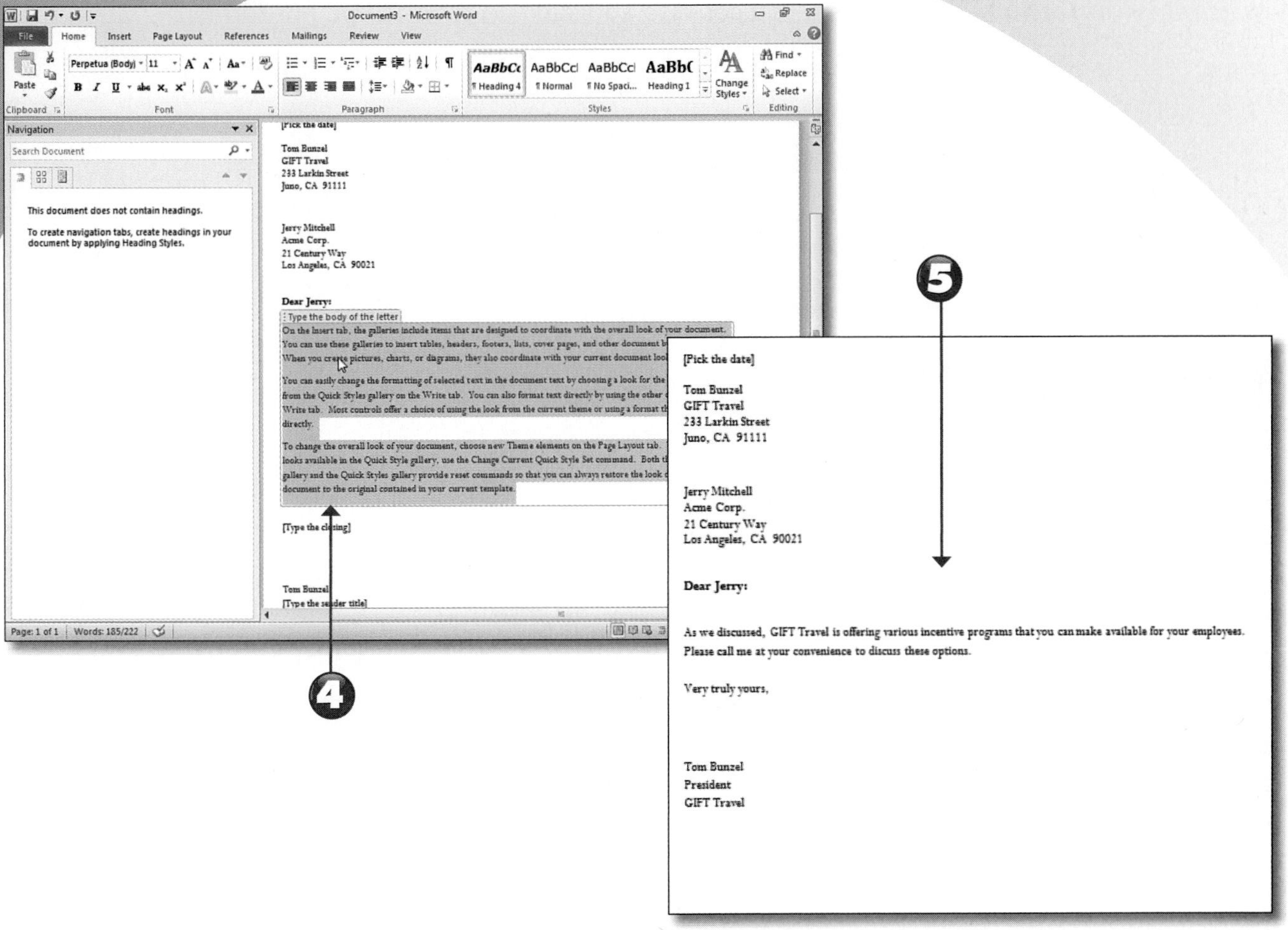

4. Click in the body of the letter to select the text and then replace it with your own version of the letter.

5. Fill in the rest of the placeholders to complete your first letter.

End

TIP

Removing Content Controls If you don't want a Content Control in the current template, the easiest way to get rid of it is to right-click and select **Remove Content Control**.

TIP

Filling in the Date The date is a special Content Control with a calendar. You can click the drop-down arrow to open the calendar to the current month and select the current date, or you can select another date on the calendar.

19

FORMATTING TEXT IN YOUR DOCUMENT

The Home tab in Office 2010 lets you quickly apply formatting changes to selected text in your document. You can change the Font, Font size, or Case and apply bold, italic, underscore, or strikethrough text. You can also add sub and superscript. For former formatting options, click the Dialog Launch Icon in the Font group.

Start

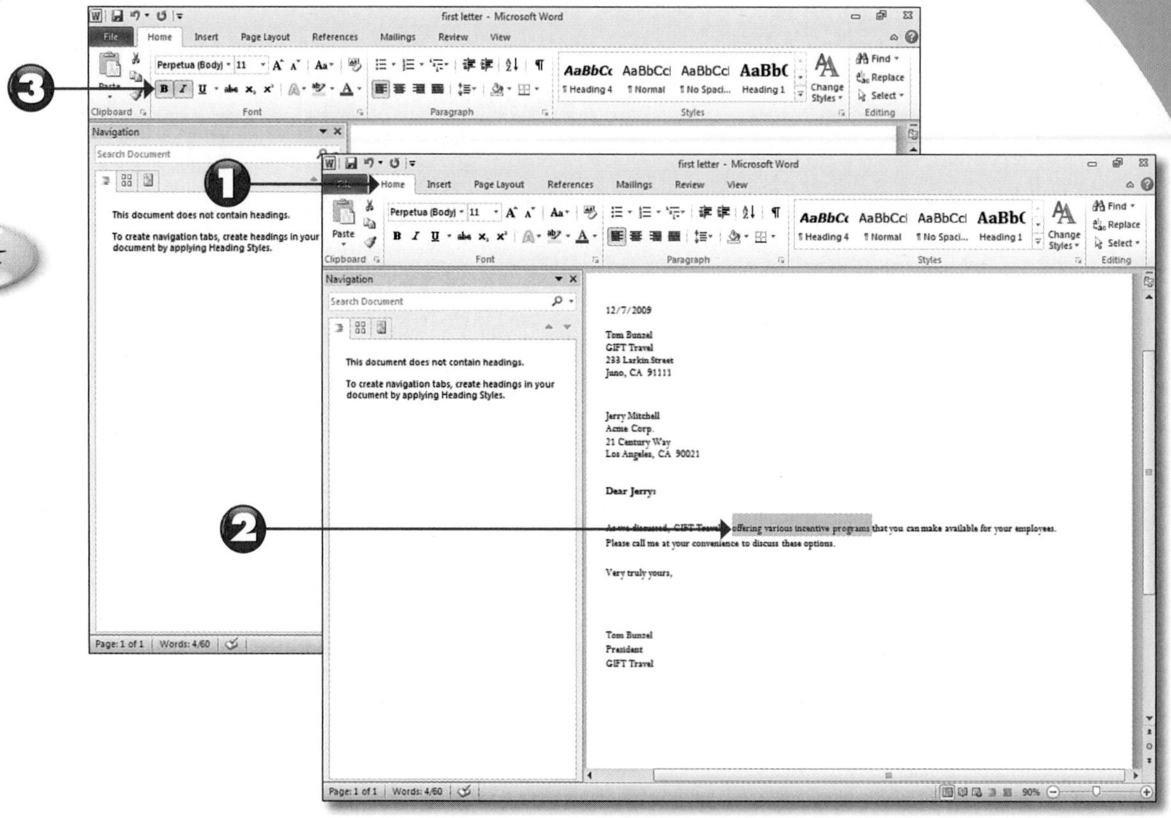

1. Click to make sure you are in the Home tab of the Ribbon.
2. Drag through the typed text to select text to reformat.
3. Click to select Bold, Italic, and/or Underline in the Font group.

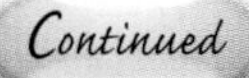

NOTE

Quick Formatting With your text selected, you can right-click it to bring up a set of menus with options for many of your most popular formatting and style options. ■

TIP

Quick Selection For quick selection, press the **Shift+Ctrl** keys with the right arrow on the keyboard to select by word. Double-click a word to select it or triple-click to select a whole paragraph. ■

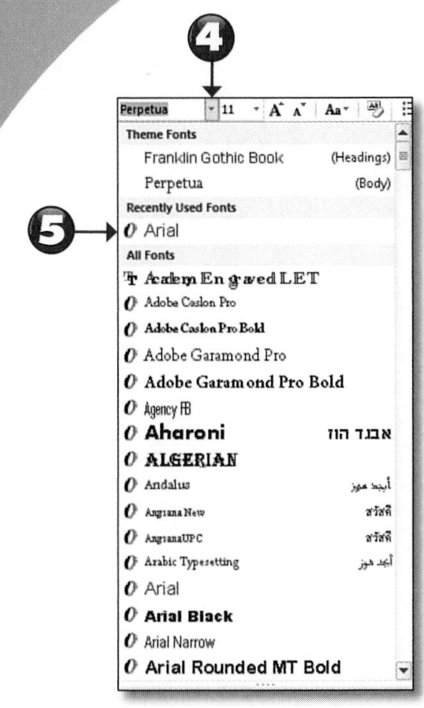

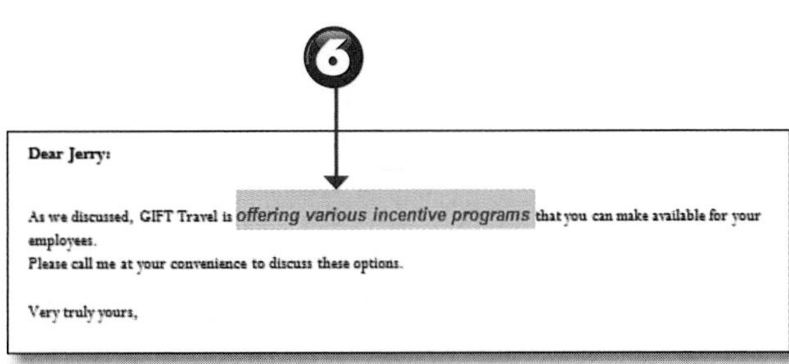

Dear Jerry:

As we discussed, GIFT Travel is offering various incentive programs that you can make available for your employees.

Please call me at your convenience to discuss these options.

Very truly yours,

4 Click the **Fonts** drop-down arrow.

5 Click to select a different font for the selected text.

6 Your text is formatted with the choices you made.

End

TIP

Clear Formatting In addition to Undo (Ctrl+Z), clicking the **Clear Formatting** button in the Fonts group also removes all formatting from a selected block of text and returns it to its original format. ■

TIP

Additional Advanced Formats You click the **Dialog Launch** icon (small diagonal arrow) at the lower right of the Fonts group (or any other group in any tab of the Ribbon) to bring up additional options. For fonts, you see more Font options and Advanced options. ■

INSERTING SYMBOLS AND CHANGING THE DATE STYLE

The Insert tab of the Ribbon provides additional elements that you can add to your document. (I cover many of the elements in the Illustration group in Chapter 4) You can use the Symbols options in the Symbols group to add important notations for copyright or math and engineering symbols. You can use the Date & Time option to specify how you want a date or time formatted in your text.

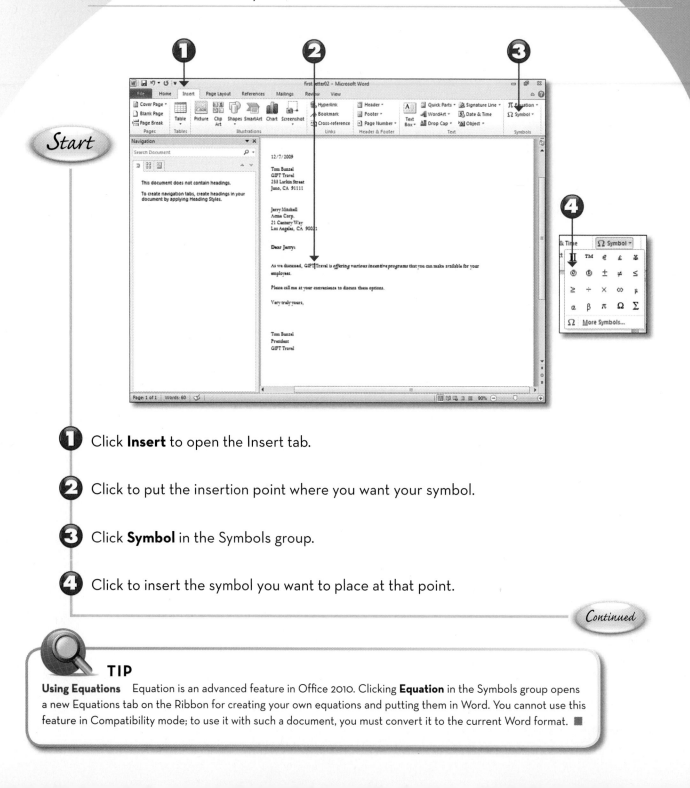

Start

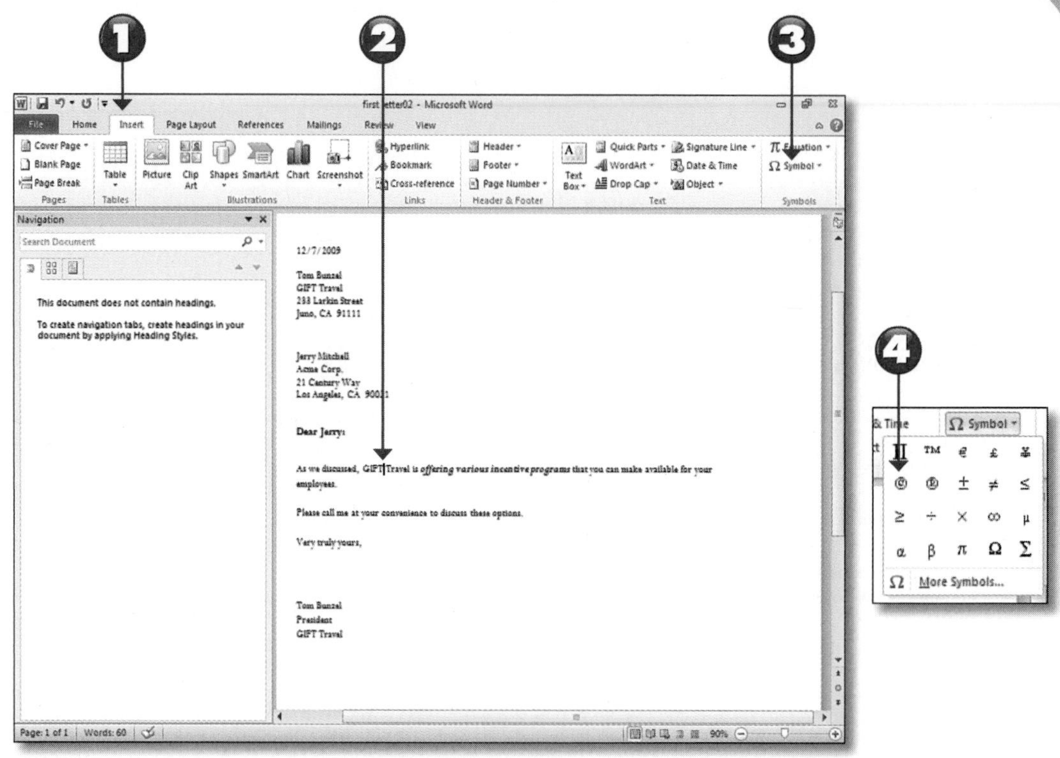

1. Click **Insert** to open the Insert tab.
2. Click to put the insertion point where you want your symbol.
3. Click **Symbol** in the Symbols group.
4. Click to insert the symbol you want to place at that point.

Continued

TIP

Using Equations Equation is an advanced feature in Office 2010. Clicking **Equation** in the Symbols group opens a new Equations tab on the Ribbon for creating your own equations and putting them in Word. You cannot use this feature in Compatibility mode; to use it with such a document, you must convert it to the current Word format. ■

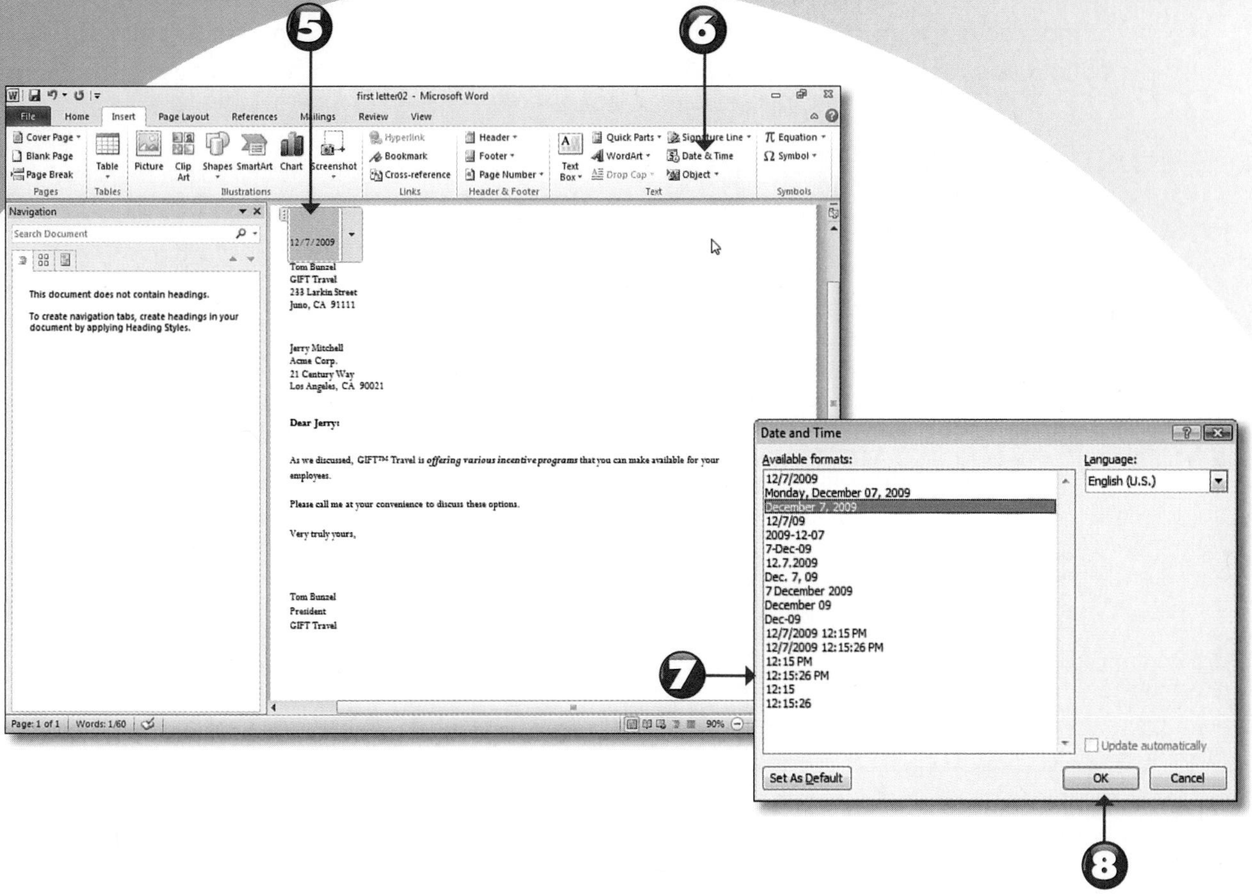

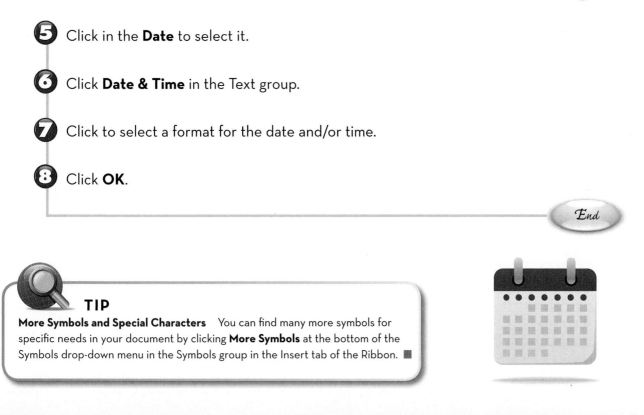

5 Click in the **Date** to select it.

6 Click **Date & Time** in the Text group.

7 Click to select a format for the date and/or time.

8 Click **OK**.

End

TIP

More Symbols and Special Characters You can find many more symbols for specific needs in your document by clicking **More Symbols** at the bottom of the Symbols drop-down menu in the Symbols group in the Insert tab of the Ribbon. ■

ADDING BULLETS AND NUMBERED LISTS

To make lists of related items stand out or look more polished, you can apply a bullet or numbered list from the Paragraph group of the Home tab. You can use preset styles for bullets and numbers, or you can define your own format.

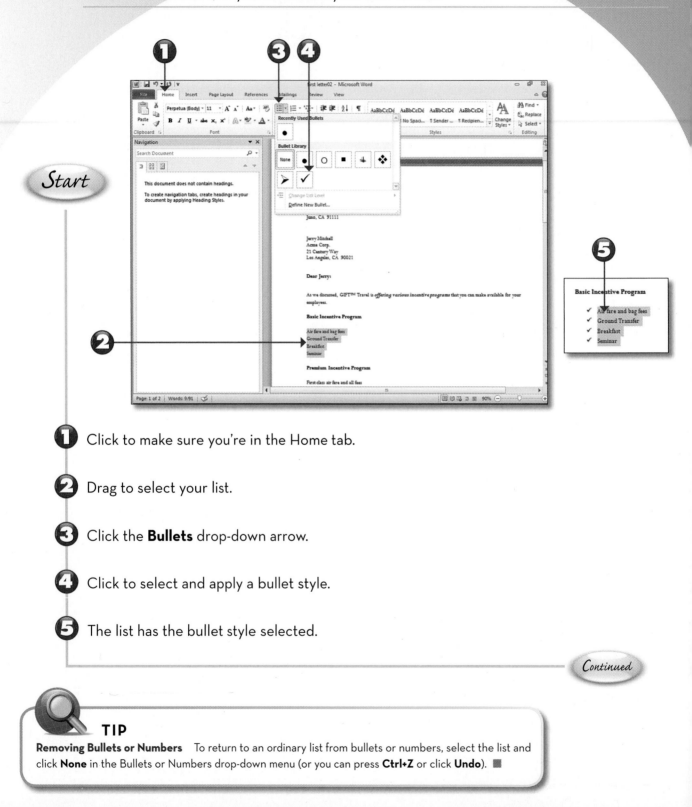

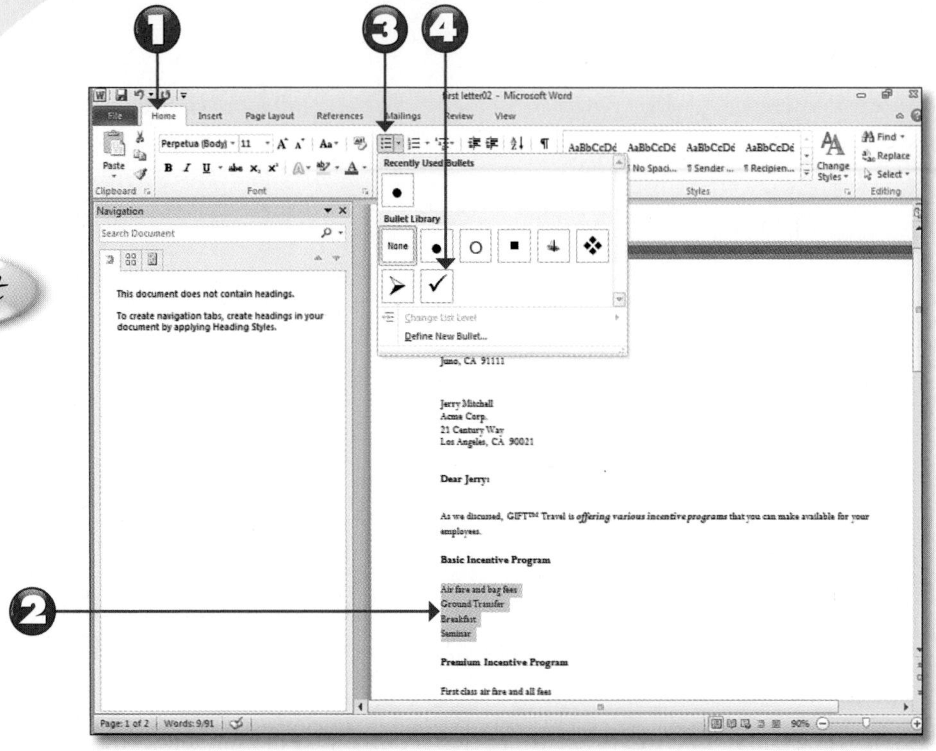

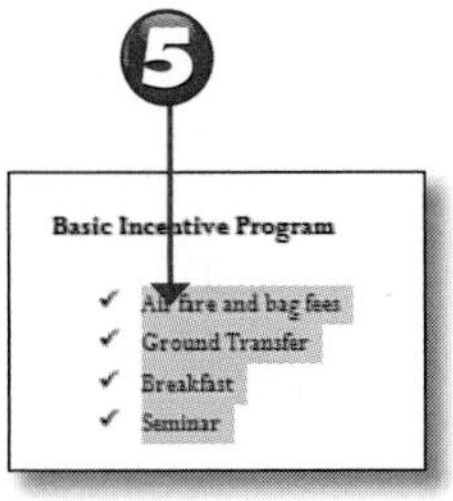

Start

1. Click to make sure you're in the Home tab.
2. Drag to select your list.
3. Click the **Bullets** drop-down arrow.
4. Click to select and apply a bullet style.
5. The list has the bullet style selected.

Continued

TIP

Removing Bullets or Numbers To return to an ordinary list from bullets or numbers, select the list and click **None** in the Bullets or Numbers drop-down menu (or you can press **Ctrl+Z** or click **Undo**).

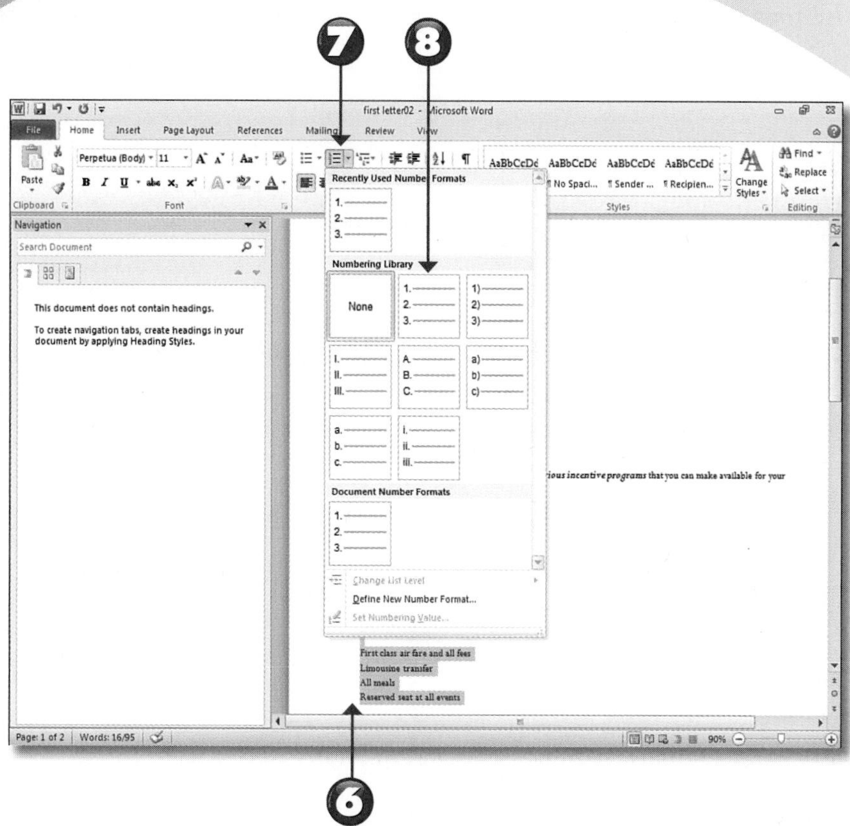

6 Select a second list.

7 Click the **Numbered List** drop-down arrow.

8 Select and click to apply a numbered list style.

End

TIP

Defining a New Bullet When you click **Define New Bullet,** you can select from a symbol, picture, or font to create your new bullet. Pictures are available from the Office clip art library when you click **Picture**, or you can also click **Import** to use your own images as bullets. ■

TIP

Defining Number Formats You can use the Define Number Format options to add or delete periods, commas, or parentheses from your numbered lists and change the alignment of numbers. ■

SEARCHING AND REPLACING IN THE DOCUMENT

Clicking Find in the Editing group of the Home tab lets you quickly locate instances of a particular word or phrase from the Navigation pane. Clicking Replace lets you search for and substitute a new word or phrase for the next instance of the search term, or click Replace All to do a global replace.

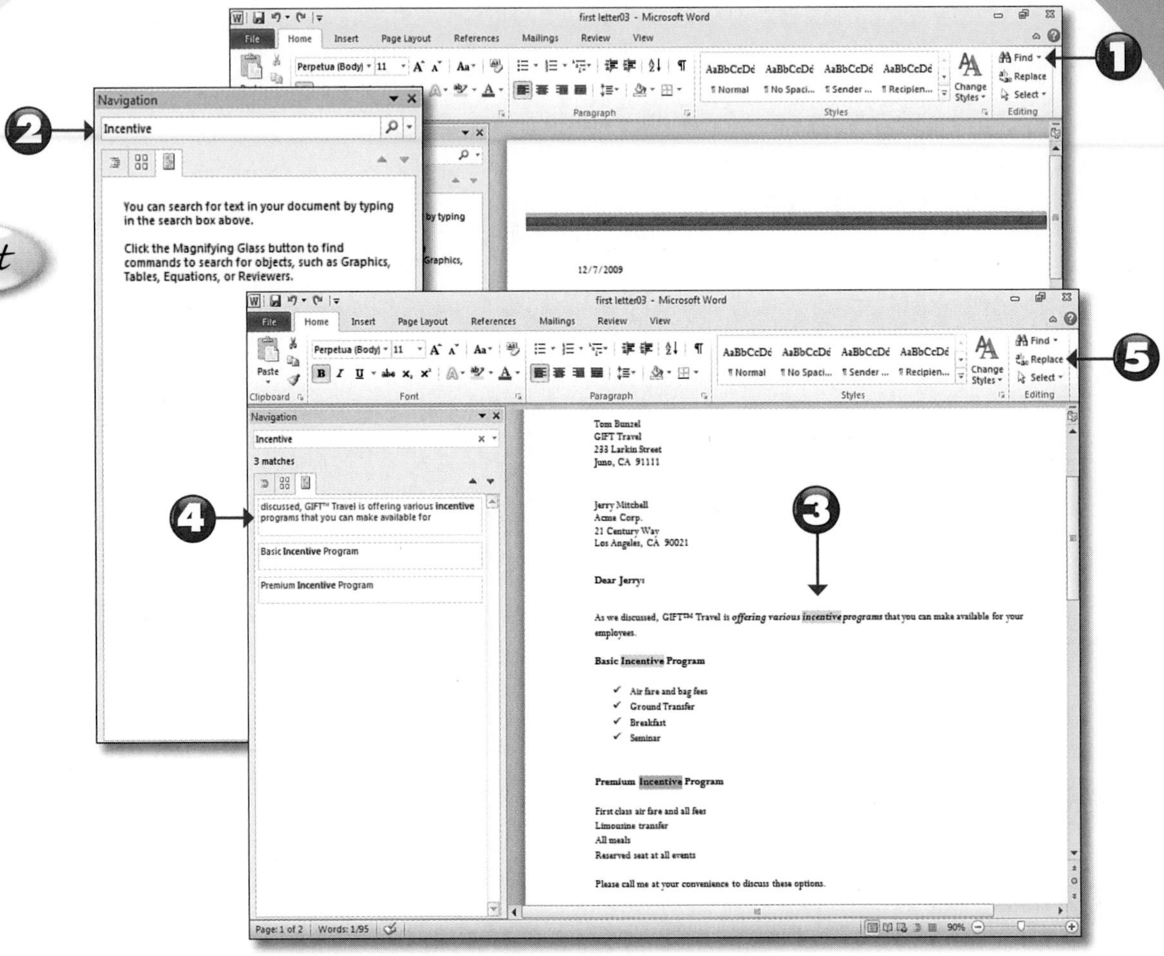

1. Click **Find** in the Home tab.
2. Type your search term in the Navigation panel and press **Enter**.
3. The instances of your search term are highlighted in the document.
4. The instances of your search term are shown in the Navigation panel, and you can click to navigate to that part of the document.
5. Click **Replace** in the Editing group of the Home tab.

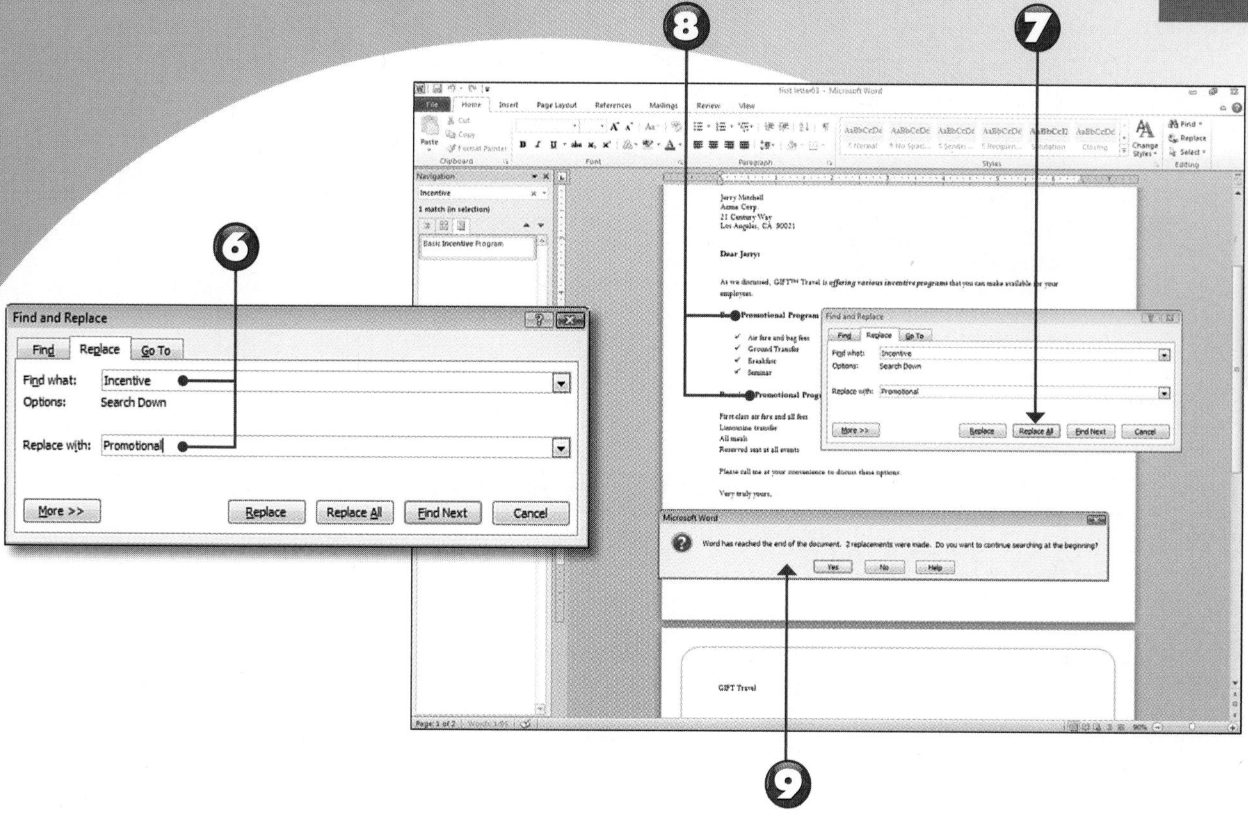

6 The word you selected is already in the Find what field. Enter a word you want to replace it with in the Replace with field.

7 Click Replace All to find and replace all instances of the chosen word.

8 The multiple instances are replaced.

9 A dialog box tells you the number of replacements.

End

TIP

Find and the Navigation Pane If the Navigation pane is closed, clicking **Find** in the Editing group of the Home tab opens it and puts your cursor into the Search panel. If this pane is already open, this action simply enables the search. ■

TIP

Changing Search Parameters When you click the magnifying glass icon in the Search panel of the Navigation pane, you are shown options to fine-tune your search. You can search by various parts of your document, such as comments, headings, graphics, and more. ■

ADJUSTING THE STRUCTURE OF YOUR DOCUMENT

Opening a document and typing text are only the start of creating a finished project in Word. It is also important to be able to change the document's appearance for print or other distribution and determine how margins and other page elements work.

When you want to maneuver in your document, the Ribbon provides instant access to various formatting and other features. On the Ribbon, the View tab gives you options to work in the document in the way it will print, for readers on computer screens, as a web page, or on a larger screen without a Ruler. There is also an Outline view to help you organize your text.

After you begin a document in Word, the program provides numerous features to let you view it in different ways and change its layout and orientation. You also can add page numbers, headers, and footers.

You can add reference materials like footnotes or endnotes and reshape a page into columns.

CHANGING THE VIEW OF YOUR DOCUMENT

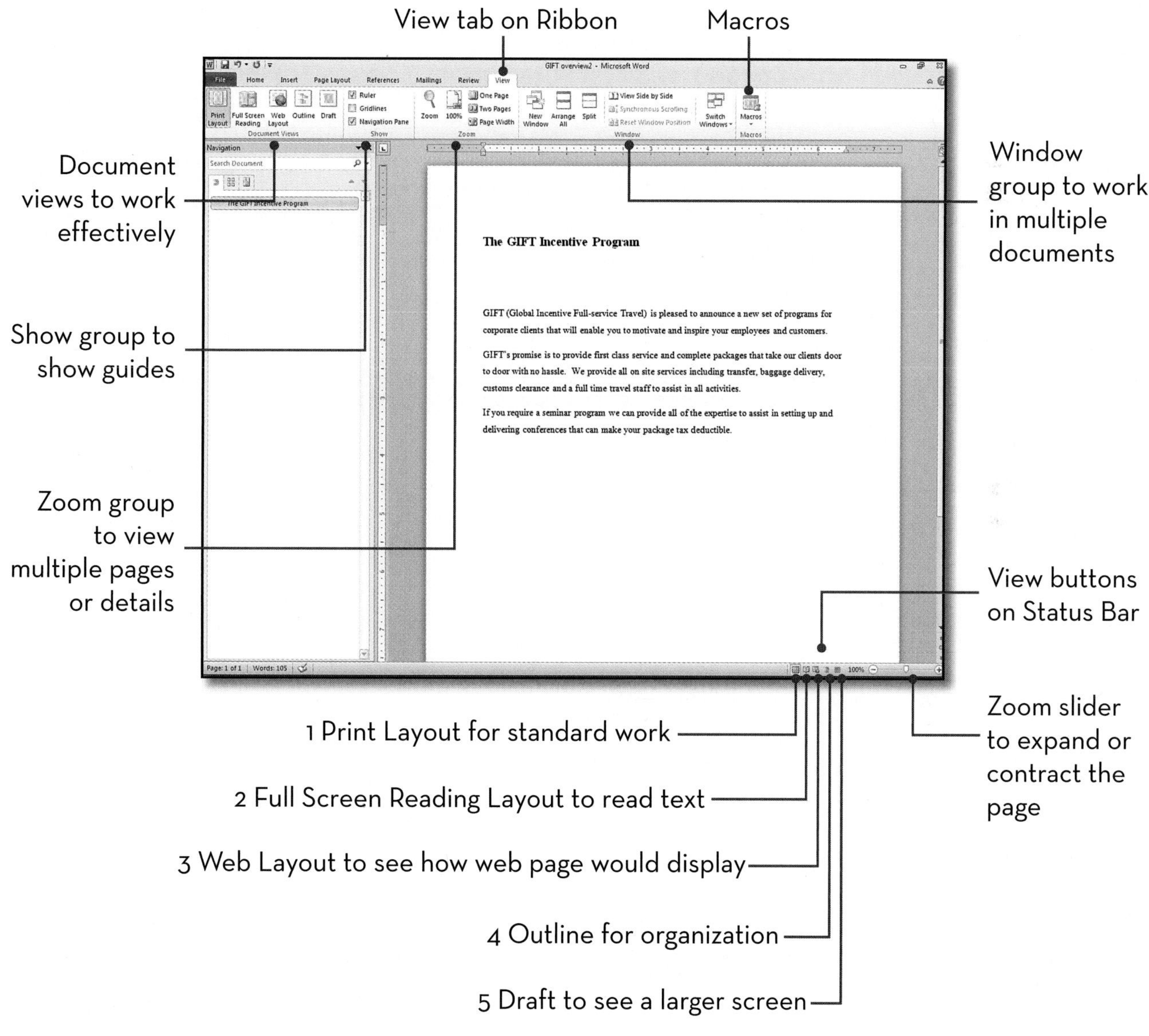
View tab on Ribbon
Macros
Document views to work effectively
Show group to show guides
Zoom group to view multiple pages or details
Window group to work in multiple documents
View buttons on Status Bar
Zoom slider to expand or contract the page
1 Print Layout for standard work
2 Full Screen Reading Layout to read text
3 Web Layout to see how web page would display
4 Outline for organization
5 Draft to see a larger screen
The GIFT Incentive Program
GIFT (Global Incentive Full-service Travel) is pleased to announce a new set of programs for corporate clients that will enable you to motivate and inspire your employees and customers.
GIFT's promise is to provide first class service and complete packages that take our clients door to door with no hassle. We provide all on site services including transfer, baggage delivery, customs clearance and a full time travel staff to assist in all activities.
If you require a seminar program we can provide all of the expertise to assist in setting up and delivering conferences that can make your package tax deductible.

CHANGING THE MARGINS IN YOUR PROJECT

By using the Page Layout tab of the Ribbon, you can make various changes to the appearance of your document. Probably the most basic change is to alter the margins in the document.

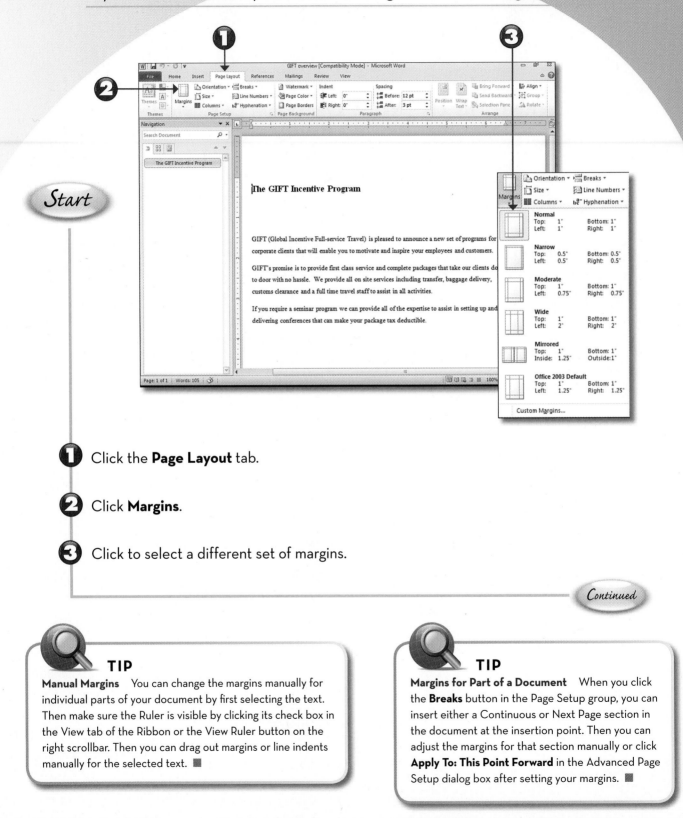

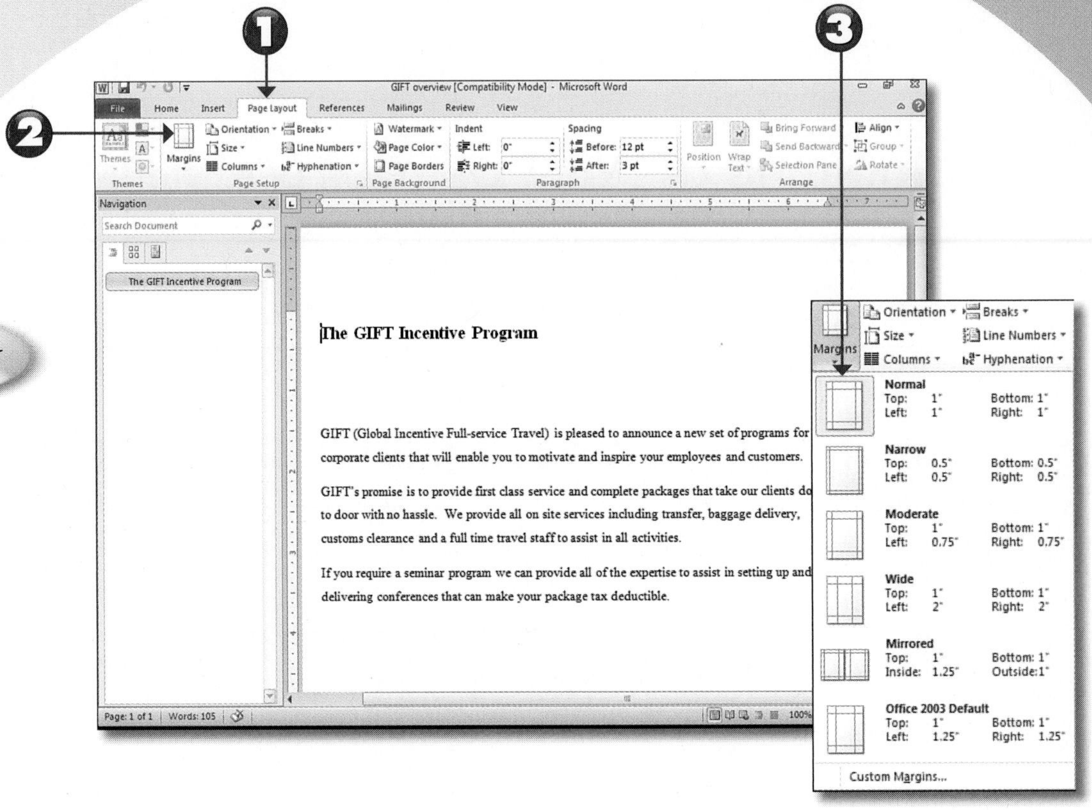

Start

1. Click the **Page Layout** tab.
2. Click **Margins**.
3. Click to select a different set of margins.

Continued

TIP

Manual Margins You can change the margins manually for individual parts of your document by first selecting the text. Then make sure the Ruler is visible by clicking its check box in the View tab of the Ribbon or the View Ruler button on the right scrollbar. Then you can drag out margins or line indents manually for the selected text. ■

TIP

Margins for Part of a Document When you click the **Breaks** button in the Page Setup group, you can insert either a Continuous or Next Page section in the document at the insertion point. Then you can adjust the margins for that section manually or click **Apply To: This Point Forward** in the Advanced Page Setup dialog box after setting your margins. ■

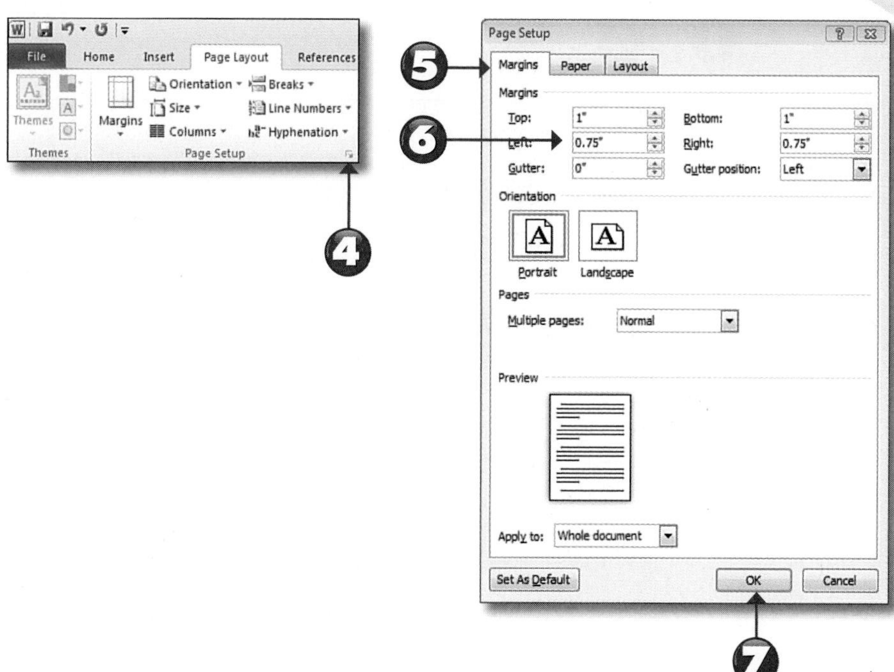

4 Click the **Dialog Launch** icon in the Page Setup group.

5 Click the **Margins** tab.

6 Change the margins.

7 Click **OK**.

End

TIP

Recent Templates The Recent Templates area shows you the various templates you've opened in the past. Using it is a good way to locate popular templates, particularly from Office.com, without searching through the various folders for them again. ■

CHANGING PAGE ORIENTATION

Some documents, like slide printouts or manuals, may look better in Landscape orientation so that they are wider than they are high. You can quickly change the page orientation in the Page Setup tab of the Ribbon.

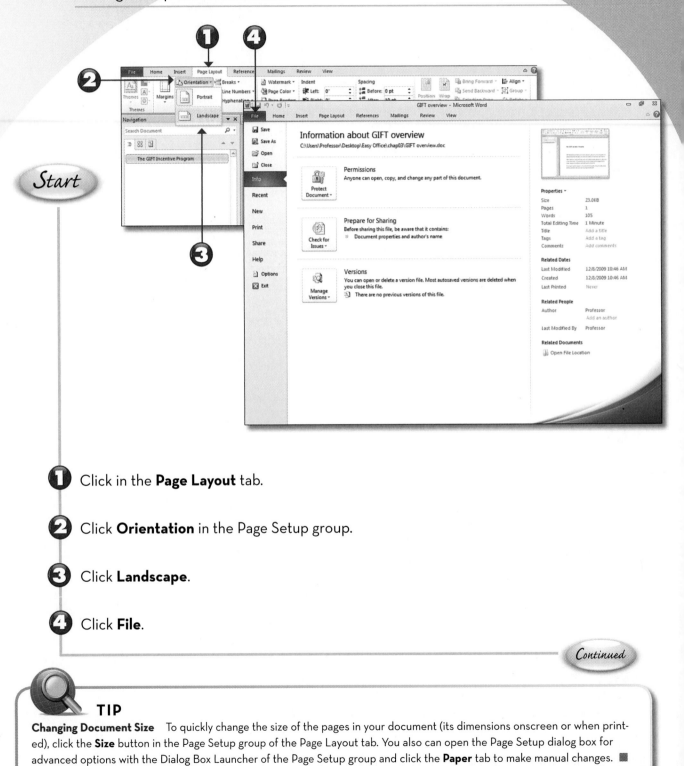

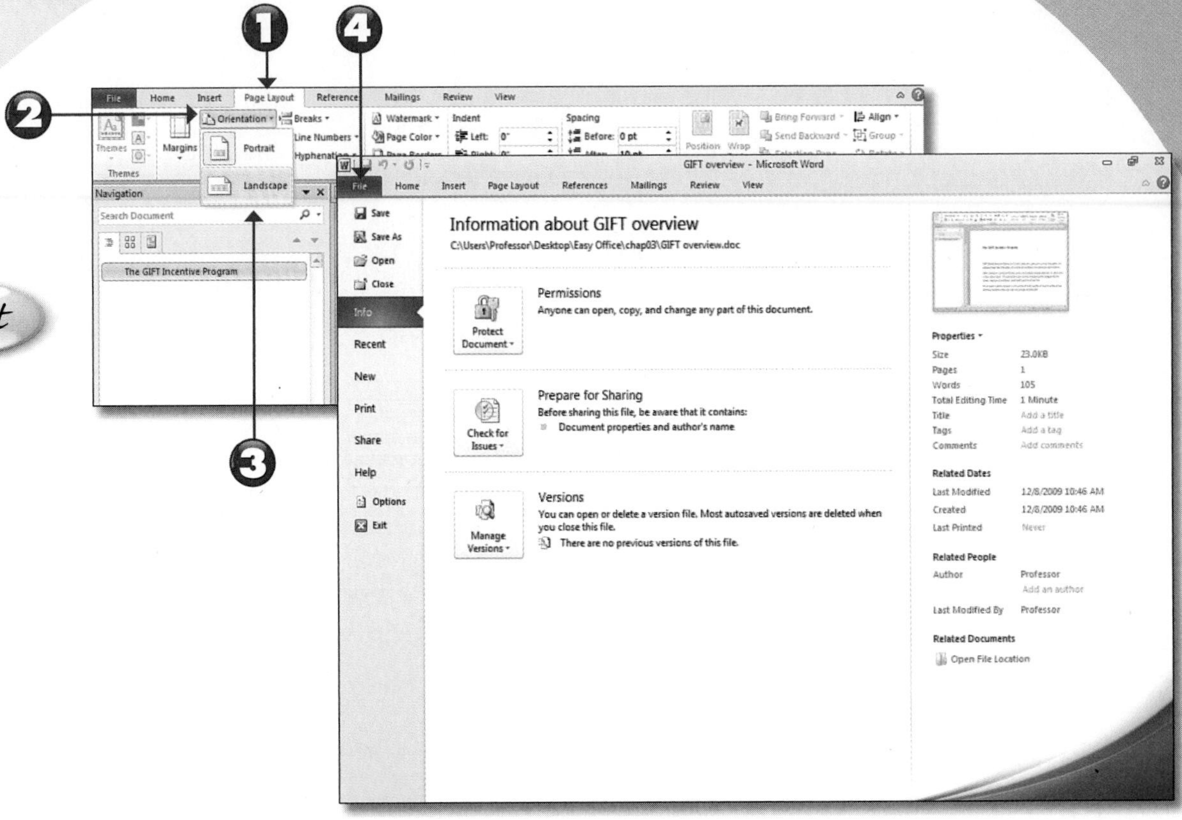

Start

1. Click in the **Page Layout** tab.
2. Click **Orientation** in the Page Setup group.
3. Click **Landscape**.
4. Click **File**.

Continued

TIP

Changing Document Size To quickly change the size of the pages in your document (its dimensions onscreen or when printed), click the **Size** button in the Page Setup group of the Page Layout tab. You also can open the Page Setup dialog box for advanced options with the Dialog Box Launcher of the Page Setup group and click the **Paper** tab to make manual changes.

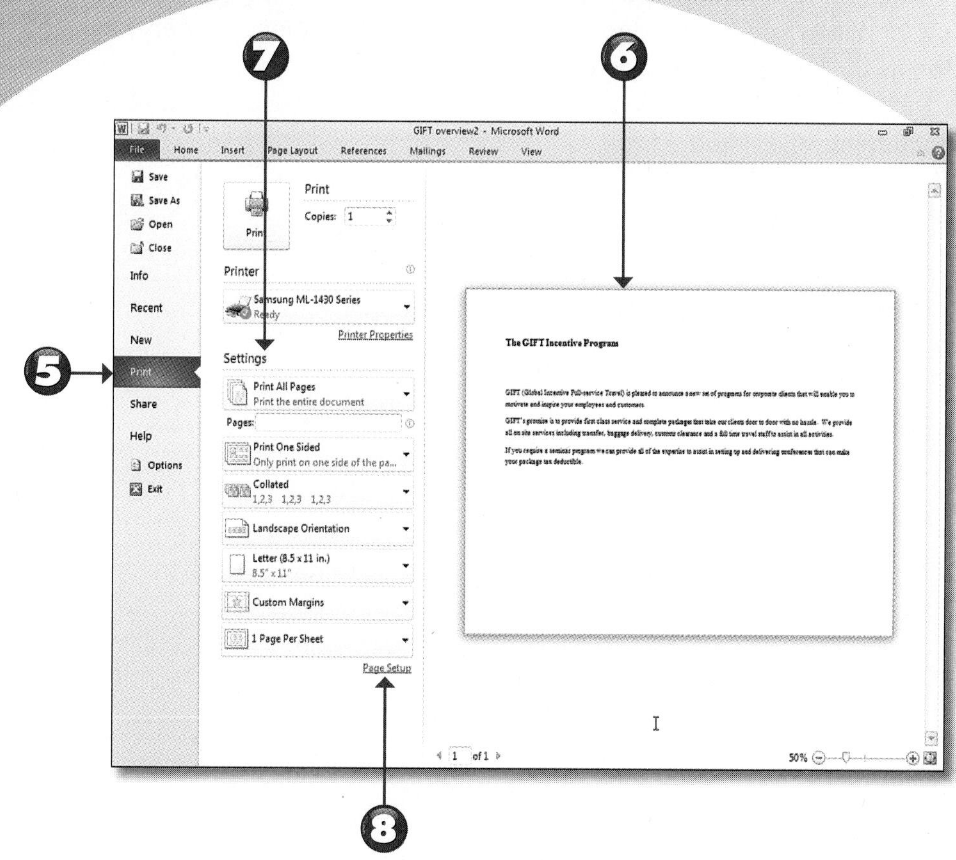

5 Click **Print**.

6 Print Preview confirms your document is in Landscape orientation.

7 Document settings are available for further revisions.

8 You can reopen Page Setup in Print Preview to change the setup of your document.

End

TIP

Viewing Multiple Pages If you have other pages in the document and want to see how two or more pages will look in the new orientation, click the **View** tab and select **Two Pages** in the Zoom group or use the zoom slider in the lower right of the document to zoom away from the document (decreasing the page display size). You can click **Page Width** in the Zoom group of the View tab to make your preview page fill the window again. ■

INSERTING PAGE NUMBERS

The Insert tab of the Ribbon gives you the option to quickly add page numbers at the bottom or at any place your documents. Page numbers become part of the footer (or header, as the case may be) and can be changed and repositioned in the Header & Footer Tools tab of the Ribbon, which opens when you create the page number or double-click in the document.

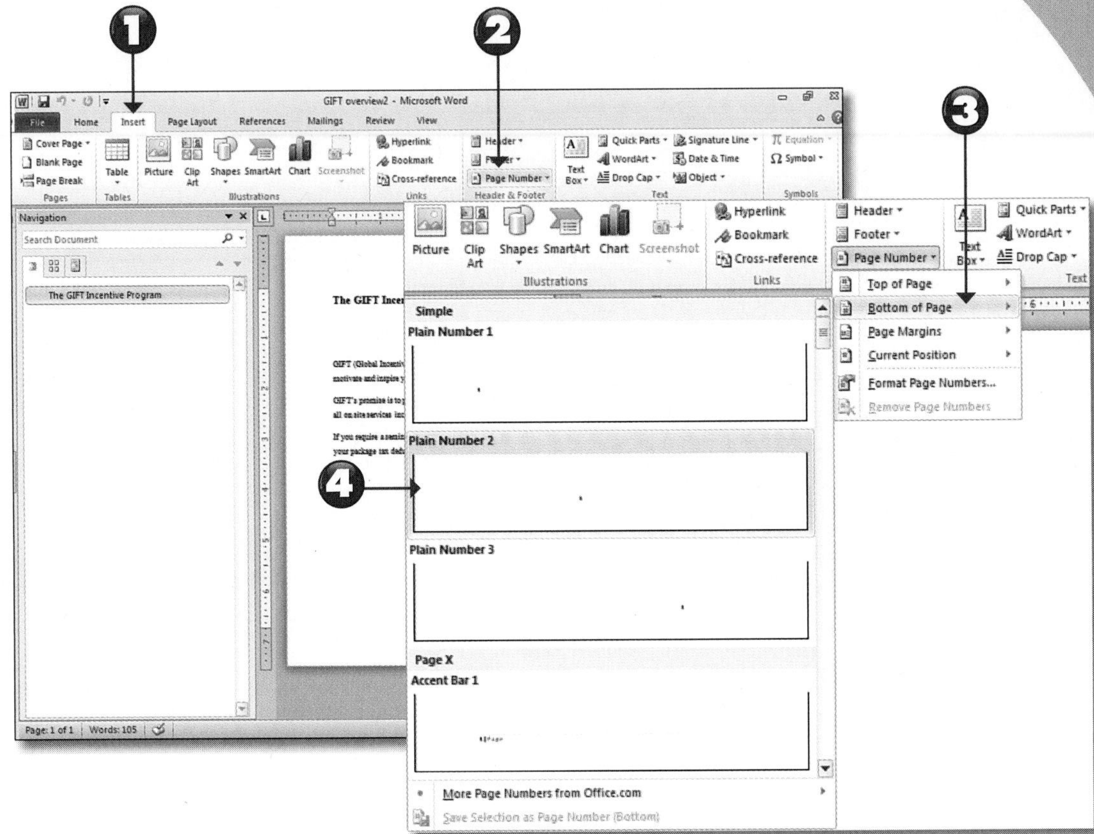

Start

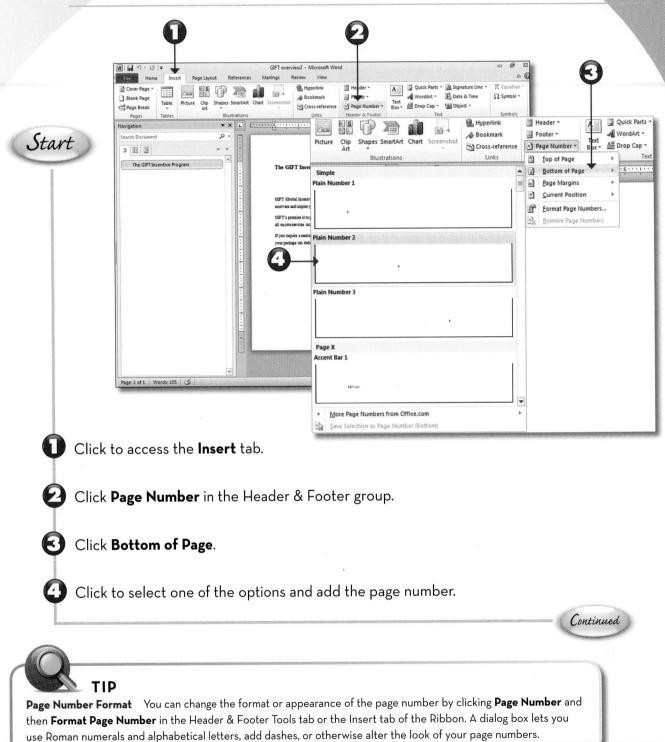

1. Click to access the **Insert** tab.
2. Click **Page Number** in the Header & Footer group.
3. Click **Bottom of Page**.
4. Click to select one of the options and add the page number.

Continued

TIP

Page Number Format You can change the format or appearance of the page number by clicking **Page Number** and then **Format Page Number** in the Header & Footer Tools tab or the Insert tab of the Ribbon. A dialog box lets you use Roman numerals and alphabetical letters, add dashes, or otherwise alter the look of your page numbers.

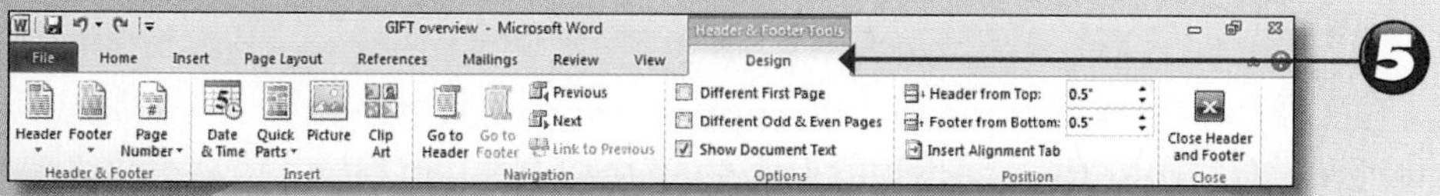

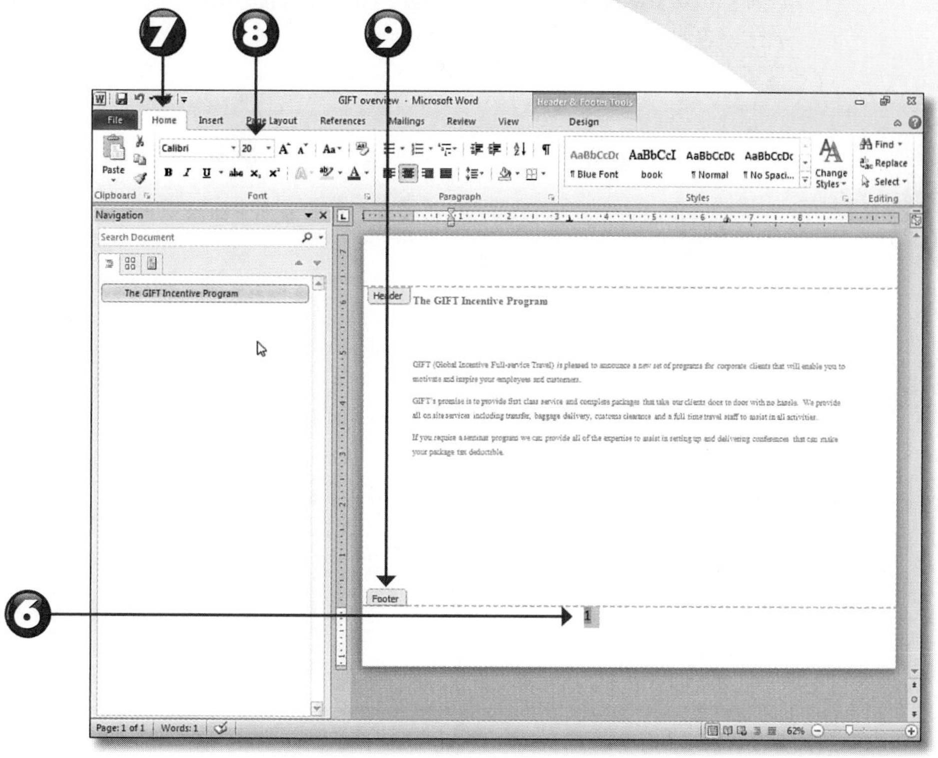

5 The Header & Footer Tools tab of the Ribbon opens in the Design tab.

6 Select the page number.

7 Click the **Home** tab of the Ribbon.

8 Click to change the font, font color, or font size of the page number.

9 Double-click the Footer or Header tabs (or click back in the main document) to close the Header & Footer.

End

TIP

Removing a Page Number The easiest way to remove a page number is to click **Footer** and then **Remove Footer** in the Header & Footer Tools tab.

35

INSERTING HEADERS AND FOOTERS

The Insert tab of the Ribbon gives you the option to quickly add headers and/or footers to your documents. A footer (or header, as the case may be) can be changed and repositioned in the Header & Footer Tools tab of the Ribbon, which opens when you create the header or footer or double-click it in the document.

Start

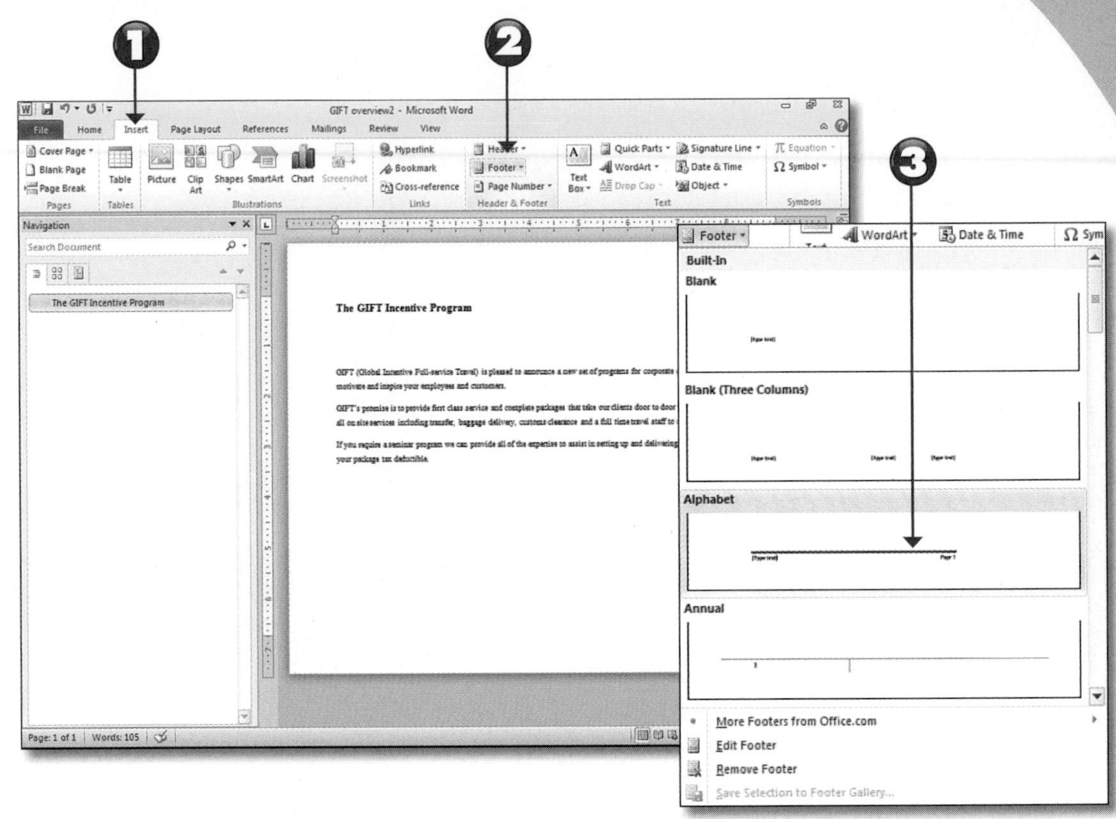

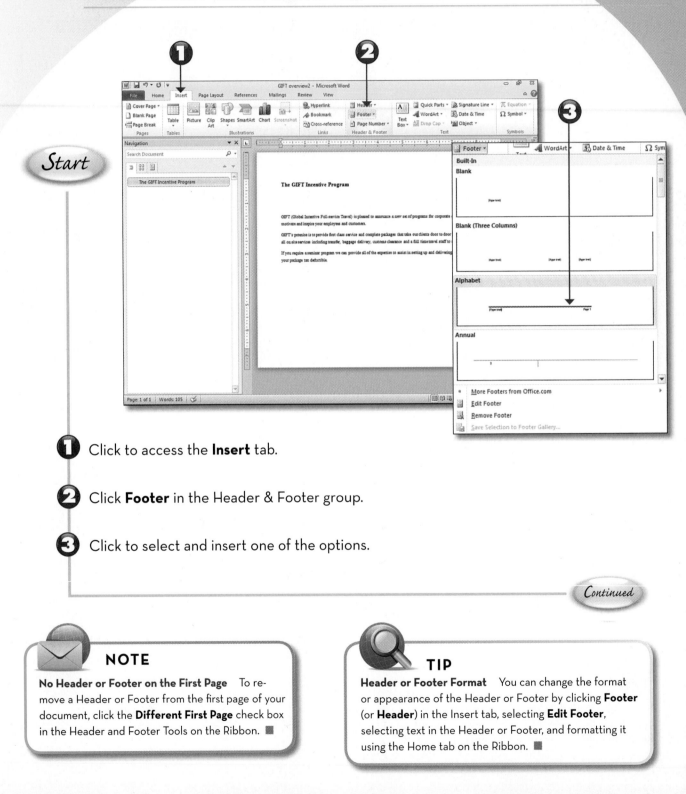

1. Click to access the **Insert** tab.

2. Click **Footer** in the Header & Footer group.

3. Click to select and insert one of the options.

Continued

NOTE

No Header or Footer on the First Page To remove a Header or Footer from the first page of your document, click the **Different First Page** check box in the Header and Footer Tools on the Ribbon. ■

TIP

Header or Footer Format You can change the format or appearance of the Header or Footer by clicking **Footer** (or **Header**) in the Insert tab, selecting **Edit Footer**, selecting text in the Header or Footer, and formatting it using the Home tab on the Ribbon. ■

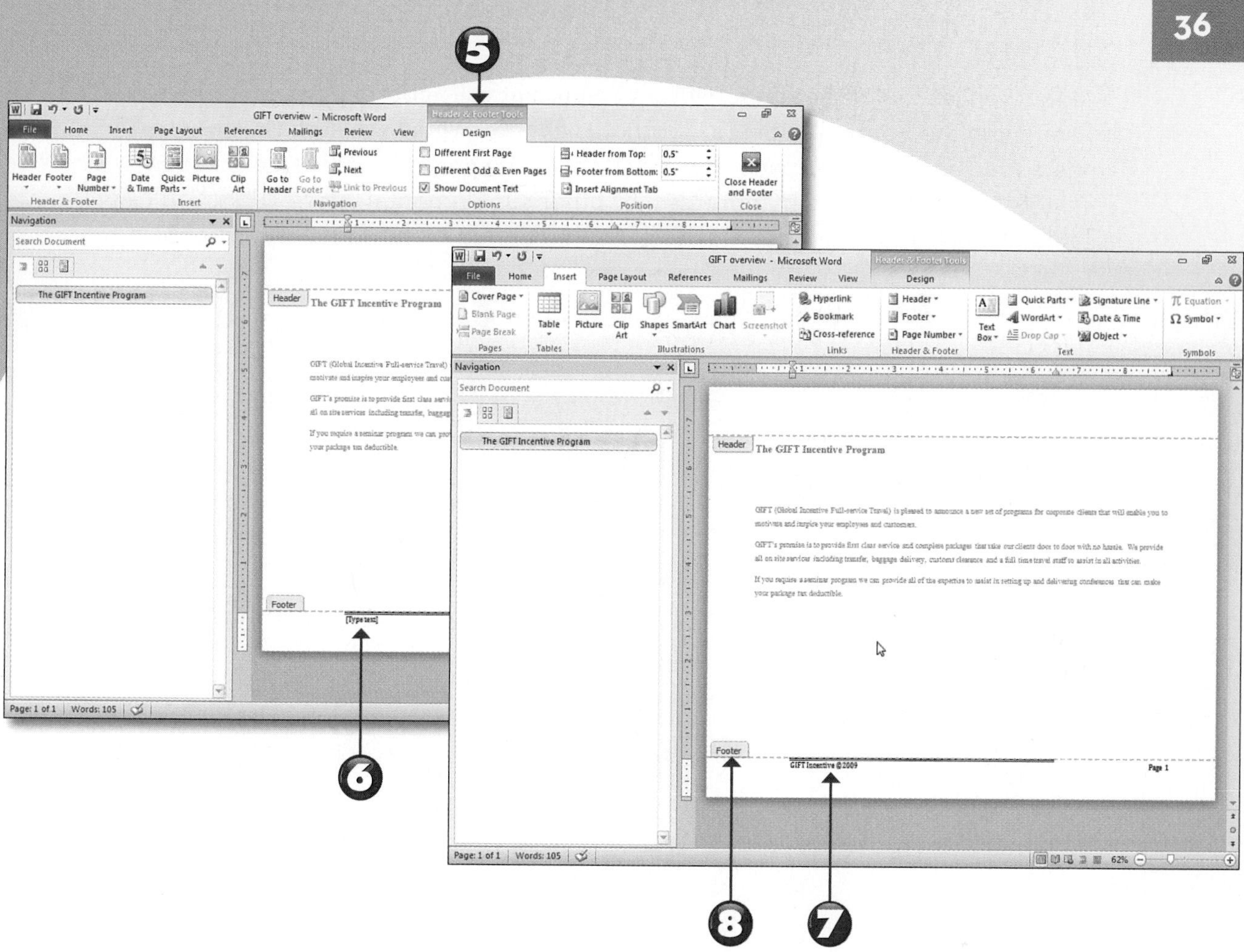

5 The Header & Footer Tools tab of the Ribbon opens in the **Design** tab.

6 Select the **Type Text** Content Control and replace the text.

7 Use your keyboard to replace or delete the Content Control text.

8 Double-click the **Footer** (or **Header**) tab or click in the main document to close the Header & Footer Tools tab.

End

TIP

More Page Header, Footer, and Number Styles Headers, footers, and page numbers are part of the Building Blocks Quick Parts in Office 2010. You can access more options by clicking **Quick Parts** in the Text group of the Insert tab and opening the Building Blocks Organizer. We cover this feature in more detail in Chapter 4, "Changing Project Appearance."

TIP

Removing a Header or Footer To a remove a footer (or header), click **Footer** and **Remove Footer** (or click **Header** and **Remove Header**).

ADDING FOOTNOTES AND ENDNOTES

The References tab of the Ribbon lets you automatically add footnotes or endnotes to your document in the Footnotes group. Footnotes and Endnotes will automatically renumber when added and provide space at the bottom of the page (Footnote) or end of the document (Endnote) for citations, web addresses, or other supplemental information. You can also add a Table of Contents using your Headings from features in the Table of Contents group.

Start

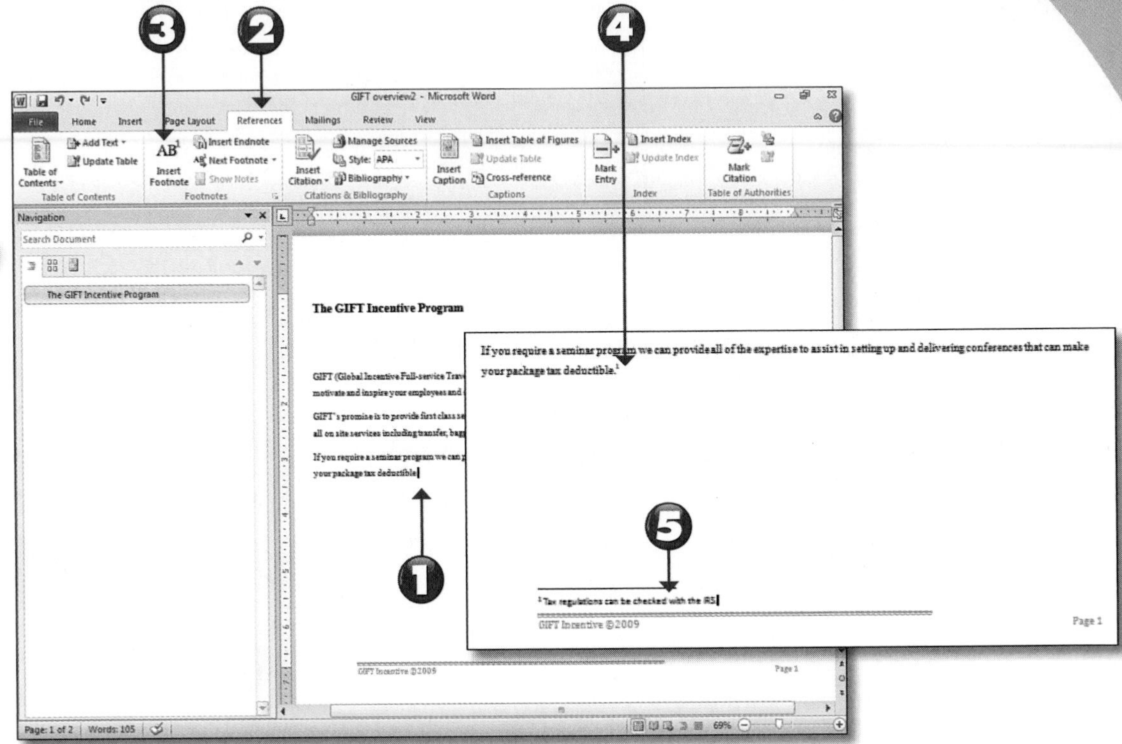

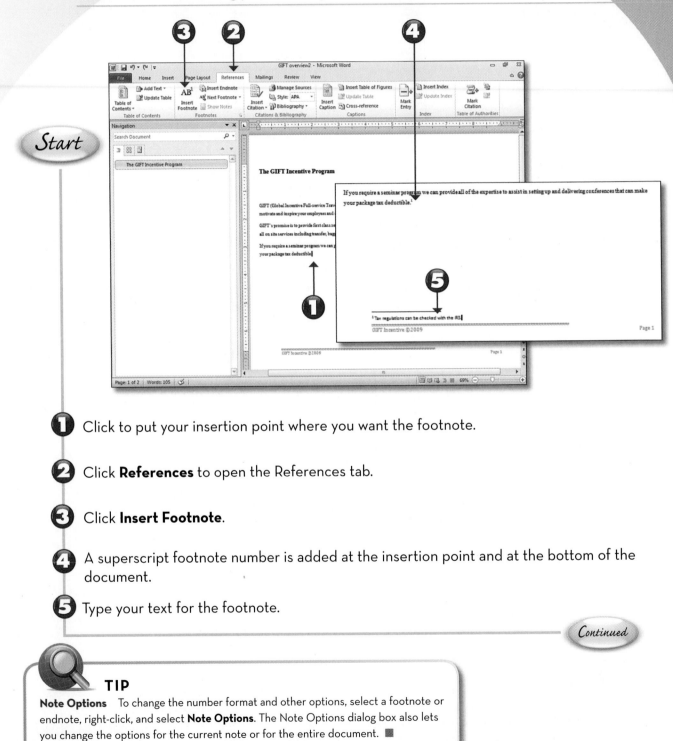

1. Click to put your insertion point where you want the footnote.
2. Click **References** to open the References tab.
3. Click **Insert Footnote**.
4. A superscript footnote number is added at the insertion point and at the bottom of the document.
5. Type your text for the footnote.

Continued

TIP

Note Options To change the number format and other options, select a footnote or endnote, right-click, and select **Note Options**. The Note Options dialog box also lets you change the options for the current note or for the entire document. ■

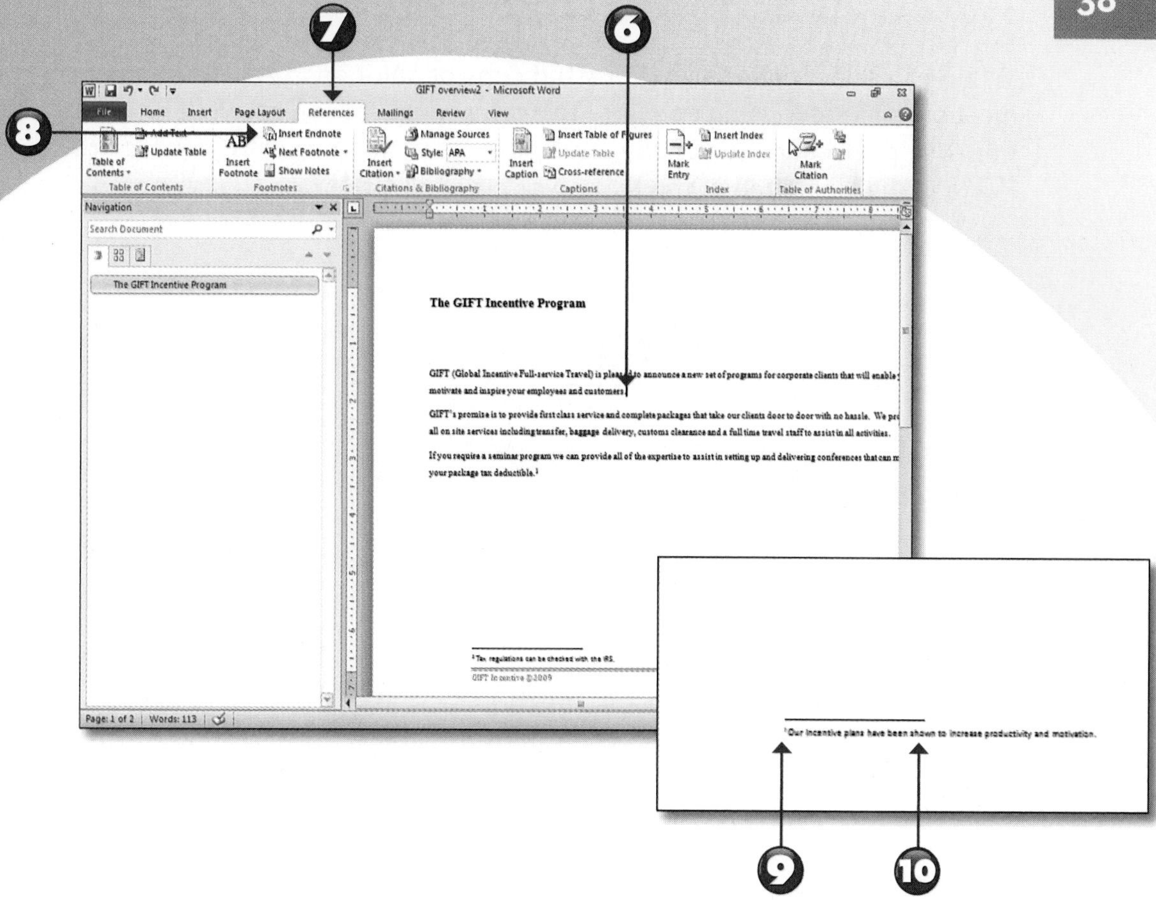

6 Click to put your insertion point where you want the endnote.

7 Click **References** to open the References tab.

8 Click **Insert Endnote**.

9 A superscript endnote number is added at the insertion point at the end of the document.

10 Type your text for the endnote.

End

TIP

Moving Through Your Footnotes or Endnotes You can move through the document by the next footnote or endnote by clicking the drop-down arrow next to **Next Footnote** in the Footnotes group in the References tab of the Ribbon.

USING COPY AND PASTE PREVIEW

When you select material in Word and copy or cut it and then click to paste it in another location, a context menu appears. You can choose Keep Source Formatting, Merge Formatting, Use the Destination Theme, or Keep Text Only. You can use Paste Preview by clicking **Paste** in the Home tab of the Ribbon or pressing **Ctrl+V** on the keyboard.

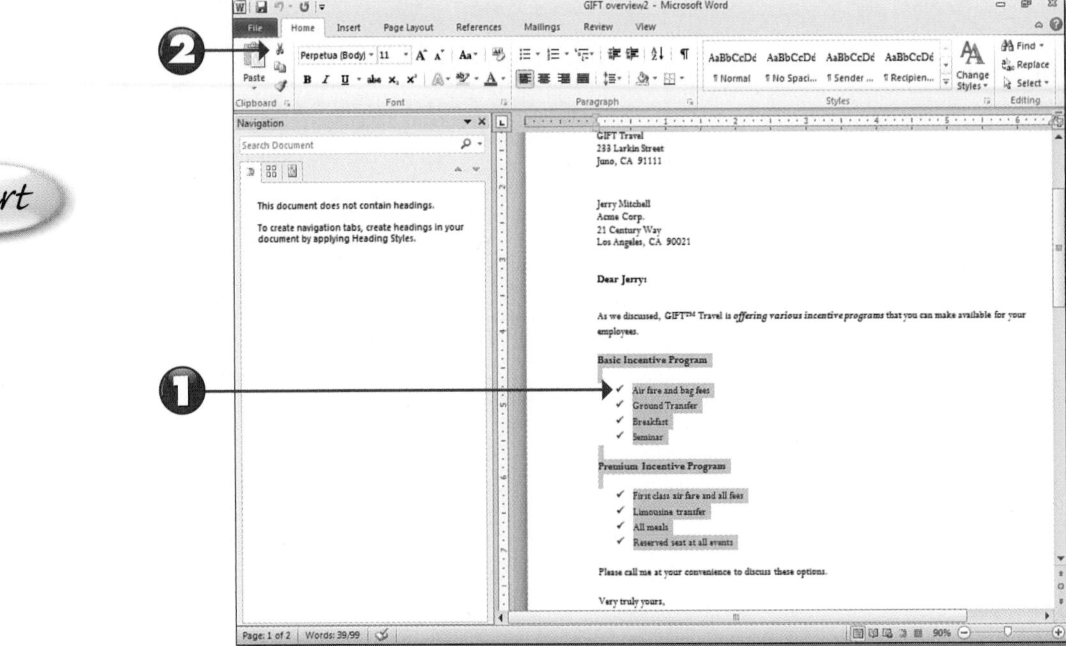

Start

1. Select the text you want to copy or cut.

2. Click **Copy** or click **Cut** on the Home tab of the Ribbon (or press **Ctrl+C** for Copy or **Ctrl+X** for Cut).

Continued

TIP

Taking Advantage of Text If the preview options shown in the Paste Preview don't work, **Keep Text Only** is the easiest way to use the formatting features of Word for more changes. ■

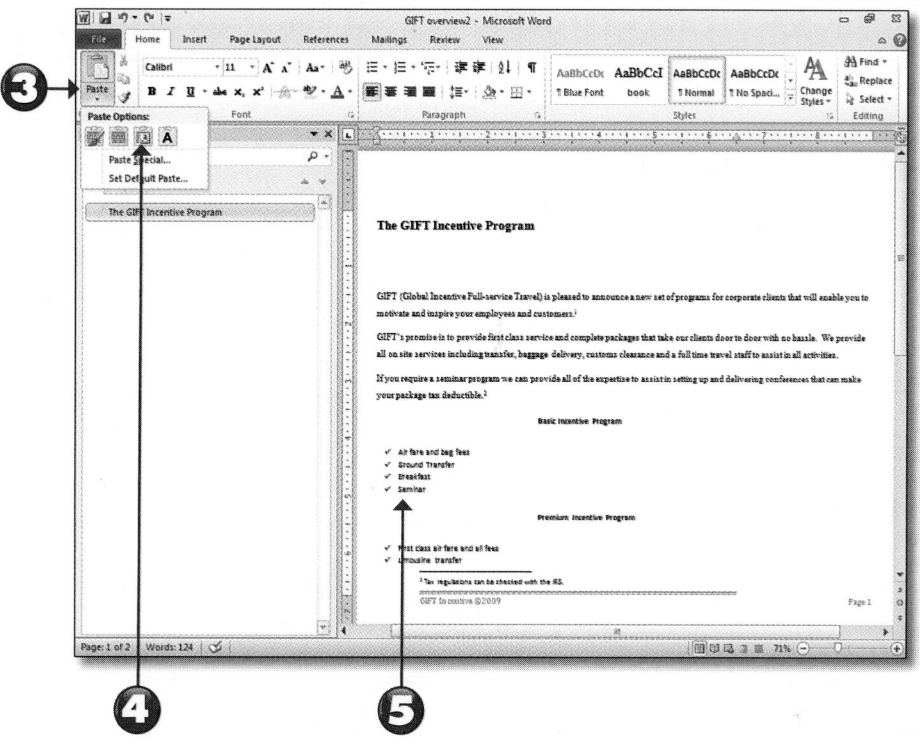

3 Where you want to put the text, click **Paste** in the Home tab of the Ribbon.

4 In the Paste Preview pop-up menu, hover your mouse over Keep Source Formatting, Merge Formatting, Use the Destination Theme, and Keep Text Only for a live preview of how the pasted text will look.

5 Watch the previews change and click the icon for your choice to paste the text.

Continued

TIP

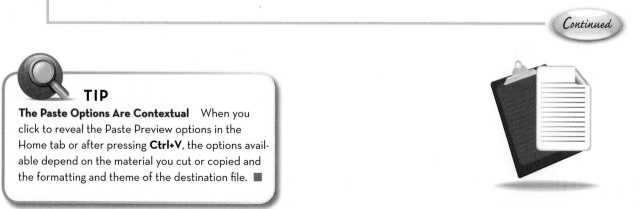

The Paste Options Are Contextual When you click to reveal the Paste Preview options in the Home tab or after pressing **Ctrl+V**, the options available depend on the material you cut or copied and the formatting and theme of the destination file.

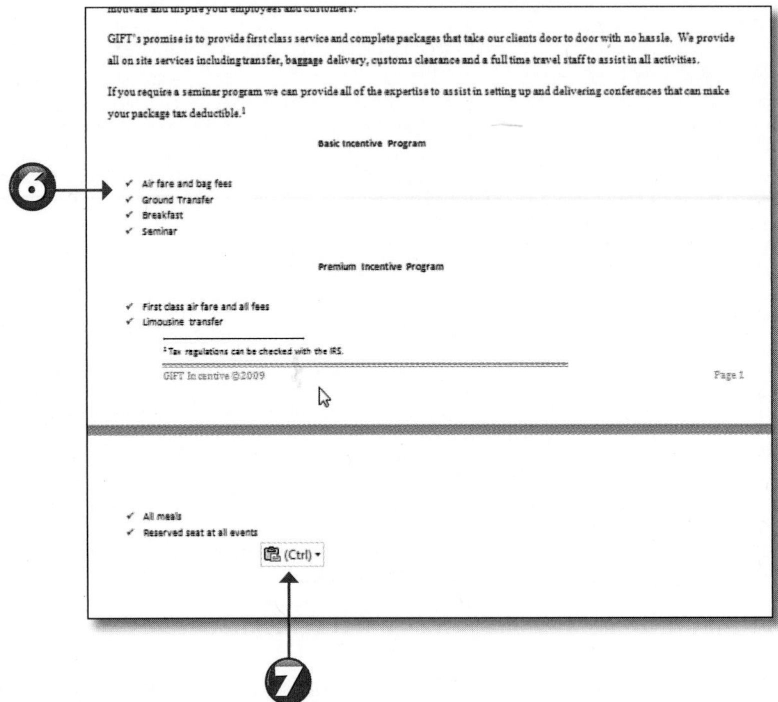
GIFT's promise is to provide first class service and complete packages that take our clients door to door with no hassle. We provide all on site services including transfer, baggage delivery, customs clearance and a full time travel staff to assist in all activities.

If you require a seminar program we can provide all of the expertise to assist in setting up and delivering conferences that can make your package tax deductible.[1]

Basic Incentive Program

- Air fare and bag fees
- Ground Transfer
- Breakfast
- Seminar

Premium Incentive Program

- First class air fare and all fees
- Limousine transfer

[1] Tax regulations can be checked with the IRS.

GIFT Incentive ©2009 Page 1

- All meals
- Reserved seat at all events

6 To use the keyboard instead of the Ribbon, at the location where you want the copied or cut text, press **Ctrl+V**.

7 Click the **Clipboard** icon or its arrow.

Continued

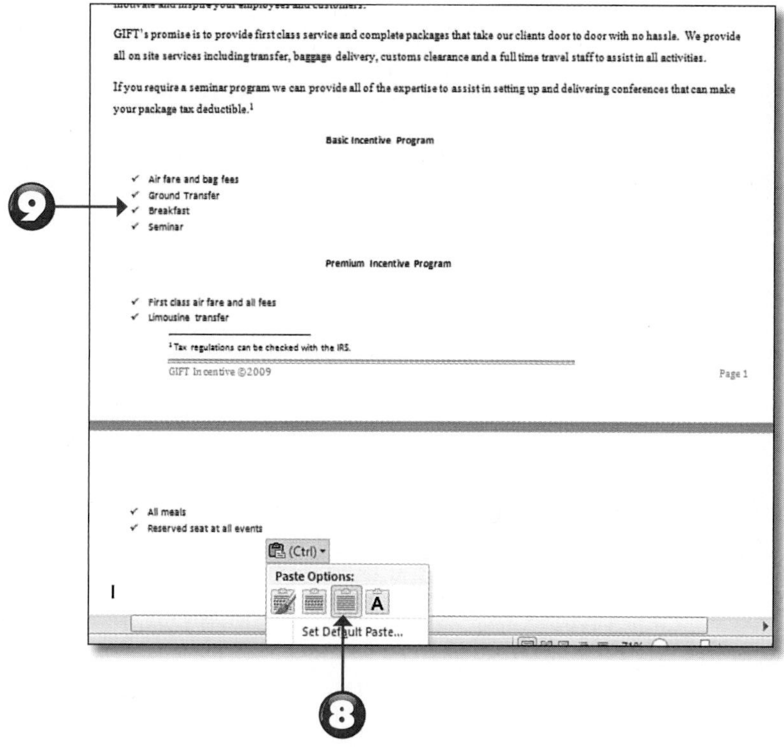

GIFT's promise is to provide first class service and complete packages that take our clients door to door with no hassle. We provide all on site services including transfer, baggage delivery, customs clearance and a full time travel staff to assist in all activities.
If you require a seminar program we can provide all of the expertise to assist in setting up and delivering conferences that can make your package tax deductible.
Basic Incentive Program
Air fare and bag fees
Ground Transfer
Breakfast
Seminar
Premium Incentive Program
First class air fare and all fees
Limousine transfer
Tax regulations can be checked with the IRS.
GIFT Incentive ©2009
Page 1
All meals
Reserved seat at all events
(Ctrl)
Paste Options:
Set Default Paste...
9
8

8 In the Paste Preview pop-up menu, hover your mouse over Keep Source Formatting, Merge Formatting, Use the Destination Styles, and Keep Text Only.

9 See a live preview of how the pasted text will look and then click the icon for your choice to paste the text.

End

TIP

Set Default Paste You can choose the various options that happen by default when you click Paste by choosing **Set Default Paste**. You can also access and change these options by clicking **File**, choosing **Options** in Backstage view, and clicking **Advanced**. You can select options for the default action when clicking Cut, Copy, or Paste. ■

CREATING COLUMNS IN A LONGER DOCUMENT OR NEWSLETTER

To break up the text into columns for a newsletter or brochure, you can use the Columns presets in the Page Setup group of the Page Layout tab of the Ribbon or fine-tune the look of your columns by using the options in More Columns.

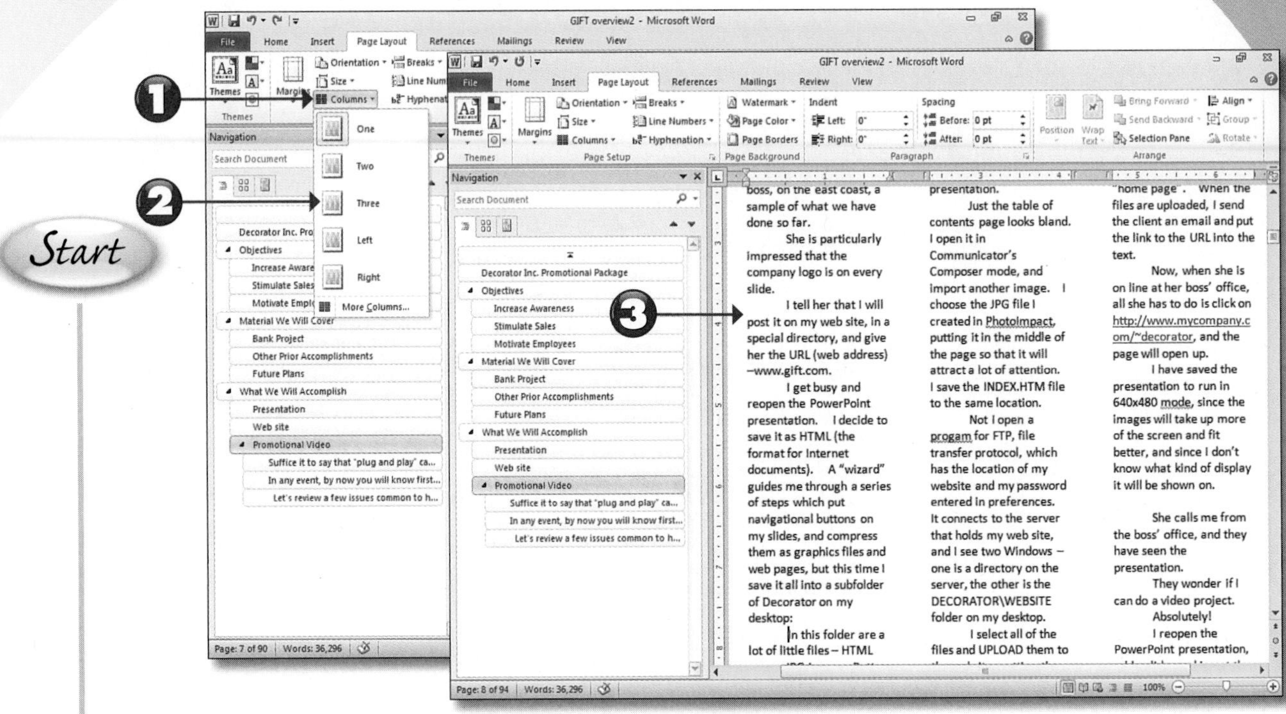

Start

1. Click **Columns** in the Page Layout tab of the Ribbon.
2. Select to apply one of the column presets.
3. The document is broken up into the columns you selected.

Continued

TIP

Adjusting Columns Manually When columns are created in a document, you can drag to adjust their widths manually in each of their individual segments in the Ruler at the top of the page. (If the Ruler is not open, click the View tab of the Ribbon and click the **Ruler** check box. ■

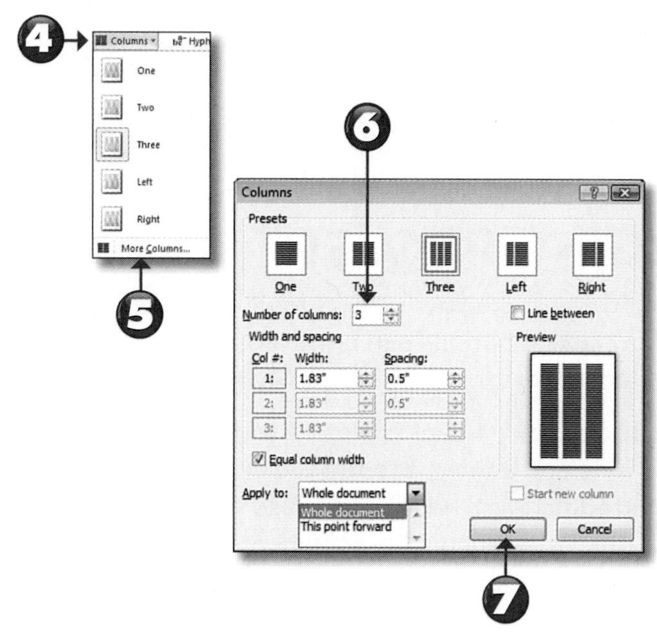

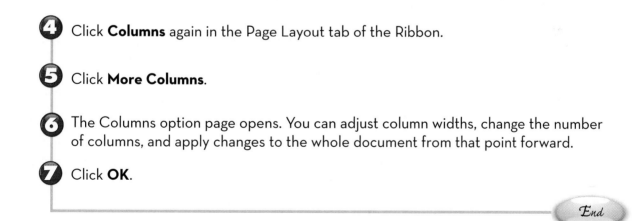

4. Click **Columns** again in the Page Layout tab of the Ribbon.
5. Click **More Columns**.
6. The Columns option page opens. You can adjust column widths, change the number of columns, and apply changes to the whole document from that point forward.
7. Click **OK**.

End

TIP

More Columns Options In the More Columns options page, you can click a check box to place lines between your columns and preview the look of your columns as you change the options.

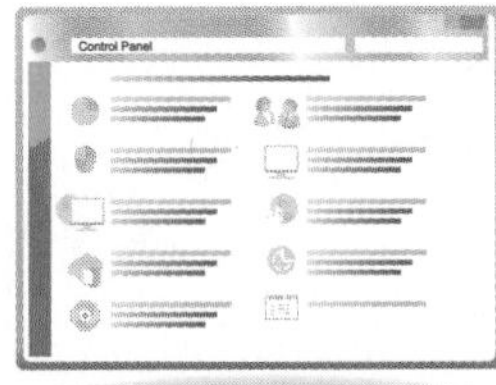

CHANGING PROJECT APPEARANCE

Microsoft Word can make your project look like much more than an ordinary document. Formatting options can be saved and reused as styles and quickly applied to selected text from the Quick Styles gallery.

You can create your own Quick Styles by formatting your own text and then saving it as a style and adding it to the Quick Styles gallery. You can also select certain formatted text as a heading and use it in the Navigation pane to see main topics or move through your document. Or you can generate a Table of Contents in the References tab of the Ribbon.

Formatting that you have applied in one area of the document can be copied elsewhere by using the Format Painter, a very handy tool.

Portions of a document can also be added from the Quick Parts gallery, including AutoText selections and cover pages. After you've put a project together, you can apply a theme, which is composed of fonts, colors, and effects (more about effects in Chapter 6, "Working with Graphics and Effects"), to change the look of the entire document from the Page Layout tab of the Ribbon.

WORKING WITH STYLES

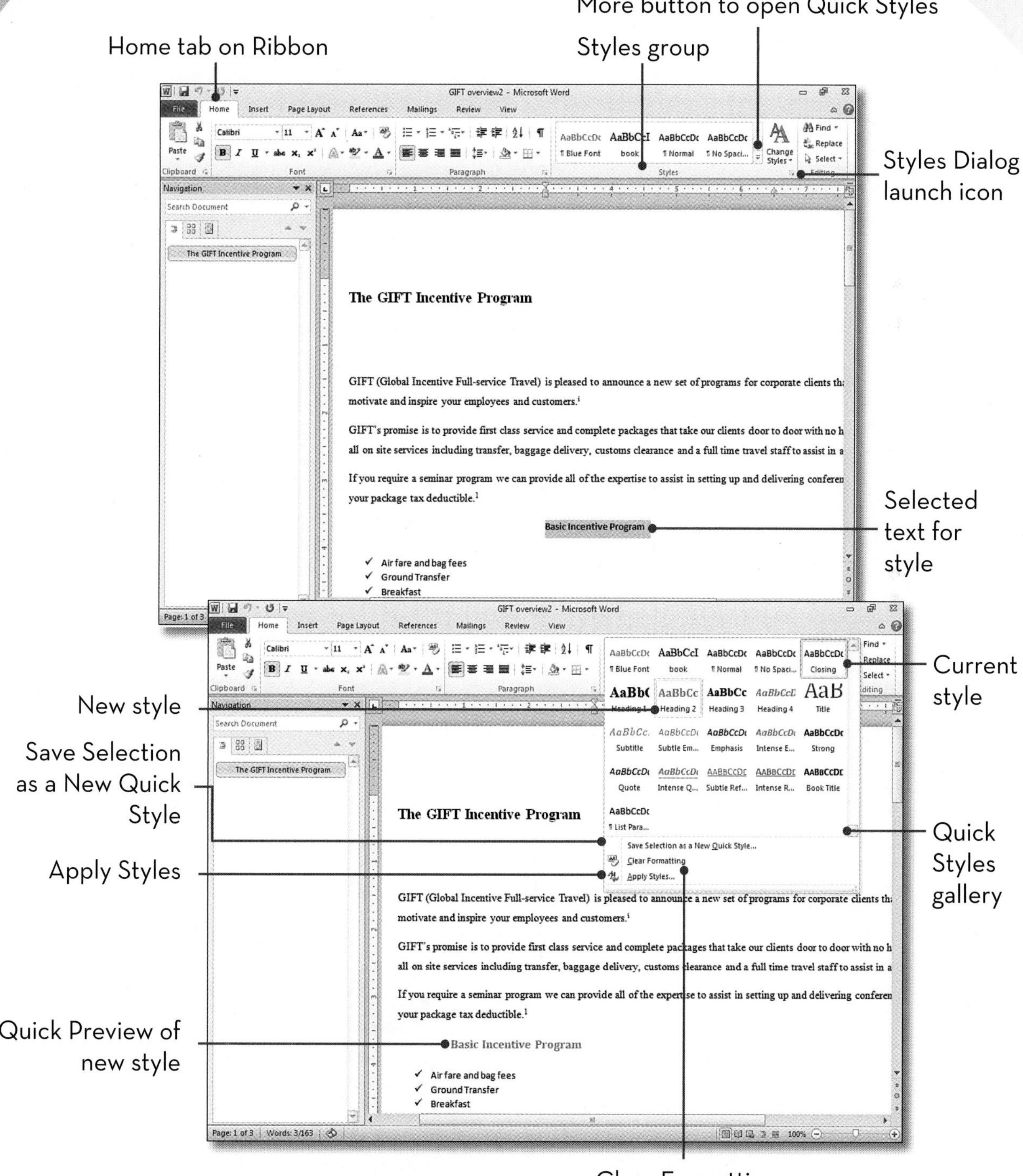

More button to open Quick Styles
Home tab on Ribbon
Styles group
Styles Dialog launch icon
Selected text for style
Current style
New style
Save Selection as a New Quick Style
Apply Styles
Quick Styles gallery
Quick Preview of new style
Clear Formatting
GIFT overview2 - Microsoft Word
The GIFT Incentive Program
GIFT (Global Incentive Full-service Travel) is pleased to announce a new set of programs for corporate clients th
motivate and inspire your employees and customers.
GIFT's promise is to provide first class service and complete packages that take our clients door to door with no h
all on site services including transfer, baggage delivery, customs clearance and a full time travel staff to assist in a
If you require a seminar program we can provide all of the expertise to assist in setting up and delivering conferen
your package tax deductible.
Basic Incentive Program
Air fare and bag fees
Ground Transfer
Breakfast
Save Selection as a New Quick Style...
Clear Formatting
Apply Styles...

APPLYING A QUICK STYLE

The easiest way to apply a style is to select your text and choose a style from the Quick Styles gallery. Before clicking to a apply a style, hover your mouse over the styles to see a Quick Preview of how the selected text would look if the style is applied. You can also click the **Dialog Launch** icon for the Styles Group to open all the styles available for the document. Here you can apply a style or add or remove a style from the Quick Styles gallery.

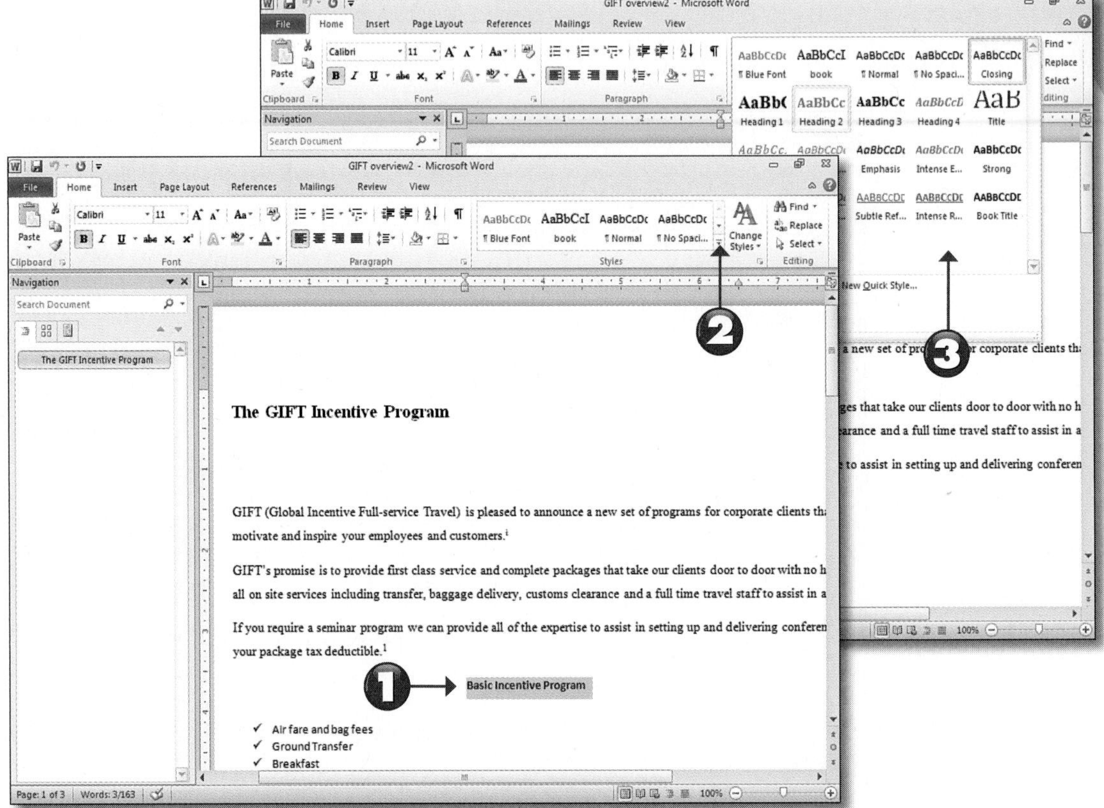

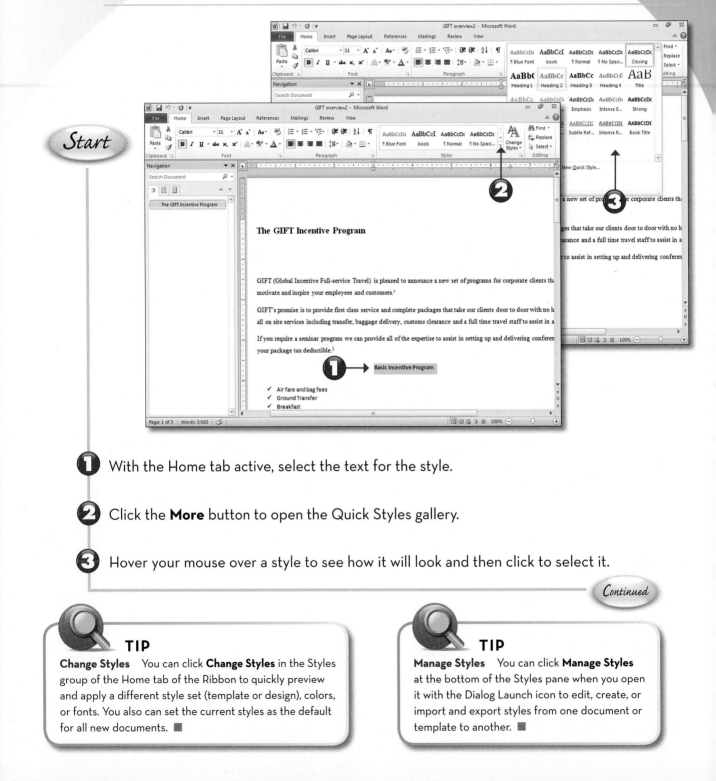

Start

1. With the Home tab active, select the text for the style.
2. Click the **More** button to open the Quick Styles gallery.
3. Hover your mouse over a style to see how it will look and then click to select it.

Continued

TIP

Change Styles You can click **Change Styles** in the Styles group of the Home tab of the Ribbon to quickly preview and apply a different style set (template or design), colors, or fonts. You also can set the current styles as the default for all new documents. ■

TIP

Manage Styles You can click **Manage Styles** at the bottom of the Styles pane when you open it with the Dialog Launch icon to edit, create, or import and export styles from one document or template to another. ■

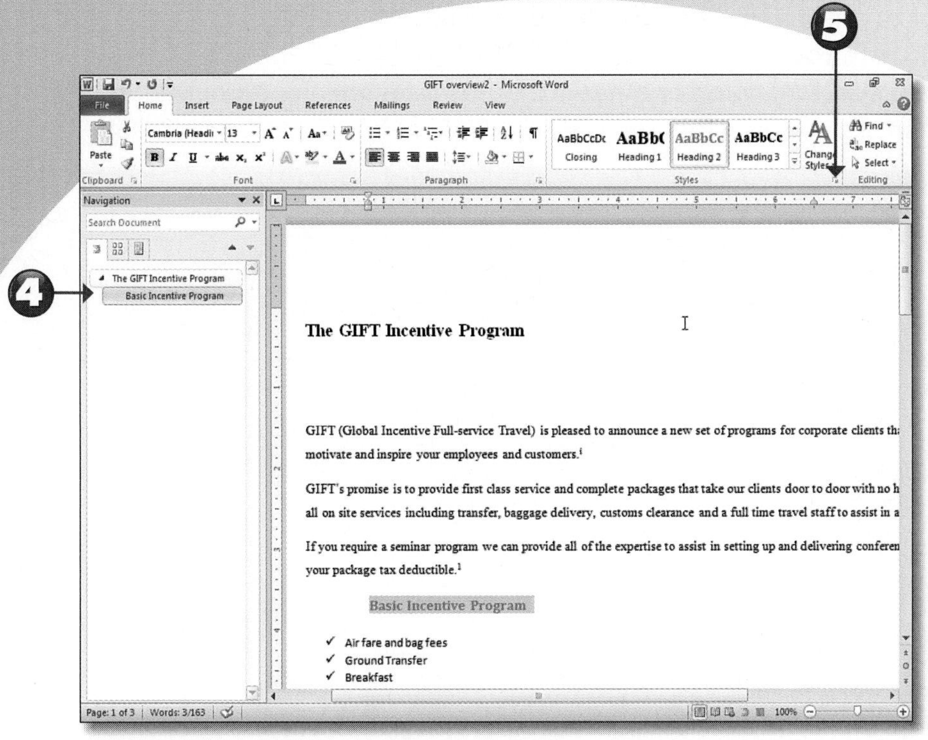

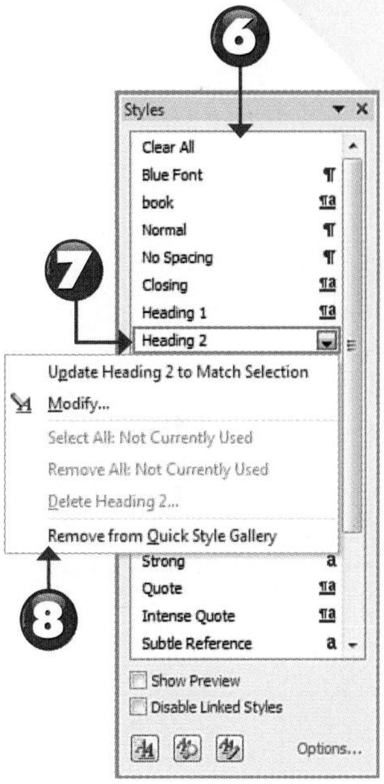

4 The Heading 2 text appears in the Navigation pane indented below Heading 1.

5 Click the **Styles Dialog Launch** icon.

6 All available styles are shown for the document in a manner similar to earlier versions of Word.

7 Click the drop-down arrow for a style.

8 Options include adding or removing the style from the Quick Styles gallery and modifying the style.

End

TIP

Style Pane Options To revise settings for how styles are displayed in the Styles pane, you can click **Options** at the bottom of the window. You can change the list from Recommended to All Styles to see a greater set of all possible styles. ■

CREATING A QUICK STYLE

Select the text for the new style. You can create your own styles to include in the Quick Styles gallery. To create your own style, select the text you want to be in the new style, modify its font, font size, font color, or other attributes using the Font group of the Home tab of the Ribbon. Then click **Save Selection as a New Quick Style** from the Quick Styles gallery.

Start

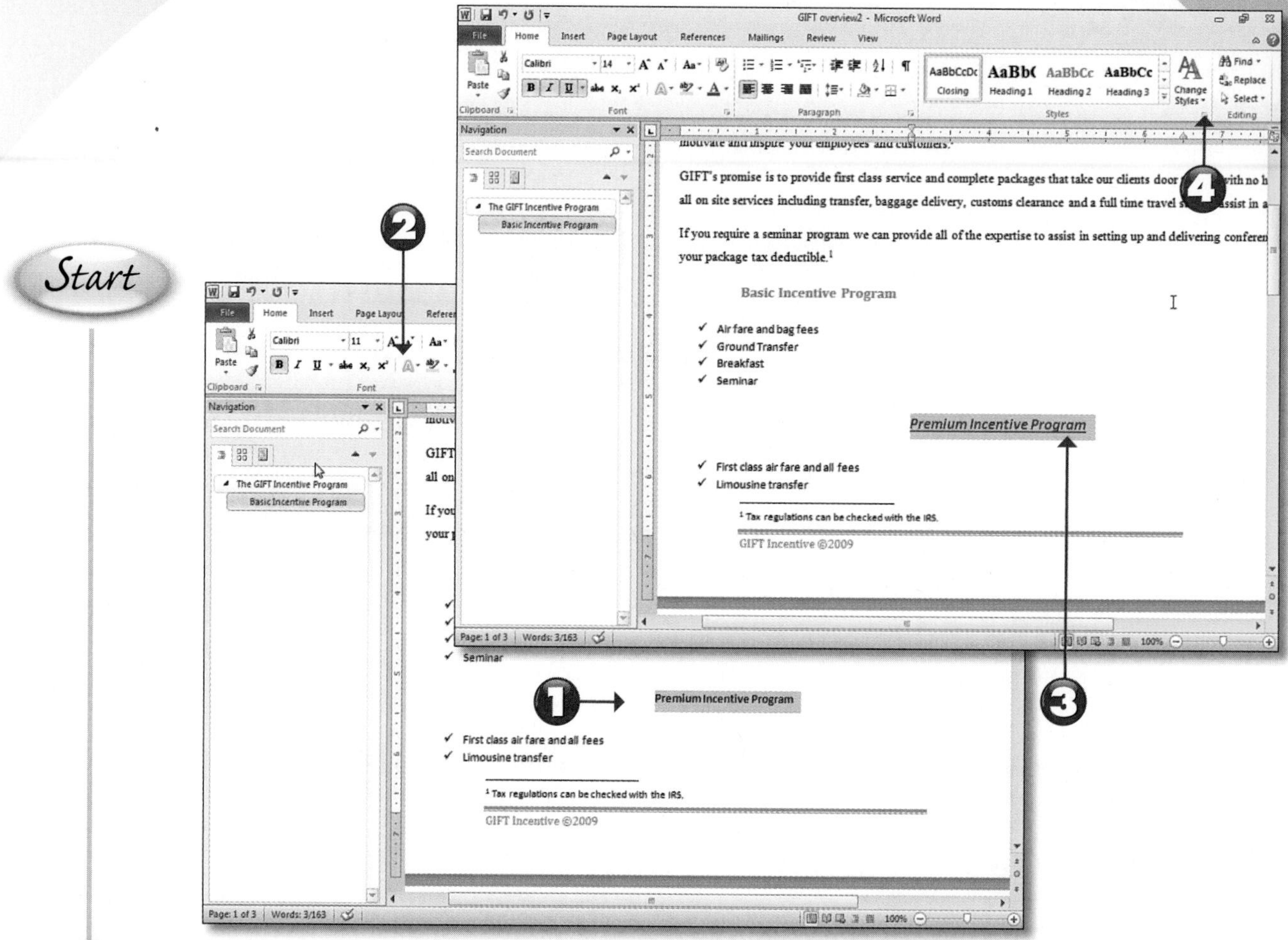

1. Select the text for the new style.
2. In the Home tab, change the text format by using the features of the Font group.
3. The text reflects the changes for the new style.
4. Click the **More** button to open the Quick Styles gallery.

Continued

TIP

Remove Styles from the Quick Styles Gallery To quickly remove a style from the gallery, right-click it and click **Remove from Quick Styles Gallery**. The new style will still be in the Styles pane if you click the **Dialog Launch** icon for Styles. ■

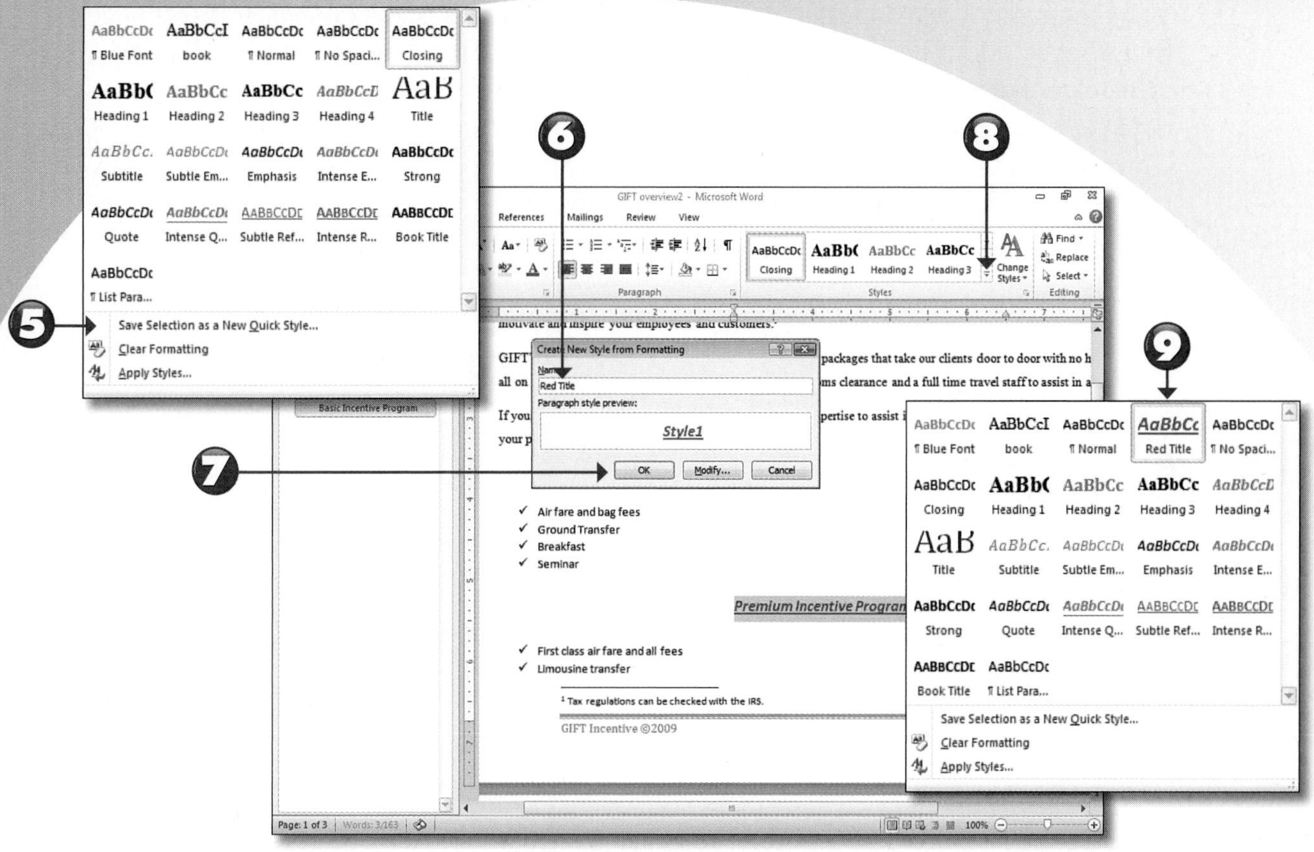

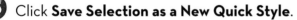

5. Click **Save Selection as a New Quick Style**.

6. Name your new style.

7. Click **OK**.

8. Click the **More** button to open the Quick Styles gallery.

9. Your new Quick Style is available to use in your document.

End

TIP

Creating a New Style from Formatting When you open the window to name your new style or click **Save Selection as a New Quick Style** in the Quick Styles gallery, you can click **Modify** to change the attributes of your newly named style. In the Create a New Style from Formatting expanded window, you can choose to add or not add the style to the Quick Styles gallery, keep the style only in the current document, or update any documents based on a template created from the current document. ■

MODIFYING A QUICK STYLE

You can modify the attributes of any Quick Style in the Quick Styles gallery to change the font, font size, font color, its name, or any other attributes of the style. After changing the style, click **Automatically Update** so that all instances of that style in the document update to reflect those changes. You can also create a template based on the document (see "Revising the Letter Template" in Chapter 2, "Beginning a New Word Project") so that documents based on that template also reflect the newly formatted style.

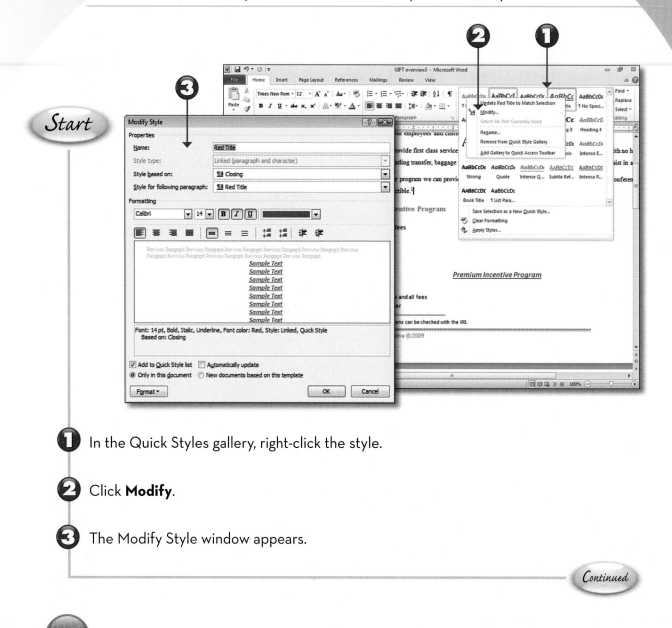

Start

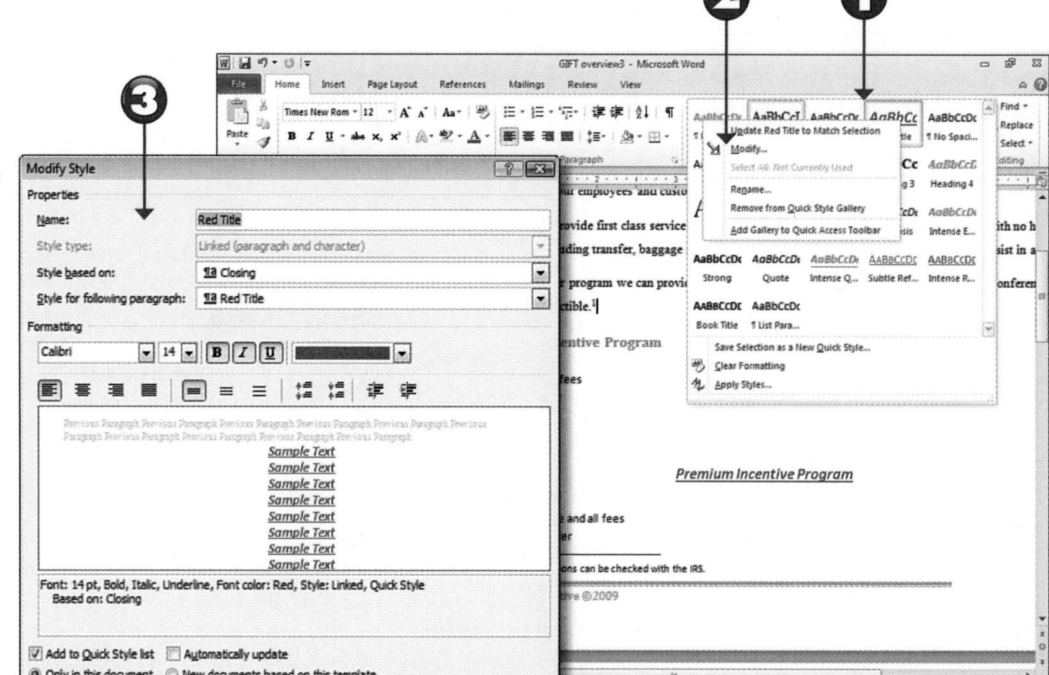

1. In the Quick Styles gallery, right-click the style.
2. Click **Modify**.
3. The Modify Style window appears.

NOTE

Update Style to Match Selection You can also modify a style by selecting it in the document, modifying its formatting, and then right-clicking the style in the Quick Styles gallery and choosing **Update Style to Match Selection**. ■

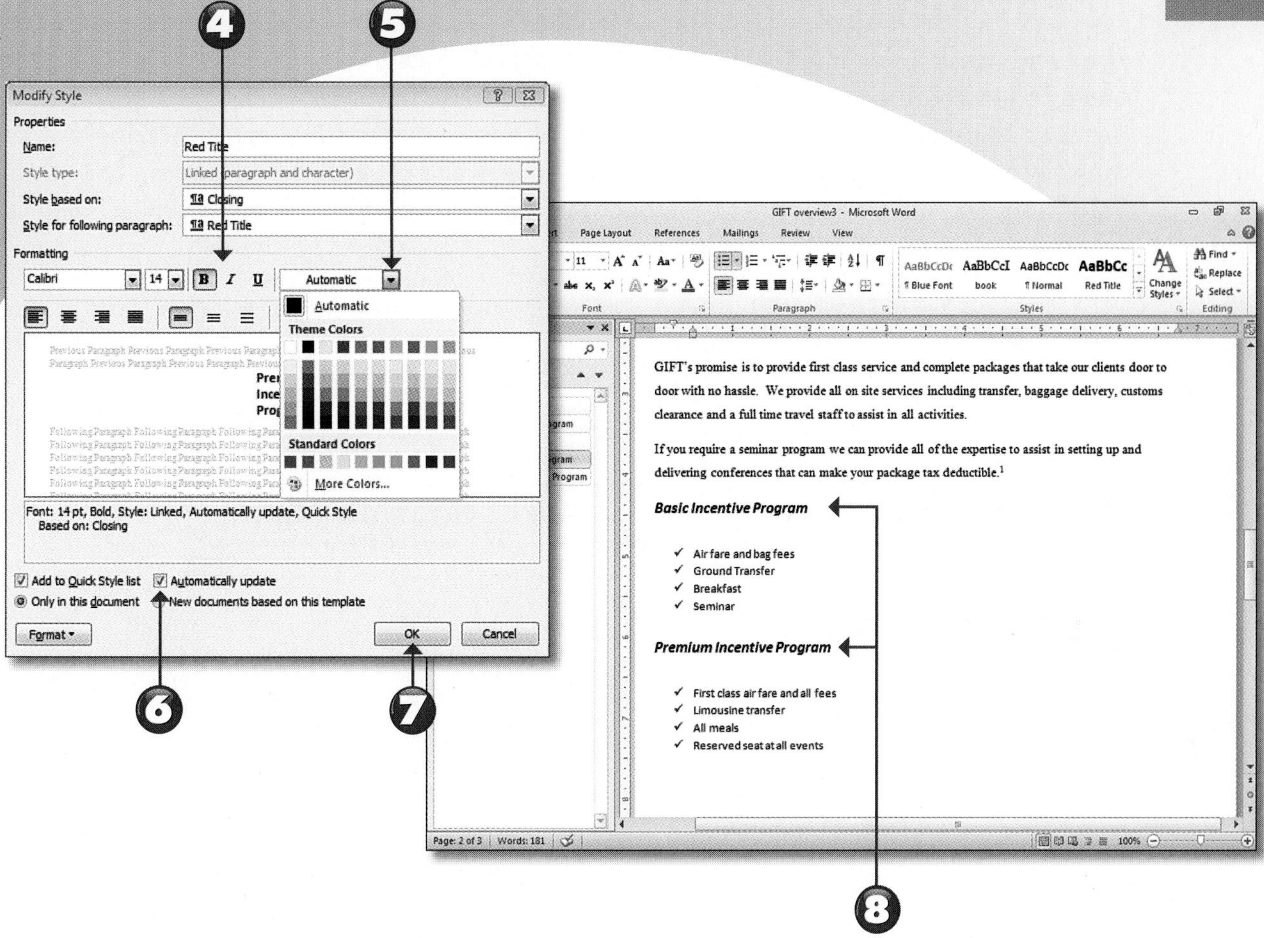

4. Remove the underline and italic or change any other attributes of the Quick Style.

5. Click the drop-down arrow to change the color of the Quick Style. The Preview window shows you how the new style will look.

6. Click **Automatically update**.

7. Click **OK**.

8. All instances of the Quick Style in the document reflect the changes.

End

TIP

Checking the Margins When you change the justification in the Modify Style window, the change sometimes is not reflected in the document. Return to the document and check the Ruler for the selected text; you may need to drag the margins for the text back to the left edge of the document. ■

UPDATING HEADINGS TO MATCH A SELECTION

The headings in a document have a special quality: They appear as topics in the Navigation pane. To get your headings to appear the way you want, format them first and then select the text. Another option is to select text that already reflects how they should look and then right-click a heading in the Quick Styles gallery and click **Update Heading to Match Selection**. The heading's format then becomes consistent with your other similar headings, and the topic appears in the Navigation pane.

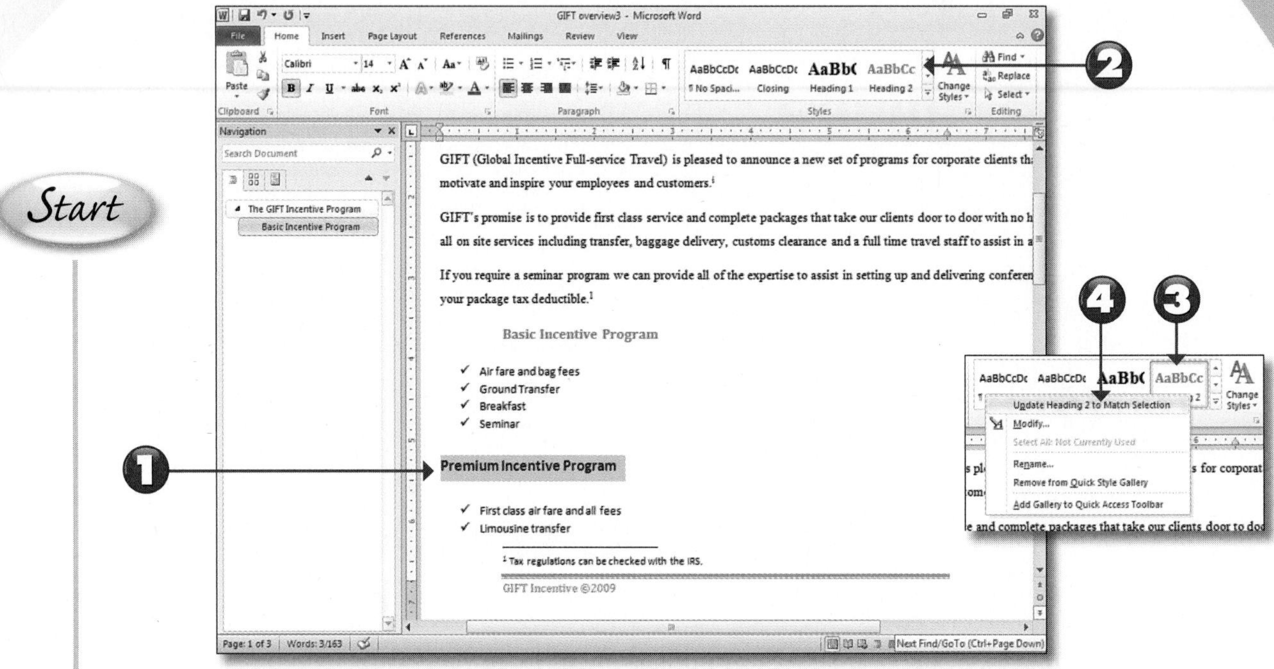

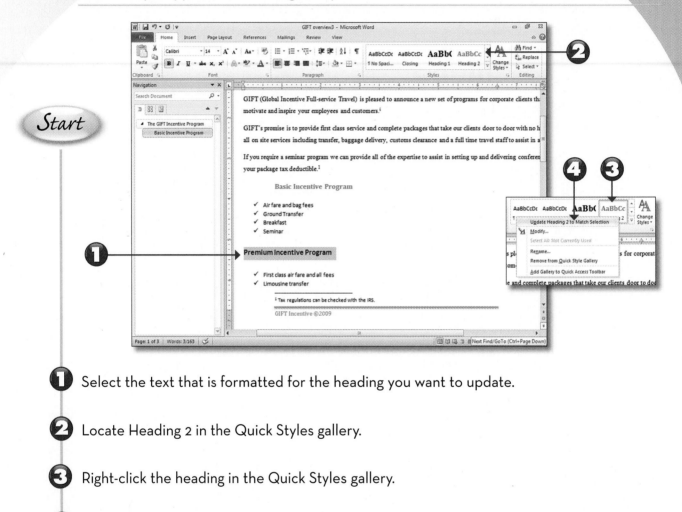

1. Select the text that is formatted for the heading you want to update.
2. Locate Heading 2 in the Quick Styles gallery.
3. Right-click the heading in the Quick Styles gallery.
4. Click **Update Heading 2 to Match Selection**.

TIP

Getting More Headings If there are no headings in the Quick Styles gallery for your document, click the **Dialog Launch** icon for Styles and locate the headings you want in the Styles pane. Click the drop-down arrow next to a heading and then click **Add to Quick Styles**. For more headings, click **Options** in the Styles pane and choose **All Styles** from the Styles to Show drop-down list. ■

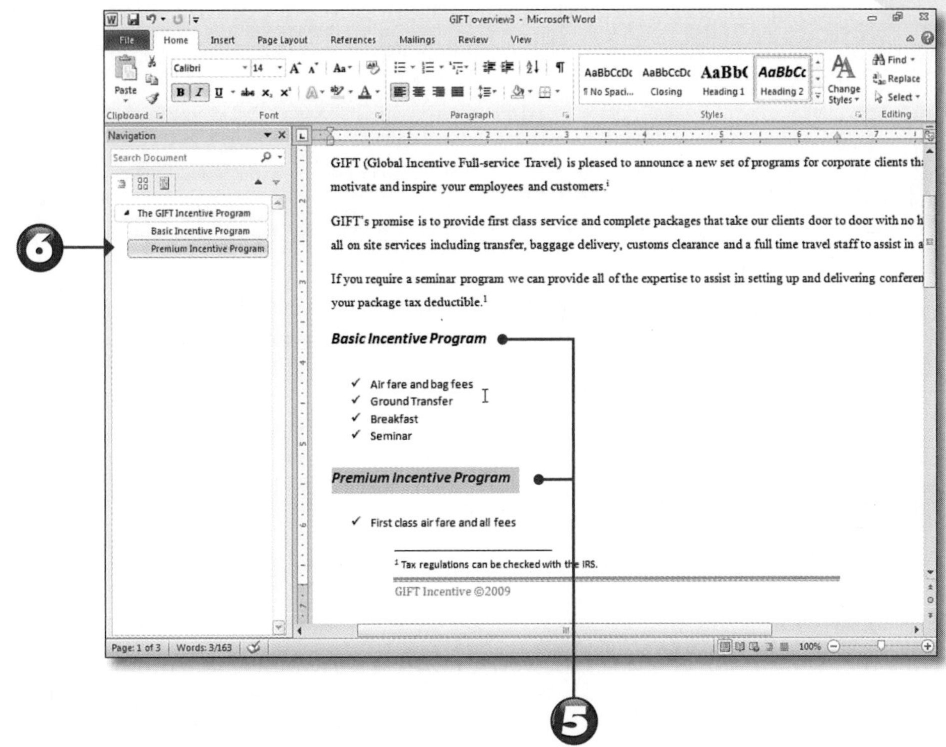

5 The text previously set as Heading 2 now reflects the new chosen format.

6 Both topics set as Heading 2 appear in the Navigation pane.

End

TIP

Show Preview in Styles Pane To see how styles will look in the document directly from the Styles pane, click the check box to enable **Show Preview**.

COPYING STYLES AND/OR FORMATTING WITH FORMAT PAINTER

The Format Painter in the Clipboard group of the Home tab of the Ribbon lets you "pick up" the format from one part of your document and "paint," or apply, it to another. For example, you can take a style and heading from one portion of your text and apply it to a differently formatted portion, in the process adding a heading to your Navigation pane.

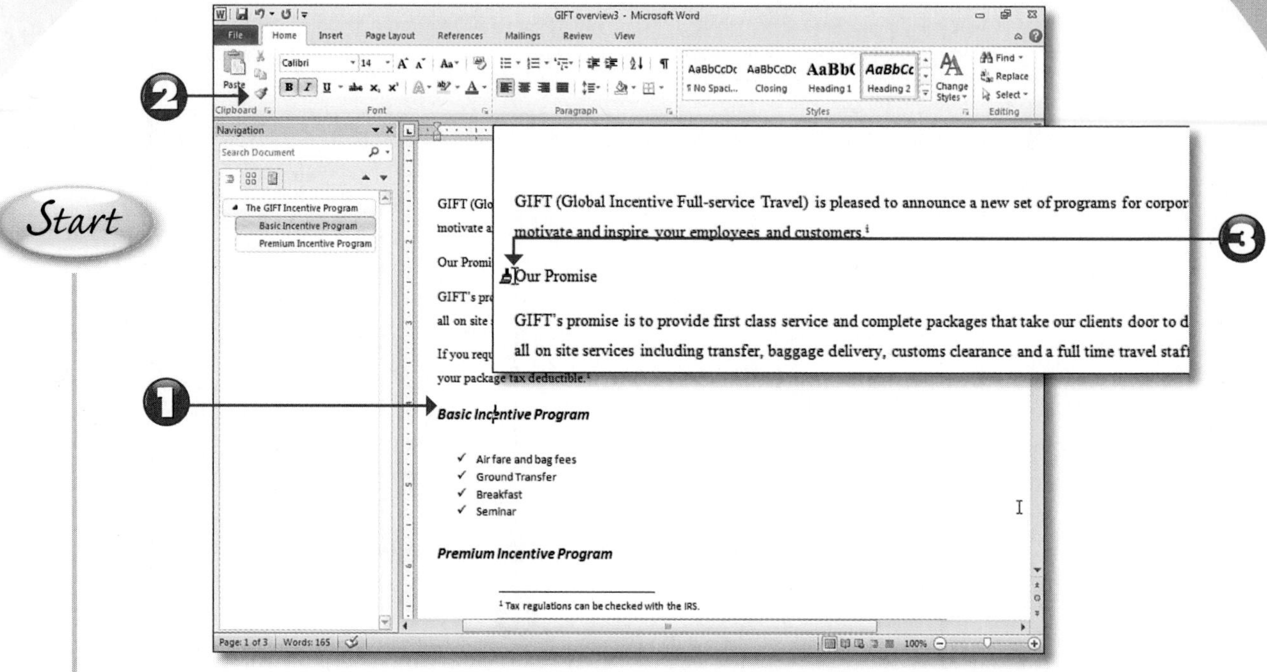

Start

1. Place your insertion point in (or select) the text with the Heading 2 style you want to copy.

2. Click the **Format Painter** in the Clipboard group of the Home tab of the Ribbon.

3. Place your mouse cursor next to the text to which you want to copy the Heading 2 style; it turns into a little paintbrush.

Continued

TIP

Painting Other Formats Besides styles and headings, the Format Painter can also pick up and apply formats and effects from one shape, picture, or other object to another. You can experiment with the Format Painter when you create tables in the next chapter or add graphics and pictures in Chapter 6, "Working with Graphics and Effects." ■

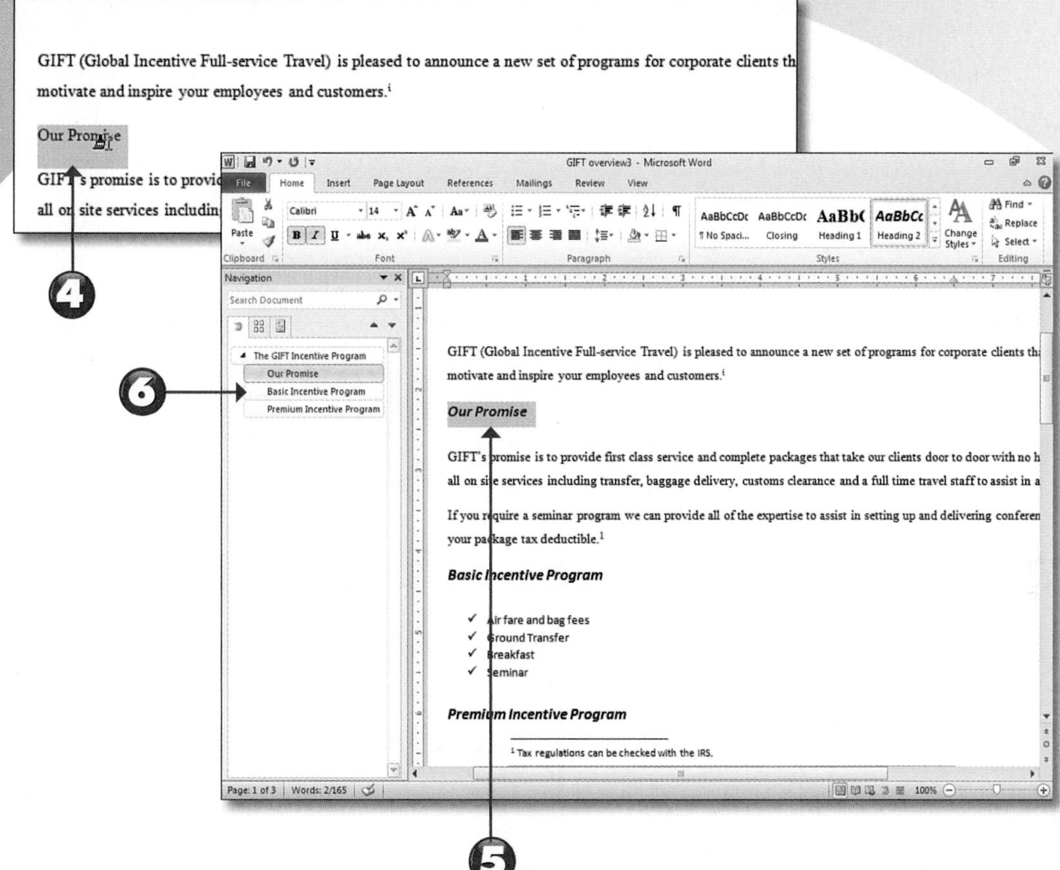

4 Drag to apply your format through the destination text.

5 When you release the left mouse button, the new format is "painted" or applied.

6 The painted text is now a Heading 2, so it appears in the Navigation pane.

End

TIP

Quick Access Toolbar The Quick Access Toolbar is a drop-down menu that you can open and use next to the Re-Do arrow at the top of the Word window. You can add the Format Painter to the Quick Access Toolbar by right-clicking it and choosing that option. You can also right-click on the Format Painter to open **Word Options** (directly in Backstage view) to customize the Quick Access Toolbar and add or remove commands. ■

INSERTING A COVER PAGE

Inserting a cover page can make an ordinary document look more professional and stand out. Word 2010 comes with preset cover pages that you can use and customize. You can download more cover pages from Office.com, or you can create your own cover pages.

Cover pages are *Building Blocks* that are saved blocks of preformatted content that can be inserted into documents and customized. Another example of a Building Block is a header or footer, which are also stored in Word as Building Blocks.

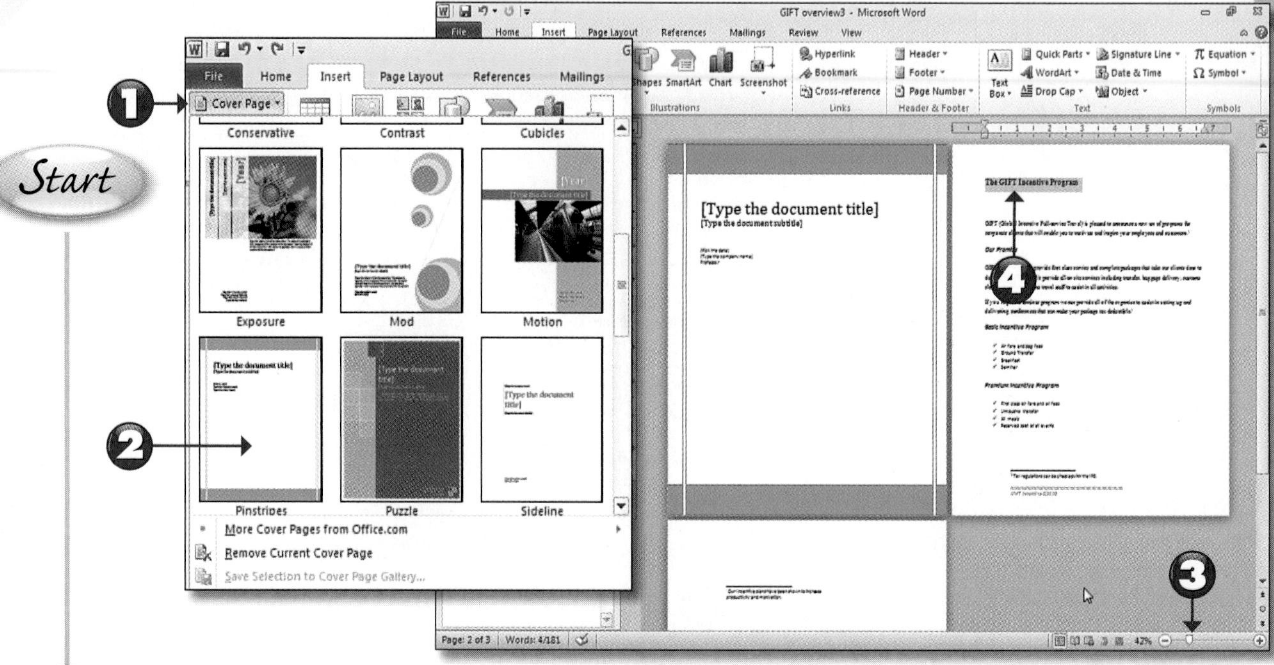

1. In the Insert tab of the Ribbon, click **Cover Page** in the Pages group.
2. Click a cover page, such as Pinstripes, to insert it in the document.
3. Slide the zoom slider to zoom out to see the cover page as part of the document.
4. Select the title text from inside your document and copy the text to the Clipboard (press **Ctrl+C**).

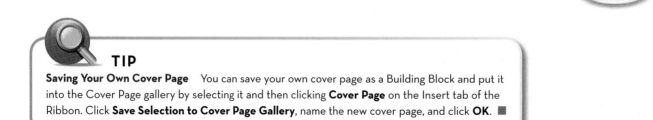

Continued

TIP

Saving Your Own Cover Page You can save your own cover page as a Building Block and put it into the Cover Page gallery by selecting it and then clicking **Cover Page** on the Insert tab of the Ribbon. Click **Save Selection to Cover Page Gallery**, name the new cover page, and click **OK**.

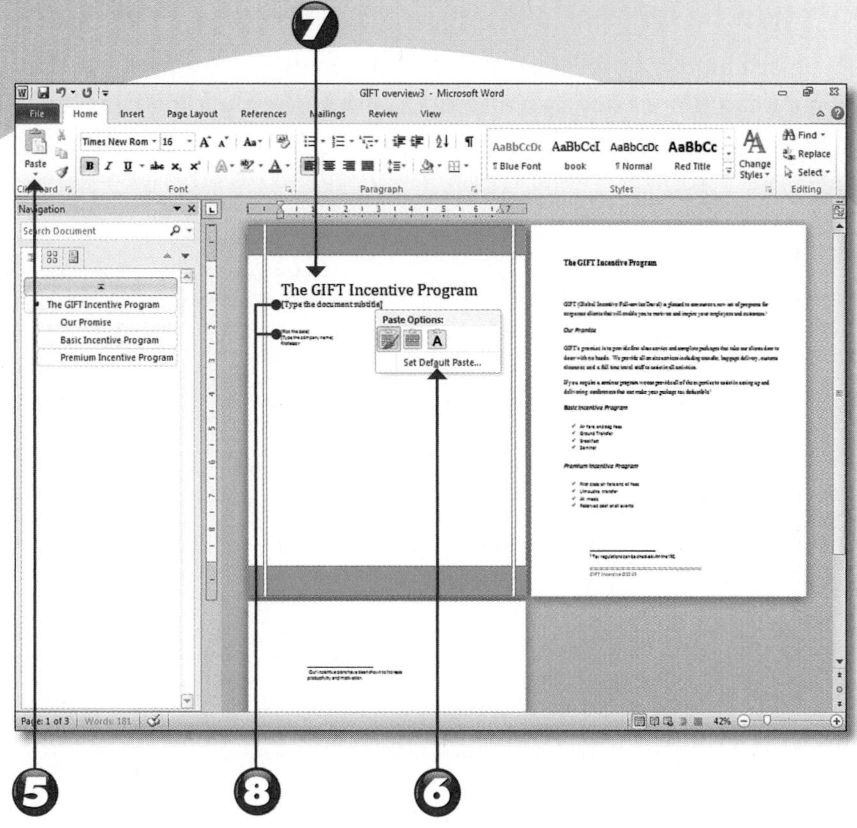

5. By using the **Paste** button on the Home tab of the Ribbon or pressing **Ctrl+V** on the keyboard, paste the copied text onto the cover page's title field.

6. In the Paste Options pop-up menu, click either **Merge Formatting** or **Keep Text Only**.

7. The title is copied to the new cover page.

8. Click in the remaining Content Controls of the cover page to fill them in or delete them.

End

TIP

Cover Pages as Organized Building Blocks If you saved your own cover page, you saw a table in which to name your cover page and save it as a Cover Page Building Block. For more information, see "Using the Building Blocks Organizer" later in this chapter. ■

TIP

Delete a Content Control To delete a Content Control from a cover page or other Building Block with content controls, click inside the control to select the prompt text, select the Content Control name tab, and then press **Delete** on your keyboard. ■

CREATING A NEW QUICK PARTS ENTRY

Quick Parts are blocks of formatted text that you can reuse and insert into a document. They are Building Blocks and can also be found in the Building Blocks Organizer, which is covered in the next section.

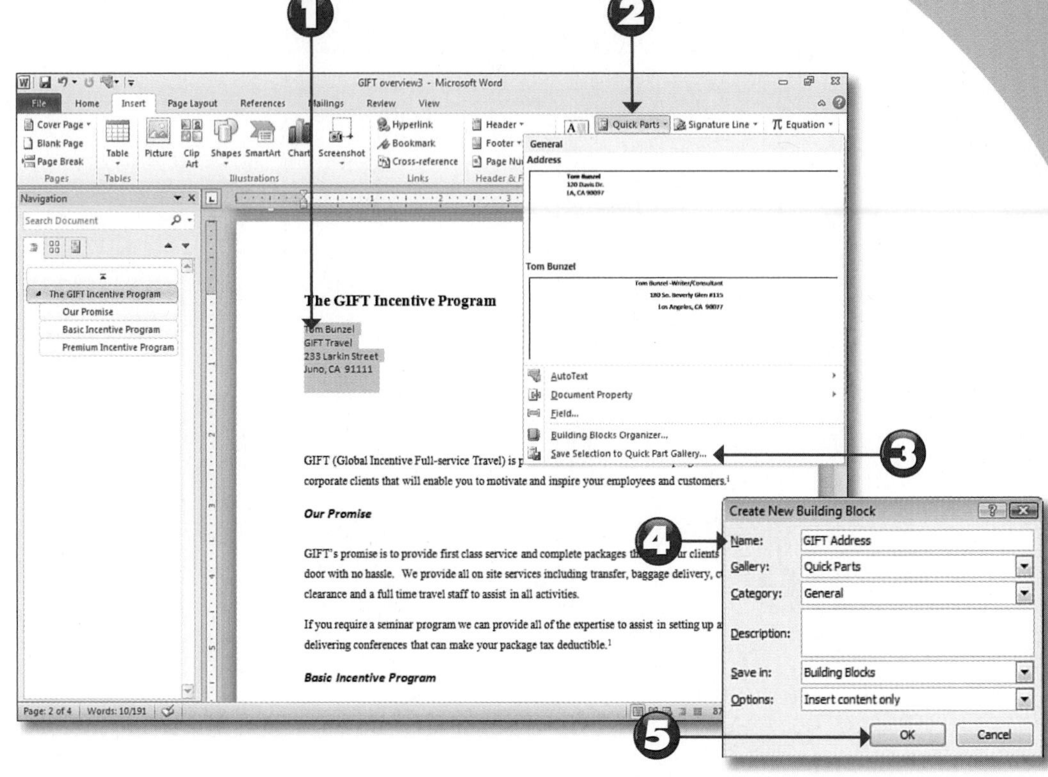

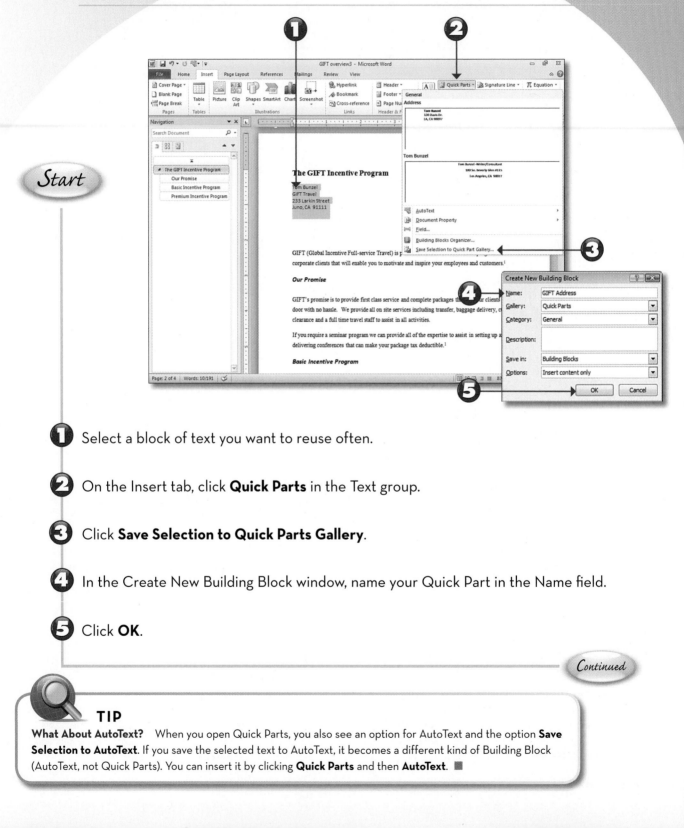

Start

1. Select a block of text you want to reuse often.
2. On the Insert tab, click **Quick Parts** in the Text group.
3. Click **Save Selection to Quick Parts Gallery**.
4. In the Create New Building Block window, name your Quick Part in the Name field.
5. Click **OK**.

Continued

TIP

What About AutoText? When you open Quick Parts, you also see an option for AutoText and the option **Save Selection to AutoText**. If you save the selected text to AutoText, it becomes a different kind of Building Block (AutoText, not Quick Parts). You can insert it by clicking **Quick Parts** and then **AutoText**. ■

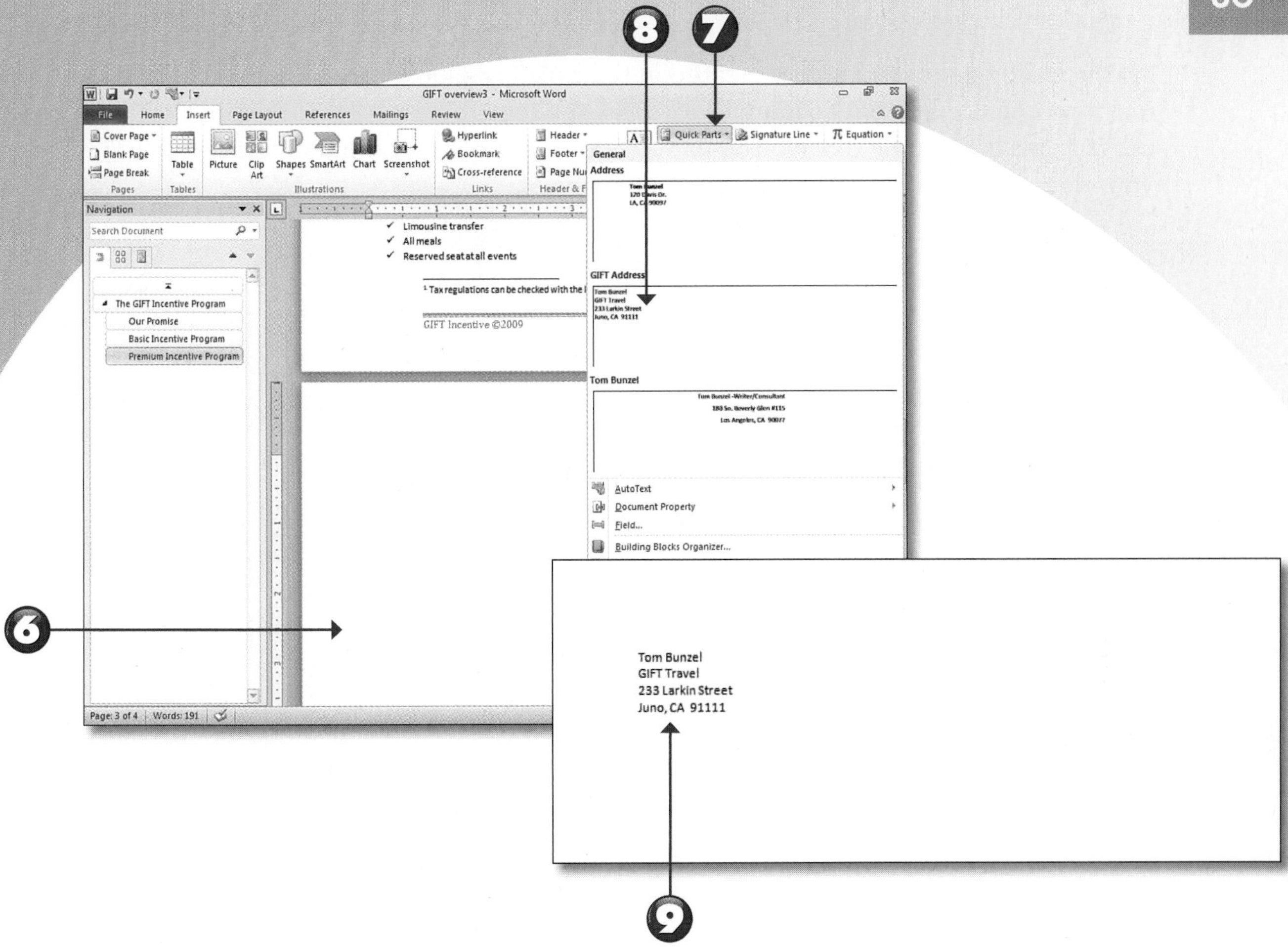

6. Move to a point in a document where you want to insert the Quick Part.

7. In the Insert tab of the Ribbon, click **Quick Parts**.

8. Click the Quick Part you want (or just created).

9. The Quick Part is inserted in the document.

End

TIP

Saving Quick Parts Quick Parts are saved in a special Building Blocks template by default in Word 2010. They are also available through the Building Blocks Organizer (see the next section). After you add a Building Block like a Quick Part, Word asks whether you want to save it to the Building Blocks template when you close the document. Click **Yes**. ■

USING THE BUILDING BLOCKS ORGANIZER

All the Building Blocks are also located in the Building Blocks Organizer, which lets you maintain and create new Building Blocks like headers, footers, Quick Parts, cover pages, and other types of Building Blocks. You can also locate and insert Building Blocks directly into your document from the Building Blocks Organizer.

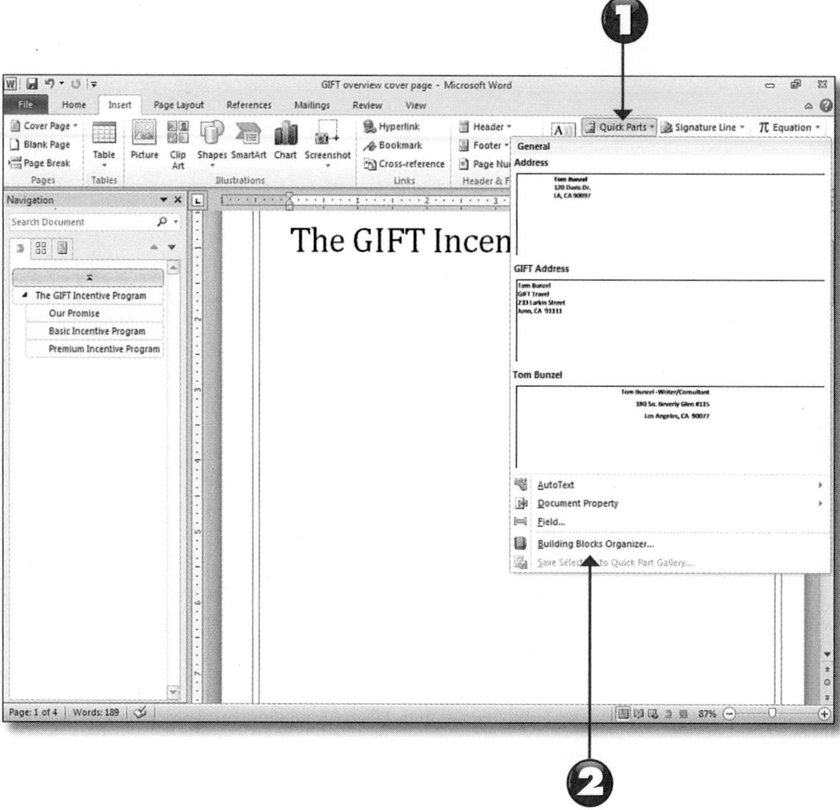

1. In the Insert tab of the Ribbon, click **Quick Parts**.

2. Click **Building Blocks Organizer**.

Continued

TIP

Building Blocks Organizer As you scroll through the Building Blocks Organizer, you see all the various galleries in Word 2010 and the preset and saved Building Blocks available in the current document. They are organized by Category, Gallery, and Template. ■

TIP

Moving a Building Block If a Building Block is not available in the current document, open the Building Block Organizer in the document where it is saved, click **Edit Properties** in the Organizer, and save it to the default Normal Word template for all documents. ■

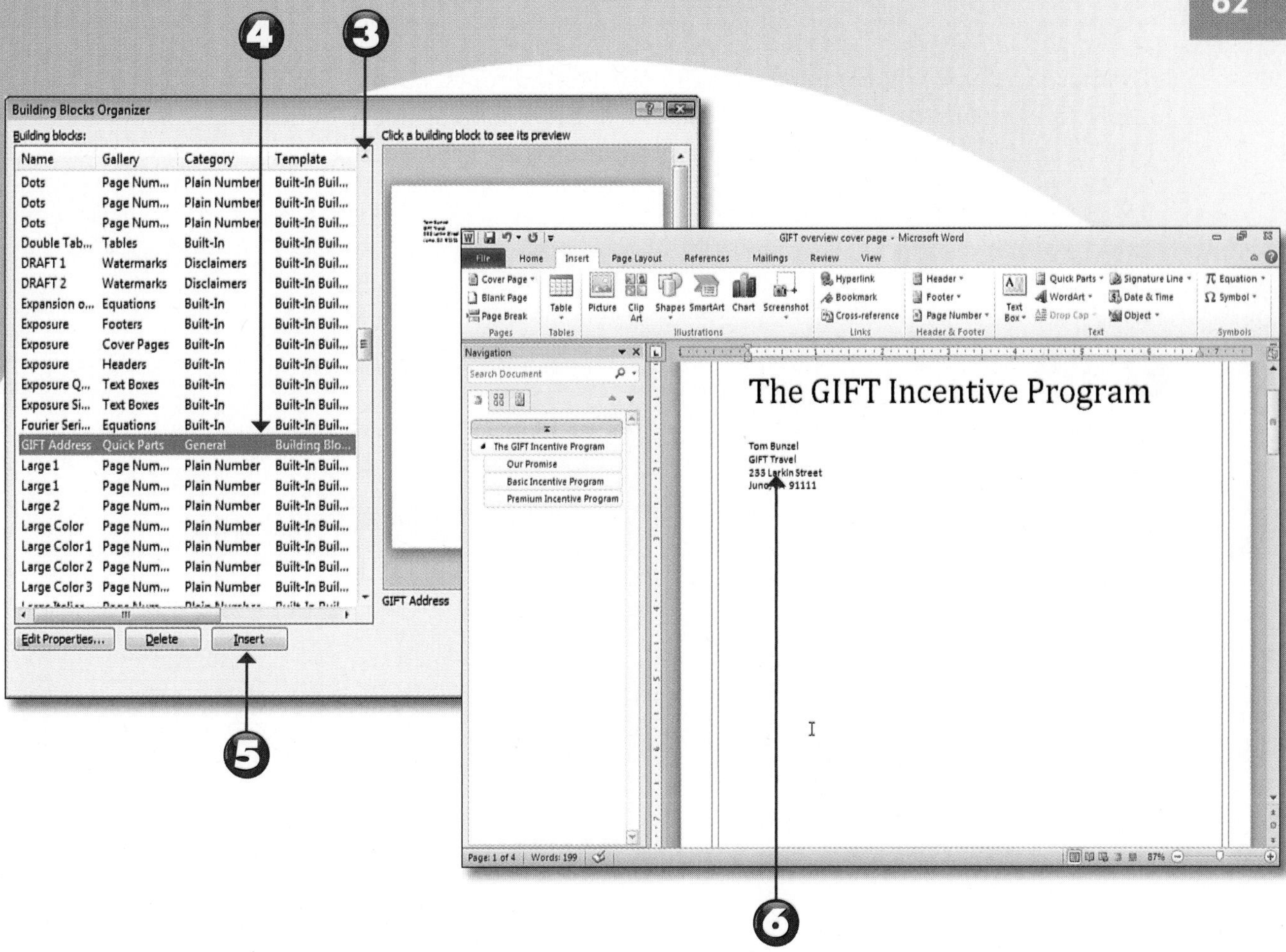

3 Scroll through the Building Blocks Organizer to find your new Quick Part by name.

4 Click to select and preview the Quick Part you created.

5 Click **Insert**.

6 The Quick Part is inserted in the document.

End

TIP

Creating Your Own Category You can create your own category (for example, for a client) to organize your Building Blocks efficiently. Select a Building Block in the Organizer, click **Edit Properties**, and click the drop-down arrow beside the Categories field and then click Create New Category from the drop-down list. Name your new category and save your customized Building Blocks to it to locate them later by category in the Building Blocks Organizer.

APPLYING A THEME TO A DOCUMENT

Themes are packaged combinations of coordinated fonts, colors, and effects that you can apply to a document. Themes are available in the Themes gallery in the Page Layout tab of the Ribbon. (Effects are enhancements to pictures and graphics that we cover in Chapter 6).

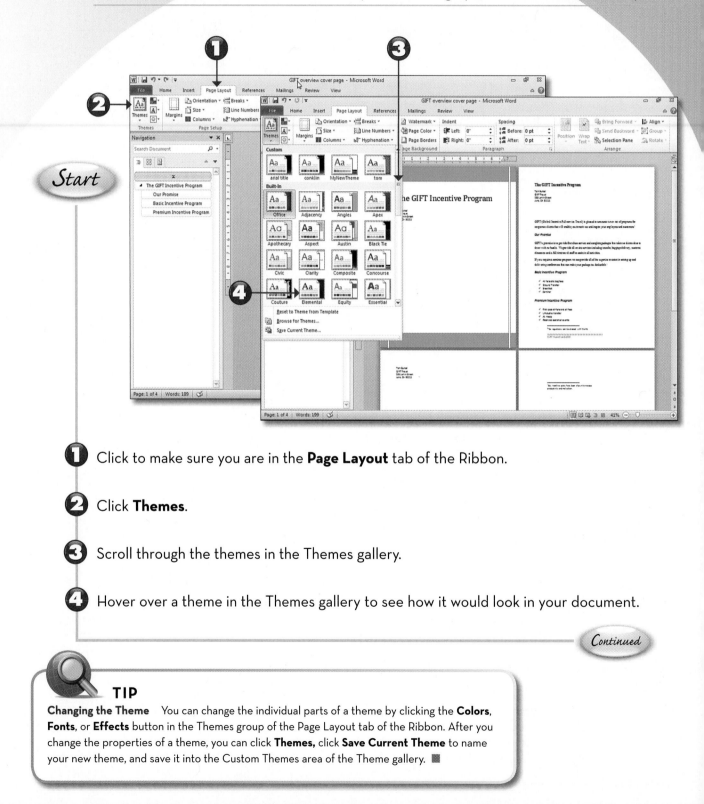

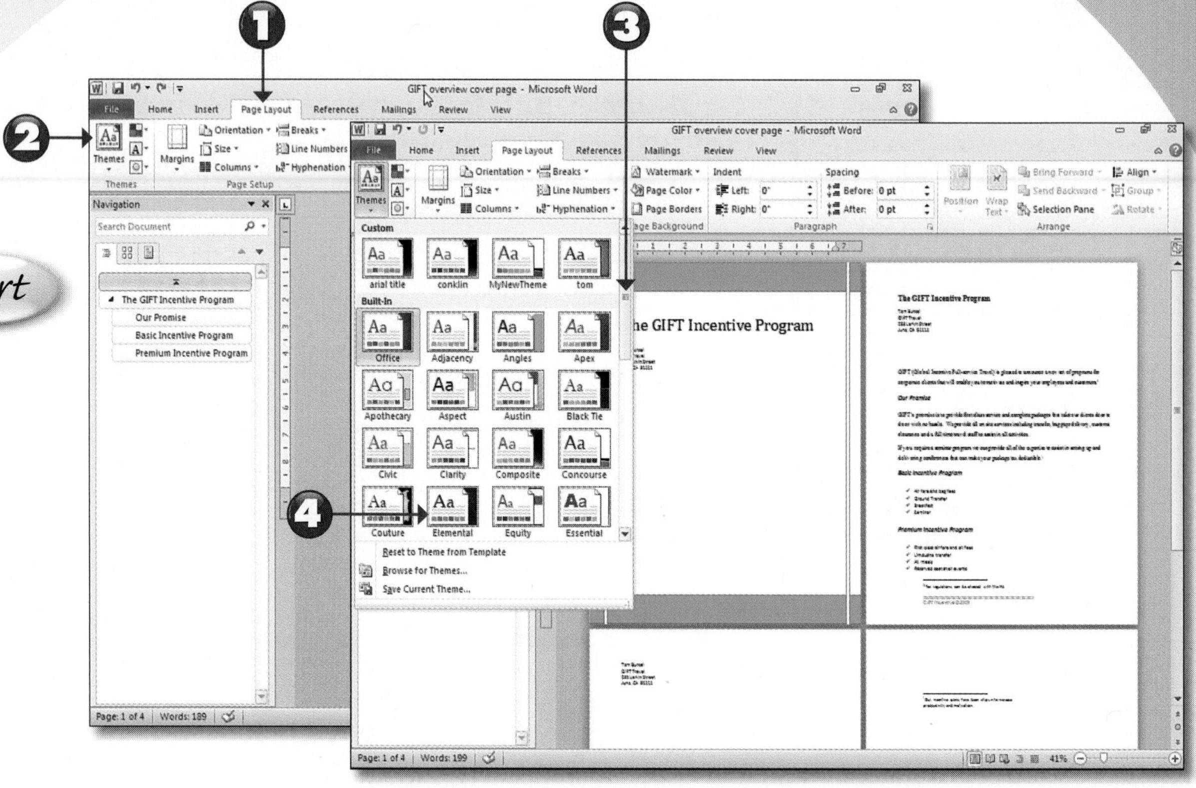

Start

1. Click to make sure you are in the **Page Layout** tab of the Ribbon.

2. Click **Themes**.

3. Scroll through the themes in the Themes gallery.

4. Hover over a theme in the Themes gallery to see how it would look in your document.

TIP

Changing the Theme You can change the individual parts of a theme by clicking the **Colors**, **Fonts**, or **Effects** button in the Themes group of the Page Layout tab of the Ribbon. After you change the properties of a theme, you can click **Themes,** click **Save Current Theme** to name your new theme, and save it into the Custom Themes area of the Theme gallery. ■

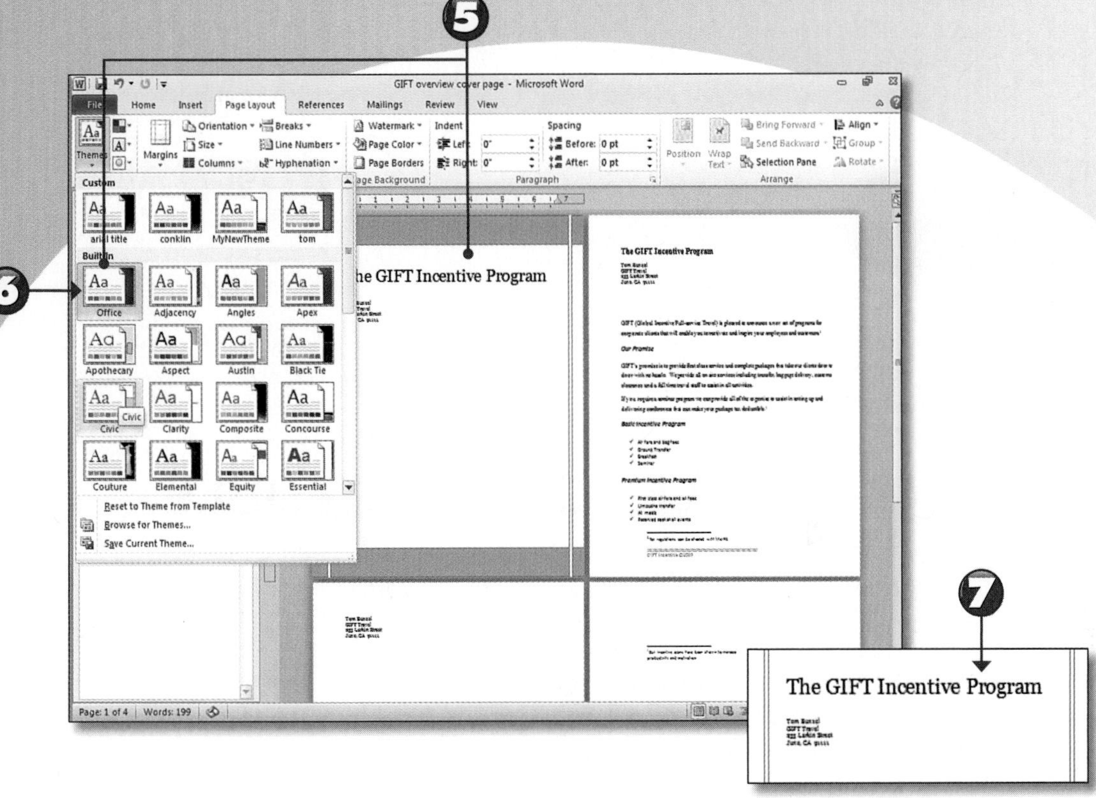

5 As you hover your mouse cursor over a theme, the Quick Preview in the document shows the new colors and font that would be applied.

6 Click to apply the new theme to the document.

7 Elements in the document reflect the fonts, colors, and effects of the selected theme.

End

TIP

Restoring the Original Themes If you've applied and changed a few themes and want to return to the way the document originally looked, you can click **Themes** and choose **Reset to Theme from Template**.

TIP

Themes Between Programs By noting the name of a specific theme in Word, you can apply the same theme in Excel or PowerPoint to maintain a consistent set of colors, fonts, and effects among various files.

CREATING A TABLE FOR A SCHEDULE

One of the best ways to organize information in Word so that it can be easily read and understood is to use a table. A table breaks up your content into easily digestible chunks of information.

You can use a table for many different types of content, from a calendar to a tabular list. A table consists of a set of columns and rows meeting to form cells that contain the information in text or numeric format.

When you create and select a table, Word's Table Tools tabs are available on the Ribbon, with one tab for design and the other to change the layout of your table. By selecting individual cells, columns, and rows, you can reformat the look of your table, or you can use the Table Styles gallery in the Design tab to quickly add a specific format to your table.

USING TABLES TO PRESENT INFORMATION

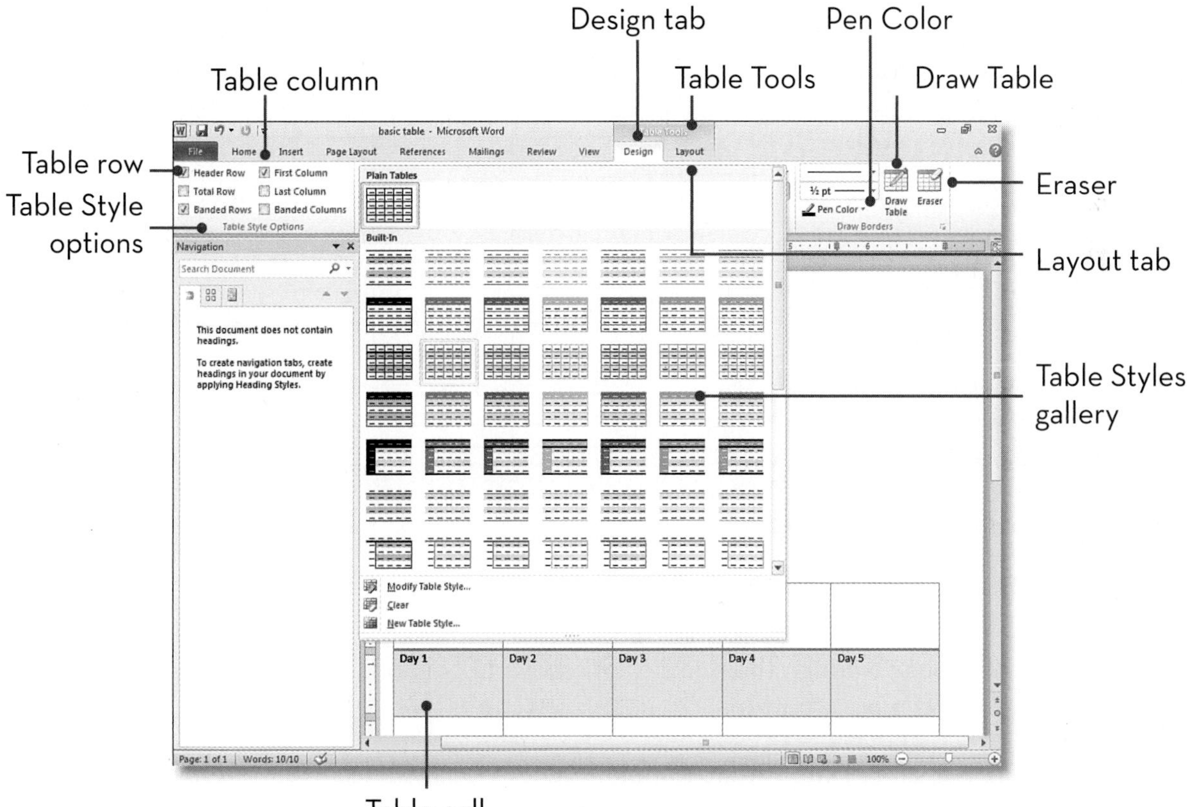

CREATING A TABLE

The easiest way to create a table is first to place your cursor where you want the table. Then use the **Table** button on the Insert tab to drag out the configuration of the table you want, setting up the number of columns and rows. After you create the table, the Table Tools tab of the Ribbon is available to let you change its layout or design.

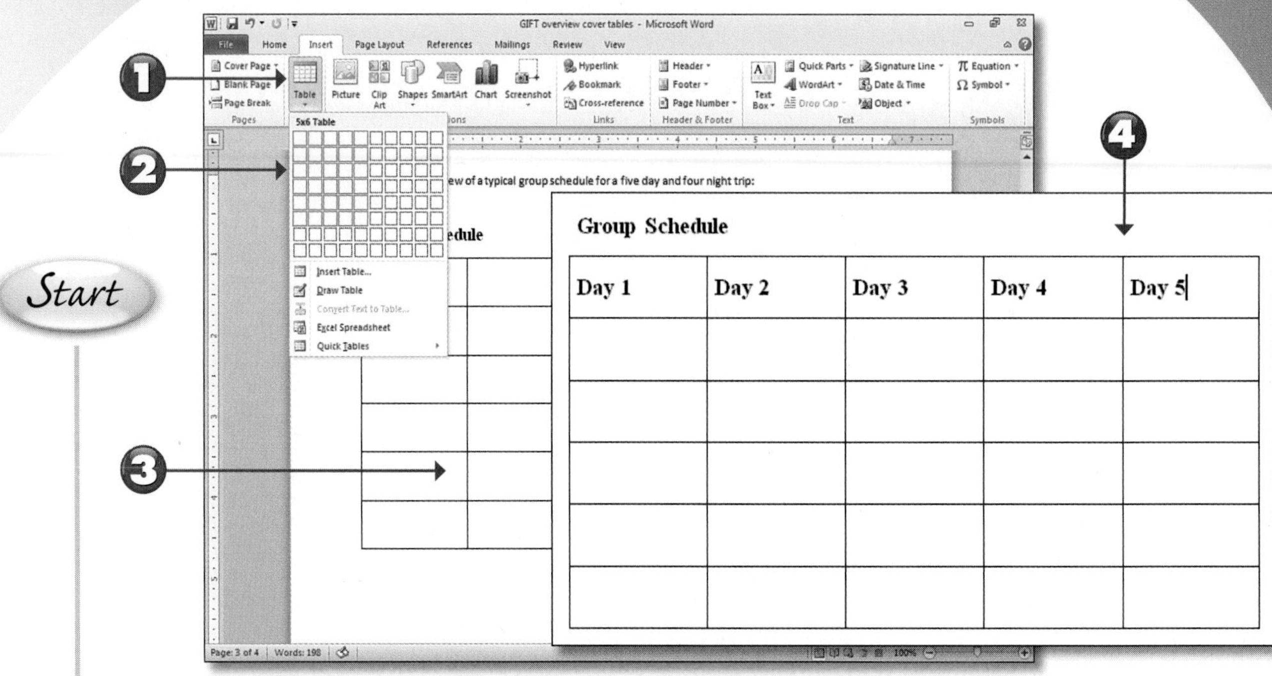

Start

1. On the Insert tab, click **Table**.
2. Drag your mouse through the number of rows and columns you want in your table and release the left mouse button.
3. The table is inserted into the document.
4. Begin typing your information into the table.

End

TIP

Draw Table You can use the Draw Table option when you click the **Tables** button in the Insert tab to create a free-form table. When you click **Draw Table**, your cursor turns into a pen, and you can draw lines for borders. You also can create your own rows and columns by dragging and releasing the left mouse button. ■

TIP

Adjusting Cell Size You can use the Cells Size group of the Layout tab of the Table Tools to automatically adjust the width and height of columns and rows. ■

SELECTING AND CHANGING TEXT ALIGNMENT

With the table active, you can select the text in the header row and use the Layout tab of the Table Tools to change its alignment and also make other changes to its appearance.

Start

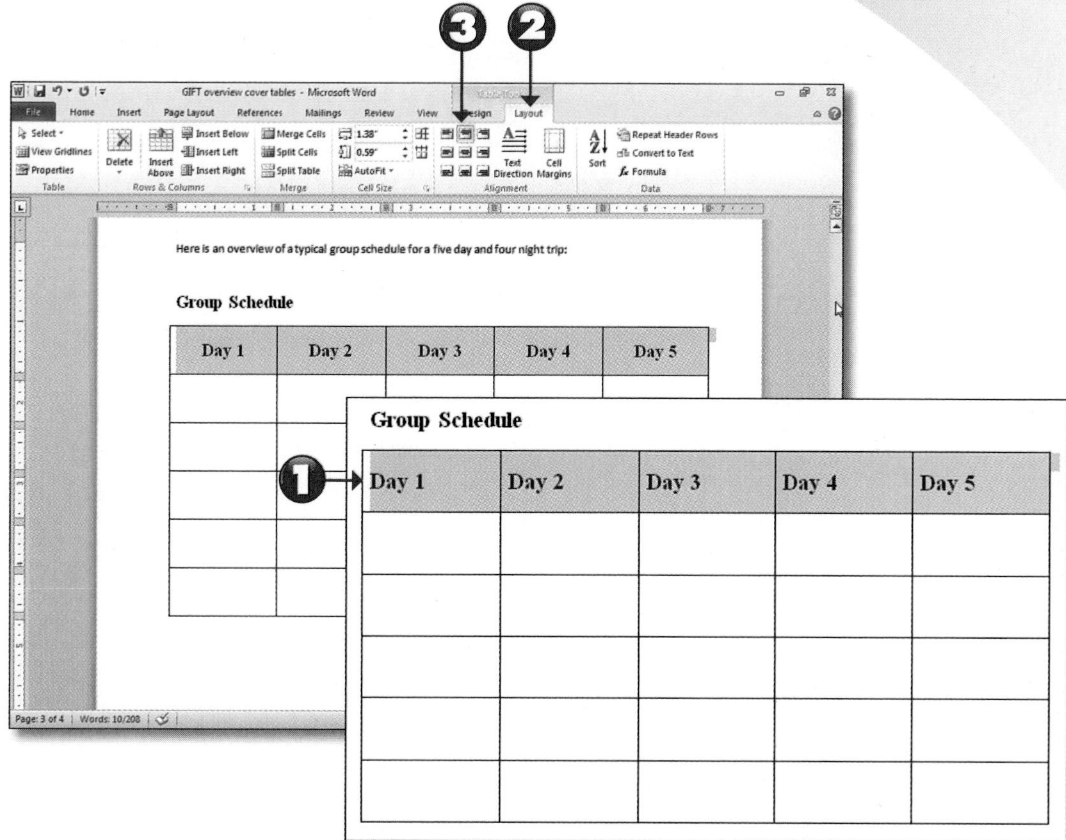

1 Drag through a row of text to select it.

2 Click the **Layout** tab of the Table Tools of the Ribbon.

3 Click the **Center Middle** icon in the Alignment group to center your column headings.

End

TIP

Paragraph Indent Issues When you begin to type text into your table, sometimes it runs vertically in the cells. If selecting the **Text Direction** button of the Layout tab does not correct the problem, select the **Table** group of the Layout tab, click the **Home** tab of the Ribbon, click the **Dialog Launch** icon of the Paragraph group, and in the Indents and Spacing Tab, change the Indentation for the cells to 0. ■

ADDING OR DELETING ROWS OR COLUMNS

You can add or remove rows or columns from your table by first selecting an adjacent row or column. Then click the **Insert Below** or **Insert Above** options in the Rows & Columns group of the Table Tools Layout tab.

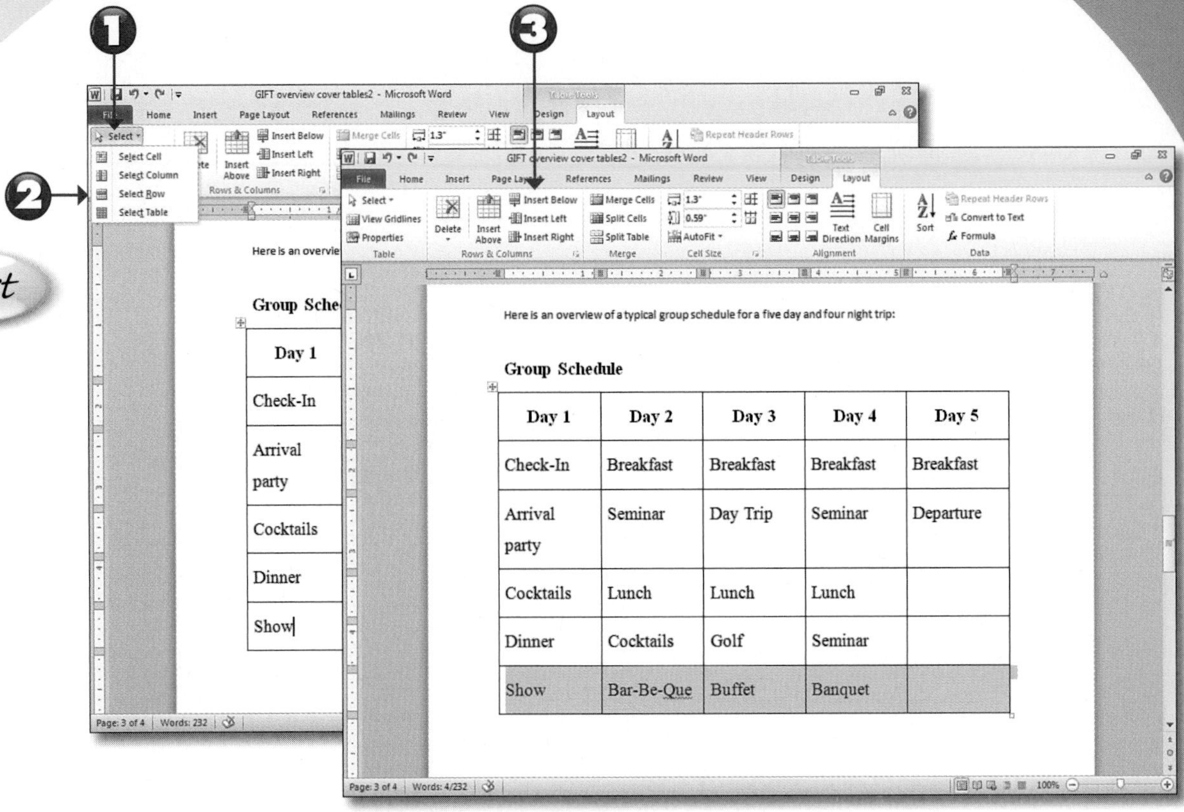

1. With your cursor in the row to which you want add another row, click **Select** in the Table group of the Layout tab of the Table Tools.
2. Click **Select Row**. You can also just place your cursor anywhere in the row above where you want the new row inserted.
3. With the Row selected, click **Insert Below** in the Rows & Columns group.

TIP

Removing Cells, Rows, or Columns You can select any cell, row, or column and click the **Delete** button to delete it. Or you can delete the entire table this way. You can also use the **Dialog Launch** icon in the Rows & Columns group to shift cells, rows, or columns in a desired direction to add more cells, rows, or columns. ■

MERGING CELLS

You can combine a group of formatted cells into one larger cell by using the Merge Cells button in the Layout tab of the Table Tools. This gives you more room within the table for more text and possible summaries of information.

Start

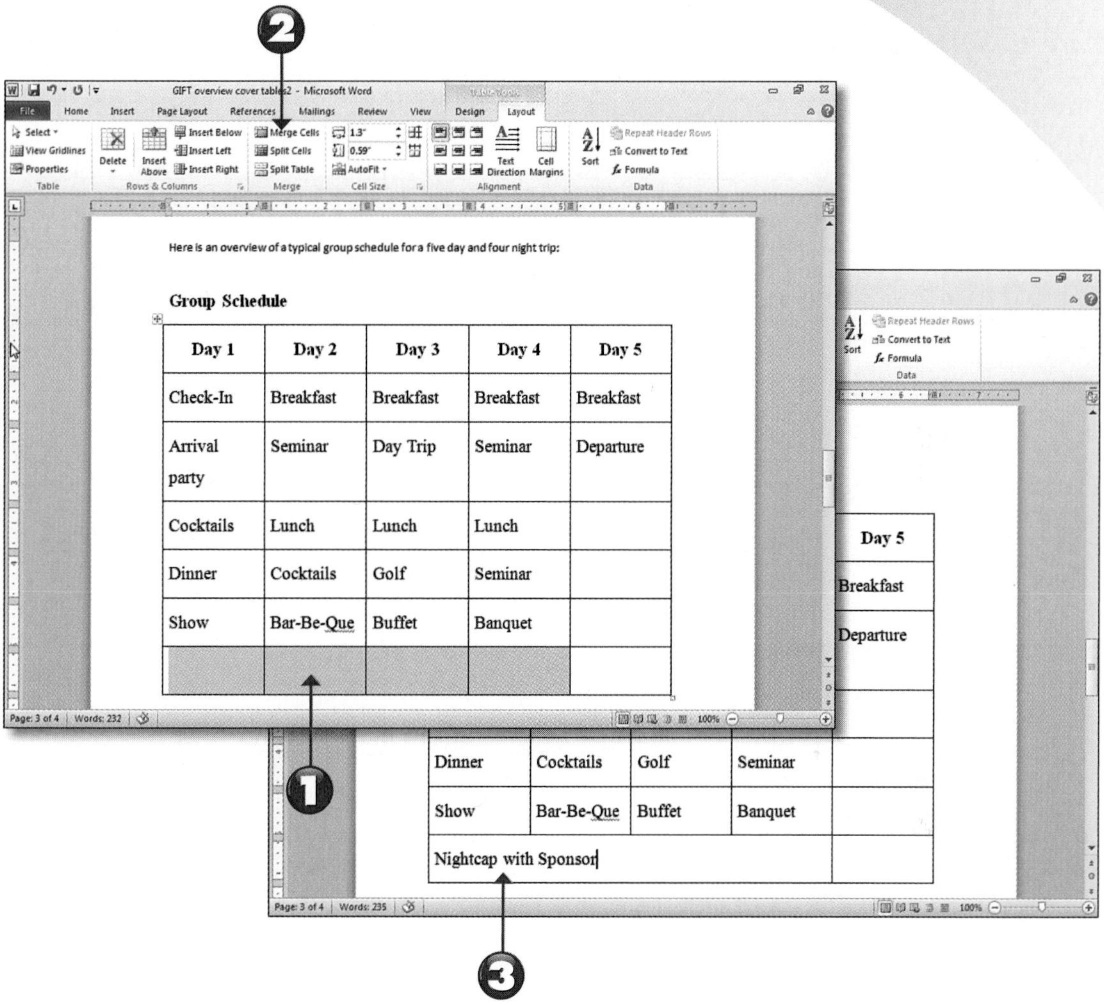

1. In the new row, drag through cells you want to combine to select them.
2. Click **Merge Cells**.
3. Type new information in the merged cells.

End

TIP

Splitting a Column or Row If you need to divide the information in a column or row, you can select it and click the **Split Cells** button in the Merge group of the Layout tab of Table Tools.

MODIFYING BORDERS

You can add or remove the borders of all or part of the table you have created and also adjust the thickness and line color of the borders using the Design tab of the Table Tools.

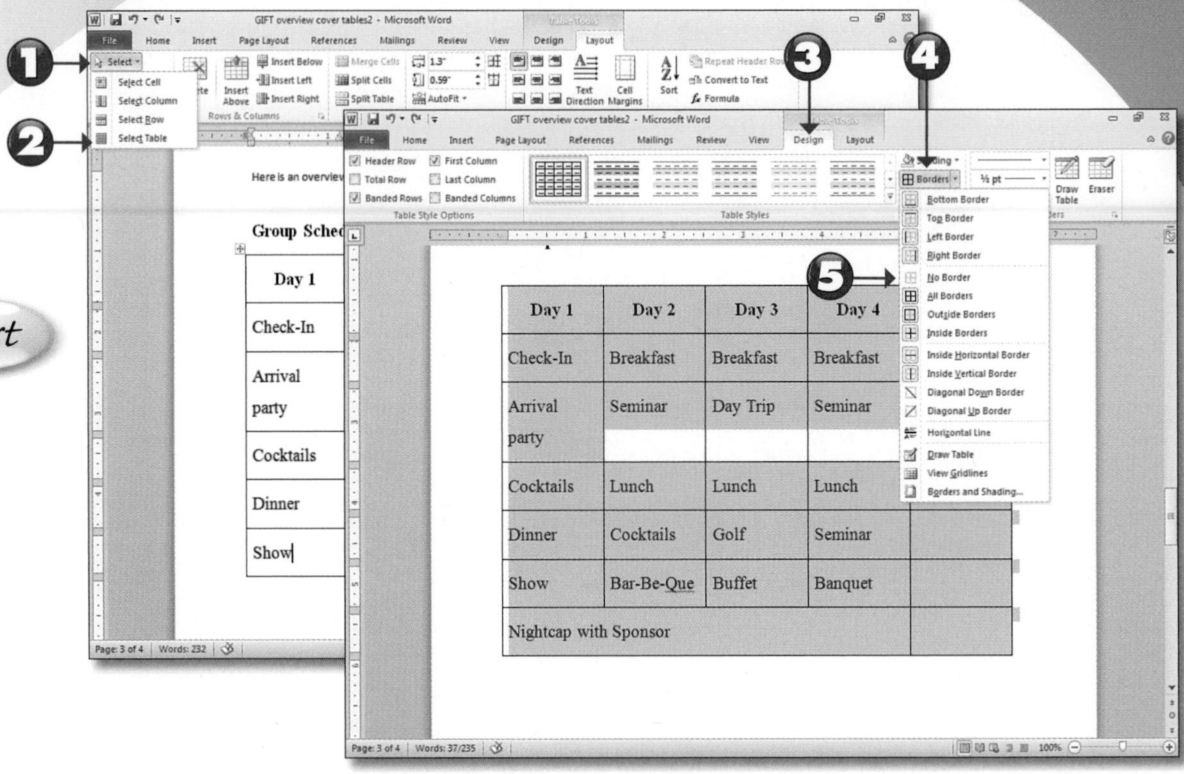

Start

1. With your cursor in the table, click **Select** in the Table group of the Layout tab of the Table Tools.
2. Click **Select Table**.
3. Click the **Design** tab of Table Tools.
4. Click the **Borders** drop-down arrow.
5. Click **No Border**.

Continued

NOTE

Adding Shading You can also add shading to the background of selected cells by using the **Shading** drop-down arrow in the Table Styles group of the Design tab. ■

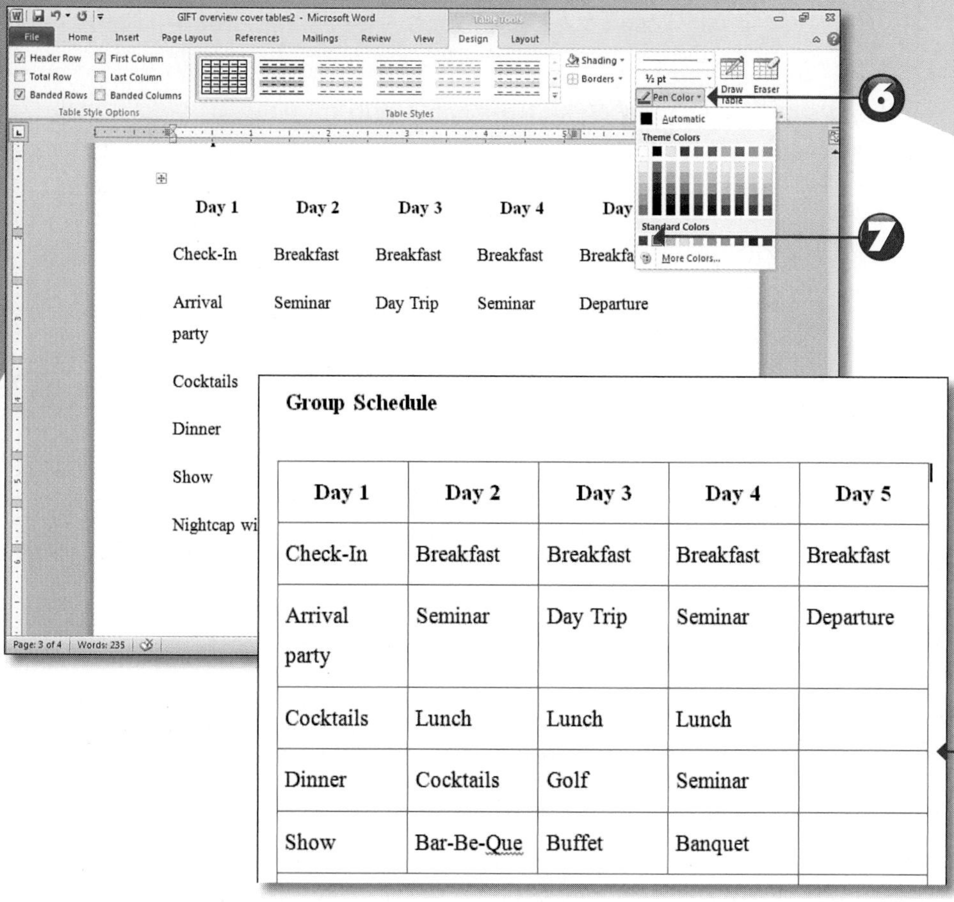

Group Schedule

Day 1	Day 2	Day 3	Day 4	Day 5
Check-In	Breakfast	Breakfast	Breakfast	Breakfast
Arrival party	Seminar	Day Trip	Seminar	Departure
Cocktails	Lunch	Lunch	Lunch	
Dinner	Cocktails	Golf	Seminar	
Show	Bar-Be-Que	Buffet	Banquet	

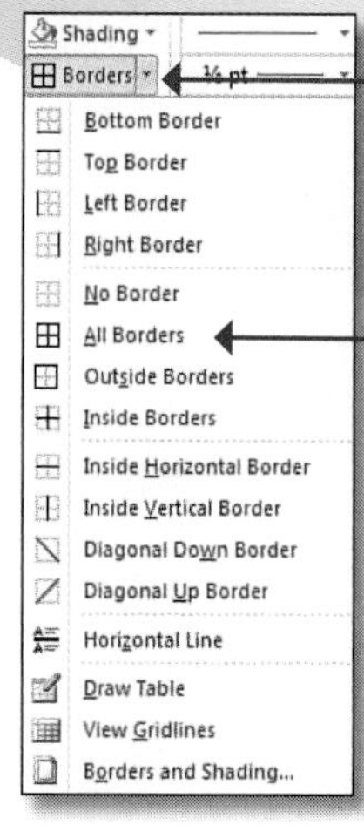

6 Click the **Pen Color** drop-down arrow.

7 Choose a new color for the borders. Make sure the entire table is selected (as in steps 1 and 2).

8 Click the **Borders** drop-down arrow.

9 Click **All Borders**.

10 The new colored borders are in the table.

End

TIP

Borders and Shading Options When you click the **Dialog Launch** icon in the Draw Borders group, you get an entire window for adjusting the borders, colors, line thickness, and shading for your table. You can select a border style for the lines and change the shading and border color.

USING THE TABLE STYLES GALLERY

Word allows you to quickly change the appearance of a table using the Table Styles in the Design tab of the Table Tools on the Ribbon. Select the table and then see a Quick Preview of one or more styles in the Table Styles Gallery and click to apply the style. You can make further adjustments like using Banded Columns in the Table Style Options group of the Design tab.

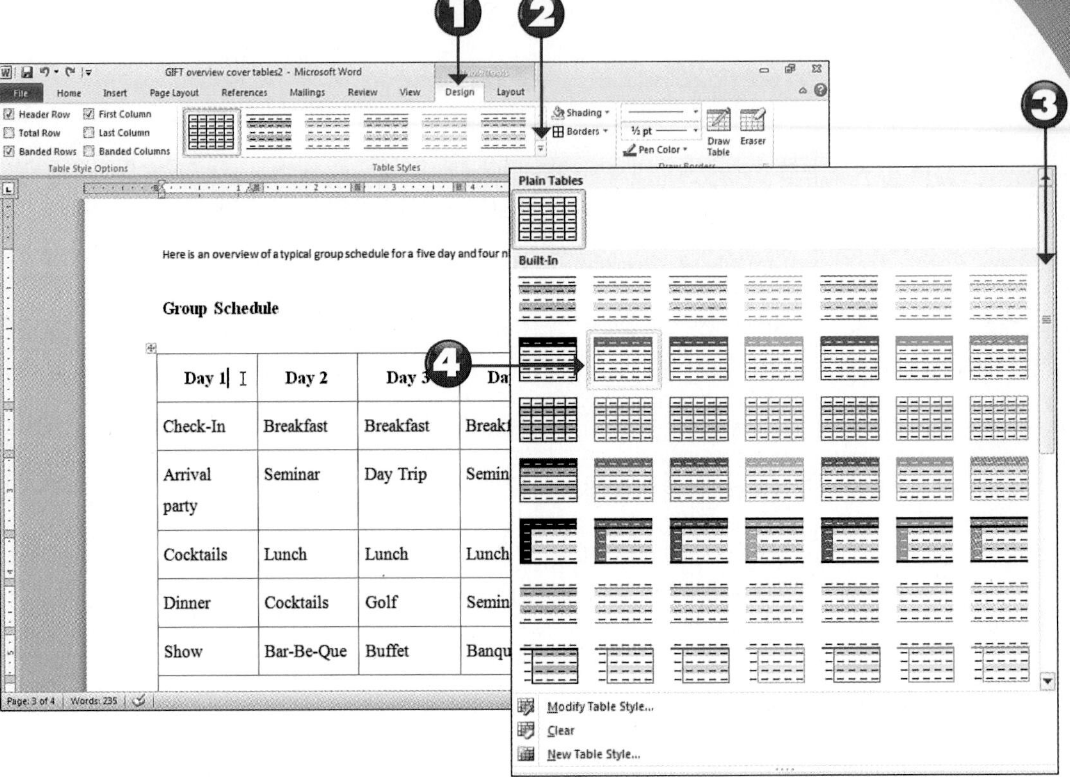

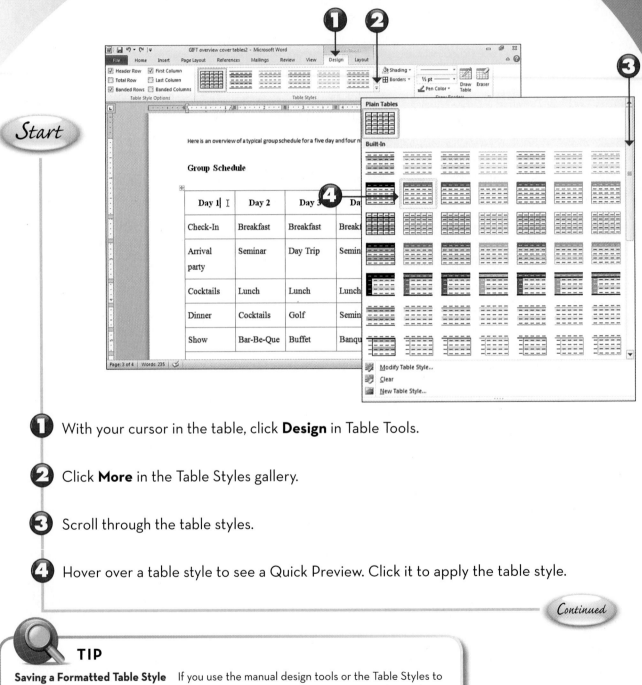

Start

1. With your cursor in the table, click **Design** in Table Tools.
2. Click **More** in the Table Styles gallery.
3. Scroll through the table styles.
4. Hover over a table style to see a Quick Preview. Click it to apply the table style.

Continued

TIP

Saving a Formatted Table Style If you use the manual design tools or the Table Styles to create a table with a style you want to save and reuse, you can click **More** in Table Styles and save that style by clicking **New Table Style**. Then give it a name and click **OK**. ■

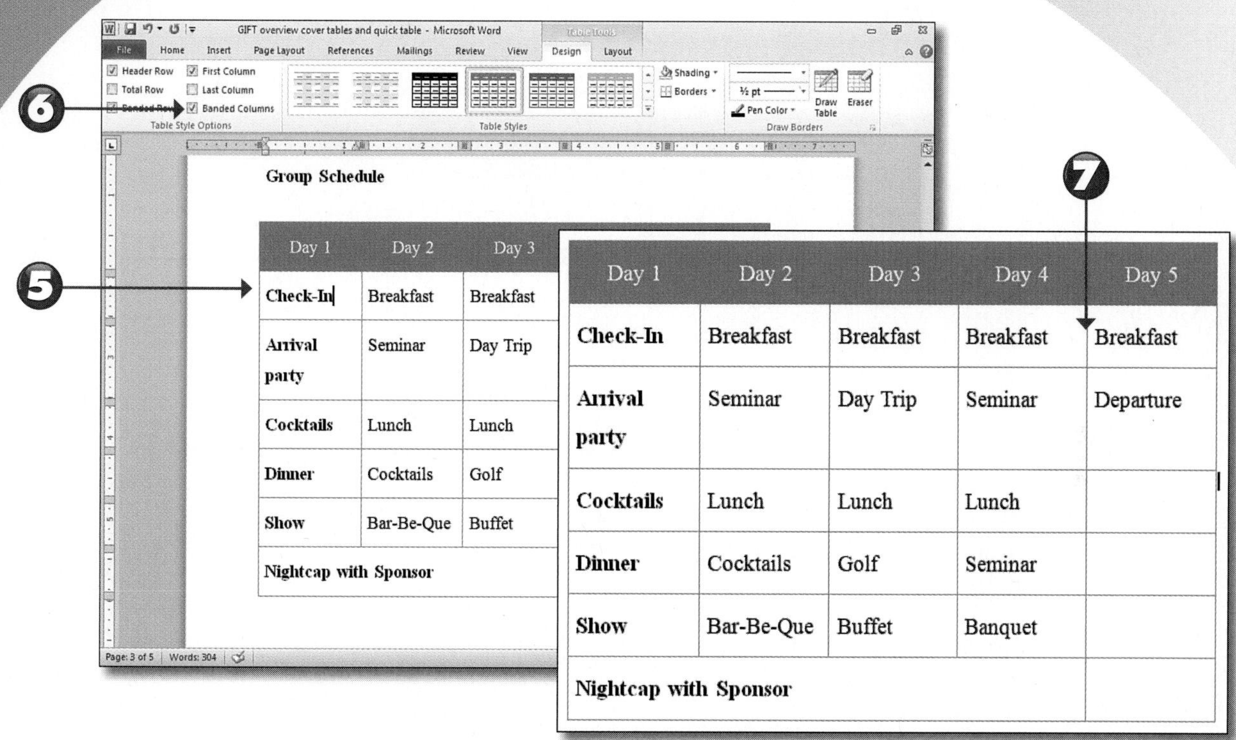

5 The new style is applied to the table.

6 Click the **Banded Columns** check box in Table Style Options.

7 Column borders are added to the table.

End

TIP

Creating a New Table Style You can create an entirely new table style from scratch by clicking **More** in Table Styles and setting up a new style from the formatting options, naming the new style, and clicking **OK**. ■

USING QUICK TABLES

Quick Tables are sample tables that already have been filled in with content so that when you put them into your document, you can revise the text in the table for your own purposes.

Start

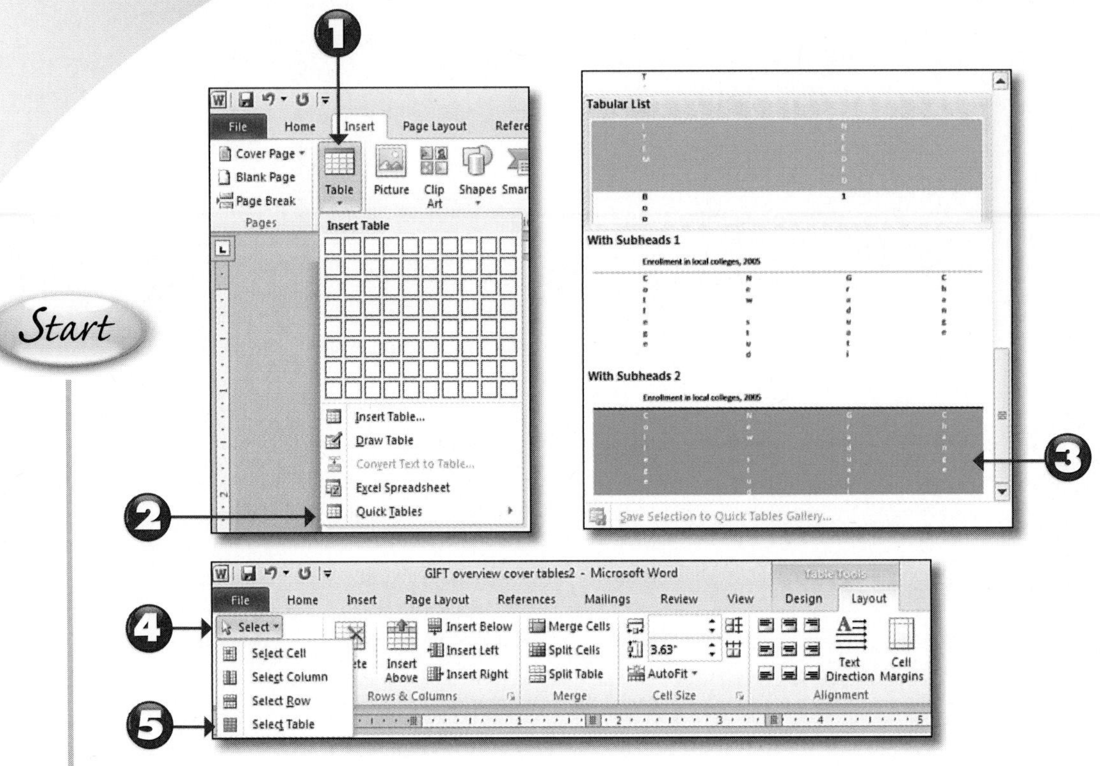

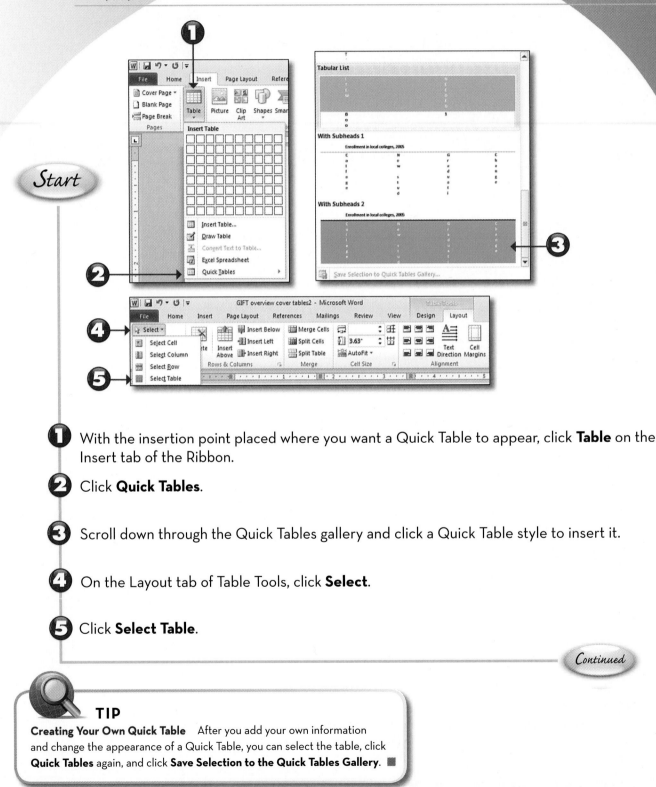

1. With the insertion point placed where you want a Quick Table to appear, click **Table** on the Insert tab of the Ribbon.
2. Click **Quick Tables**.
3. Scroll down through the Quick Tables gallery and click a Quick Table style to insert it.
4. On the Layout tab of Table Tools, click **Select**.
5. Click **Select Table**.

TIP

Creating Your Own Quick Table After you add your own information and change the appearance of a Quick Table, you can select the table, click **Quick Tables** again, and click **Save Selection to the Quick Tables Gallery**. ■

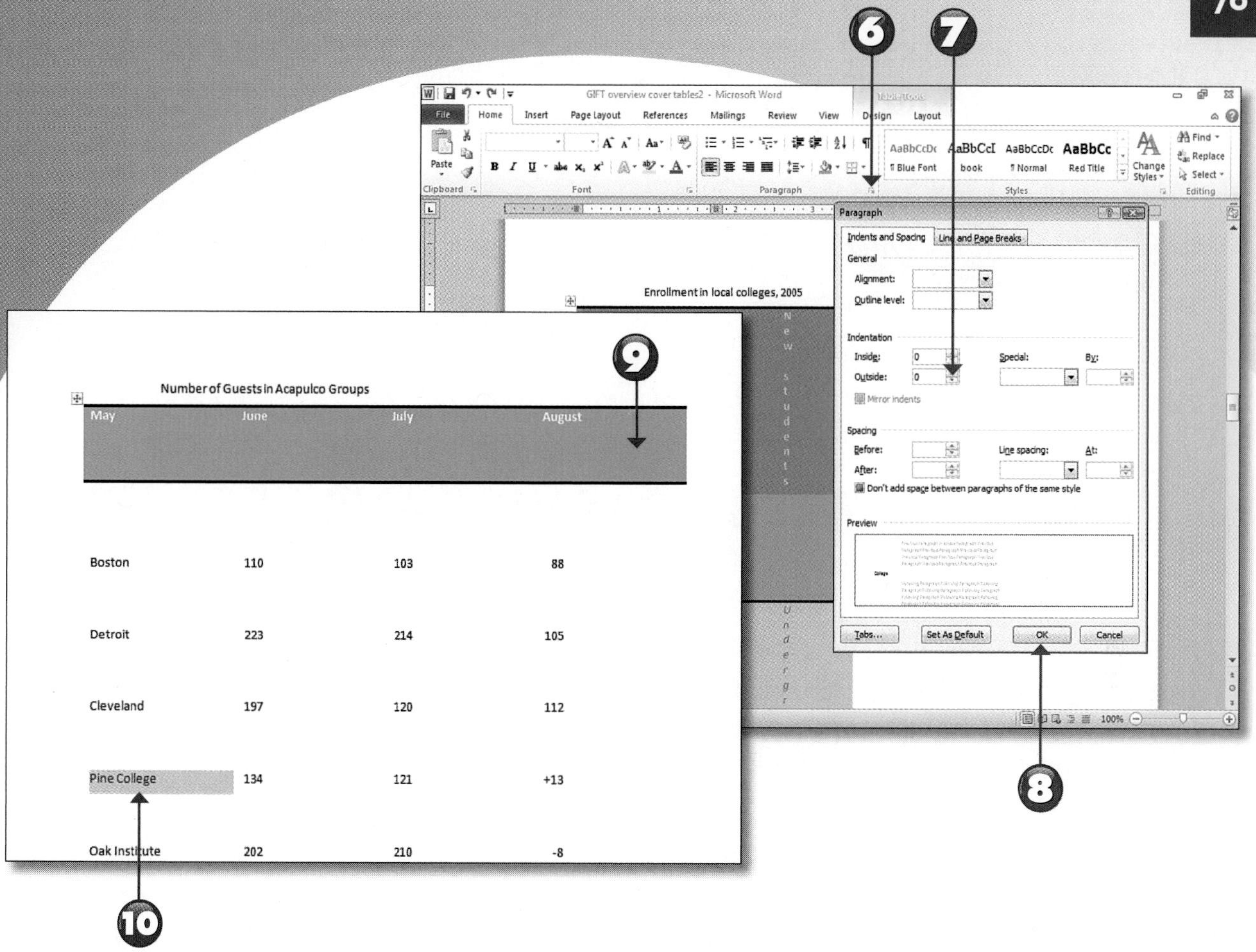

6 On the Home tab of the Ribbon, click the **Dialog Launch** icon in the Paragraph group.

7 Set the Indentation to 0.

8 Click **OK**.

9 The Quick Table is ready to be edited.

10 Replace the content in the Quick Table with your own information.

End

TIP

Sorting a Table You can sort the information in your table by selecting a column and clicking **Sort** in the Data group of the Layout tab of Table Tools. You can choose sort order by selecting **Ascending** or **Descending by Text** (alphabetical), Number or Date (if applicable).

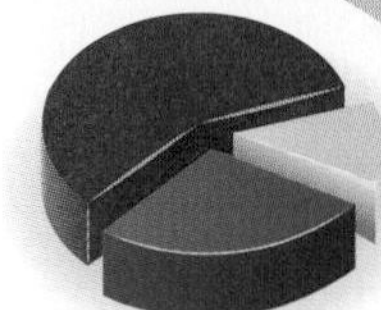

WORKING WITH GRAPHICS AND EFFECTS

Word comes with a wide array of graphics tools that let you put illustrations and diagrams into your document to enhance its appearance and to communicate more clearly.

When you add a graphic, a Picture Tools tab becomes active on the Ribbon, letting you add styles, borders, and effects to an image in the document. The Picture Styles gallery allows you to instantly add preset looks to your image that include borders, shadows, and rotation. You can also use the Picture Tools to crop the image, resize the graphic, or add a picture layout that can include a caption.

Shapes and SmartArt graphics are a good way to make concepts more visual with diagrams that help you tell your story.

Word 2010 also has Advanced Typography and the capability to capture a screen from a window in an open program and insert it into your document, which is a good way to create training materials.

USING PICTURE STYLES TO ENHANCE AN IMAGE

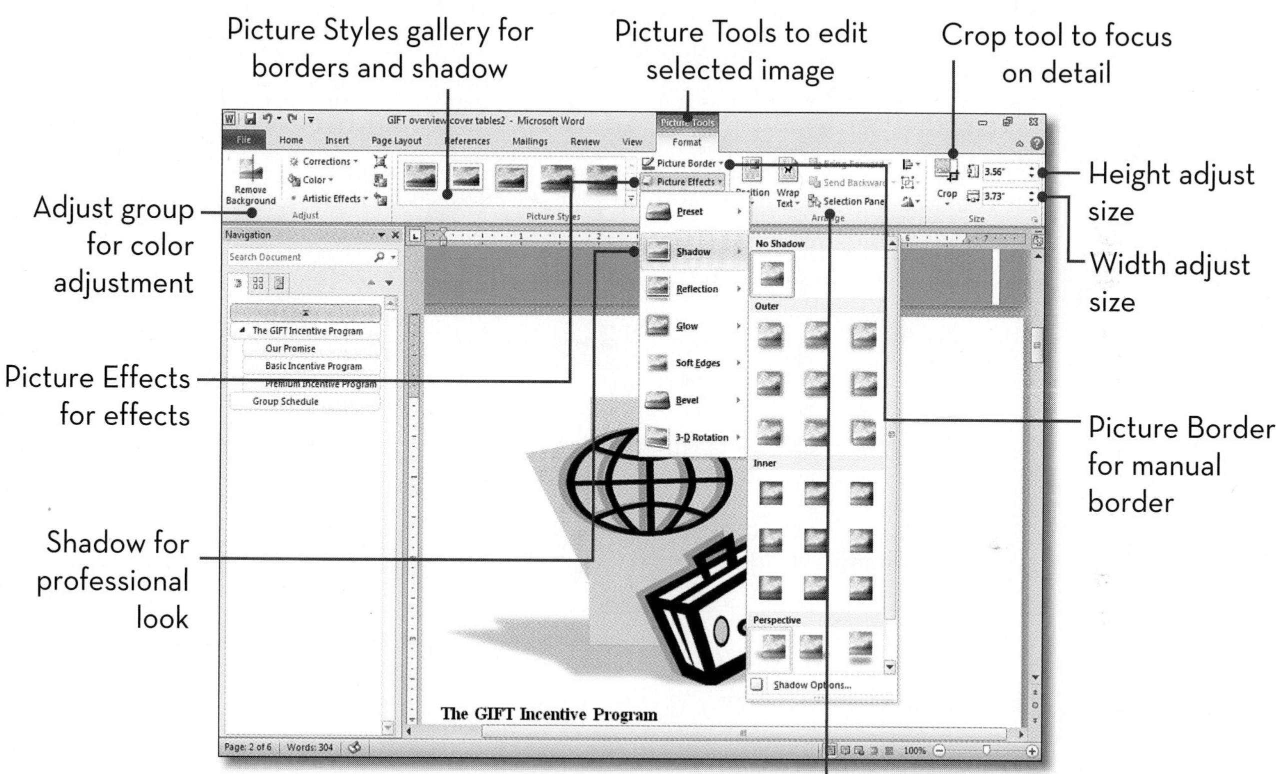

INSERTING A PICTURE

You can use a picture to illustrate a point or to be a logo for letterhead. To insert a picture, you need to know where on your computer it is located. By default, pictures are saved or located in the Pictures folder under your username. Word can acquire images from a wide variety of sources, including from scanners, digital cameras, or downloads from the Internet.

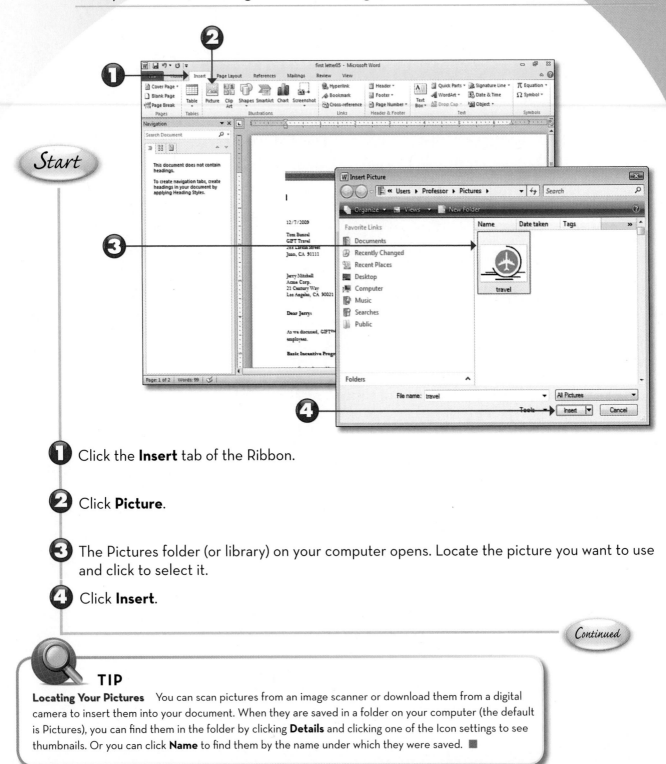

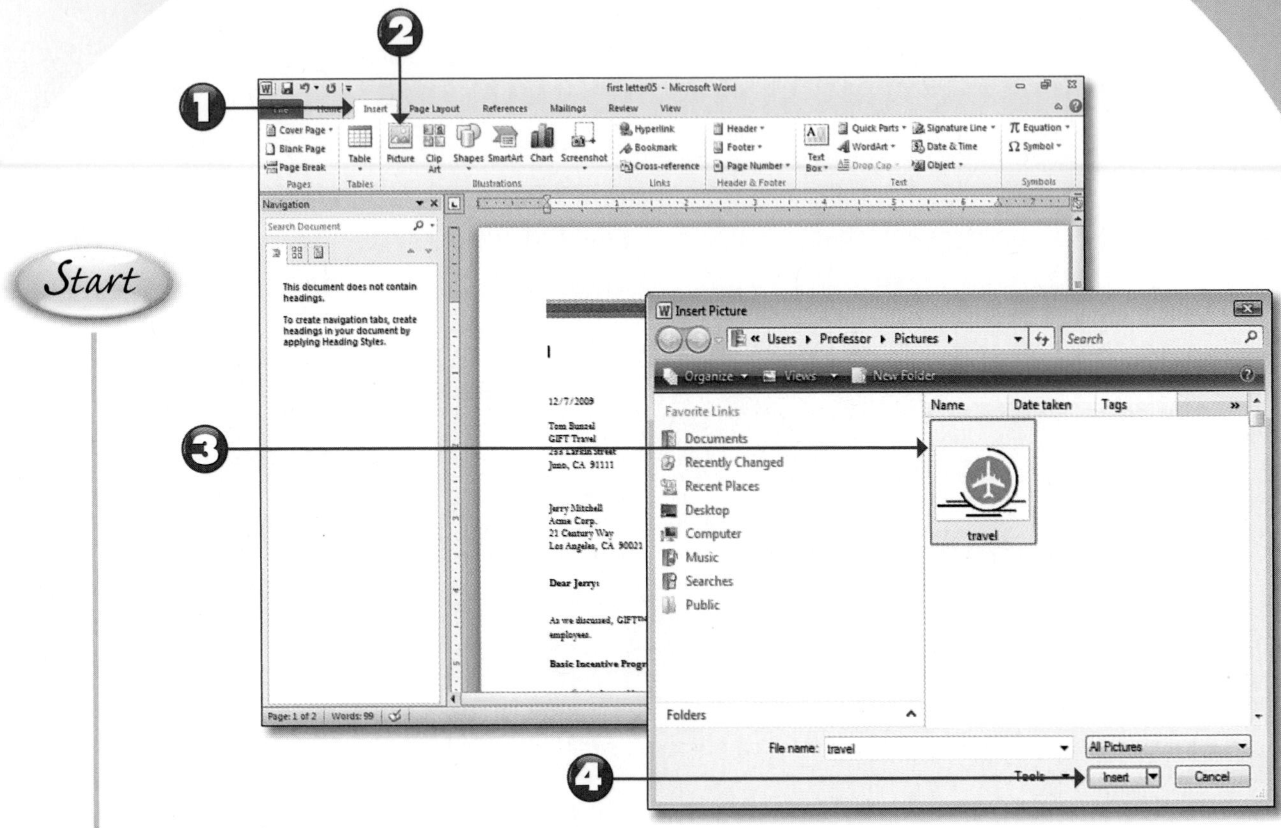

Start

1. Click the **Insert** tab of the Ribbon.
2. Click **Picture**.
3. The Pictures folder (or library) on your computer opens. Locate the picture you want to use and click to select it.
4. Click **Insert**.

Continued

TIP

Locating Your Pictures You can scan pictures from an image scanner or download them from a digital camera to insert them into your document. When they are saved in a folder on your computer (the default is Pictures), you can find them in the folder by clicking **Details** and clicking one of the Icon settings to see thumbnails. Or you can click **Name** to find them by the name under which they were saved.

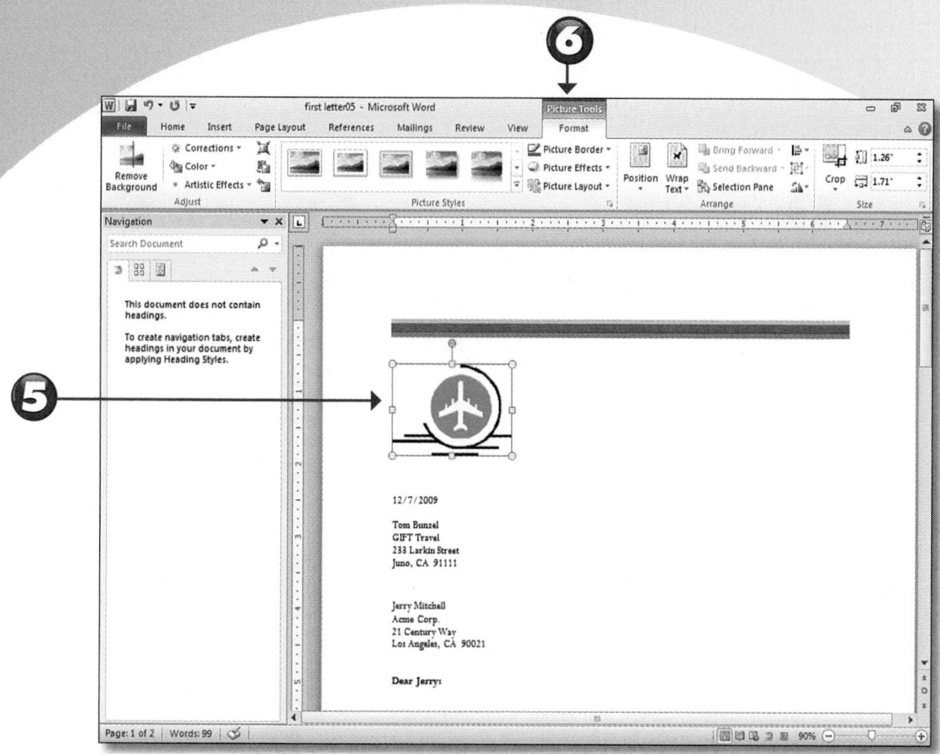

5. The picture is inserted into the document.

6. When a picture is selected in a document, the Picture Tools tab of the Ribbon is active.

End

TIP

Picture File Formats When you click All Pictures in the Insert Picture window, you can review a list of all the picture formats Word accepts. The most common formats are JPEG (.JPG) for digital cameras and the Web and Tagged Image File (.TIF) for larger uncompressed images. ■

TIP

Organizing Pictures in Folders If you have several images for a particular project or client, you might want to keep them all in a specific folder, either in Pictures, in your Documents folder, or on your Desktop. You can create a new folder by right-clicking in an existing folder or on your Desktop, clicking **New**, selecting **Folder**, and then naming your new folder. ■

ADDING A CLIP ART IMAGE

By inserting clip art, you access the Microsoft Office Clip Organizer, which is a catalog of all media on your computer. It lets you search for content in your computer or on the Office website.

Start

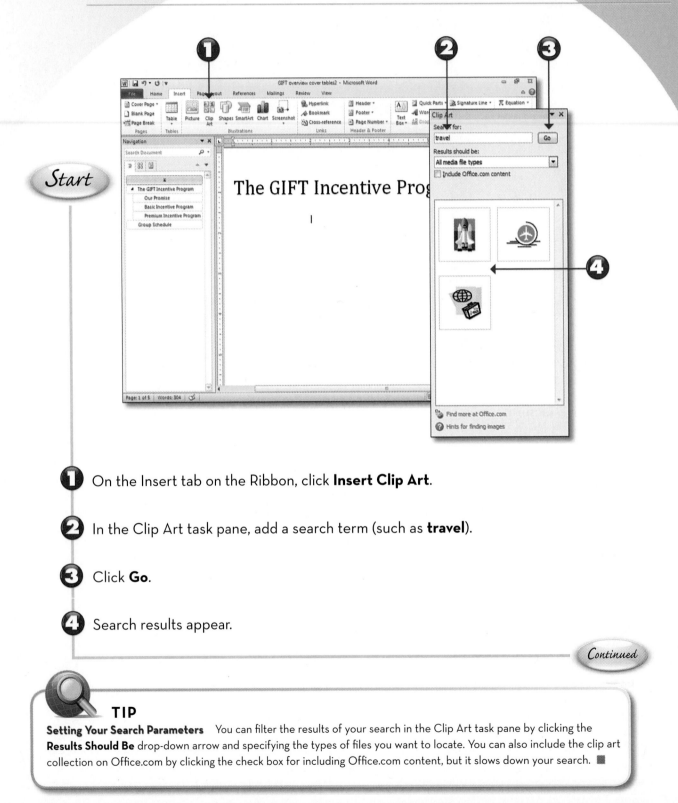

1. On the Insert tab on the Ribbon, click **Insert Clip Art**.
2. In the Clip Art task pane, add a search term (such as **travel**).
3. Click **Go**.
4. Search results appear.

Continued

TIP

Setting Your Search Parameters You can filter the results of your search in the Clip Art task pane by clicking the **Results Should Be** drop-down arrow and specifying the types of files you want to locate. You can also include the clip art collection on Office.com by clicking the check box for including Office.com content, but it slows down your search. ■

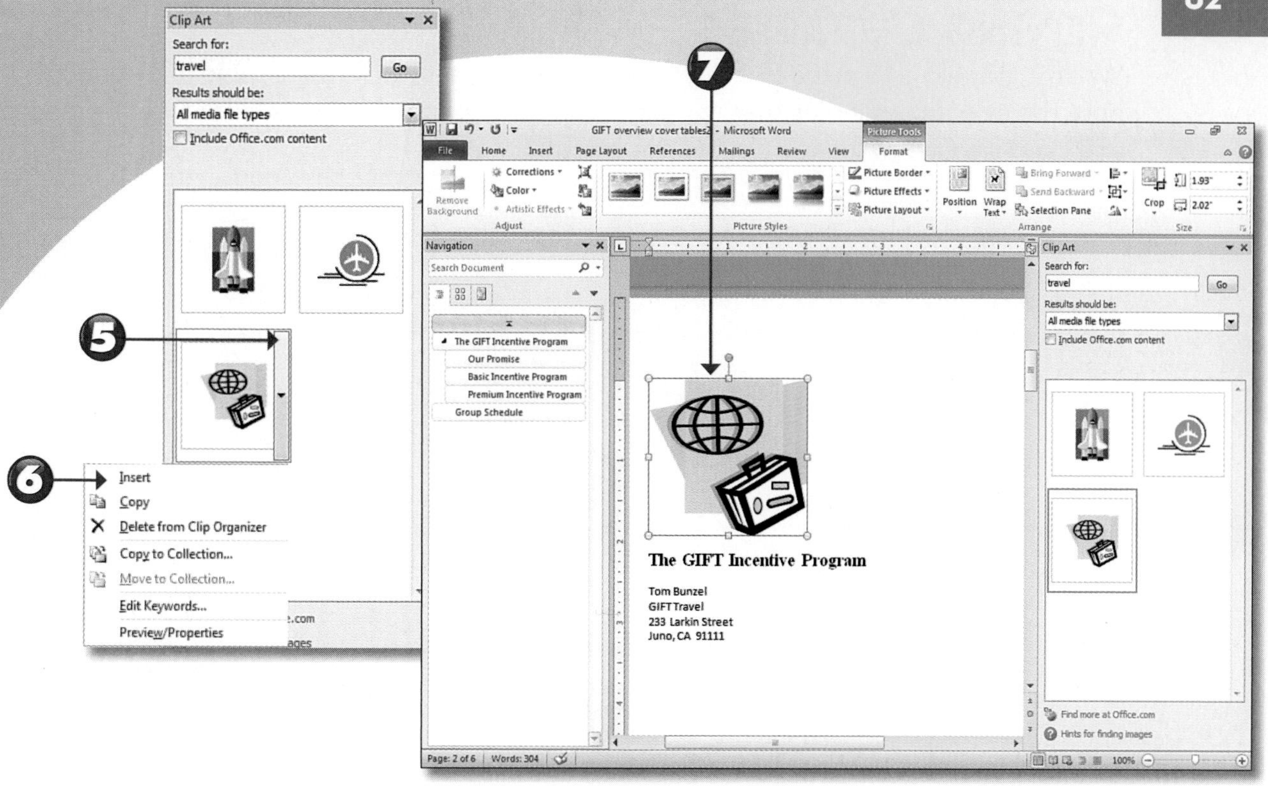

5 Place your cursor over the right side of the image you want to insert and click the drop-down arrow.

6 Click **Insert**.

7 The image is placed into your document and selected, activating the Picture Tools on the Ribbon.

End

TIP

Adding Search Capabilities If you click the drop-down arrow next to a clip art image in the Clip Art task pane, you can choose **Edit Keywords** to tag the image for future searches. You can click **Copy to Collection** to add it to another part of the Clip Organizer.

TIP

Using the Clip Organizer If you like the cataloging features of the Clip Organizer, you can find it under Microsoft Office Tools in your Windows Start menu. To add media to your Clip Organizer (and locate it later in the Clip Art task pane), click **File** in the Clip Organizer and click **Add Clips to Organizer**.

MOVING A GRAPHIC

When a graphic is inserted in a document and selected (click the graphic to select it and note the selection handles that appear around the graphic), you can grab a border and drag and drop it to a new location in the document.

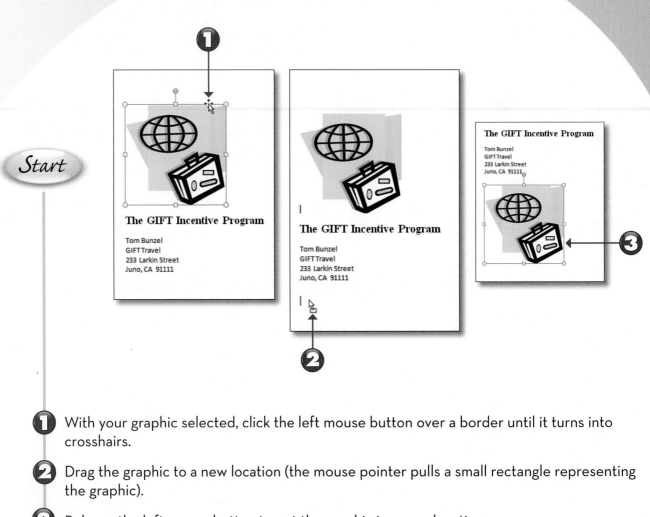

Start

1. With your graphic selected, click the left mouse button over a border until it turns into crosshairs.
2. Drag the graphic to a new location (the mouse pointer pulls a small rectangle representing the graphic).
3. Release the left mouse button to put the graphic in a new location.

End

TIP

Using Paragraph Alignment You can select a graphic and use the Paragraph Alignment options in the Paragraph group of the Home tab to reposition a graphic relative to the page and other text. ■

TIP

Wrapping Text To change the way text is wrapped around a graphic, click the Wrap Text button in the Format tab of the Picture Tools when the graphic is selected. Alternatively, right-click the graphic and select Wrap Text. As you select the various options in Wrap Text, the graphic and text show you a preview of what each option does if clicked. ■

RESIZING A GRAPHIC

When a graphic is inserted into a document and selected (click the graphic to select it and see the selection handles around the graphic), you can grab a corner to pull it in or out to resize the graphic.

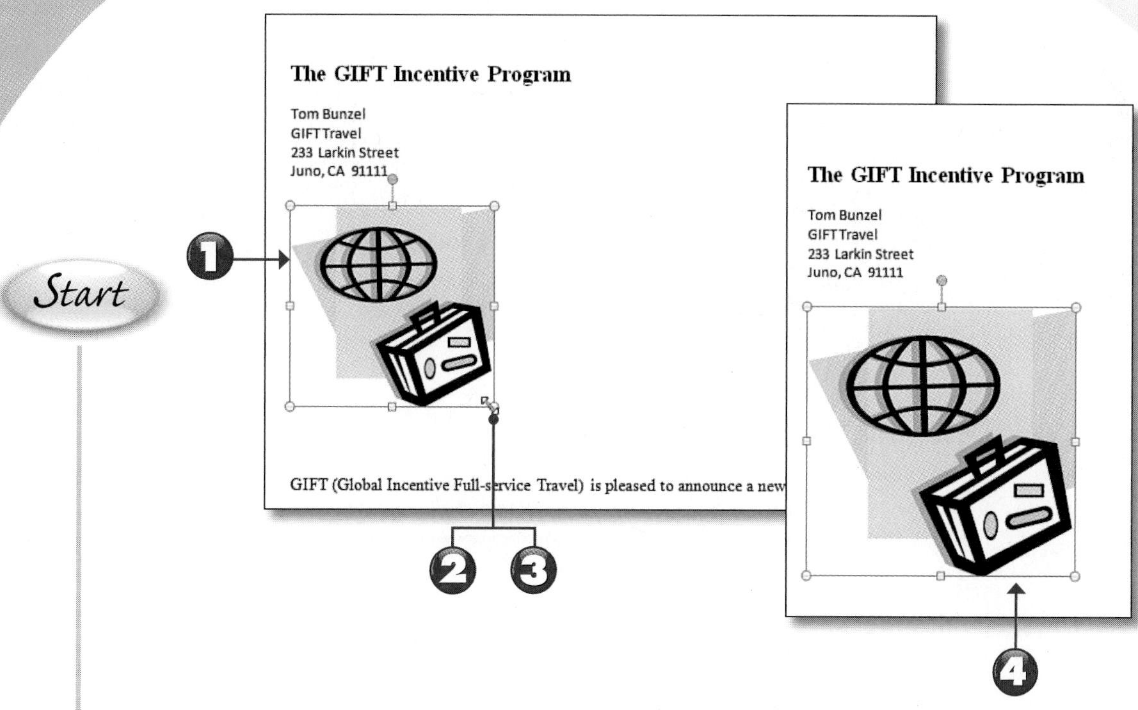

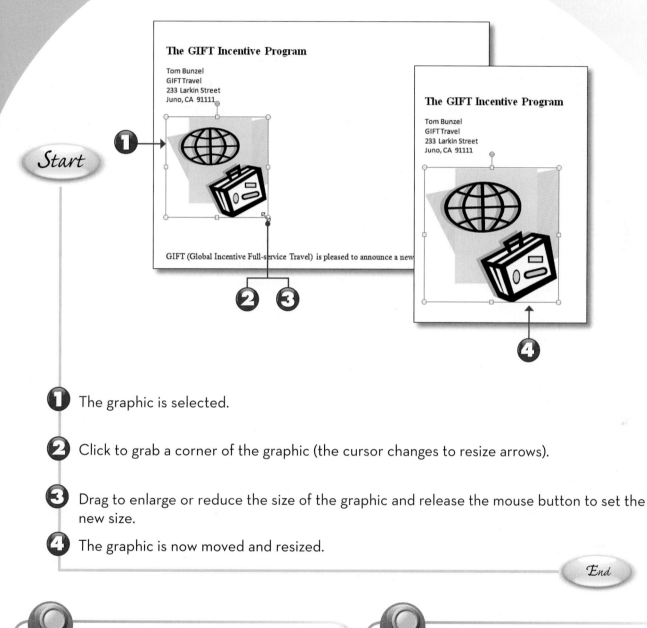

1. The graphic is selected.
2. Click to grab a corner of the graphic (the cursor changes to resize arrows).
3. Drag to enlarge or reduce the size of the graphic and release the mouse button to set the new size.
4. The graphic is now moved and resized.

End

TIP

More Exact Resizing To preserve the aspect ratio of the graphic, hold down the Shift key as you drag a corner. You can resize exactly in inches using the Height and Width fields in the Size group of the Picture Tools Format tab when the graphic is selected. You can also click the Dialog Launch icon in the Size group for more resizing options. ■

TIP

Images or Objects Obscuring Others If you find an image or another object obscuring one another, click to select it and then either click **Bring Forward** or **Send Backward** in the Arrange group of the Picture Tools Format tab to make the obscured object fully visible in front of the other object or image. ■

CROPPING AN IMAGE

Sometimes you want to use only one particular part or portion of an image in your document. Using the Crop tool in Picture Tools, you can select the part of the image you want to display and make the other parts of the image disappear from the document.

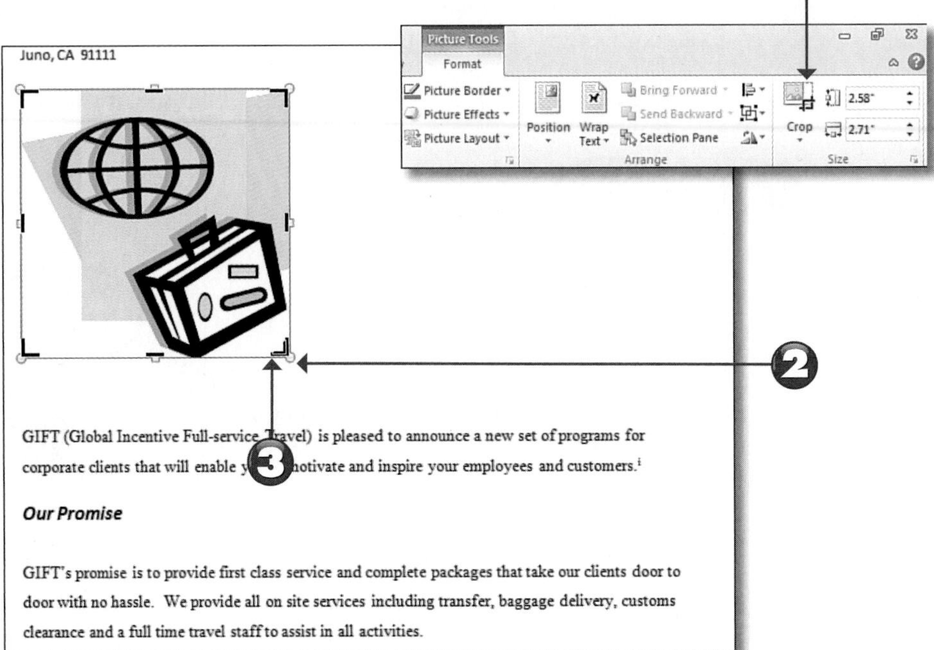
Picture Tools
Format
Picture Border
Picture Effects
Picture Layout
Position
Wrap Text
Bring Forward
Send Backward
Selection Pane
Arrange
Crop
2.58"
2.71"
Size
Juno, CA 91111
GIFT (Global Incentive Full-service Travel) is pleased to announce a new set of programs for corporate clients that will enable y otivate and inspire your employees and customers.
Our Promise
GIFT's promise is to provide first class service and complete packages that take our clients door to door with no hassle. We provide all on site services including transfer, baggage delivery, customs clearance and a full time travel staff to assist in all activities.
1
2
3

Start

1. With your image selected, click **Crop** in the Size group of the Picture Tools Format tab on the Ribbon.
2. Crop handles appear around the image.
3. Grab a corner until a smaller crop handle appears; then drag in to get rid of the unwanted part of the image.

Continued

TIP

Cropping Options Clicking the drop-down arrow under the Crop tool opens other options. You can crop to specific shapes, select an aspect ratio between the height and width, and change the contents of the cropped area by fitting or filling it with the image. ■

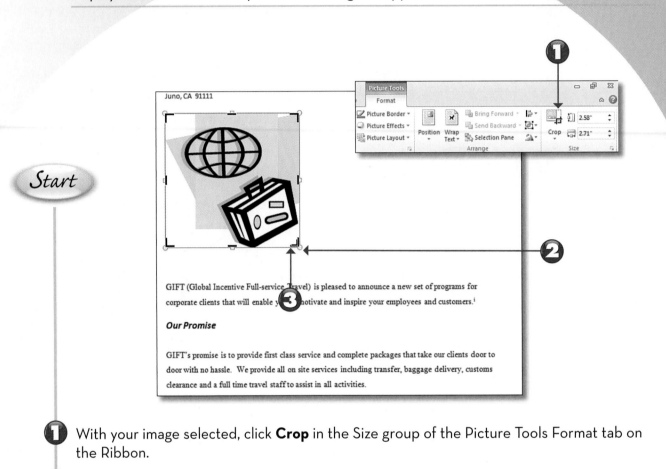

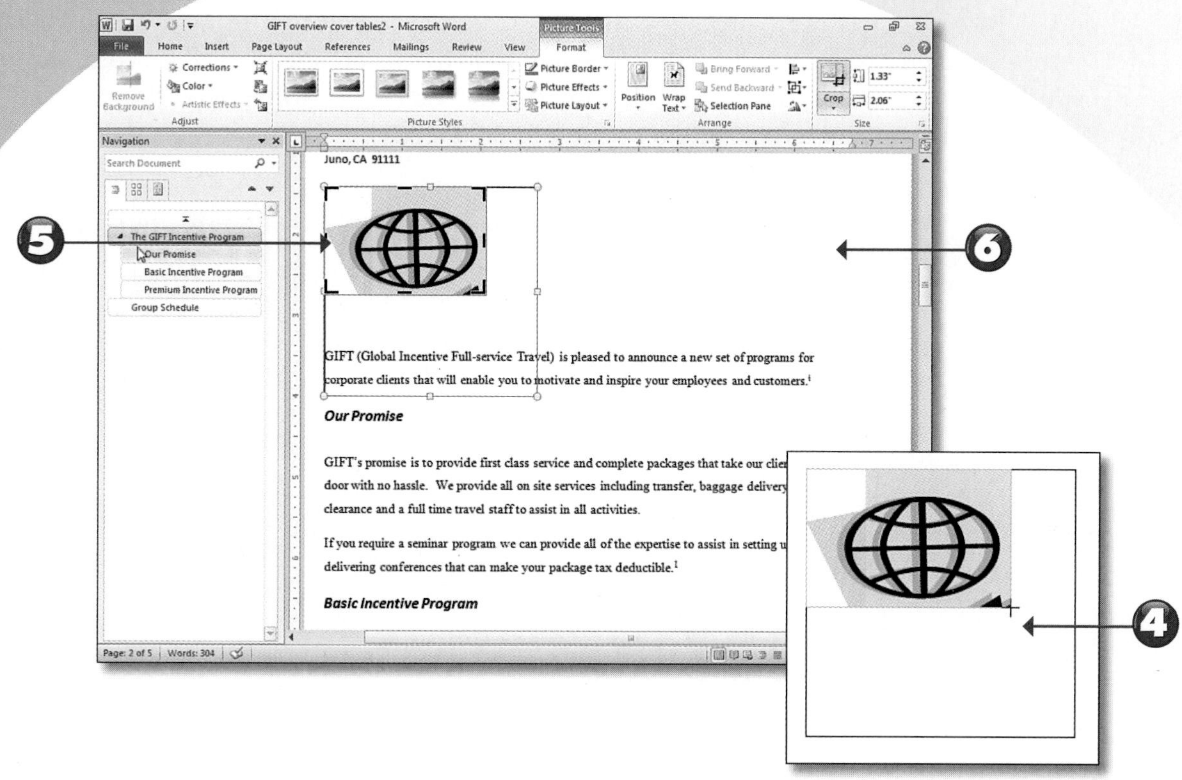

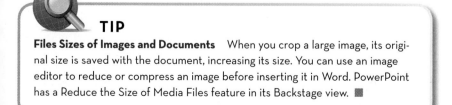

4 The corner of the image turns into a cross shape as you drag. Release the mouse when only the part of the image you want to keep is showing.

5 Only the part of the image you want to show remains visible.

6 Click away from the image to deselect it in the document.

End

TIP

Files Sizes of Images and Documents When you crop a large image, its original size is saved with the document, increasing its size. You can use an image editor to reduce or compress an image before inserting it in Word. PowerPoint has a Reduce the Size of Media Files feature in its Backstage view.

APPLYING PICTURE STYLES AND EFFECTS

Using the Office 2010 Picture Tools, you can quickly apply a coordinated set of special effects to a picture from the Picture Styles gallery. You can also add picture borders and picture effects directly from the Picture Border and Picture Effects drop-down lists. Picture borders can be adjusted by color, line thickness, and line style. Picture effects include Reflections, Glows, 3D Effects, Bevels, Soft Edges, and Shadows. You can use the Picture Layout feature to add a caption to an image.

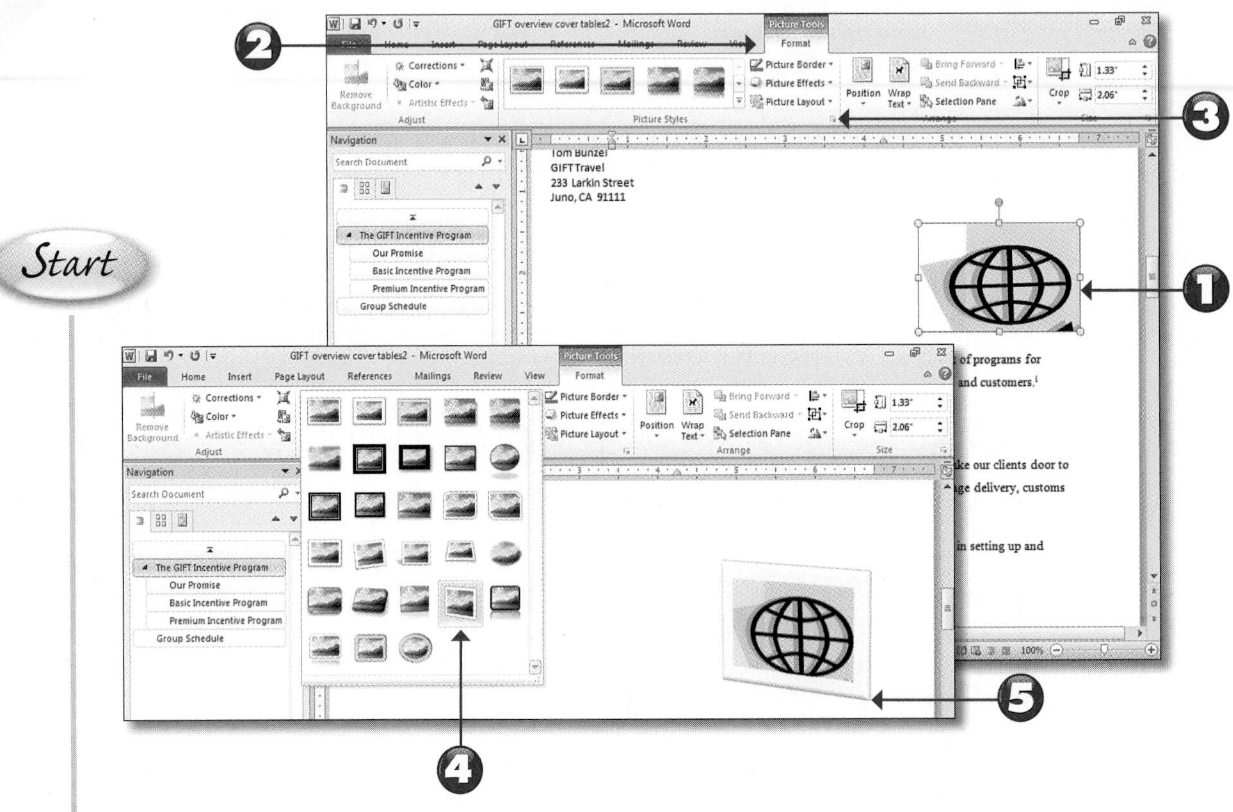

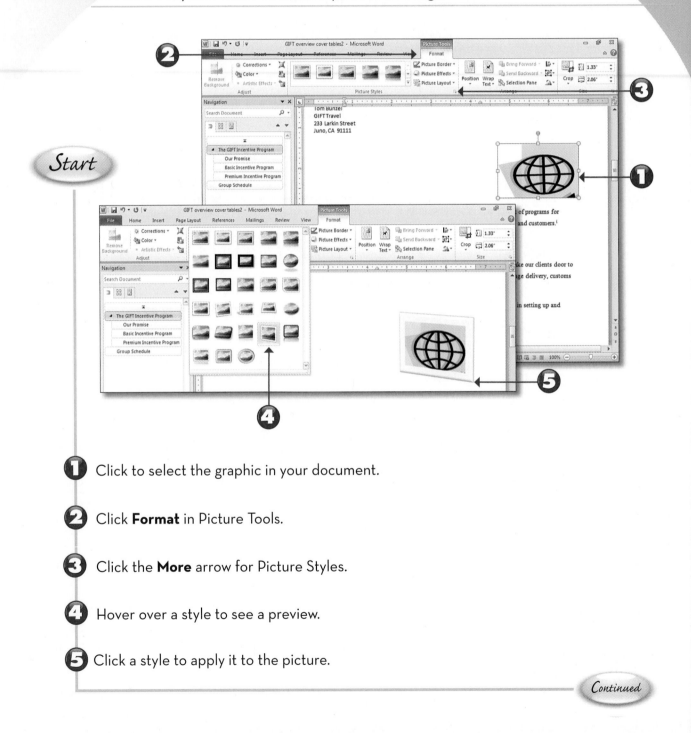

1. Click to select the graphic in your document.

2. Click **Format** in Picture Tools.

3. Click the **More** arrow for Picture Styles.

4. Hover over a style to see a preview.

5. Click a style to apply it to the picture.

Continued

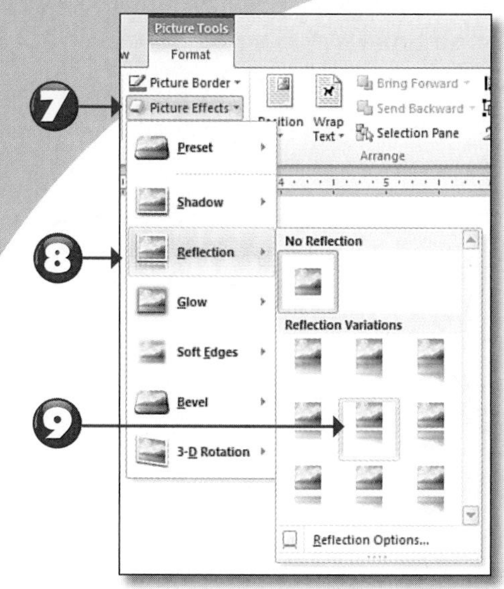

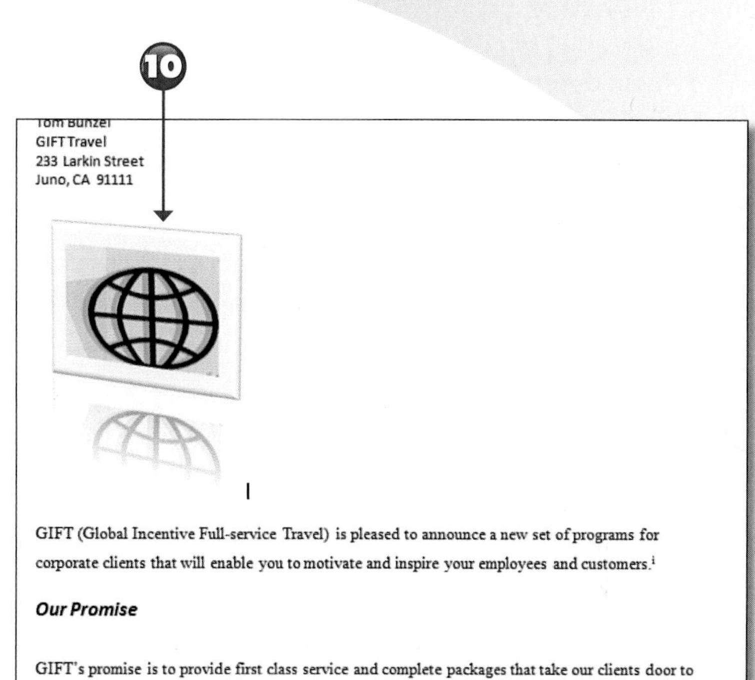

Tom Bunzel
GIFT Travel
233 Larkin Street
Juno, CA 91111

GIFT (Global Incentive Full-service Travel) is pleased to announce a new set of programs for corporate clients that will enable you to motivate and inspire your employees and customers.[i]

Our Promise

GIFT's promise is to provide first class service and complete packages that take our clients door to door with no hassle. We provide all on site services including transfer, baggage delivery, customs clearance and a full time travel staff to assist in all activities

7. Click **Picture Effects**.

8. Click an effect such as **Reflection**.

9. Hover over an effect to see a preview and then click to apply the desired effect (in this example, **Reflection**).

10. The picture is set with the new style and effect.

End

TIP

Effects and Themes The effects available are part of the theme applied to a document. If you do not see an effect (like a specific Glow color) available, consider applying a different theme or changing the colors in the current theme and saving it as a new theme (see Chapter 5, "Creating a Table for a Schedule," for more details on themes). ■

TIP

The New Picture Layout Picture Layout, a new feature in Office 2010, lets you add a text caption to a graphic. When you open the options for Picture Layout, you can see a preview of how the text and graphic will look. You can resize or uncrop the picture to add a new caption. ■

INSERTING A SMARTART DIAGRAM

SmartArt graphics are preset diagrams that let you add text to depict a concept graphically instead of just with words. SmartArt diagrams include List, Process, Cycle, Hierarchy, Relationship, Matrix, Pyramid, and Picture. You can change one SmartArt diagram into another if you determine later a different type is preferable.

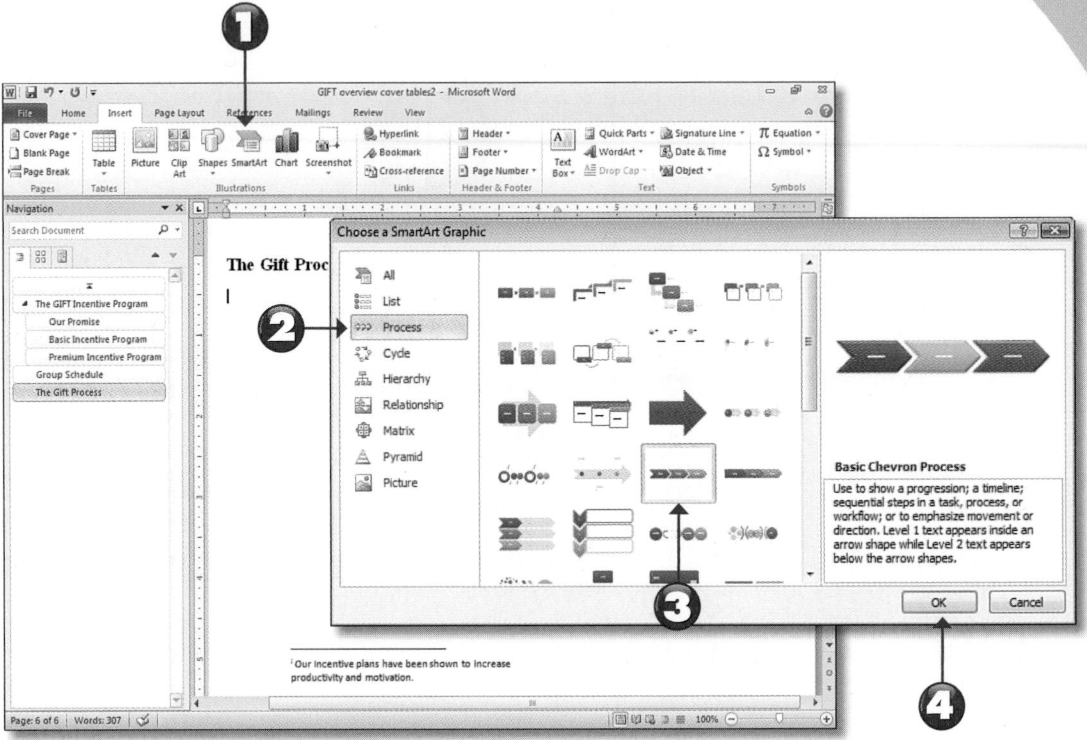

Start

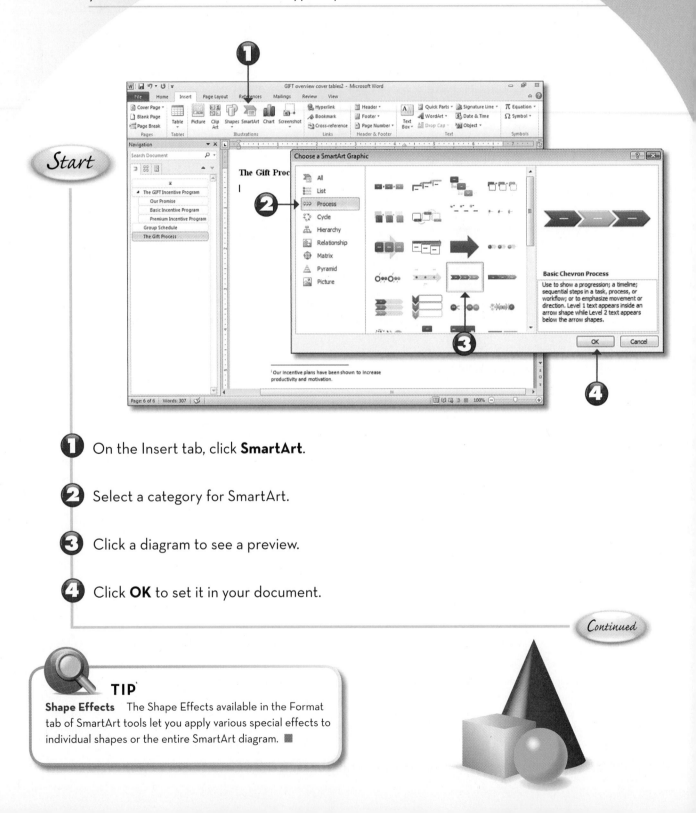

1. On the Insert tab, click **SmartArt**.
2. Select a category for SmartArt.
3. Click a diagram to see a preview.
4. Click **OK** to set it in your document.

Continued

TIP

Shape Effects The Shape Effects available in the Format tab of SmartArt tools let you apply various special effects to individual shapes or the entire SmartArt diagram.

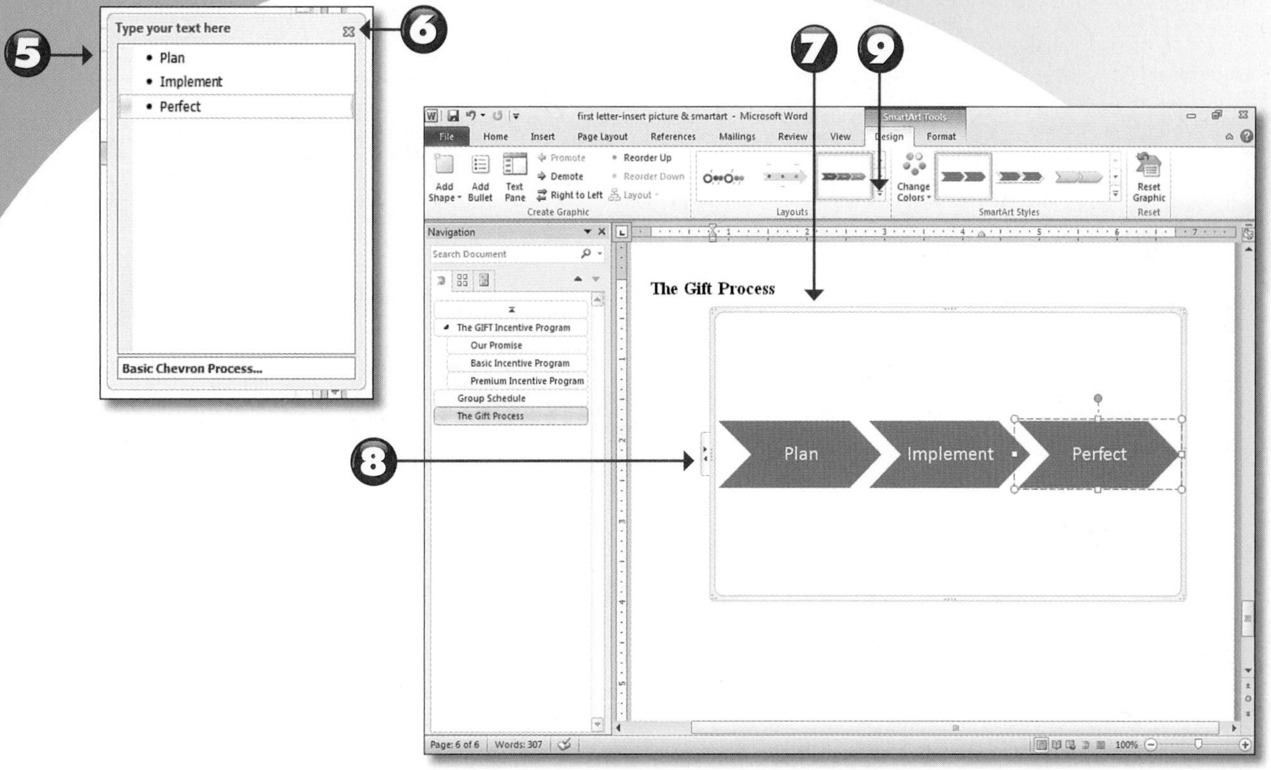

5 Fill in the text for each shape.

6 Click **x** (the close button).

7 The SmartArt diagram is set.

8 You can click the left arrow to reopen the text pane.

9 Click **More** to see other Layouts you can use to change the diagram.

Continued

TIP

Shape and Text Formats Formats available in the Format tab of SmartArt tools let you fine-tune your SmartArt diagram by changing the colors, fills, and effects of individual shapes and changing the appearance of your text, including using WordArt styles. However, when you apply a Layout or SmartArt style from the Design tab, it may overwrite your formatting choices.

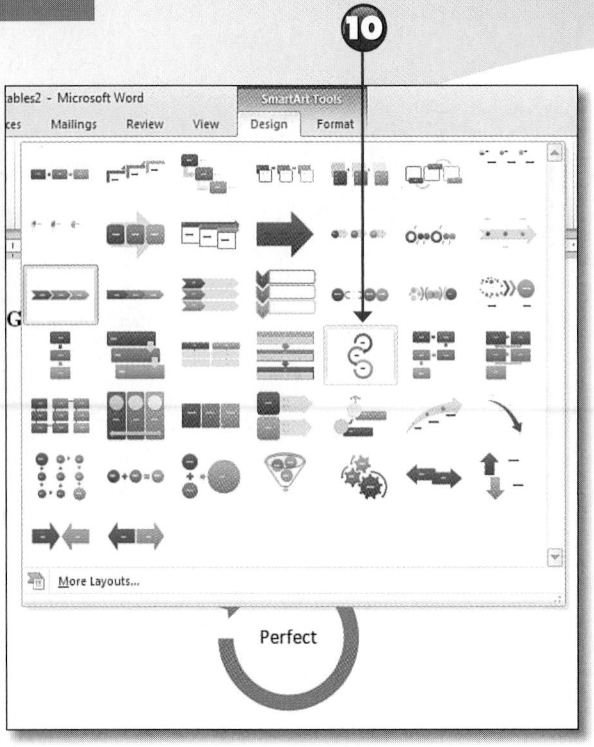

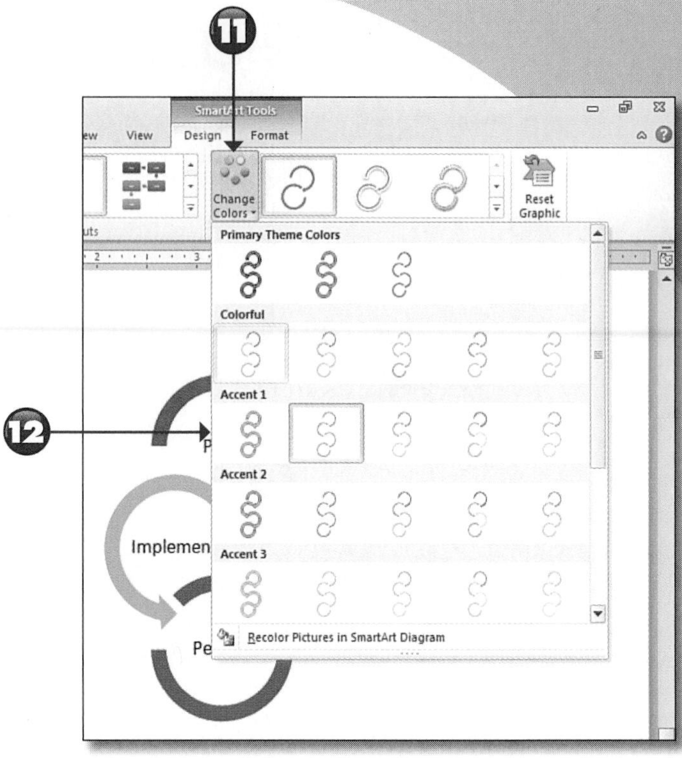

10 Hover your mouse cursor to preview another layout and click the layout to change the diagram.

11 Click **Change Colors** in the Design tab of SmartArt Tools.

12 Click to apply a Colorful color set.

Continued

TIP

Available Colors The Change Colors selections available are part of the theme applied to the document. If you do not see the colors you want available, consider applying a different theme or changing the colors in the current theme and saving it as a new theme (see Chapter 5 for more details on themes).

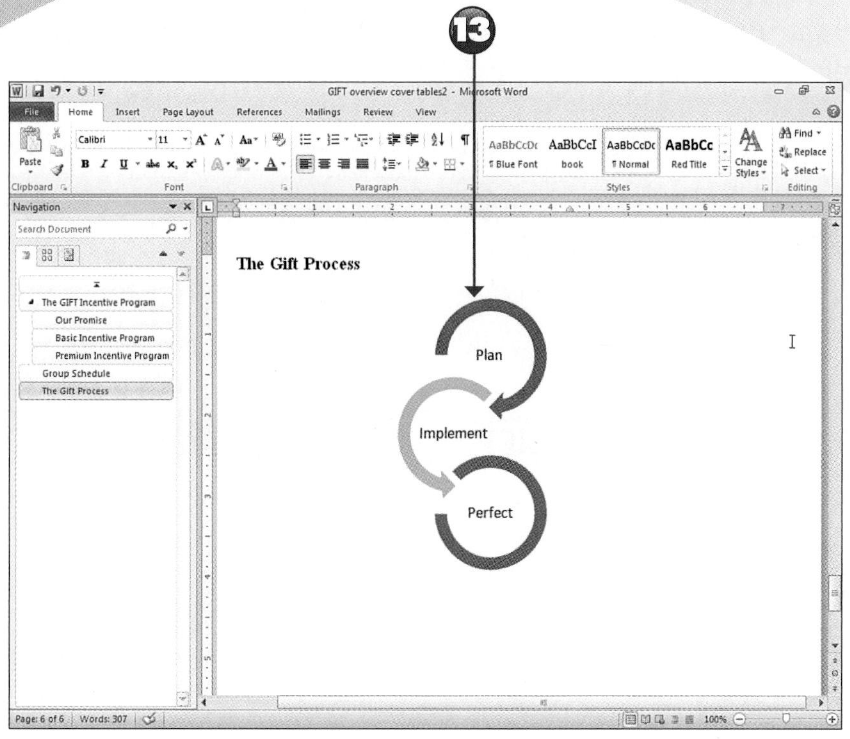

13 The new colorful diagram represents your concept in the document.

End

TIP

SmartArt and PowerPoint Bullets In Office 2010, you can convert PowerPoint bullets into SmartArt diagrams by selecting the bullets, right-clicking, and choosing **Convert to SmartArt**.

USING OPENTYPE LIGATURES

In typography, a ***ligature*** is a combination of certain letters that are joined together. Word 2010 includes the feature to enable ligatures for certain fonts, like Calibri (the default font in Word 2010), Corbel, and Cambria. This feature can give all or portions of your document (like the title) the look of fine typography.

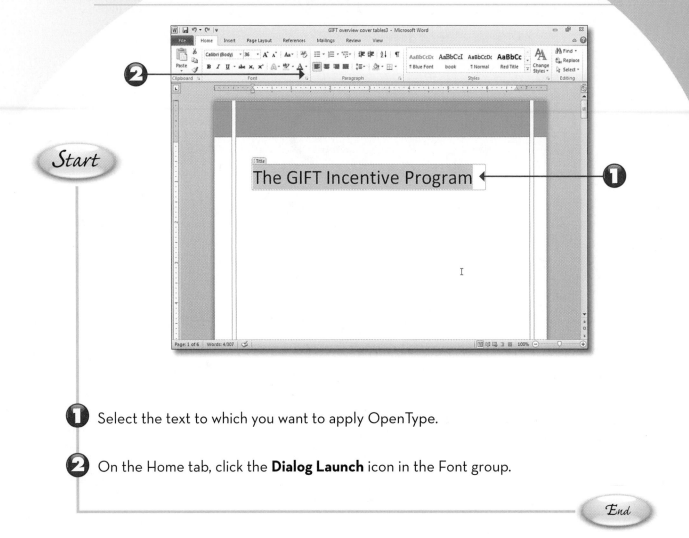

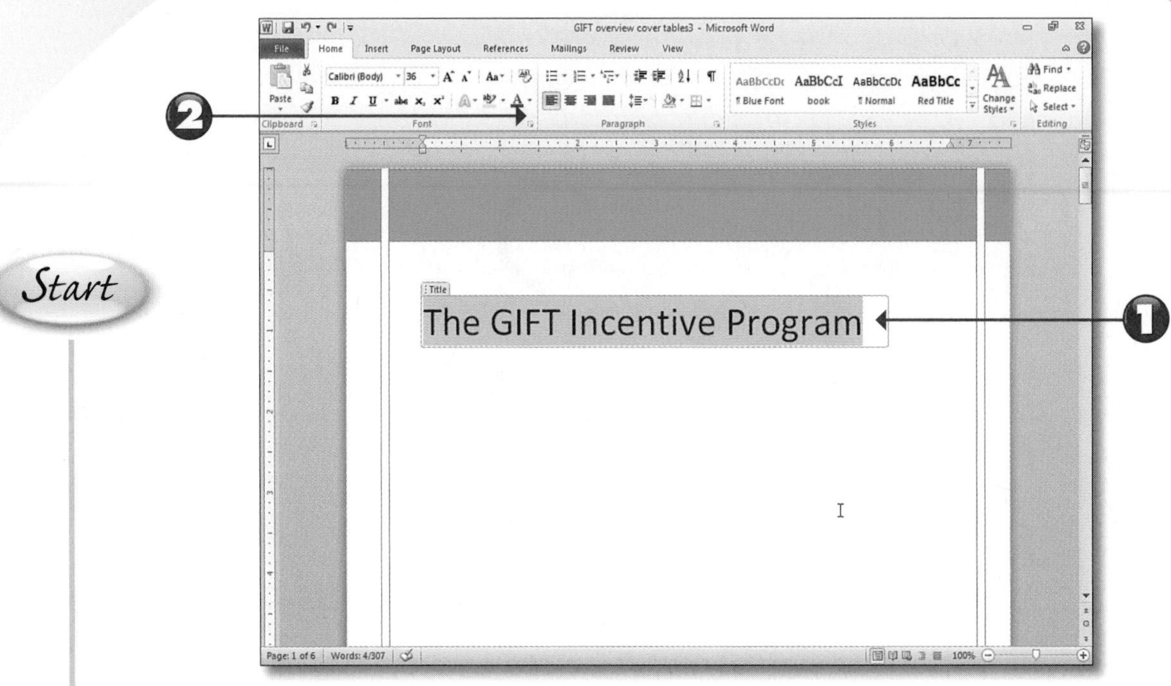

1. Select the text to which you want to apply OpenType.

2. On the Home tab, click the **Dialog Launch** icon in the Font group.

TIP

Disabling OpenType You can disable OpenType features entirely by opening **Options in Backstage** view, selecting the **Advanced tab**, and checking **Disable OpenType Font Formatting Features** under the Layout Options that are right at the bottom (click the arrow if necessary to expand the Layout Options).

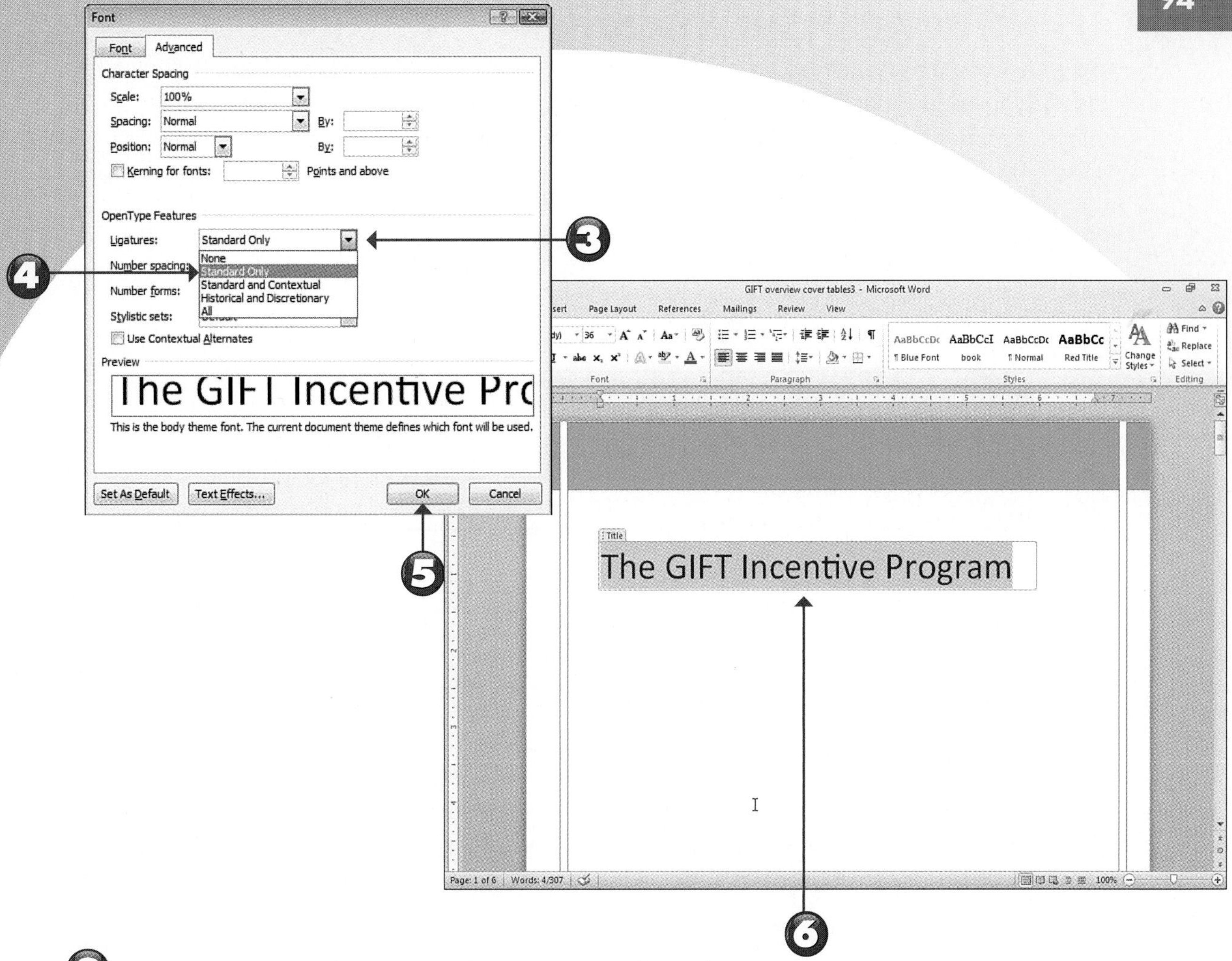

3 On the Advanced tab, click the **Ligatures** drop-down arrow.

4 Select **Standard Only**.

5 Click **OK.**

6 The OpenType combination of the letters ***t*** and ***i*** is established as the two letters are connected in fine typography.

End

TIP

Other Sets of Ligatures Other ligatures are available depending on the font being used. In some cases under Ligatures, you see refinements in your type when you choose from Standard and Contextual and Historical and Discretionary or select from the Number Spacing, Number Forms, or Stylistic Sets on the Advanced tab of the Font dialog box.

USING SCREENSHOTS OR SCREEN CLIPPINGS

Screenshots are images taken of what appears on your computer monitor. They are frequently used in computer training or help desk function but can also show web pages, blogs, or any other content that is helpful to include in a document. Word 2010 also provides a way to crop a screenshot before you insert it, using the screen clipping feature.

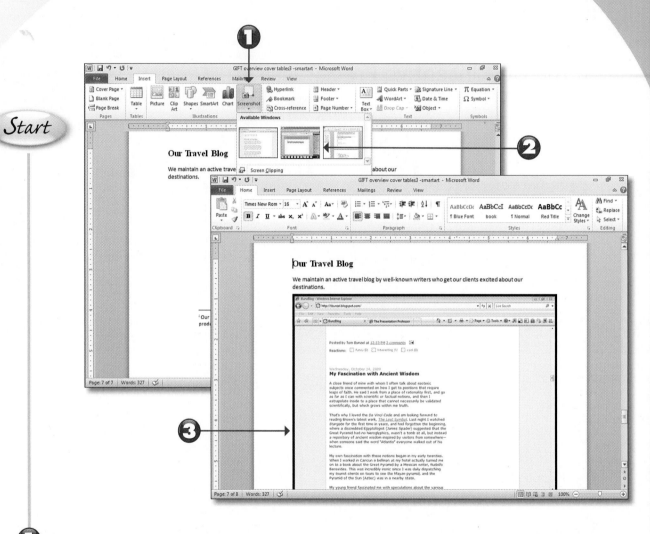

1. On the Insert tab, click **Screenshot**.
2. From the Available Windows, click the one that you want to capture and insert.
3. The screenshot is placed in the document.

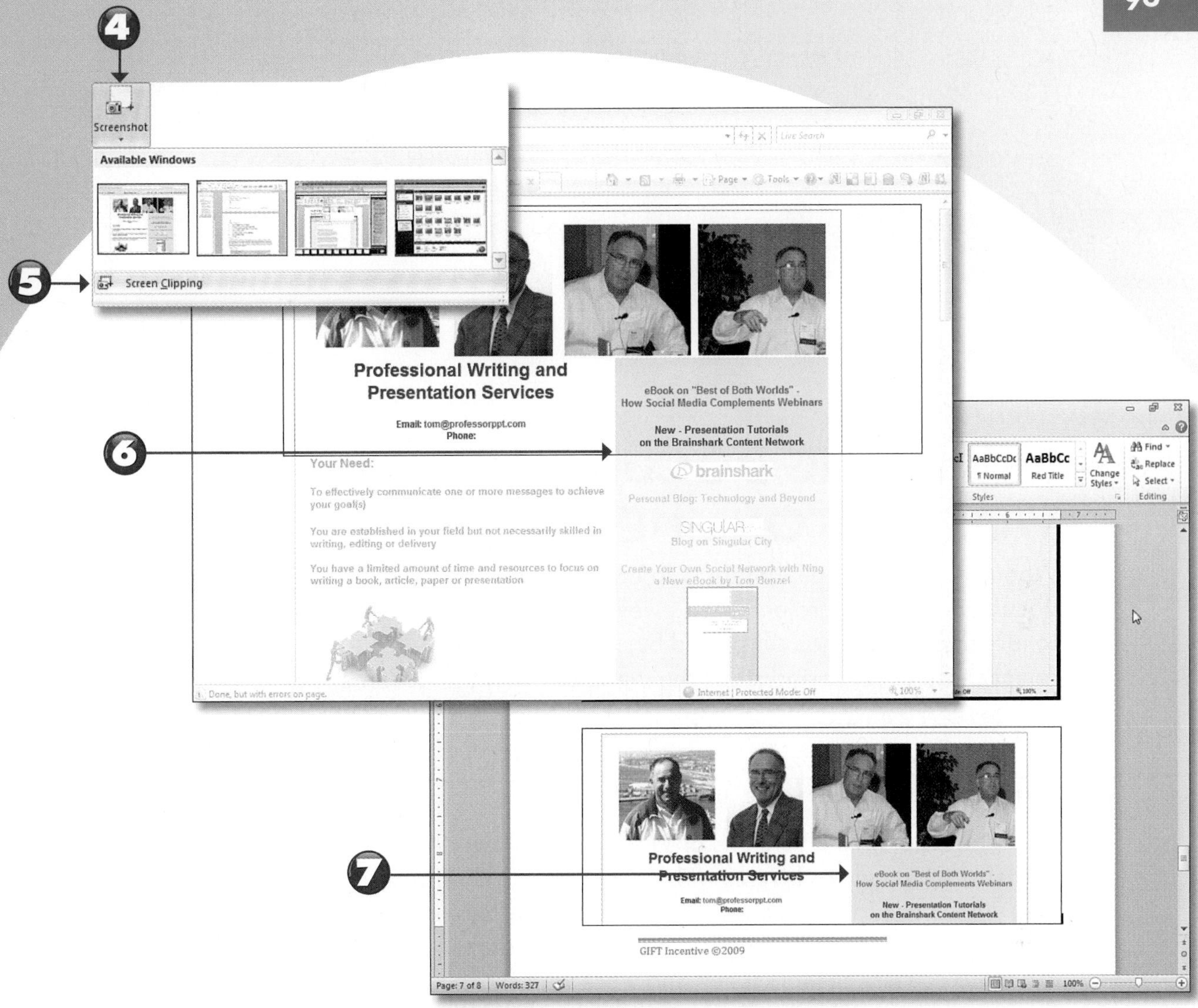

4 On the Insert tab, click **Screenshot**.

5 Click **Screen Clipping**.

6 The screen opens, and you can drag out the portion you want to clip.

7 The clipped portion of the captured screen is added to the document.

End

TIP

Editing Screenshots The Format tab of Picture Tools on the Ribbon lets you add effects or otherwise edit your screenshots or screen clippings because they are pictures that have been placed into the document.

REVIEWING DOCUMENTS AND WORKING ONLINE

When you need to collaborate with others to get feedback or approval on a document or other project, the Review tab of the Ribbon gives you the tools to identify the changes suggested by other Word users. You also can accept or reject those changes and show the markup within the document.

You can also add comments to parts of the document that will appear in the marked-up version's margin, allowing others to understand suggestions or corrections that need to be implemented.

In Office 2010, online versions of Word, Excel, PowerPoint, and OneNote are available on Windows Live as web applications. When you sign in to a Windows Live workspace (or if your company has a SharePoint site on a server), you can maintain versions of your files in various folders in your workspace, allow others to access the workspace and work with those files, and create or edit documents using the new Office 2010 web applications.

USING YOUR WINDOWS LIVE WORKSPACE

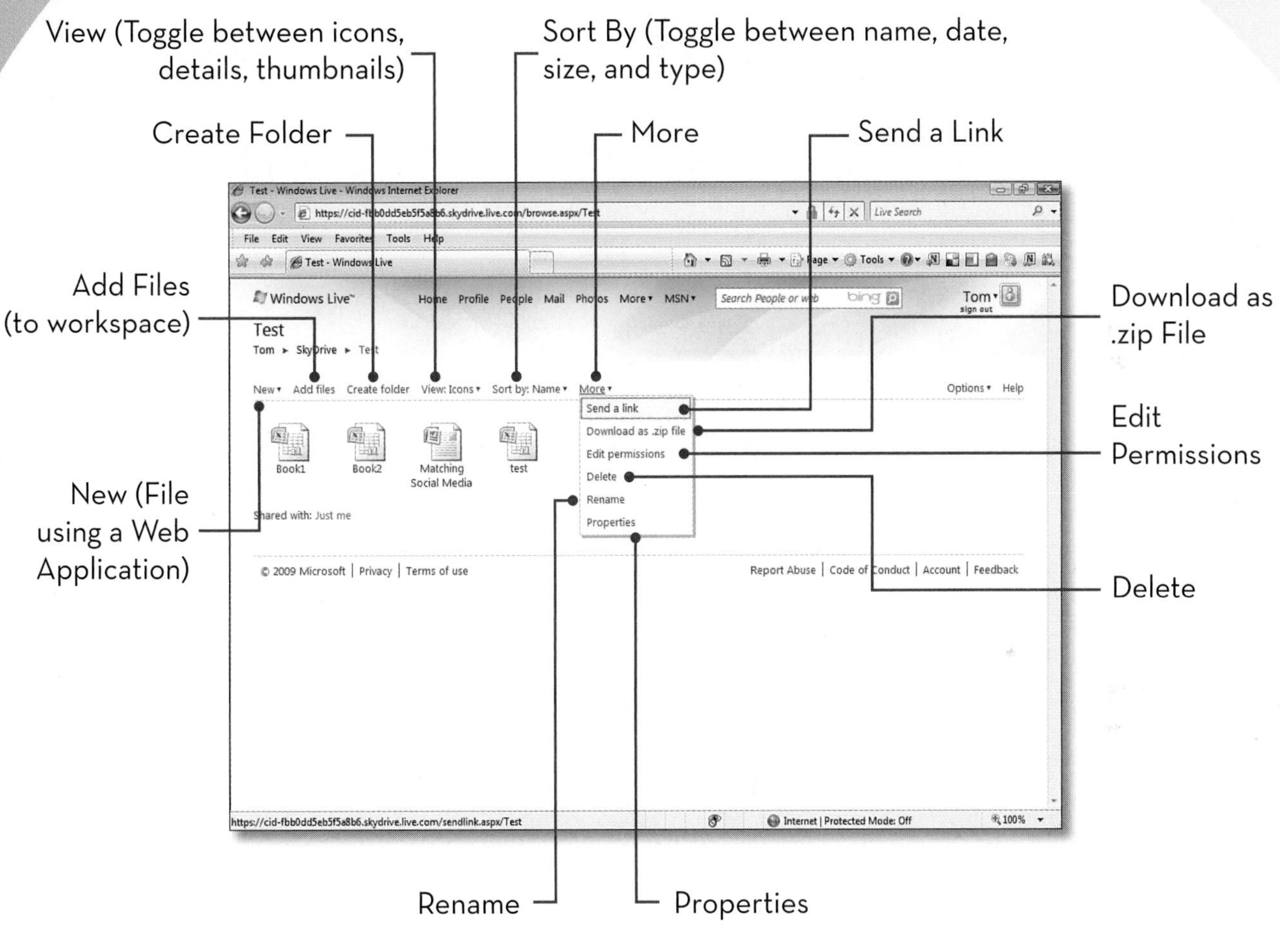

TRACKING CHANGES WITH REVIEWERS

You can enable the highlighting or tracking of any changes made to a document. Tracked changes are color-coded with the name(s) of the reviewer(s) and can be viewed in the Reviewing pane below or adjacent to the document. Reviewers can also add comments that are of a more general nature and to which the original author or any other person with permission to edit the document can respond.

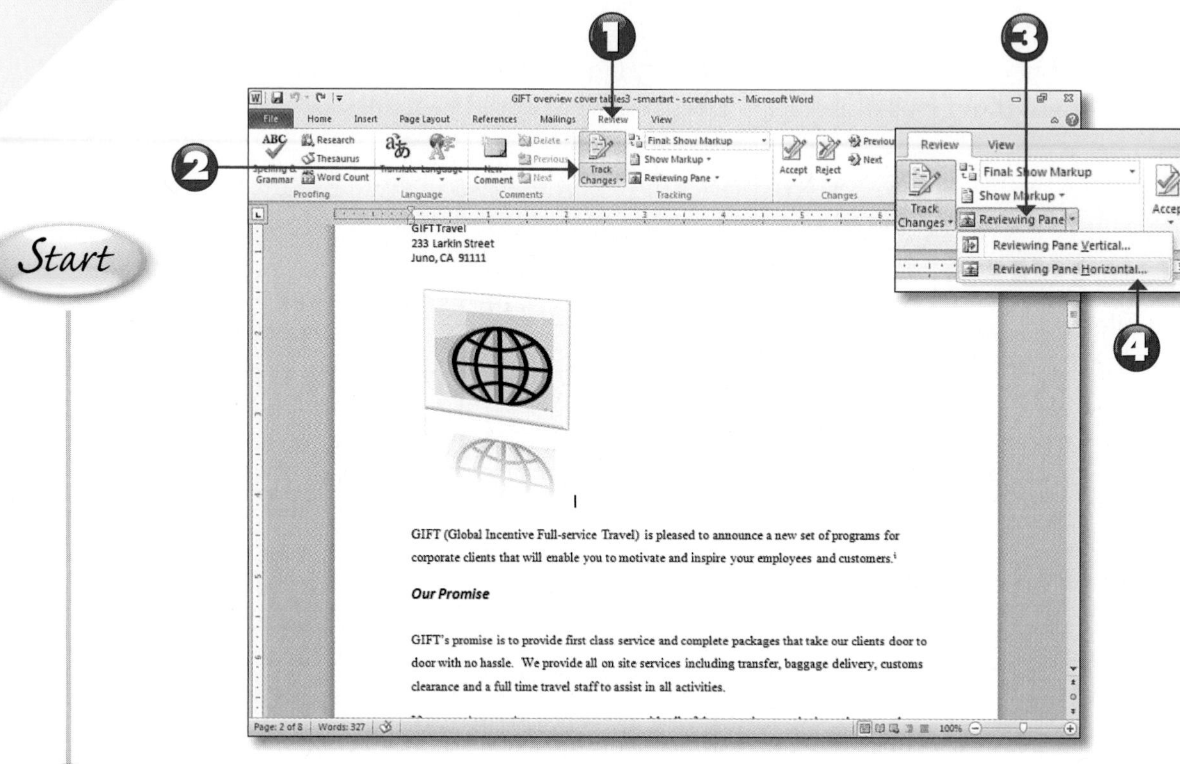

Start

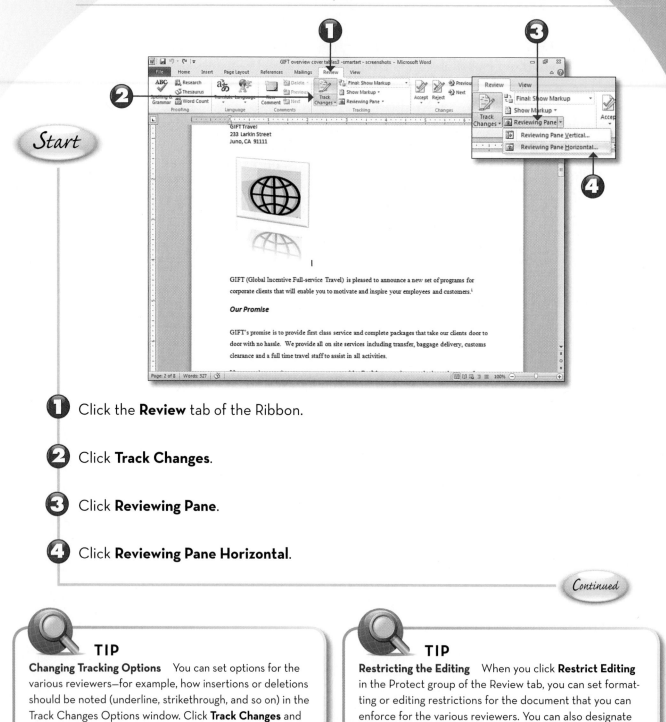

1. Click the **Review** tab of the Ribbon.
2. Click **Track Changes**.
3. Click **Reviewing Pane**.
4. Click **Reviewing Pane Horizontal**.

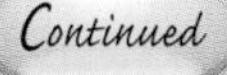

TIP

Changing Tracking Options You can set options for the various reviewers—for example, how insertions or deletions should be noted (underline, strikethrough, and so on) in the Track Changes Options window. Click **Track Changes** and select **Change Tracking Options**.

TIP

Restricting the Editing When you click **Restrict Editing** in the Protect group of the Review tab, you can set formatting or editing restrictions for the document that you can enforce for the various reviewers. You can also designate users or groups as exceptions to your restrictions.

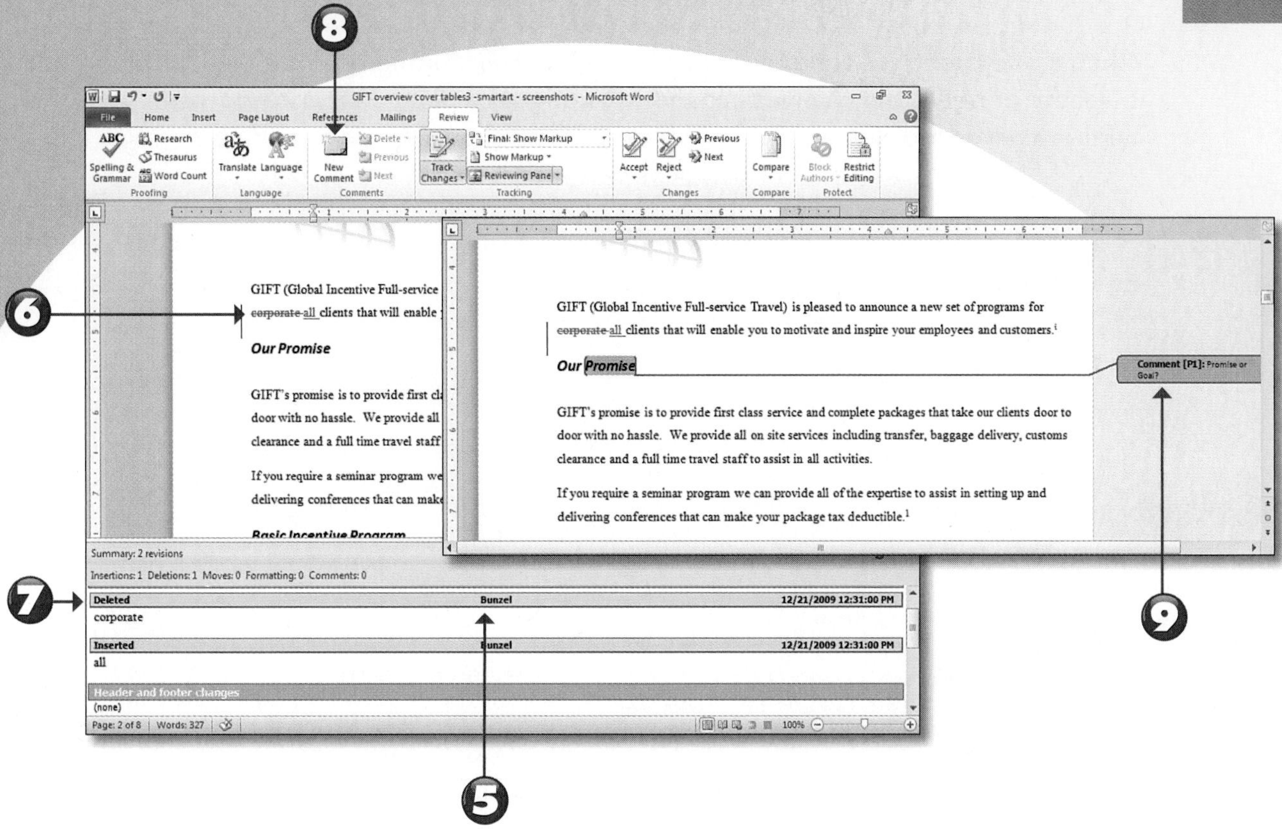

5 The Reviewing pane opens to show changes under the username associated with your version of Word.

6 Select a word and replace it with another.

7 Changes are reflected in the Reviewing pane and in the document.

8 Click **New Comment**.

9 A Comment callout is opened in the margin. You can add a comment for the author or other reviewers.

End

TIP

Comparing Documents If you have multiple documents that have been changed by different editors or reviewers, you can click the **Compare** button in the Compare group on the Review tab to open the documents side-by-side and choose the appropriate parts of either version to use in a final version. ■

101

ACCEPT AND REJECT REVIEWERS' CHANGES

When a document has gone through a set of reviews by other users, a user with permission to accept or reject the changes can move through the document and address each comment or change individually, or accept or reject all changes in the document.

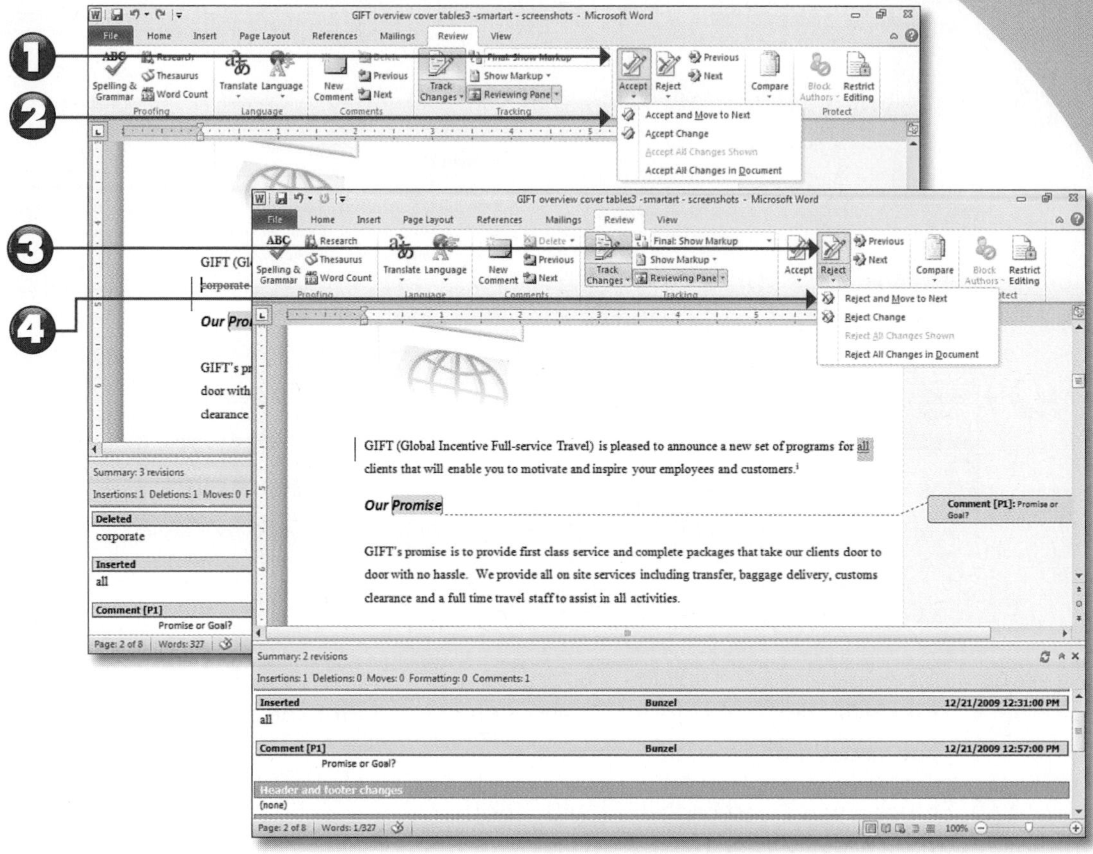

Start

1. On the Review tab, to accept a change, click the **Accept** drop-down arrow.
2. Click **Accept and Move to Next**.
3. To reject a change, click the **Reject** drop-down arrow.
4. Click **Reject and Move to Next**.

End

TIP

Inspecting the Document After your reviewers have finished their work, you can use the Prepare for Sharing window under Info in the Backstage view to select **Check for Issues** and then click **Inspect Document.** *The Document Inspection can strip out reviewer's comments, including documents and revisions, the document properties, and other extraneous data.* Once this data is removed, it is gone, so saving a version as a backup is advised. ■

HIDING AND SHOWING MARKUP

The Tracking Group in the Review tab of the Ribbon lets you see various versions of the document: Final: Show Markup, Final, Original: Show Markup, and Original. You can change the view of the document to hide or show the markup and display the Final or Original version of the document.

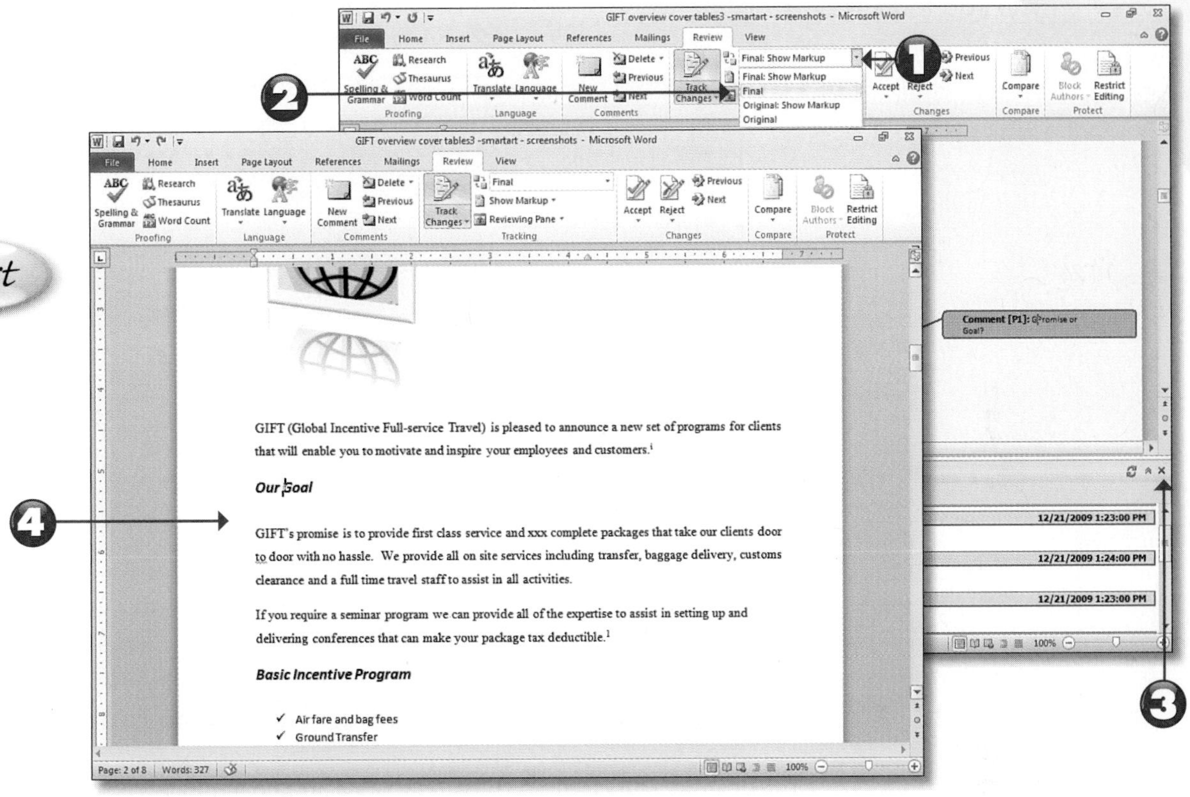

Start

1. Click the **Final: Show Markup** drop-down arrow.
2. Click **Final**.
3. Click **x** (the close button) to close the Reviewing pane.
4. The document is displayed without markup.

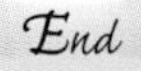

TIP

Seeing All Reviewers If you click the **Show Markup** drop-down arrow in the Tracking group of the Review tab and click the arrow by **Reviewers**, you can see a list of the document's reviewers. If you check or uncheck these reviewers' names, you can show or hide their comments and changes.

TIP

Returning to the Original If you need to get back to the version of the document that was first sent out for review without changes, click **Final: Show Markup** and then select **Original**. If desired, you can save this version to safeguard what was created before the file was sent out for review.

CREATING A FOLDER FOR WEB APPLICATIONS

Web applications of Word, Excel, PowerPoint, and OneNote 2010 are available online as part of SharePoint services if you use Windows Server or in Windows Live. In Windows Live, *when you register with a username and password,* you are provided a workspace with four folders: My Documents, for just your files; Public, for files to be shared with everyone; Favorites, for accumulating web addresses; and Shared Favorites, for use by those users you add to your personal network.

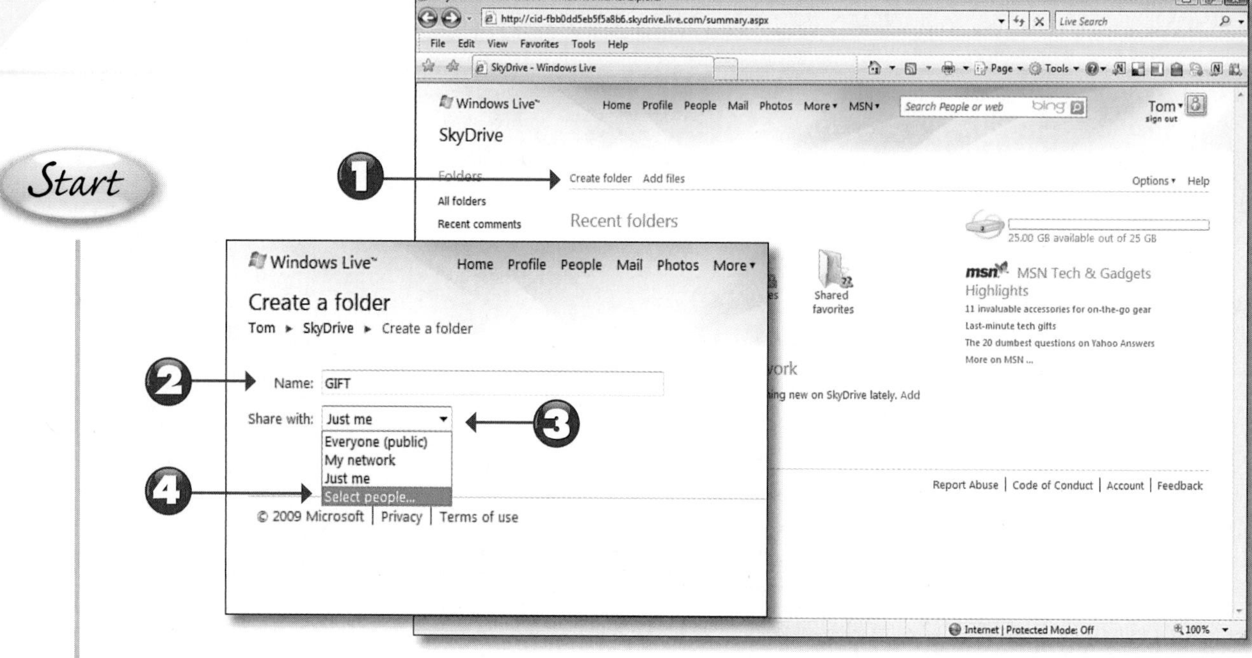

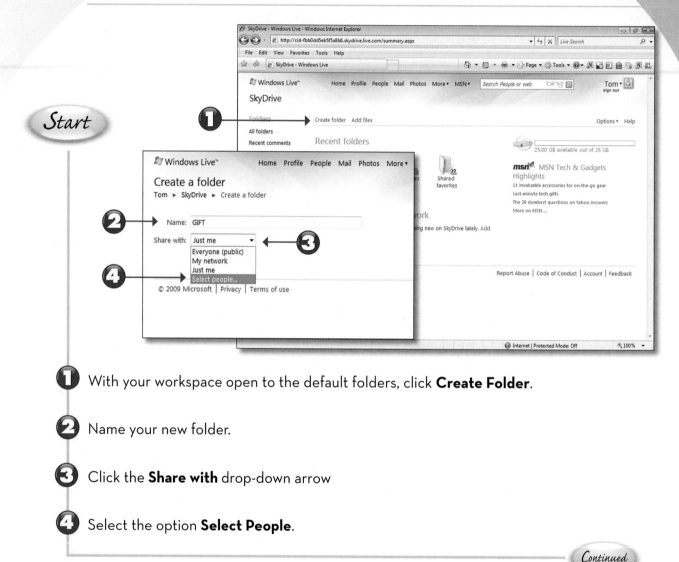

1. With your workspace open to the default folders, click **Create Folder**.
2. Name your new folder.
3. Click the **Share with** drop-down arrow
4. Select the option **Select People**.

Continued

NOTE

Adding a Network You can add people to your network and give permission to everyone in your network for a given folder. In your main workspace view, you can see recent activity for those in your network. Just click **Add People** if necessary. ■

TIP

All Folders When you start working online, your main Recent Folders view shows the same contents as All Folders. As you add folders, to access those not showing under Recent Folders, click **All Folders**. ■

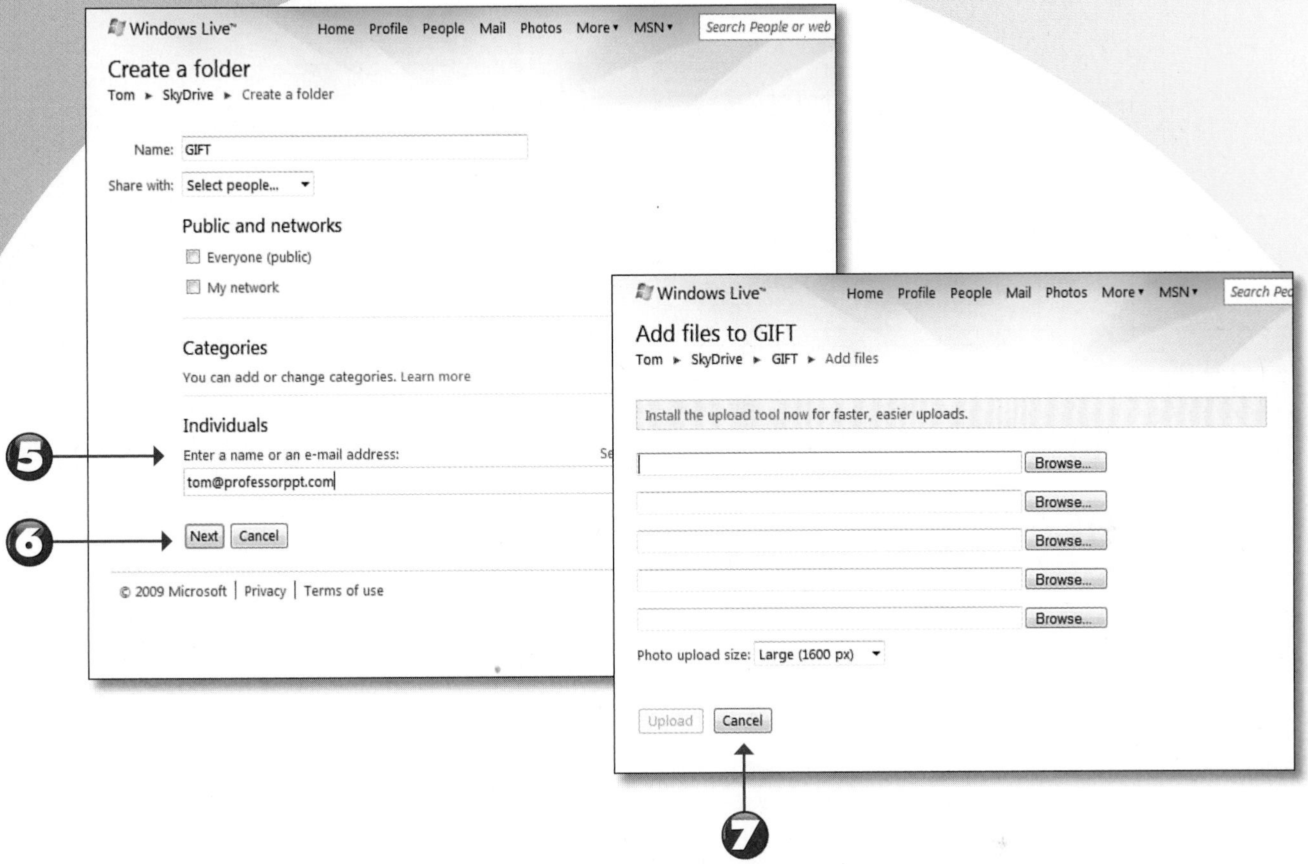

5. Add a name from your Contact list or a specific email address for a person to have access to the folder.

6. Click **Next**.

7. Click **Cancel** to proceed without uploading files to the folder (or click the **Browse** button to select files to upload files immediately and then click the **Upload** button).

End

TIP

Changing Folder Permission To let everyone in your network download and access files in a folder, double-click to open the folder; then click **More** and **Edit Permissions**. This returns you to step 3, and you can change the permission for your folder to share with people in your network. ■

TIP

Navigating the Workspace Because you access your workspace with a web browser, you can click the **Back** and **Forward** buttons to return to some pages instead of the main Workspace menu. ■

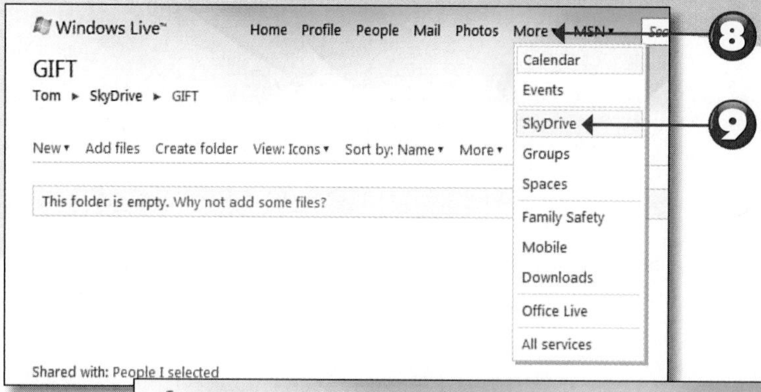

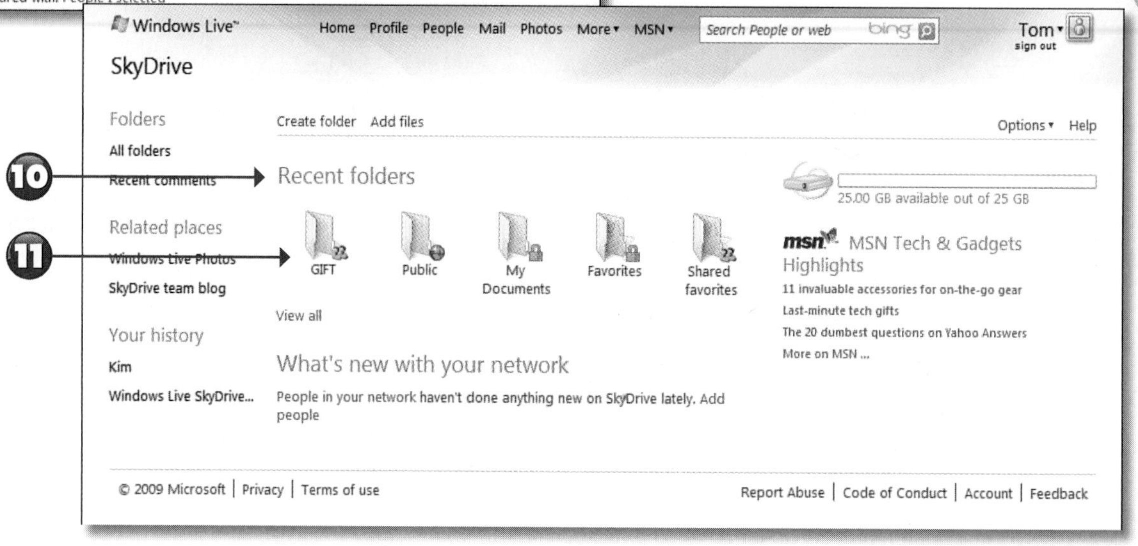

8. In the empty newly named folder, click the **More** drop-down arrow.

9. Click the name of your workspace (for example, **SkyDrive**). You can also click SkyDrive next to your user name on the top left of the window.

10. You return to your main Workspace area.

11. Your new folder is available for use.

End

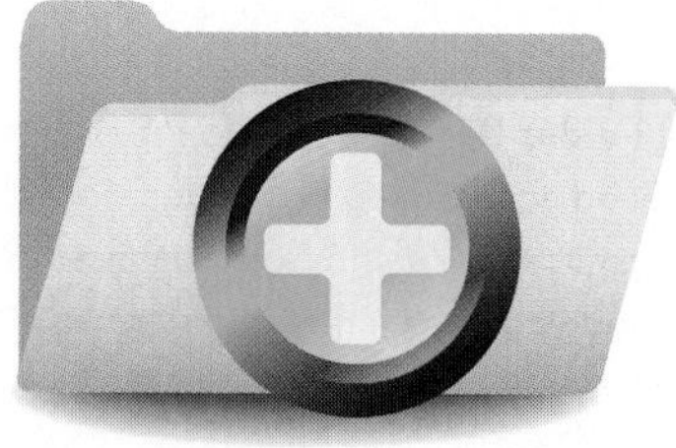

UPLOADING A FILE TO YOUR FOLDER

After you set up a folder, you can begin to populate it with files that you upload from your desktop. Depending on the permissions you have granted for the folder, people in your network can download or open these files with the web applications.

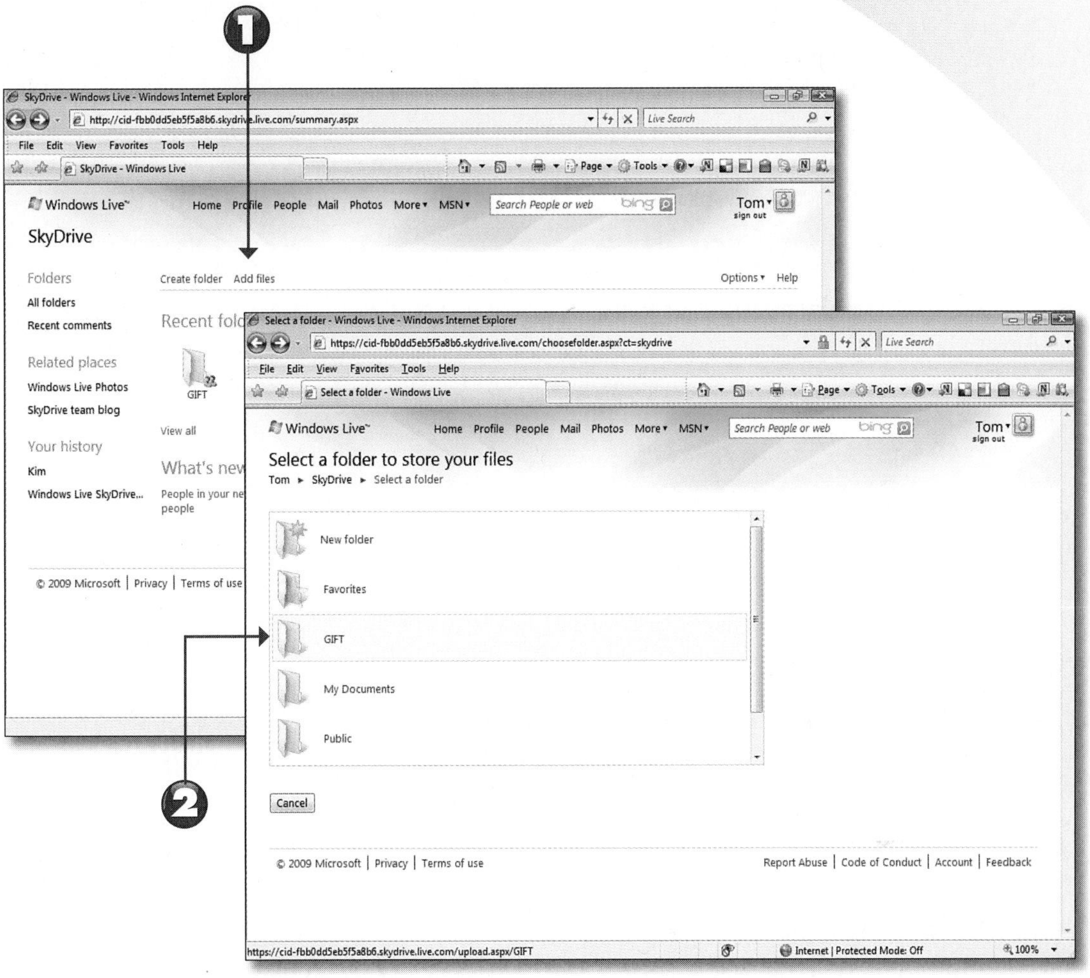

Start

1. In your workspace, click **Add Files**.
2. Click the folder to which you want to upload files.

Continued

TIP

Sending a Link To let people you have selected know that they can use your workspace folder and its files, you can send them a link. In your folder, click **More** and then **Send a Link**. In the new window, add an email address and a message. You also can check a check box to make it unnecessary for recipients to sign in to Windows Live to use the files. ■

In the Add Files window, click **Browse**.

Click to select a file to upload in the desktop folder.

Click **Open**.

Continued

TIP

Viewing Permissions To quickly check or confirm who has permission for a folder, click **People I Selected** next to **Shared With**. In the Permissions window, you can see who has access to the files in the folder, and you can change the settings by clicking **Edit Permissions**.

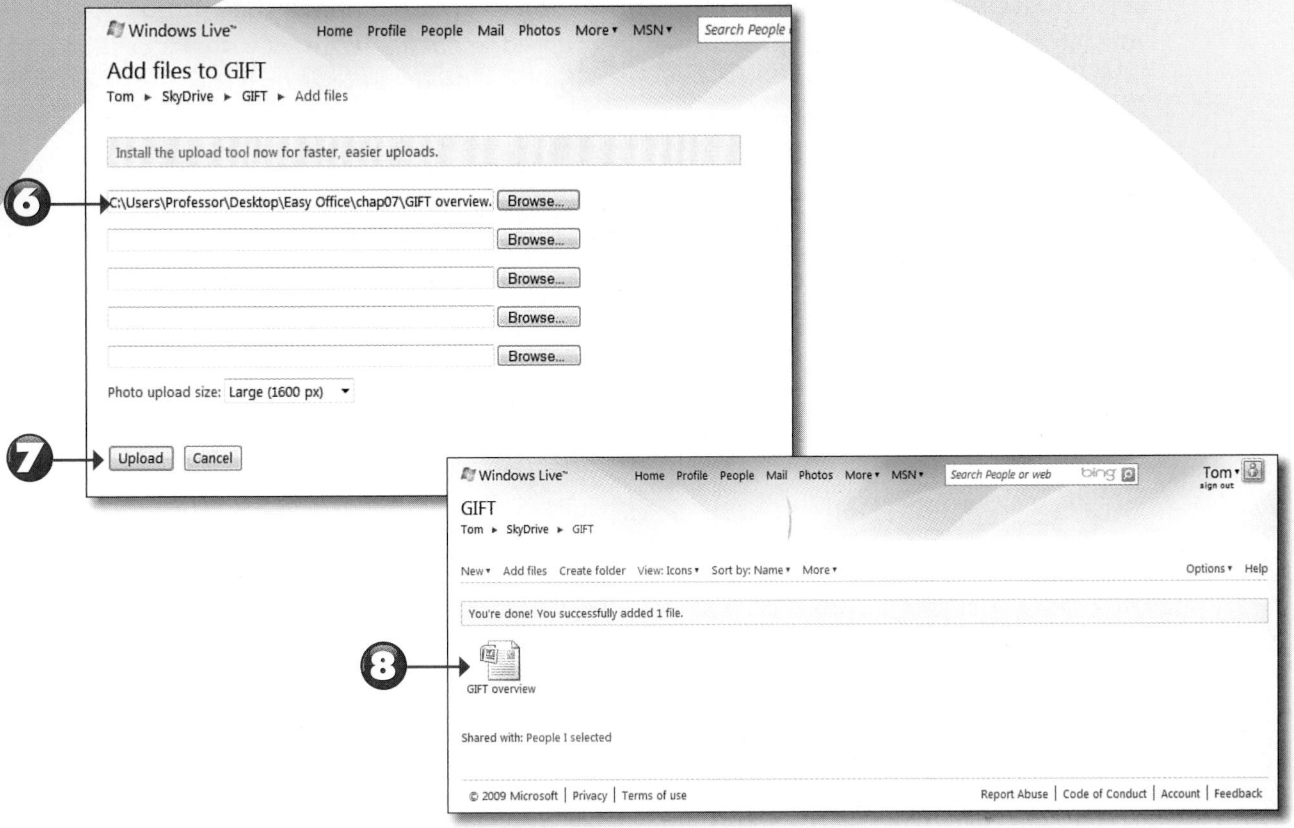

6 Your selected file is shown in the first upload field.

7 Click **Upload.**

8 Your file is available in your folder for use as a download or using a Web Application in your folder.

End

TIP

Viewing and Sorting Folder Contents Like your desktop folders, folders on the workspace can be viewed by icons, details, or thumbnails or sorted by name, date, size, and type. To change these options, click **View** or **Sort** on the main menu for any folder. ■

CREATING A NEW WEB APPLICATION FILE

Office 2010 web applications have many of the features of the regular desktop programs but work in your web browser. You can create a new file directly within your workspace and begin to use the features of the online application to create and edit the file. For example, you can create a new Excel spreadsheet in your workspace, let others with access to your folder add to it, and then continue to work with it online or on your desktop. Excel is covered in detail in the next chapter.

Start

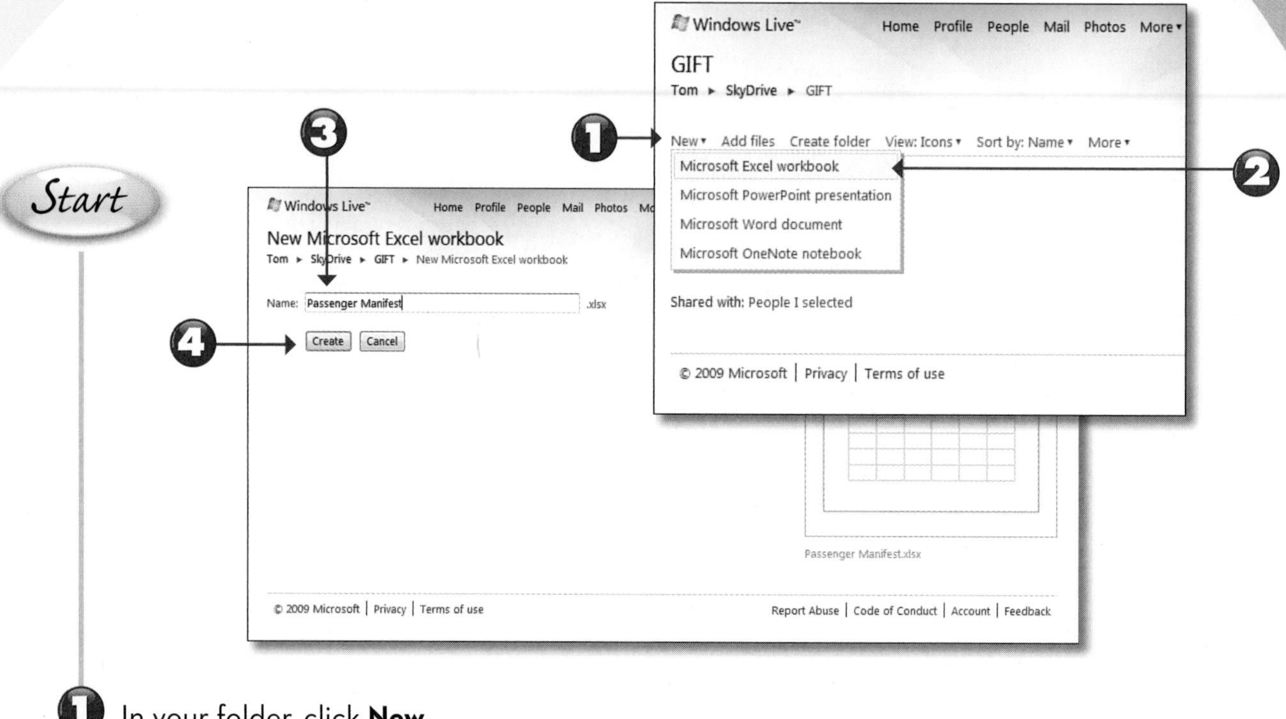

1. In your folder, click **New**.
2. Click the program and file format you want to create.
3. Type in a name for the file.
4. Click **Create**.

Continued

TIP

No Save Button There are no Save buttons in the web applications because changes and additions are saved automatically. You can click **File** for the options to open in Excel (on your desktop), save as a different filename, download a snapshot (a simple version of your file with only the values and formatting), or download a copy to download the Excel spreadsheet to your desktop to work on separately from the web application. ■

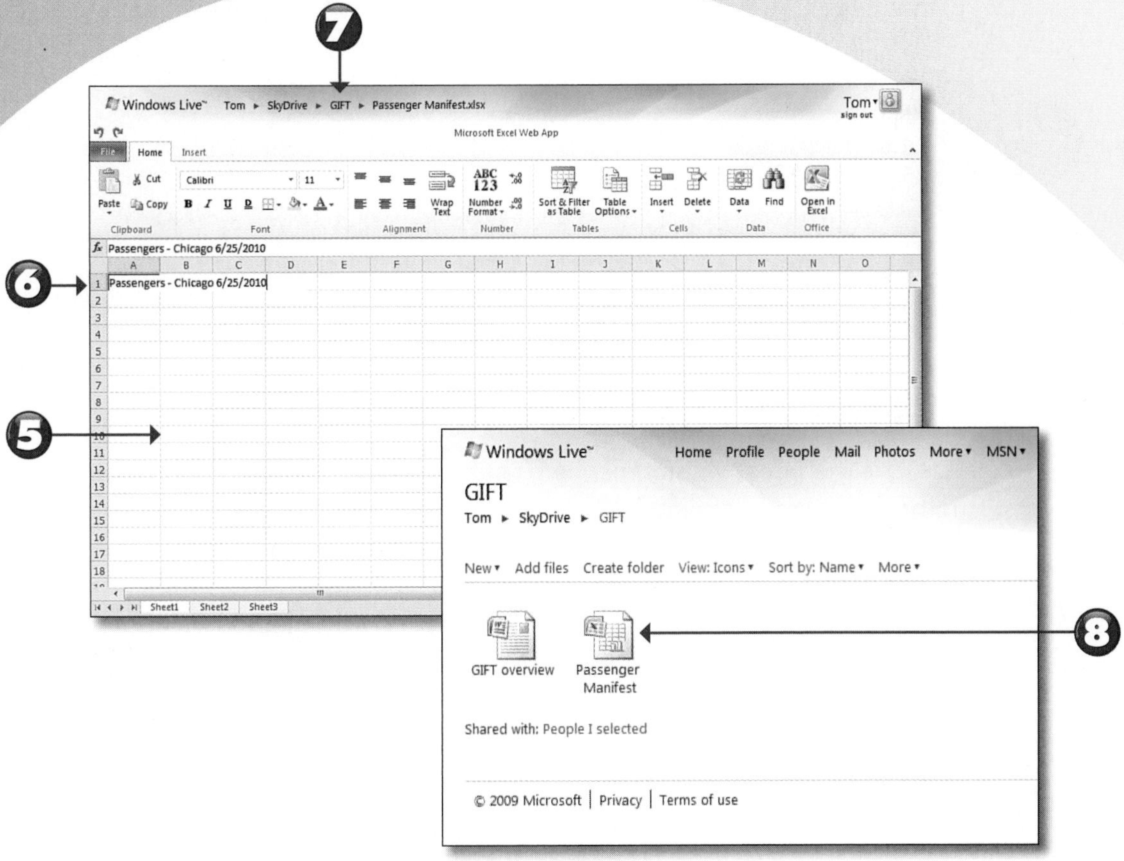

5 The web application (Excel) opens with a blank spreadsheet.

6 You can add information in the first cell.

7 Click the name of the folder (for example, **GIFT**).

8 Excel closes, and your new Excel spreadsheet is available in your folder, with the changes you made.

End

TIP

Opening in Excel Although the web applications have a limited Ribbon with features specific to each program, a button on the right of the Home tab enables you to open a file directly in the desktop program to use its full features. Then you can save the file locally, click **Save** on the desktop to save changes directly back to the web application, or save it locally and upload it back to your workspace. ■

GETTING STARTED WITH EXCEL

Excel 2010 is the latest version of the popular spreadsheet program, organizing your information and data into a series of columns and rows, which intersect to form cells. Similar to the popular game Battleship, Excel's data is placed in preset cells that are identified by their columns and rows (for example, the first cell is A1). Information contained in a cell in one worksheet can be referenced by its location elsewhere in that page or worksheet, or in another worksheet in the same workbook.

While primarily used for calculations performed with formulas and functions, Excel can also be used to create complex tables that allow for information to be sorted and filtered effectively.

Excel 2010 uses Ribbon tabs to enable a smooth workflow and expose its many features to the user. The Home tab features formatting for the look of your data, Insert provides additional features for displaying information, Page Layout lets you change the way your data is displayed or printed, Formulas helps you calculate results, Data is for importing and analyzing information, Review is for collaboration, View is for changing focus or emphasis, and Add-Ins is for extra programs. File opens Backstage view in Excel.

OVERVIEW OF EXCEL

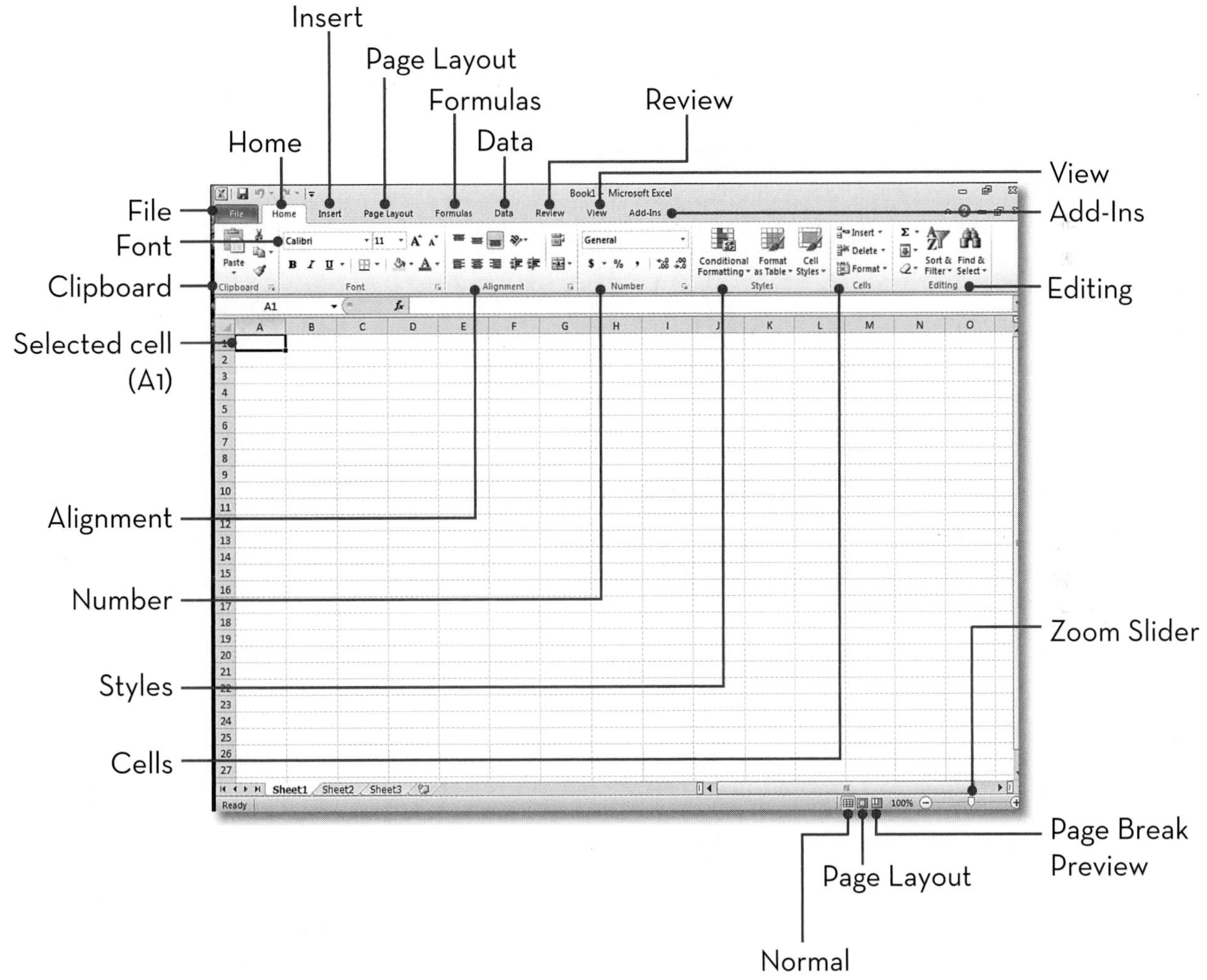

Insert
Page Layout
Formulas
Review
Home
Data
View
File
Add-Ins
Font
Clipboard
Editing
Selected cell (A1)
Alignment
Number
Zoom Slider
Styles
Cells
Page Break Preview
Page Layout
Normal

ALIGNING AND FORMATTING TEXT

As you begin to type text into cells in Excel, you might want to create a heading for your worksheet or headings and content for your columns and rows. As you do this, you may find the content you enter overruns the preset borders of the cells or that it needs to be adjusted to display your information clearly and effectively.

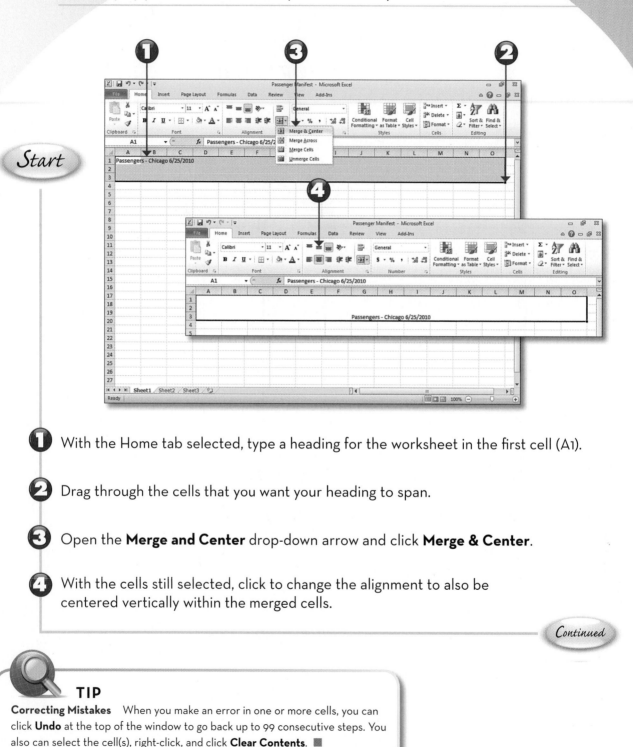

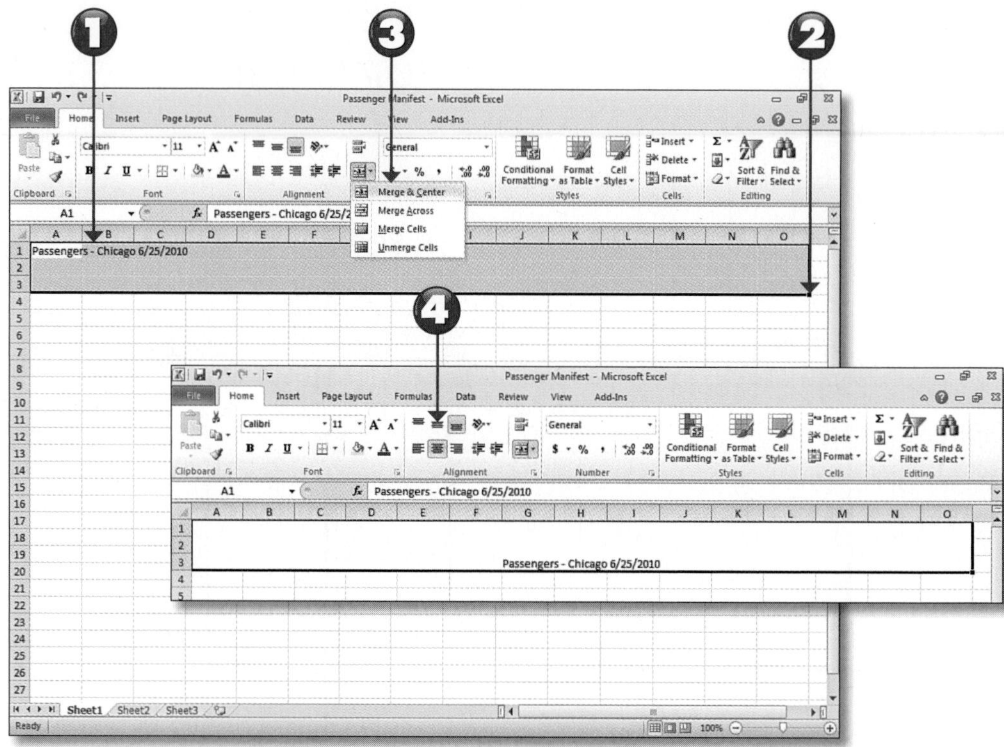

Start

1. With the Home tab selected, type a heading for the worksheet in the first cell (A1).
2. Drag through the cells that you want your heading to span.
3. Open the **Merge and Center** drop-down arrow and click **Merge & Center**.
4. With the cells still selected, click to change the alignment to also be centered vertically within the merged cells.

TIP

Correcting Mistakes When you make an error in one or more cells, you can click **Undo** at the top of the window to go back up to 99 consecutive steps. You also can select the cell(s), right-click, and click **Clear Contents**. ■

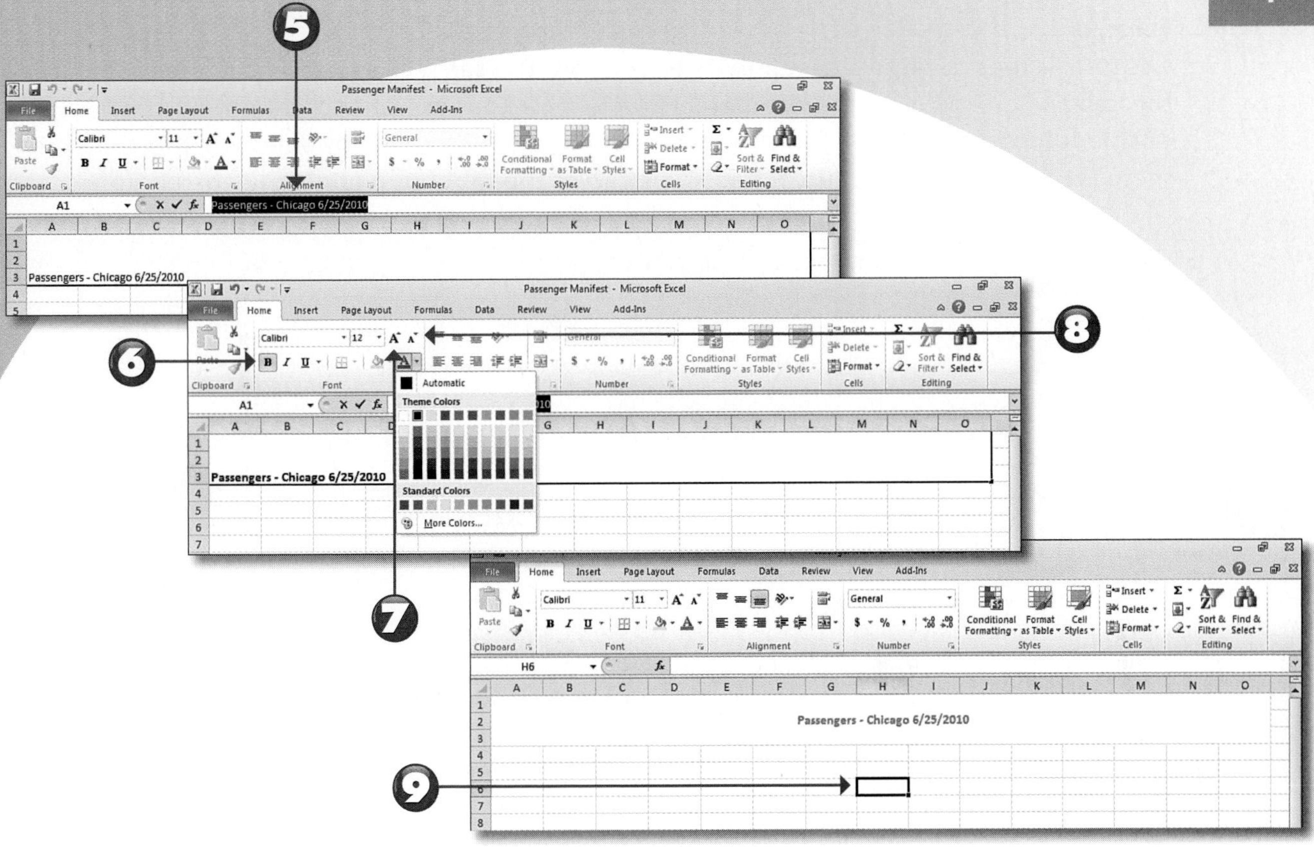

5 Select a cell with text and then drag through the text in the Formula Bar to select it.

6 In the Font group of the Home tab, change the text format to **Bold**.

7 Click the **Font Size Increase** button to increase font size.

8 Click the **Font Color** drop-down arrow to choose a different font color.

9 Click outside the merged cells to see the new alignment and format applied to the selected cells.

End

TIP

Formatting Cells If you have selected an individual or group of merged cells, you can use **Borders** drop-down options in the Font group in the Home tab to set an external or other border. Alternatively, click the **Fill Bucket** drop-down arrow to change the background fill color of the selected cells.

INPUTTING AND FORMATTING NUMBERS

The initial steps for inputting numbers to cells are the same as for text: you simply select the cell and begin typing the numbers. However, for the sake of appearance and also to enable future calculations, you should format numbers correctly by selecting them first and then using the Number group in the Home tab of the Ribbon to apply the correct format.

Start

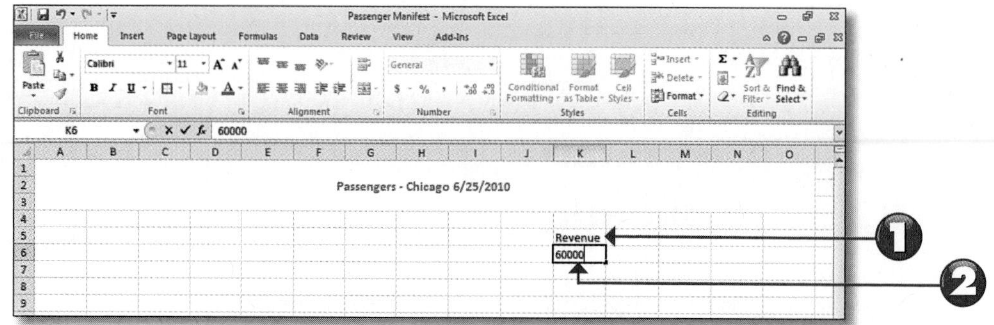

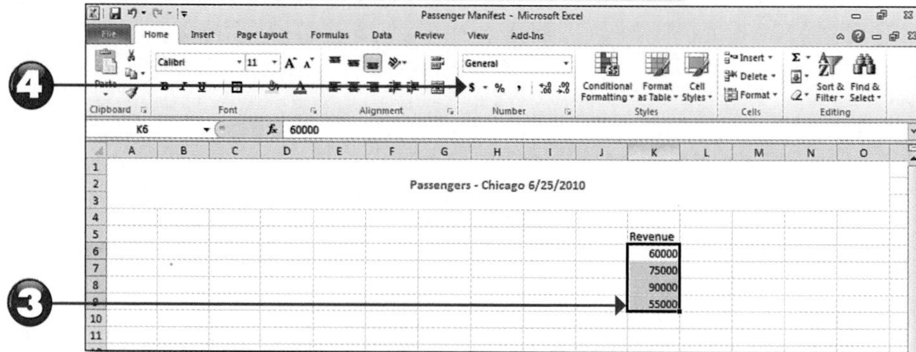

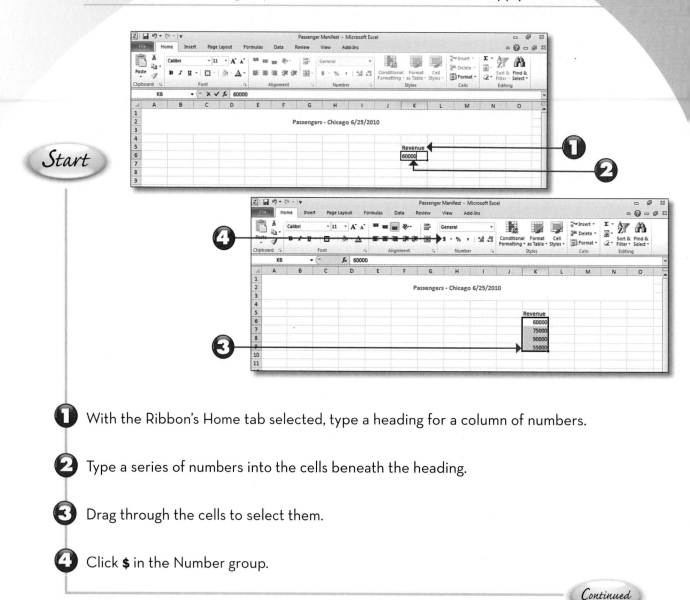

1. With the Ribbon's Home tab selected, type a heading for a column of numbers.
2. Type a series of numbers into the cells beneath the heading.
3. Drag through the cells to select them.
4. Click **$** in the Number group.

Continued

TIP

Number Formats Choosing the correct number format can be significant not just for the appearance of the document, but also for future formulas, functions, and calculations. Although the default General format permits calculation, more complex calculations may require formatting such as Time, Percentage, Fraction, or other format for correct results. ■

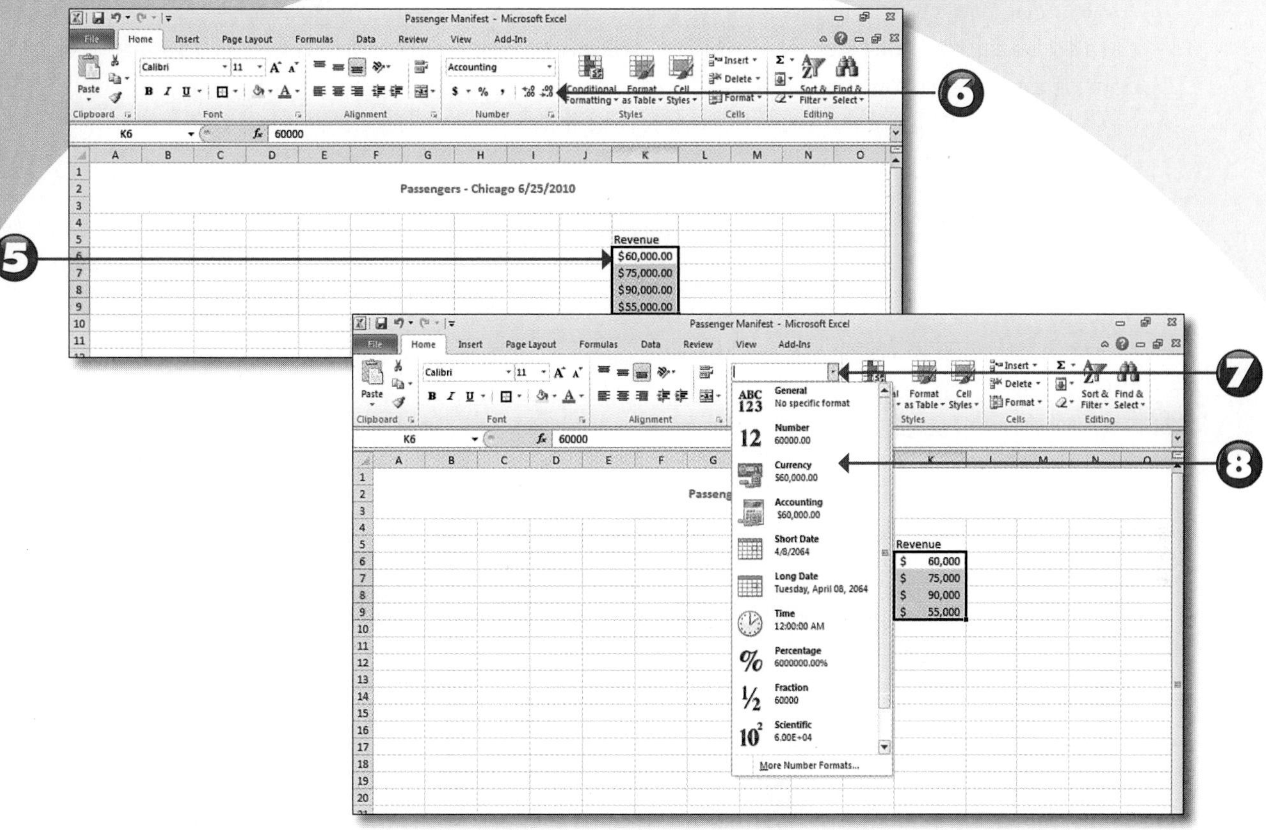

5. The number and two decimal places are applied by default.

6. Click the **Decrease Decimal** button twice to remove the decimals.

7. Click the drop-down arrow to display other number formats.

8. Select a format that suits your needs.

End

TIP

Using a Numeric Keypad For large amounts of numbers to be input quickly, you may want to use the numeric keypad to input the numbers calculator-style. To enable this, press the **NumLock** key on the keyboard and then press it again to use the normal keyboard keys. ■

TIP

Other Currencies If you need to use other currencies for your data, you can click the drop-down arrow under the $ button for other choices. ■

FILLING IN YOUR DATA

As you continue working in Excel, you can add more columns (with headings) and rows of data to begin to make the information look clean and professional. When you add data to cells, it can overrun the borders at times. You can use the Format feature in the Cells group of the Home tab to make the information fit inside the columns or rows of your worksheet.

Start

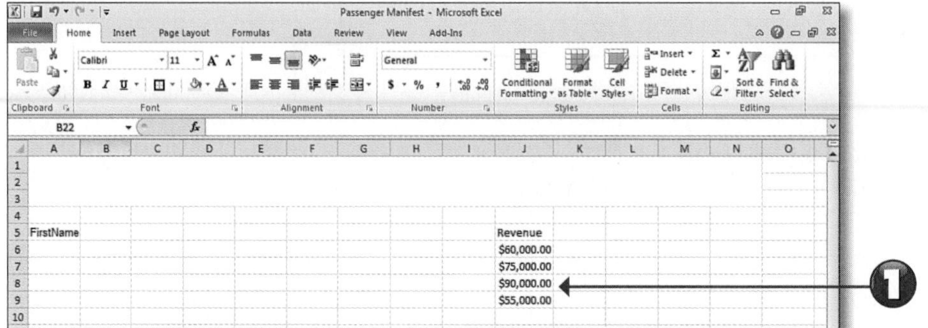

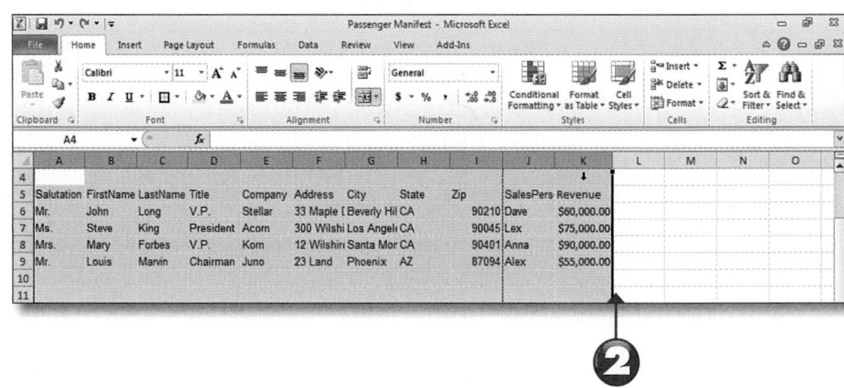

1. With the Home tab selected, fill in more cells with information.

2. With some of the columns not large enough to show all information, drag through the column headings to select the filled-in columns. (The cursor turns into a down arrow as you select a column).

Continued

NOTE

Adjusting Columns or Rows Manually You can increase or decrease the height or width of a row or column by first grabbing a border with your mouse. When the mouse turns into a vertical or horizontal line with two arrows, drag the column or row border to a new location. ■

TIP

Wrapping Text Clicking the **Wrap Text** button in the top right of the Alignment group of the Home tab wraps text to additional rows within selected cells to display all the cell's information without expanding the column width. ■

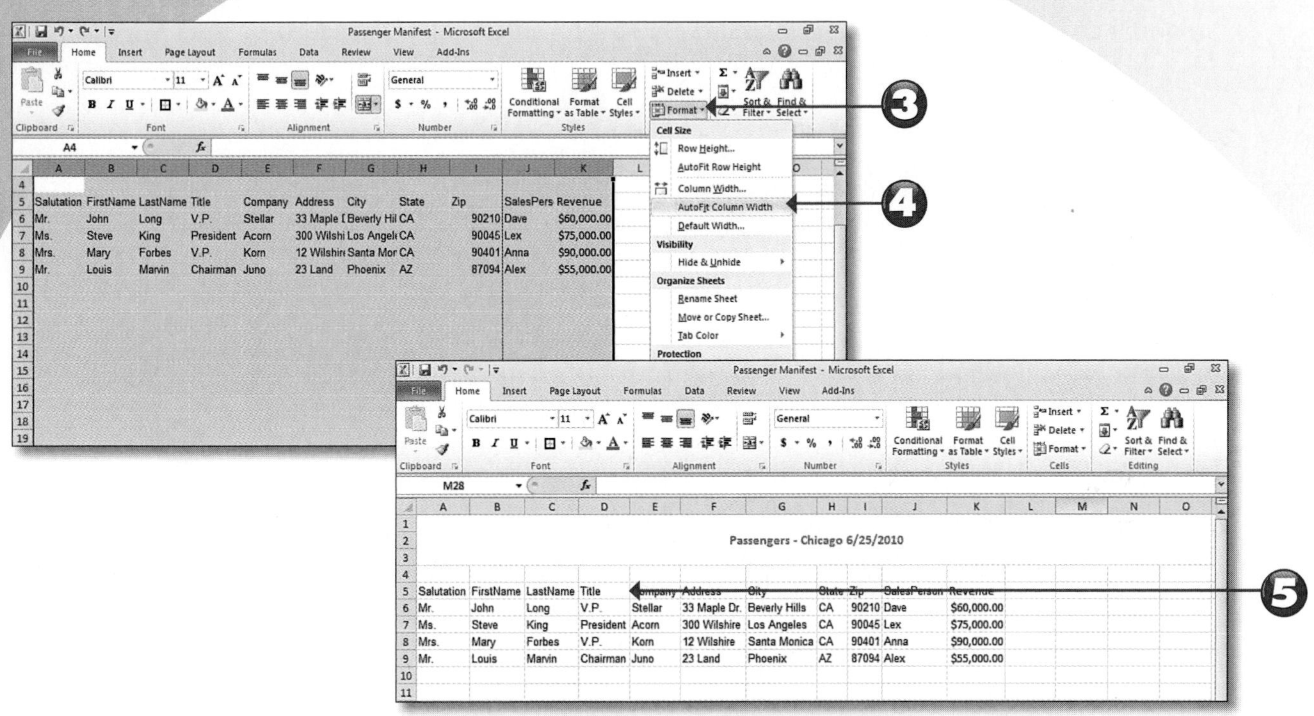

3. Click **Format**.

4. Click **AutoFit Column Width**.

5. The information in the columns fits into the newly adjusted column widths.

End

TIP

Indenting or Centering Data To further adjust the appearance of information in selected cells, click the **Paragraph** and **Indent** buttons in the Alignment group of the Home tab. ■

TIP

Setting a Column Width You can specify a uniform column width to accommodate your data by clicking **Column Width** in the Cell Size group of the Format drop-down options. ■

INSERTING A NEW COLUMN OR ROW

If you determine that you need to add more information, you can always add a column or row to your spreadsheet. After selecting a column to the right of the one to which you want insert a new column (or the row below where you want to add a row), you can click **Insert** to add a column or row, and a new column or row for information is inserted.

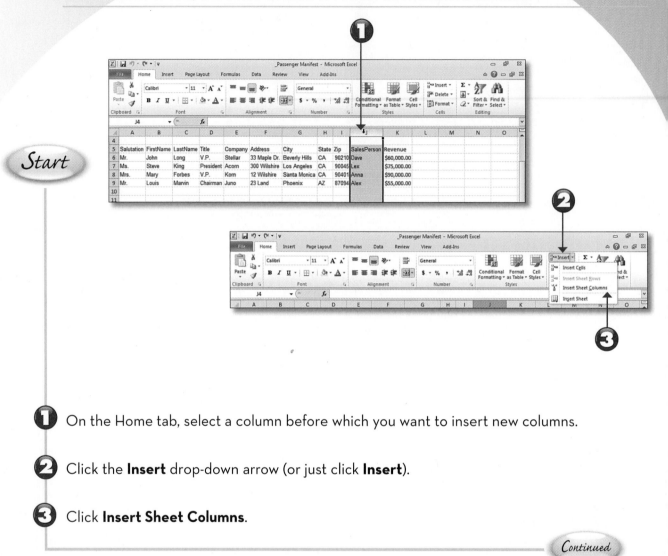

Start

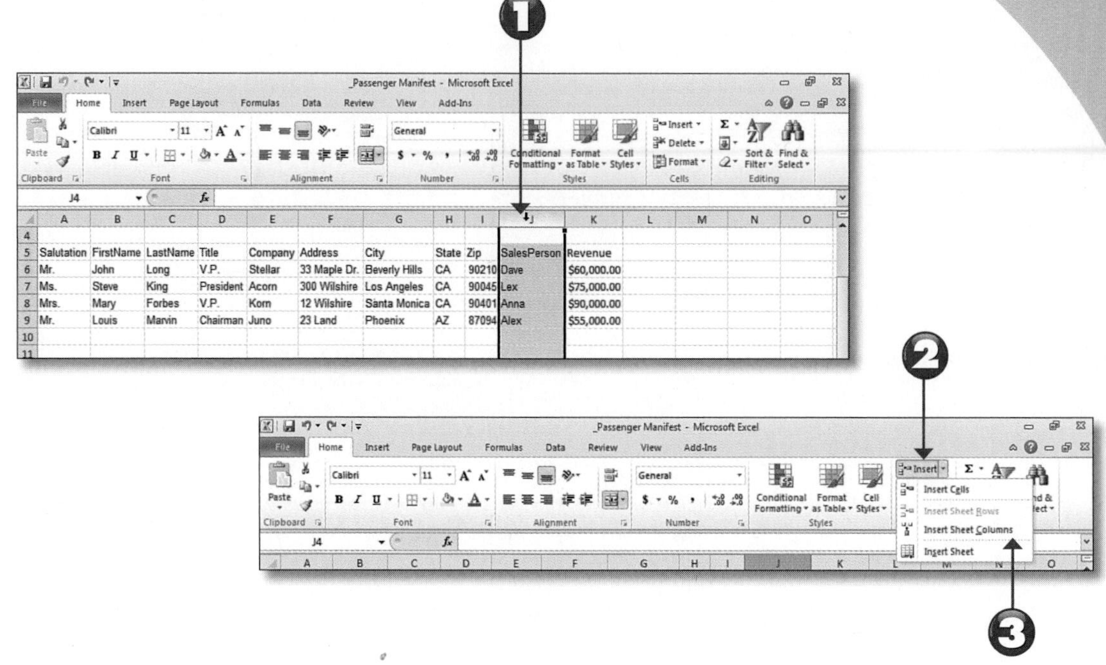

1. On the Home tab, select a column before which you want to insert new columns.
2. Click the **Insert** drop-down arrow (or just click **Insert**).
3. Click **Insert Sheet Columns**.

Continued

TIP

Inserting Multiple Columns Excel inserts as many columns (or rows) as you originally select. So, for example, if you select four columns prior to clicking **Insert**, four columns are added for you.

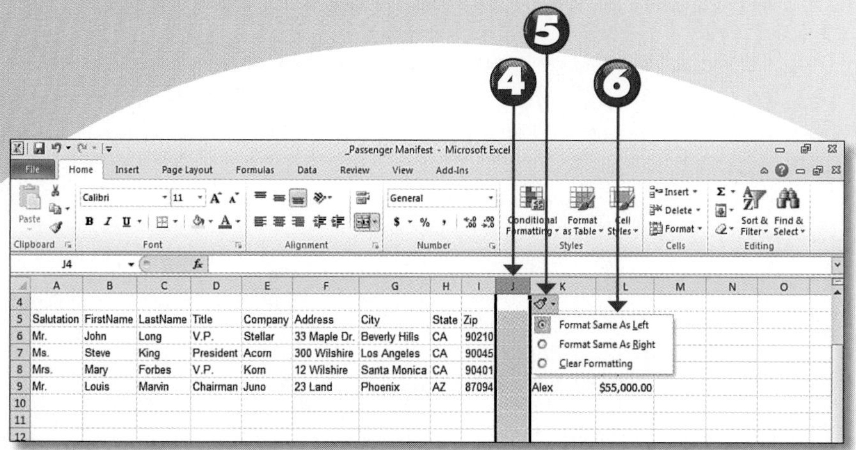

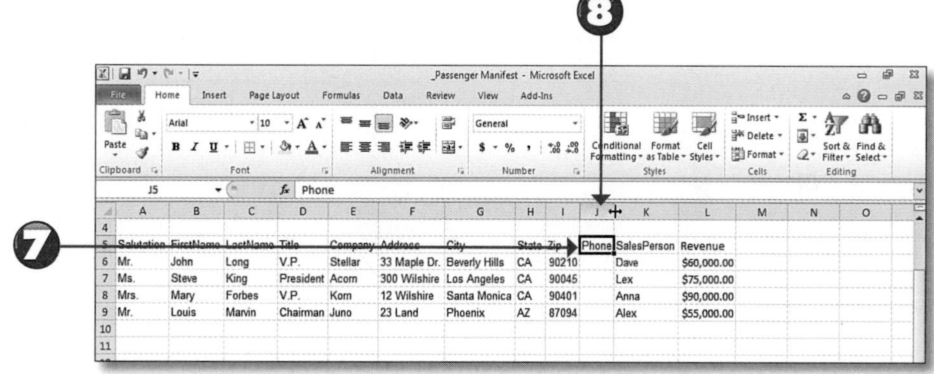

4 A new selected column is inserted.

5 Click the **Format Copy Paintbrush**.

6 Select a formatting option from adjacent columns.

7 The new column is ready to fill in.

8 You can grab the column border (the cursor turns into wide arrows) to move the border to widen the column.

End

TIP

Deleting Columns or Rows To delete one or more columns or rows, select them and click **Delete** in the Cells group of the Home tab. ■

HIDING AND UNHIDING COLUMNS

Sometimes you might want to print or display a worksheet without certain information, although you want to maintain that information for future use. Although you could save the workbook under a different name and then delete the column, Excel lets you hide a column and later reveal (or unhide) it.

Start

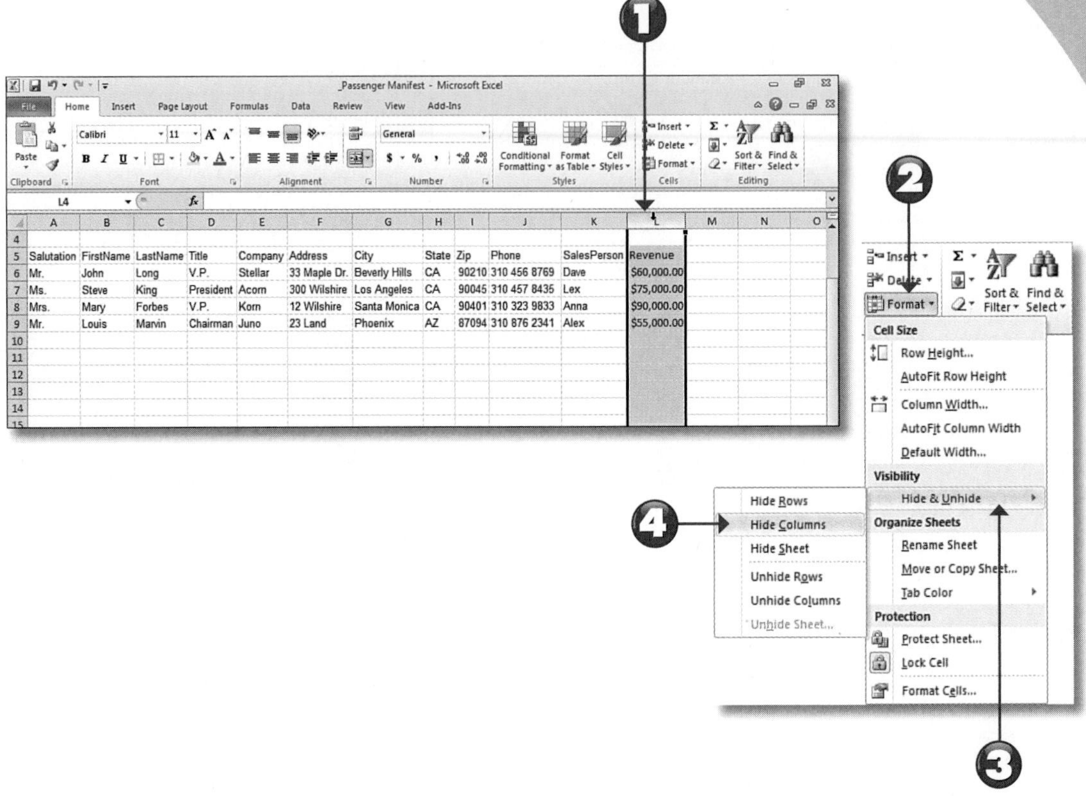

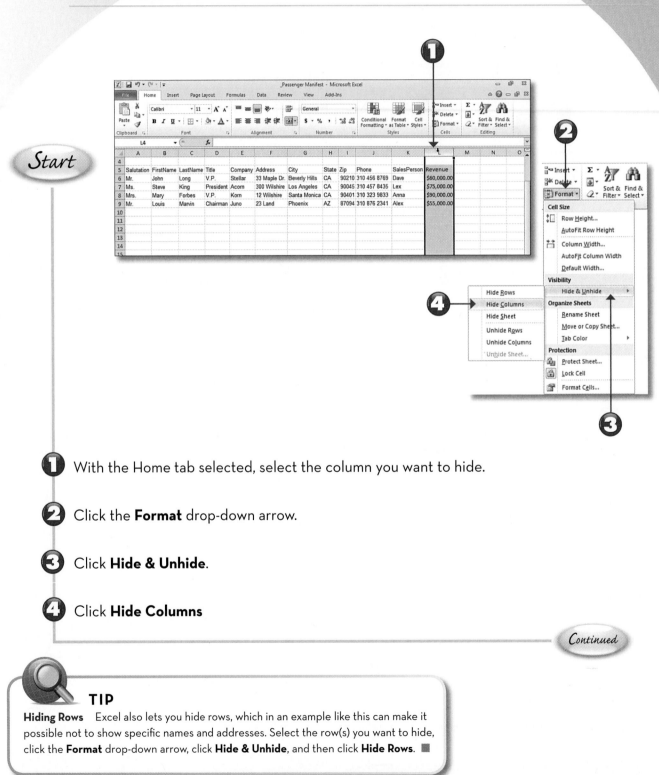

1. With the Home tab selected, select the column you want to hide.
2. Click the **Format** drop-down arrow.
3. Click **Hide & Unhide**.
4. Click **Hide Columns**

Continued

TIP

Hiding Rows Excel also lets you hide rows, which in an example like this can make it possible not to show specific names and addresses. Select the row(s) you want to hide, click the **Format** drop-down arrow, click **Hide & Unhide**, and then click **Hide Rows**. ■

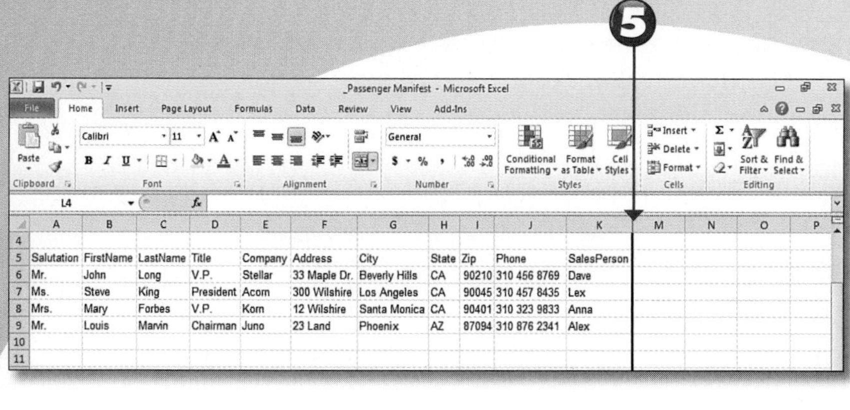

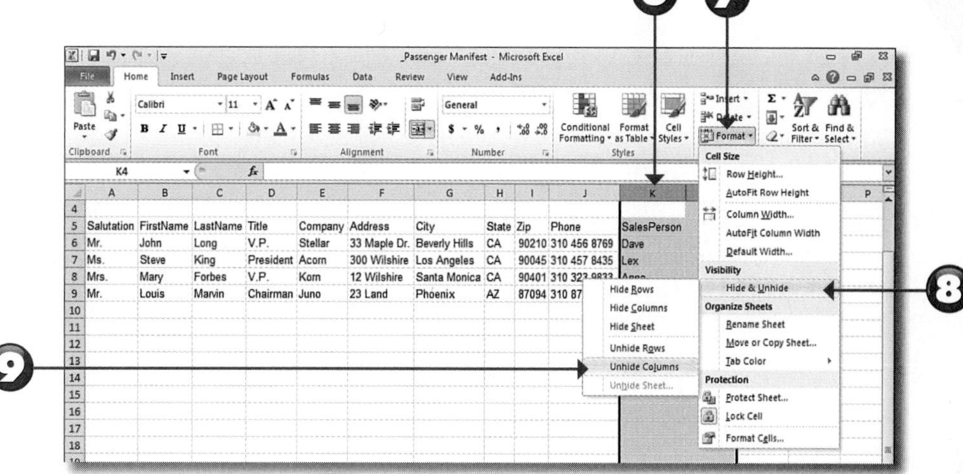

5 The column is hidden for display or print.

6 Click the column names to select columns on both sides of the hidden column (the cursor points down when columns are selected).

7 Click the **Format** drop-down arrow.

8 Click **Hide & Unhide**.

9 Click **Unhide Columns**.

End

TIP

Hiding a Sheet You can also hide an entire worksheet in Excel. Use the **Hide & Unhide** feature of Format in the Cells group to hide and unhide sheets. ■

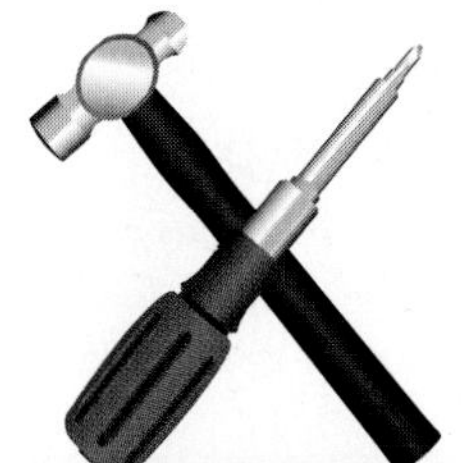

ADDING AND RENAMING A WORKSHEET

Every Excel workbook comes with three worksheets by default, named Sheet1, Sheet2, and Sheet3. You can add new worksheets to the workbook and rename existing or new sheets to reflect the information contained on those worksheets.

Start

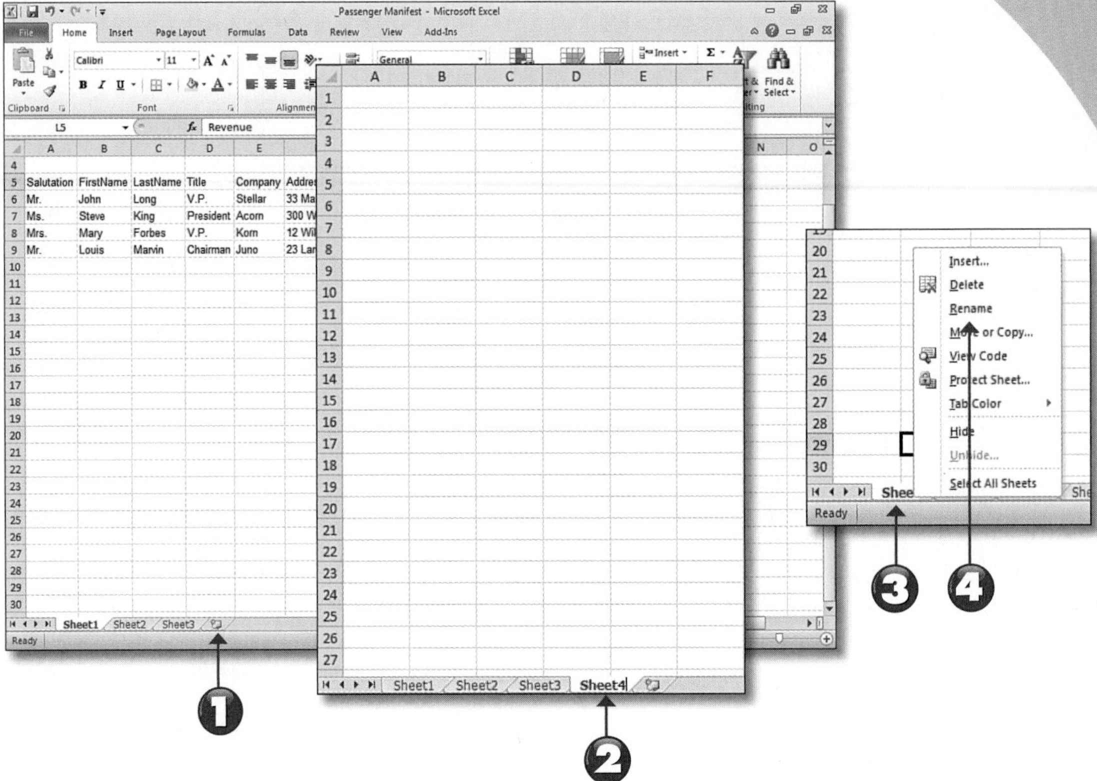

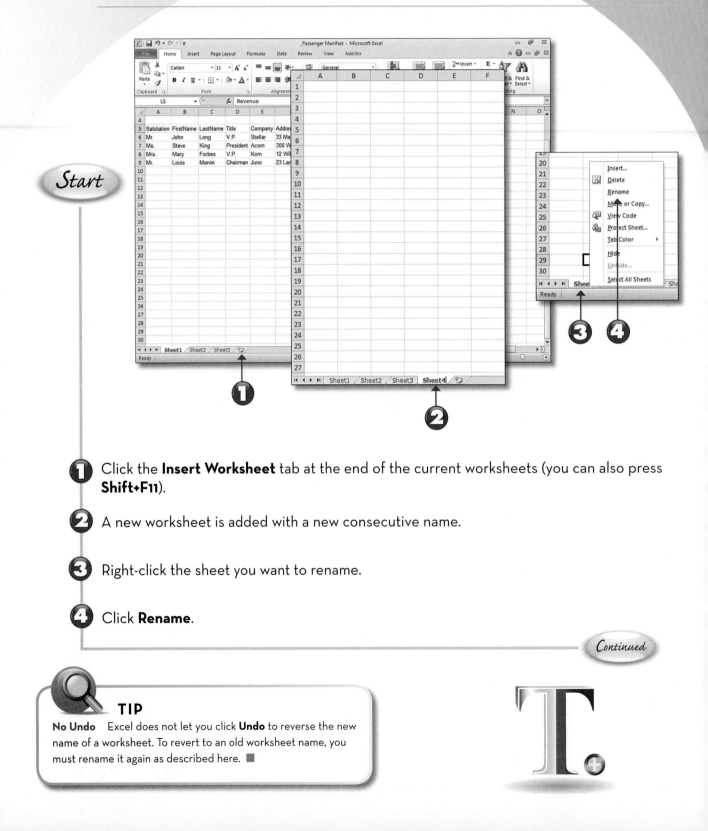

1. Click the **Insert Worksheet** tab at the end of the current worksheets (you can also press **Shift+F11**).
2. A new worksheet is added with a new consecutive name.
3. Right-click the sheet you want to rename.
4. Click **Rename**.

Continued

TIP

No Undo Excel does not let you click **Undo** to reverse the new name of a worksheet. To revert to an old worksheet name, you must rename it again as described here. ■

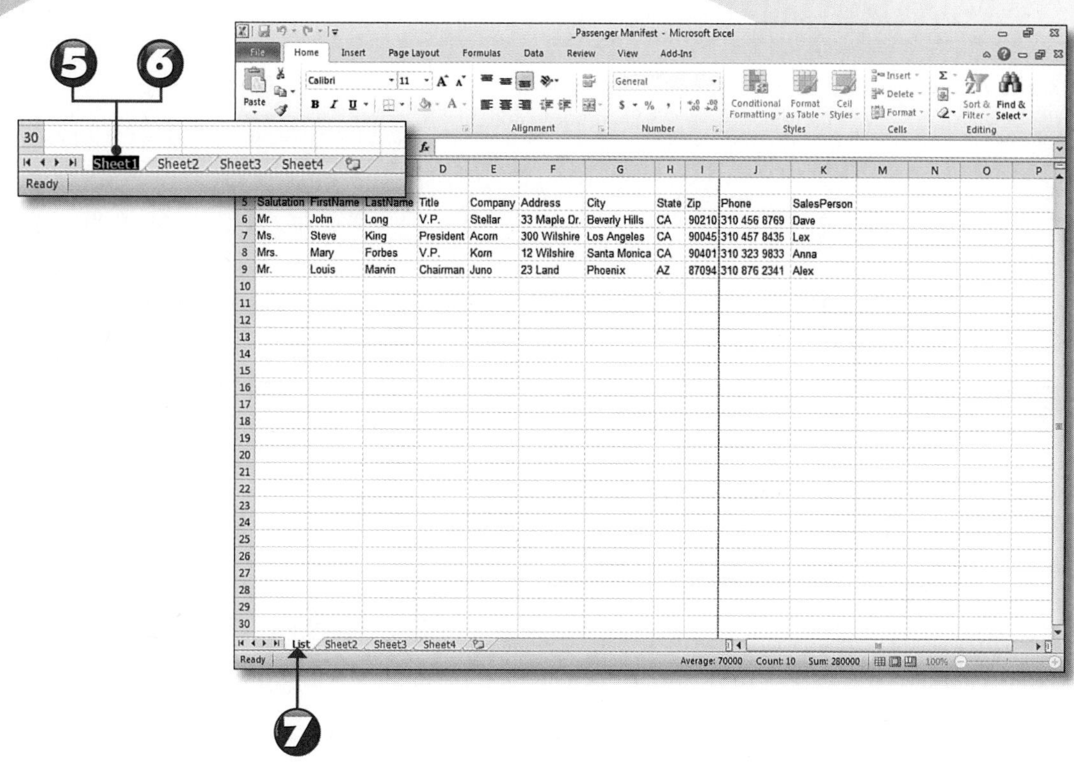

5 The old name is highlighted.

6 Type a new name.

7 The sheet is renamed.

End

TIP

Duplicate Names You cannot give a worksheet the same name as an existing sheet. Attempting to do so produces an error message.

USING CELL STYLES

You can enhance the appearance of your worksheet by using Cell Styles to give certain cells a background color and definitive font. You also can apply a different color and/or font to other cells.

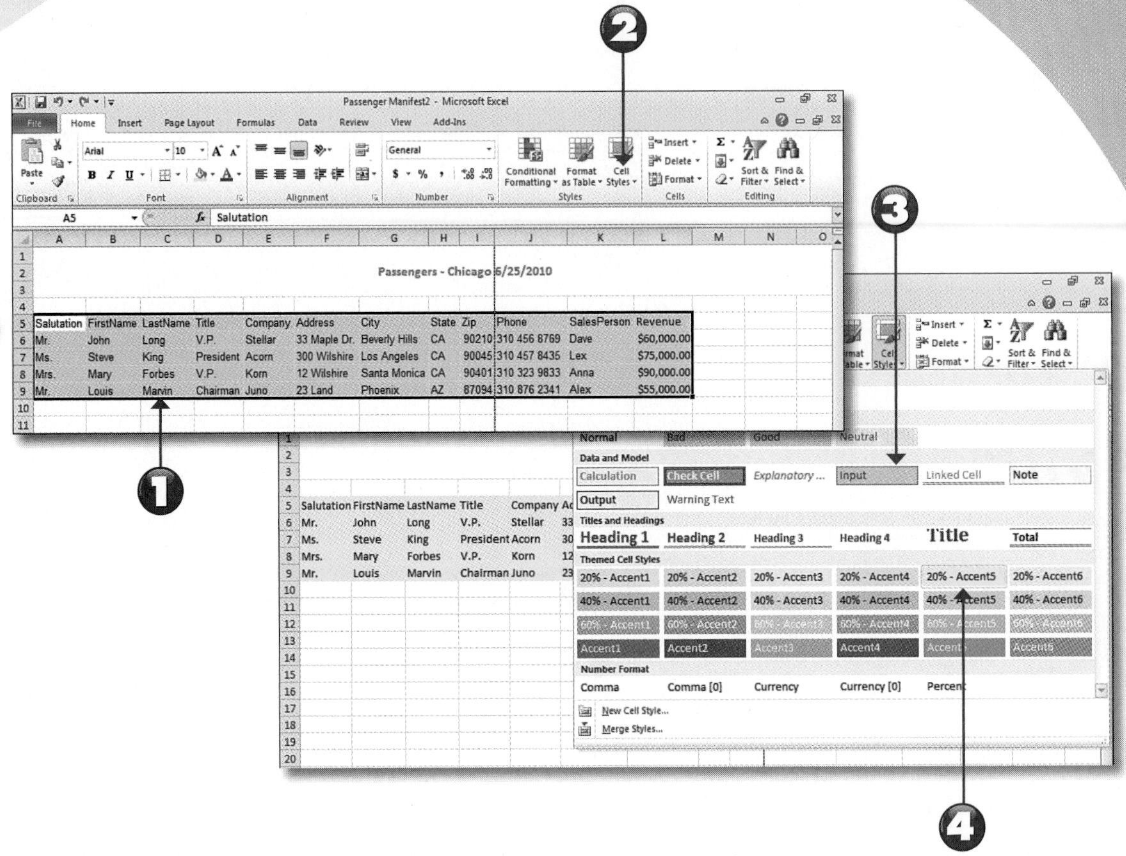

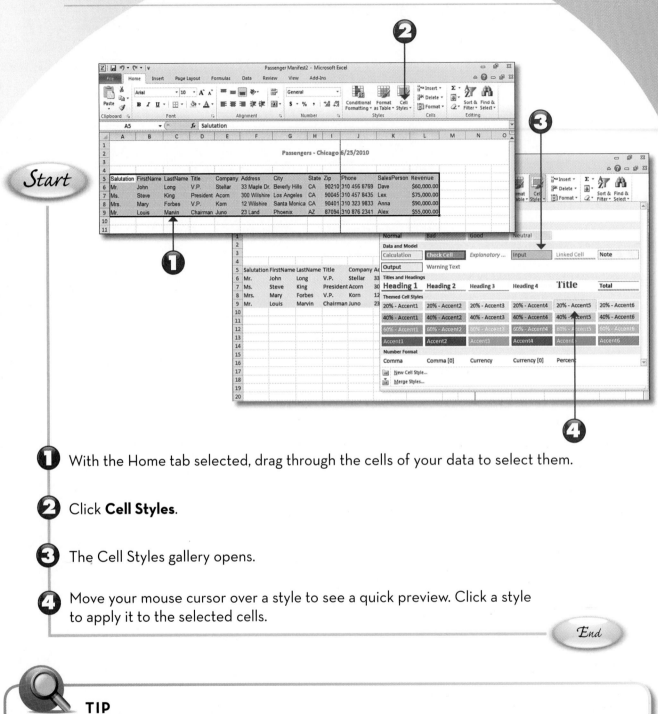

Start

1. With the Home tab selected, drag through the cells of your data to select them.
2. Click **Cell Styles**.
3. The Cell Styles gallery opens.
4. Move your mouse cursor over a style to see a quick preview. Click a style to apply it to the selected cells.

End

TIP

Adjusting Cells to Styles Some Cell Styles, require you to readjust your cells to display the data fully after the style is applied. Click the **AutoFit Column Width** option in the Format button of the Cells group and the **Wrap to Cell** feature in the Alignment group to make all cell data visible. ■

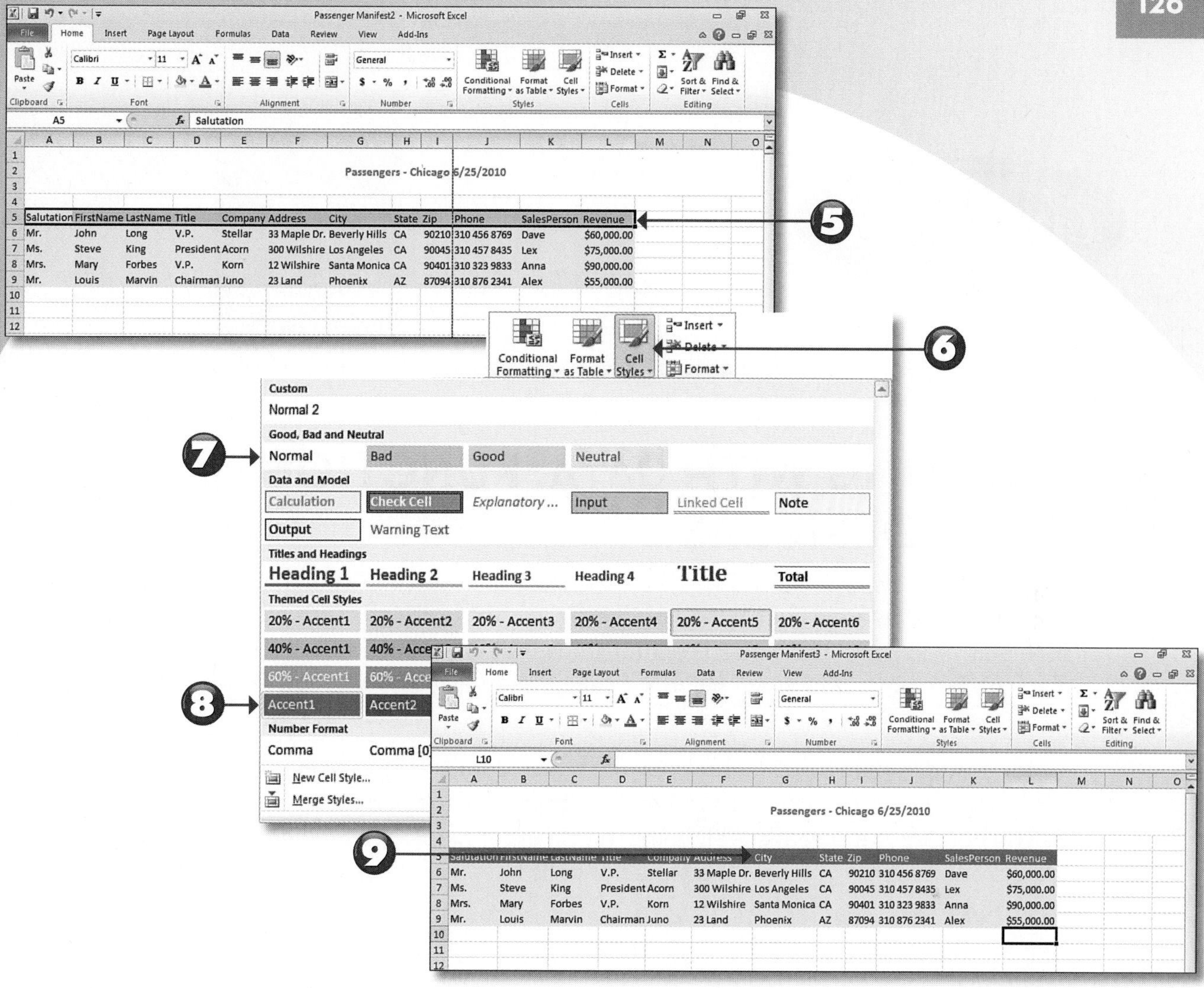

5. Drag through a specific group of cells to select those cells.

6. Click **Cell Styles**.

7. The Cell Styles gallery opens.

8. Mouse over a style to see a quick preview. Click a style to apply it to the selected cells.

9. The top row of column headings is now differentiated with a different cell style.

End

TIP

Creating Your Own Cell Style You can create your own cell style by formatting one or more cells in the way you want clicking **Cell Styles**, and choosing **New Cell Style**. You can name and save your new cell style to make it available in the Custom area of the Cell Styles gallery.

WORKING WITH DATA, FUNCTIONS, AND FORMULAS

Excel 2010 is a very powerful spreadsheet program, which means that it can be used to calculate values based on the figures entered into the cells, using formulas, which are customized relationships that are placed into the Formula Bar, and functions, which are standard calculations, like the average of a set of numbers.

Excel provides numerous features to work with data effectively. In a large spreadsheet, you can use the Find feature to locate specific items in cells. And as you construct a spreadsheet, you can use Excel's artificial intelligence to fill in blank cells and complete a series of cells based on data that has already been entered.

The Formulas tab of the Excel 2010 Ribbon provides a wide array of functions, from very simple calculations like averages or maximum values, to complex and specialized functions for financial and other types of applications. The Excel Function Library contains the many Excel function options, broken down by category.

THE FORMULA TAB OF THE RIBBON

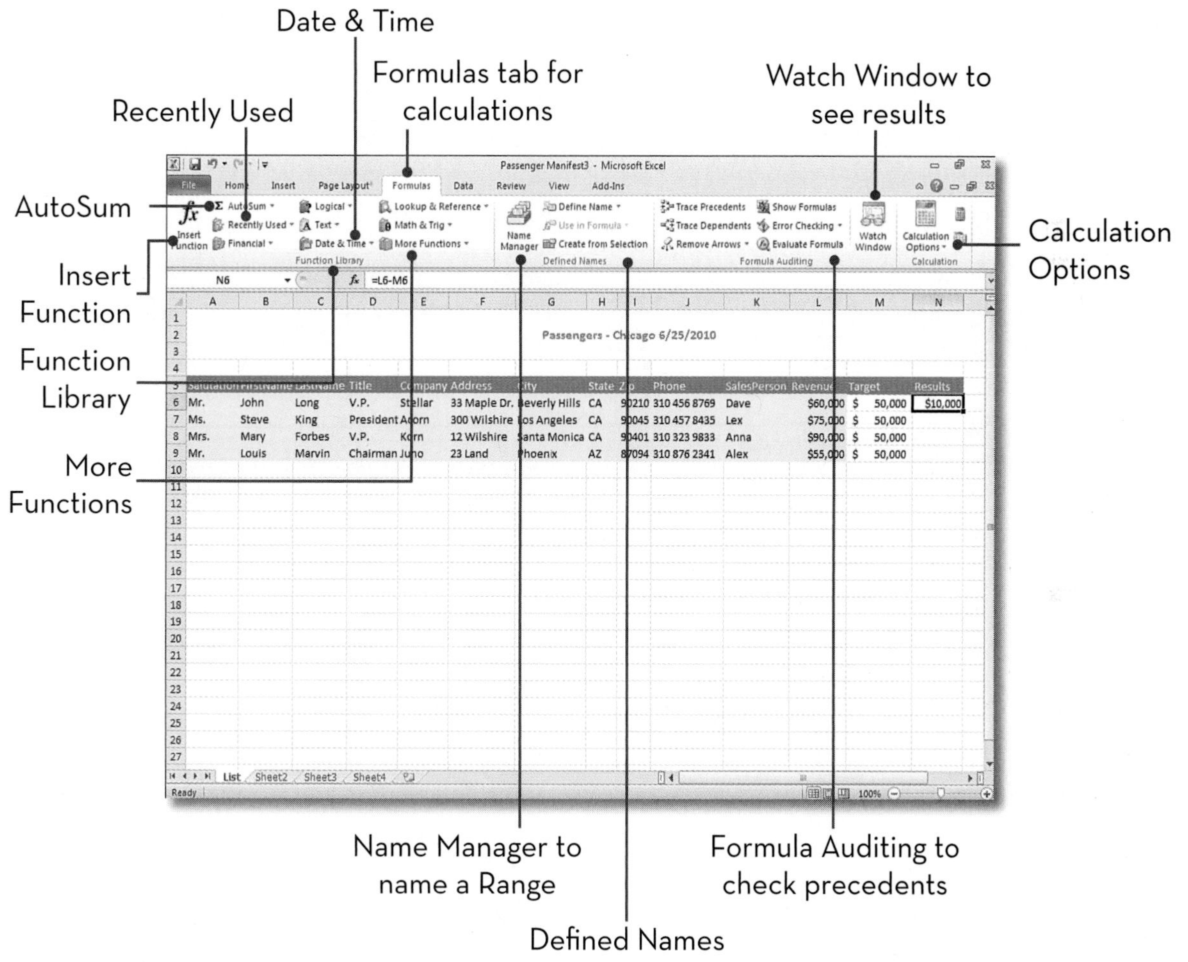

FINDING DATA

As you create large spreadsheets, you might need to locate specific words, phrases, or numbers on a complex worksheet. In the Editing group of the Home tab, the Find & Select tool lets you enter search parameters and quickly locate specific items in your worksheet.

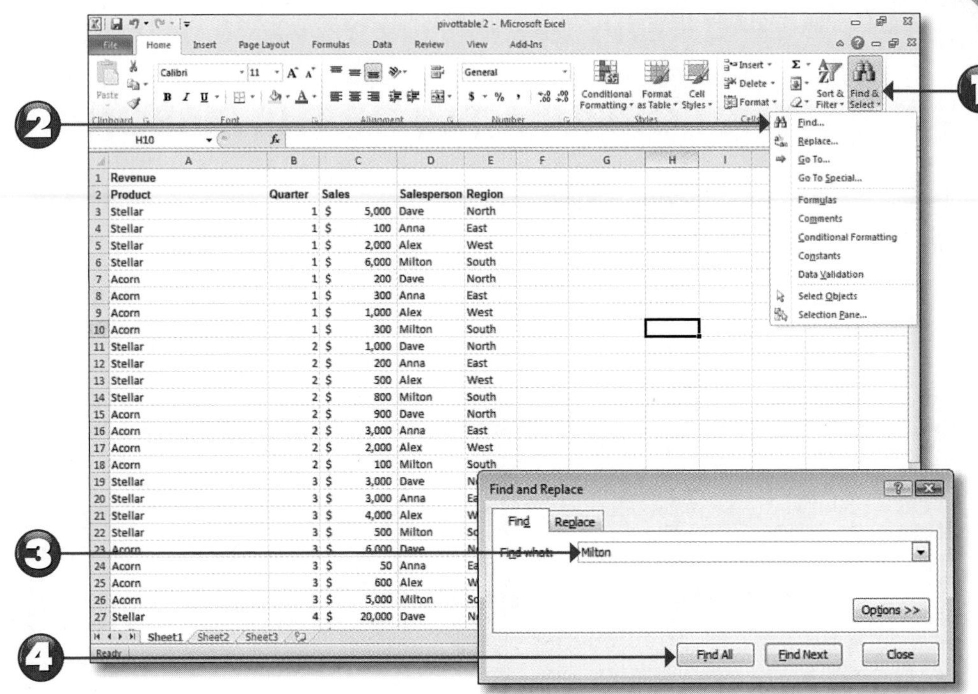

Start

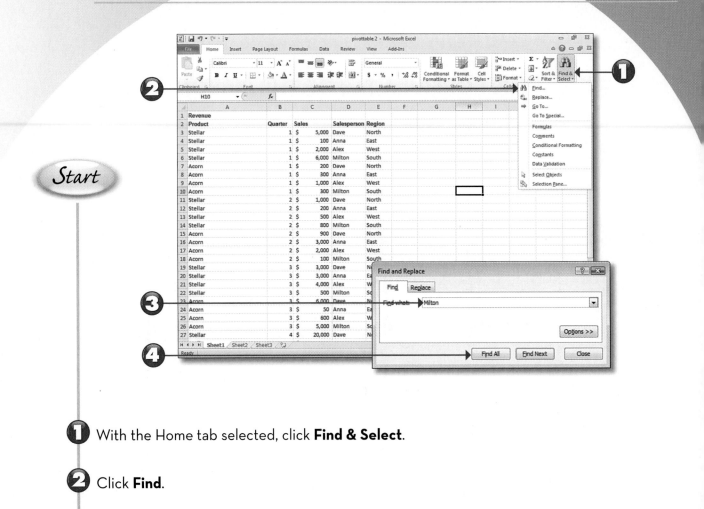

1. With the Home tab selected, click **Find & Select**.
2. Click **Find**.
3. Enter a search term.
4. Click **Find All**.

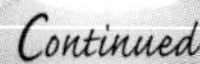
Continued

TIP

Special Searches By clicking the **Options** button in the Find and Replace window, you can narrow down your search. For example, you can determine whether to match upper and lowercase in words that you search for. ■

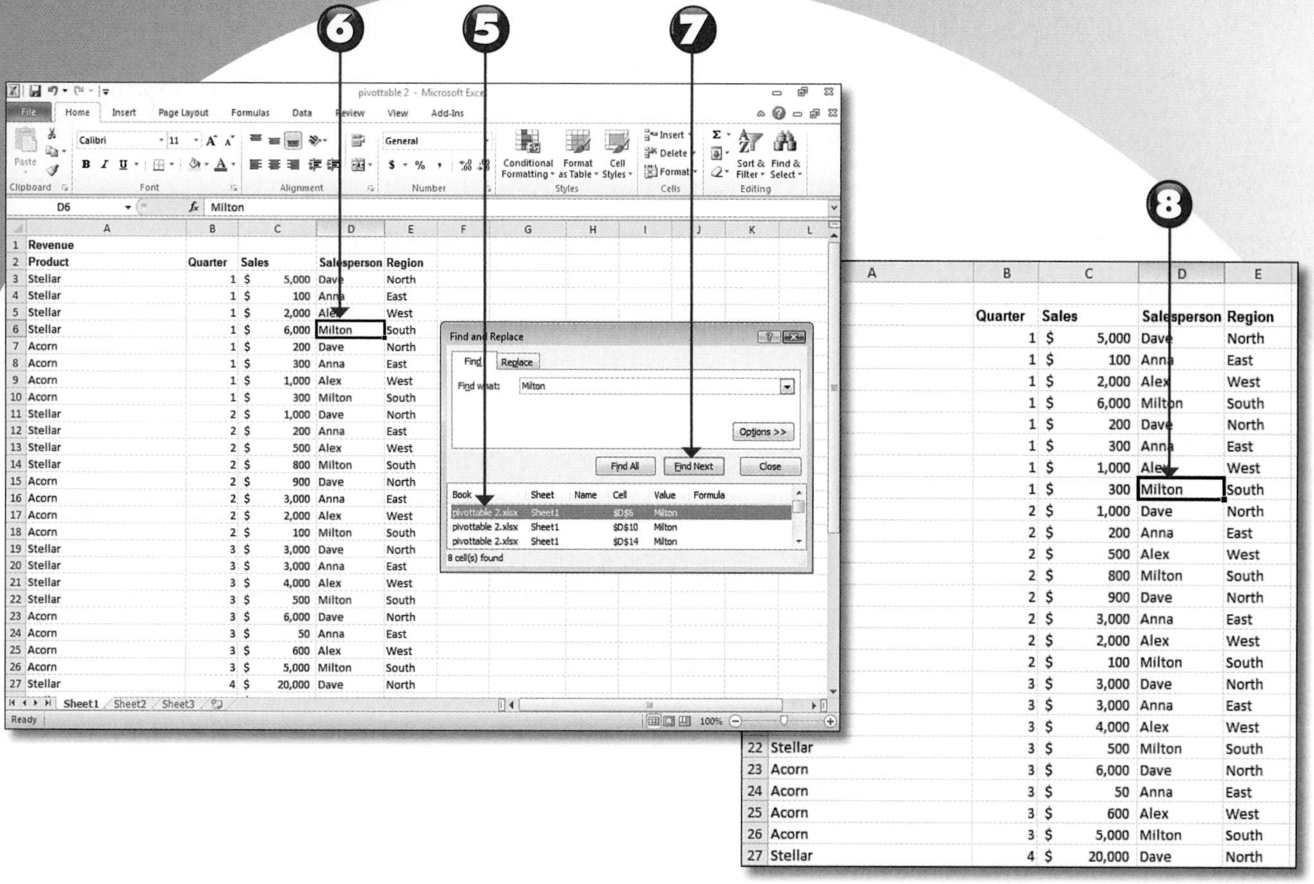

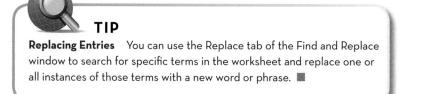

5 Instances of the search term are listed in the Find and Replace window.

6 The first instance in a cell is selected in the worksheet.

7 Click **Find Next**.

8 The next instance of the search term is selected in the worksheet.

End

TIP

Replacing Entries You can use the Replace tab of the Find and Replace window to search for specific terms in the worksheet and replace one or all instances of those terms with a new word or phrase. ■

FILLING A SERIES

Excel has its own way of guessing what you might want in the rest of a group of cells in which you have already entered some data and automatically filling in those cells based on your entries. Filling a series simply copies the data from one cell through a group of cells that you drag through; in the case of formulas, the cell references are adjusted accordingly. AutoComplete extrapolates from your previous entries to guess the results.

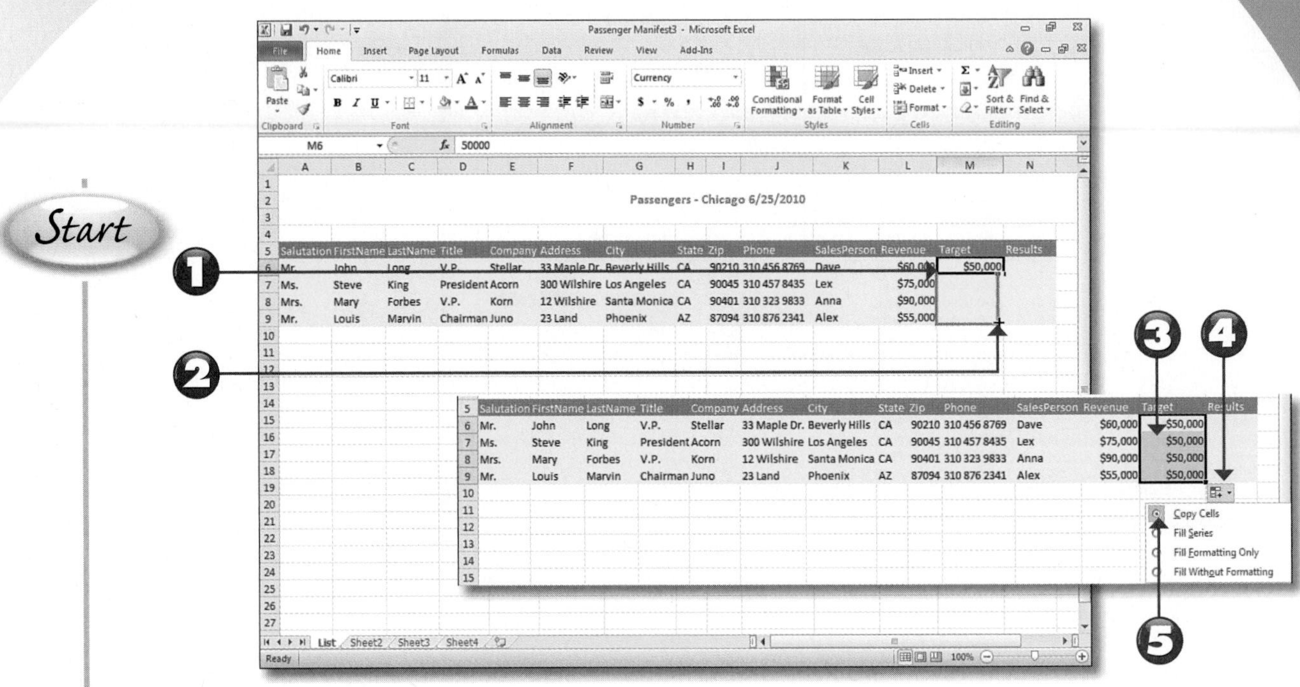

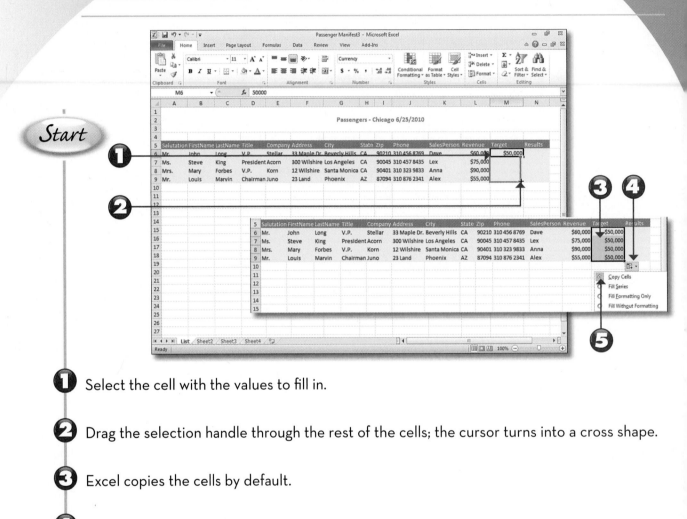

1. Select the cell with the values to fill in.
2. Drag the selection handle through the rest of the cells; the cursor turns into a cross shape.
3. Excel copies the cells by default.
4. Click the **AutoFill Options** drop-down arrow.
5. Select from the options to fill the series or formatting or both. Click **Copy Cells**.

Continued

TIP

Creating Your Own Lists You can select a series of entries in a worksheet and reuse them as a custom list. When the cells are selected, click **File**; then click **Advanced**. Click the **Custom Lists** button, verify the cell references and values for your new list, click **Import**, and then click **Add**. Your new custom list becomes available in other workbooks. ■

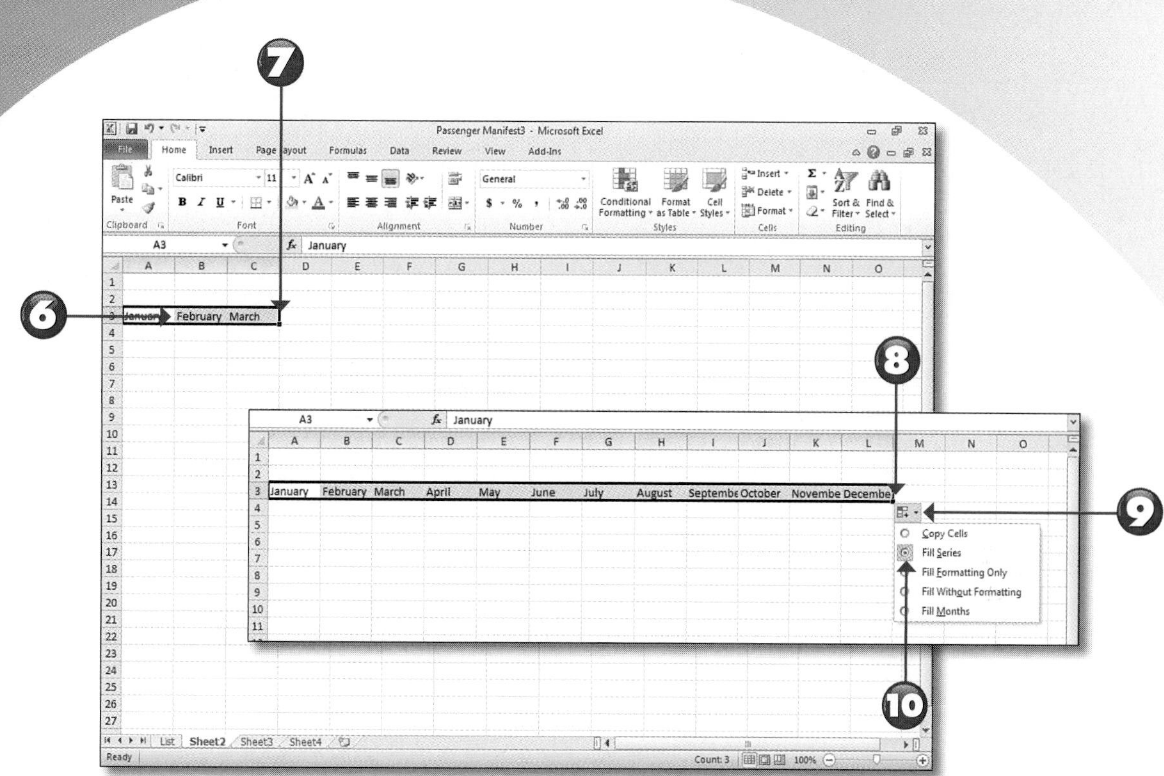

6 Enter the beginning of sequence of cells that have a probable order.

7 Grab the selection handle and begin dragging through the next set of cells.

8 Excel fills in the values of the cells based on the previous entries.

9 Click the **AutoFill Options** drop-down arrow.

10 Select from the options to fill the series or formatting or both. Click **Fill Series**.

End

TIP

Using AutoComplete As you type in cells directly after or below those in which you've typed data, Excel fills in the remainder with possible entries based on what you have entered previously. You can accept by pressing the down arrow or **Tab** key on your keyboard or simply type in your own new entry. ■

ENTERING DATES AND TIMES

Dates and time are specific numbers that you can enter into Excel cells, and the default formats for dates and times are used. You can adjust the formats by using the Number group in the Home tab of the Ribbon.

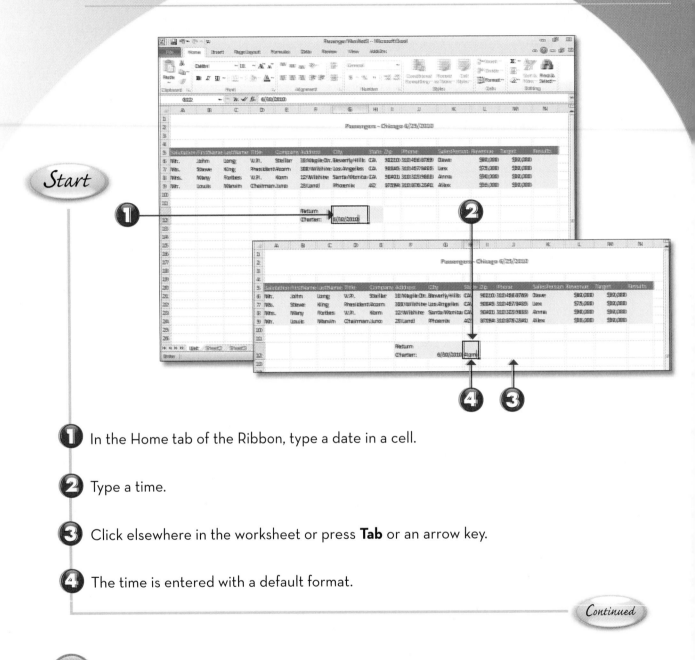

Start

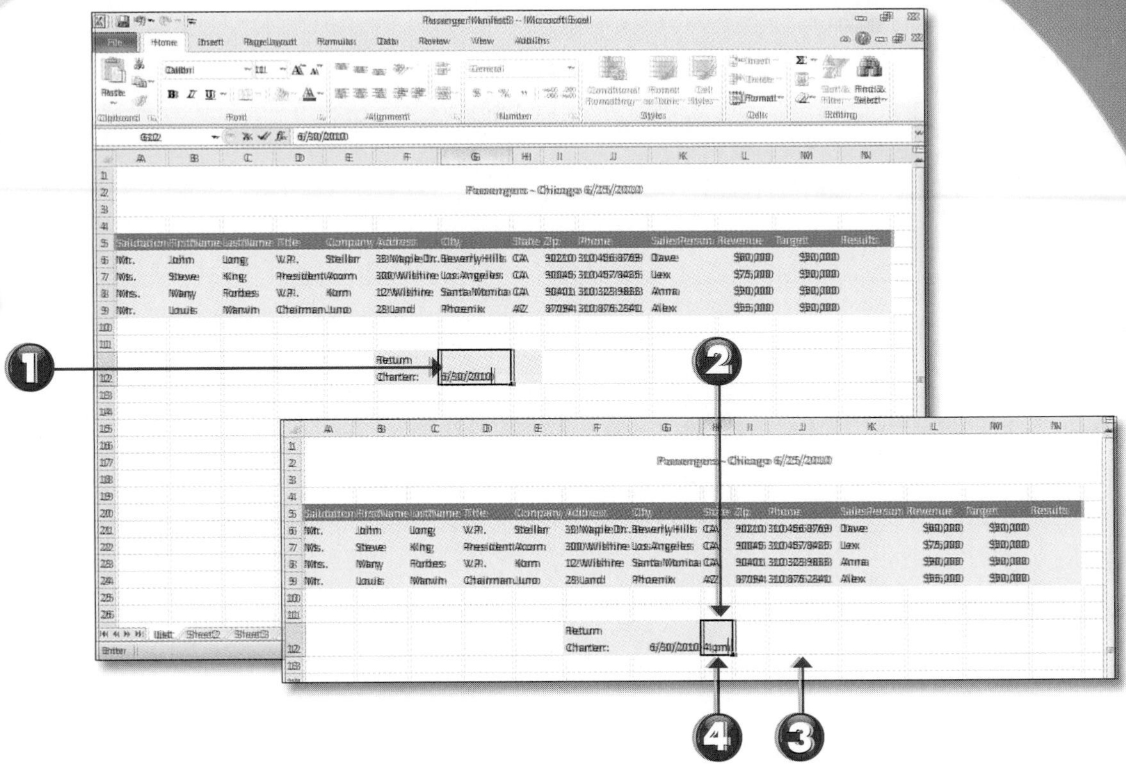

1. In the Home tab of the Ribbon, type a date in a cell.
2. Type a time.
3. Click elsewhere in the worksheet or press **Tab** or an arrow key.
4. The time is entered with a default format.

Continued

NOTE

How Dates Can Work in Excel Even when the formats for dates and times are changed, the numeric values are available in Excel for formulas and functions to use in calculations. For example, you can subtract one date from another to get the interval.

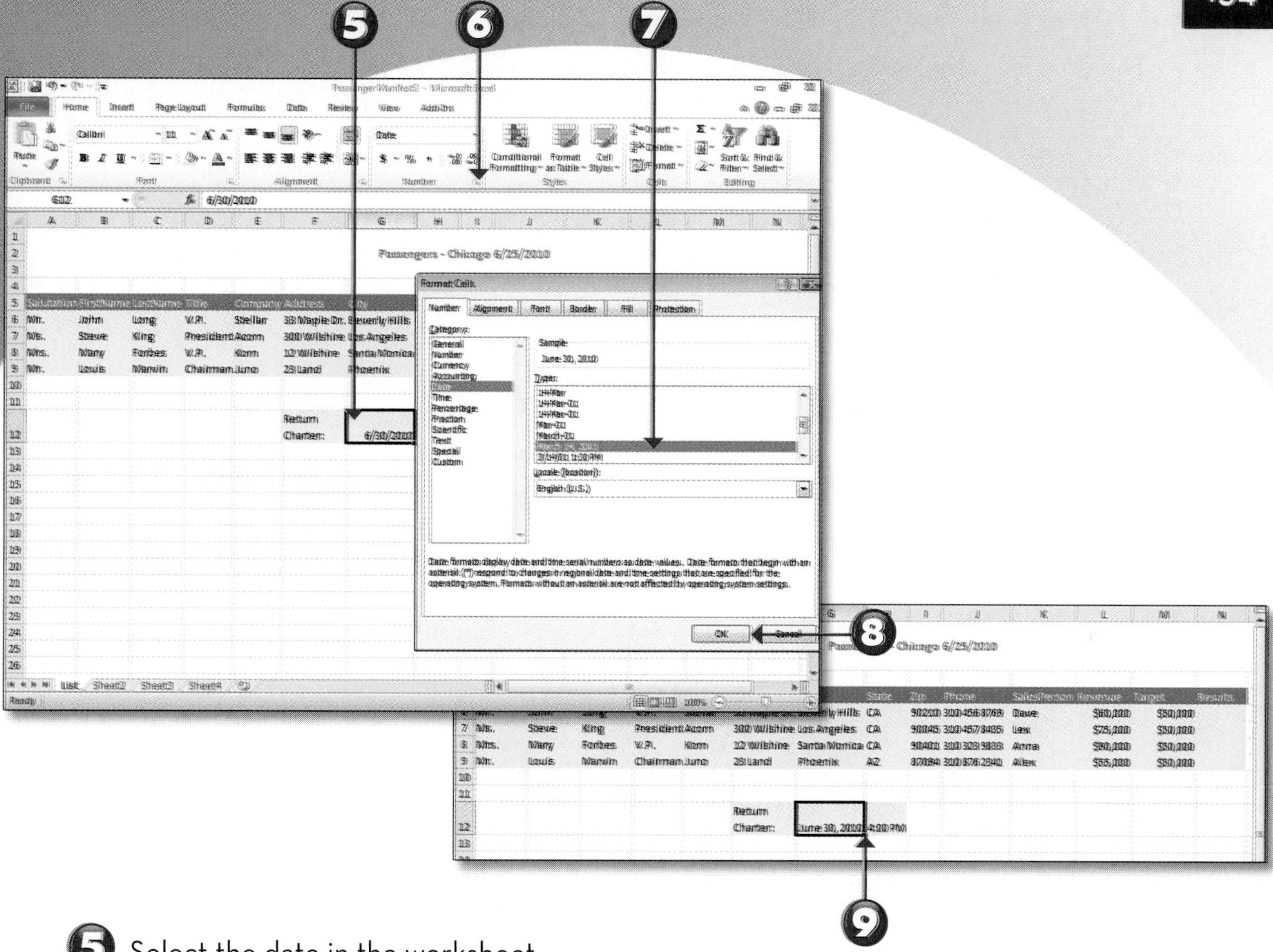

5 Select the date in the worksheet.

6 Click the **Dialog Launch** icon for the Number group in the Home tab.

7 In the Number tab of the Format Cells dialog, select the date format you want.

8 Click **OK**.

9 The date and time are set. You can repeat the process to reformat the time.

End

TIP

Entering the Current Date You can quickly enter the current date into a cell by pressing **Ctrl+;** (semicolon).

TIP

Calculating Time Excel stores time values in fractions of a 24-hour day. You can use time values in formulas and functions to calculate intervals and other parameters involving time in a worksheet.

USING FUNCTIONS: AUTOSUM

The quickest calculation that Excel can make is to add a set of selected cells or numbers with the AutoSum feature. AutoSum is really the easiest function in the Excel Function Library of the Ribbon's Formulas tab.

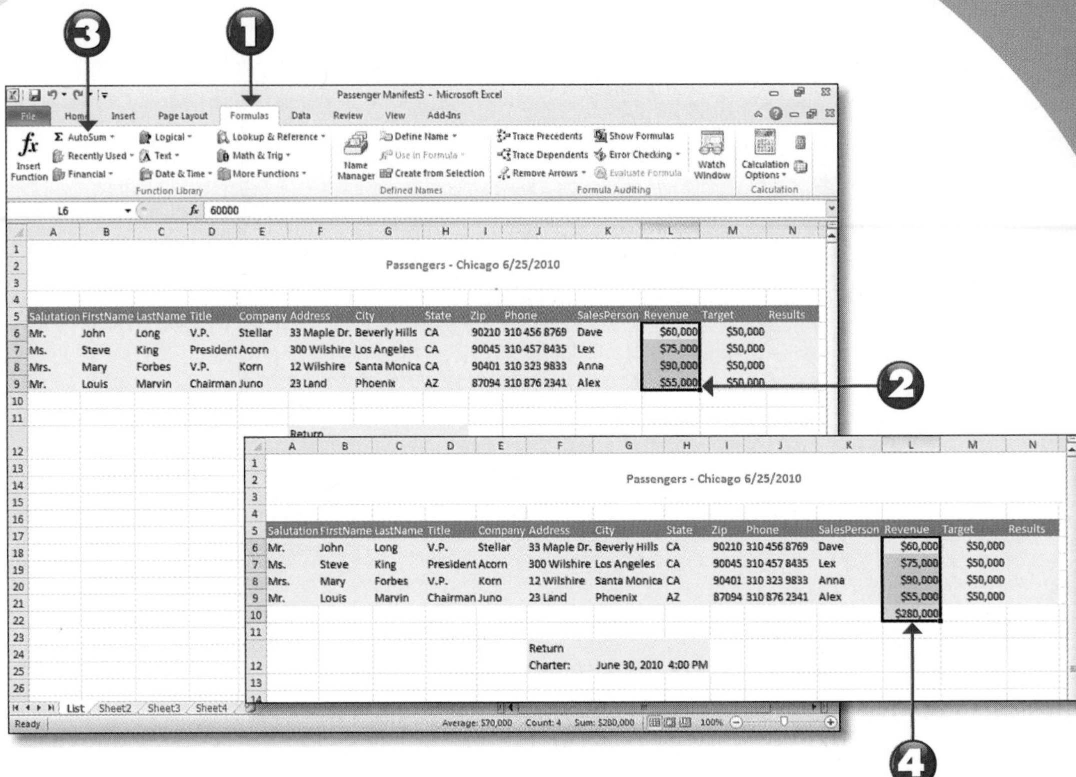

Start

1. Click the **Formulas** tab of the Ribbon.
2. Drag through to select the cells you want to add.
3. Click **AutoSum**.
4. The column of figures is added with the sum placed in the next cell below those selected.

End

TIP

Checking the Status Bar Excel displays values that you calculate on its status bar at the bottom of the window. For example, both the average and sum of the selected number are still available on the status bar even if you have cleared some of the results. ■

TIP

Exploring the Function Library Excel's Function Library has functions available for virtually any purpose or application. Each function has a pop-up tip to explain its use and purpose. You can press **F1** to get further help for using a function. ■

USING FUNCTIONS: AVERAGE

Excel can also calculate as a Function the average of a selected set of numbers. Other common functions include Count, or the number of cell instances in a selected group, Max, or the maximum value of those selected, or Min, the minimum value of those selected.

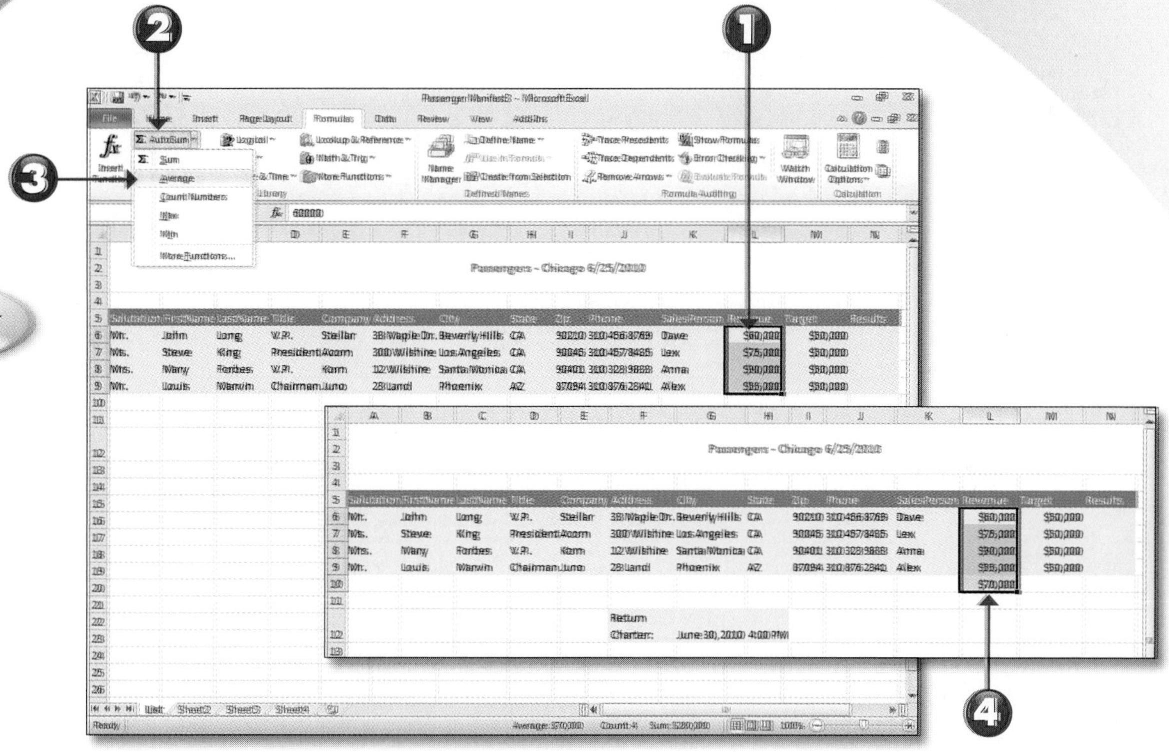

Start

1. Undo (**Ctrl+Z**) the AutoSum action from step 3 and reselect the original cells.
2. Click the **AutoSum** drop-down arrow.
3. Click **Average**.
4. The average of the selected values is placed in the next cell below the selected cells.

End

TIP

Using Insert Function To access all functions in Excel in one place, select the cell where you want the function calculated and click the **Insert Function** button. In the Insert Function window, you can select **All for Category** and choose from all functions. After you click **OK**, you can set the function based on *function arguments*. You are able to use the *Range Selector* to choose cells within the worksheet that will be used to calculate the results of the chosen function. ■

USING FORMULAS FOR CALCULATIONS

The real power of Excel comes from being able to make calculations based on your data and having the results displayed in other cells. For example, you can subtract a target for sales or revenue from actual sales to see how various salespeople performed.

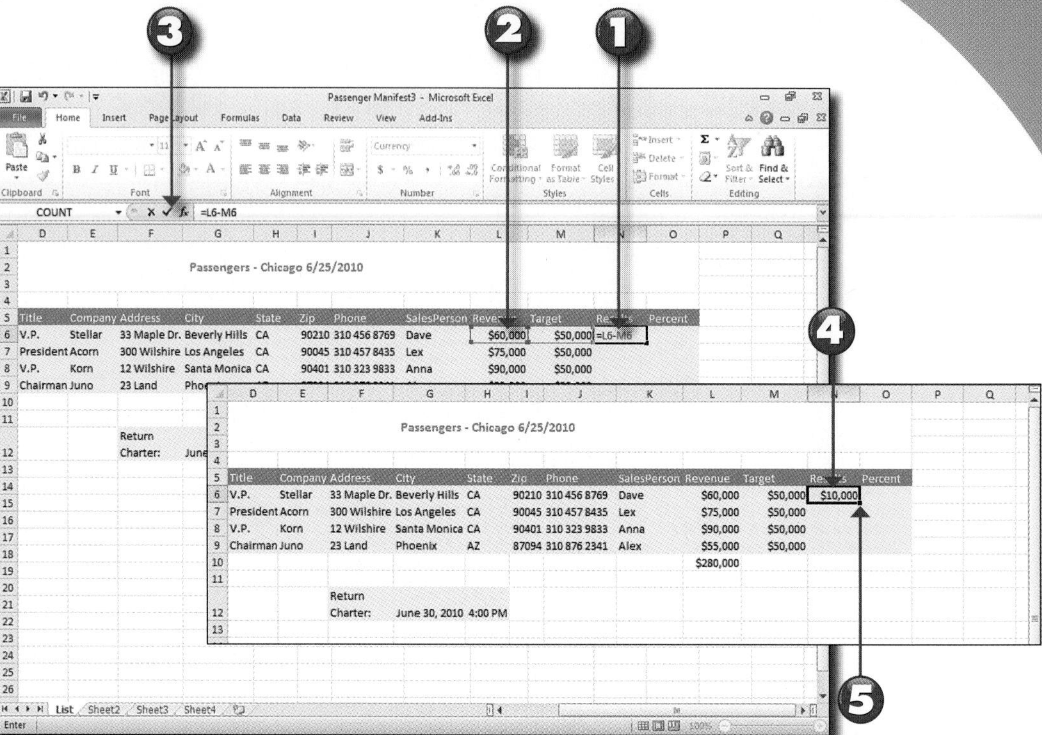

Start

1. Click to select the cell where the formula should show results and enter **=** (an equal sign) in the Formula Bar followed by the arguments for the formula. For example, subtract cell M6 (Target revenue) from cell L6 (Actual revenue).

2. The referenced cells in the formula are highlighted in the worksheet.

3. Click the check mark on the **Formula Bar** to apply the formula.

4. The formula result is shown in the cell.

5. Click to grab the corner handle of the formula cell.

Continued

TIP

Editing a Formula If the formula returns an incorrect value or does not fulfill the task you wanted, you can select the cell to place the formula in the Formula Bar, revise the formula, and click the check mark again to reset the formula. ■

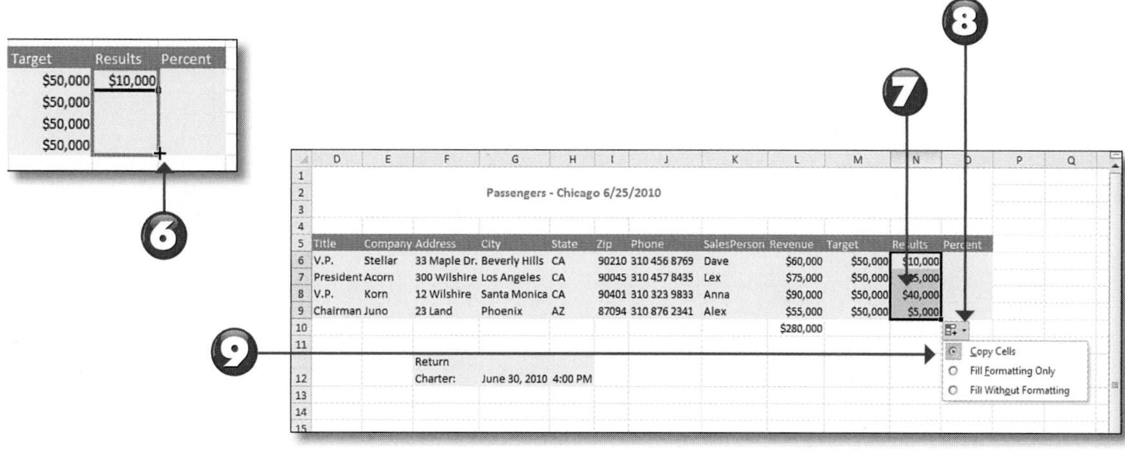

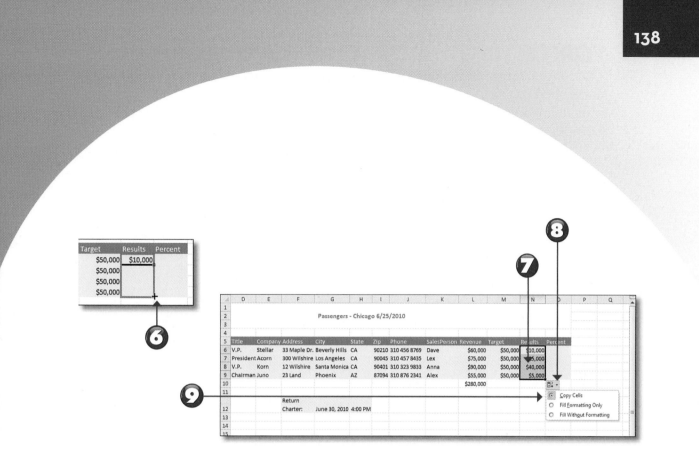

6 The cursor turns into crosshairs, and you can drag through the other cells where results are desired.

7 The formula is copied with the correct results reflecting the appropriate cell references.

8 Click the **AutoFill Options** drop-down arrow.

9 Click **Copy Cells**.

End

TIP

Absolute References In this example the formula adjusts as it is filled to reflect the current row value. To use an absolute reference to a specific cell rather than have the formula adjust, enter **$** before both the row number and column letter that you want to make absolute.

FORMATTING AND TRACING FORMULA RESULTS

After entering a formula, you can use the same formatting features of the Home tab's Number group to show the values in the way you want. You can also use the features of the Formula tab's Formula Auditing group to trace the cells that lead to the results of your formula (Precedents) or to locate the formulas that result from values in those cells (Dependents).

Start

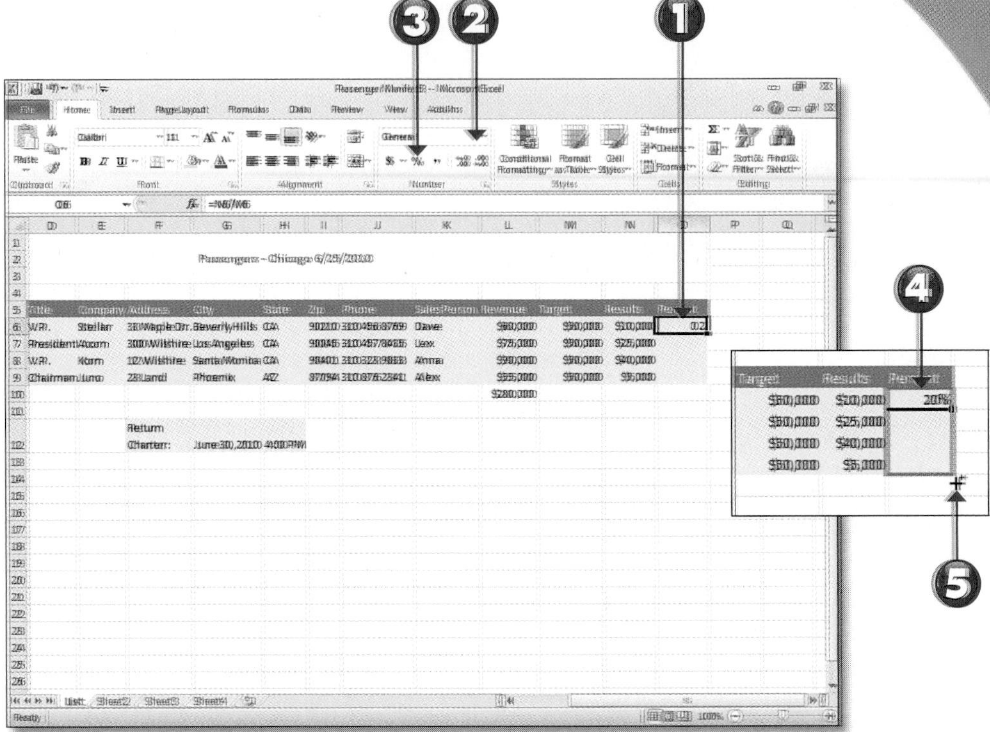

1. Enter a formula that represents a percent or fraction in the Formula Bar (for example, the percentage of Results from the Target Revenue).
2. In the Home tab, set the Number format as **General** to see the fraction as a decimal.
3. Click the **%** button to set it as a percentage.
4. The cell formula result reflects the number formatted as a percentage.
5. Drag through the other cells to fill in the formula.

Continued

TIP

Referencing Other Worksheets Enter **!** after a sheet name in the Formula Bar reference. For example, List!A1 refers to the first cell in the worksheet called "List" and can be used in other worksheets in the workbook.

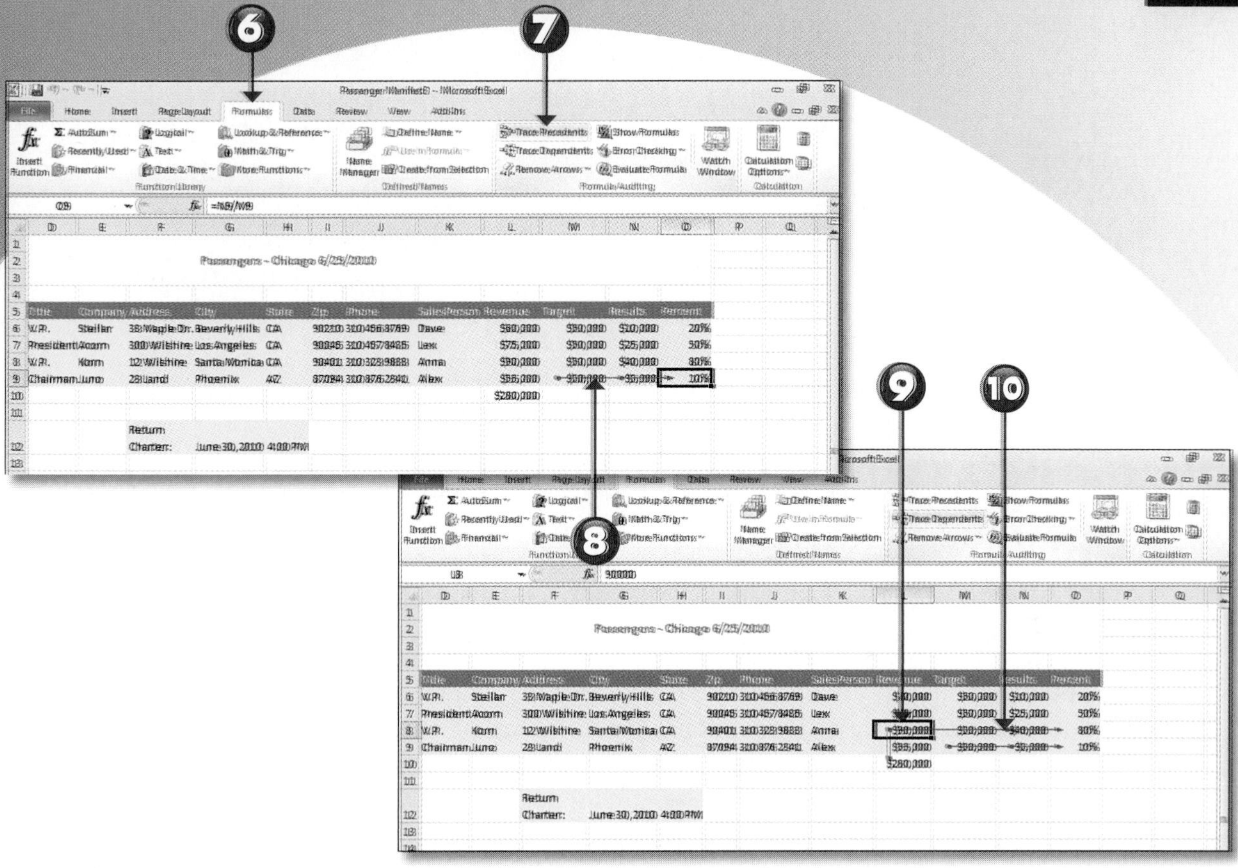

6 Click the **Formulas** tab of the Ribbon.

7 Click to select a cell with a formula value and click **Trace Precedents**.

8 The cells resulting in that formula value are traced.

9 Click to select a cell that is part of a formula and click **Trace Dependents**.

10 The other cells comprising the formula and the formal result cell are traced.

End

TIP

Referencing Other Workbooks Use brackets **[]** around the filename of another workbook to identify it in the formula, and also use an **!** after the sheet name in the Formula Bar reference. For example, [PassengerManifest.xlsx]List!A1 refers to the first cell in the worksheet called "List" in the workbook saved as Passenger Manifest.xlsx (Excel Workbook format). As an Excel 97–2003 file, the same file would be saved as PassengerManifest.xls.

CREATING CHARTS, DATA TABLES, AND PIVOT TABLES

Excel 2010 provides various ways that you can enter, view, analyze, and reorganize your data when it is in a worksheet.

The Insert tab on the Ribbon lets you create a visual representation of your data using a variety of preset chart types, including column, bar, pie, and more. The Chart Tools on the Ribbon let you modify the design, layout, and format of the various elements in your chart.

After selecting parts of your worksheet and converting those cells to a data table, you can sort and filter the various columns. The Table Tools on the Ribbon let you format your table with Table Styles and Table Style Options.

You can also reorganize your data in a pivot table to see relationships differently or use the Conditional Format feature to view results graphically or according to rules. New features in Excel 2010 include the capability to search in tables for pivot tables, filter pivot tables with the Slicer, and add Sparklines to visualize data in your worksheet.

THE DATA TABLE TOOLS

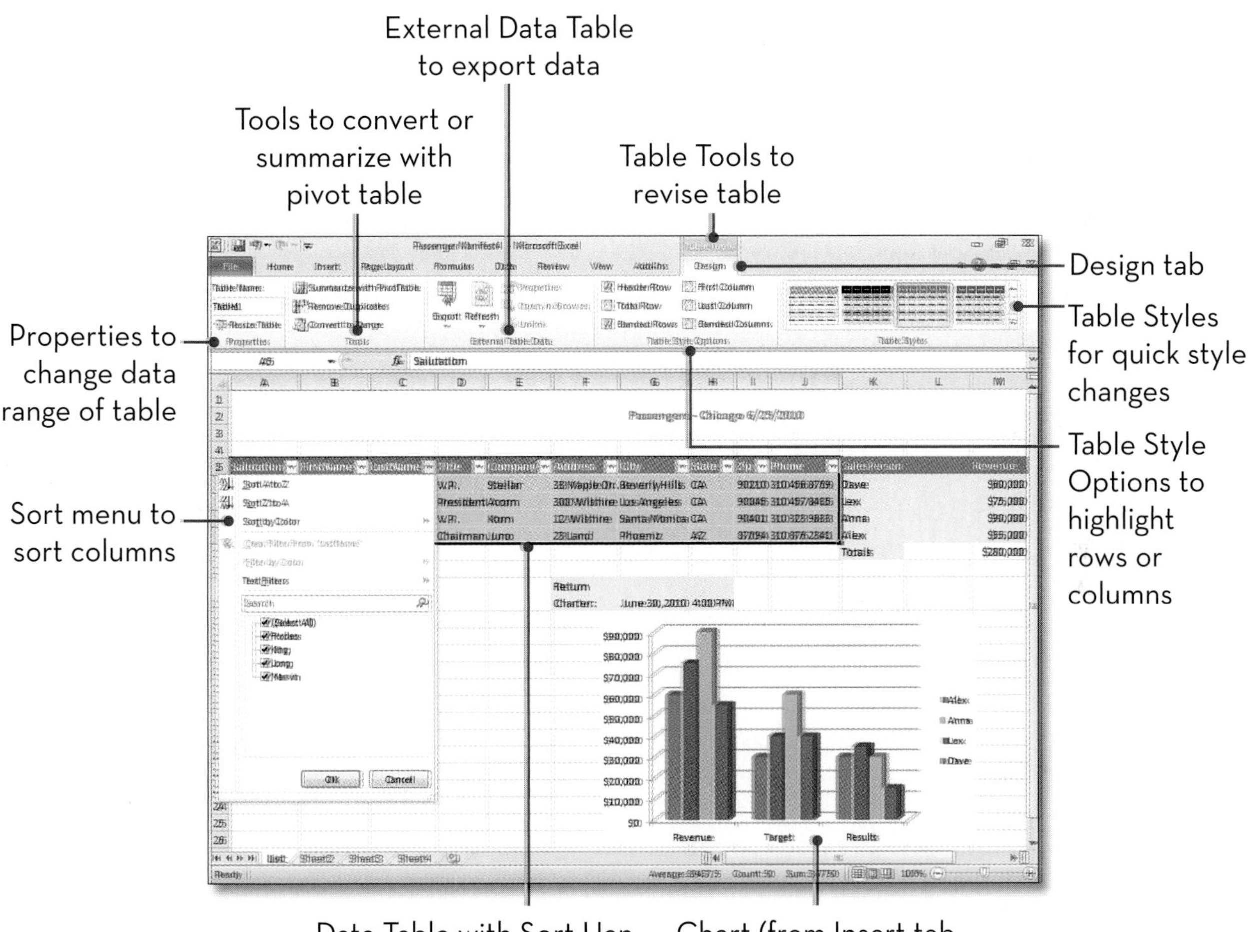

External Data Table to export data
Tools to convert or summarize with pivot table
Table Tools to revise table
Design tab
Properties to change data range of table
Table Styles for quick style changes
Table Style Options to highlight rows or columns
Sort menu to sort columns
Data Table with Sort Handles to open Sort menu
Chart (from Insert tab of Ribbon)

CREATING A CHART USING THE RIBBON

A chart creates a visual representation of your data that you can use in a presentation or to analyze results. Chart map your data along a set of coordinates to display values for a data series according to various categories, which can include a span of time. When a chart is created, the Chart Tools become available on the Ribbon to change the design, layout, or format of chart elements.

Start

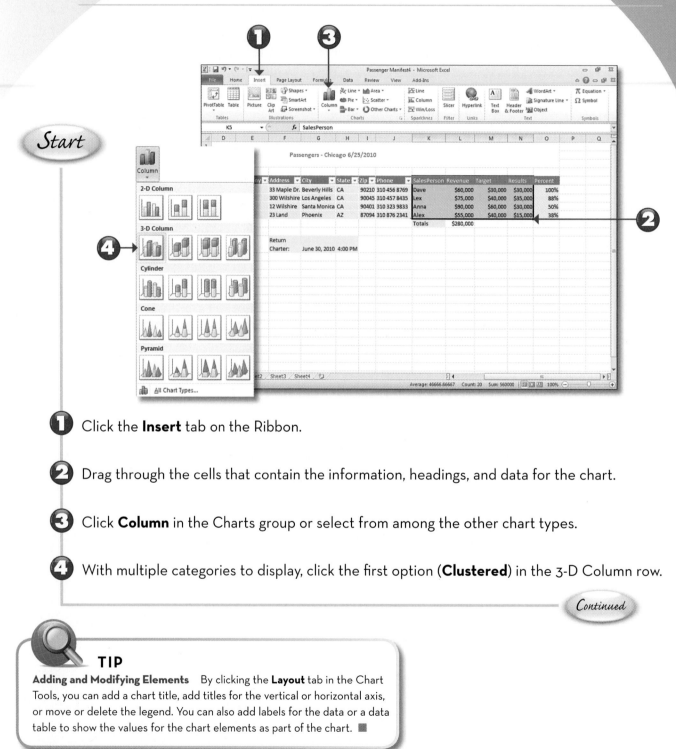

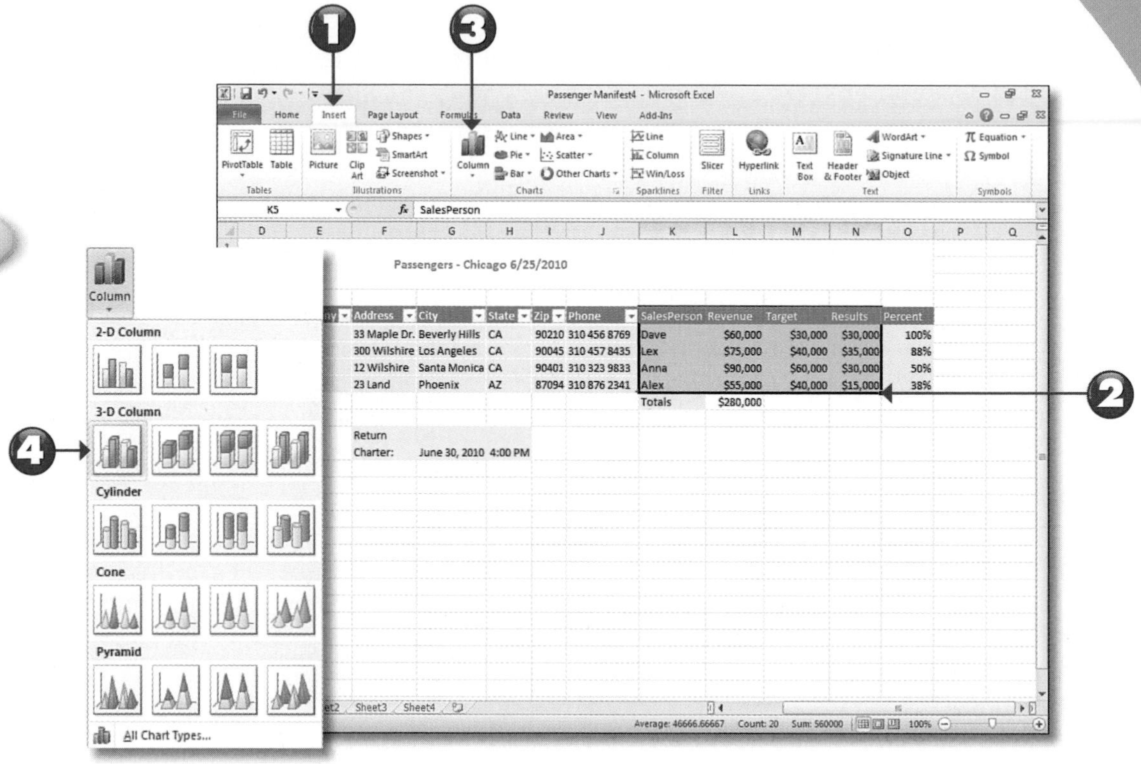

1. Click the **Insert** tab on the Ribbon.
2. Drag through the cells that contain the information, headings, and data for the chart.
3. Click **Column** in the Charts group or select from among the other chart types.
4. With multiple categories to display, click the first option (**Clustered**) in the 3-D Column row.

Continued

TIP

Adding and Modifying Elements By clicking the **Layout** tab in the Chart Tools, you can add a chart title, add titles for the vertical or horizontal axis, or move or delete the legend. You can also add labels for the data or a data table to show the values for the chart elements as part of the chart. ■

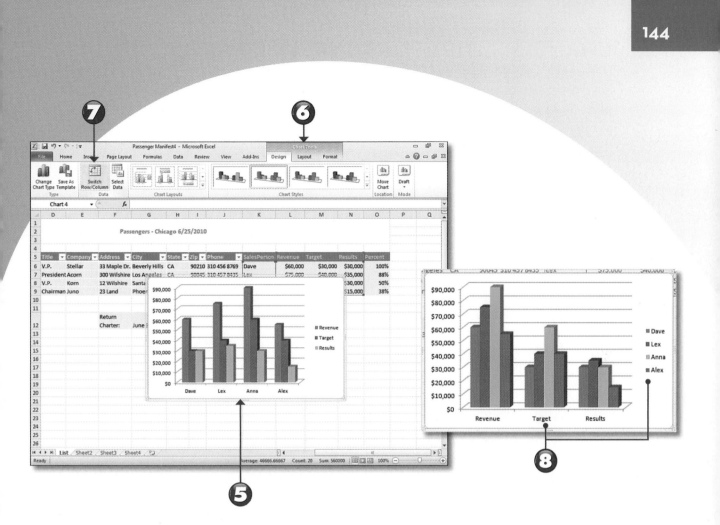

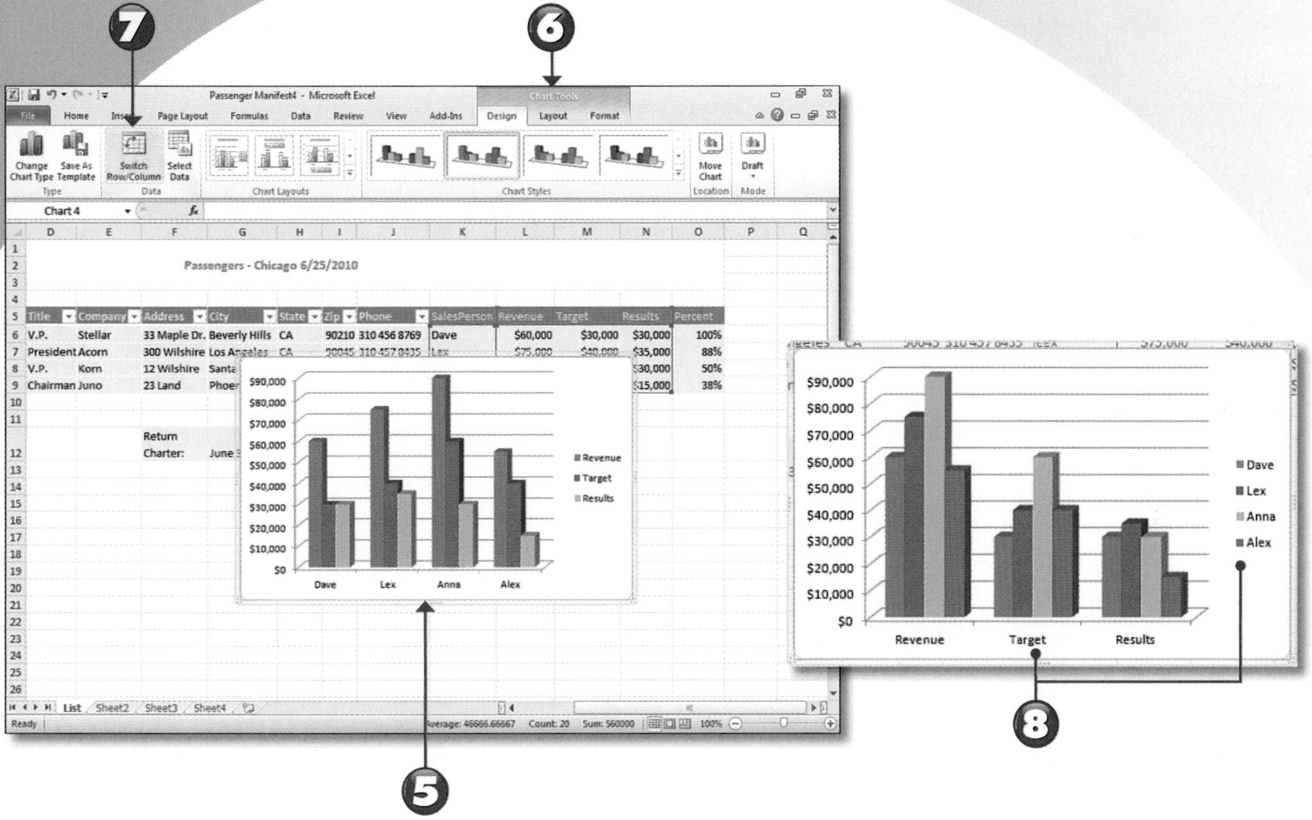

5 The chart is created in the worksheet.

6 The Chart Tools open on the Ribbon.

7 Click **Switch Row/Column** to reorient the display of values in the chart by switching the categories with the series.

8 The chart is altered to put different parameters in the legend and change the contents of the horizontal access or series and the categories in the legend.

End

TIP

Adding and Modifying Data By clicking the **Select Data** button in the Data group on the Design tab, you can add another series to the information being plotted in the chart or edit the information in the legend. ■

TIP

Changing the Chart Layout You can use the Chart Layouts in the Design tab to apply any one of 10 preset layouts to the chart and then modify the layout further using the Design, Layout, and Format tabs of the Chart Tools. ■

CHANGING THE CHART TYPE

Different charts have various capabilities to display data for specific purposes. After you have created a basic chart, you can use the All Charts window to change the chart type to plot values over time to show them in various shapes like a doughnut, area, scatter, bubble, pyramid, and more.

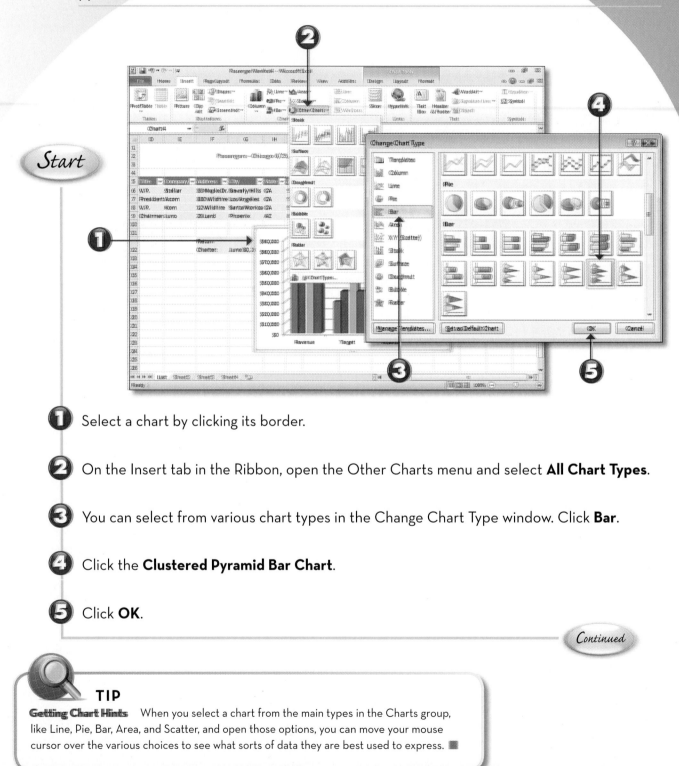

Start

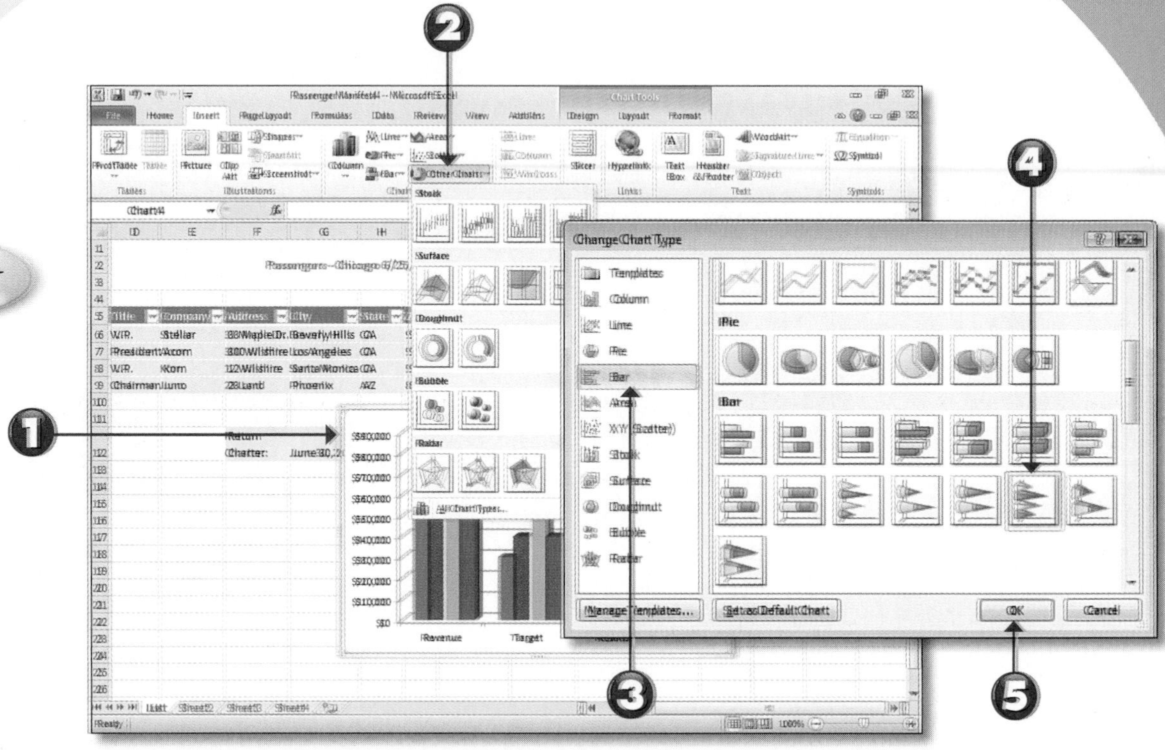

1. Select a chart by clicking its border.
2. On the Insert tab in the Ribbon, open the Other Charts menu and select **All Chart Types**.
3. You can select from various chart types in the Change Chart Type window. Click **Bar**.
4. Click the **Clustered Pyramid Bar Chart**.
5. Click **OK**.

Continued

TIP

Getting Chart Hints When you select a chart from the main types in the Charts group, like Line, Pie, Bar, Area, and Scatter, and open those options, you can move your mouse cursor over the various choices to see what sorts of data they are best used to express.

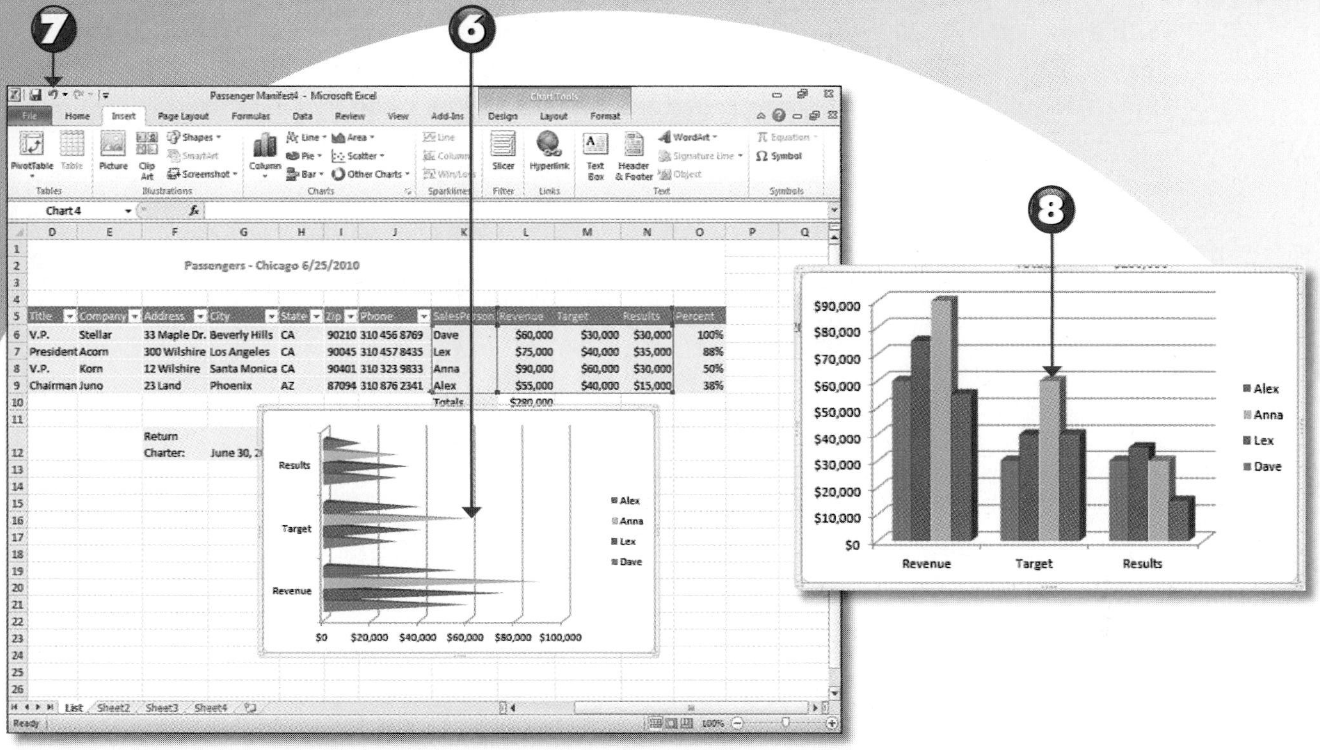

6 The chart is transformed into the type you selected.

7 Click **Undo** if you don't care for the results.

8 The chart reverts to your original selection.

End

TIP

Reusing Favorites When you use a specific chart type frequently, you can make that the default chart by clicking **Set as Default Chart** in the Change Chart Type window. You can also save your worksheet with a chart as an Excel template using Backstage view and then select **Manage Templates** in the Change Chart Type window to reuse such charts in a new project. ■

TIP

Using Pie Charts and Doughnut Charts A pie chart is a very specific chart type used to express *parts of a whole*, so you can display only one data series in a pie chart, which is displayed by percentages. You can use a doughnut chart to display multiple such series, with each forming one ring of the doughnut. ■

FORMATTING CHART ELEMENTS

With any chart type, the Format tab in the Chart Tools provides a way to change the appearance of any element in the chart. You can also use the Shape Styles gallery and Shape Effects to add dramatic effects to selected graphics in your chart.

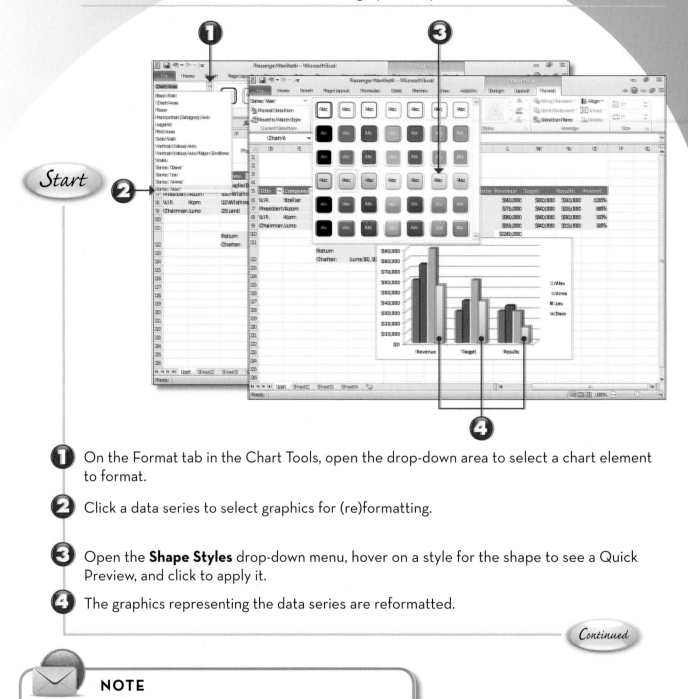

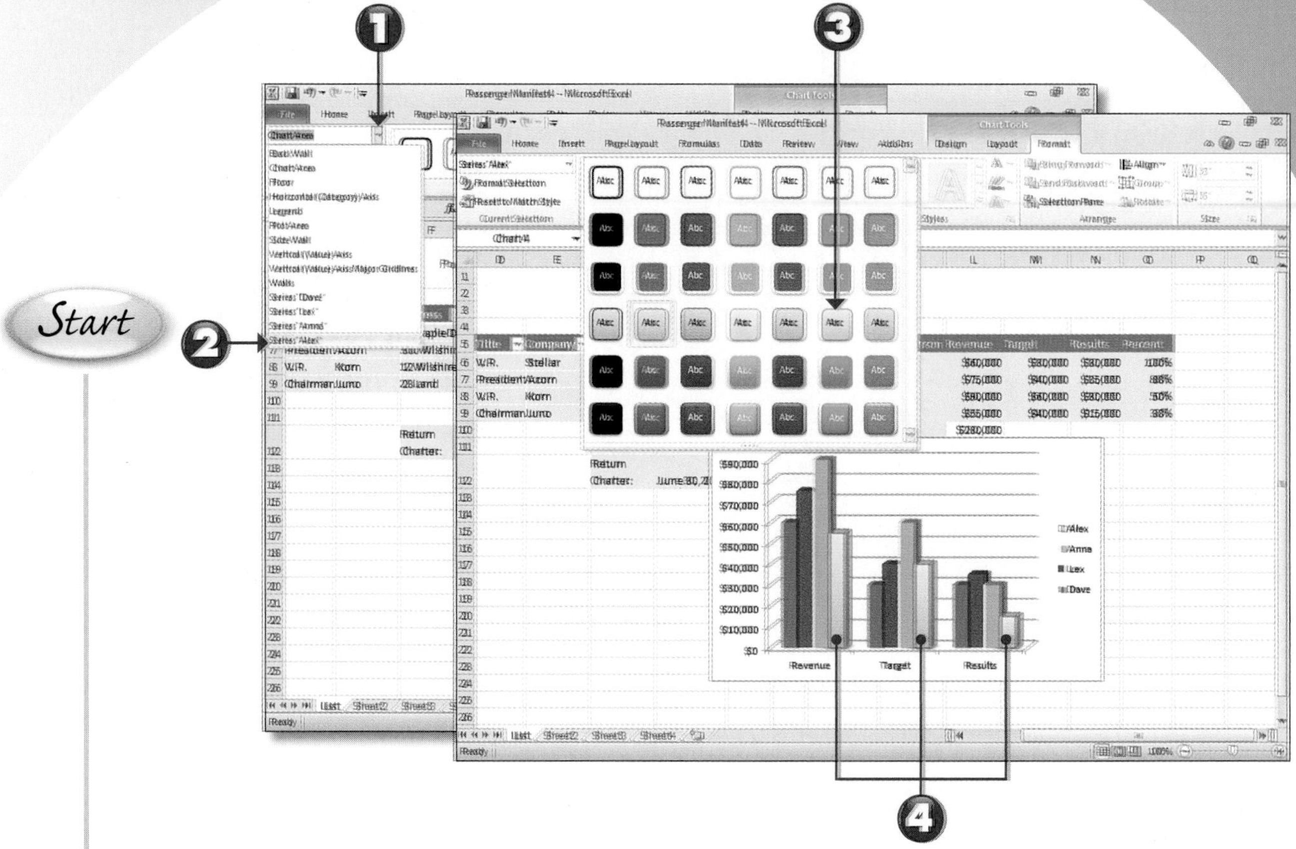

Start

1. On the Format tab in the Chart Tools, open the drop-down area to select a chart element to format.
2. Click a data series to select graphics for (re)formatting.
3. Open the **Shape Styles** drop-down menu, hover on a style for the shape to see a Quick Preview, and click to apply it.
4. The graphics representing the data series are reformatted.

Continued

NOTE

Changing Font Size or Color Although changing the look of the graphics is nice, you may want to change the size of a font on an axis or in the legend. You can select the axis or legend manually from the drop-down menu in the Current Selection group of the Format tab of Chart Tools. Then you can use the formatting features on the Home tab of the Ribbon.

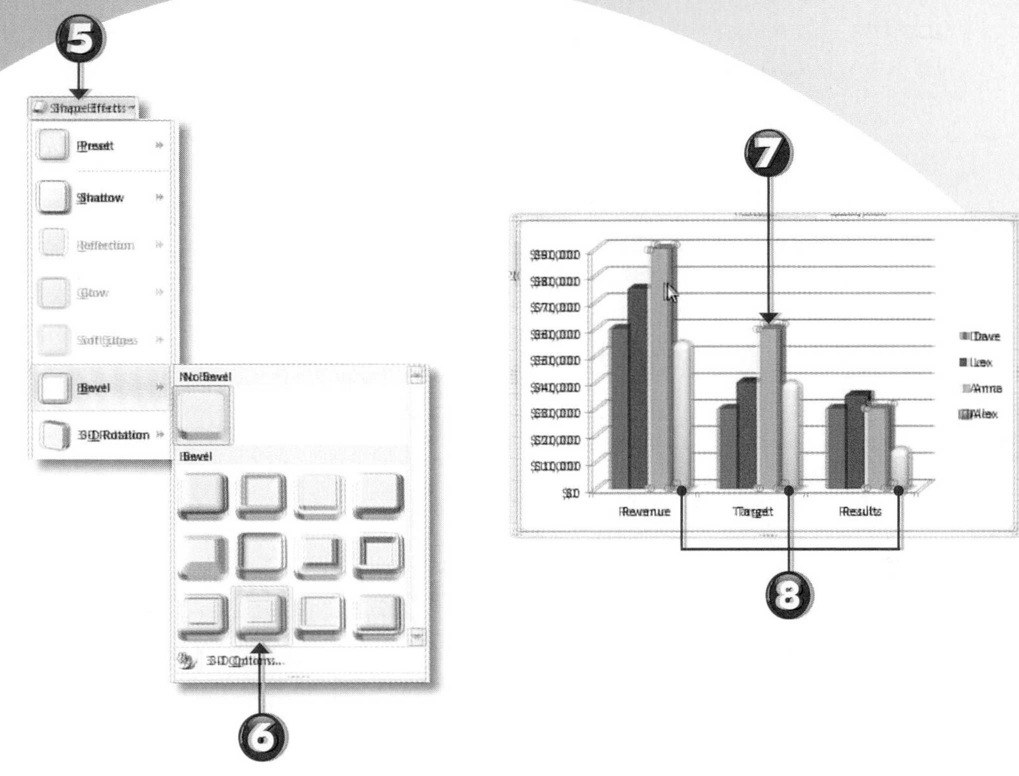

5. With the shape still selected, click the **Shape Effects** drop-down arrow.

6. Hover on an effect for the shape to see a Quick Preview and click to apply that shape effect.

7. The style and effect are applied to all elements in the series.

8. You can also click to manually select another series to change its format, shape, or effect.

End

TIP

Using WordArt Styles You can select text elements in the chart and use the Word Art Styles in the Format tab to change the appearance of the legend, title, axis text, or labels. ■

TIP

Chart Styles With the chart selected (click its border), you can use the Chart Style in the Design tab on the Chart Tools to apply an entire design or look to your chart. (Applying Chart Styles removes individual element formatting you have applied to graphics in the chart). ■

MOVING A CHART

You can move a chart within the current worksheet or to its own worksheet. Then you can use the zoom slider to change its relative size in the new worksheet and the formatting tools to change its appearance on the full page.

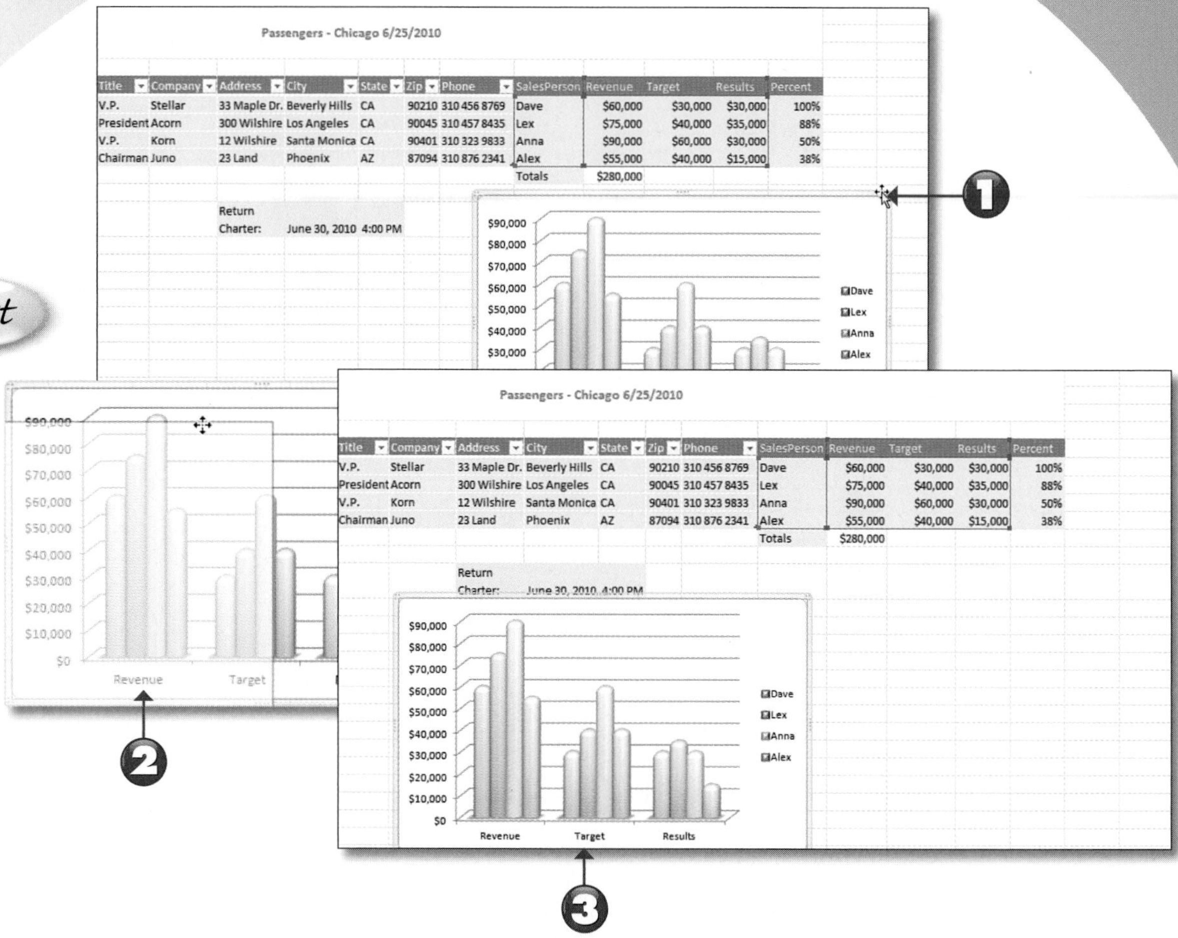

Start

1. Click the border of a selected chart until your cursor turns to a cross shape.
2. Drag and drop the chart to a new place on the worksheet.
3. The chart is repositioned on the worksheet.

Continued

TIP

Resizing a Chart You can resize a chart by clicking on the corner of the chart until your cursor changes into a two-headed arrow. Then you can drag the corner out to make the chart larger or in to reduce its size. ■

TIP

Moving a Slice of a Pie Chart In a pie chart, you can "break out" one of the pieces by selecting it and dragging it away from the rest of the pie. ■

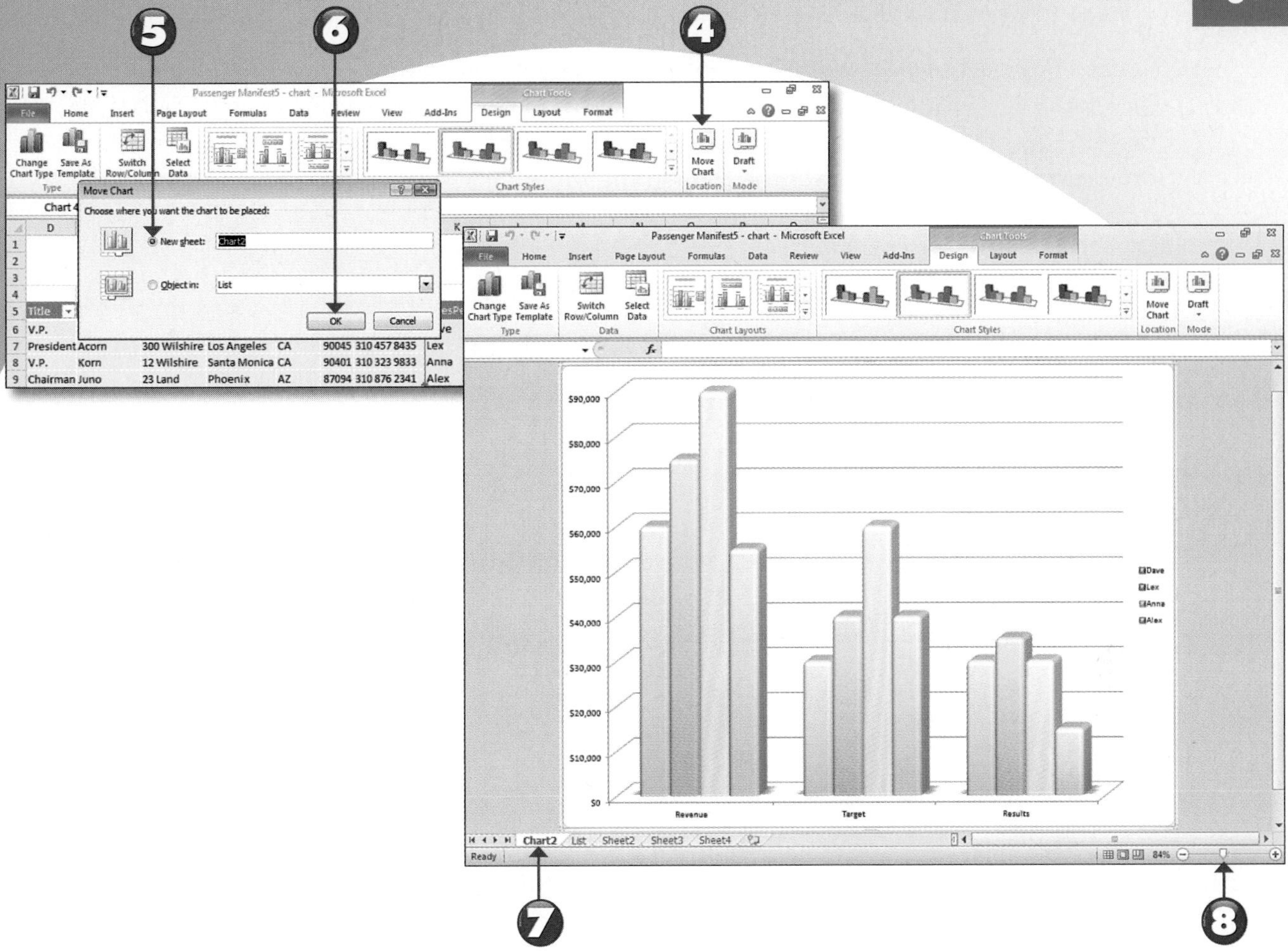

4 With the chart still selected, click **Move Chart** on the Design tab in Chart Tools.

5 Click **New Sheet** (with the sheet name selected, you can change it).

6 Click **OK**.

7 The chart is moved to its own sheet.

8 You can use the zoom slider to adjust its display size in the new sheet.

End

TIP

Reformatting the Chart Moving a chart to its own sheet changes its appearance and makes the text appear smaller. To change the font size select a chart element and use the formatting tools of the Home tab. ■

TIP

Copying a Chart You can select a chart and click **Copy** in the Home tab of the Ribbon (or press **Ctrl+C**) and then click **Paste** (**Ctrl+V**) to place the chart into another worksheet. ■

SORTING DATA IN A TABLE

Converting part of your worksheet into a table by first selecting the cells you want for the table and then using the Insert tab on the Ribbon enables you to analyze that set of data. A table puts sort handles into the header row of the columns, allowing you to use the drop-down arrows to sort and filter the data in the table.

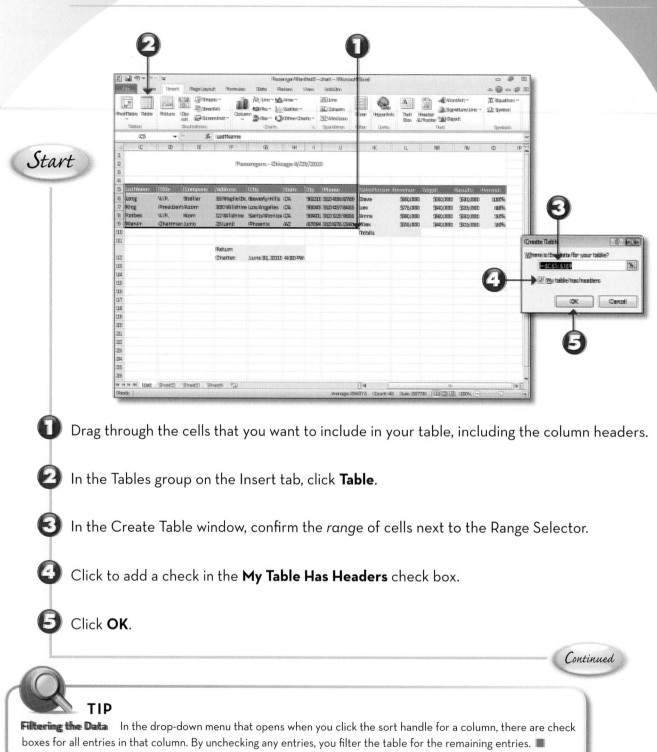

Start

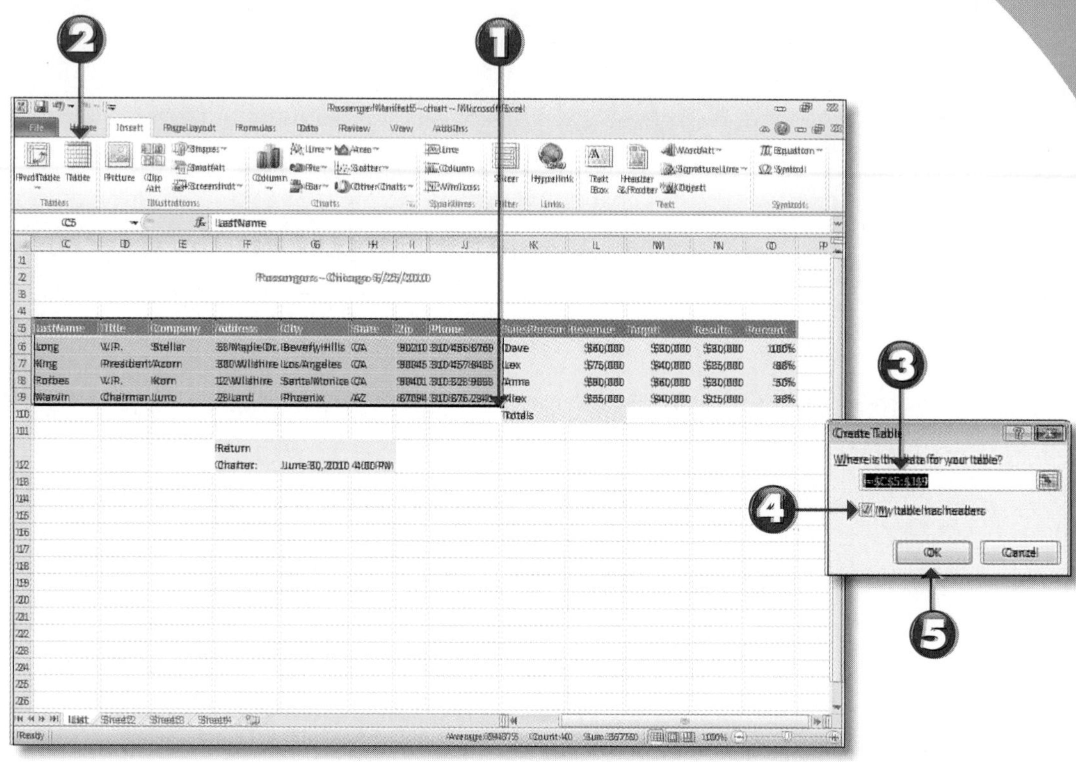

1. Drag through the cells that you want to include in your table, including the column headers.
2. In the Tables group on the Insert tab, click **Table**.
3. In the Create Table window, confirm the *range* of cells next to the Range Selector.
4. Click to add a check in the **My Table Has Headers** check box.
5. Click **OK**.

Continued

TIP

Filtering the Data In the drop-down menu that opens when you click the sort handle for a column, there are check boxes for all entries in that column. By unchecking any entries, you filter the table for the remaining entries.

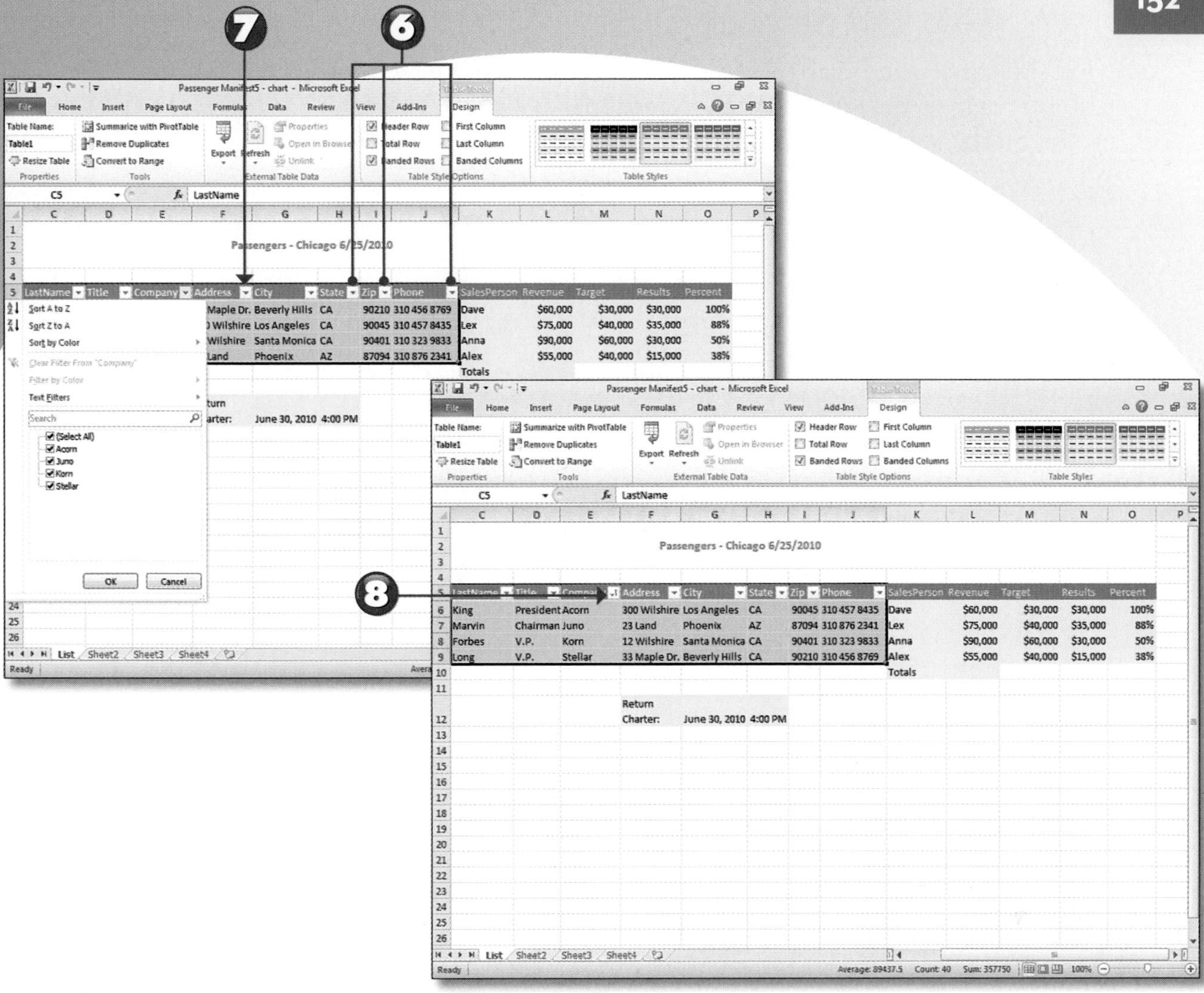

6 Sort handles are added to the header row.

7 Click one of the sort handles for a column heading.

8 Select a sorting method to sort table columns according to the option selected (Ascending shown here) with an up arrow indicating the sort selection (Ascending).

End

TIP

Clearing Filter Handles To remove the filter handles and deselect the cells in a table, click in the table to open Table Tools and then click **Convert to Range** in the Tools group of the Design tab.

TIP

Using Text Filter Parameters Text filters in the drop-down filter options let you fine-tune your filter using parameters such as Equals, Does Not Equal, Begins With, Ends With, Contains, and Does Not Contain.

ADDING SPARKLINES

Sparklines are tiny charts within one cell that visually show trends or data relationships. Depending on the type of data plotted, Sparklines can show a Line chart (trend), Column chart (relationship), and Win/Loss (for teams).

Start

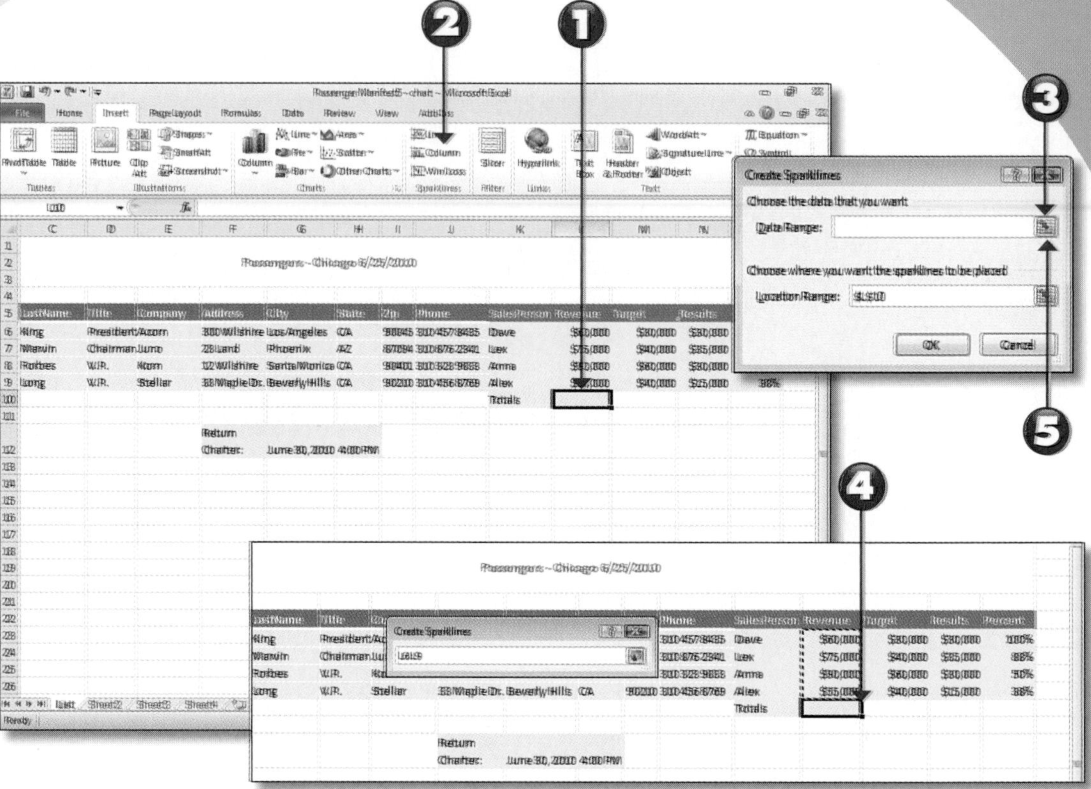

1. Click to select a cell where you want to add Sparklines.
2. On the Insert tab, click a Sparkline—**Column**, for example.
3. In the Create Sparklines window, click the **Range Selector** for Data Range.
4. Drag through the cells for the Sparklines to put them into the Data Range box.
5. Click the **Range Selector** again to return to the full Create Sparklines window.

Continued

TIP

Referencing Key Points You can use the Show group of the Sparklines Tools to indicate high and low points and other key aspects of your Sparklines. To do so, you click a check box. You can change the color of the shown points by clicking on **Marker Color** and selecting different colors for various points. ■

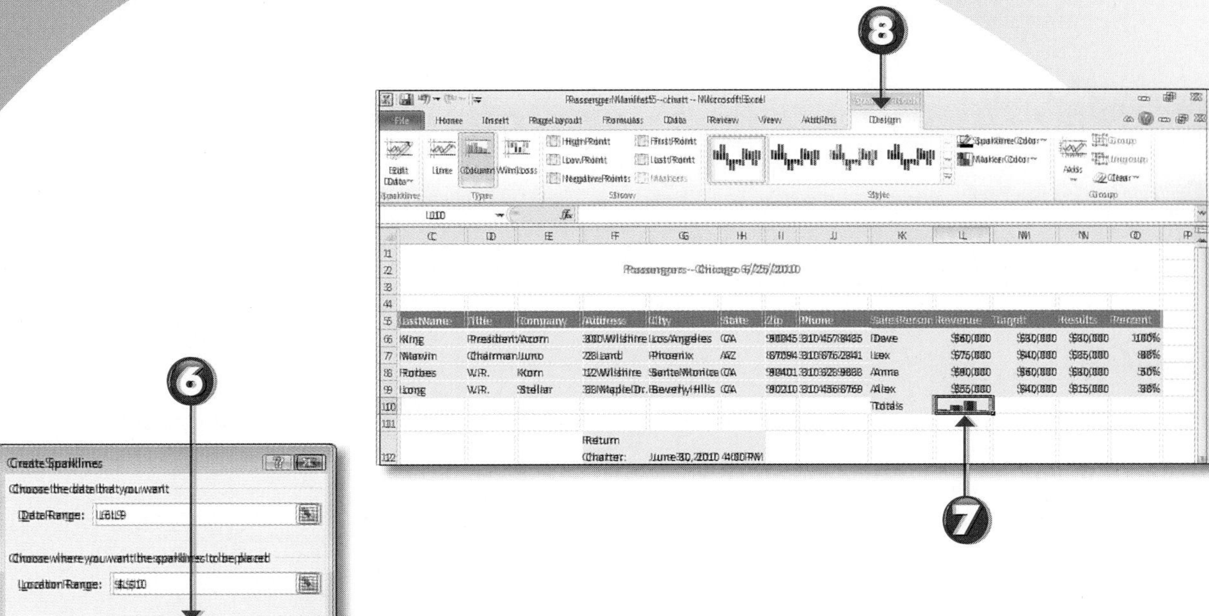

6. With the Data Range selected, click **OK**.

7. The Sparklines, in the form of a small chart, appear in the selected cell.

8. A new Sparkline Tools section opens on the Ribbon. It has just one tab: Design.

End

TIP

Changing the Sparkline Type and Style Use the Type group in the Sparklines Design tab to change to another type of Sparkline. Click the **Style** drop-down arrow to select a different color and style for the Sparklines. ■

USING A PIVOT TABLE

You can use a pivot table to reorganize your data to more clearly see various relationships. For example, with your sales data in ordinary columns or rows, with columns listing the various categories, it's hard to see who sold what, when it was sold, or where. By putting your categories into a pivot table, you can display all these relationships more clearly.

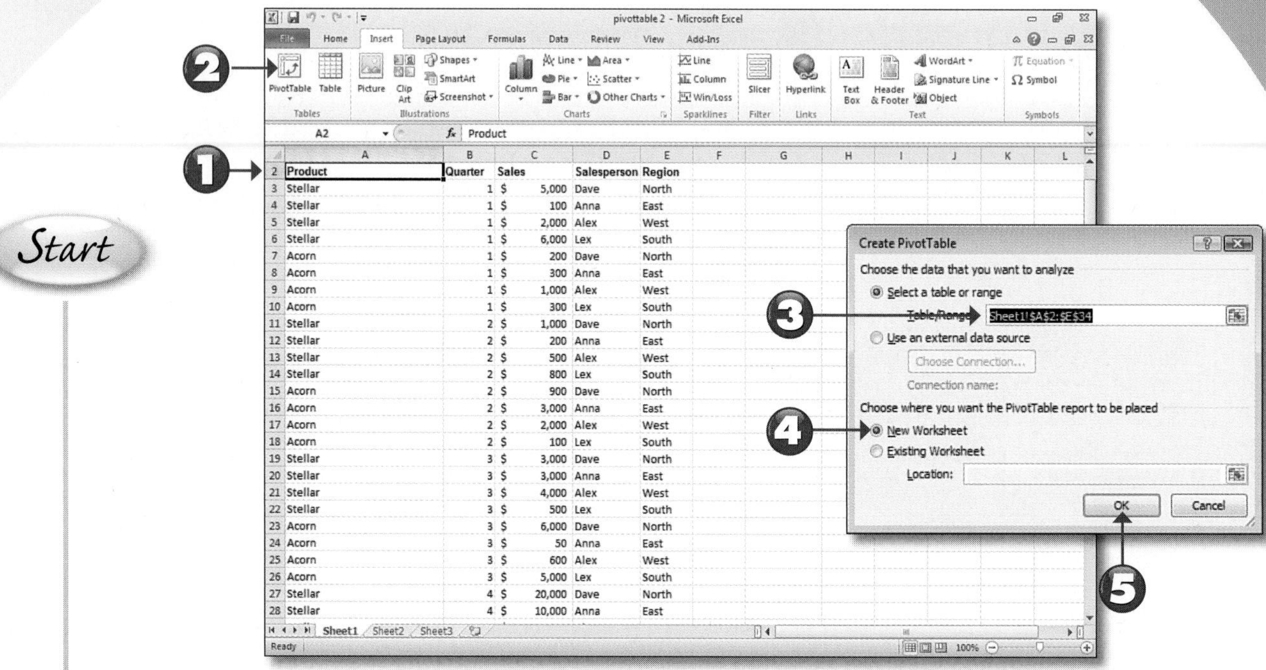

Start

1. Click in the data that you want to make a pivot table.
2. Click **Pivot Table** on the Ribbon's Insert tab.
3. In the Create Pivot Table window, check that the Table/Range shows all your data (use the Range Selector to drag through the data again to modify it).
4. Accept the default setting for placing the pivot table into a new worksheet.
5. Click **OK**.

Continued

TIP

Choosing Your Fields Laying out your fields is usually just a matter of asking a question, such as how much of which product was sold where or by whom? Separating those categories into columns and rows is a good first step. Values answer the question "How much?" and generally go in the middle. Then you can decide what might be a helpful filter—for example, which product, which area, by whom, or when. To adjust the pivot table, uncheck fields to remove them or drag and drop them to other areas. ■

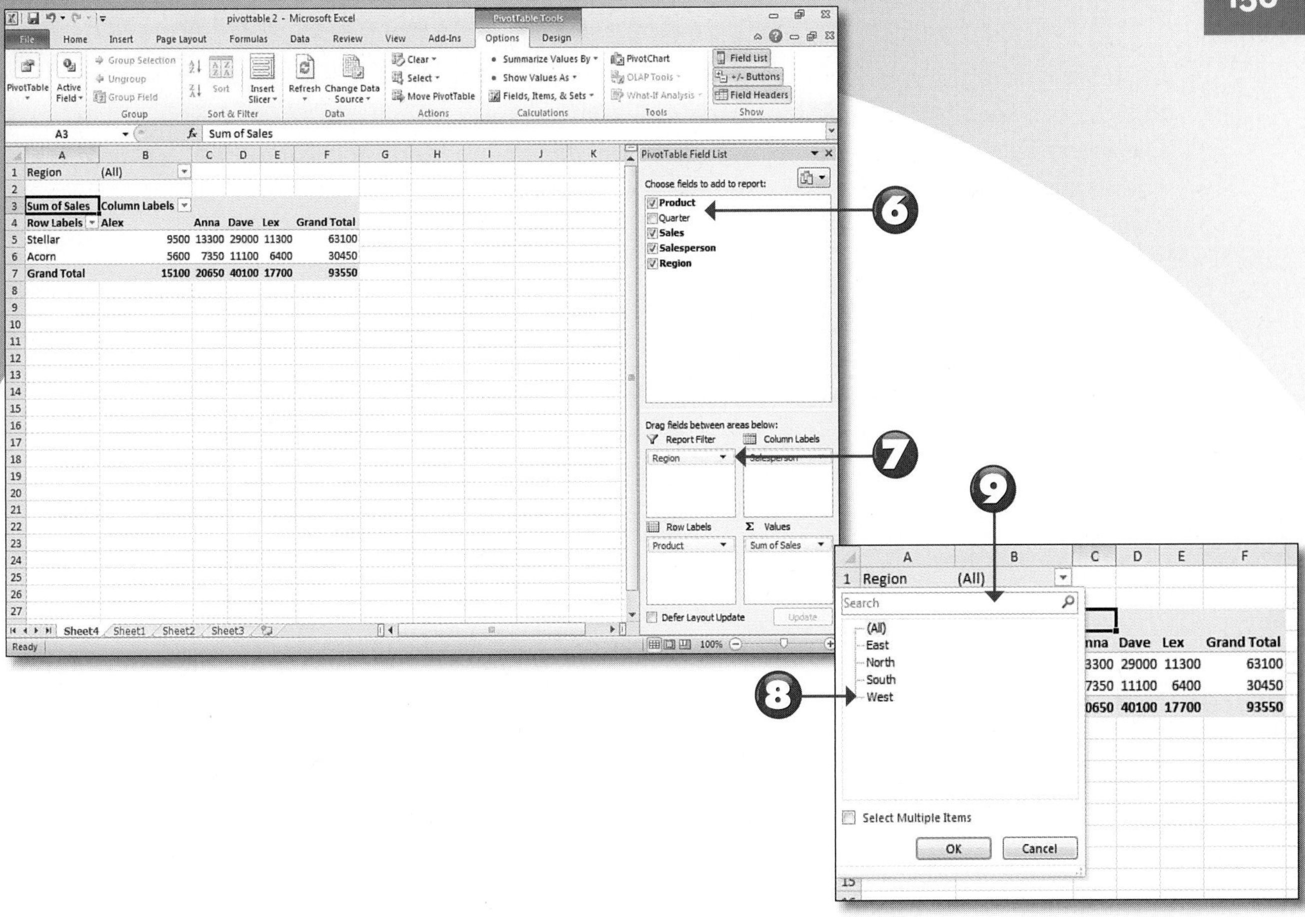

6. Check the boxes for the fields you want to report or display in the Pivot Table Field List. Note how they are laid out in the pivot table. (Drag and drop fields to other parameters like Column, Row, or Values if the display is not what you want).

7. Click the drop-down arrow for a field you have added as a Report Filter.

8. You can click to filter the items in the pivot table for another parameter (Region).

9. You can use the **Search** feature to locate any item in a large pivot table.

End

TIP

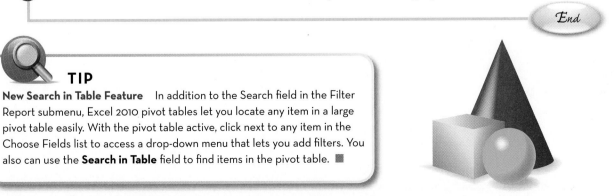

New Search in Table Feature In addition to the Search field in the Filter Report submenu, Excel 2010 pivot tables let you locate any item in a large pivot table easily. With the pivot table active, click next to any item in the Choose Fields list to access a drop-down menu that lets you add filters. You also can use the **Search in Table** field to find items in the pivot table. ■

FILTERING A PIVOT TABLE WITH THE SLICER

In your pivot table, you can use the Slicer panel to quickly drill down or filter through your data to see specific "slices" of information. For example, with a sales report, you can use the Slicer to see how the sales played out by quarter for the fields and values you already have added to the pivot table.

Start

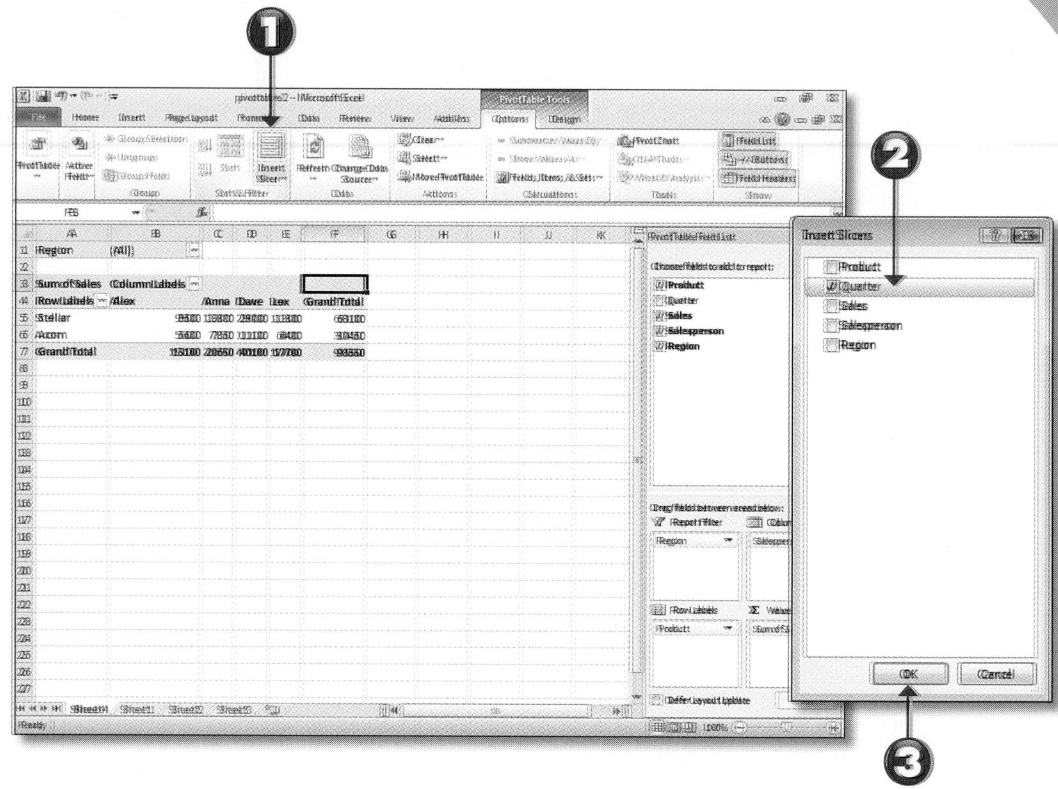

1. With the pivot table active (click in the pivot table), click **Insert Slicer** in the Option tab of the PivotTable Tools.
2. Click to select a parameter to "slice" or filter in the Insert Slicers window.
3. Click **OK**.

Continued

TIP

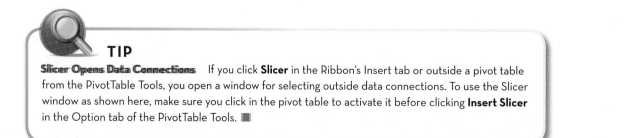

Slicer Opens Data Connections If you click **Slicer** in the Ribbon's Insert tab or outside a pivot table from the PivotTable Tools, you open a window for selecting outside data connections. To use the Slicer window as shown here, make sure you click in the pivot table to activate it before clicking **Insert Slicer** in the Option tab of the PivotTable Tools.

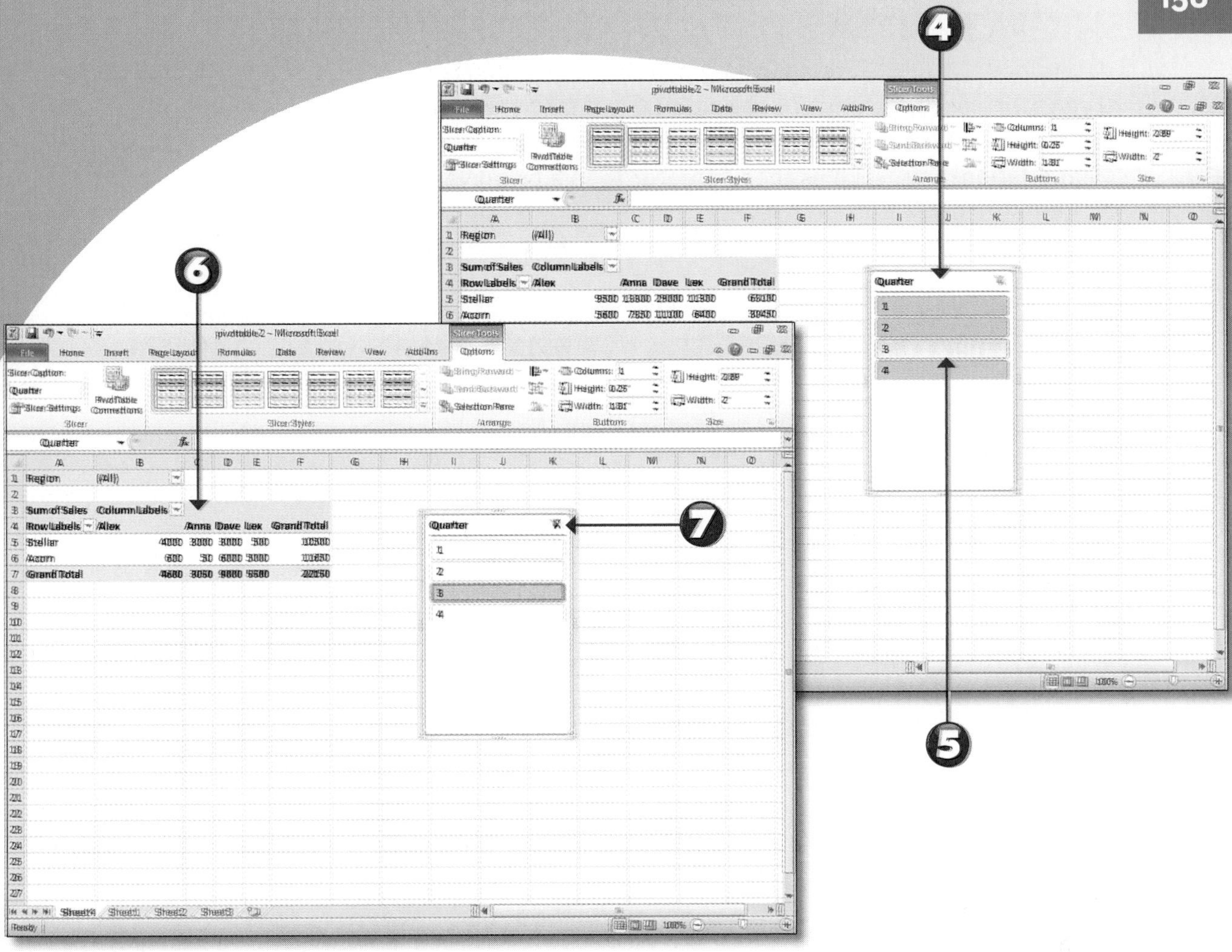

4. A graphic window opens with buttons for your Slicer, so you can quickly choose one of the selections for a filter. The Slicer Tools Options tab also opens on the Ribbon.

5. Click one of the Slicer options to “slice,” or filter, your data for that selection.

6. The data reflects the selection you made.

7. You can remove the selected filter by clicking the **X** on the Filter icon.

End

TIP

Slicer Settings Using the Slicer Settings in the Slicer group of the Options tab of the Slicer Tools, you can change the caption and sort parameters as well as other options for the Slicer window.

TIP

Removing a Slice You can remove the Slicer by right-clicking its border and selecting **Remove [Name of Slicer]**.

HIGHLIGHTING DATA WITH CONDITIONAL FORMATS

Conditional formats are another way to display important aspects of your data. You can use the graphical capabilities of conditional formats to display the relative values of data such as a bar, gradients, or icons, or you can create rules to highlight which cells represent certain relationships, such as those greater than a given value.

Start

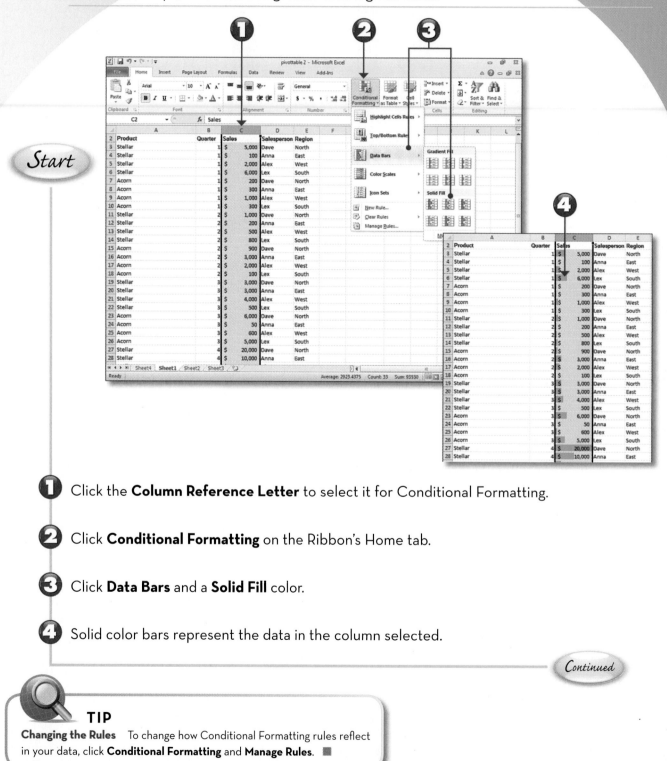

1. Click the **Column Reference Letter** to select it for Conditional Formatting.
2. Click **Conditional Formatting** on the Ribbon's Home tab.
3. Click **Data Bars** and a **Solid Fill** color.
4. Solid color bars represent the data in the column selected.

Continued

TIP

Changing the Rules To change how Conditional Formatting rules reflect in your data, click **Conditional Formatting** and **Manage Rules**.

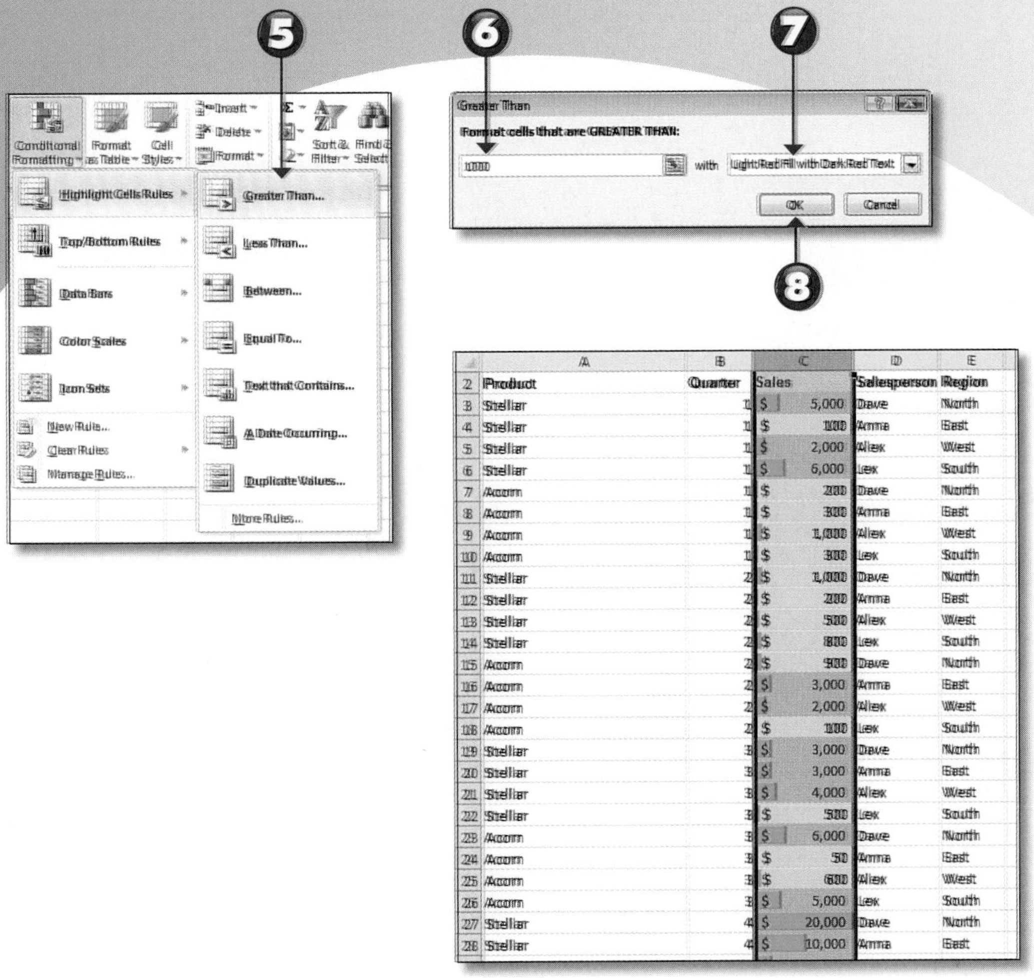

	A	B	C	D	E
2	Product	Quarter	Sales	Salesperson	Region
3	Stellar	1	$ 5,000	Dave	North
4	Stellar	1	$ 100	Anna	East
5	Stellar	1	$ 2,000	Alex	West
6	Stellar	1	$ 6,000	Lex	South
7	Acorn	1	$ 200	Dave	North
8	Acorn	1	$ 300	Anna	East
9	Acorn	1	$ 1,000	Alex	West
10	Acorn	1	$ 300	Lex	South
11	Stellar	2	$ 1,000	Dave	North
12	Stellar	2	$ 200	Anna	East
13	Stellar	2	$ 500	Alex	West
14	Stellar	2	$ 800	Lex	South
15	Acorn	2	$ 900	Dave	North
16	Acorn	2	$ 3,000	Anna	East
17	Acorn	2	$ 2,000	Alex	West
18	Acorn	2	$ 100	Lex	South
19	Stellar	3	$ 3,000	Dave	North
20	Stellar	3	$ 3,000	Anna	East
21	Stellar	3	$ 4,000	Alex	West
22	Stellar	3	$ 500	Lex	South
23	Acorn	3	$ 6,000	Dave	North
24	Acorn	3	$ 50	Anna	East
25	Acorn	3	$ 600	Alex	West
26	Acorn	3	$ 5,000	Lex	South
27	Stellar	4	$ 20,000	Dave	North
28	Stellar	4	$ 10,000	Anna	East

5. Click **Conditional Formatting**, **Highlight Cell Rules**, and **Greater Than**.
6. Set a Greater Than Rule for the cells—for example, greater than 1000.
7. Accept the highlighting option (or select a different highlight option by using the drop-down arrow).
8. Click **OK**.
9. The cells now also reflect values greater than 1000.

End

TIP

Creating Your Own Rule You can use the **New Rule** option in Conditional Formatting to set up your own rule for a specific parameter and how the selected cells that meet that condition will be formatted.

SHARING YOUR PROJECT ONLINE WITH MICROSOFT OFFICE WEB APPLICATIONS

The Microsoft web applications are scaled-down versions of the main programs created to allow users to collaborate and share information online.

You can create an entire spreadsheet in Excel's online application, or, for example, you can upload the project that has been used as an example for Excel 2010 to the web workspace and view and modify it using the Excel web application. (See "Creating a Folder for Web Application" and "Uploading a File to Your Folder" at the end of Chapter 7, "Reviewing Documents and Working Online").

In the case of a data table, information can be modified and added to the web application to supplement what was originally entered. For cells with formulas, functions, and other calculations, you can adjust figures so that they have different results and affect the display of charts based on the information.

Working with the online web application means not having to save your work; it is automatically stored online. From the web application, you can return directly to the desktop version of Excel 2010 to continue revising your work and use all the features of the Ribbon to complete your project.

THE EXCEL WEB APPLICATION

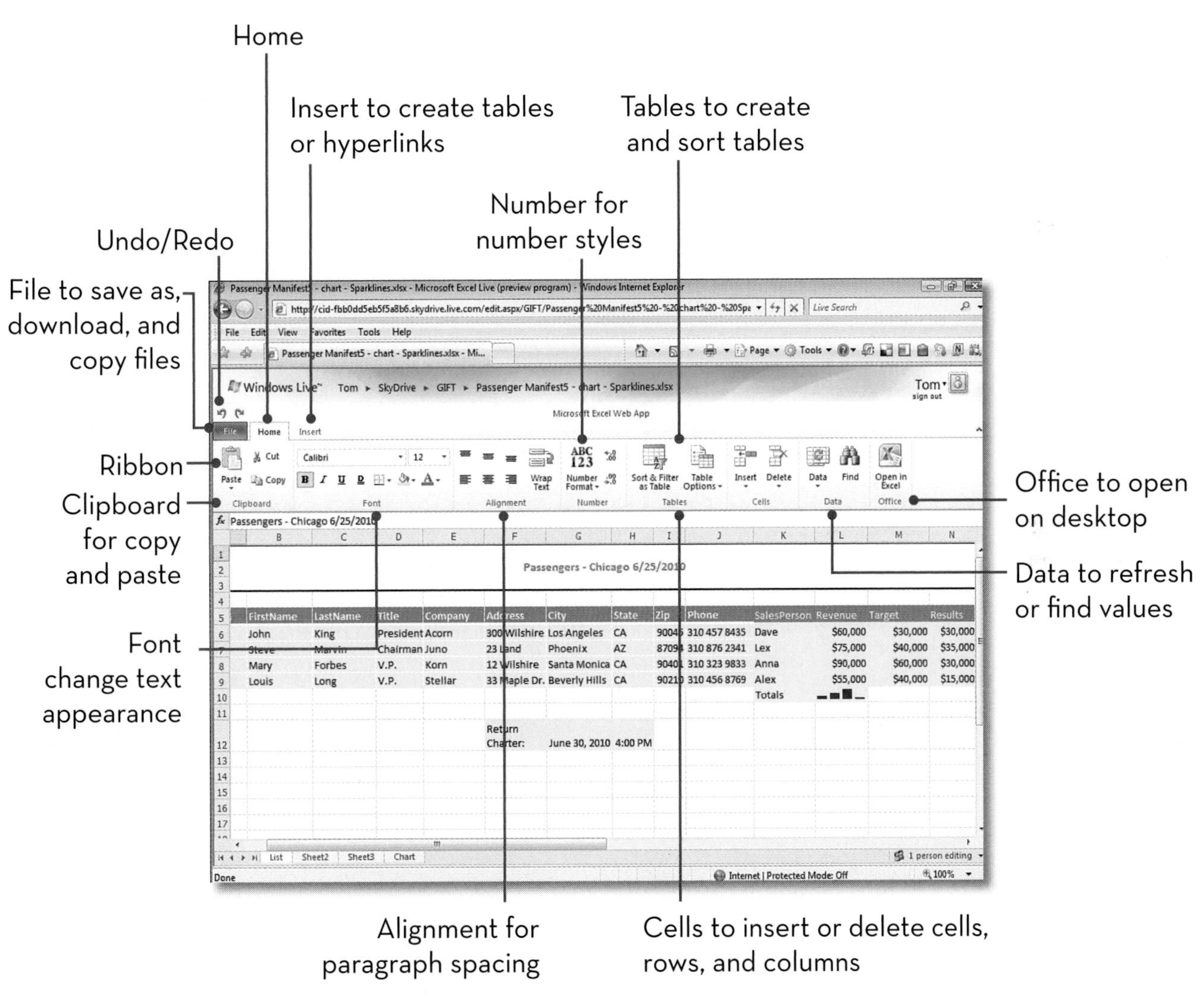
Home
Insert to create tables or hyperlinks
Tables to create and sort tables
Number for number styles
Undo/Redo
File to save as, download, and copy files
Ribbon
Clipboard for copy and paste
Font change text appearance
Office to open on desktop
Data to refresh or find values
Alignment for paragraph spacing
Cells to insert or delete cells, rows, and columns

OPENING YOUR UPLOADED PROJECT

Your workspace has default folders, and you can create your own folders with shared access for others (See "Creating a Folder for Web Application" and "Uploading a File to Your Folder" at the end of Chapter 7). With your document uploaded, you can open it in the web application so that you can begin to modify it or let others review and change some of the information in the file.

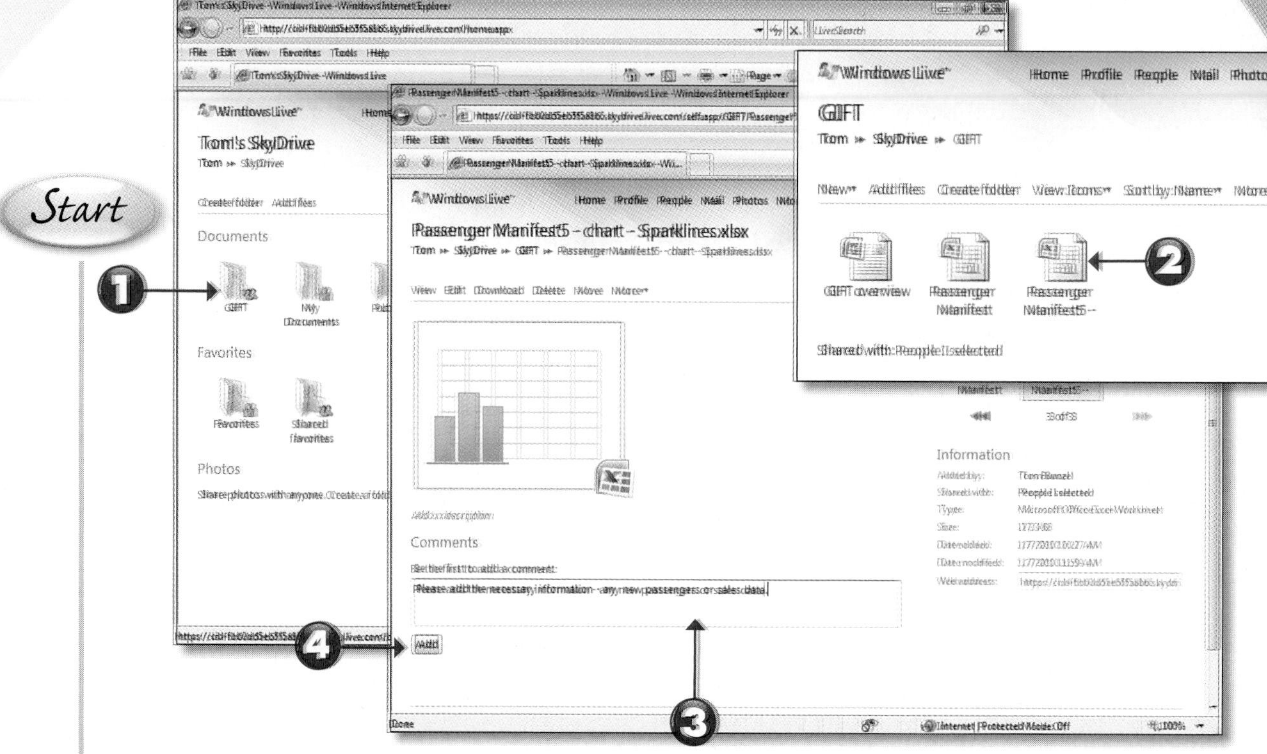

Start

1. In your online workspace, click the folder with your uploaded file(s).
2. Click to open the file with the information to review or change.
3. Add a comment to let others know what they can do in the file to complete the project.
4. Click **Add** to save the comment.

Continued

TIP

Creating Effective Comments The comments are viewed as a thread when they are added, allowing those with access to the workspace to make suggestions or point out significant aspects of their revisions.

TIP

Some Cells with Data May Appear Blank Sometimes the web application does not display data that has already been entered in certain cells until you widen the column border or refresh the page.

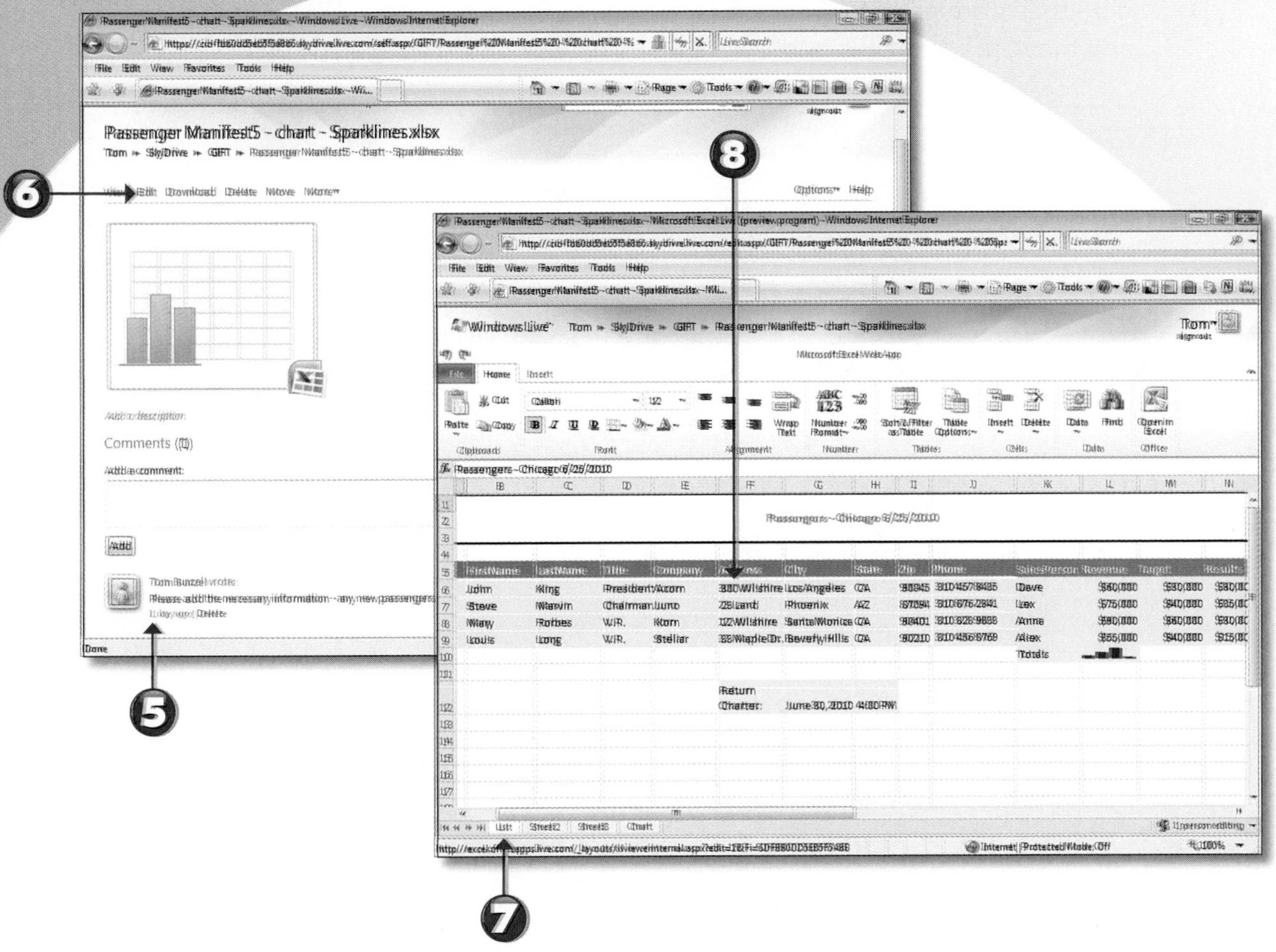

5 Your comment is added to the bottom of the page. Others with permission to access your workspace can see your comment.

6 Any users with permission can create their own comment or click **Edit** to open the spreadsheet.

7 When the spreadsheet opens online, you can click a worksheet tab to get to the information you need.

8 In the worksheet with your data, you can begin to change information.

End

TIP

Chart Effects in the Web Application A chart may not retain all its special effects (glows, bevels, and so on) when displayed within the Excel web application.

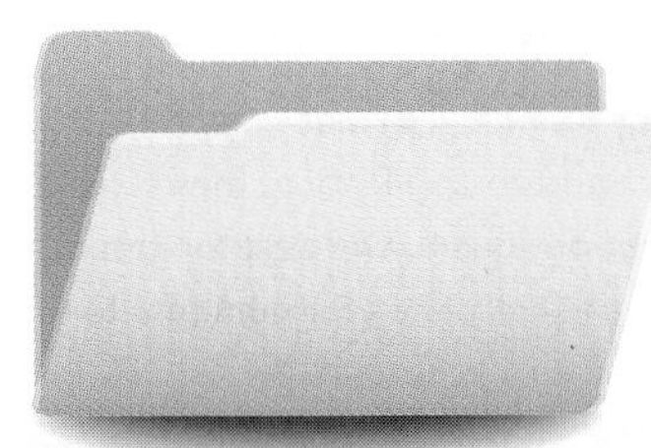

REVISING DATA IN THE WEB APPLICATION

By changing the data in the cells of a spreadsheet in the Excel web application, you can update the information for your project. Your new data is saved when you click in another cell, and functions, formulas, and charts that use your data also are updated.

Start

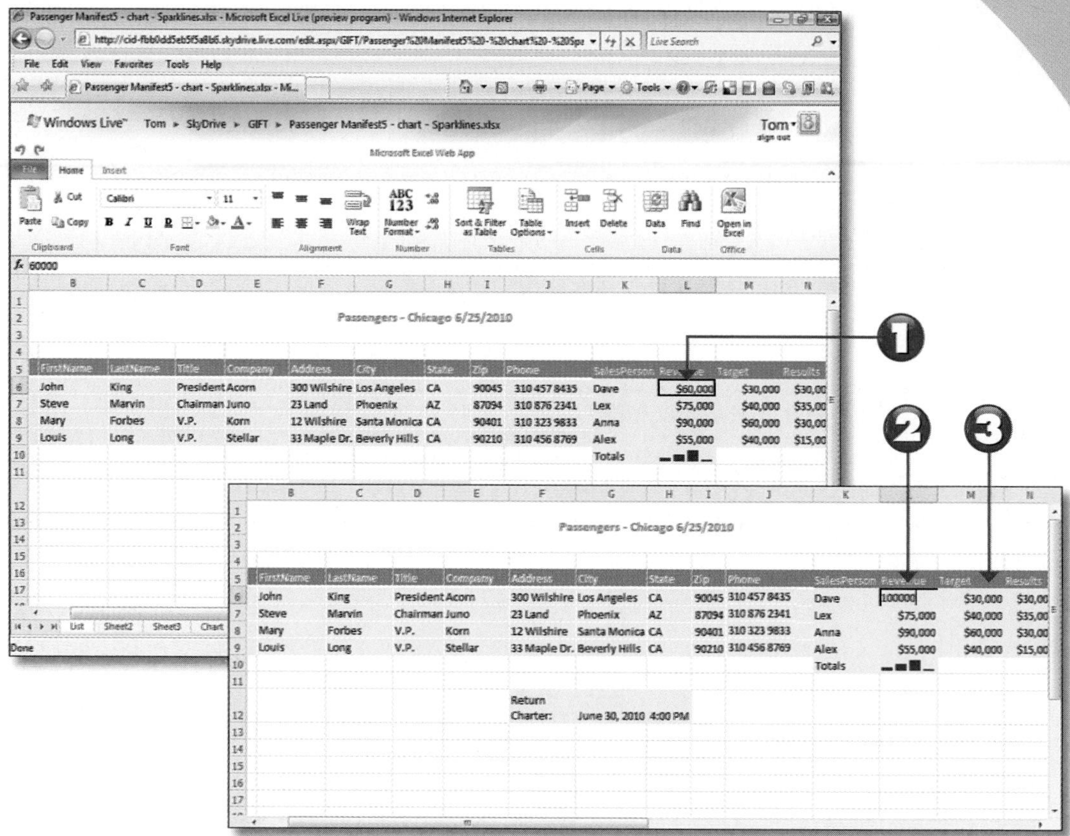

1. Click in a cell to revise the data.

2. Type in the new data.

3. Click another cell or press **Tab** to enter the data.

Continued

TIP

Changing Number Format In the Home tab of the Excel web application, the Number group has similar options to the desktop application for changing the cell styles for numbers to display them in a different format. ■

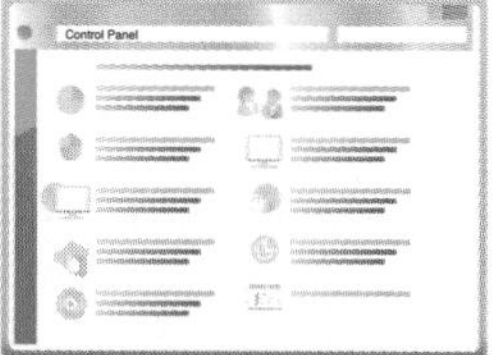

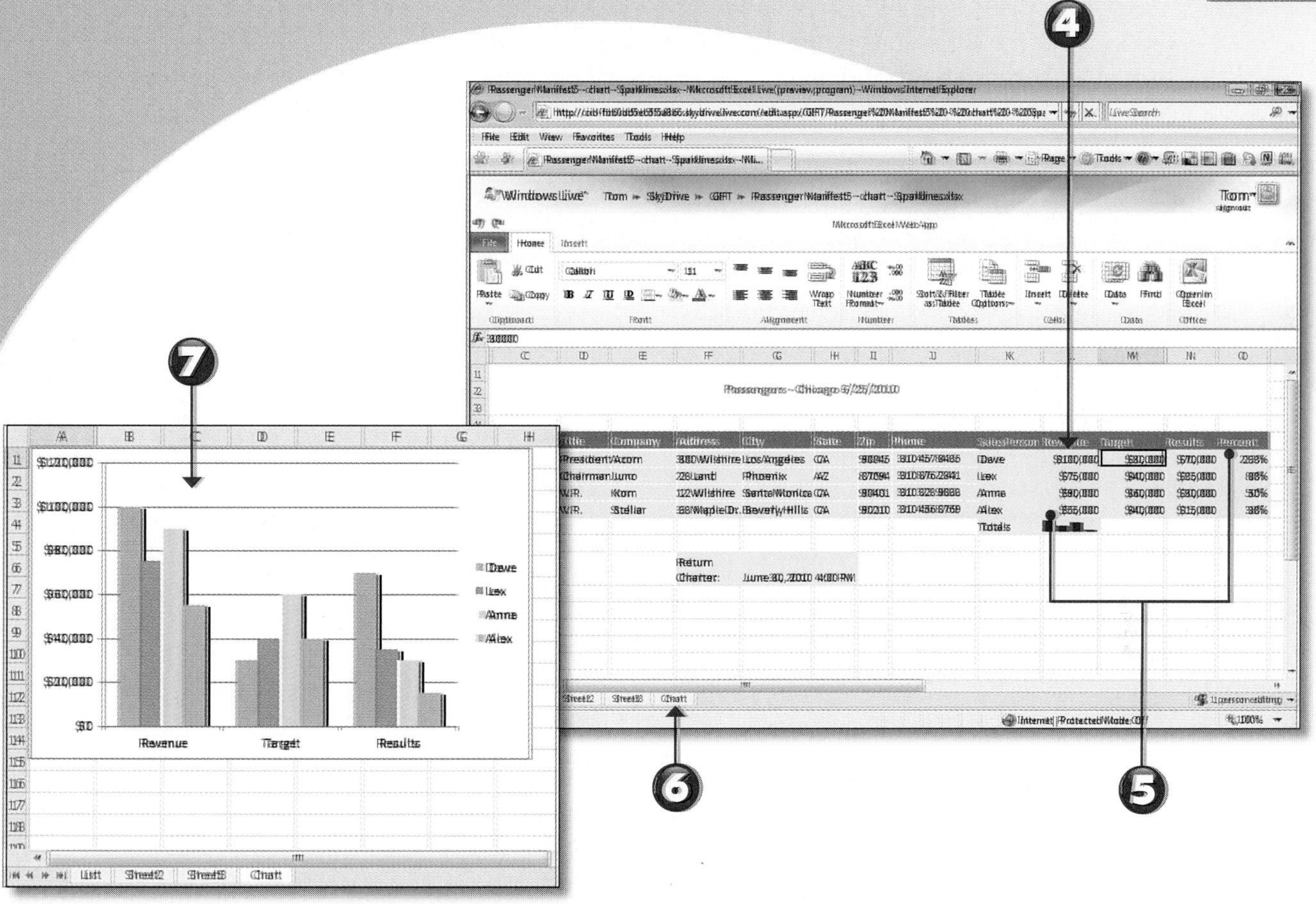

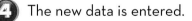

4 The new data is entered.

5 Any formulas or Sparklines reflecting your data are updated.

6 You can click another worksheet to view results in a chart.

7 A chart based on the data also reflects the new figures added.

End

TIP

New Sparklines Feature There is no Sparklines feature directly in the web application for Excel 2010, but if you upload a file with Sparklines and revise the data, the Sparklines reflect the changes.

APPENDING AND SORTING A DATA TABLE

Just as you would with the desktop version of Excel, you can insert a new row (or column) into your spreadsheet and fill in the necessary information, thereby adding data to your file. You can also create a table from your information to use the sort and filter tools.

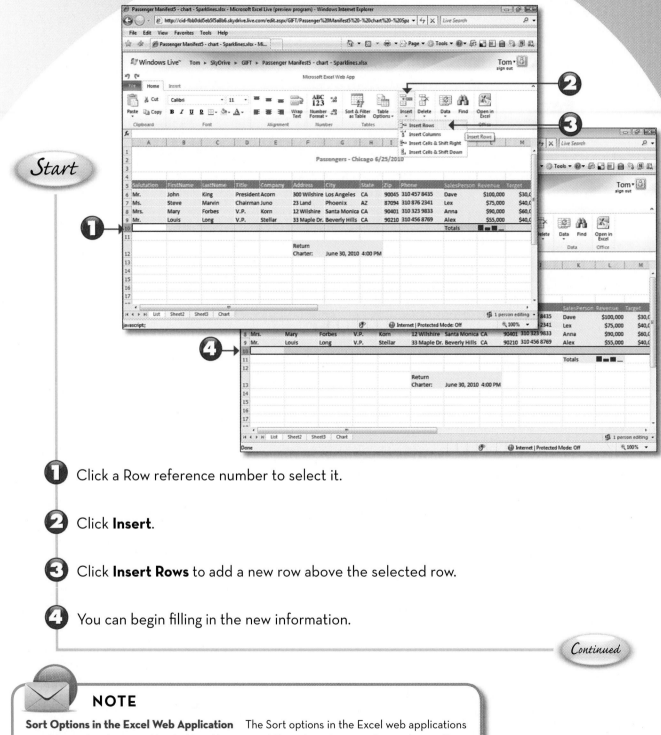

Start

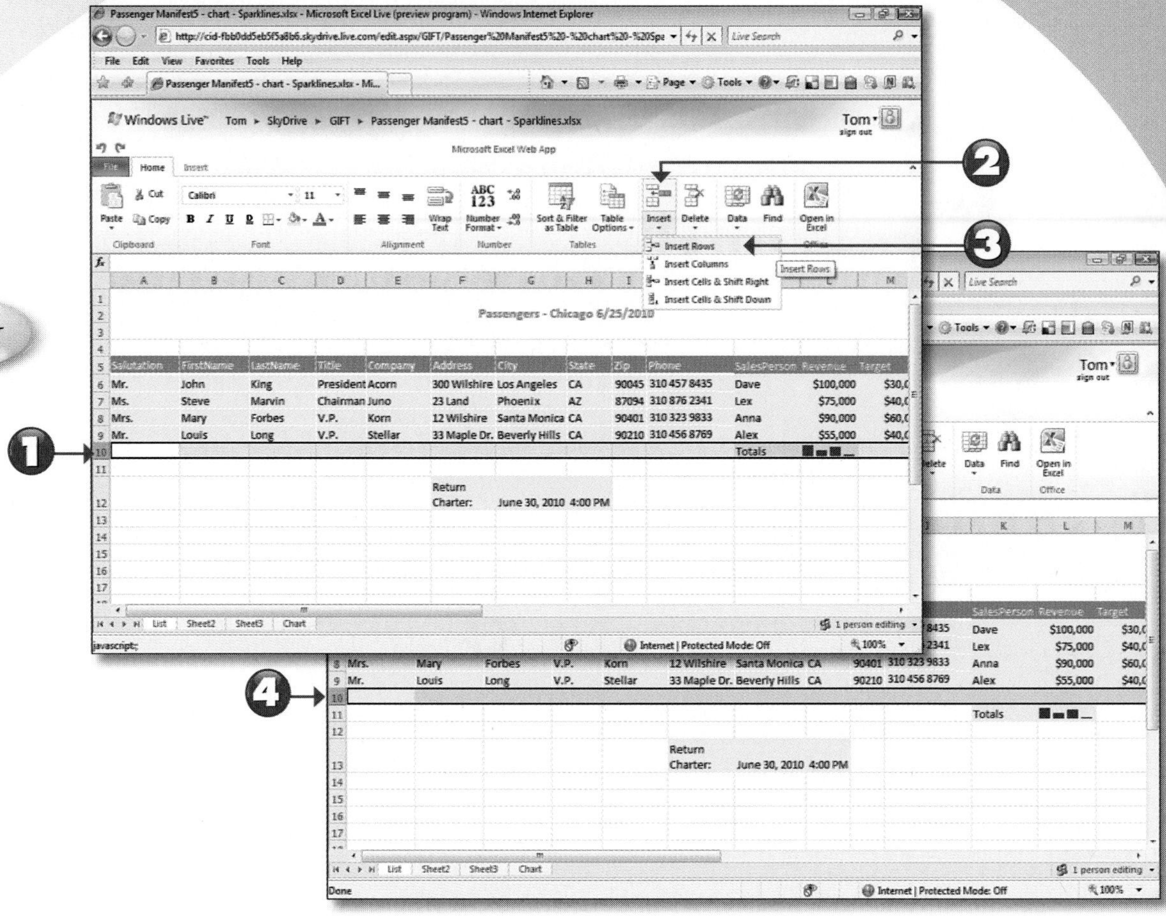

1. Click a Row reference number to select it.

2. Click **Insert**.

3. Click **Insert Rows** to add a new row above the selected row.

4. You can begin filling in the new information.

Continued

NOTE

Sort Options in the Excel Web Application The Sort options in the Excel web applications are not as extensive as on the desktop. You can sort the column in ascending or descending order and apply some basic filters under Text Filters. ■

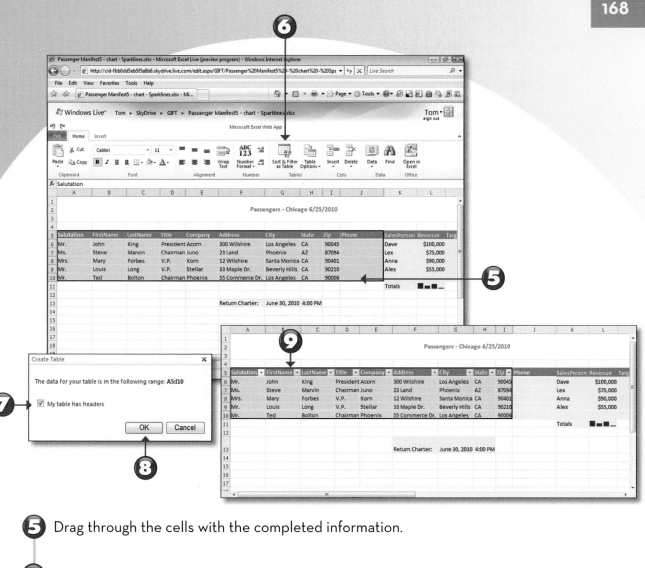

5. Drag through the cells with the completed information.

6. Click **Sort & Filter as Table**.

7. Confirm the range of your table and whether or not it has headers.

8. Click **OK**.

9. Your table has sort handles that let you use the sort options for a table. (See "Sorting Data in a Table" in Chapter 10, "Creating Charts, Data Tables, and Pivot Tables.")

End

TIP

Deleting Rows and Columns You can click the **Delete** button in the Cells group to delete selected rows, columns, and cells and shift the remaining cells left (column) or up (row).

OPENING ONLINE FILES LOCALLY

You can open the web application version of an Office file using your Office 2010 desktop version to take advantage of the full feature set of the program. For example, you can open the changed file and make more complex changes, save it directly back online (the default), or you can save it under another name, or use other options like those in Backstage view.

Start

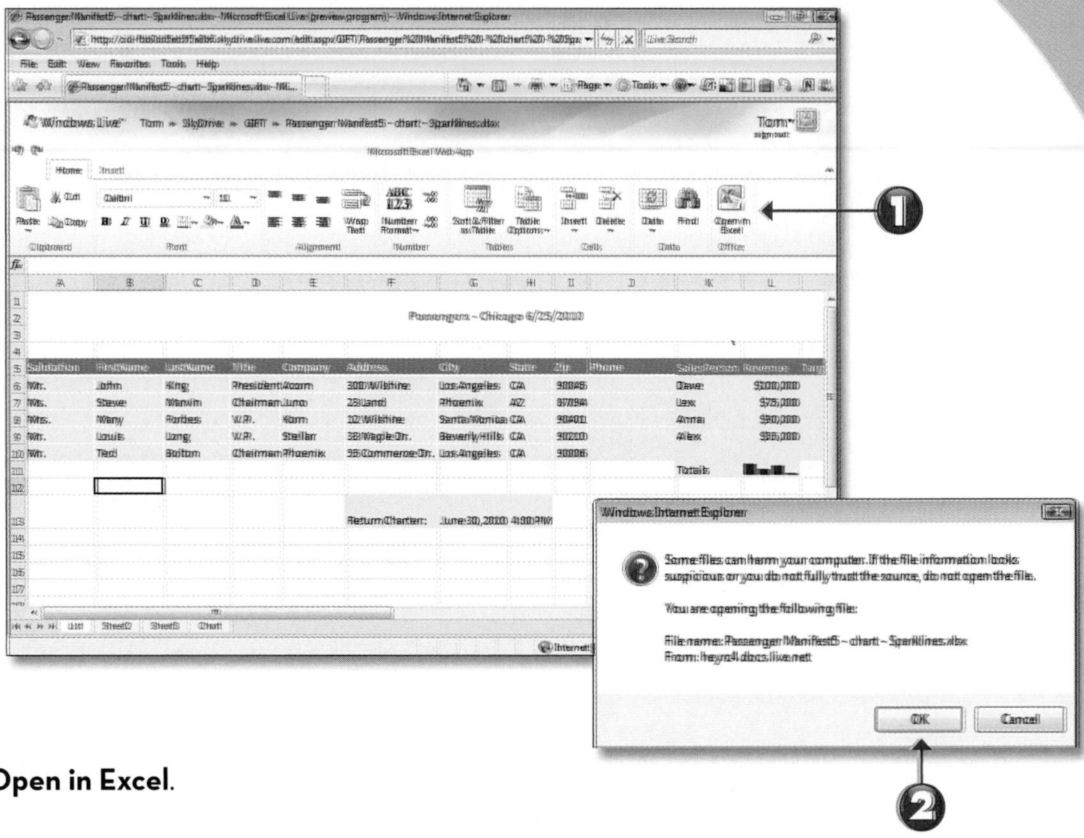

1. Click **Open in Excel**.
2. Click **OK** to accept the warning about harmful files.

Continued

TIP

Resizing a Chart You can resize a chart by clicking on a corner of the chart until your cursor changes into a two-headed arrow and then dragging the corner out to make the chart larger or in to reduce its size. ■

TIP

Locked Files When a workbook is opened locally in Excel (or Word or PowerPoint) from the web application, the online version is locked for editing. The user who opened the file must save the local changes and close the file for it to be used again within the web application. Changes are saved directly to the web application, so the user may want to also save a local version under a different name. ■

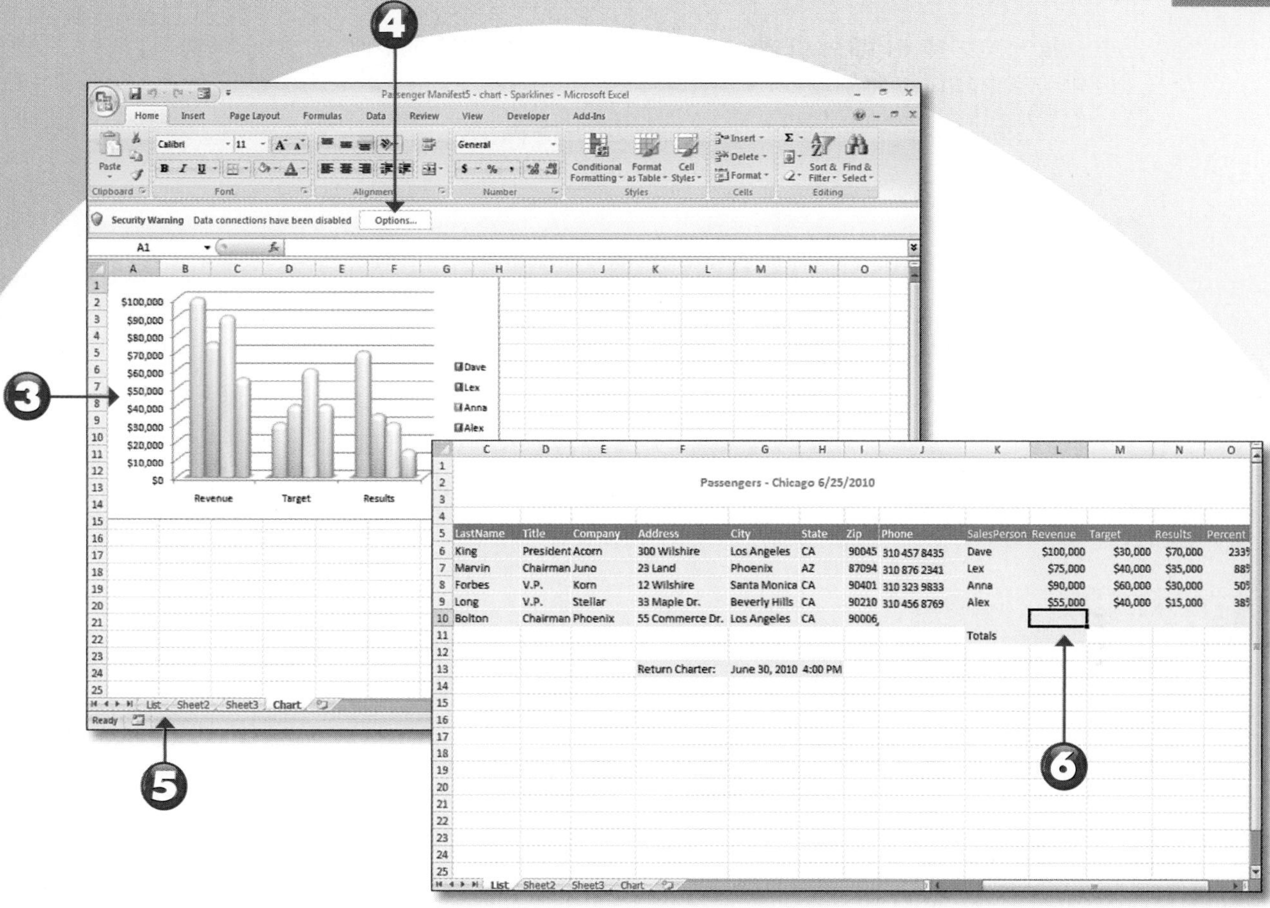

3. The file opens in the desktop application with the name from the web application. Notice that any charts in the worksheet still retain their original effects.

4. You can click **Options** to clear the Security Warning about any external data connections to other databases that the file might access.

5. You can click another worksheet to access its data.

6. You can work with the data that has been added or changed online by those with permission to access your workspace folder.

End

TIP

Saving in the Web App There is no Save button or feature in the web applications. But you can choose the **Save As** option under **File** to save the changes made online into the workspace folder under a different name. ■

TIP

Downloading from the Web App Downloading a web app version of the file keeps the web app file available for editing and lets the user work with the downloaded file locally using the full features of Excel (or Word or PowerPoint). ■

PRINTING AN EXCEL WORKSHEET

Although you can print your web application worksheet as part of your web browser, using the desktop application gives you more versatility in terms of previewing your printed page and scaling the columns to fit into a printed page.

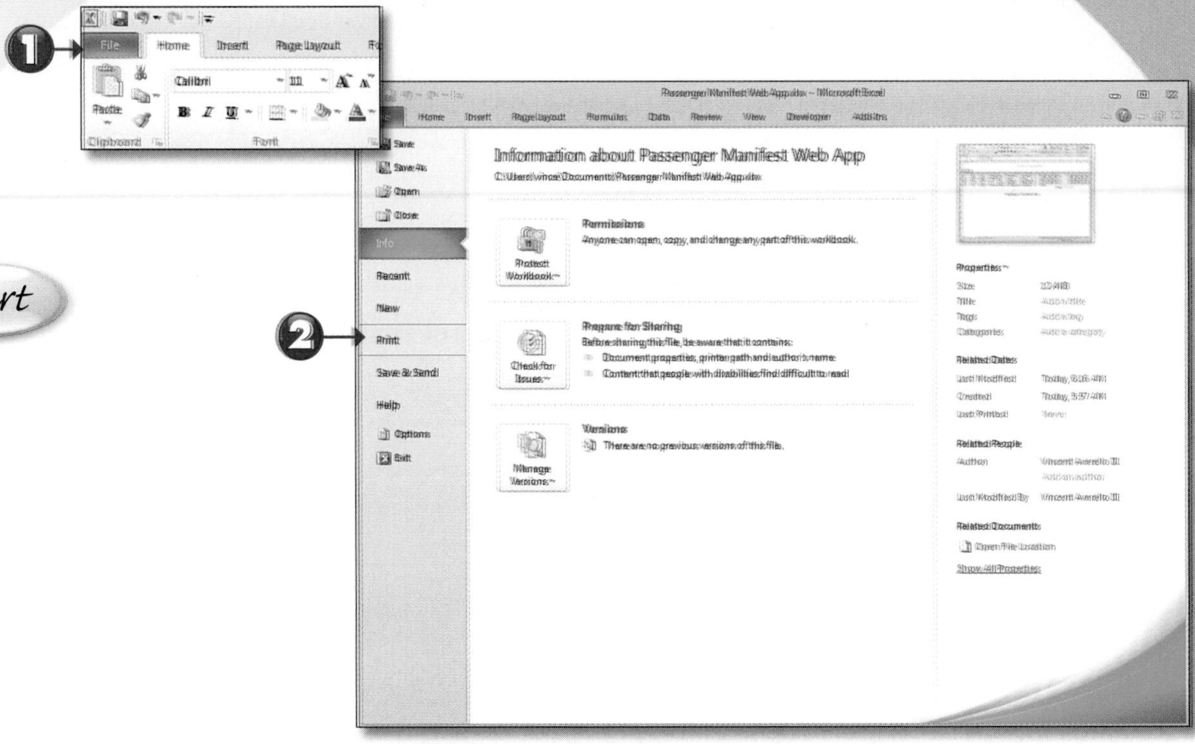

Start

1. Click **File** to open Backstage view.
2. Click **Print**.

Continued

TIP

Page Break Preview If you want to adjust which columns to print within the worksheet, you can use the Page Break Preview view at the bottom right of the Excel 2010 window. You can drag the break line to extend or contract the portion of the worksheet that will print on each page.

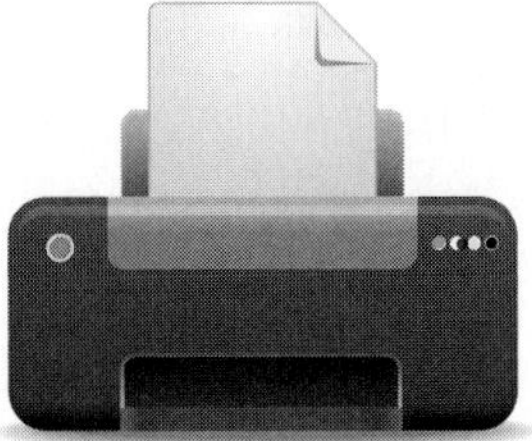

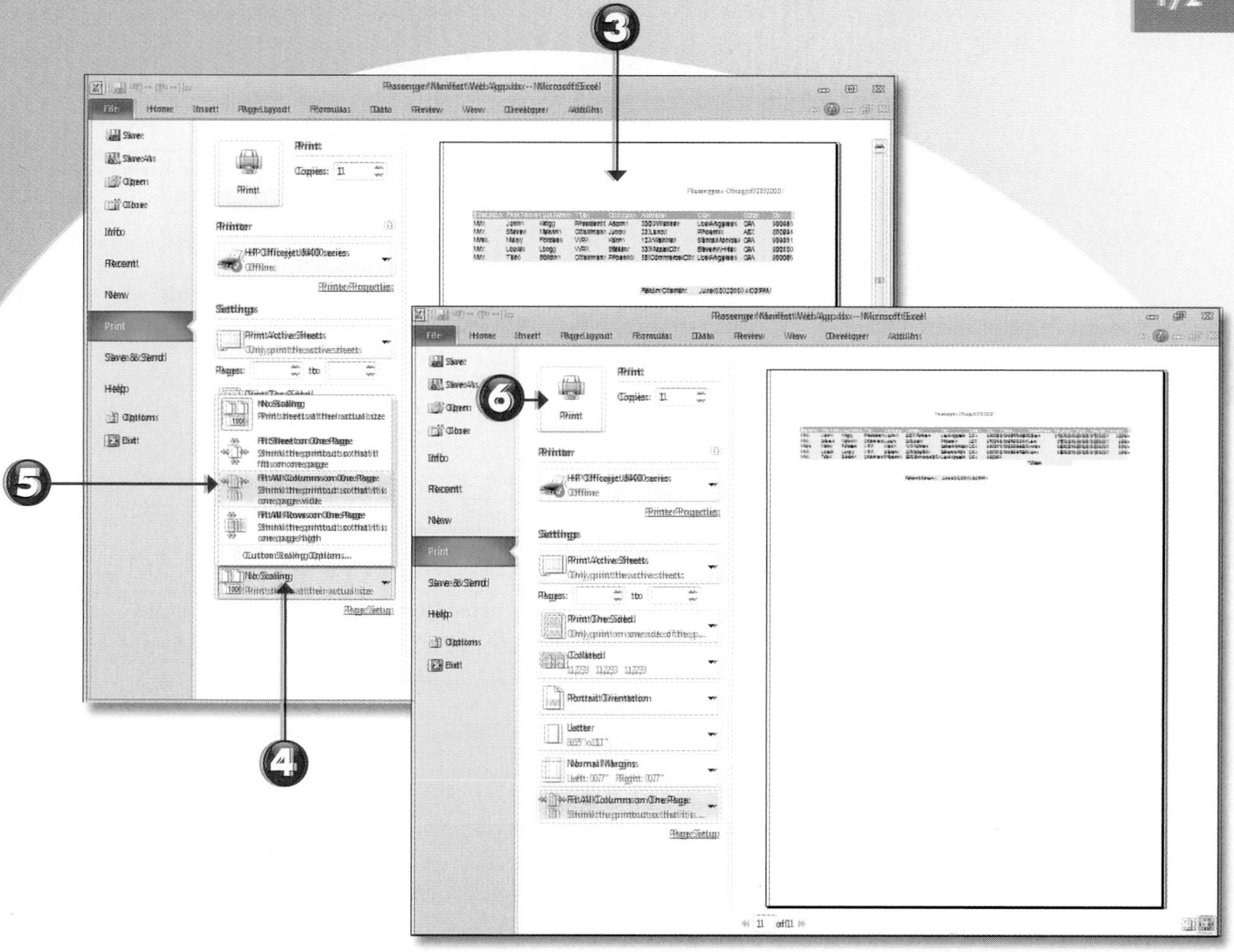

3. Check the Preview window to see whether the printed page is the way you want it to look when printed.

4. Click the **No Scaling** drop-down arrow to see other options.

5. Click **Fit All Columns on One Page**.

6. Review the effect these changes have had in the print preview and, if you're satisfied, click **Print**.

End

TIP

Returning to the Original Layout To remove the option Fit All Columns on One Page, you can readjust the Page Break Preview to reflect a different portion to fit on a page, use the Undo button, or select another option like No Scaling in the Print preview window of Backstage view. ■

GETTING STARTED WITH POWERPOINT 2010

PowerPoint is a presentation program based on the concept of a slide projector; it projects a sequence of slides that tell a story to help you accomplish a task, such as selling, educating, motivating, or conveying a message.

You can begin a new presentation from the Backstage view, which has preset templates in your Sample Templates folder, or from the Office.com online folders of templates. (See "Creating a New Blank Document" in Chapter 1, "Introducing the New Features in Office 2010.")

Your new presentation begins with a cover page. From there, you can add new slides and change their layout using different placeholders that contain text, graphics, tables, charts, or other elements to communicate your message. You can also add title and bullet text by typing directly into placeholders and can format the text using the Font group in the Home tab on the Ribbon.

You can use slides from previous presentations or change the view of your presentation to see the entire presentation in Slide Sorter view. Slide Sorter view lets you see how a new theme affects your entire presentation, whereas Slide Master view lets you control formatting of all your layouts.

THE POWERPOINT WINDOW

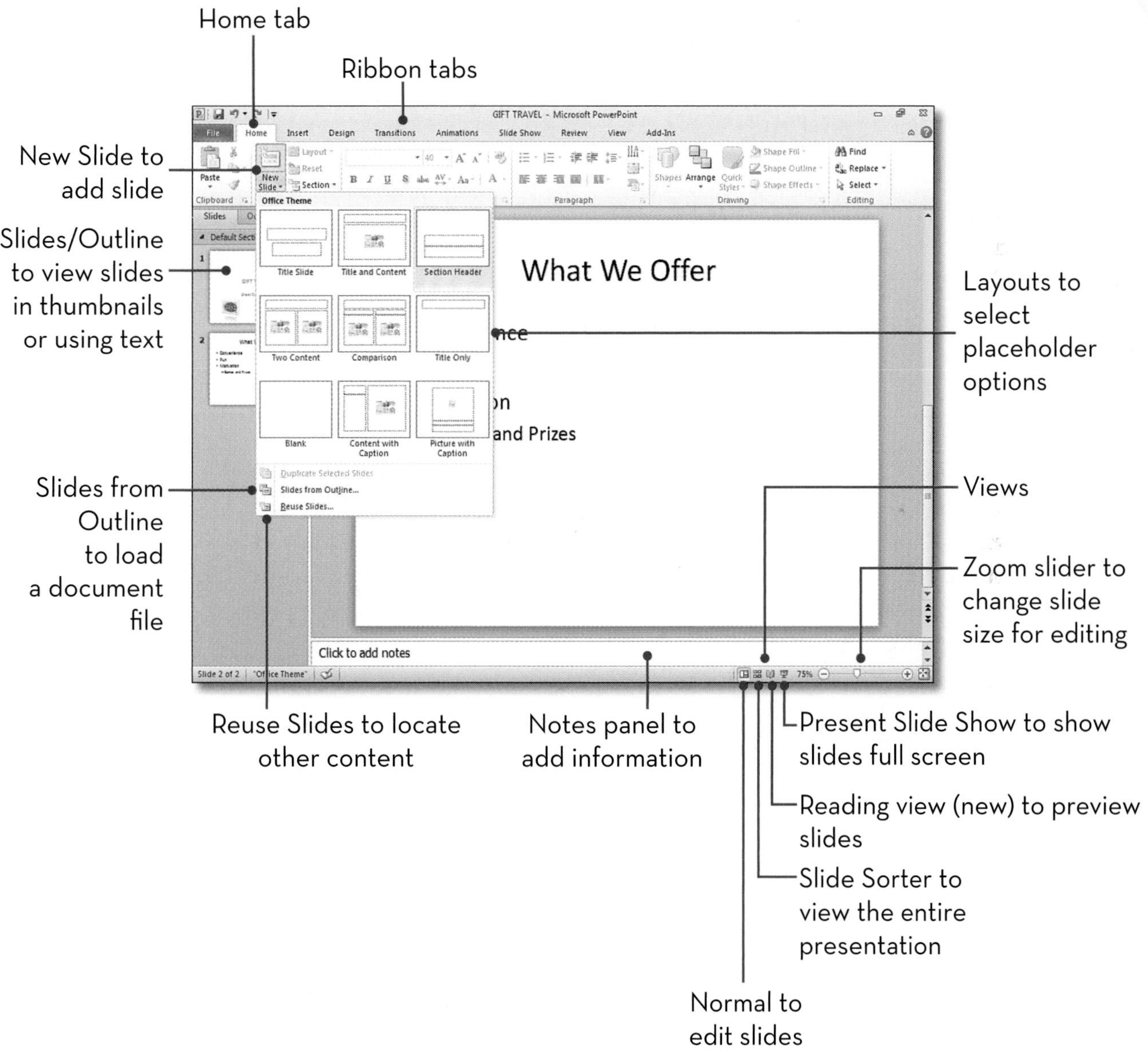
Home tab
Ribbon tabs
New Slide to add slide
Slides/Outline to view slides in thumbnails or using text
Slides from Outline to load a document file
Layouts to select placeholder options
Views
Zoom slider to change slide size for editing
Reuse Slides to locate other content
Notes panel to add information
Present Slide Show to show slides full screen
Reading view (new) to preview slides
Slide Sorter to view the entire presentation
Normal to edit slides
What We Offer

ADDING AND EDITING TEXT

The first slide in any new presentation is a Title slide with two placeholders: one for the main title and the other for a subtitle. With any text placeholder, just click inside it to add your text; then you can use the Font group on the Ribbon's Home tab to change its appearance.

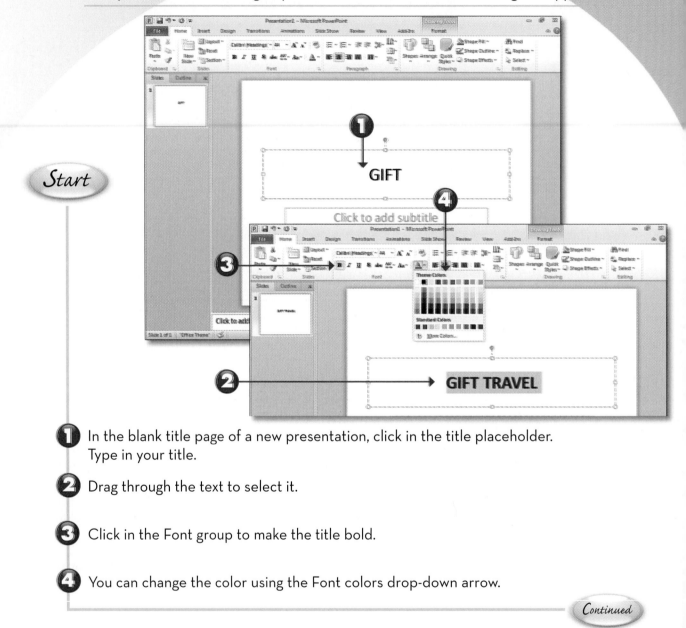

Start

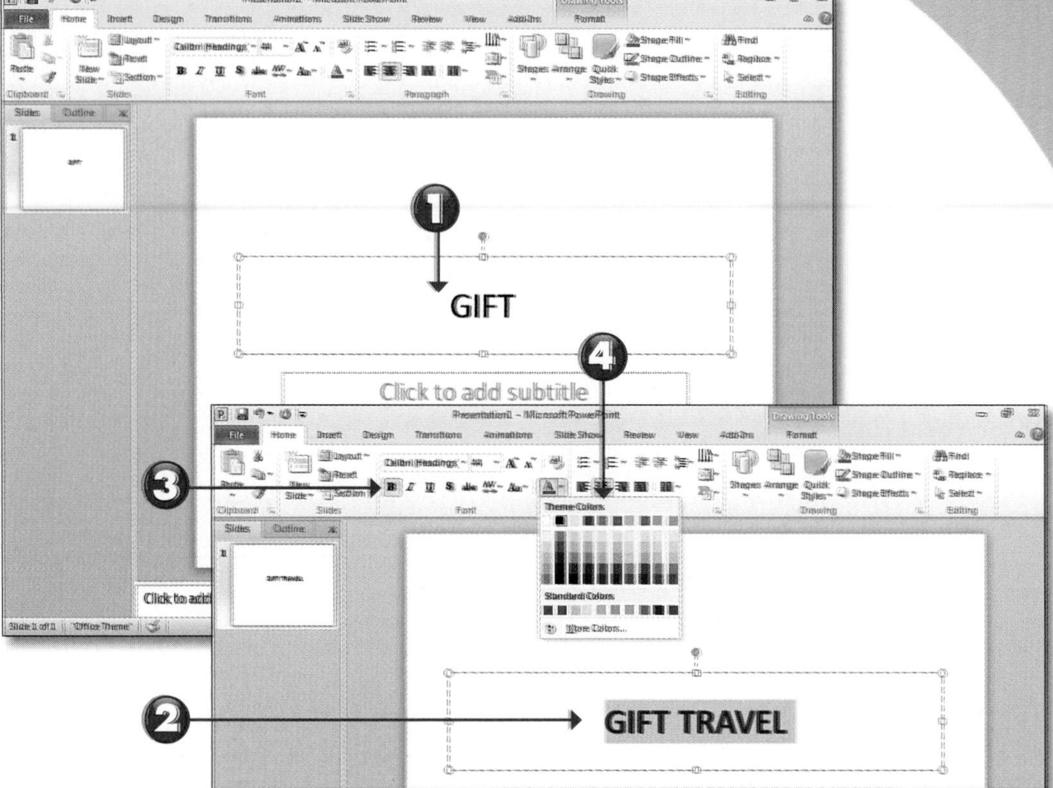

1. In the blank title page of a new presentation, click in the title placeholder. Type in your title.
2. Drag through the text to select it.
3. Click in the Font group to make the title bold.
4. You can change the color using the Font colors drop-down arrow.

Continued

TIP

Using the New Presentations in Backstage View You can begin a new presentation using the Sample Templates folder in Backstage view or the Office.com online templates. Some of the templates are for specific purposes such as Sales and already have slides in them to revise, along with designs for the slides.

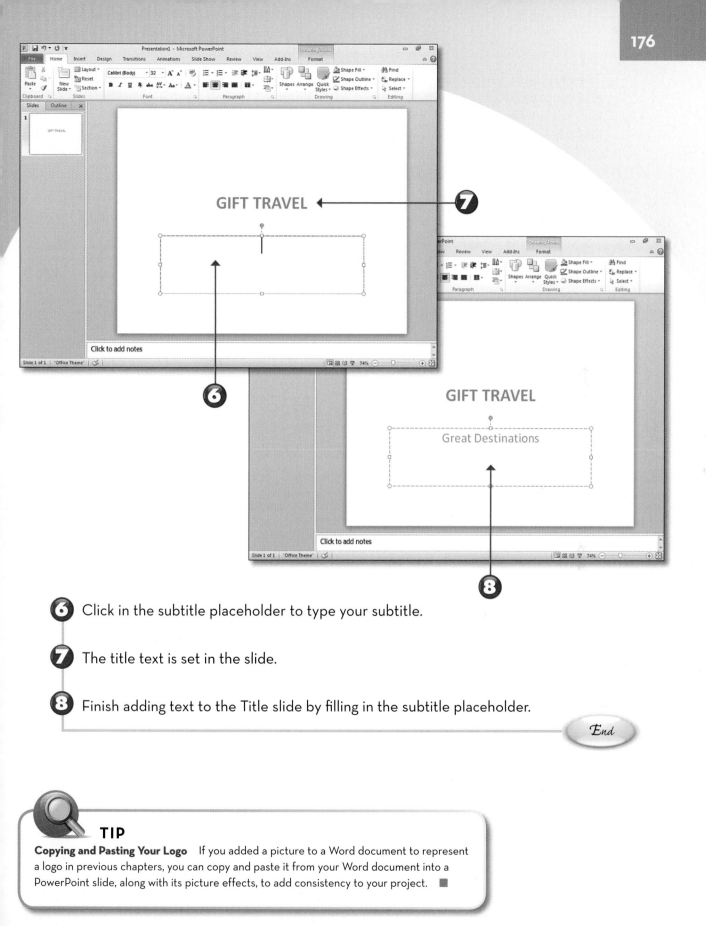

6 Click in the subtitle placeholder to type your subtitle.

7 The title text is set in the slide.

8 Finish adding text to the Title slide by filling in the subtitle placeholder.

End

TIP

Copying and Pasting Your Logo If you added a picture to a Word document to represent a logo in previous chapters, you can copy and paste it from your Word document into a PowerPoint slide, along with its picture effects, to add consistency to your project. ■

ADDING A SLIDE WITH BULLETS

The most basic layout for a slide is Title and Content, which lets you add bullet text to the slide or use one of the content icons to add a different type of element, like Table, Chart, Clip Art, Picture, SmartArt, and Media. You also can add and change bullets from the Outline tab next to the Slide tab in the left panel.

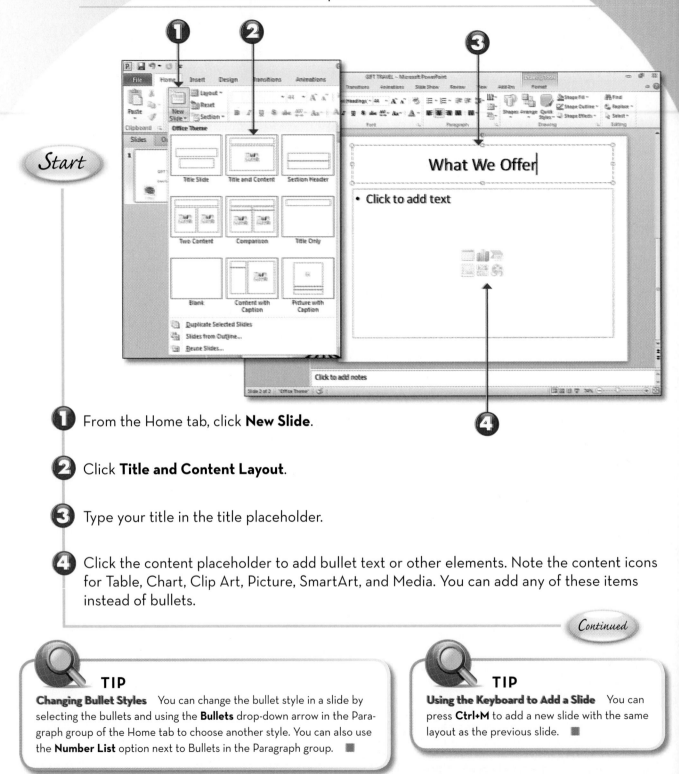

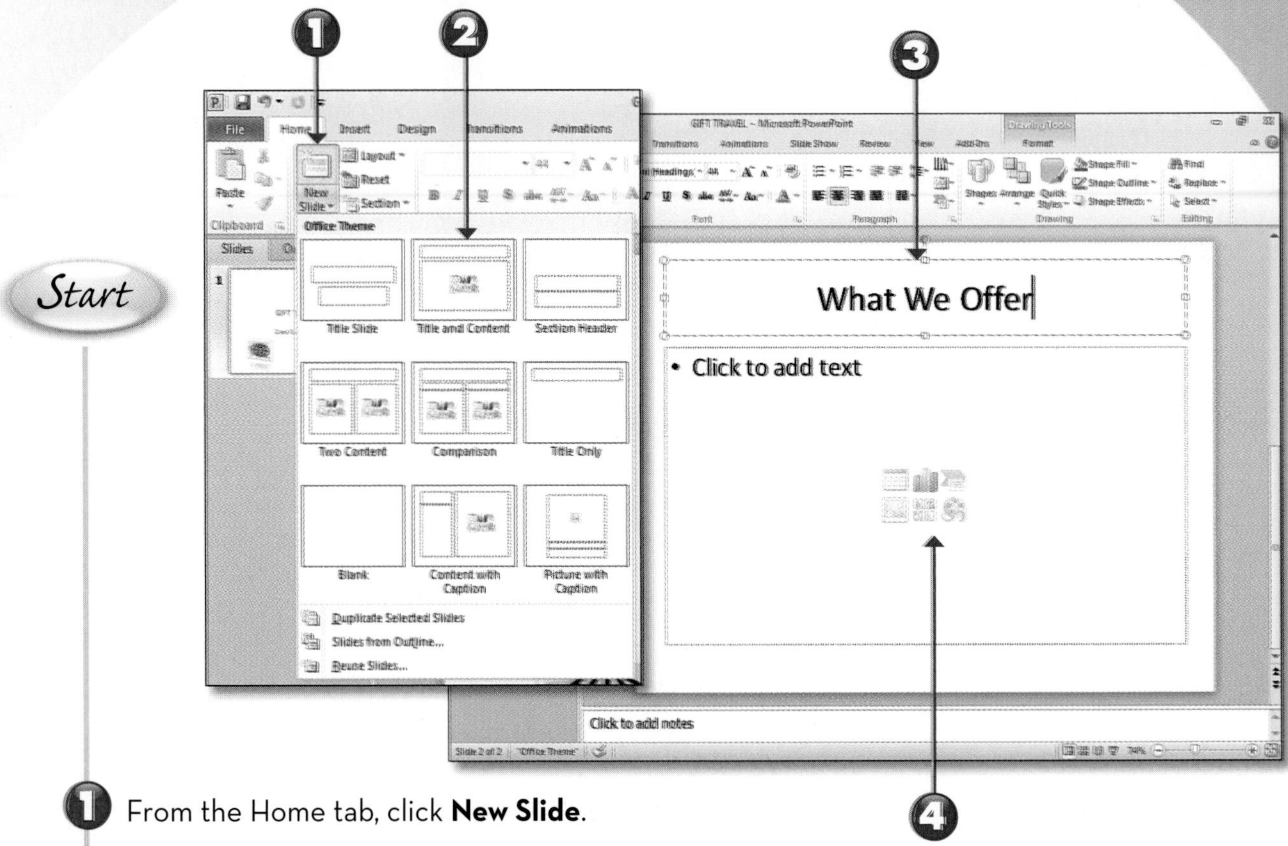

Start

1. From the Home tab, click **New Slide**.
2. Click **Title and Content Layout**.
3. Type your title in the title placeholder.
4. Click the content placeholder to add bullet text or other elements. Note the content icons for Table, Chart, Clip Art, Picture, SmartArt, and Media. You can add any of these items instead of bullets.

Continued

TIP

Changing Bullet Styles You can change the bullet style in a slide by selecting the bullets and using the **Bullets** drop-down arrow in the Paragraph group of the Home tab to choose another style. You can also use the **Number List** option next to Bullets in the Paragraph group.

TIP

Using the Keyboard to Add a Slide You can press **Ctrl+M** to add a new slide with the same layout as the previous slide.

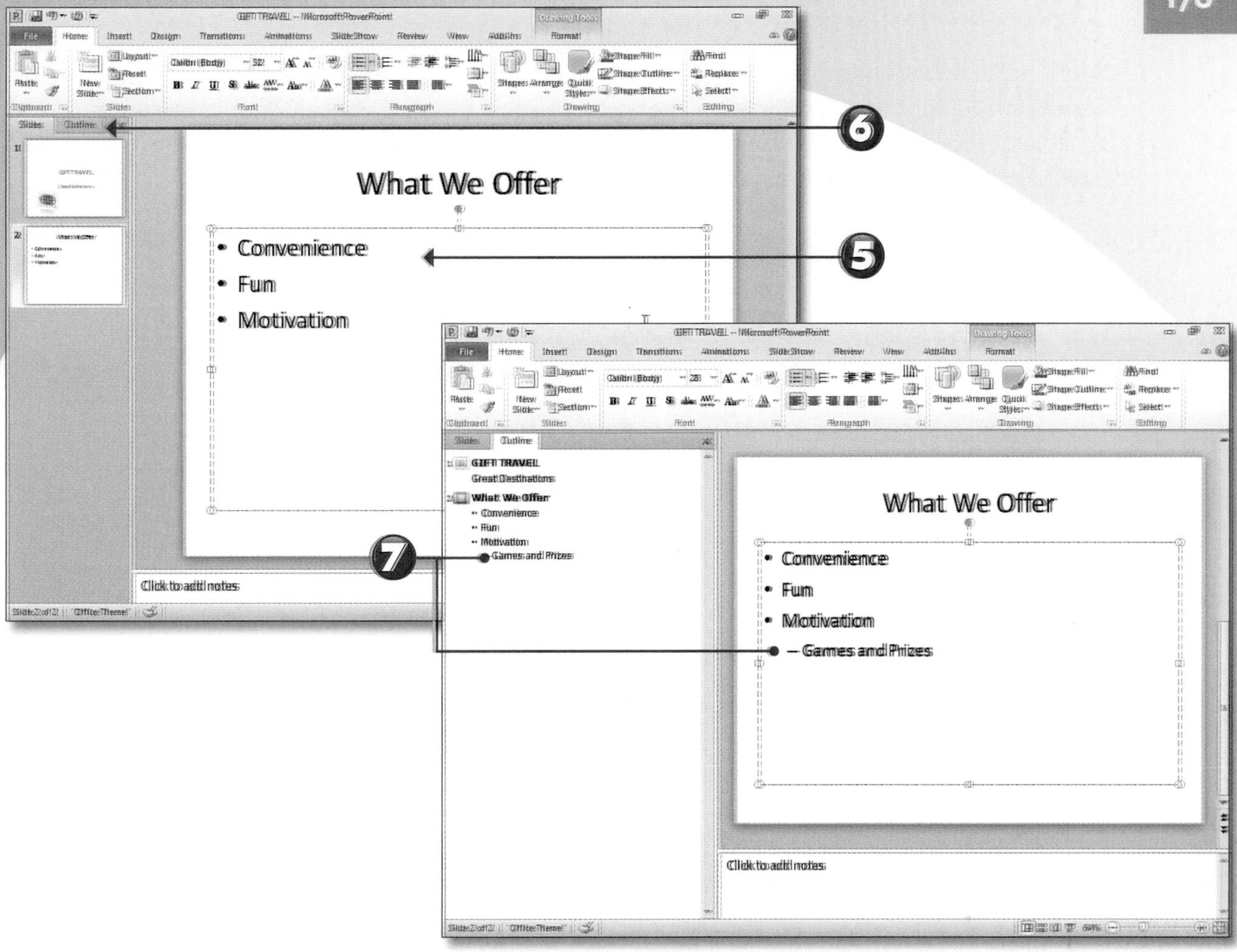

5 Type your bullets into the content placeholder, pressing **Enter** between each bullet. The other content icons for Table, Chart, Clip Art, Picture, SmartArt, and Media disappear.

6 Click to open the Outline tab.

7 Press **Tab** to enter a sub-bullet under the last bullet. Notice how adding a bullet in the Outline tab is reflected in the actual slide (and vice versa).

End

TIP

Changing the Layout If you want to change the layout of a slide, click **Layout** again and choose another layout. For example, you can combine your bullets using a second content placeholder with more content icons or to add a second set of bullets.

TIP

Creating Your Own Layout If you want to create your own layout, you can use Slide Master view. (See "Using Slide Masters" later in this chapter.) Right-click any layout in the left panel of Slide Master view, click **Copy**, right-click it again, and click **Rename Layout**. Then adjust the layout in the Slide Master view and click **Close Master View**. The new Layout is made available when you click **New Slide**.

ADDING A NEW SECTION

Sections, which are new in PowerPoint 2010, let you organize your presentation into subject areas with Section Header slides. When you use this feature, your audience members get an idea of the structure of your slide show. When you add a Section Header slide from the Layouts panel, a new section is created that you can rename.

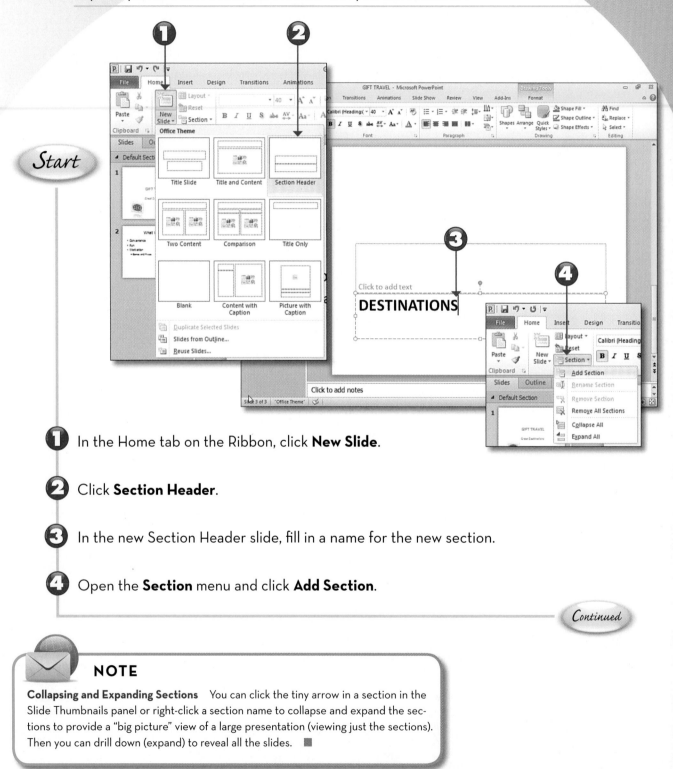

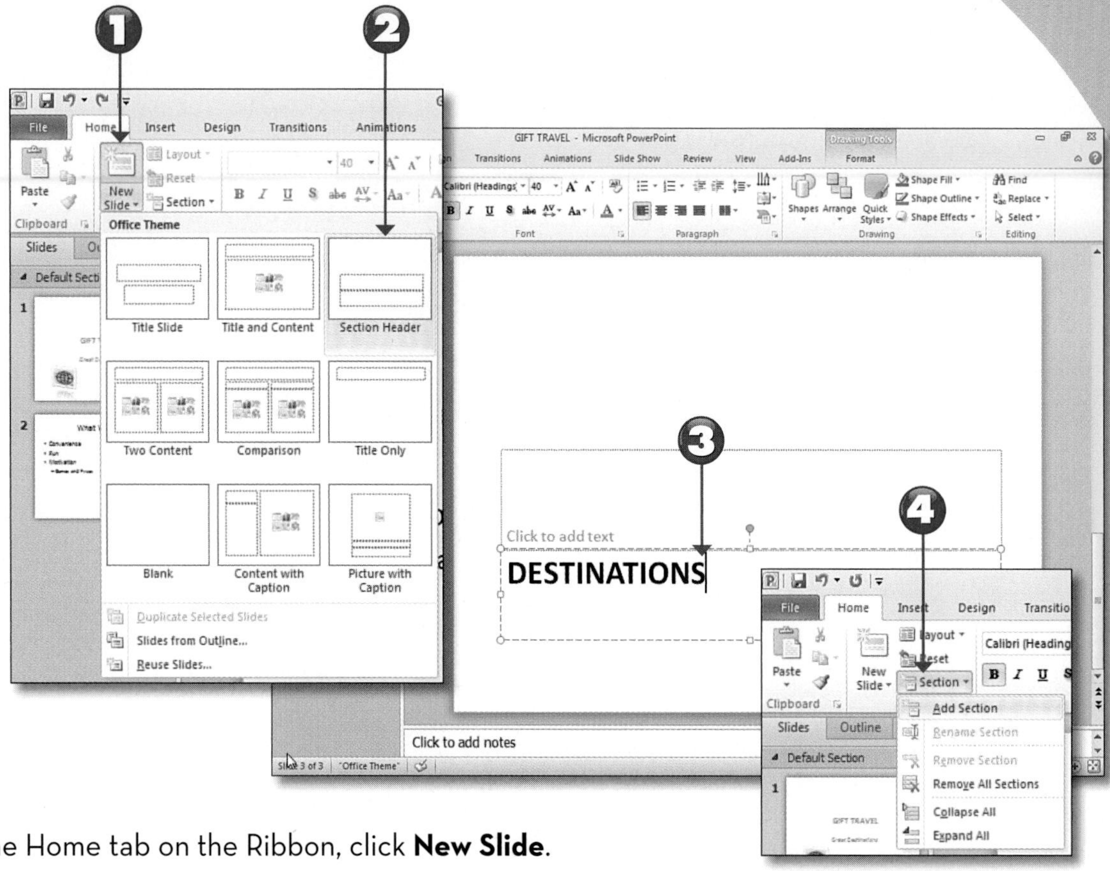

Start

1. In the Home tab on the Ribbon, click **New Slide**.
2. Click **Section Header**.
3. In the new Section Header slide, fill in a name for the new section.
4. Open the **Section** menu and click **Add Section**.

Continued

NOTE

Collapsing and Expanding Sections You can click the tiny arrow in a section in the Slide Thumbnails panel or right-click a section name to collapse and expand the sections to provide a "big picture" view of a large presentation (viewing just the sections). Then you can drill down (expand) to reveal all the slides. ■

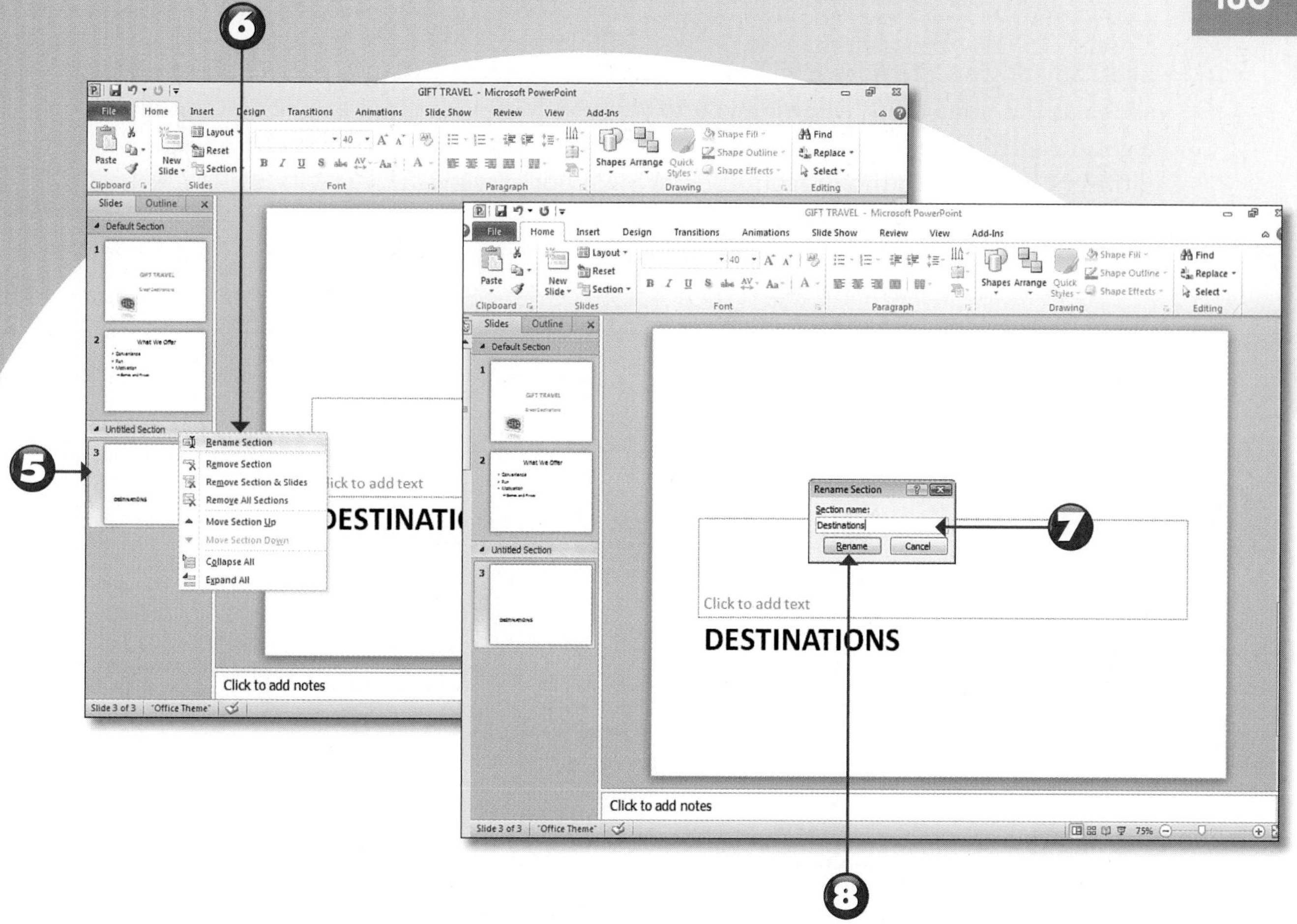

5 A new untitled section is added, setting off a new section before the Section Header slide.

6 Right-click **Untitled Section** and click **Rename Section** in the context menu that appears.

7 Type a new name for the section.

8 Click **Rename**.

End

TIP

Moving Sections To move a section, right-click it and choose either **Move Section Up** or **Move Section Down**. The sections are simply markers, so you should generally also move the Section Header slides with your sections to change where sections begin.

MOVING SLIDES (SLIDE SORTER VIEW)

Slide Sorter view provides a valuable overview of your entire presentation by showing your slides as thumbnails and allowing you to view both their content and titles. This gives you a good way to evaluate the flow of your message, and you can drag and drop your slides to different positions in the presentation in Slide Sorter view.

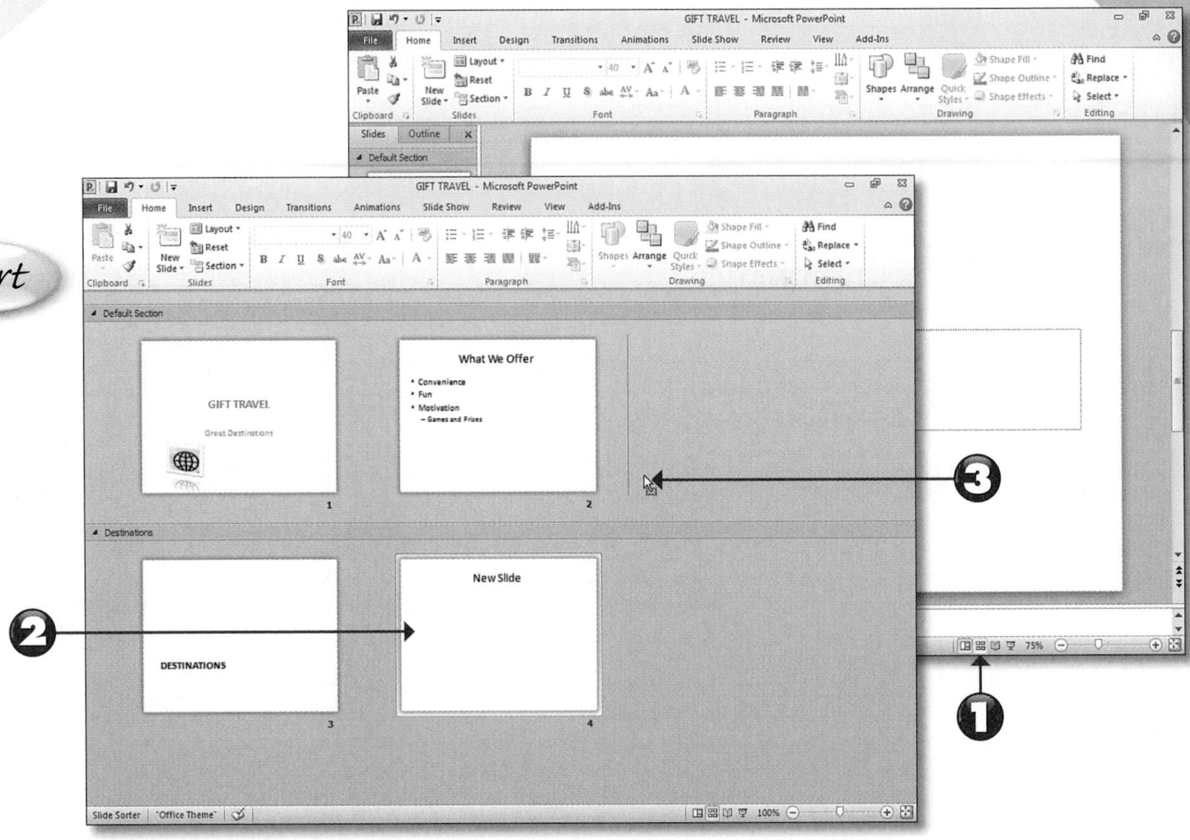

Start

1. Click **Slide Sorter View** to open the Slide Sorter view, which also divides slides into their separate sections.
2. Grab a slide using your left mouse button.
3. Drag and drop the slide onto a new location in the presentation. (While you're dragging, a vertical line shows where it will go based on the mouse pointer's current location on the screen.)

Continued

TIP

Slide Thumbnails You can drag and drop slides in the Slide Thumbnails panel, and you can drag the border of the Slide Thumbnails panel to make the Slide Thumbnails larger. ■

TIP

Returning to Normal View From Slide Sorter view, you can return to Normal view by double-clicking a slide. ■

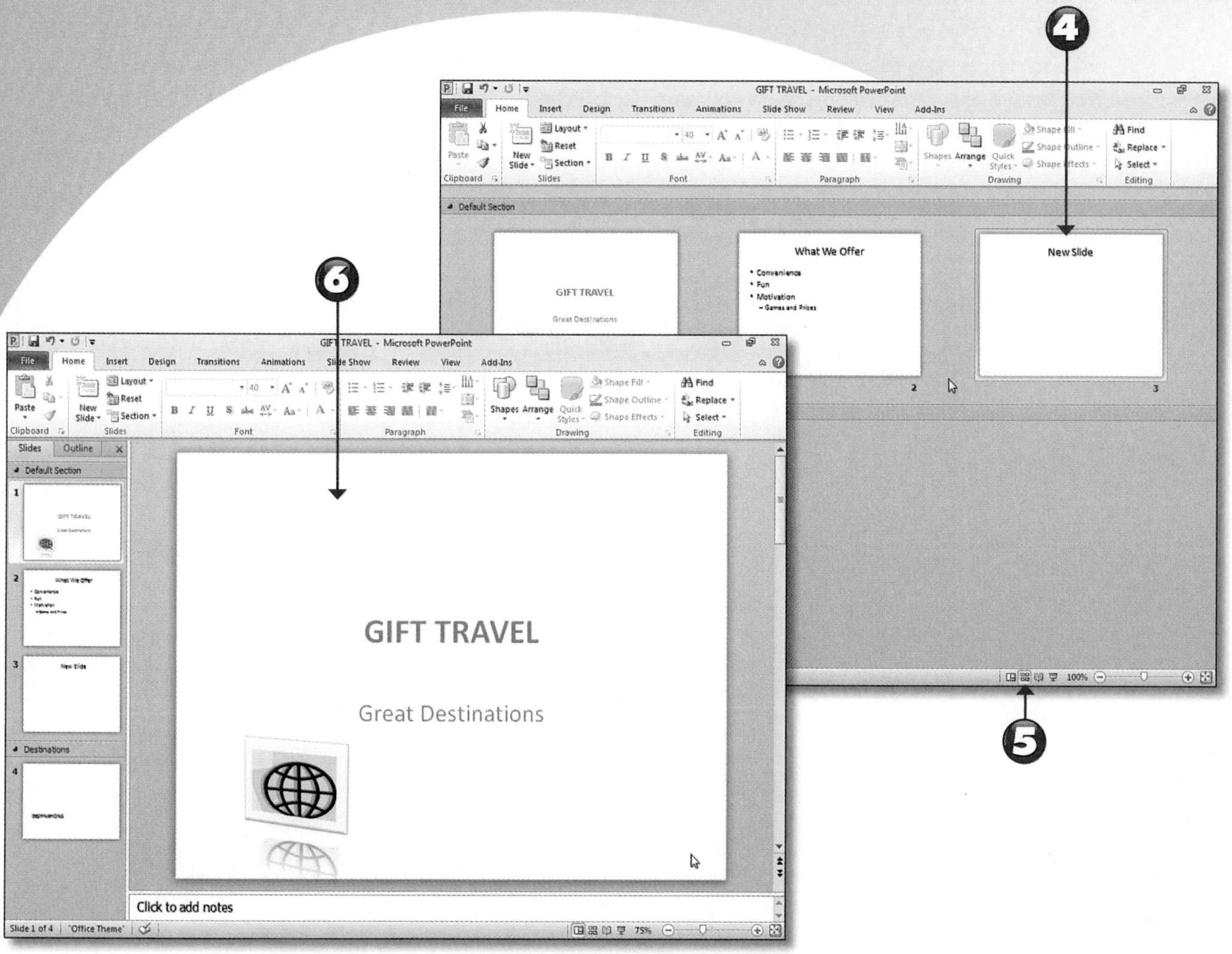

4 The slide is moved within the presentation and is now shown after Slide.

5 Click **Normal View**.

6 You return to the Normal view to work with individual slides.

End

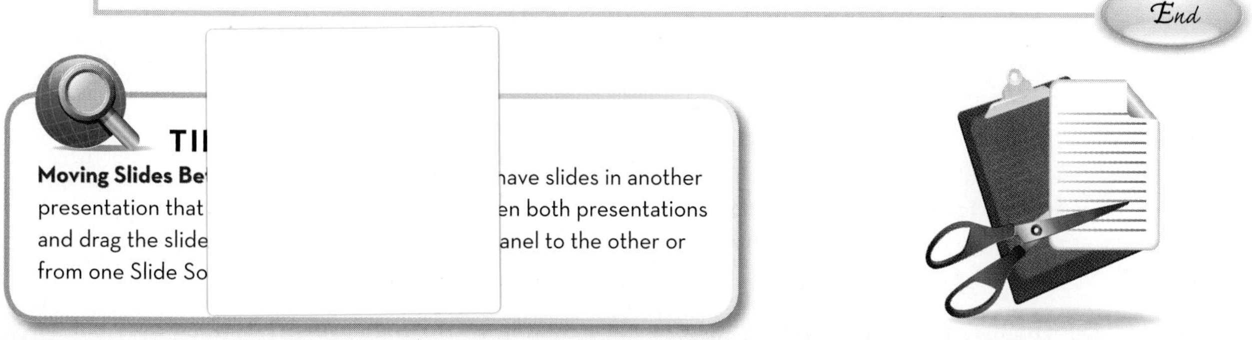

TI
Moving Slides Be
have slides in another
presentation that
en both presentations
and drag the slide
anel to the other or
from one Slide So

APPLYING A THEME FROM THE DESIGN TAB

To make your presentation stand out or give it more color, you can apply a theme from the Ribbon's Design tab. Each theme has its own coordinated set of fonts, colors, and effects. For more information on themes, see "Applying a Theme to a Document" in Chapter 4, "Changing Project Appearance."

Start

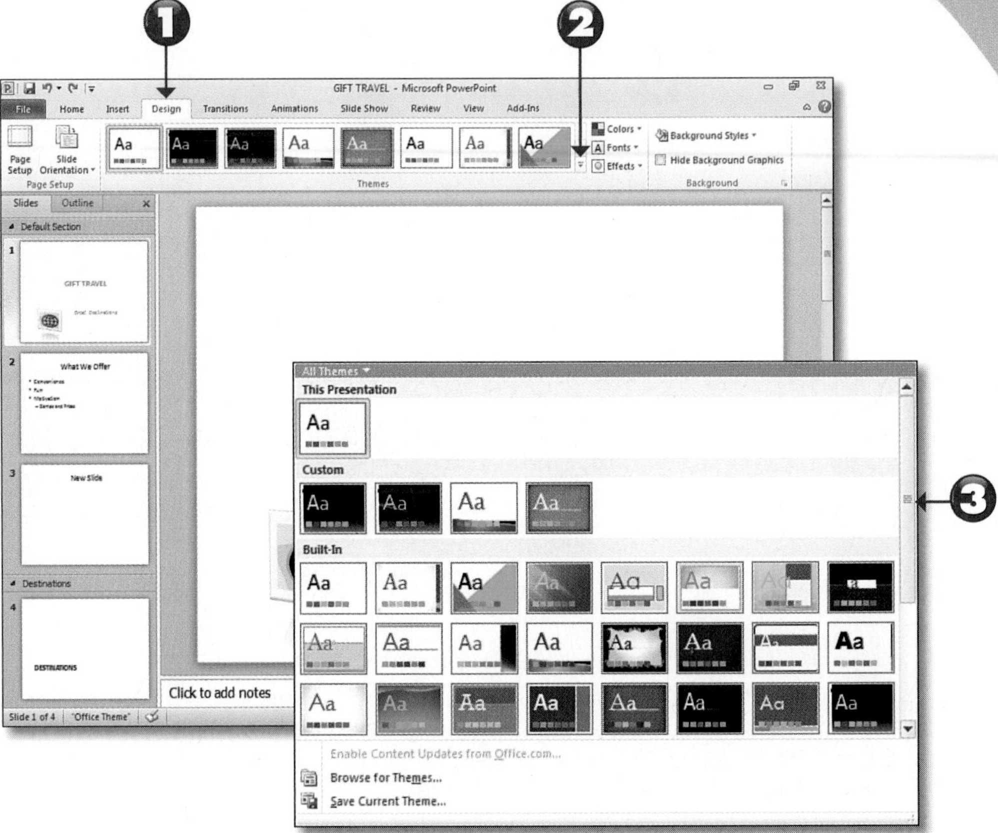

1. Click the **Design** tab on the Ribbon.
2. Click the More drop-down arrow for **Themes**.
3. Scroll through the Themes Gallery, which shows This Presentation, Custom, and Built-in themes.

Continued

TIP

Different Themes for Different Slides If you want to apply different themes to different slides, click **Slide Sorter View** and use your mouse to select individual slides (**Ctrl+click**) or sequential slides (**Shift+click**). With the slides selected, you can choose a different theme for them. ■

4. Hover over a theme to see how it will look when applied to a presentation. Click a theme to apply it.

5. The theme is applied to the entire presentation. (Different *masters* control the appearance of different layouts, so the Title slide is different from the Title and Content slides with a lighter background.)

End

TIP

Saving Your Own Custom Theme When you change any elements in your slide—for example, the font for bullets; colors for a font or shape fill; or effects for a picture, shape, or WordArt—you can save that coordinated combination to reuse in other presentations by opening the Theme Gallery and choosing **Save Current Theme**.

USING SLIDE MASTERS

Slide masters are like blueprints for different layouts in your presentation. You can control the appearance of different elements; for example, when you change the title font color of the main master that controls all Title and Content slides, all slides with that layout are automatically changed to that title font color. You can also use a slide master to add content (such as a logo) to all slides with the layout that the master controls.

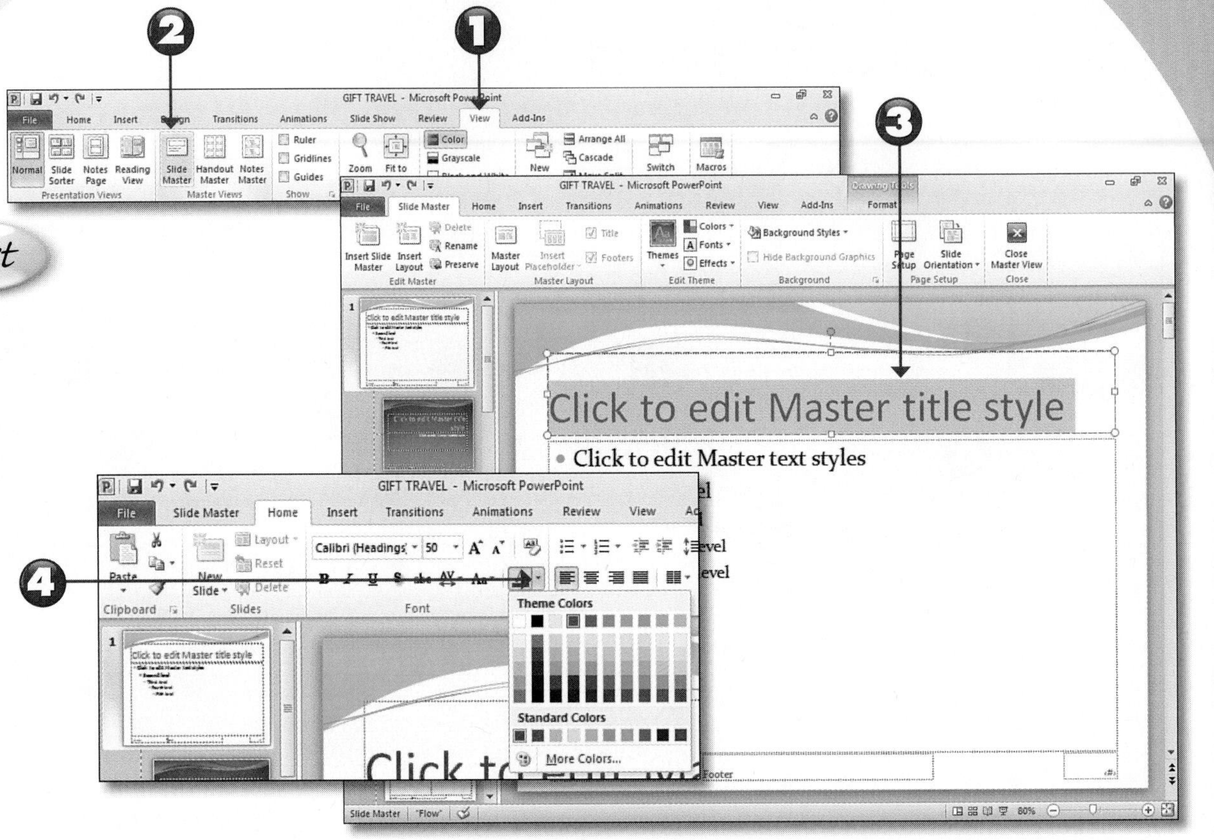

Start

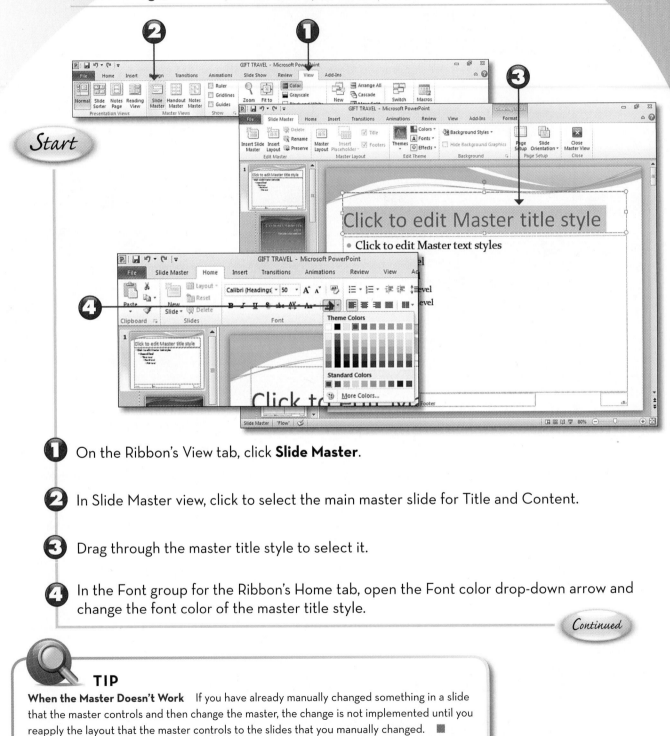

1. On the Ribbon's View tab, click **Slide Master**.
2. In Slide Master view, click to select the main master slide for Title and Content.
3. Drag through the master title style to select it.
4. In the Font group for the Ribbon's Home tab, open the Font color drop-down arrow and change the font color of the master title style.

Continued

TIP

When the Master Doesn't Work If you have already manually changed something in a slide that the master controls and then change the master, the change is not implemented until you reapply the layout that the master controls to the slides that you manually changed. ■

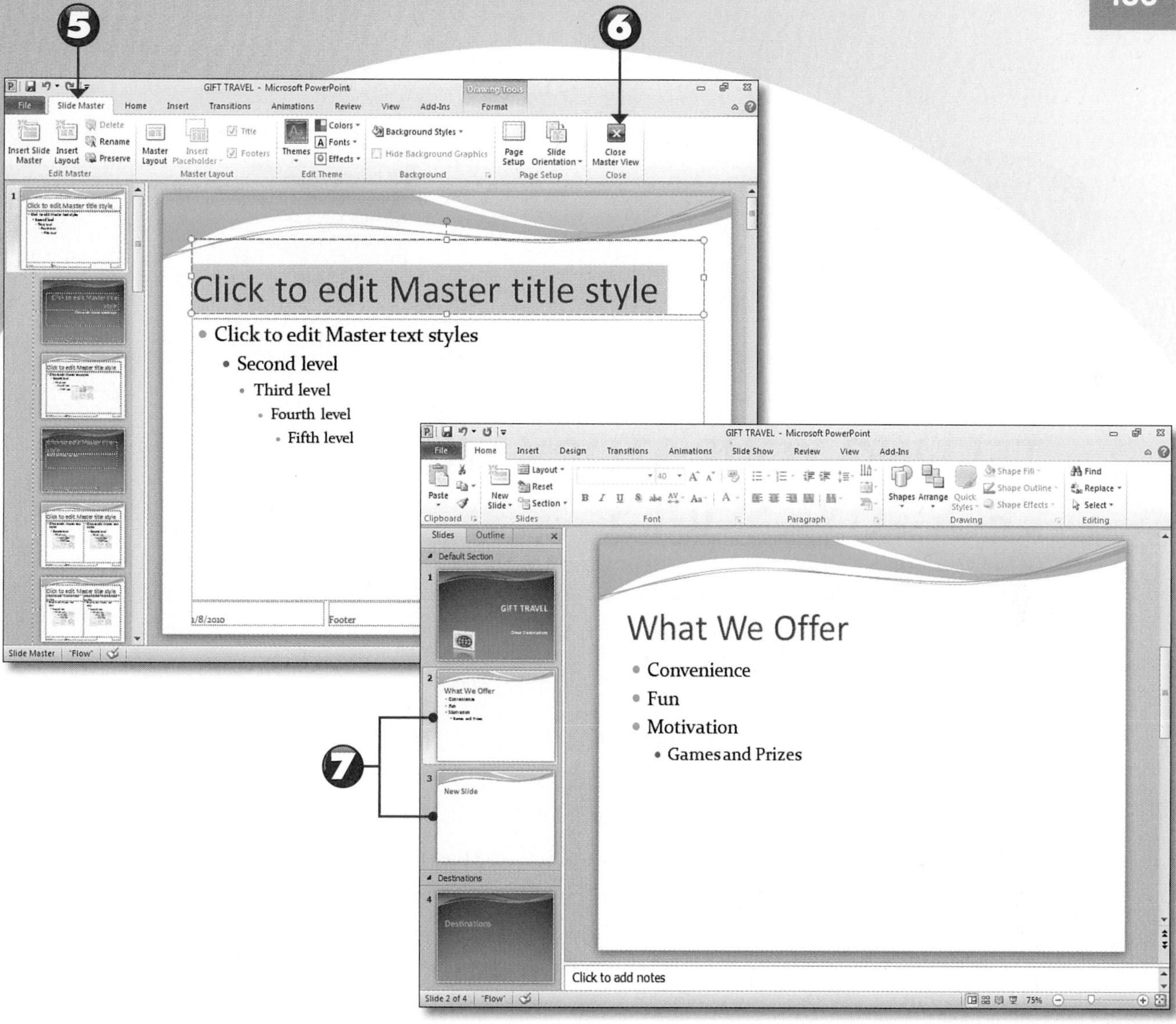

5 Click the **Slide Master** tab on the Ribbon.

6 Click **Close Master View**.

7 All slides with the layout of the master you altered now reflect those changes.

End

TIP

Masters Did Not Affect Footers or Slide Numbers Masters control only the formatting, not the content itself. To get footers or slide numbers to appear on your slides where you may have formatted the master for them, make sure you check those options. Click the **Insert** tab of the Ribbon, click **Header and Footer**, click to check (enable) **Footer and/or Slide Number** for the slides, and then click either **Apply** or **Apply to All**. ■

TELLING YOUR STORY WITH EFFECTIVE SLIDES

After you begin to create your presentation with a Title slide, putting text in bullets and perhaps setting up sections of slides for topics, it's time to create slides that tell your story effectively with the content and graphics features of PowerPoint.

In Chapter 12, "Getting Started with PowerPoint 2010," when you added the Title and Content slide to enter bullets, you saw how PowerPoint provides content icons to add specific elements to your slides. You can choose from the Table, Chart, SmartArt Diagram, Picture, ClipArt, and Media Clip icons.

Tables enable you to lay out information in a way that lets the audience quickly grasp it. Charts, on the other hand, are for numerical information to be viewed visually. SmartArt diagrams can help you visually present concepts (using bullets, for example). Pictures, clip art, and media clips can illustrate a point more dramatically.

All these graphical elements come with their own specific tabs on the Ribbon to provide more formatting options and enable you to add final touches and special effects.

SMARTART TOOLS

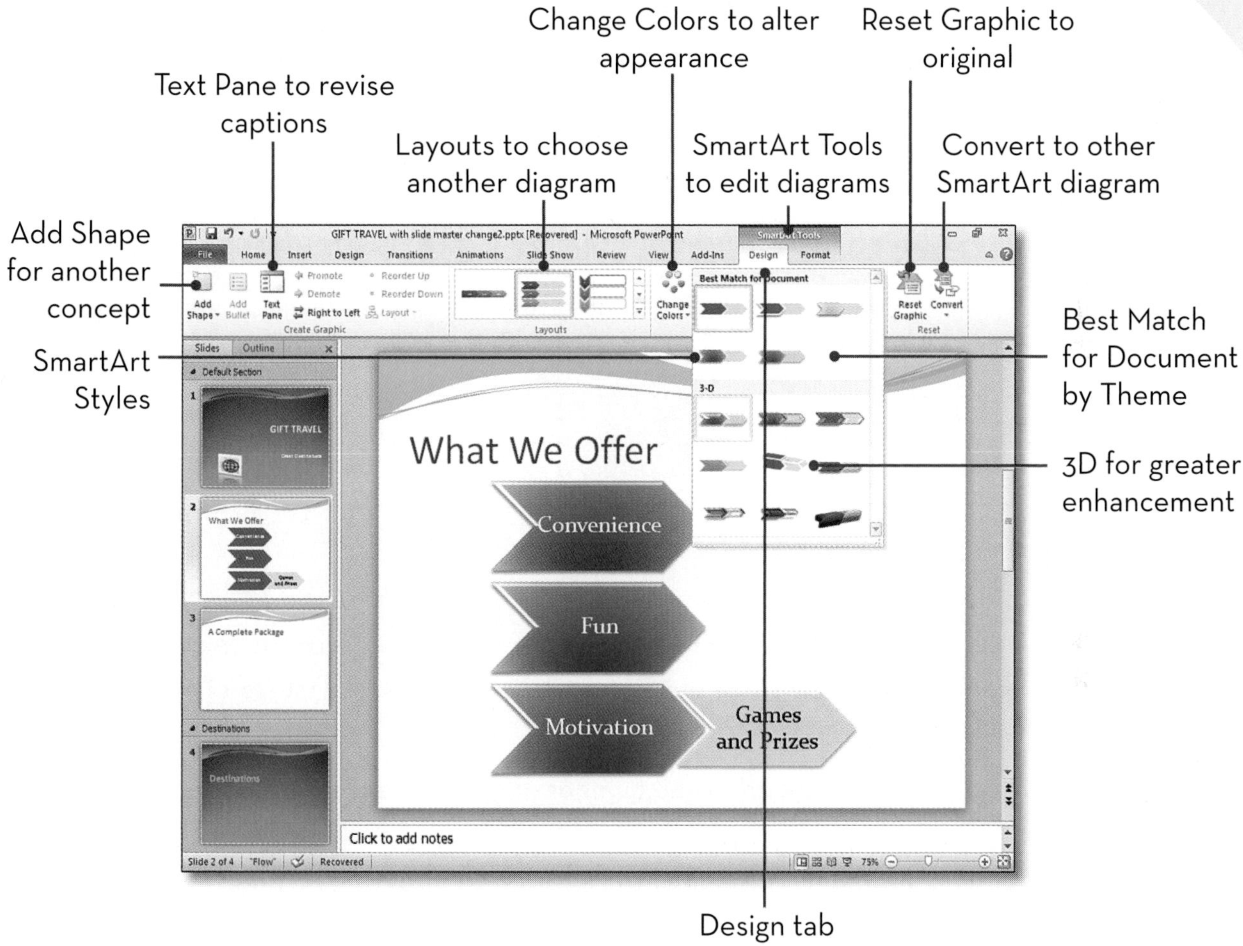

Change Colors to alter appearance
Reset Graphic to original
Text Pane to revise captions
Layouts to choose another diagram
SmartArt Tools to edit diagrams
Convert to other SmartArt diagram
Add Shape for another concept
SmartArt Styles
Best Match for Document by Theme
3D for greater enhancement
Design tab
What We Offer
Convenience
Fun
Motivation
Games and Prizes
Click to add notes

CREATING A TABLE FOR INFORMATION

A table is a great way to lay out text information in a way that an audience can grasp quickly and easily. A table is simply a grid with columns and rows that combine to form cells that you can use to hold text. You can format it using the Table Tools on the Ribbon.

Start

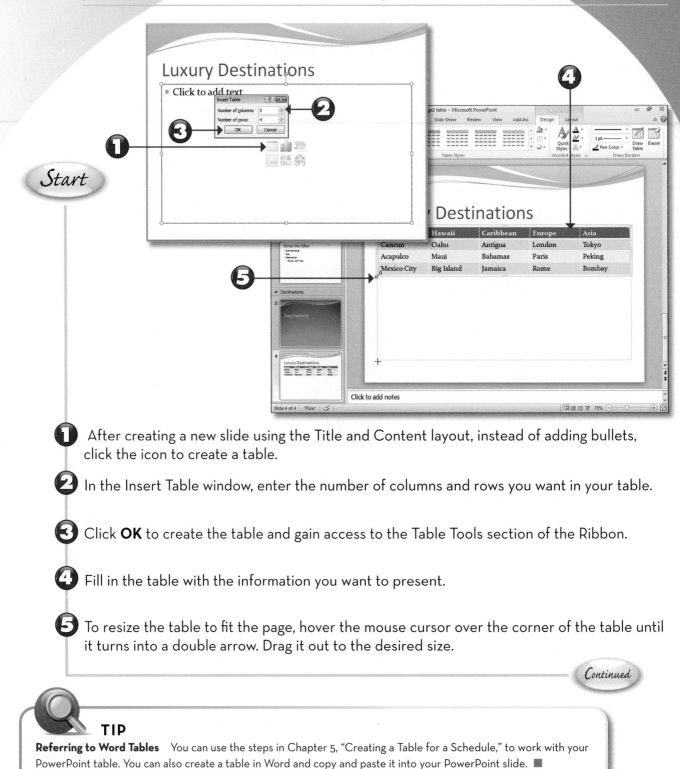

1. After creating a new slide using the Title and Content layout, instead of adding bullets, click the icon to create a table.
2. In the Insert Table window, enter the number of columns and rows you want in your table.
3. Click **OK** to create the table and gain access to the Table Tools section of the Ribbon.
4. Fill in the table with the information you want to present.
5. To resize the table to fit the page, hover the mouse cursor over the corner of the table until it turns into a double arrow. Drag it out to the desired size.

Continued

TIP

Referring to Word Tables You can use the steps in Chapter 5, "Creating a Table for a Schedule," to work with your PowerPoint table. You can also create a table in Word and copy and paste it into your PowerPoint slide. ■

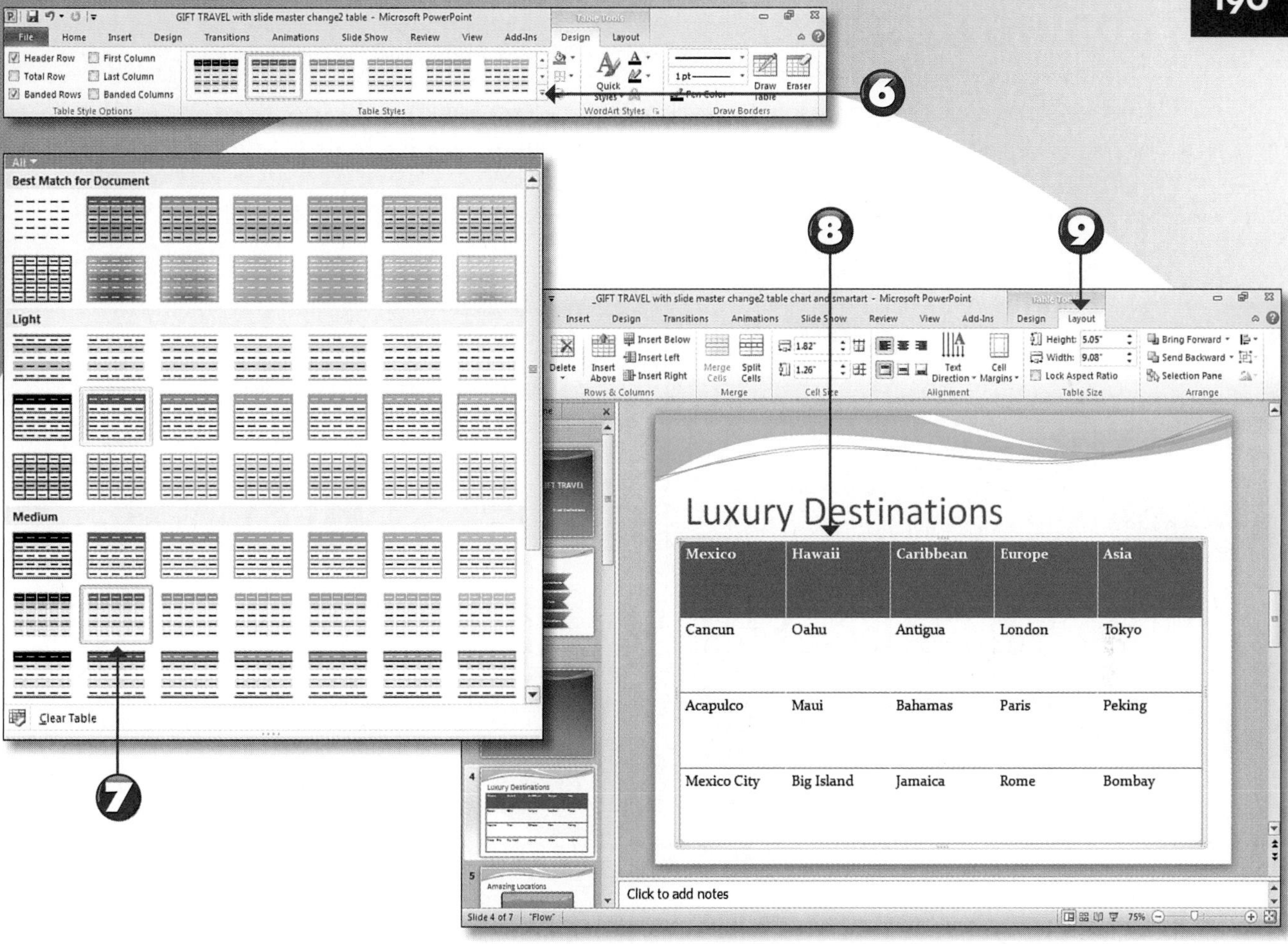

6 In the Table Styles section of the Ribbon's Table Tools Design tab, click **More**.

7 Hover over a table style for a Quick Preview. Click to apply the desired table style.

8 The table presents your information in an effective slide.

9 You can finish formatting the table using the Table Tools Design and Layout tabs.

End

TIP

Inserting a Table from the Ribbon Using the Ribbon's Insert tab (for example, on a title only or a blank slide), you can click **Table** and then drag out a table with the number of columns and rows that you want. ■

TIP

Drawing a Table You can use the Ribbon's Insert tab to access the pencil tool to manually draw a table in your slide. When the table is selected and the Table Tools are active, there is also a Draw Table pencil tool in the Design tab of Table Tools. ■

ADDING A CHART

A chart enables you to present numerical data in a graphic form that lets your audience see relationships quickly and easily. PowerPoint uses Excel as its data source, so you can create or use an Excel worksheet to hold the data for a chart that is created, edited, and displayed in PowerPoint.

Start

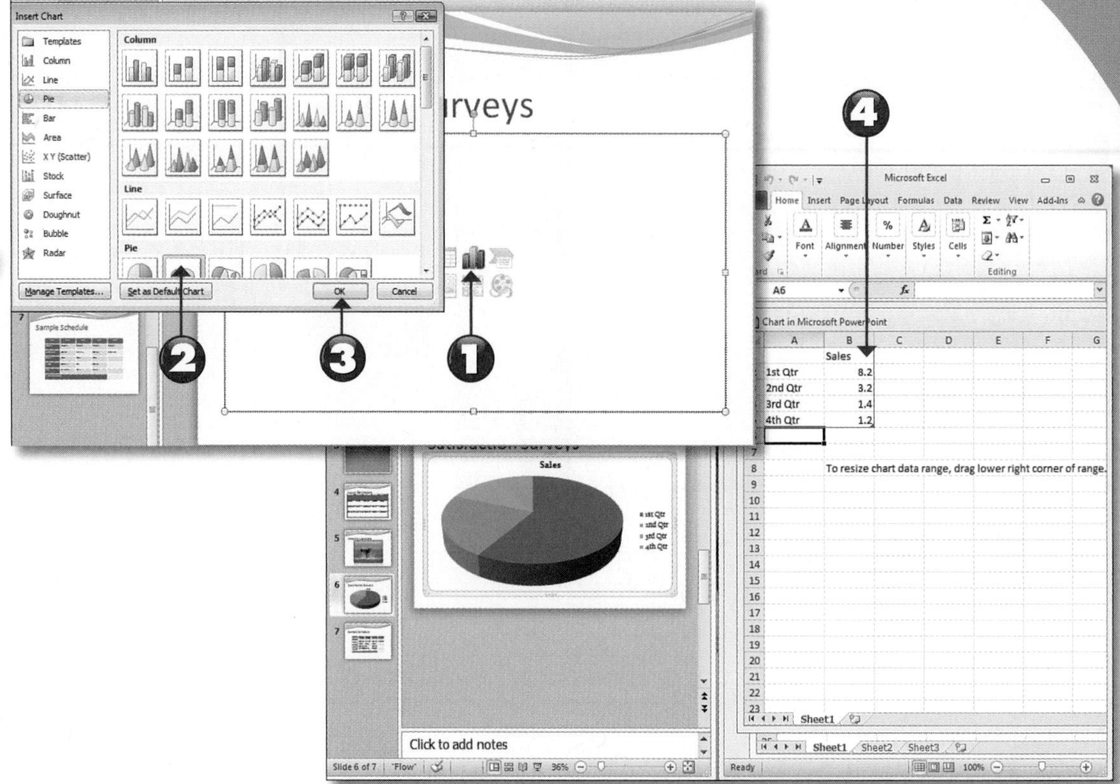

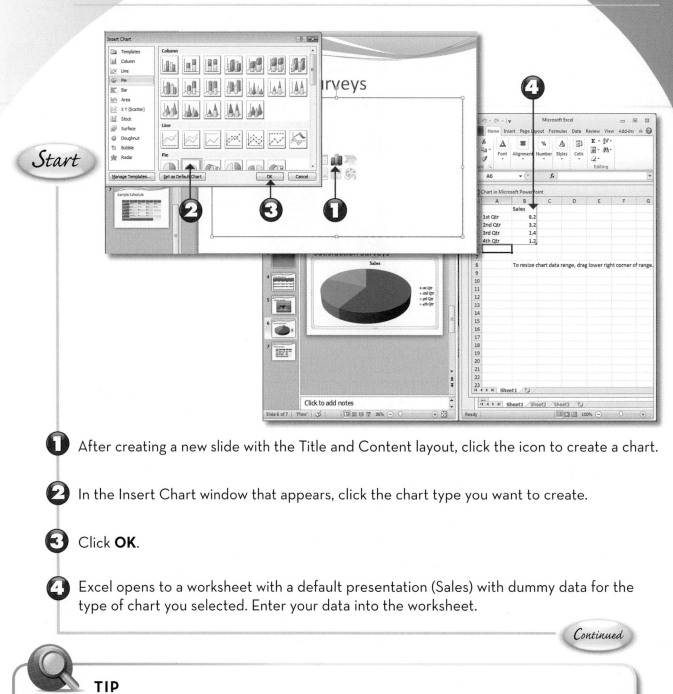

1. After creating a new slide with the Title and Content layout, click the icon to create a chart.

2. In the Insert Chart window that appears, click the chart type you want to create.

3. Click **OK**.

4. Excel opens to a worksheet with a default presentation (Sales) with dummy data for the type of chart you selected. Enter your data into the worksheet.

Continued

TIP

Creating a Chart in Excel You can create a chart in Excel and copy and paste it into your PowerPoint slide. The Paste Preview feature lets you determine whether to keep the Word formatting options (Keep Source Formatting) or the PowerPoint theme (Destination Styles). See "Using Copy and Paste Preview" in Chapter 3, "Adjusting the Structure of Your Document."

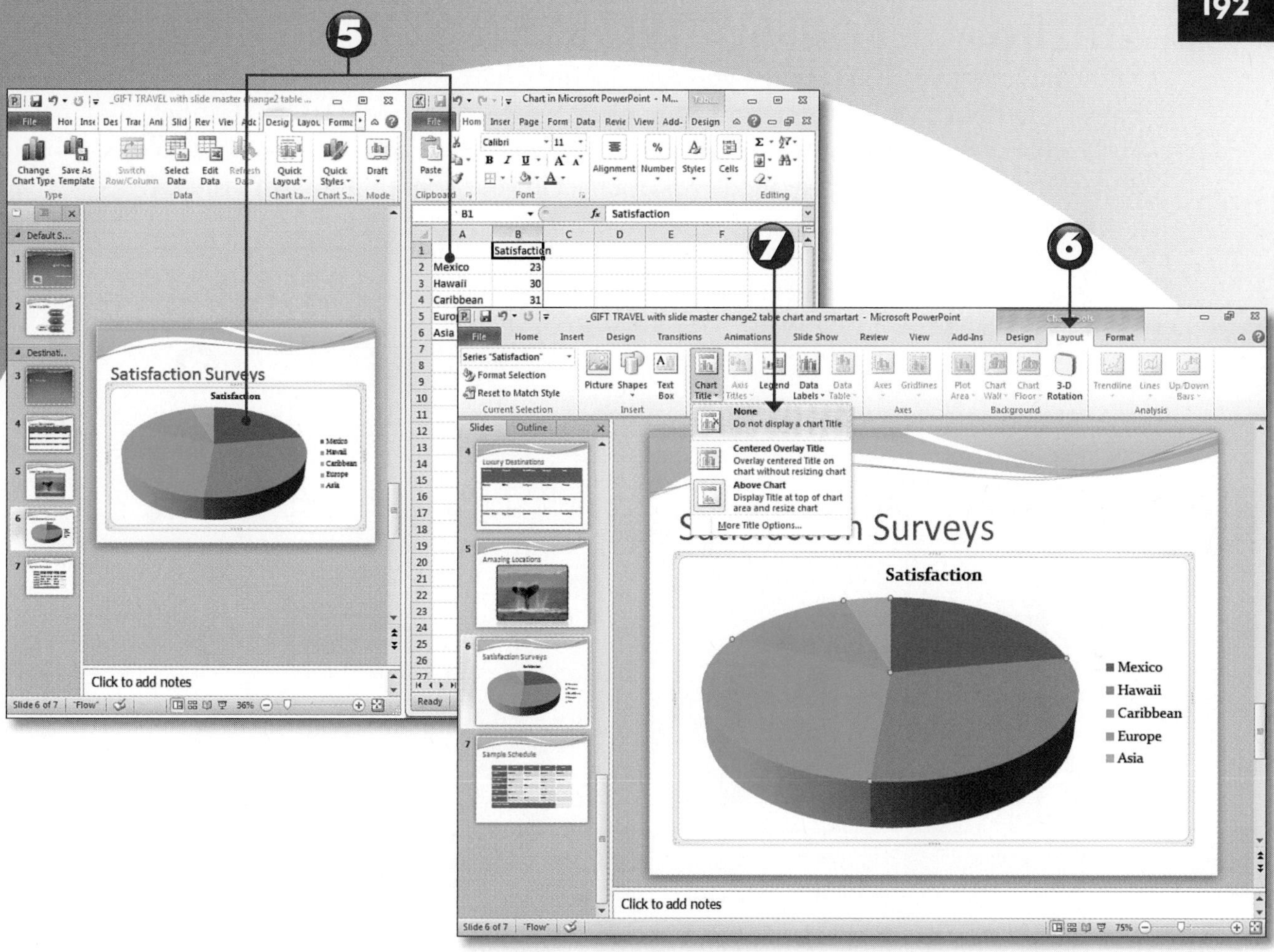

5 With the correct data in Excel, the chart in PowerPoint reflects the information. (The title can be changed.) Save the chart in PowerPoint and save your Excel file with a new name to keep your data available.

6 Return to PowerPoint and click the **Layout** tab of the Chart Tools.

7 You can use the **Chart Title** button in the Layout tab to remove a redundant chart title from the chart (if the title is already part of the slide).

End

TIP

Changing the Chart Type If you want to change the type of chart you are using to display data, select the Chart Tools Design tab on the Ribbon and click **Change Chart Type.** ■

EDITING OR FORMATTING A CHART

With your chart set in your slide, you can use the Chart Tools on the Ribbon to make it look better and reflect your information more effectively. You can add labels to show data values in the chart, select and format different parts of your chart by changing fonts and colors, and further refine the appearance of your chart in your presentation with the Layout tab of the Chart Tools.

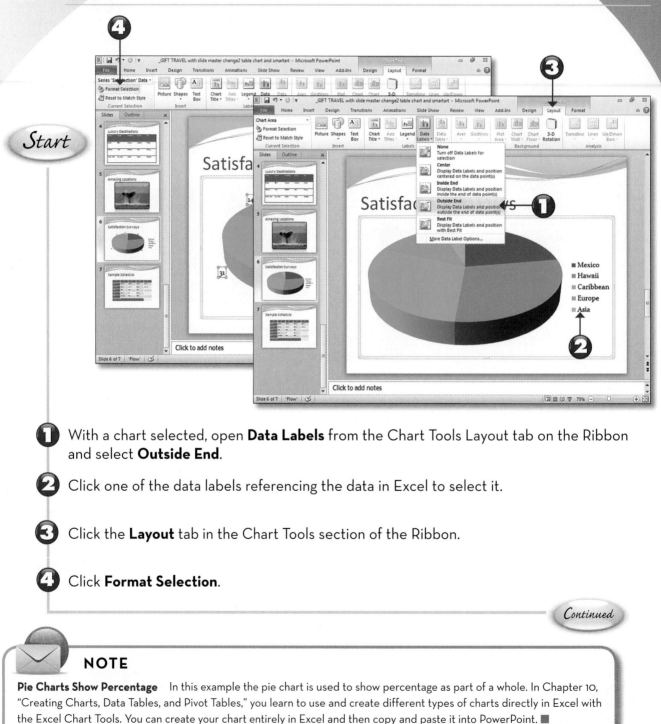

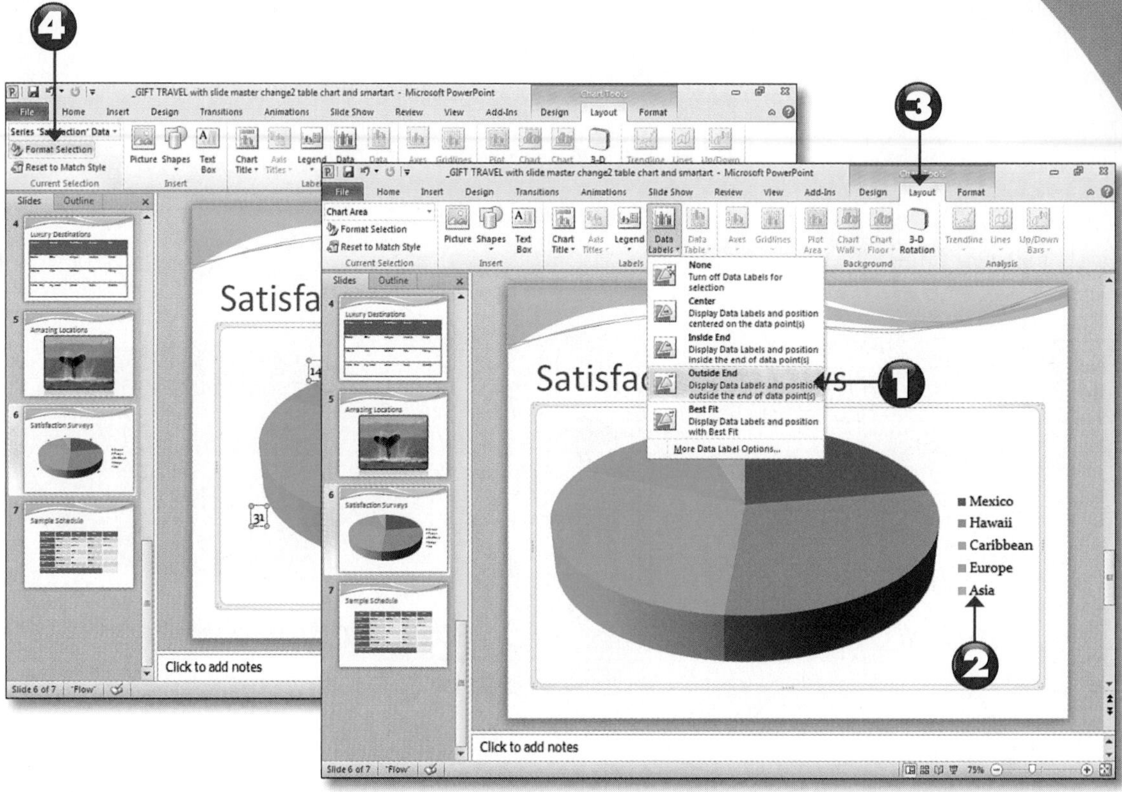

1. With a chart selected, open **Data Labels** from the Chart Tools Layout tab on the Ribbon and select **Outside End**.
2. Click one of the data labels referencing the data in Excel to select it.
3. Click the **Layout** tab in the Chart Tools section of the Ribbon.
4. Click **Format Selection**.

Continued

NOTE

Pie Charts Show Percentage In this example the pie chart is used to show percentage as part of a whole. In Chapter 10, “Creating Charts, Data Tables, and Pivot Tables,” you learn to use and create different types of charts directly in Excel with the Excel Chart Tools. You can create your chart entirely in Excel and then copy and paste it into PowerPoint. ■

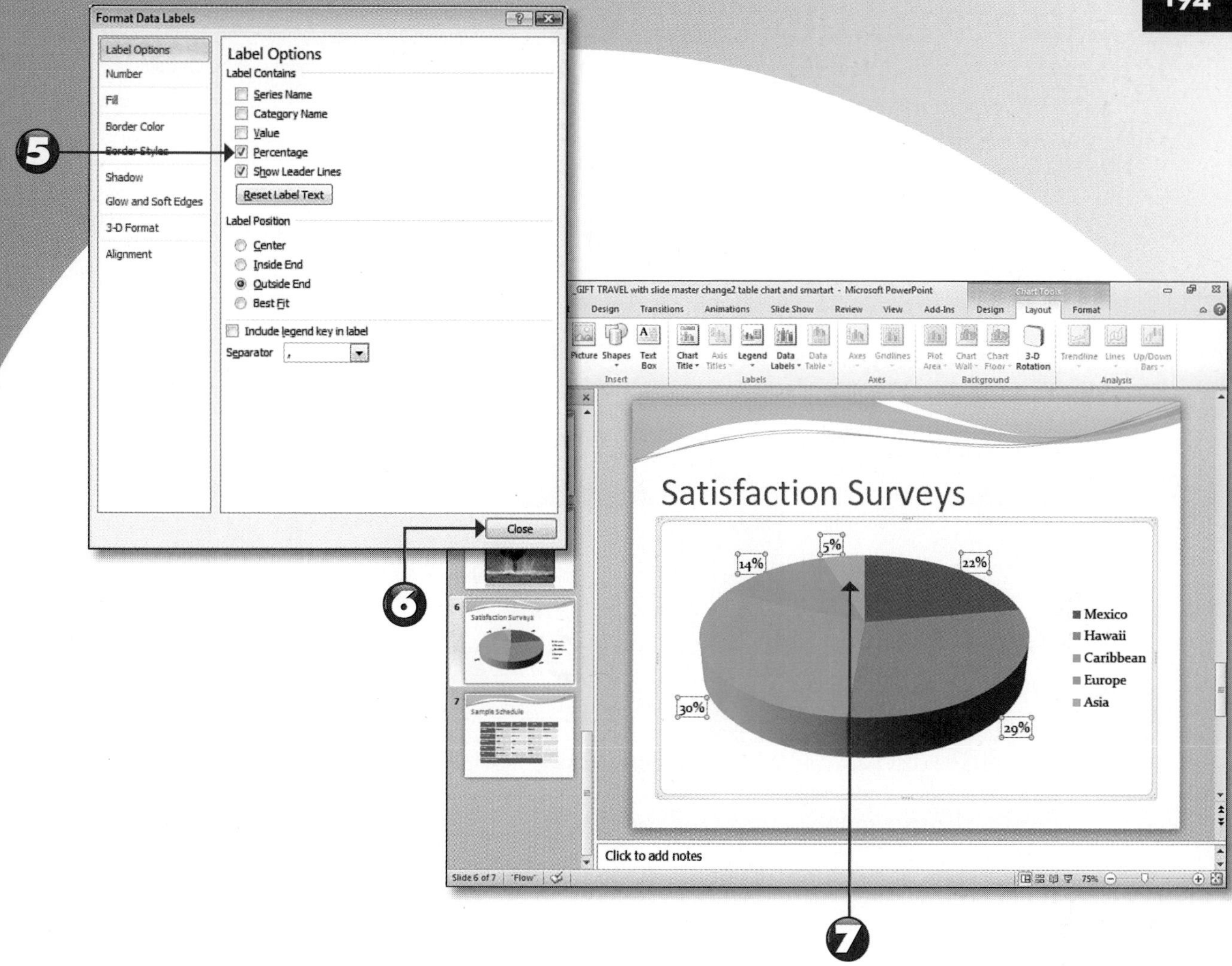

5 In Label Options, click to enable the type of label you want—for example, **Percentage**.

6 Click **Close**.

7 The chart shows the values as percentages. With the data labels still selected, you can use the **Font Size** button on the Ribbon's Home tab to adjust the size of the data labels.

End

TIP

Chart Styles To change the appearance of the chart more dramatically, use the Chart Styles in the Design tab of the Chart Tools to quickly apply a more artistic style to the chart. ■

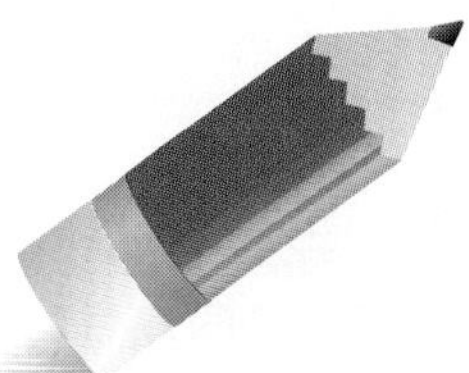

INSERTING A PICTURE

A great way to tell your story or enhance the appearance of your slides is to insert a picture, using the Picture content icon in a new slide. With the picture selected in your slide, you can use the Format tab in the Picture Tools to apply a style from the gallery and crop the image or otherwise change its appearance in the slide.

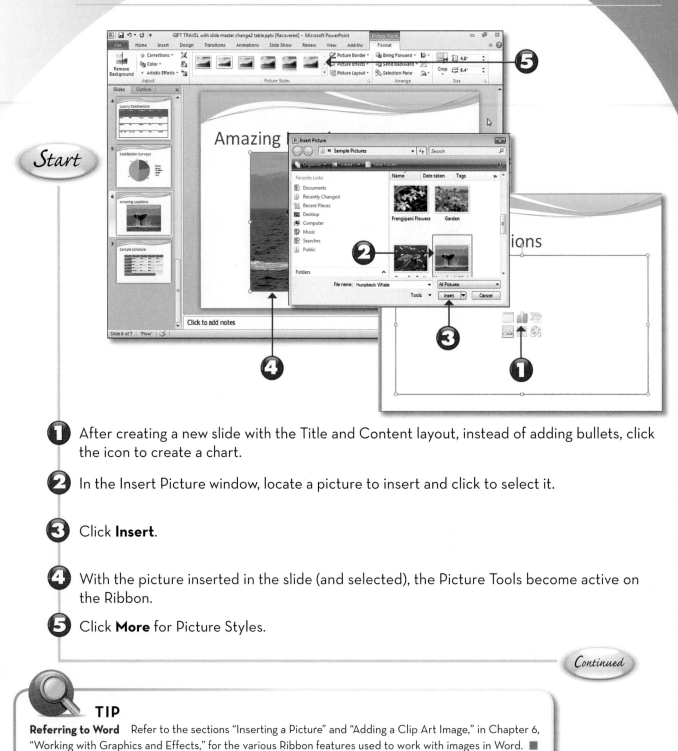

Start

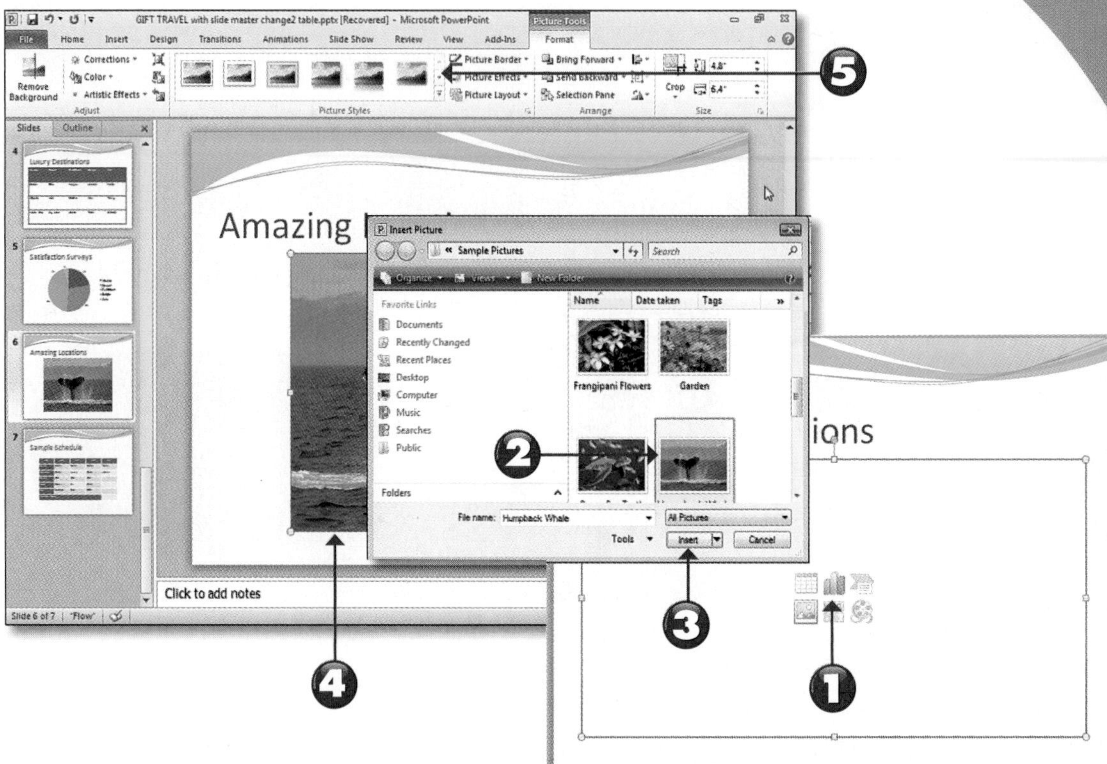

1. After creating a new slide with the Title and Content layout, instead of adding bullets, click the icon to create a chart.
2. In the Insert Picture window, locate a picture to insert and click to select it.
3. Click **Insert**.
4. With the picture inserted in the slide (and selected), the Picture Tools become active on the Ribbon.
5. Click **More** for Picture Styles.

Continued

TIP

Referring to Word Refer to the sections "Inserting a Picture" and "Adding a Clip Art Image," in Chapter 6, "Working with Graphics and Effects," for the various Ribbon features used to work with images in Word. ■

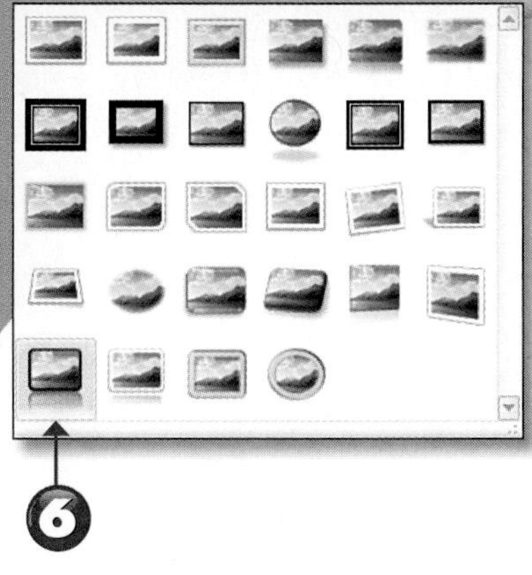

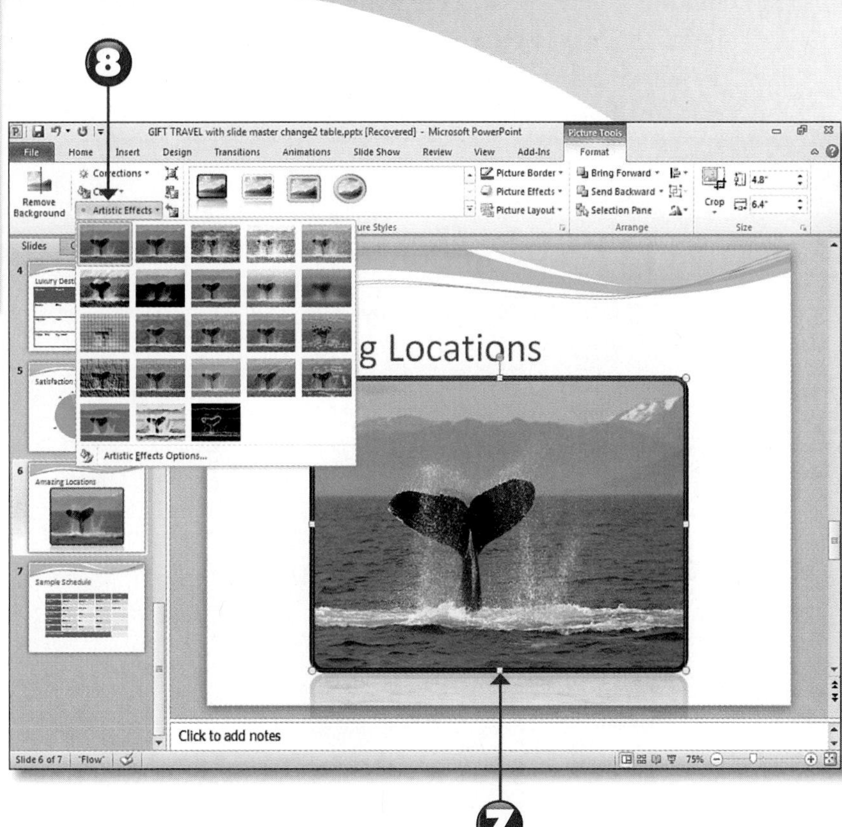

6 Hover over a picture style to see a Quick Preview. Click a picture style to apply it.

7 The picture is set in the slide with the picture style applied.

8 You can continue to add enhancements to the picture. For example, you can use the **Artistic Effects** in the Adjust group of the Format tab of Picture Tools to change how the image is rendered.

End

TIP

Screenshots and Screen Clippings To capture screens on your computer for PowerPoint slides, you can use the new Insert Screenshots and Screen Clippings feature. It is covered in "Using Screenshots or Screen Clippings" in Chapter 6. ■

TIP

Working with Large Images Large images from digital cameras and scanners can overwhelm your slide. Use the zoom slider in the lower right to zoom out so that you can grab a corner of the image and drag it into the viewable area and resize it. If you want an image to be behind another object, text, or shape, select the image and use the **Send Backward** feature of the Format tab of the Picture Tools to put it behind the other object. ■

CONVERTING BULLETS TO SMARTART

Because PowerPoint has been around for a long time, audiences have grown tired of bullets in slides. Their overuse results in what some people refer to as "Death by PowerPoint." To avoid this problem, you can select a set of bullets and use a SmartArt diagram to quickly convert them into a visual representation of your ideas.

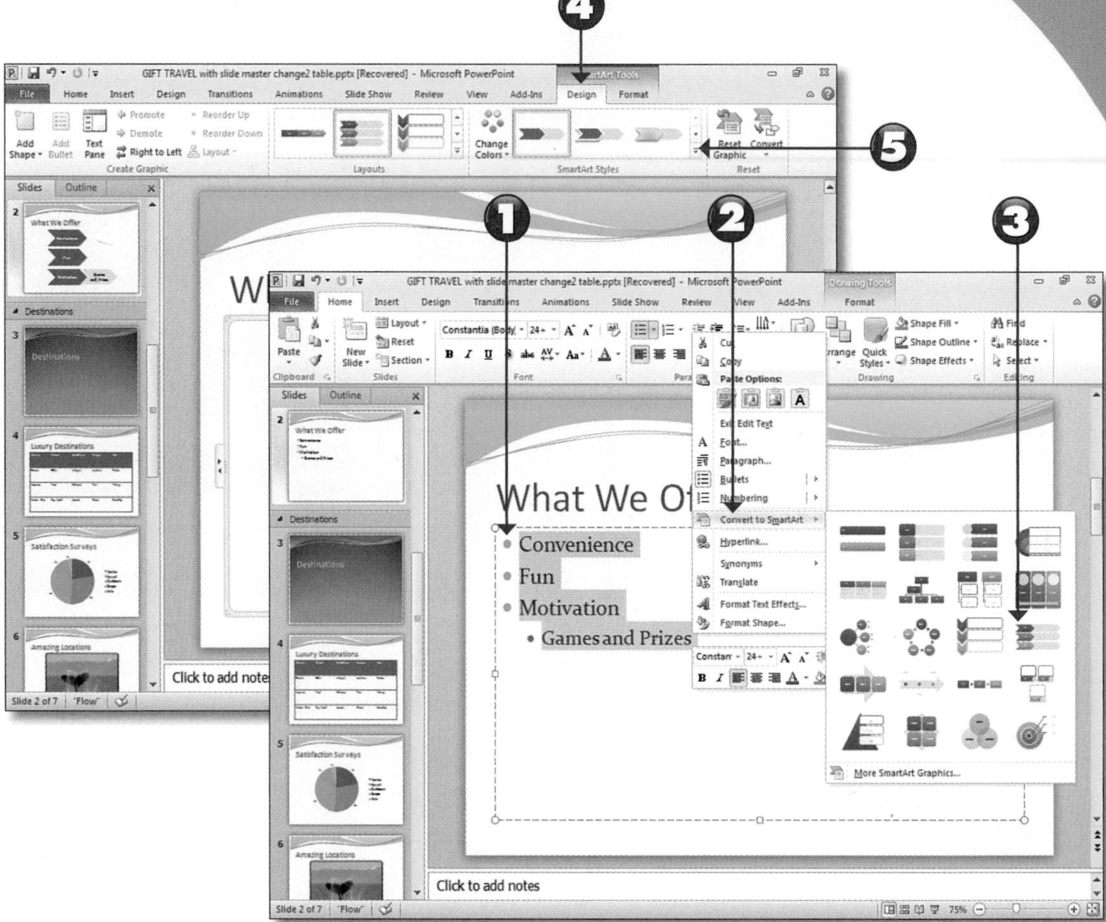

Start

1. Drag through your bullet text to select it.
2. Right-click the text and select **Convert to SmartArt**.
3. Click to apply a SmartArt diagram (or you can click **More SmartArt Graphics** to see more options).
4. The SmartDiagram is selected, and the SmartArt Tools become active on the Ribbon.
5. On the SmartArt Tools **Design** tab on the Ribbon, click **More** in the SmartArt Styles section.

Continued

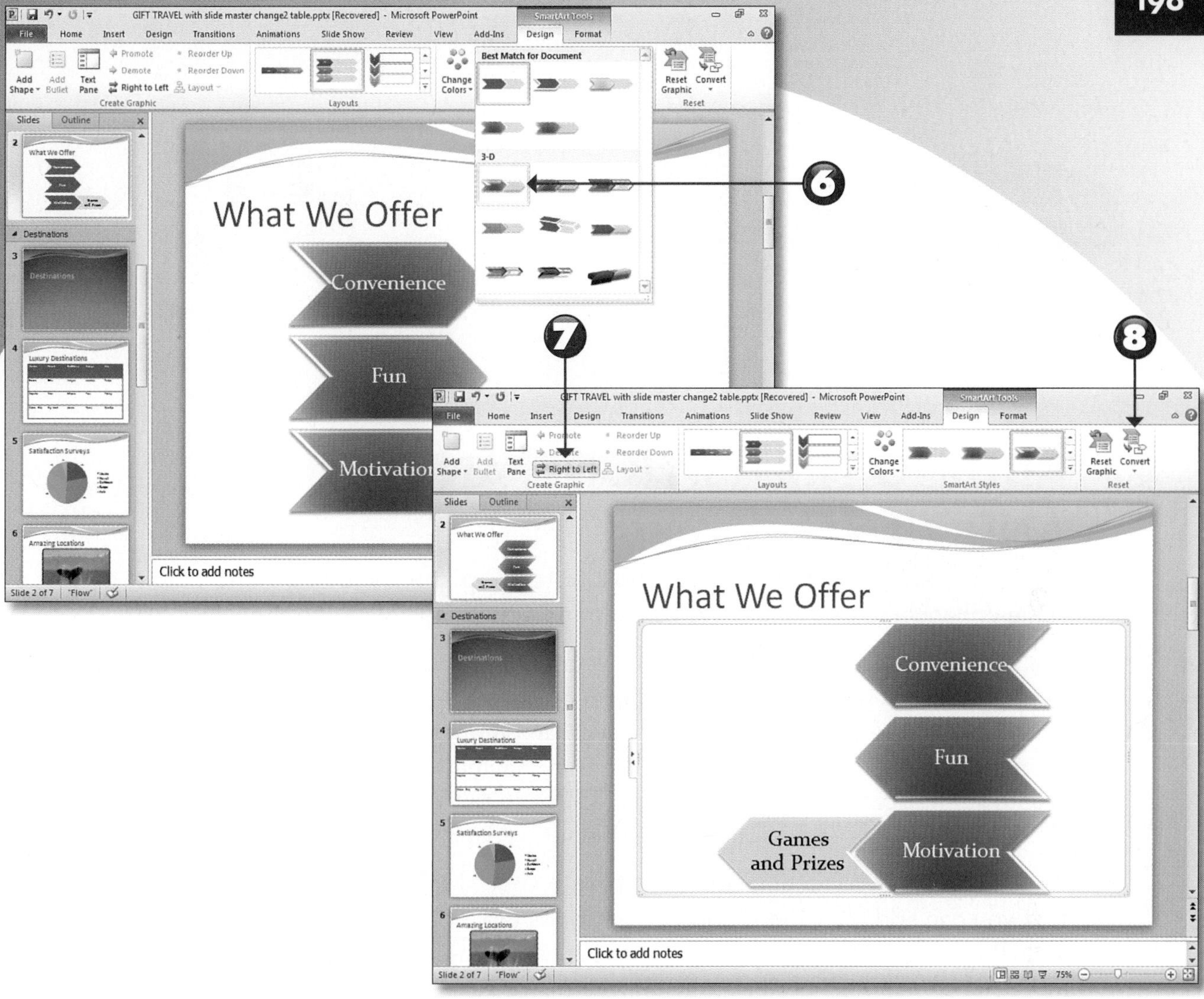

6 Hover over a SmartArt Style to see a Quick Preview. Click a SmartArt Style to select it.

7 You can use the SmartArt Tools Design tab on the Ribbon to refine your SmartArt diagram; for example, select **Right to Left** to change the arrows' direction.

8 You can click **Convert** to change your SmartArt diagram into another visual representation of your idea.

End

TIP

Changing or Adding Text To add or change text in a SmartArt diagram, click within the shape to select the text or click **Text Pane** in the Design tab of the SmartArt tools to access the text itself for revision. ■

TIP

More Color Options When you click the **Change Colors** button of the Design tab of the SmartArt Tools, your options reflect the theme that is currently applied to that slide in the presentation. For more or different color options, apply a different theme. See "Applying a Theme from the Design Tab " in Chapter 12. ■

ADDING TRANSITIONS, ANIMATION, AND VIDEO

Now that you have content in your slides to tell your story, you may want to add some enhancements that add movement and activity to your slides.

Animation can provide various parts of your slide with a separate "entrance" like an actor in a movie or play would use. Besides an entrance effect, you can also give a selected object in your slide an Emphasis, Exit, or Motion Path animation. Using the Animation pane and new Animation Painter tool, you can create sophisticated movements within a slide to tell your story sequentially by showing and hiding text, pictures, and shapes.

Transitions are eye-catching movements with special effects between slides that you can add from the Ribbon's Transitions tab. For transitions as well as animation, you can set the timing to happen when the presenter clicks the mouse or to happen automatically at preset intervals.

You can also add movies from your local hard drive or directly from the Internet; plus, you can add recording narration for your slides.

THE ANIMATIONS TAB

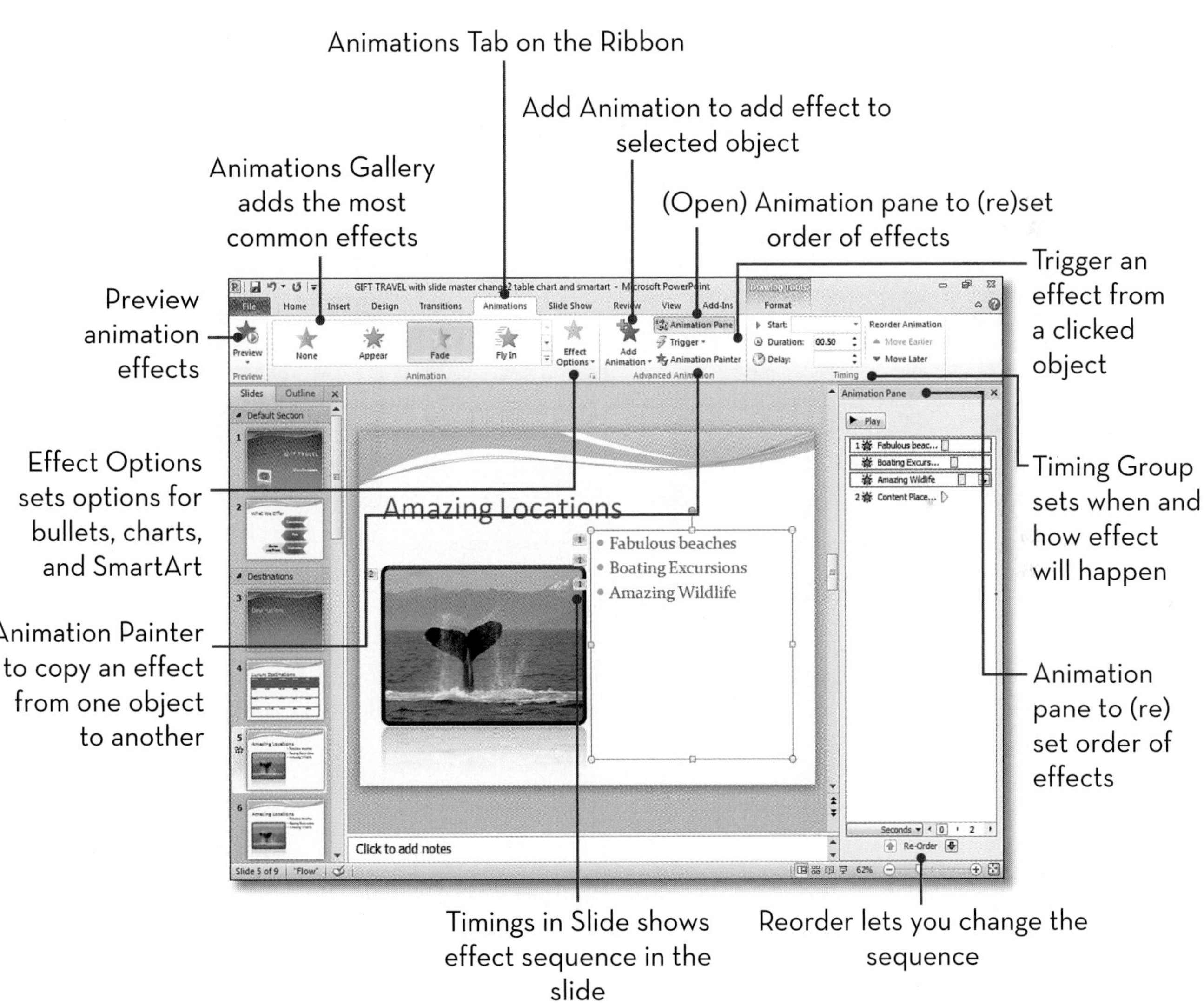

ADDING SLIDE TRANSITIONS

Transitions are movements such as fades, wipes, or other special effects that blend one slide into the next. You can apply transitions to some or all slides, determine how long they last, and determine whether they will happen with a mouse click by the presenter or automatically for a self-running show.

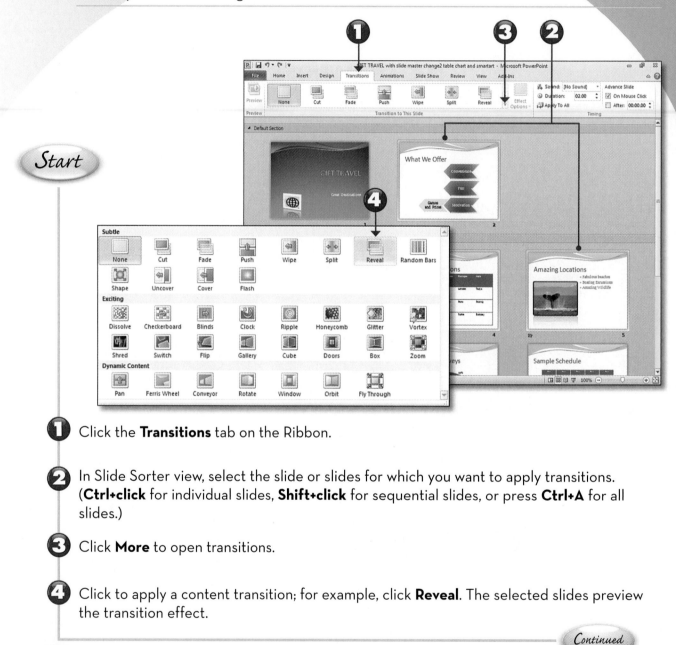

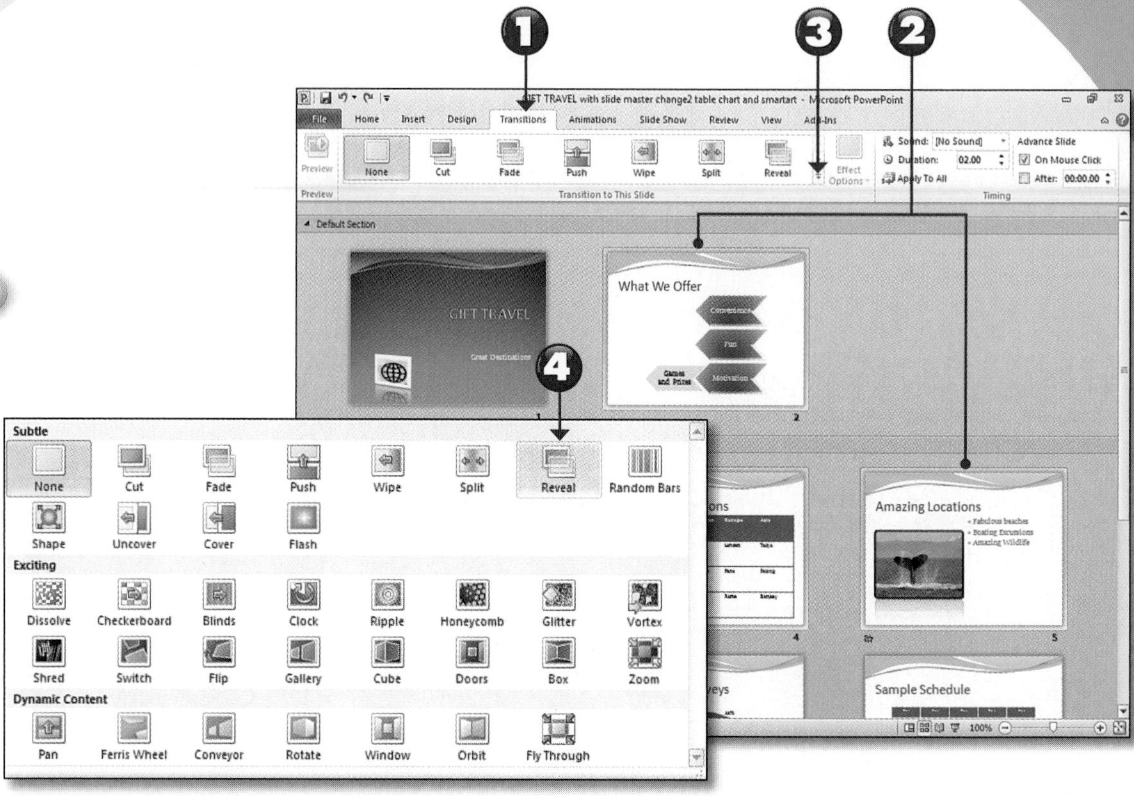

Start

1. Click the **Transitions** tab on the Ribbon.
2. In Slide Sorter view, select the slide or slides for which you want to apply transitions. (**Ctrl+click** for individual slides, **Shift+click** for sequential slides, or press **Ctrl+A** for all slides.)
3. Click **More** to open transitions.
4. Click to apply a content transition; for example, click **Reveal**. The selected slides preview the transition effect.

Continued

TIP

Removing Transitions You can clear transitions from all slides by clicking **None** in the Transitions gallery and then clicking **Apply to All**. ■

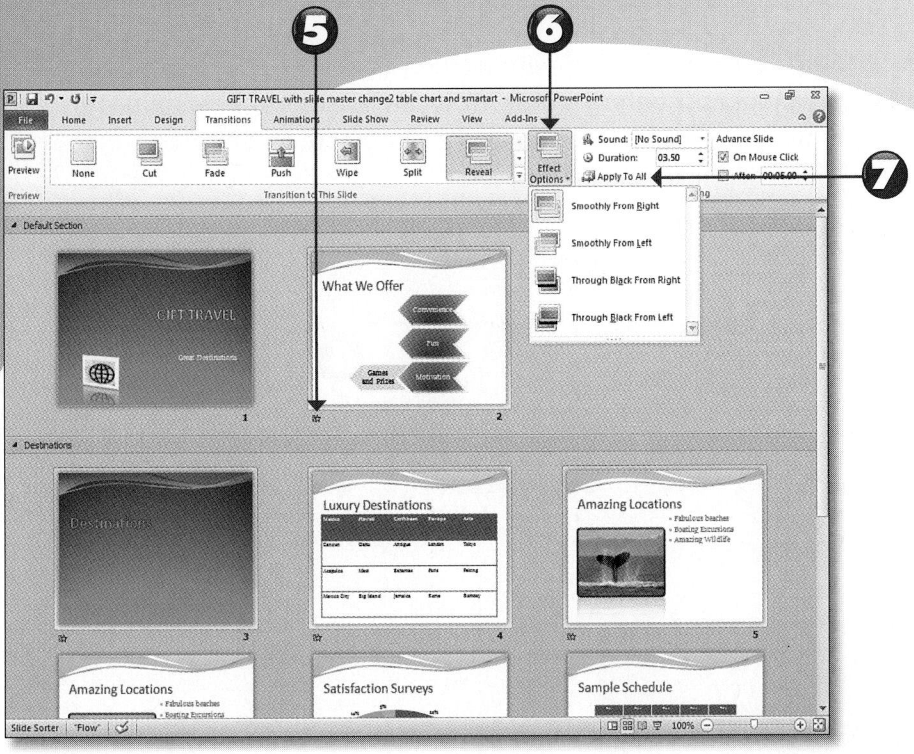

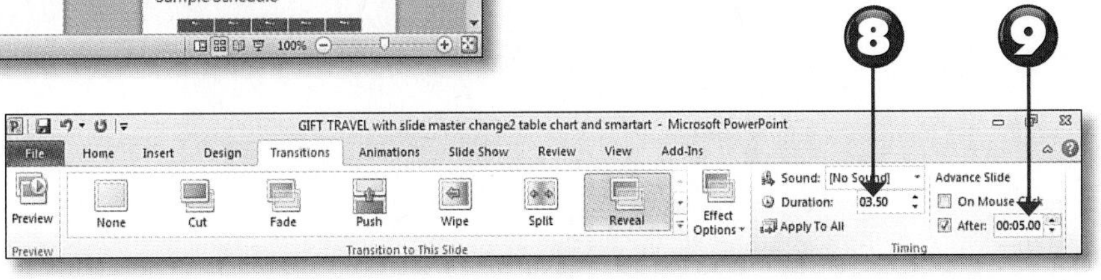

5 Each slide with a transition has a small star icon.

6 Click **Effect Options** to fine-tune the movement of some transitions.

7 You can click **Apply to All** to make the transition you selected apply to all slides.

8 You can using the Timing group to change the length of the transition for the selected slides.

9 You can using the Timing group to change whether the slides advance *automatically* after a set time (rather than on a mouse click) for the selected slides.

End

TIP

Using Rehearse Timings to Save Timings for Your Show You can use the Rehearse Timings feature in the Ribbon's Slide Show tab to present your show to an imaginary audience. At the end, you have the option to save those timings (as automatic) with the show. ■

ADDING ANIMATION TO CONTENT

Entrance animations can help you present information (such as bullets) in a sequential way and draw attention to each object as it enters a slide. You can use the Animation pane to change the order of the Animation effects. You can also give objects an Emphasis, Exit, or Motion Path animation to build sophisticated slides.

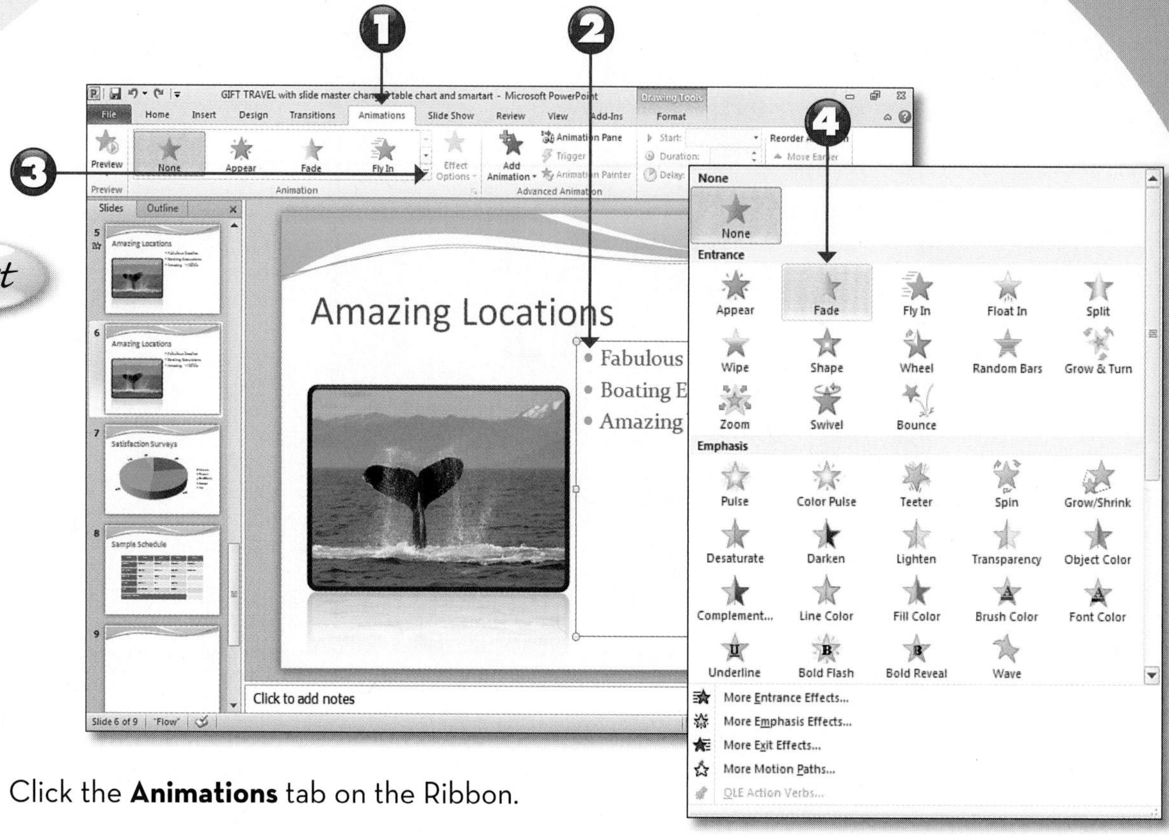

Start

1. Click the **Animations** tab on the Ribbon.
2. Select an object (such as your bullets) to which you want add an Animation effect.
3. Click **More** in the Animation group to open the animations.
4. Click to apply an Entrance effect; for example, click **Fade.** The chosen effect is previewed in the slide.

Continued

TIP

Changing the Order of Effects As you add effects to various objects in a slide, they appear in the Animation pane. When you click the **Reorder** arrows at the bottom of the Animation pane, you can change the sequence of the events by moving one above (before) or below (after) another. ■

TIP

Animating Charts and SmartArt When you apply an Entrance effect to a chart or SmartArt diagram, it applies to the entire object. But when it is selected in the Animation pane, you can click **Effect Options** in the Animation group or use the drop-down arrow beside the effect in the Animation pane to select specific options regarding how the components of the object appears. ■

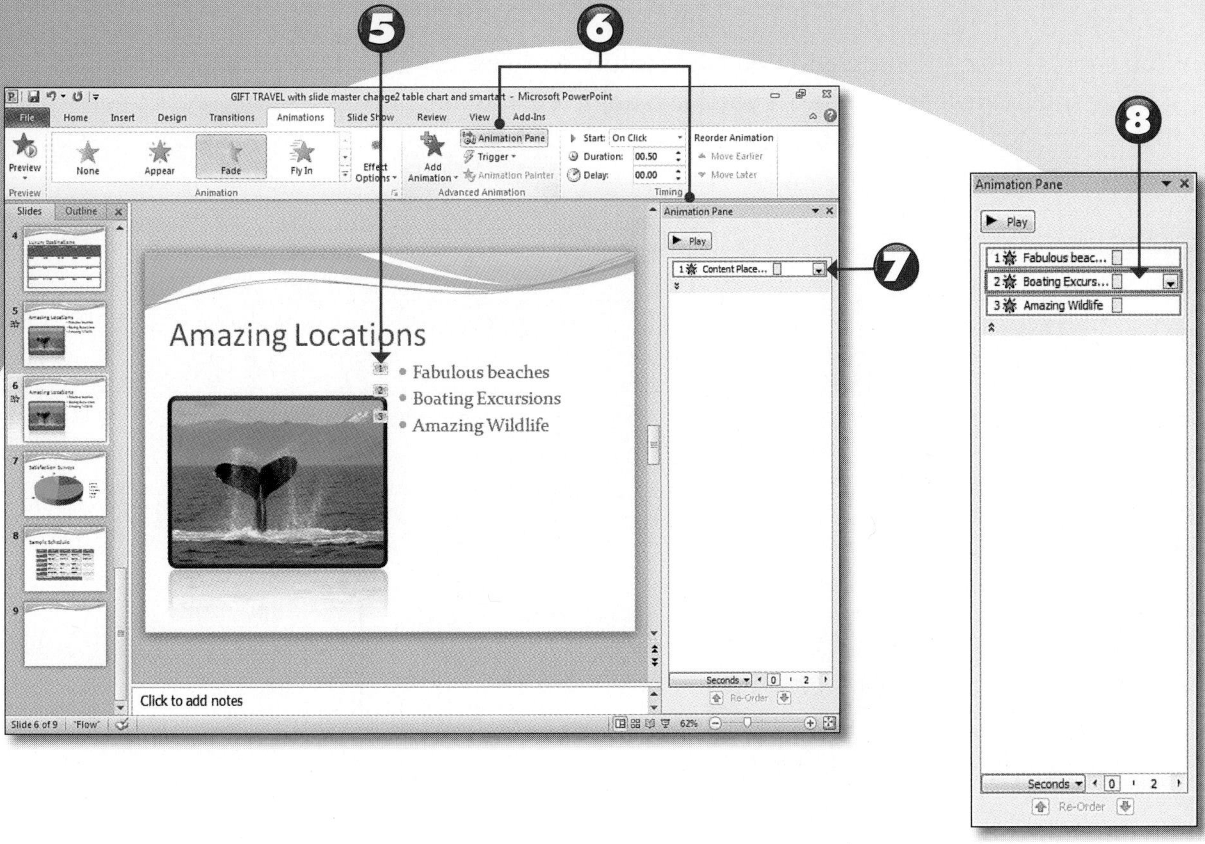

5. The sequential entrance of the bullets is shown in the slide.

6. You can click the **Animation Pane** button in the Advanced Animation group to open the Animation pane on the right side of the screen. The Animation pane shows the order of your Animation effects.

7. Click the drop-down arrow to expand the bullets.

8. In the Animation pane, the duration of each bullet entrance is shown as a small bar; you can move or resize the bars to adjust the timings.

End

TIP

Changing the Timings You can change the duration of an Animation effect by dragging out its icon in the Animation pane. You also can drag one effect to happen after the other. You can use the **Start** drop-down arrow in the Timing group to adjust the delay, duration, and whether an effect is to occur when the presenter clicks the mouse or after a certain period after the previous effect has happened or with the previous effect. ■

USING THE ANIMATION PAINTER TOOL

You can use the new Animation Painter feature to "pick up" an Animation effect from one object and apply it to another. If you have adjusted specific timings to your favorite effects, this can be a time-saving tool.

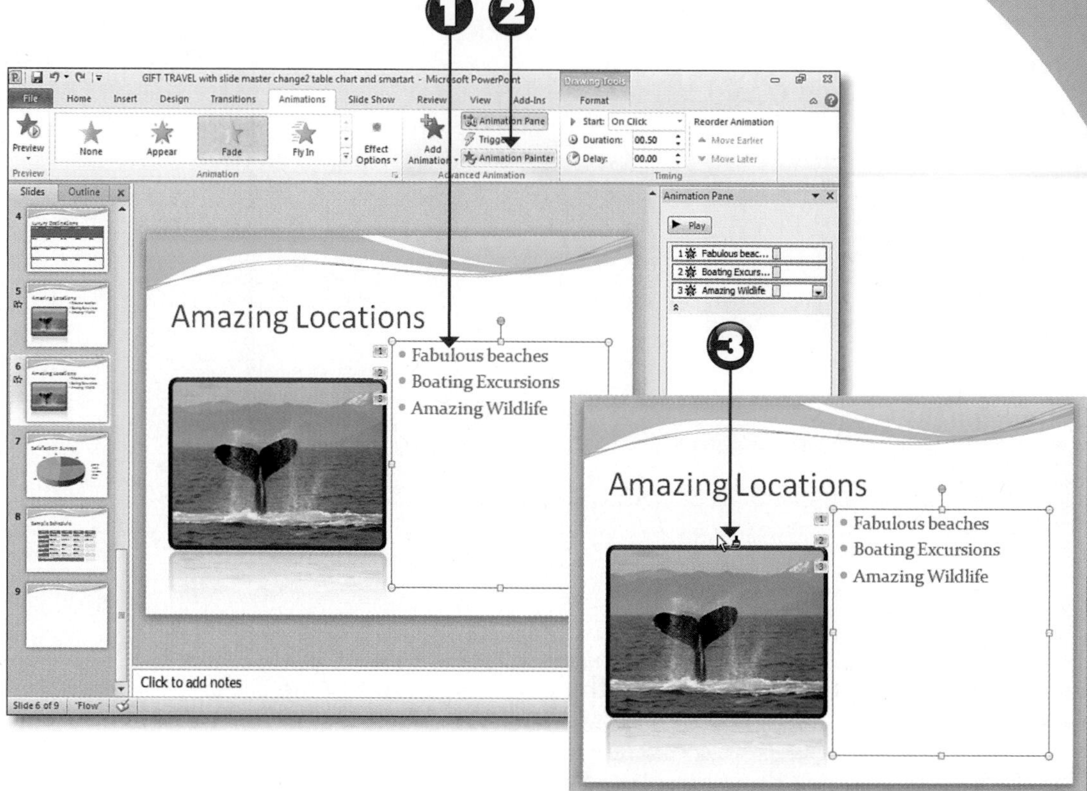

Start

1. Select the object with the Animation effect you want to use.

2. Click **Animation Painter** in the Ribbon's Animations tab.

3. After the mouse cursor turns into a small paintbrush, click the object to which you want to apply the effect.

Continued

NOTE

Using Preview You can click **Preview** any time to see how the animations you've added will play in the slide. You can also press **Shift+F5** to play the current slide full screen to see how the animations will work in the actual presentation. ■

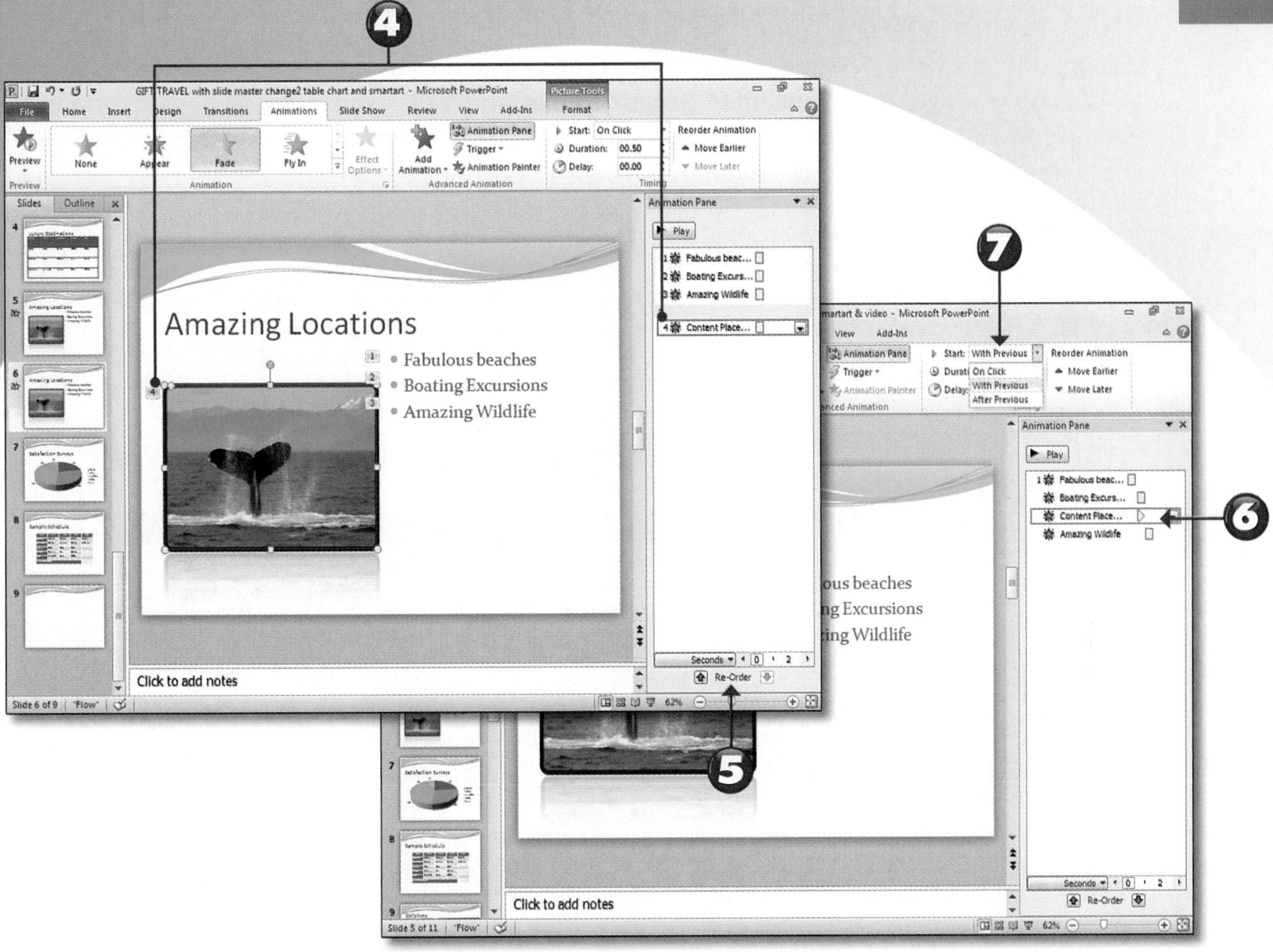

4. With the effect applied, it is added to the Animation pane.

5. You can click the **Re-Order** up arrow to move it to appear before the last bullet.

6. You can expand its duration icon to make the animation take more time.

7. You can change its start from On Click to With Previous to have it appear in concert with the bullet that describes it.

End

TIP

Using Triggers After you add an effect to an object, you can select that effect to be triggered by the click of another object. To do so, click **Trigger** in the Advanced Animation group and select the object you want to serve as the trigger for the effect. ■

INSERTING AND TRIMMING VIDEO

Using video or movies is a great way to tell your story, and PowerPoint can present video in a slide show, allowing the presenter to click to play and pause the video or have it play automatically. You can also "trim" the video in PowerPoint 2010, which means setting new begin and end points for the clip to eliminate unwanted portions of the video.

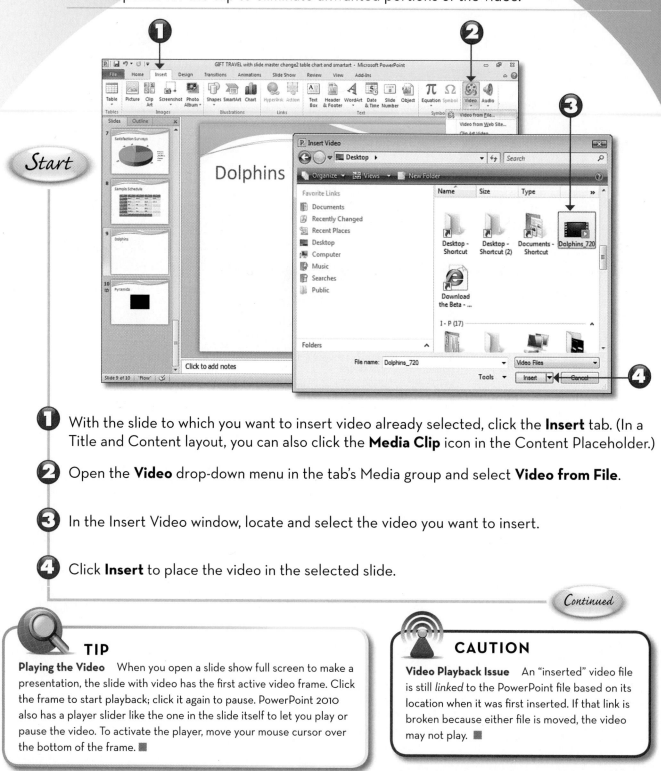

Start

1. With the slide to which you want to insert video already selected, click the **Insert** tab. (In a Title and Content layout, you can also click the **Media Clip** icon in the Content Placeholder.)
2. Open the **Video** drop-down menu in the tab's Media group and select **Video from File**.
3. In the Insert Video window, locate and select the video you want to insert.
4. Click **Insert** to place the video in the selected slide.

Continued

TIP

Playing the Video When you open a slide show full screen to make a presentation, the slide with video has the first active video frame. Click the frame to start playback; click it again to pause. PowerPoint 2010 also has a player slider like the one in the slide itself to let you play or pause the video. To activate the player, move your mouse cursor over the bottom of the frame. ■

CAUTION

Video Playback Issue An "inserted" video file is still *linked* to the PowerPoint file based on its location when it was first inserted. If that link is broken because either file is moved, the video may not play. ■

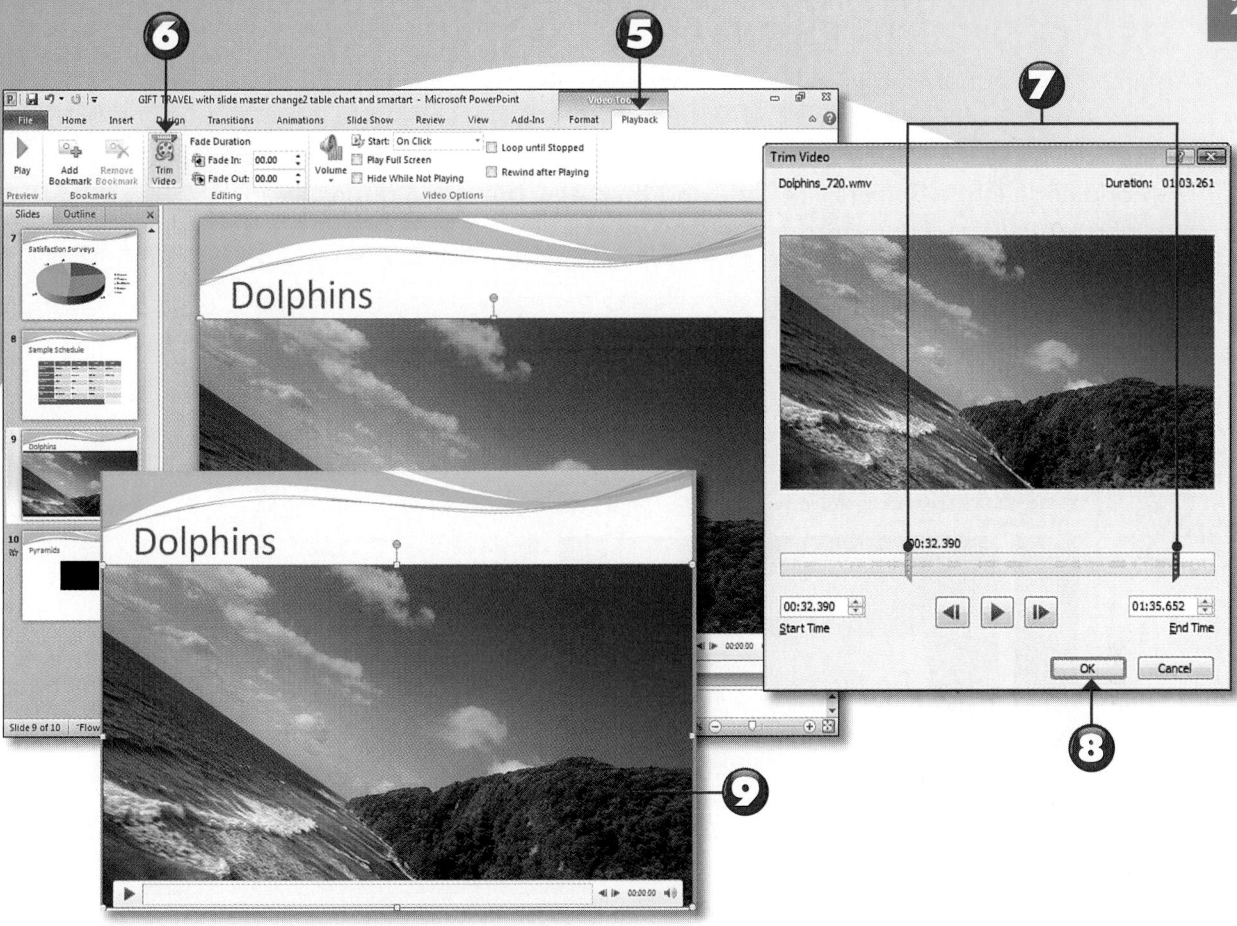

5 The Video Tools tabs appear on the Ribbon. Click the **Playback** tab if it isn't already selected.

6 Click **Trim Video**.

7 Drag the sliders to create new begin and end points for the clip. (You can use the Preview window to help you find the right frames or set the start and end times.)

8 Click **OK**.

9 The video plays the selected segment when played in the slide. To play the video full screen from that slide, press **Shift+F5**.

End

TIP

Video Enhancements You can use the **Format** tab in the Ribbon's Video Tools to add a border or styles to the appearance of your video in the slide. ■

TIP

Video File Formats PowerPoint natively supports the *.WMV (Windows Media), *.AVI, and *.MPG video formats. It can also import *.MOV and *.SWF (Adobe Flash Media) formats under **Insert Video from File**. ■

USING ONLINE VIDEO

Many *video hosting* services are available online where you can share videos and display them in web pages using their *embed code*, which is the HTML that references the video location and tells the web browser how to display it. You can also copy and paste this embed code into a PowerPoint slide and then play the video during a slide show *as long as you are reliably connected to the Internet*.

Start

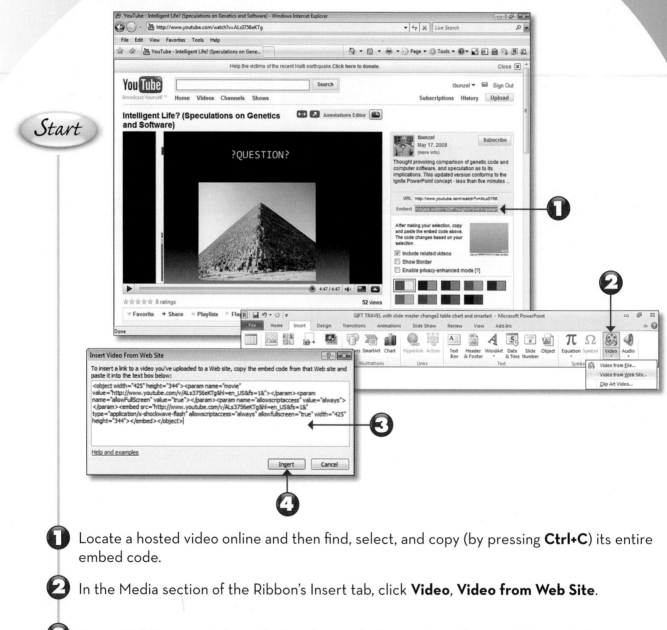

1. Locate a hosted video online and then find, select, and copy (by pressing **Ctrl+C**) its entire embed code.
2. In the Media section of the Ribbon's Insert tab, click **Video**, **Video from Web Site**.
3. Press **Ctrl+V** to paste the embed code into the Insert Video from Web Site window.
4. Click **Insert**.

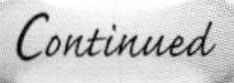

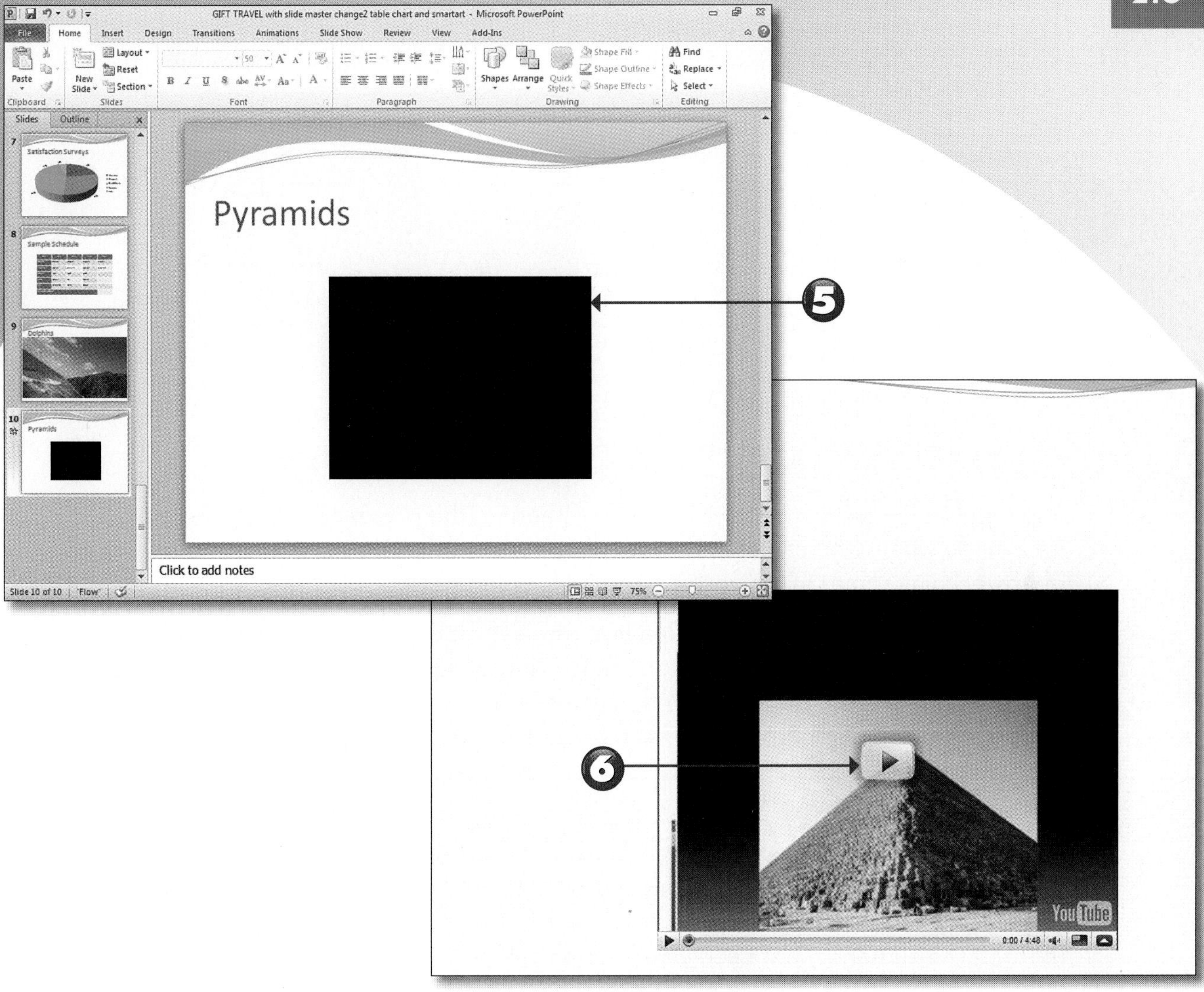

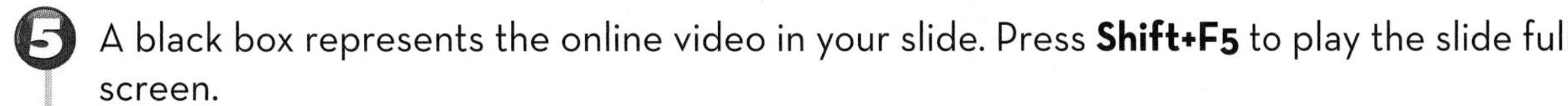

5 A black box represents the online video in your slide. Press **Shift+F5** to play the slide full screen.

6 With your web connection active, the video will load into the slide and allow you to play it during a slide show.

End

TIP

Previewing in the Slide You can right-click an online video within a slide and select **Preview** to see it play within the slide in PowerPoint. ■

COMPLETING THE PRESENTATION

The focus in PowerPoint 2010 thus far has been on the program itself or the editing mode where you can create slides to tell your story. But the actual impact of PowerPoint comes in delivering the presentation itself.

PowerPoint 2010 features a new Reading view, which lets you preview the presentation while you are still in the editor. In addition to rehearsing your slides, you also can record a slide show with narration and timings so that you can save and send that show to others and have them watch it as you deliver it. In addition, you can use Backstage view to create a video of your show to upload to the Web or send to others.

For your audience, you can print handouts or put supplemental information in your notes to distribute as a booklet after a presentation or as follow-up. When you make your presentation, you can use a dual monitor setup that lets you (but not the audience) both see what's coming next and refer to your notes.

With the PowerPoint web application, you can collaborate with your colleagues on a presentation and even deliver it online to those with a web browser.

THE SLIDE SHOW TAB

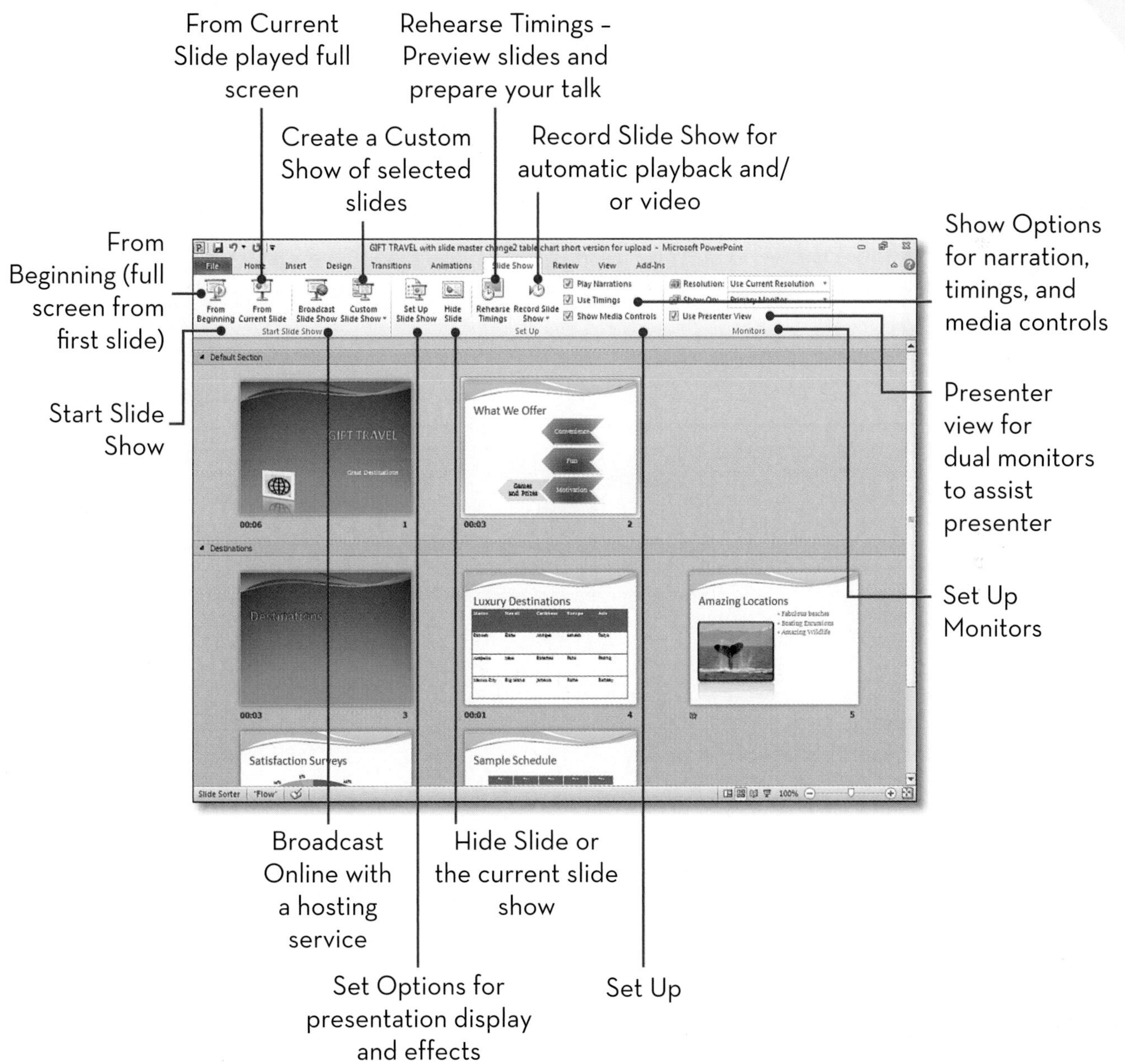

PREVIEWING SLIDES IN READING VIEW

PowerPoint 2010 provides a Reading view, which lets you move through your slides, including the animations and transitions, so that you can check any media without opening the show full screen. Reading view has forward and back buttons for navigation, along with a menu that lets you move through the presentation to specific slides.

Start

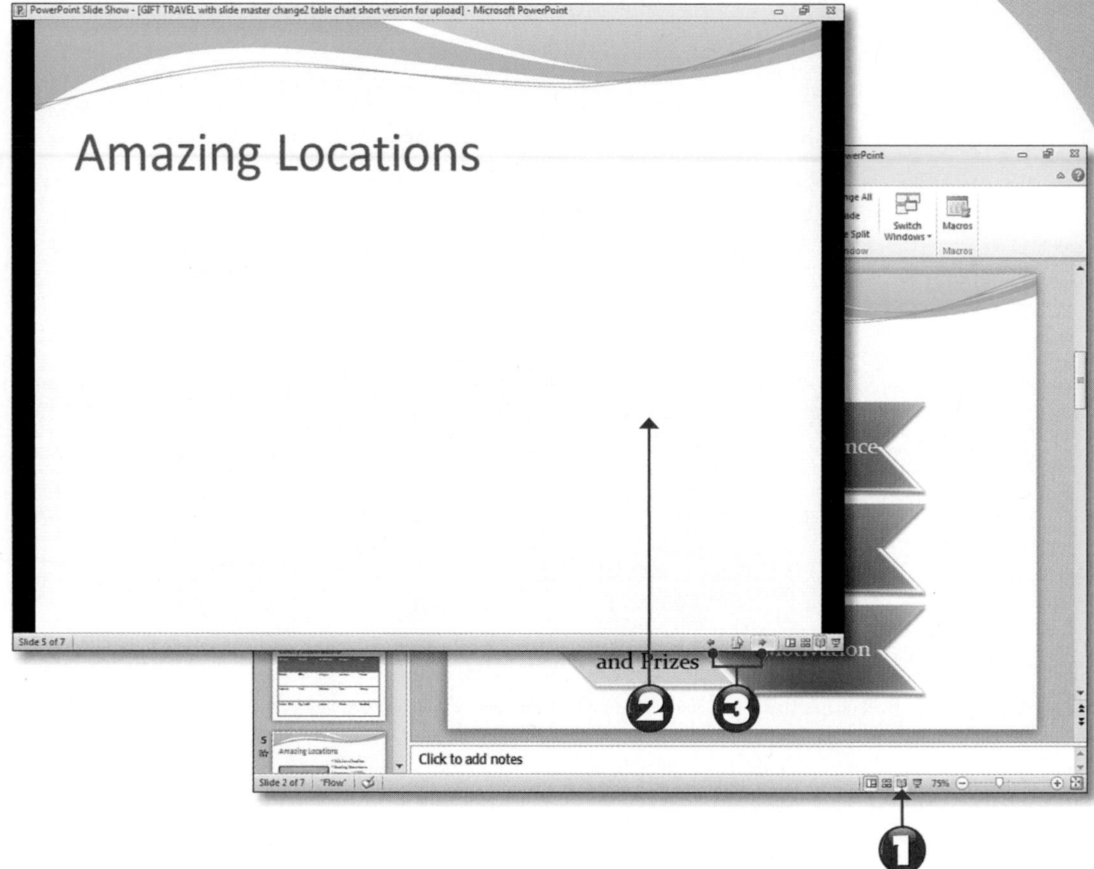

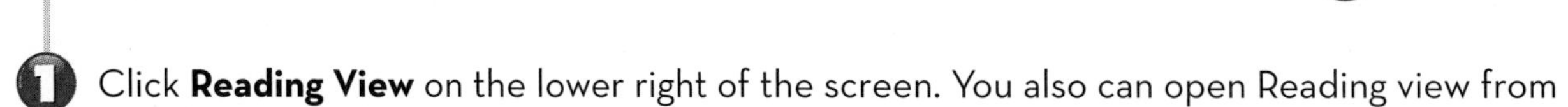

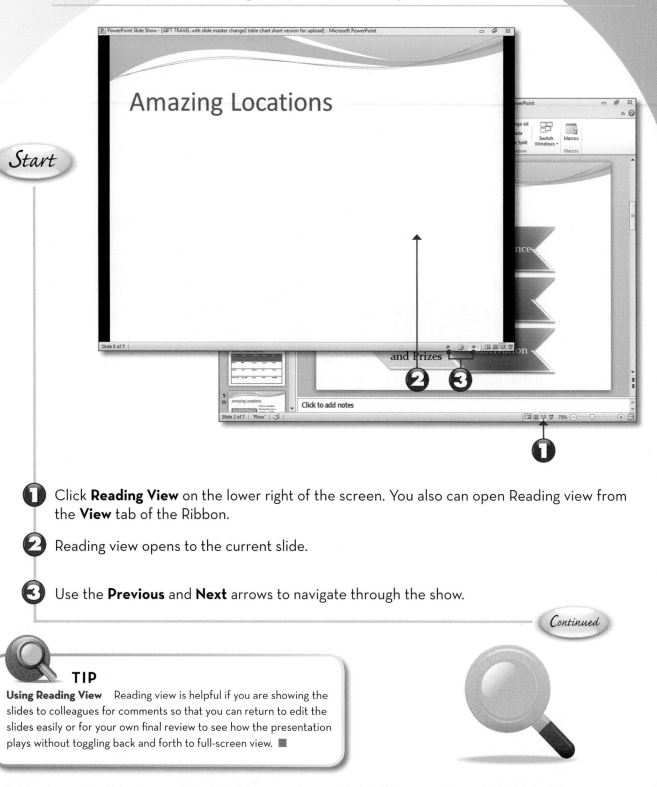

1. Click **Reading View** on the lower right of the screen. You also can open Reading view from the **View** tab of the Ribbon.
2. Reading view opens to the current slide.
3. Use the **Previous** and **Next** arrows to navigate through the show.

Continued

TIP

Using Reading View Reading view is helpful if you are showing the slides to colleagues for comments so that you can return to edit the slides easily or for your own final review to see how the presentation plays without toggling back and forth to full-screen view. ■

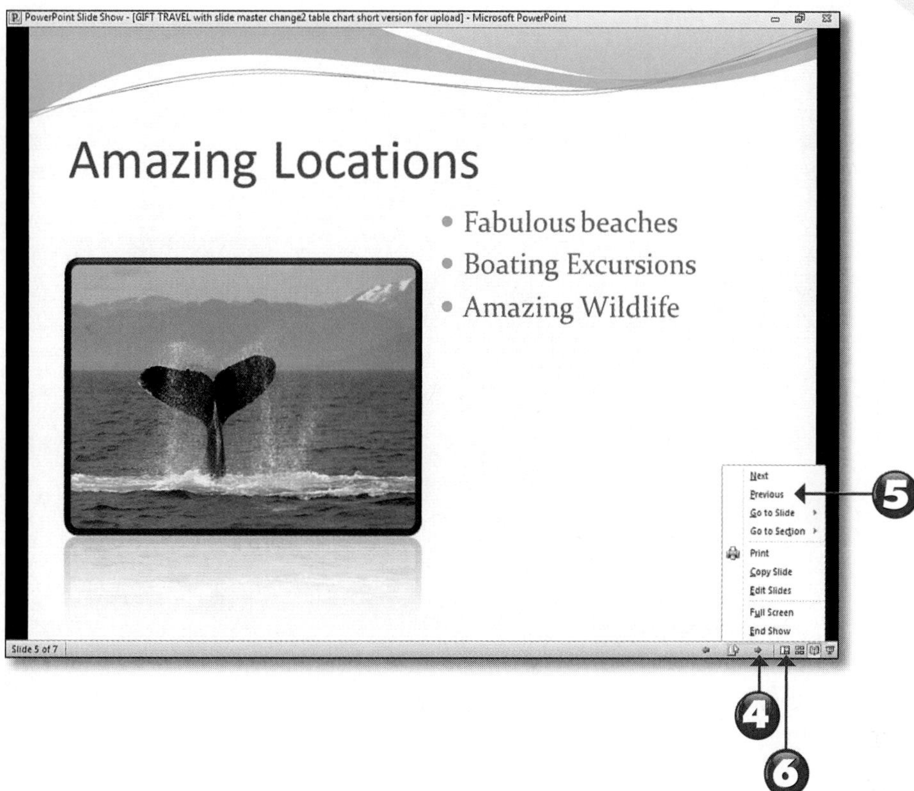

4 Click the **Forward** arrow to play the next animation.

5 You can click **Menu** to navigate to a slide (by title) or section, along with other options.

6 Click **Normal View** to return to the current slide (or press the **Esc** key).

End

TIP

Projecting Reading View With a simple projector setup, you can show Reading view to your audience and use it to make your presentation. Note that the filename of the presentation appears on a small strip at the top of the screen.

RECORDING YOUR PRESENTATION

Record Slide Show is a feature that lets you go through the show as you would present it, narrate your slides, and save all the transition and animation timings with your show. To record narration, you need to have a working microphone set up in Windows. Then, as you play each slide, you can speak into the microphone, and your narration is saved as an embedded audio file with each slide.

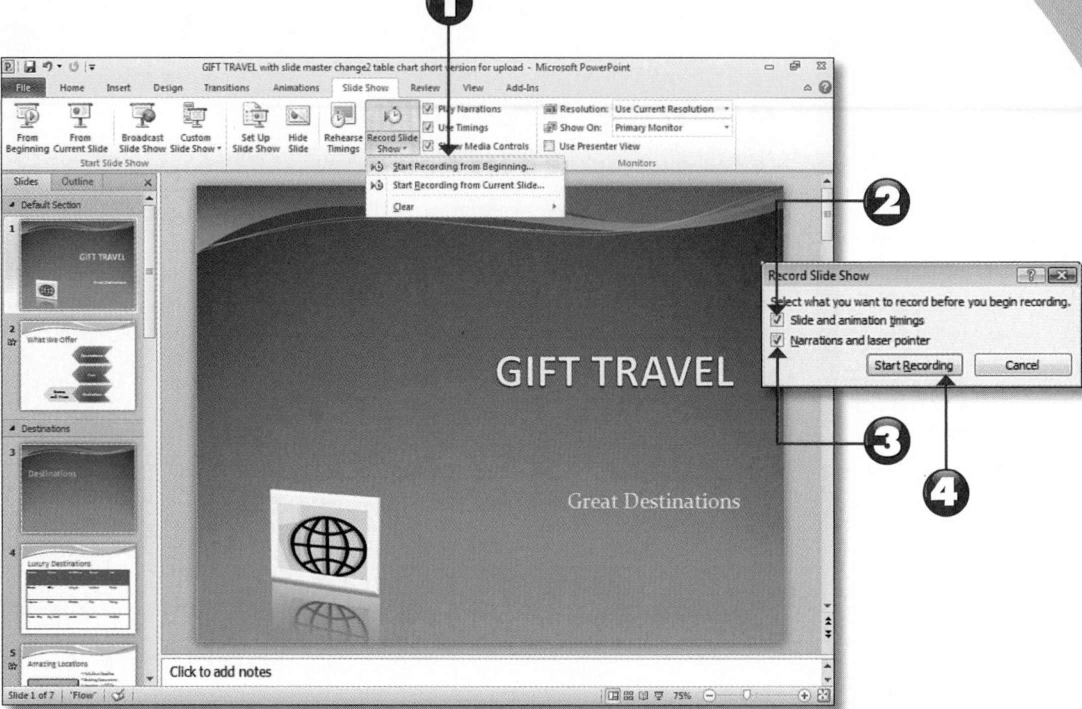

Start

1. On the Ribbon's Slide Show tab, click **Record Slide Show**, **Start Recording from Beginning**.
2. Enable the **Slide and Animation Timings** check box if you want to record the amount of time each slide should remain on the screen.
3. Enable the **Narrations and Laser Pointer** check box to record audio for your presentation and use Ctrl + click to record a laser pointer to highlight areas of the slides.
4. Click **Start Recording**.

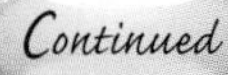

TIP

Getting Rid of Recorded Elements Because your recorded timings and narration would interfere if you were to play the show to an audience with a presenter, you can clear narration and timings by clicking **Record Slide Show**. You can also present the show and uncheck **Play Narrations**, Use **Timings and Show Media Controls** in the Set Up group of the Ribbon's Slide Show tab. ■

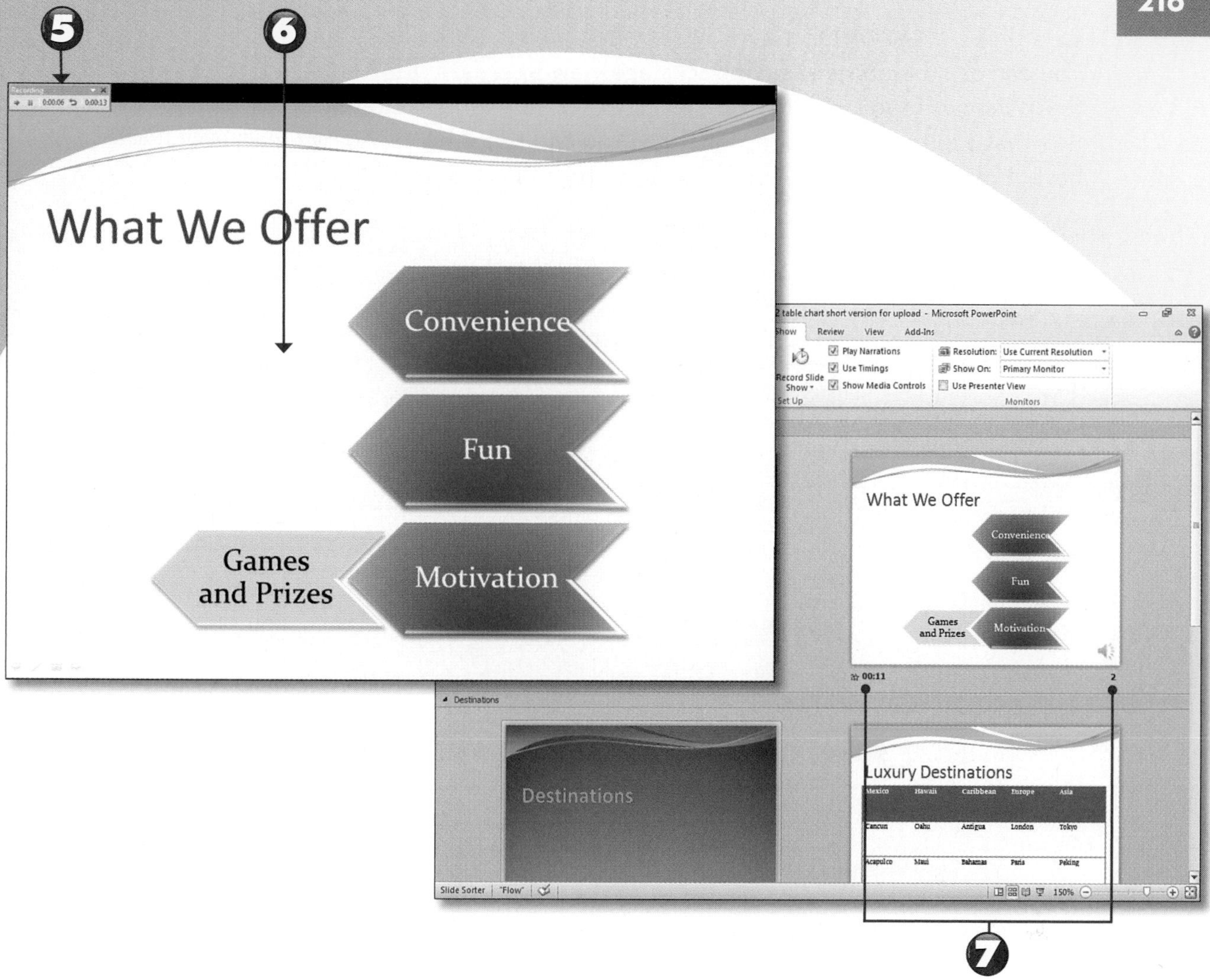

5 Your presentation opens full screen with a timer showing your progress. You can also end your recording using these controls.

6 Click through your slides and animations normally as you narrate through the show. You can click to the end of the show or press **Esc** to end on another slide.

7 You can see your timings (duration of slides), transitions, and an icon representing your audio in the narrated slides in Slide Sorter view.

End

TIP

Saving the Show You can save a special version of your show to maintain your saved timings and narration by clicking **File** and choosing **Save As in Backstage view**. You can choose to save as a PowerPoint Show file that will play full screen when sent to the others who have PowerPoint. ■

CREATING A VIDEO OF YOUR SHOW

You can use the Share area of Backstage view to create self-running video of your show in the Windows Media (*.WMV) file format. This video incorporates all the timings and narration that you recorded with your show. You can send the movie by email, post it online, or have it hosted on a video hosting website to show to others.

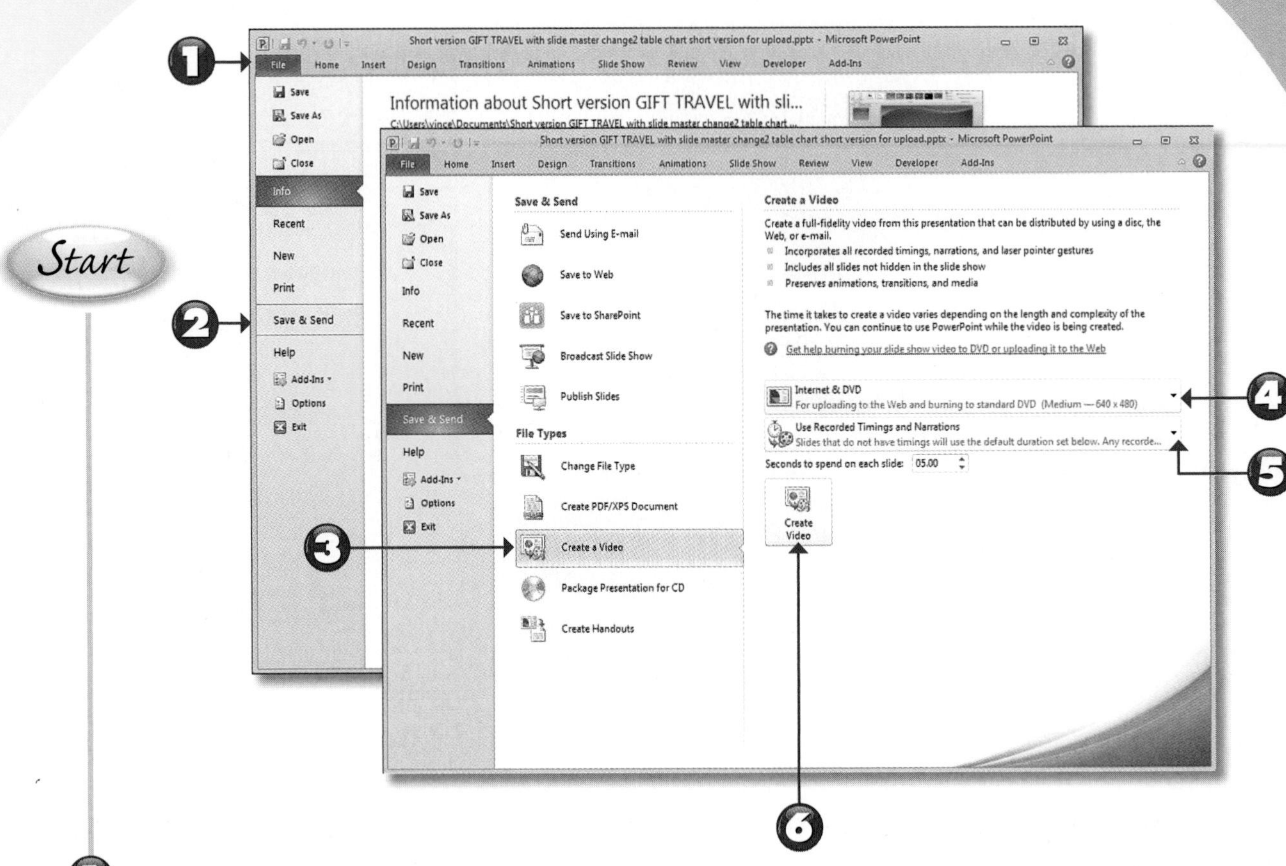

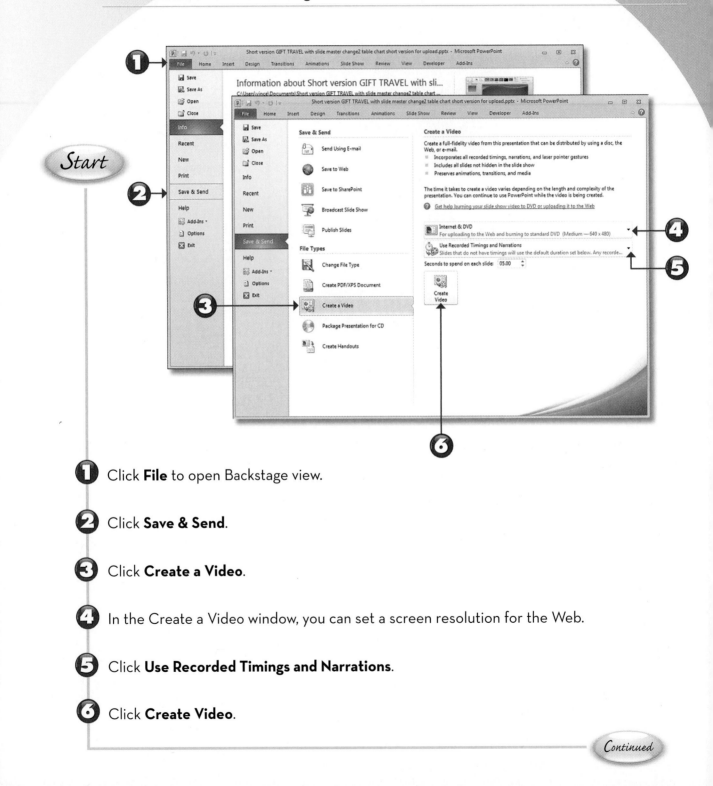

1. Click **File** to open Backstage view.
2. Click **Save & Send**.
3. Click **Create a Video**.
4. In the Create a Video window, you can set a screen resolution for the Web.
5. Click **Use Recorded Timings and Narrations**.
6. Click **Create Video**.

Continued

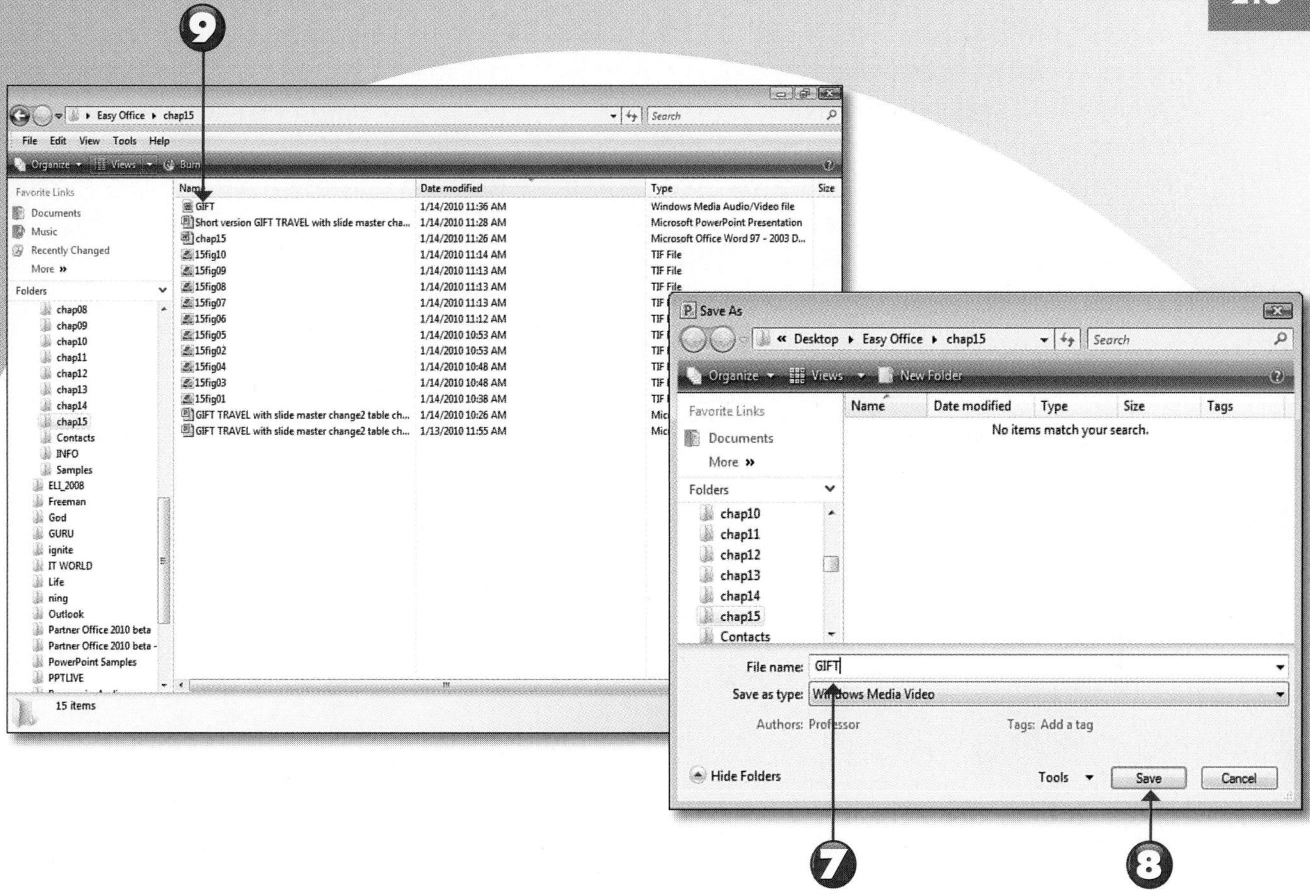

7. In the Save As window, choose a folder location for the video file and enter a filename.

8. Click **Save**. A progress bar at the bottom of the PowerPoint window indicates the approximate time to completion; creating the video may take some time, depending on the complexity of the slides.

9. After the video is created, it is available in the folder where it was saved.

End

TIP

Hosting Video and Recorded Slide Shows Most video hosting sites such as YouTube accept an upload (and convert) your *.WMV file to YouTube's video format. There are also presentation hosting sites such as AuthorSTREAM.com that accept the recorded presentation to host and allow you to link to or embed the show in a web page or blog. ■

TIP

Broadcast Slide Show The **Broadcast Slide Show** button in the Set Up group of the Ribbon's Slide Show tab lets you access an online conferencing service from Microsoft to present your show online and invite others to watch. ■

PRINTING NOTES AND HANDOUTS

When you print your slides in Backstage view, you can also include notes that you wrote in your Notes panel in Normal view. You can use these notes yourself to prepare your presentation, or you can add supplemental information to print for your audience as a handout. (You may want to save different versions of your file for each purpose.) You can also use the Notes Master to format the look of your notes. (See "Using Slide Masters" in Chapter 12, "Getting Started with PowerPoint 2010.")

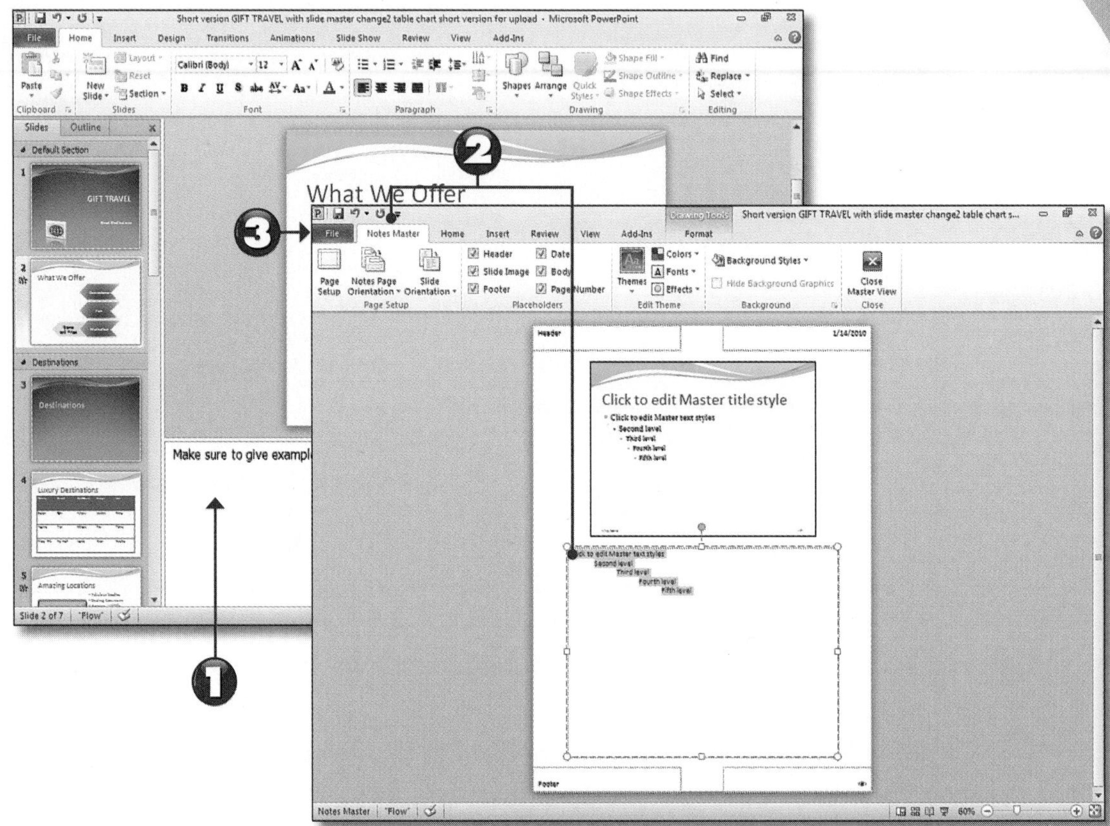

1. In your slide, enter information in the Notes panel.
2. Notes Master view lets you format your notes page before printing To open Notes Master view, click the Ribbon's **View** tab and then click **Notes Master view**.
3. Click the **File** tab.

Continued

TIP

Providing Audience Notes Area The 3 Slides configuration for printing lets you print blank lines for an audience to take notes in handouts. ■

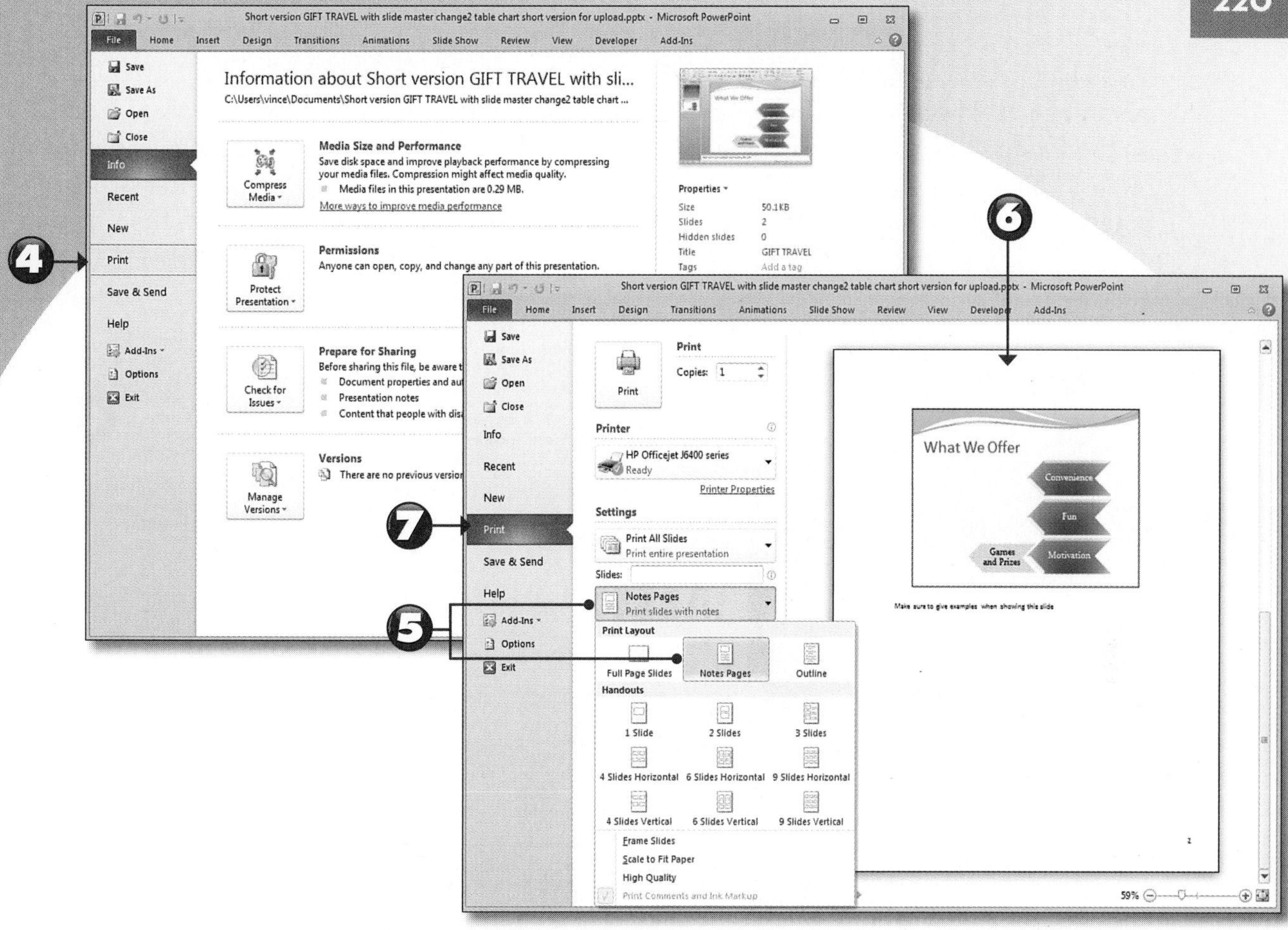

4. In Backstage view, click **Print**.

5. Select **Notes Pages** from the drop-down menu.

6. Check the print preview on the right to ensure the overall look of your print job matches your expectations.

7. Click **Print**.

End

TIP

Printing as PDF You can use the **Save As** button in Backstage view to save your presentation as a PDF file (click the **Save as Type** drop-down arrow and select PDF). When the PDF file is created, you can open it in a PDF reader program and print it. ■

USING PRESENTER VIEW

If you have multiple displays available to your system during a presentation, you can take advantage of PowerPoint's Presenter View. By using Presenter view in the Monitors group on the Ribbon's Slide Show tab, you can use one display to show you what's coming next and remind you what to say, while at the same time controlling your presentation and making annotations, as the actual presentation projects on a projector or is viewed on another monitor.

Start

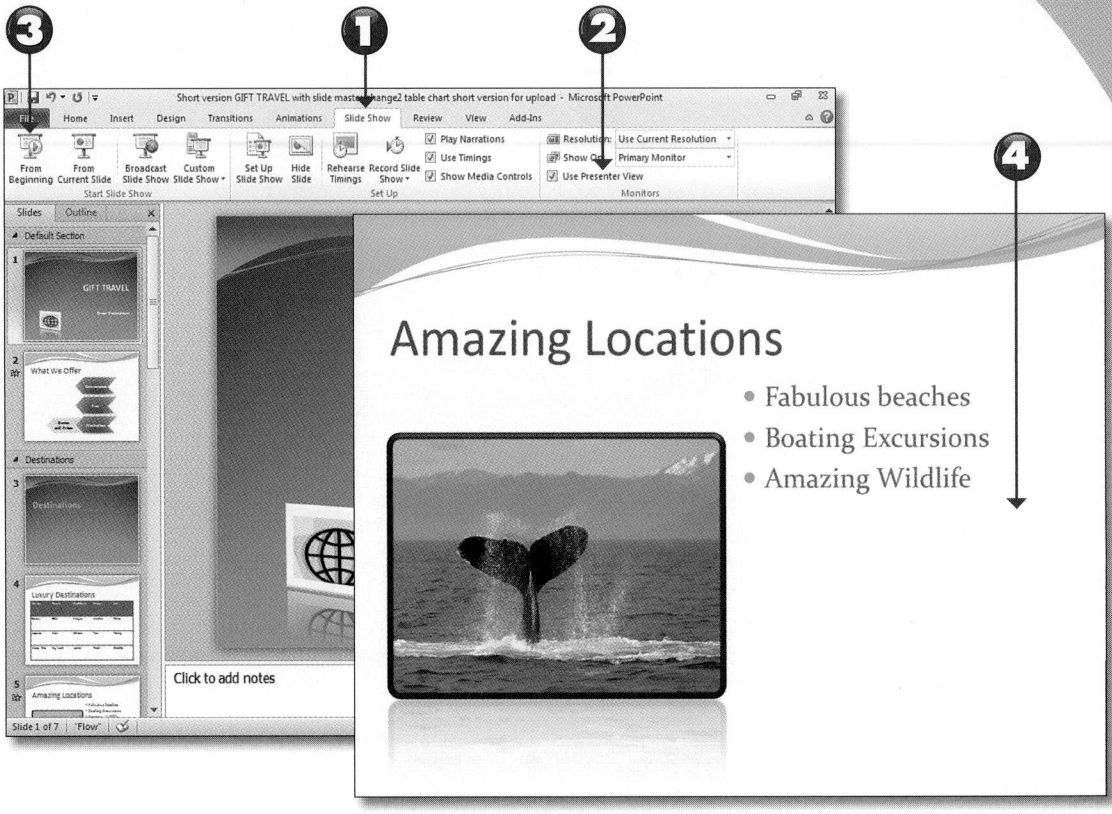

1. Click the **Slide Show** tab on the Ribbon.
2. Click to enable Presenter View.
3. Click **From Beginning** to start the show.
4. The slide show appears full screen on your main monitor or projector.

TIP

Going to Slide Thumbnails You can click a slide thumbnail at the bottom of Projector view to jump to another slide. ■

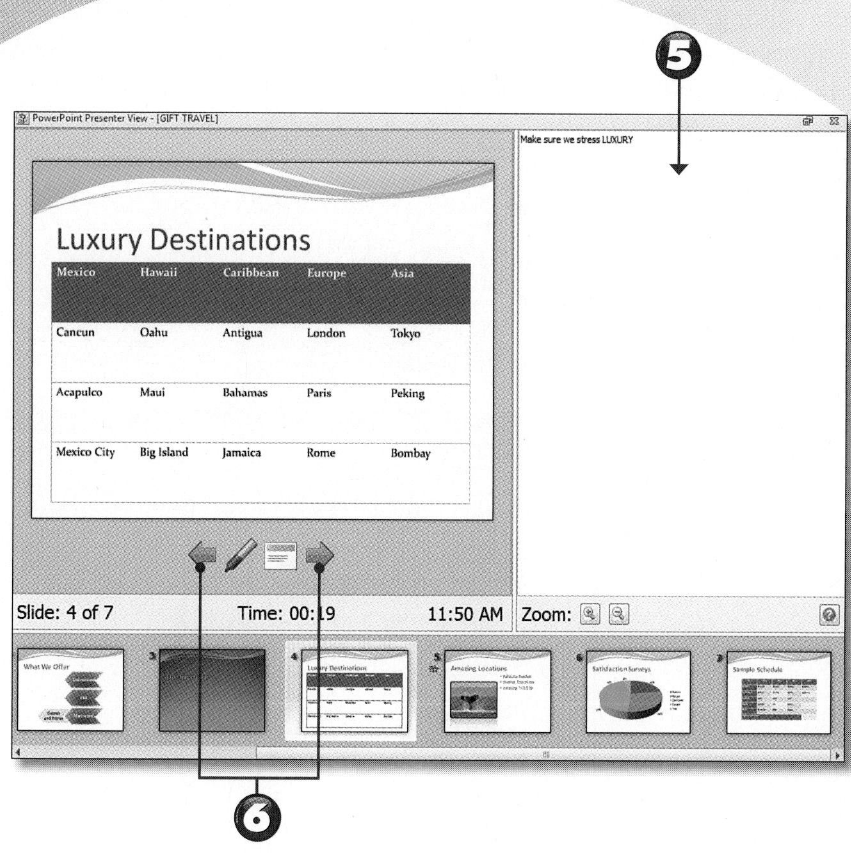

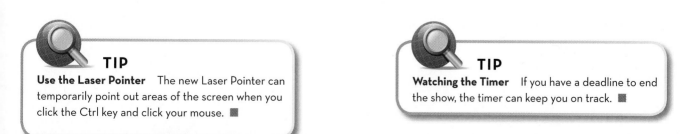

5 Presenter View is a control panel for your show that is visible only on your screen and not the presentation's display device. It includes a view of the slide presentation, notes for the presenter, and some other information and controls.

6 You can advance slides or use arrows to go back and use the Annotation tool to highlight significant parts of your slide(s). Press **Esc** to end the presentation and return to the PowerPoint editor.

End

TIP

Use the Laser Pointer The new Laser Pointer can temporarily point out areas of the screen when you click the Ctrl key and click your mouse. ■

TIP

Watching the Timer If you have a deadline to end the show, the timer can keep you on track. ■

PRESENTING FROM THE POWERPOINT WEB APP

PowerPoint 2010 has a light version that works as a web application, or *web app*. You can do simple editing from the Home and Insert tabs on the web app's Ribbon; add a picture, SmartArt, or hyperlink from the Insert tab; and view notes, use the Reading view, or actually watch the presentation from the View tab.

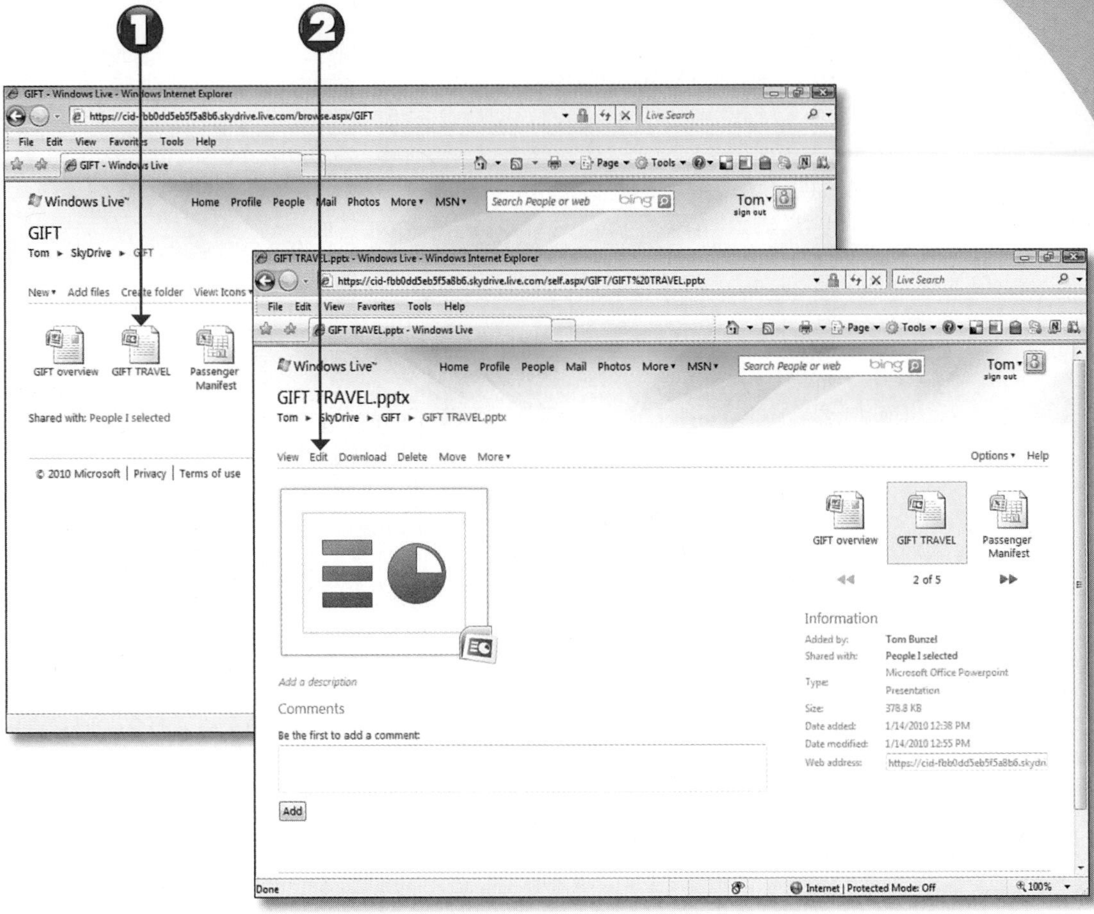

Start

1. In your online workspace, click an uploaded PowerPoint file. (See "Uploading a File to Your Folder" in Chapter 7, "Reviewing Documents and Working Online.")
2. Click **Edit**.

Continued

TIP

Saved Timings If you have saved a rehearsed or recorded version of your presentation and uploaded it to the web application, when it is played full screen, it will use those automatic timings. ■

3 You can do simple editing in the PowerPoint web app.

4 Click the **View** tab.

5 Click **Slide Show**.

6 The slide show plays full screen in the web browser with any transitions, animations, and timings. You can press **Esc** or use the **Back** button in your browser to return to the PowerPoint web app.

End

TIP

Playing Narration or Video If you have recorded narration or used a video file in your presentation, it does not play presently in the web applications. Consider using the features covered in "Creating a Video of Your Show" and uploading the video to an online hosting service.

ORGANIZING YOUR PROJECT WITH ONENOTE

OneNote is a note-taking program originally designed to read ink on tablet PCs, but it is a remarkably efficient way to keep track of a wide variety of different information and data and even share your information with others. The model for OneNote is the format of a day planner or loose-leaf notebook, with main tabs for separate notebooks on the left panel, tabs for sections within the currently open notebook on the top of the window, and pages within each section, with named tabs for specific topics on the right panel.

Like the other Office applications, OneNote 2010 uses a Ribbon to access its various features, and there is a OneNote web application available to share your notes directly online. OneNote also puts an icon on your taskbar that lets you immediately open and create a note with formatting. Such Side Notes go into an Unfiled Notes section of your notebook, but you can move them into another section to keep them organized.

One of the best ways to use OneNote is to collect information from the Web by copying and pasting material into named OneNote pages. OneNote pastes not only the content itself, but also a reference URL, or web address, so that you can easily return to the source material.

OneNote also provides robust capability for searching through your notebooks using a Search panel and Navigation pane. There are tags to help you organize items and quick links to send items to and from other Office programs; for example, tasks can be sent and received from Outlook.

THE ONENOTE WINDOW

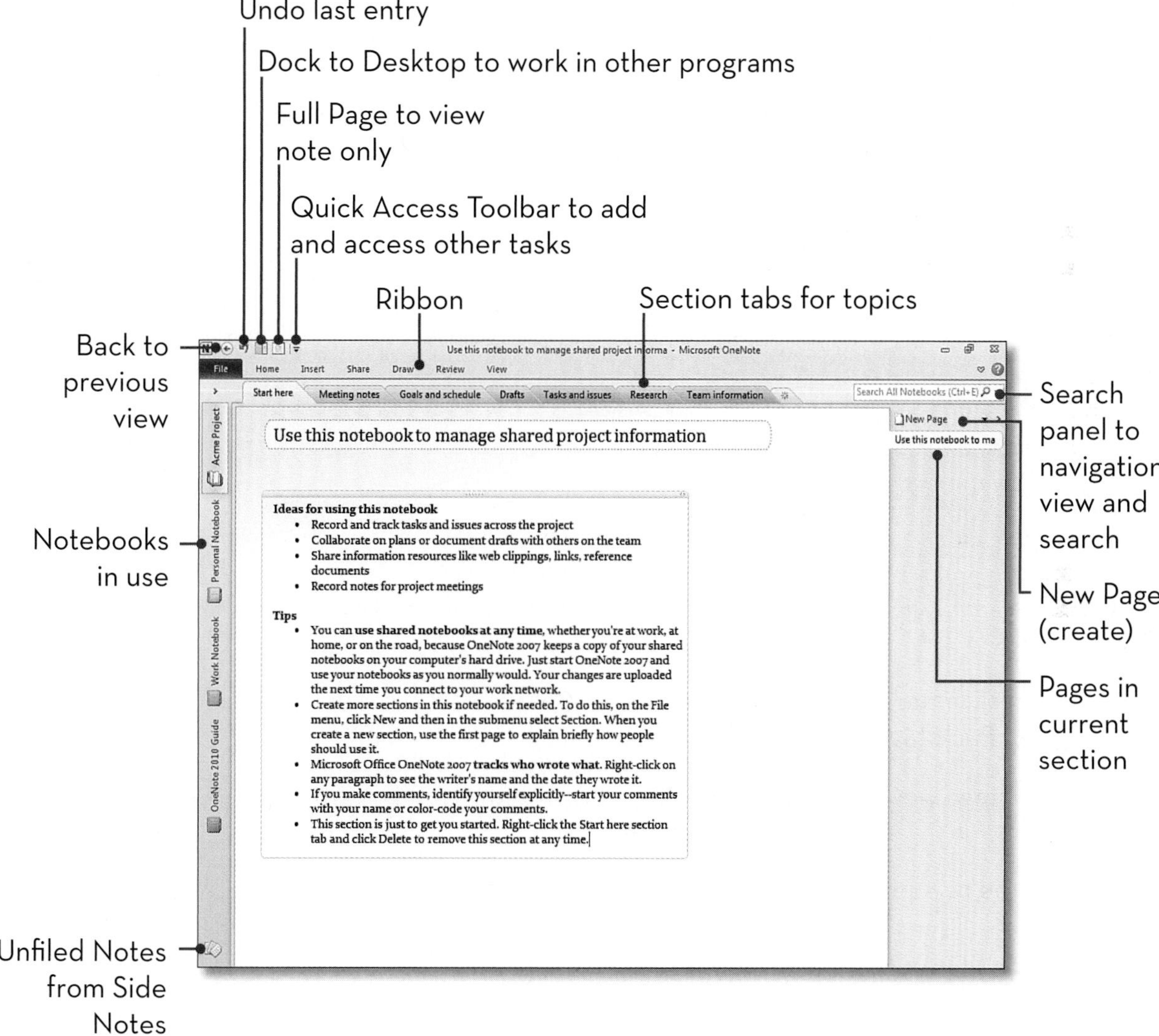

STARTING A NEW NOTEBOOK

A notebook is a collection of named sections, each with its own set of named pages. For a specific project, you can create a new notebook or designate a section in a current notebook, depending on the amount of information you expect to add.

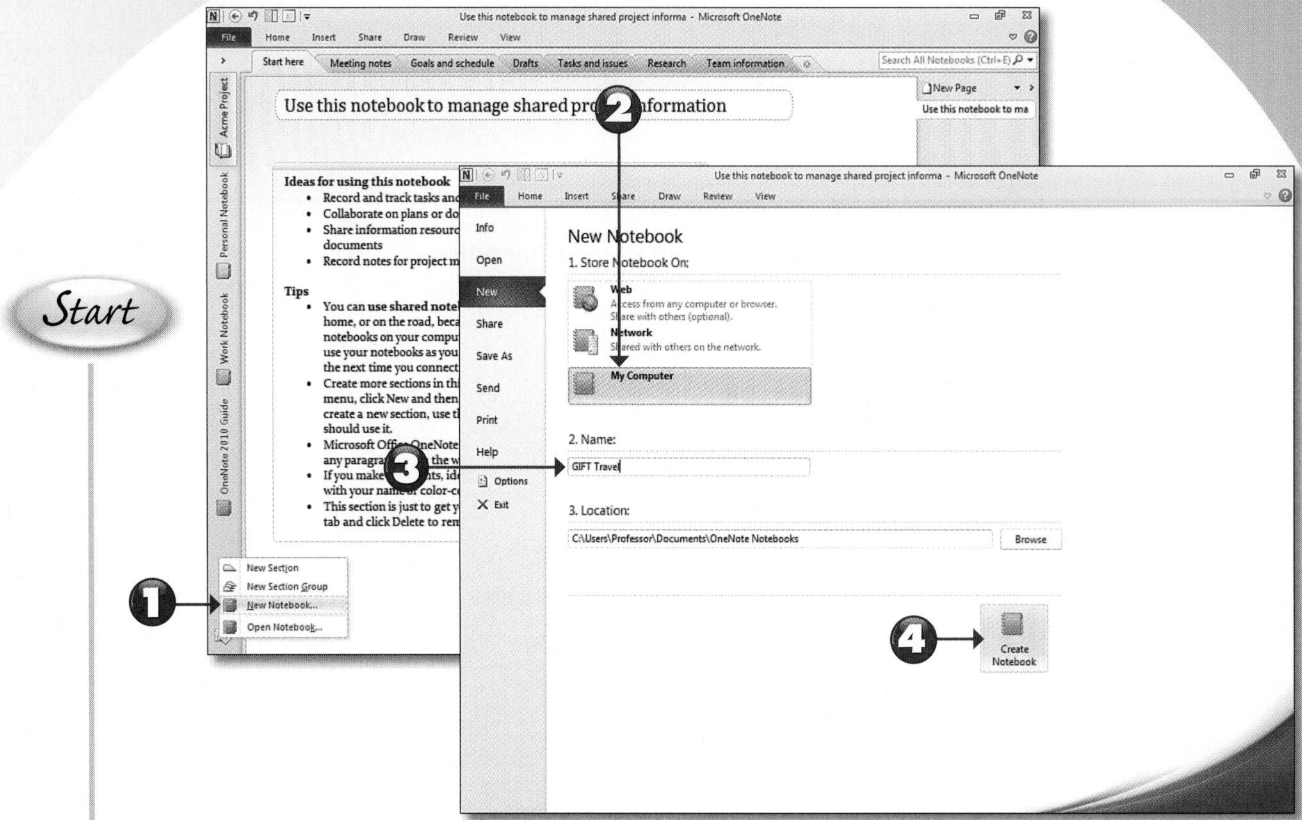

1. Right-click in the Notebooks panel on the left side of the screen and click **New Notebook** to open Backstage view.
2. In Backstage view, click **My Computer** to create the notebook there.
3. Name the new notebook.
4. Click **Create Notebook**.

TIP

Creating or Renaming a Section You can create a new OneNote section by clicking the star icon to the right of the last section in a notebook at the top of the window. You can rename an existing section by double-clicking its name so it is highlighted or right-clicking the tab and choosing **Rename** to type in a new name. ■

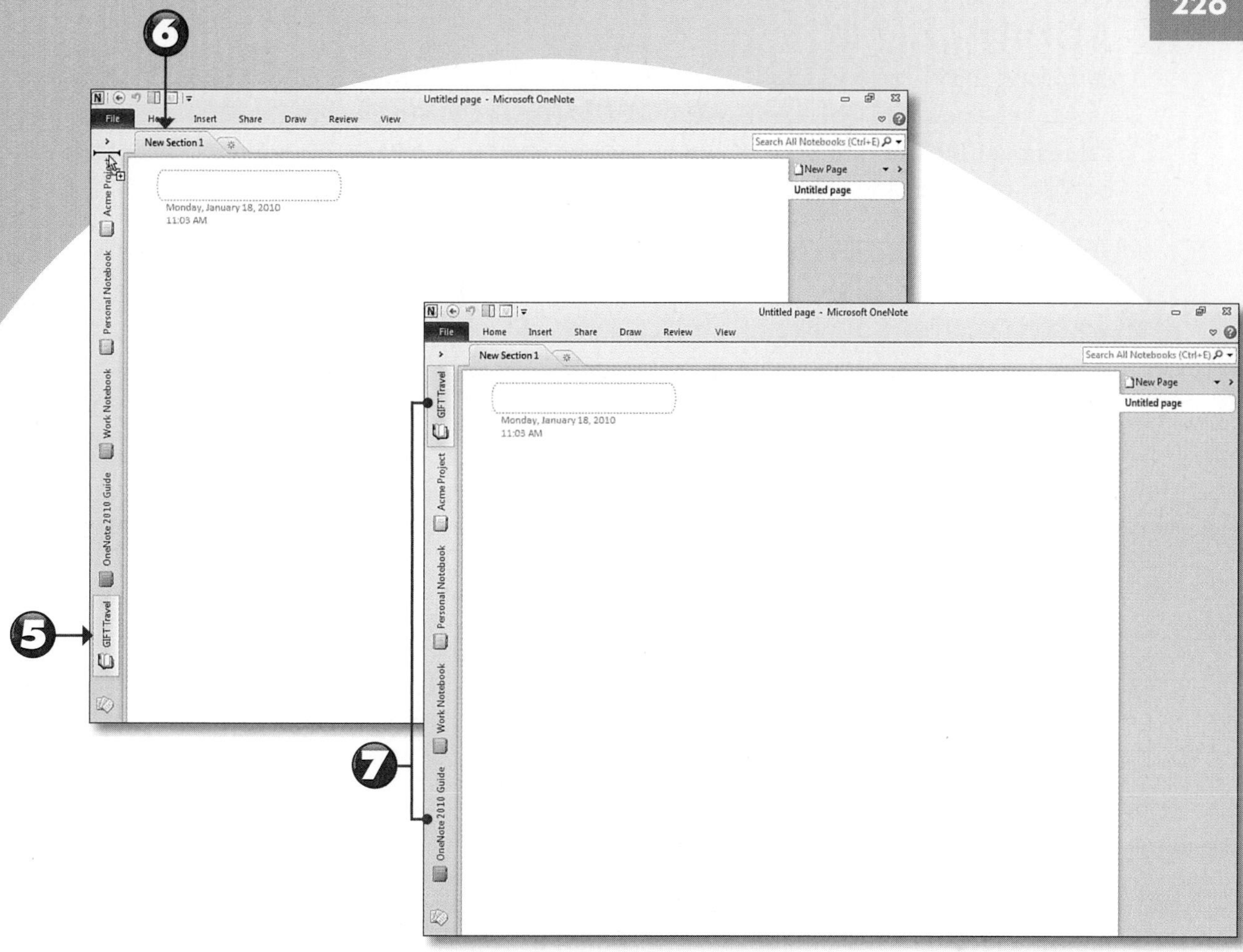

6 The new notebook is created with a tab in the left panel.

5 A New Section tab is available at the top, and a blank untitled page is open.

7 You can reorganize your notebooks by dragging and dropping the new notebook to the top of the panel.

End

TIP

Unfiled Notes The Unfiled Notes icon at the bottom of the Notebooks opens the Unfiled Notes, which are created from Side Notes added by clicking the OneNote icon in your taskbar.

TIP

Reviewing the OneNote 2010 Guide The OneNote 2010 Guide is a default notebook available when you start OneNote that has helpful examples and suggestions on how to use OneNote effectively.

ADDING A NOTE TO A PAGE

Different charts have various capabilities to display data for specific purposes. After you create a basic chart, you can use the All Charts window to change the chart type to plot values over time and to show them in various shapes such as a doughnut, area, scatter, bubble, pyramid, and more.

Start

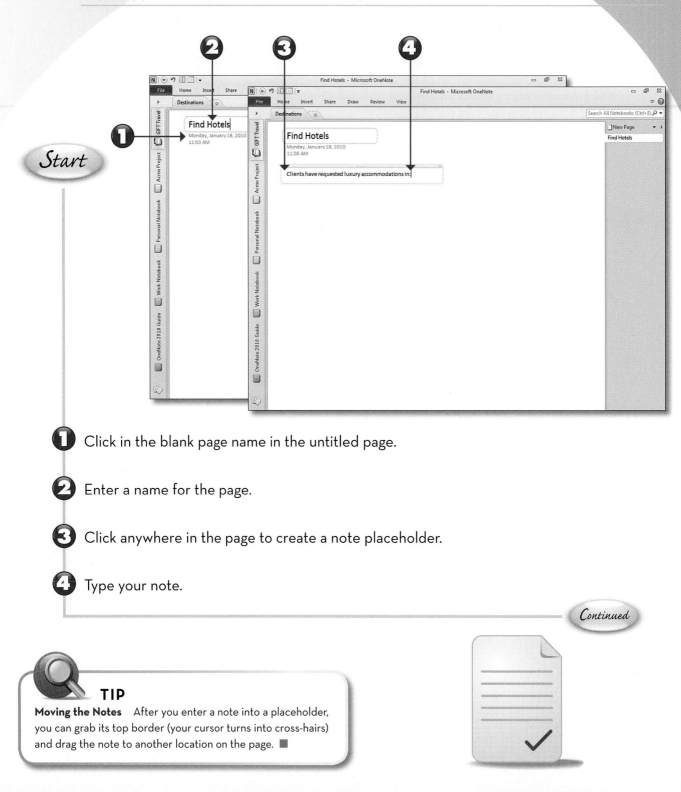

1. Click in the blank page name in the untitled page.
2. Enter a name for the page.
3. Click anywhere in the page to create a note placeholder.
4. Type your note.

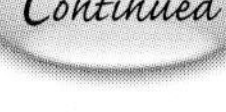

TIP

Moving the Notes After you enter a note into a placeholder, you can grab its top border (your cursor turns into cross-hairs) and drag the note to another location on the page.

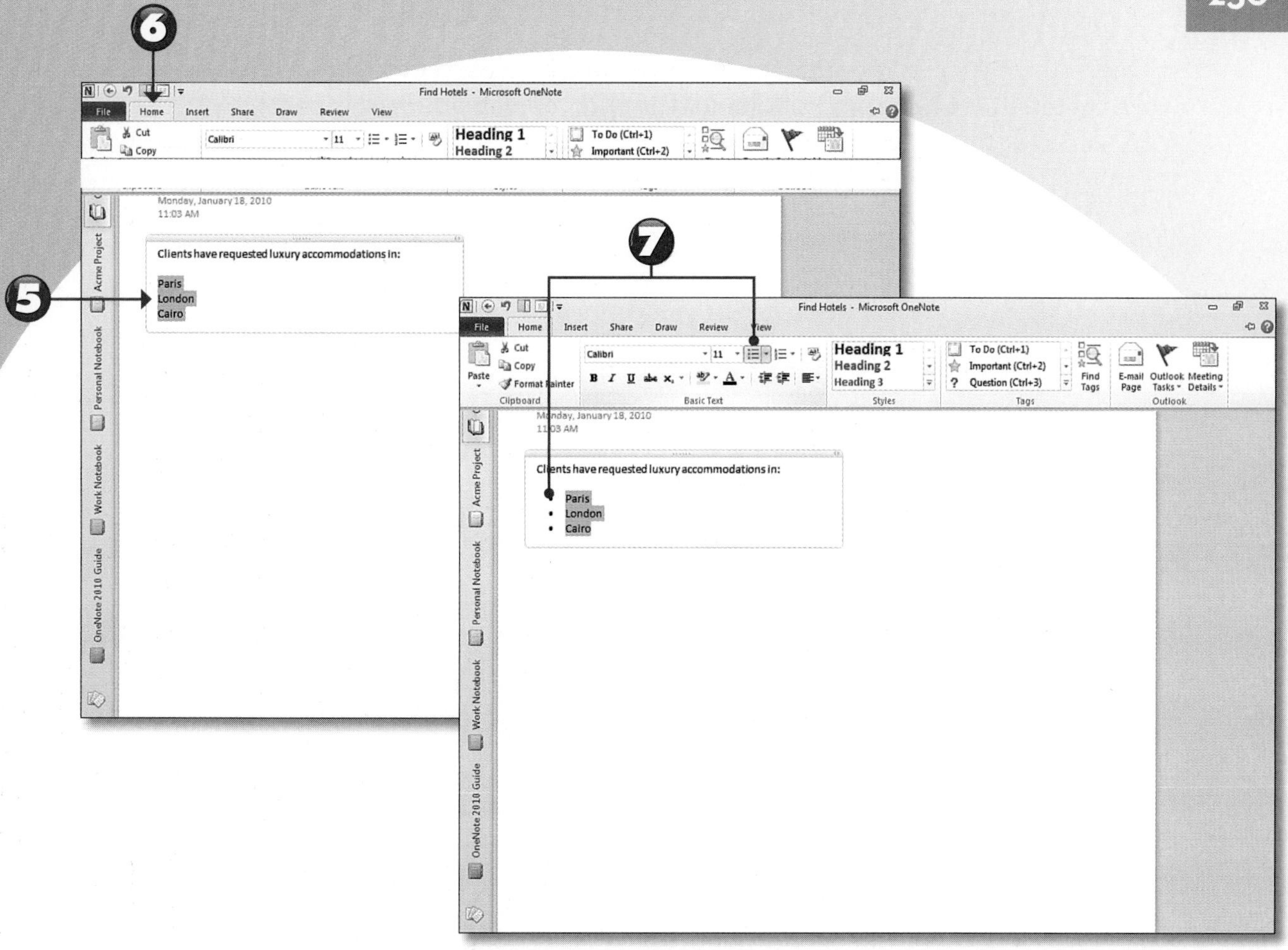

5 You can type and select a list.

6 Click the **Home** tab of the Ribbon.

7 Use the formatting options for selected text to apply bullets to the list.

End

TIP

Deleting and Moving Sections, Pages, or Notes You can delete a section, page, or note by right-clicking it and selecting **Delete**. You can move a page by dragging and dropping it into another section or by dragging and dropping it directly on the Section tab. ■

ADDING WEB CONTENT TO A NEW PAGE

OneNote pages are a great place to copy and paste web content because you can refer to the material when you are not online. The URL, or web address, is pasted with the content, so you can go back to the original page again later.

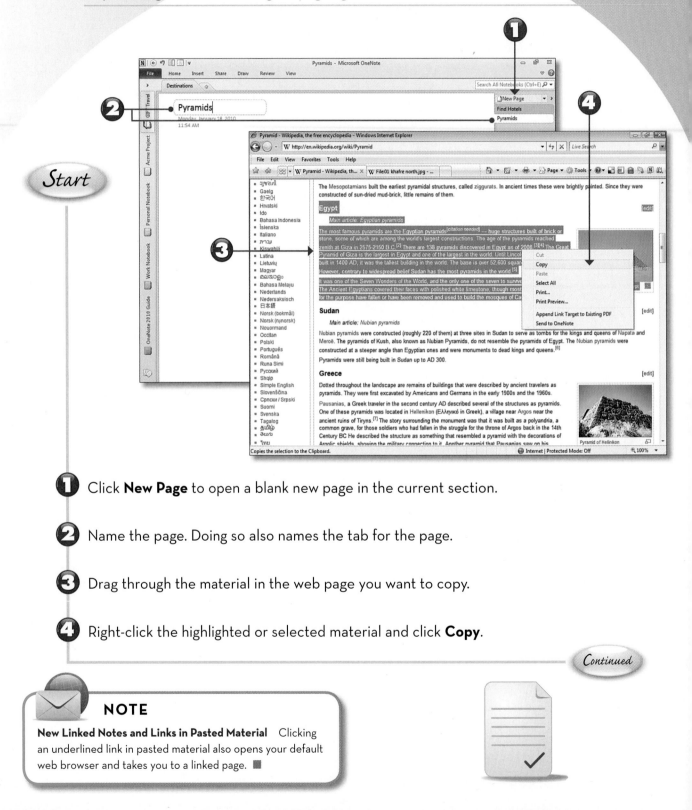

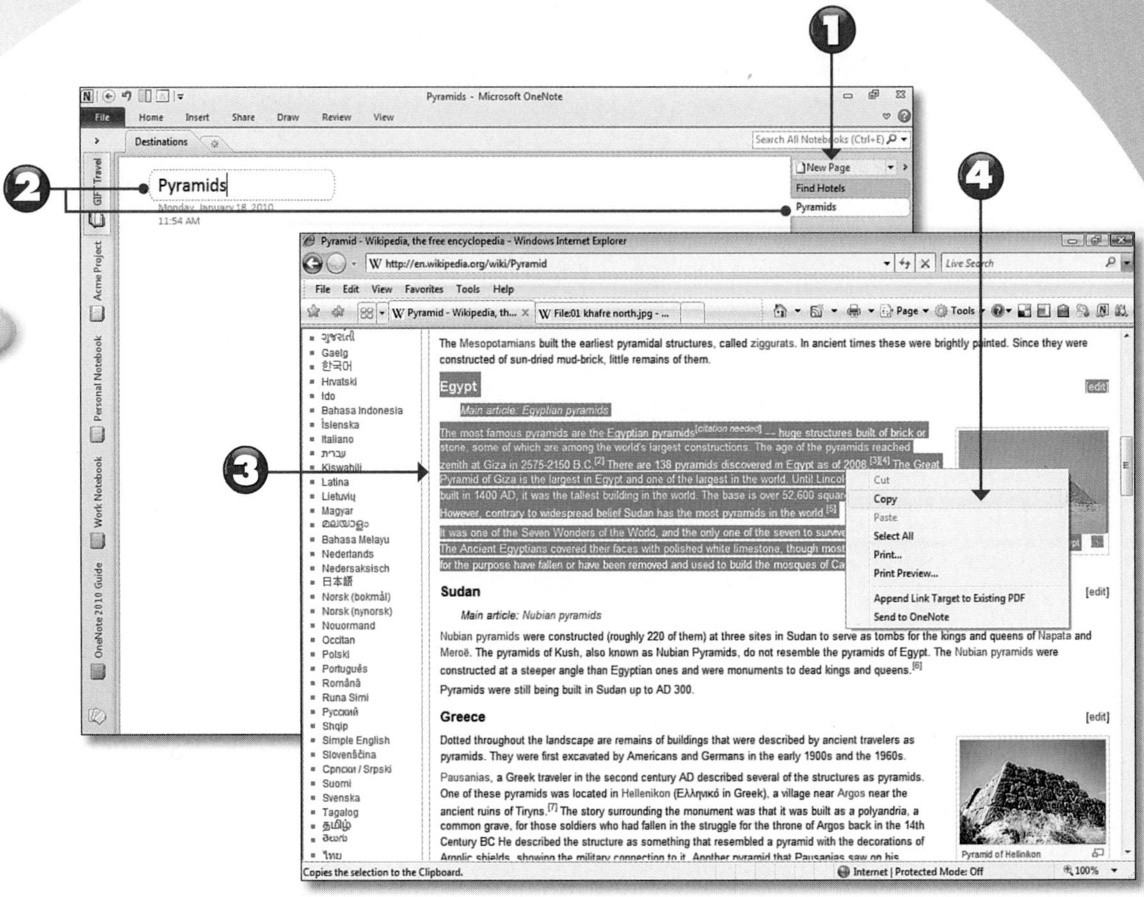

Start

1. Click **New Page** to open a blank new page in the current section.
2. Name the page. Doing so also names the tab for the page.
3. Drag through the material in the web page you want to copy.
4. Right-click the highlighted or selected material and click **Copy**.

Continued

NOTE

New Linked Notes and Links in Pasted Material Clicking an underlined link in pasted material also opens your default web browser and takes you to a linked page. ■

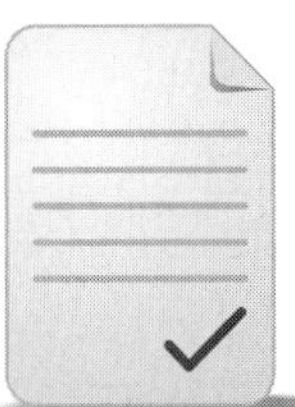

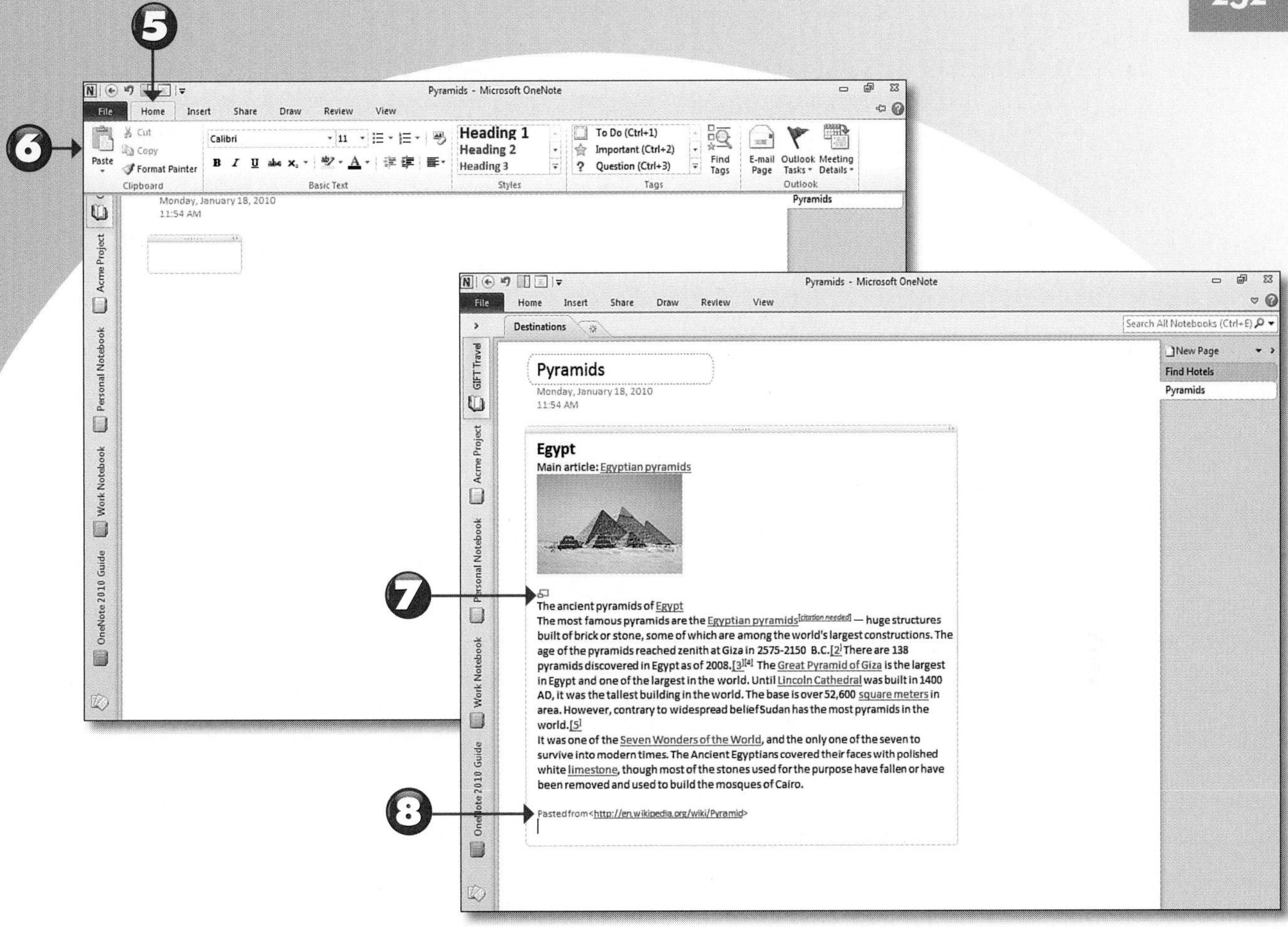

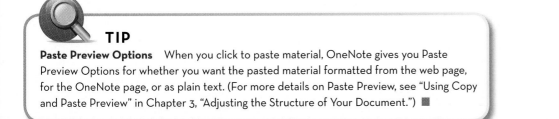

5. Click the **Home** tab on the Ribbon.

6. Click **Paste** (or click in the placeholder for a new note and press **Ctrl+V**).

7. The material from the web page is inserted in your OneNote page.

8. You can click the URL from the web page to open your default web browser and return to the web page.

End

TIP

Paste Preview Options When you click to paste material, OneNote gives you Paste Preview Options for whether you want the pasted material formatted from the web page, for the OneNote page, or as plain text. (For more details on Paste Preview, see "Using Copy and Paste Preview" in Chapter 3, "Adjusting the Structure of Your Document.") ■

USING ONENOTE SEARCH

Perhaps the most powerful feature of OneNote is the ability to find information in notebooks, sections, and pages by using the Search panel. You can use Search to open a Navigation view of all Notebooks and Sections or type a search term and see all of its instances displayed within a page and in the search panel.

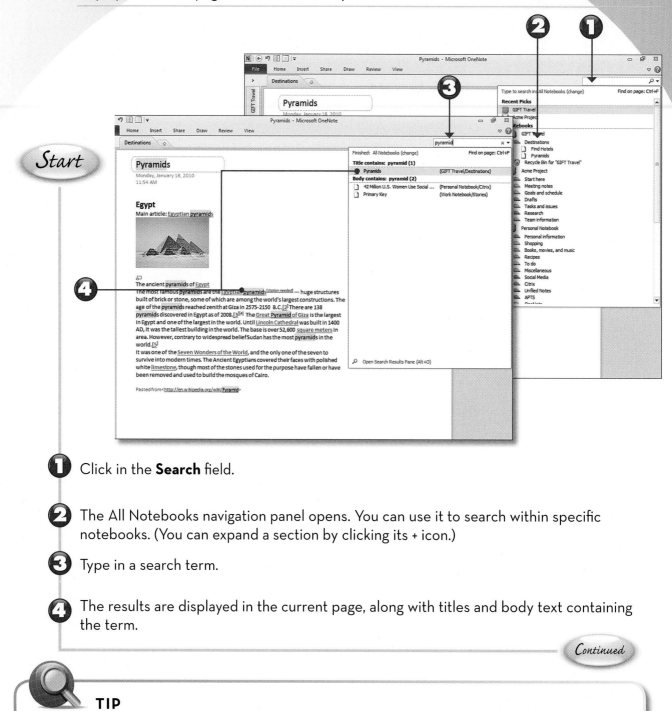

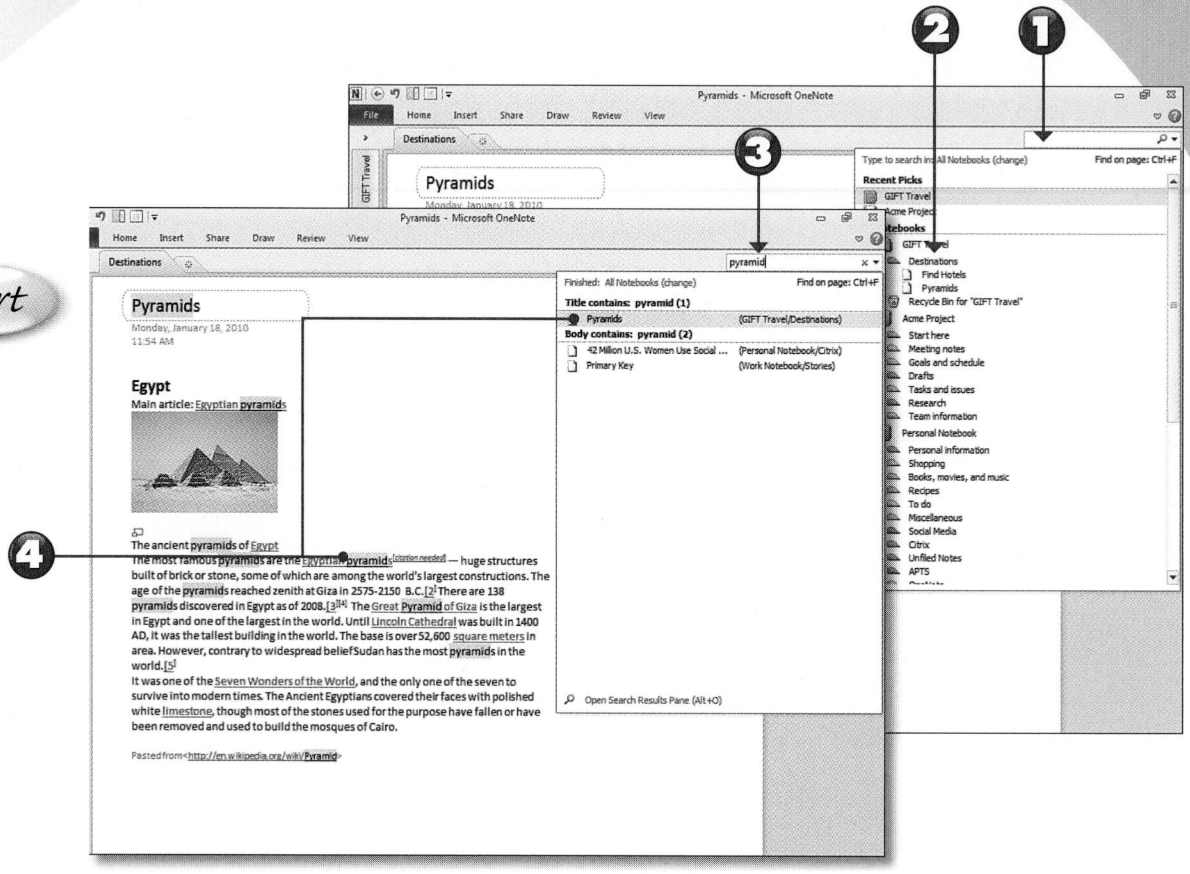

Start

1. Click in the **Search** field.
2. The All Notebooks navigation panel opens. You can use it to search within specific notebooks. (You can expand a section by clicking its + icon.)
3. Type in a search term.
4. The results are displayed in the current page, along with titles and body text containing the term.

Continued

TIP

Navigating to Found Pages You can click any page in the Search panel with a term that has been located (for example, in another notebook) and go directly to that page. Use the **Back** button at the top of the window to return to the current page. ■

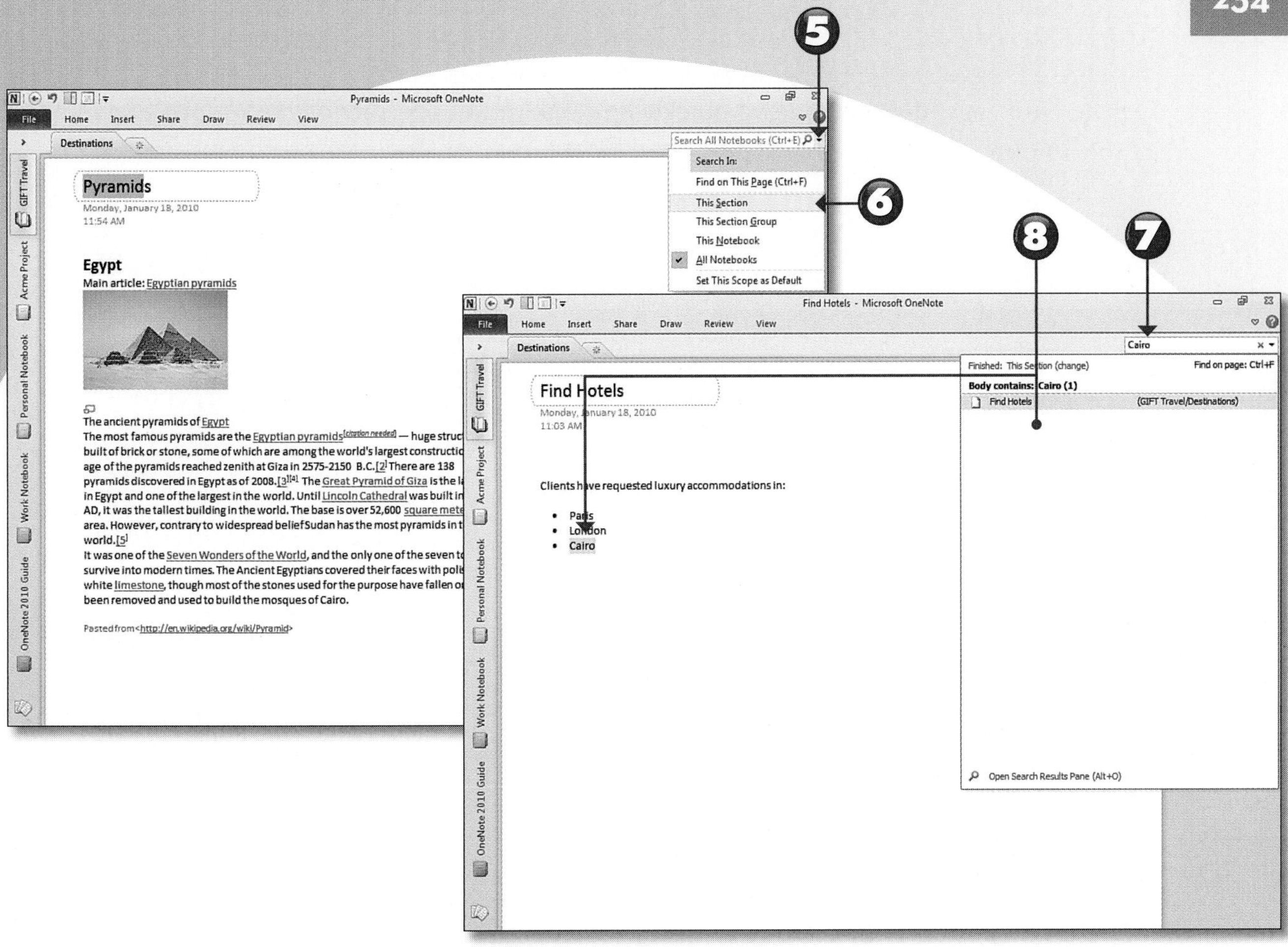

5 Click the drop-down arrow to narrow the search.

6 Click **This Section** to limit search results to the current section.

7 Type another search term.

8 The page or pages are displayed with the search parameters for only the currently open section.

End

TIP

Setting a Default Search Scope You can set OneNote to have a default scope for your searches. For example, when working in a large section, set the scope to **This Section** and then click **Set This Scope as Default**. All searches are limited to the current section unless you change the scope again. ■

USING TAGS FOR ORGANIZATION

Tags are a way to sort important topics and concepts within OneNote for future filtering using the Find Tags feature. You can quickly add one of the pre-set Tags to a Note, customize any of the tags for your own use, and then locate items by their tags with Find Tags.

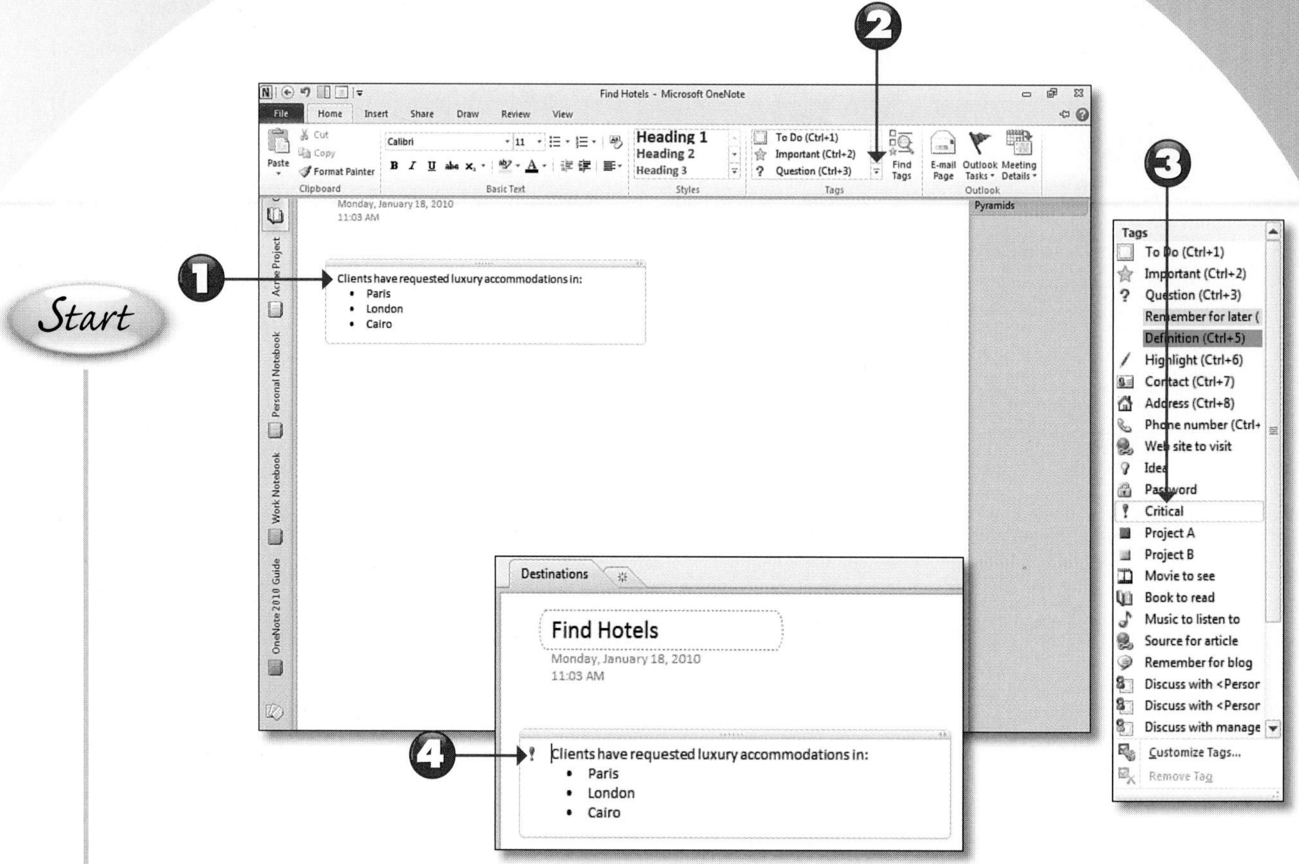

Start

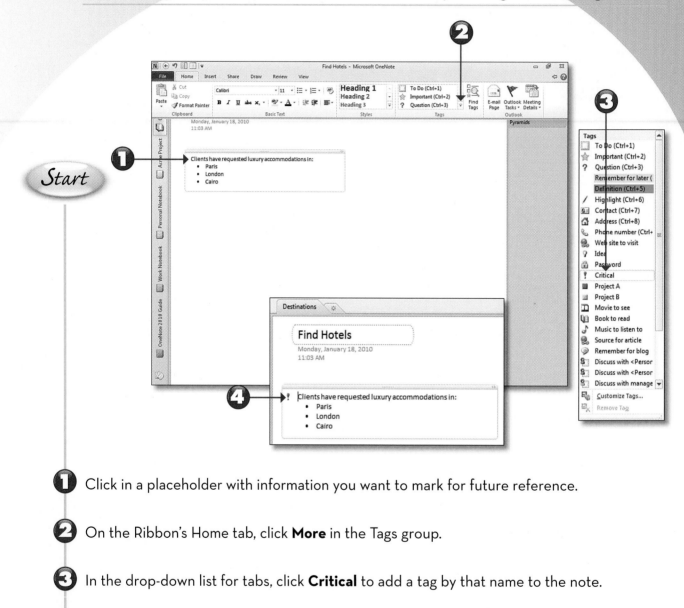

1. Click in a placeholder with information you want to mark for future reference.
2. On the Ribbon's Home tab, click **More** in the Tags group.
3. In the drop-down list for tabs, click **Critical** to add a tag by that name to the note.
4. A Critical tag is added to the note.

Continued

TIP

Create a Summary Page Clicking **Create a Summary Page** at the bottom of the Tags Summary pane creates a new OneNote page with all the displayed tags that you can rename and refer to in the future. ■

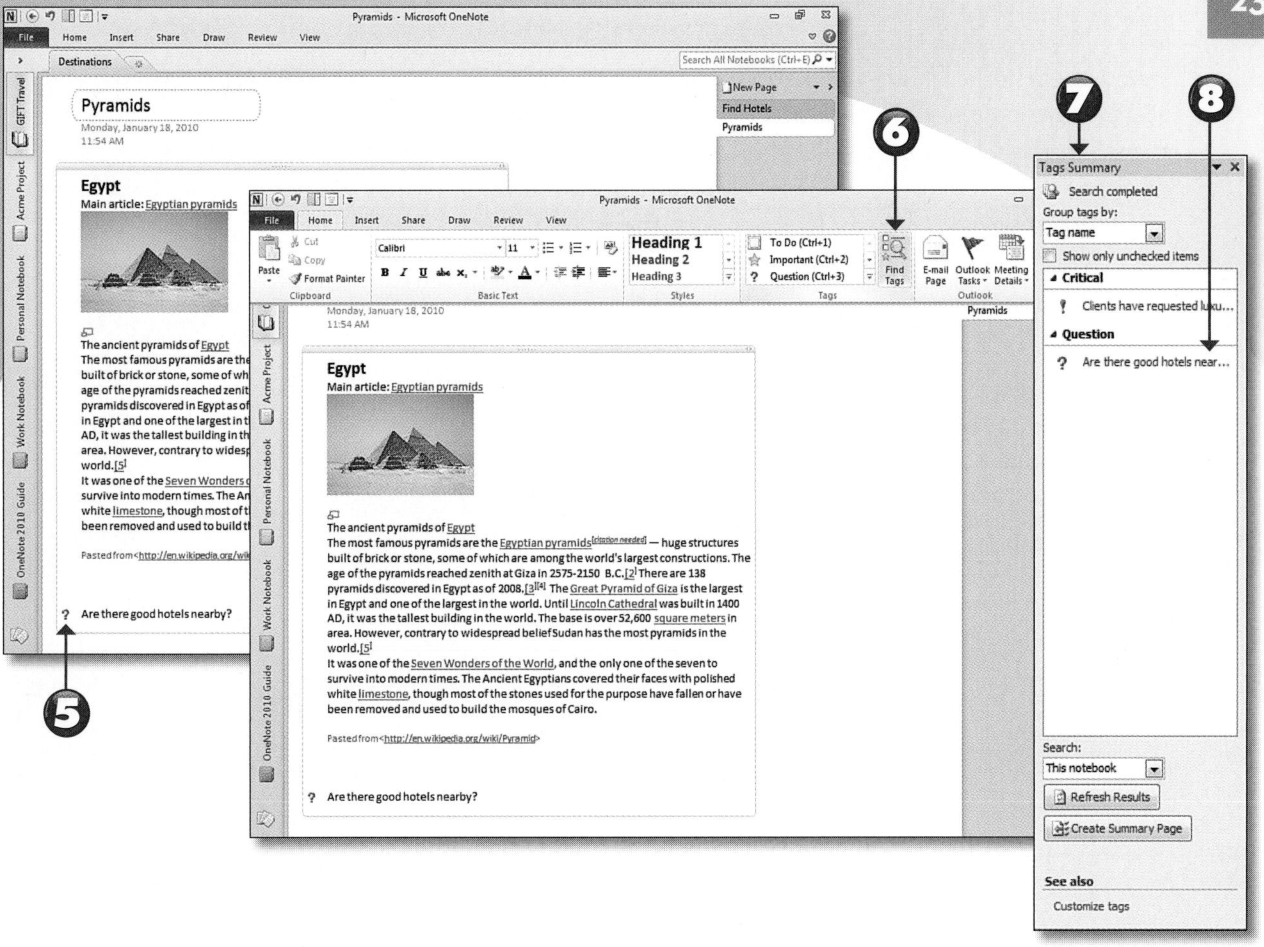

5 Add another tag in another page, such as the Question tag shown here.

6 On the Ribbon's Home tab, click **Find Tags**.

7 The Tags Summary pane opens.

8 Your tags are displayed, and you can click one to navigate to its page.

End

TIP

Show Only Unchecked Items If you have created a To Do check box, you can display only those items that have not been completed by clicking **Show Only Unchecked Items**. ■

TIP

Group Tags Besides the default, to group by tag, you can refresh the Tags Summary pane by changing **Group Tags By** to Section, Title, Date, or Note text. ■

USING A SIDE NOTE

You can click the OneNote icon on your taskbar in Windows to open a *Side Note*, which is a OneNote page with formatting capability that you can write on instantly. Side Notes are stored in the OneNote Unfiled Notes area by default, but after you create one, you can drag and drop it into a section in another notebook. Side Notes are a good way to jot down quick notes without having to work with the main OneNote application.

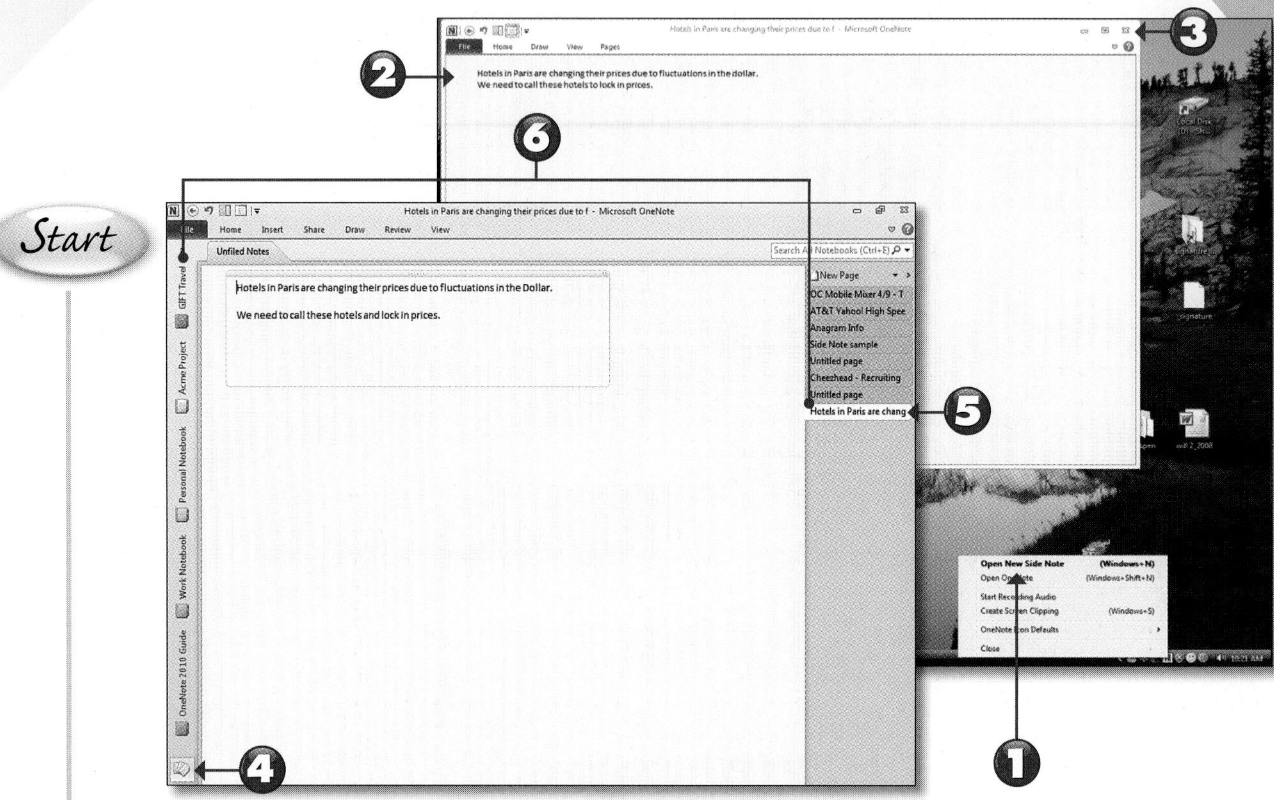

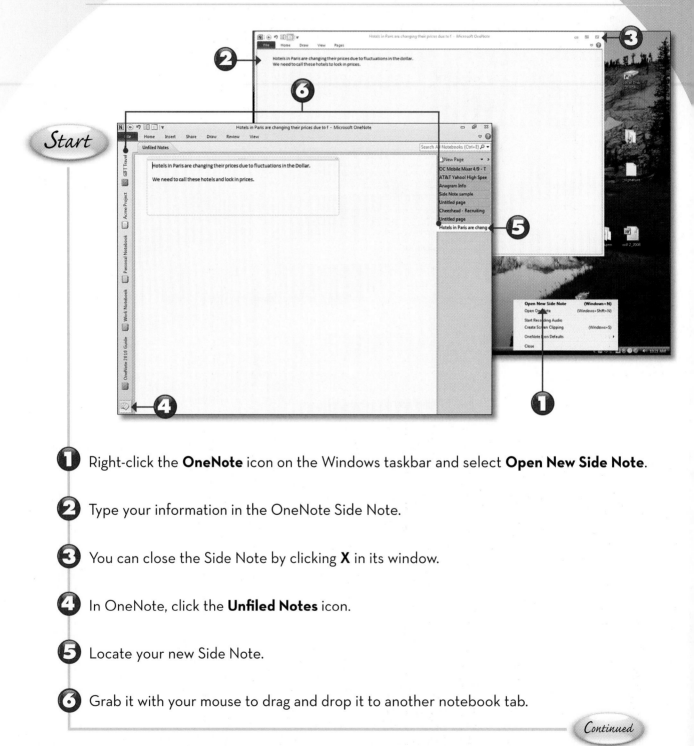

1. Right-click the **OneNote** icon on the Windows taskbar and select **Open New Side Note**.
2. Type your information in the OneNote Side Note.
3. You can close the Side Note by clicking **X** in its window.
4. In OneNote, click the **Unfiled Notes** icon.
5. Locate your new Side Note.
6. Grab it with your mouse to drag and drop it to another notebook tab.

Continued

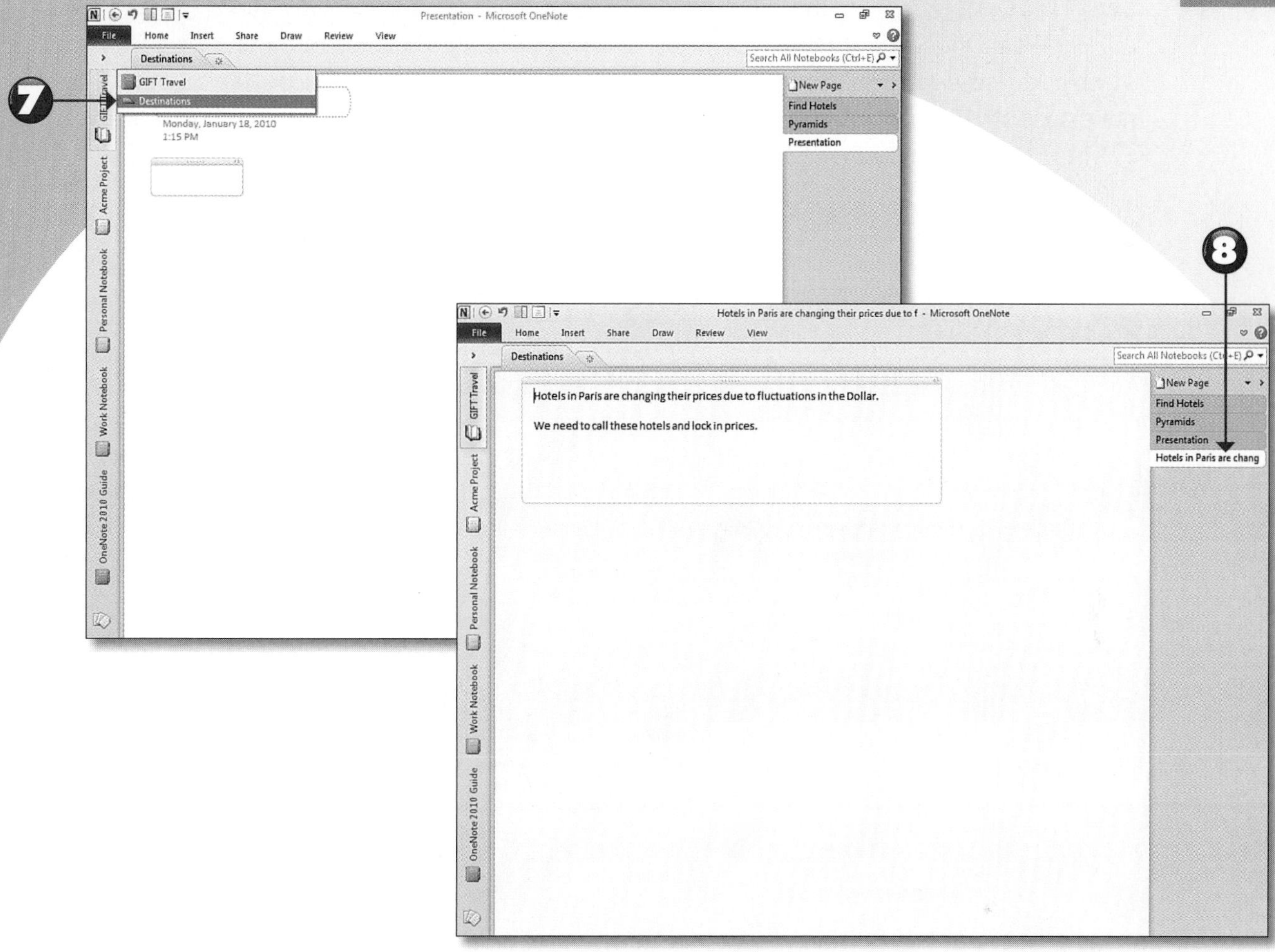

7 As you hover over the notebook, locate the section into which you want to drop the Side Note and drop it in.

8 The Side Note becomes a new page in the section where it is dropped.

End

TIP

Keep on Top You can make sure that a Side Note is always accessible as you work by clicking **View** on its Ribbon and selecting **Keep on Top**. ■

TIP

Drawing in a Side Note or in OneNote Of particular interest to pen or stylus users, the Draw tab on the Side Note Ribbon lets you create diagrams in freehand. A more extensive Draw tab on the main OneNote Ribbon lets you add shapes for diagrams. ■

SENDING A TASK TO OUTLOOK

You can use OneNote notes as Outlook tasks by sending them directly to Outlook from OneNote. You can set alarms, make others accountable, and mark notes as complete to make sure that important items do not get overlooked. (Outlook is covered in more detail in Chapter 17, "Coordinating Your Activities with Outlook.")

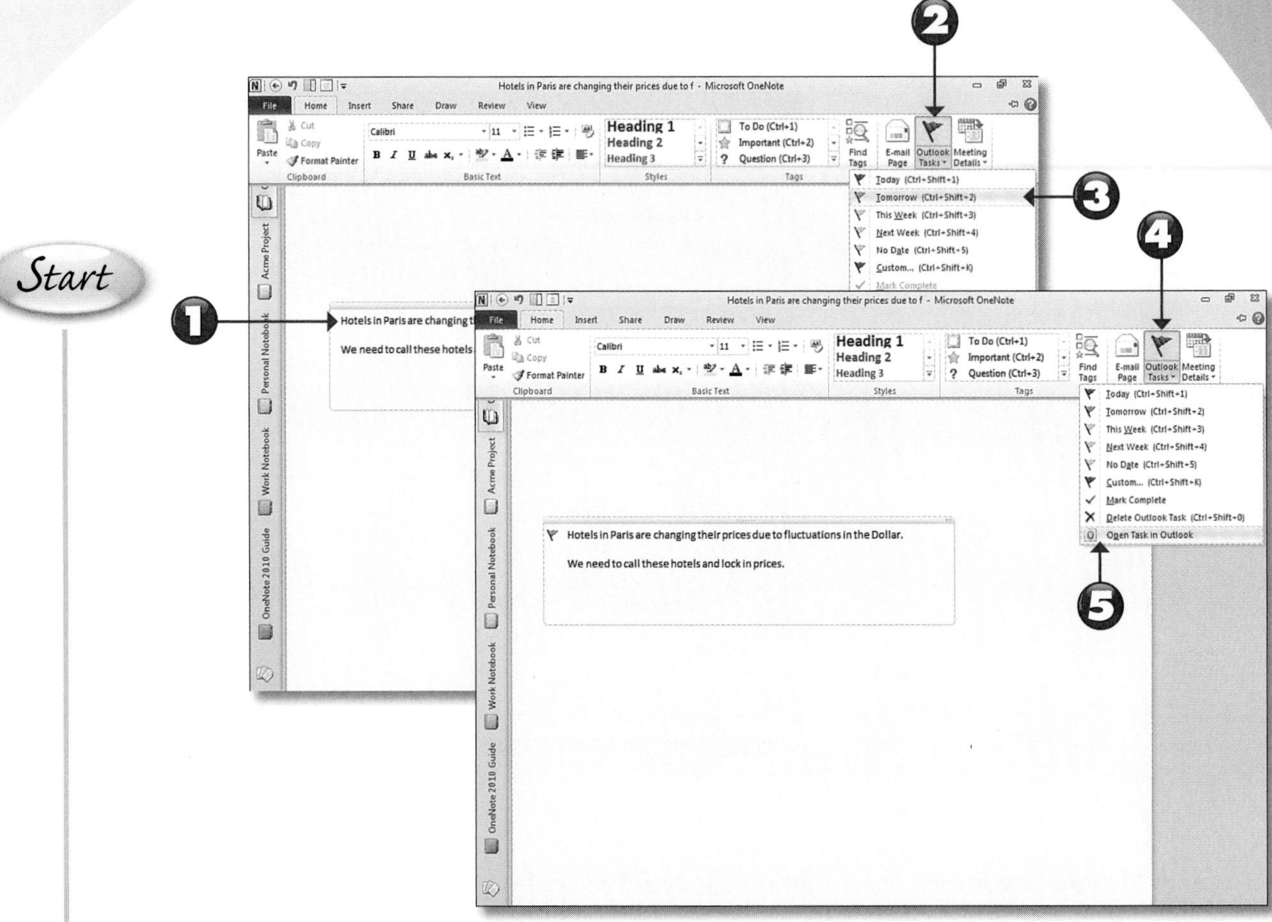

Start

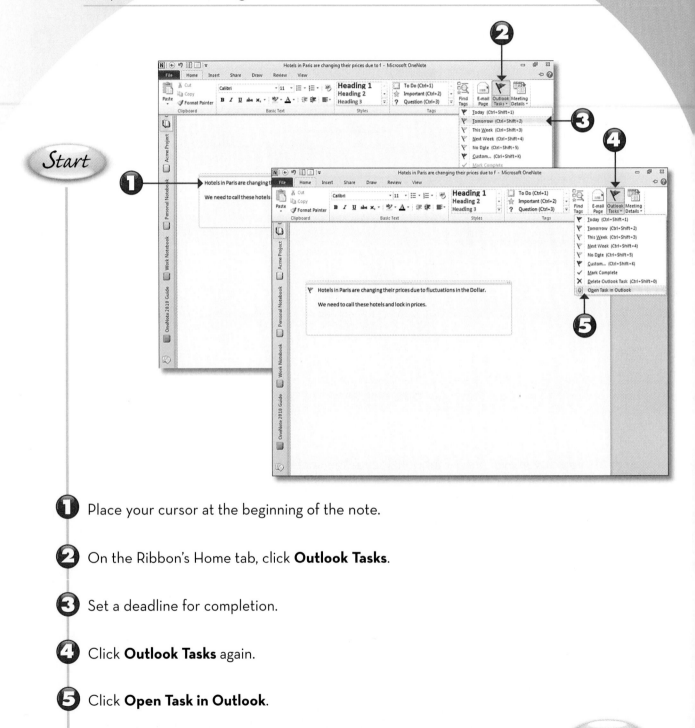

1. Place your cursor at the beginning of the note.
2. On the Ribbon's Home tab, click **Outlook Tasks**.
3. Set a deadline for completion.
4. Click **Outlook Tasks** again.
5. Click **Open Task in Outlook**.

Continued

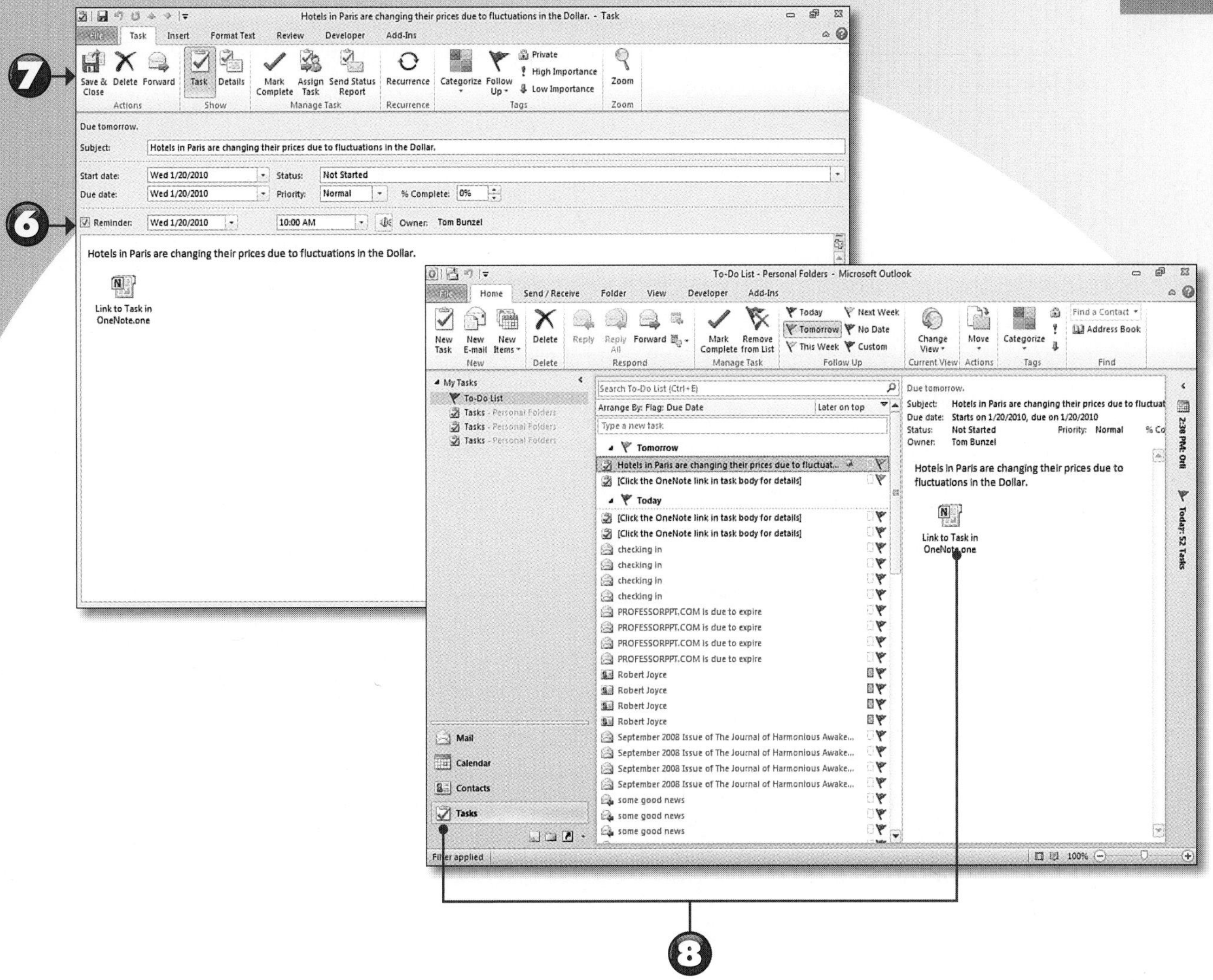

6 You can set a reminder in an Outlook task. Click the check box to enable it.

7 With the task set, click **Save & Close**.

8 The task is now available for you in Outlook (or OneNote).

End

TIP

Marking as Complete To mark a task as complete, select it and click the **Task** flag. You can also click it again to keep it active. ■

TIP

Assigning a Task or Forwarding To have someone else assigned to completing a task, you can click **Assign the Task** in Outlook and send the task to a colleague or associate by email. ■

SENDING A FILE TO ONENOTE

You can send a file—for example, a PowerPoint presentation on which you want comments made—to a specific OneNote page in a section of your notebook by printing the file and using the OneNote printer driver.

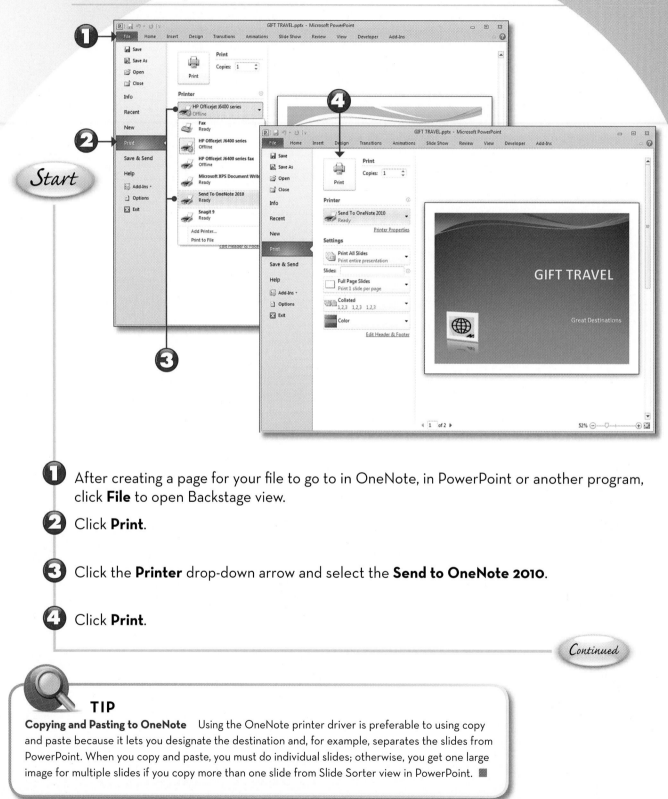

Start

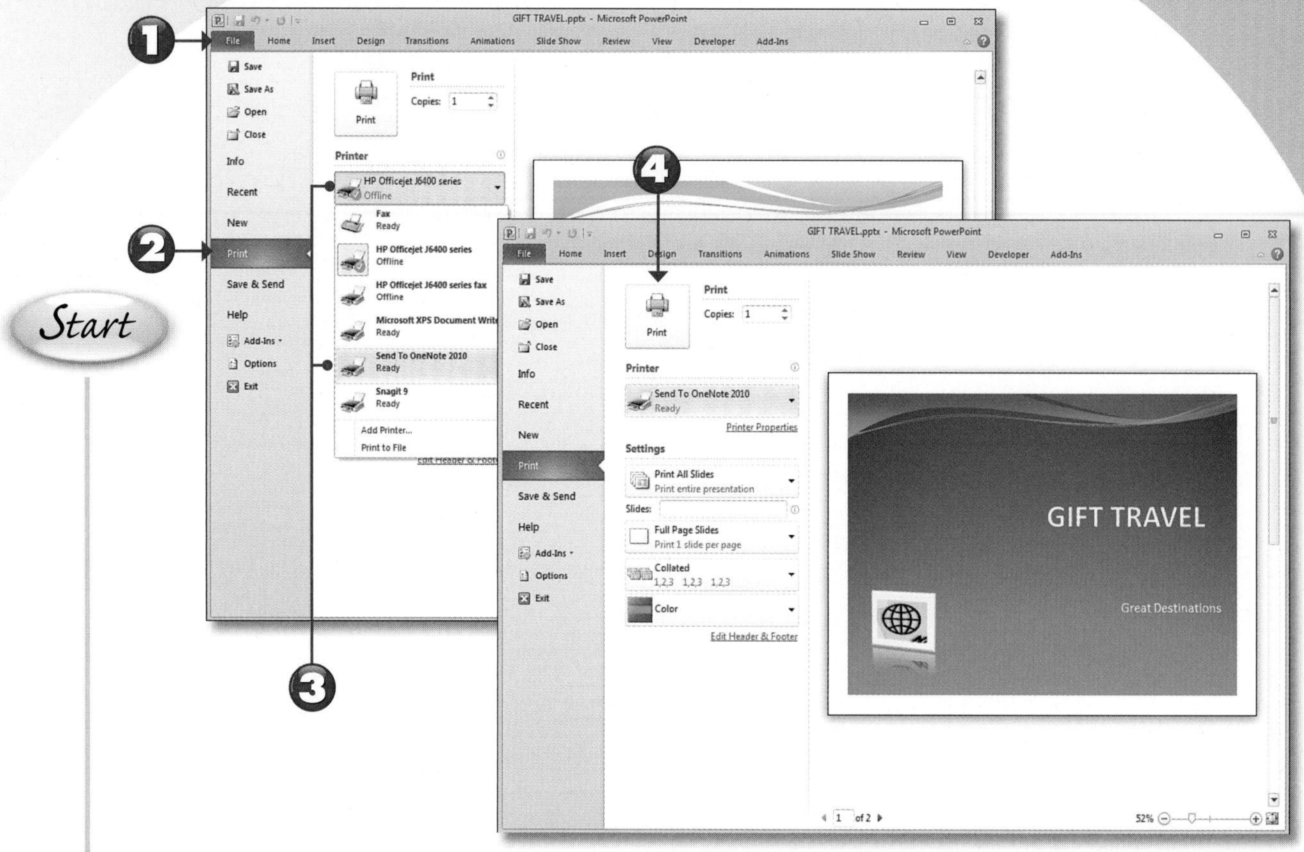

1. After creating a page for your file to go to in OneNote, in PowerPoint or another program, click **File** to open Backstage view.
2. Click **Print**.
3. Click the **Printer** drop-down arrow and select the **Send to OneNote 2010**.
4. Click **Print**.

Continued

TIP

Copying and Pasting to OneNote Using the OneNote printer driver is preferable to using copy and paste because it lets you designate the destination and, for example, separates the slides from PowerPoint. When you copy and paste, you must do individual slides; otherwise, you get one large image for multiple slides if you copy more than one slide from Slide Sorter view in PowerPoint. ■

5. Click to open the notebook, section, and page to which you want to print.

6. Click **OK**.

7. After the file is integrated into your OneNote page, you can adjust it further. For example, you can drag in a corner of a PowerPoint slide to reduce its size.

8. Work with the presentation within OneNote (for example, add tags to notes).

TIP

Recording Audio Notes To add commentary to files that you get from other programs, such as a PowerPoint presentation, consider using your microphone to dictate or narrate audio notes by clicking **Record Audio** from the Insert tab on the Ribbon. ■

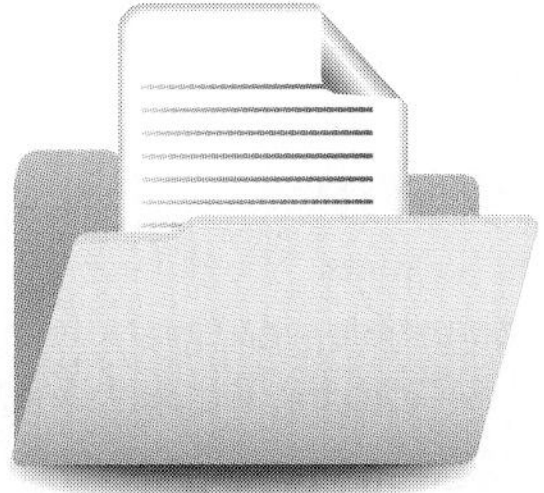

SAVING YOUR SECTION OR NOTEBOOK

You can save your OneNote page, section, or entire notebook in various formats to safeguard and back up your work or to send it to someone else. You can save OneNote pages and sections in *.DOCX (Word), *.PDF, or *.MHT (single file web page) format. Notebooks can be saved in *.PDF or packaged as a OneNote package (*.ONEPKG).

Start

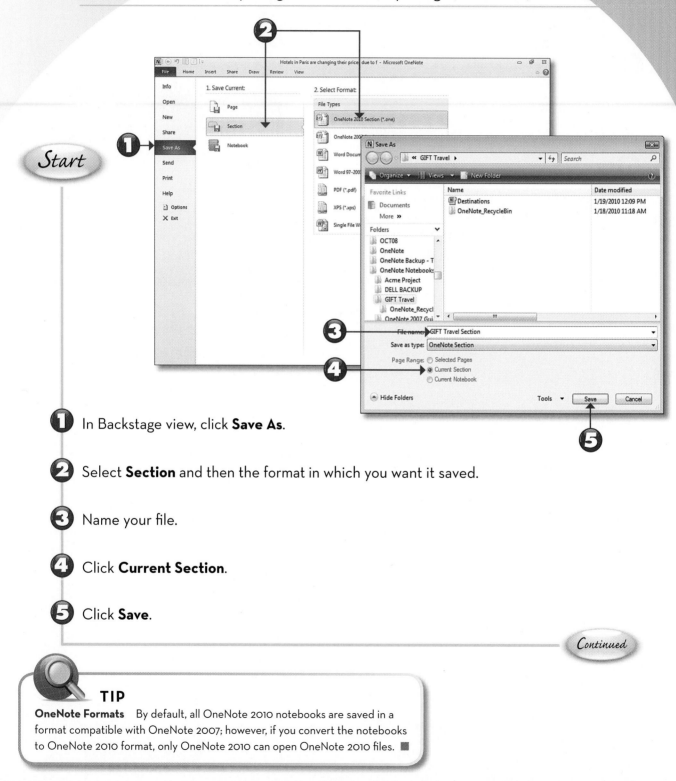

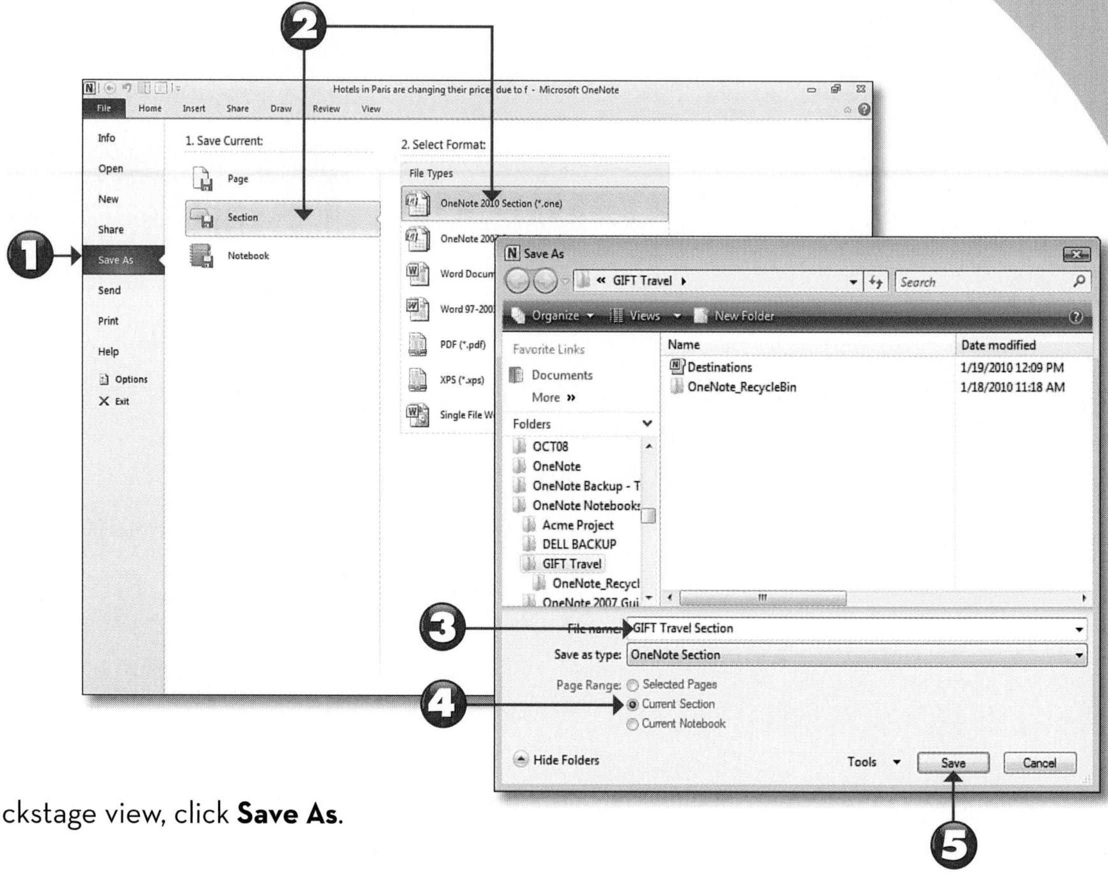

1. In Backstage view, click **Save As**.
2. Select **Section** and then the format in which you want it saved.
3. Name your file.
4. Click **Current Section**.
5. Click **Save**.

Continued

TIP

OneNote Formats By default, all OneNote 2010 notebooks are saved in a format compatible with OneNote 2007; however, if you convert the notebooks to OneNote 2010 format, only OneNote 2010 can open OneNote 2010 files.

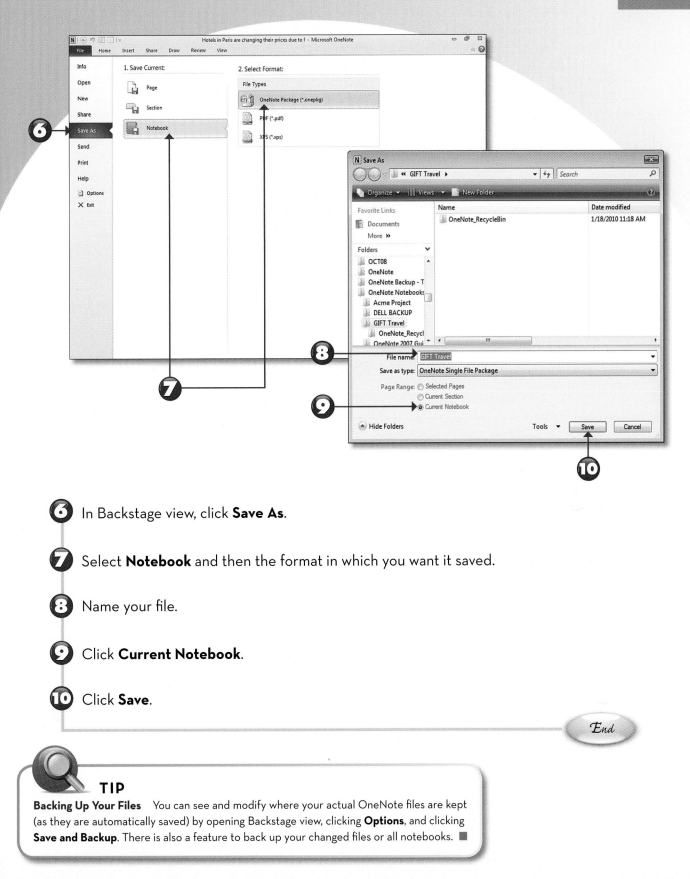

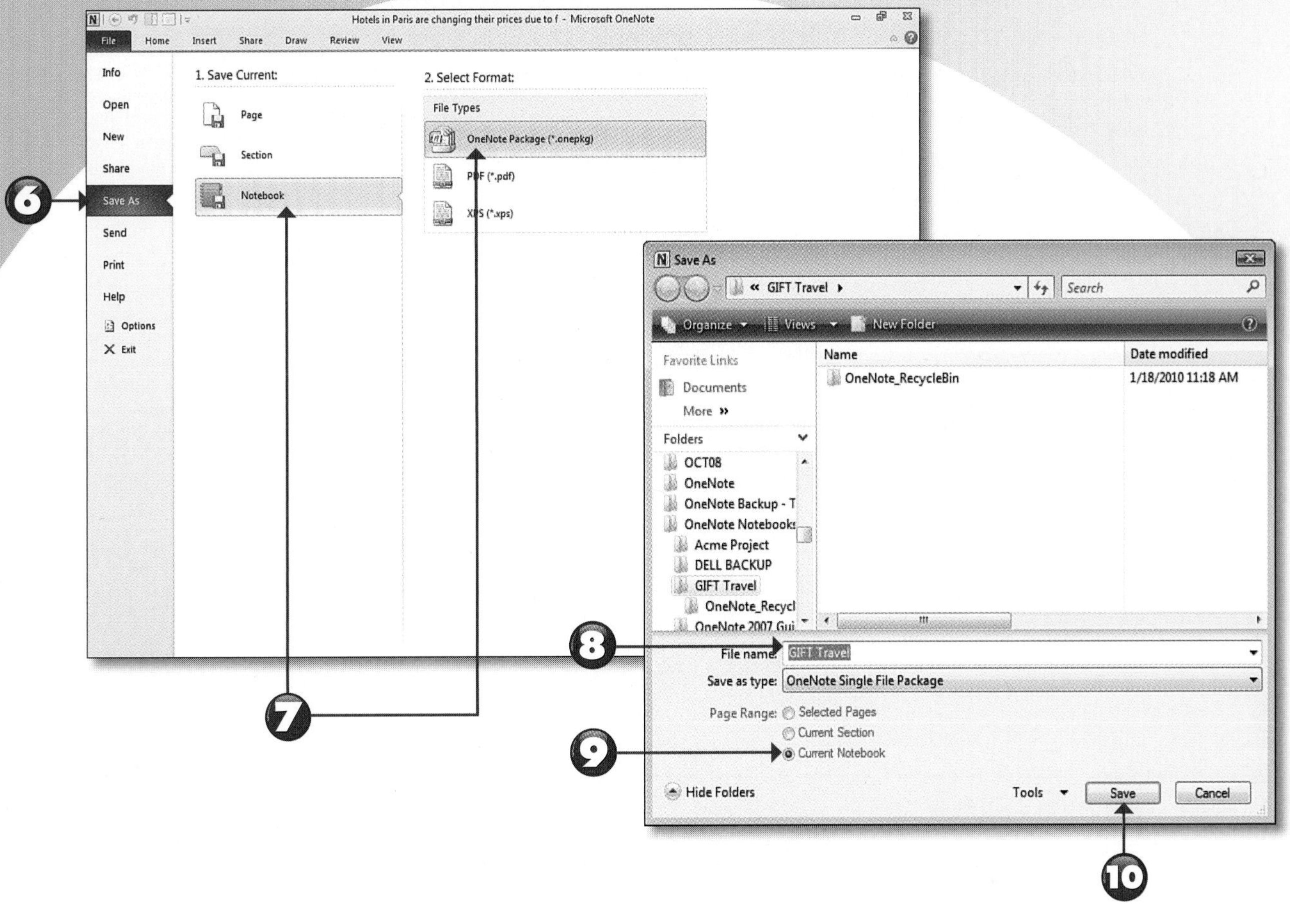

6 In Backstage view, click **Save As**.

7 Select **Notebook** and then the format in which you want it saved.

8 Name your file.

9 Click **Current Notebook**.

10 Click **Save**.

End

TIP

Backing Up Your Files You can see and modify where your actual OneNote files are kept (as they are automatically saved) by opening Backstage view, clicking **Options**, and clicking **Save and Backup**. There is also a feature to back up your changed files or all notebooks.

SHARING YOUR NOTEBOOK

You can make your notebook available as a shared resource over a local area network (with SharePoint services) or online. This synchronizes your version of the notebook with anyone who has access and permission to the network location you designate.

Start

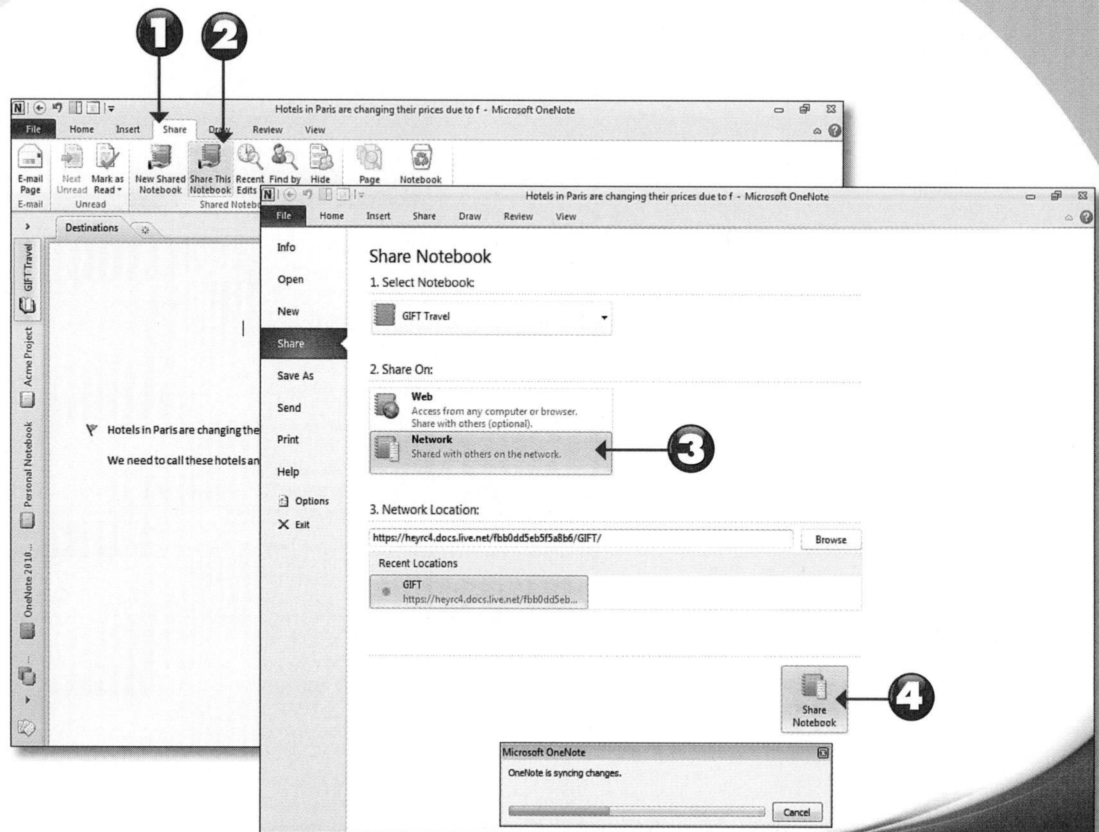

1. Click the **Share** tab on the Ribbon.
2. Click **Share This Notebook**.
3. In the **Share** part of Backstage view (which opens automatically), click **Network** (or **Web**). If you choose Network, fill in the Network location too.
4. Click **Share Notebook**. Wait till the notebook is syncing.

Continued

TIP

New Shared Notebook You can create a new notebook that is shared by clicking **New Shared Notebook** in the Share tab on the Ribbon or from the New area of Backstage view. ■

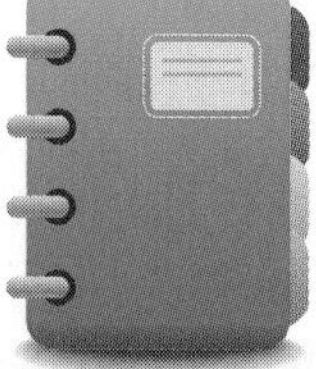

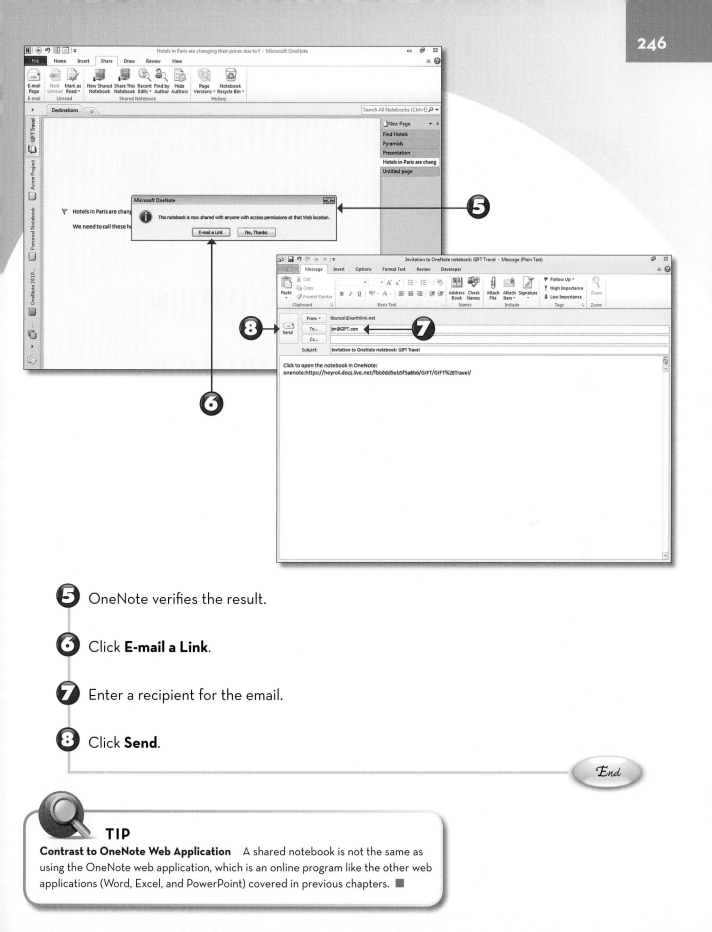

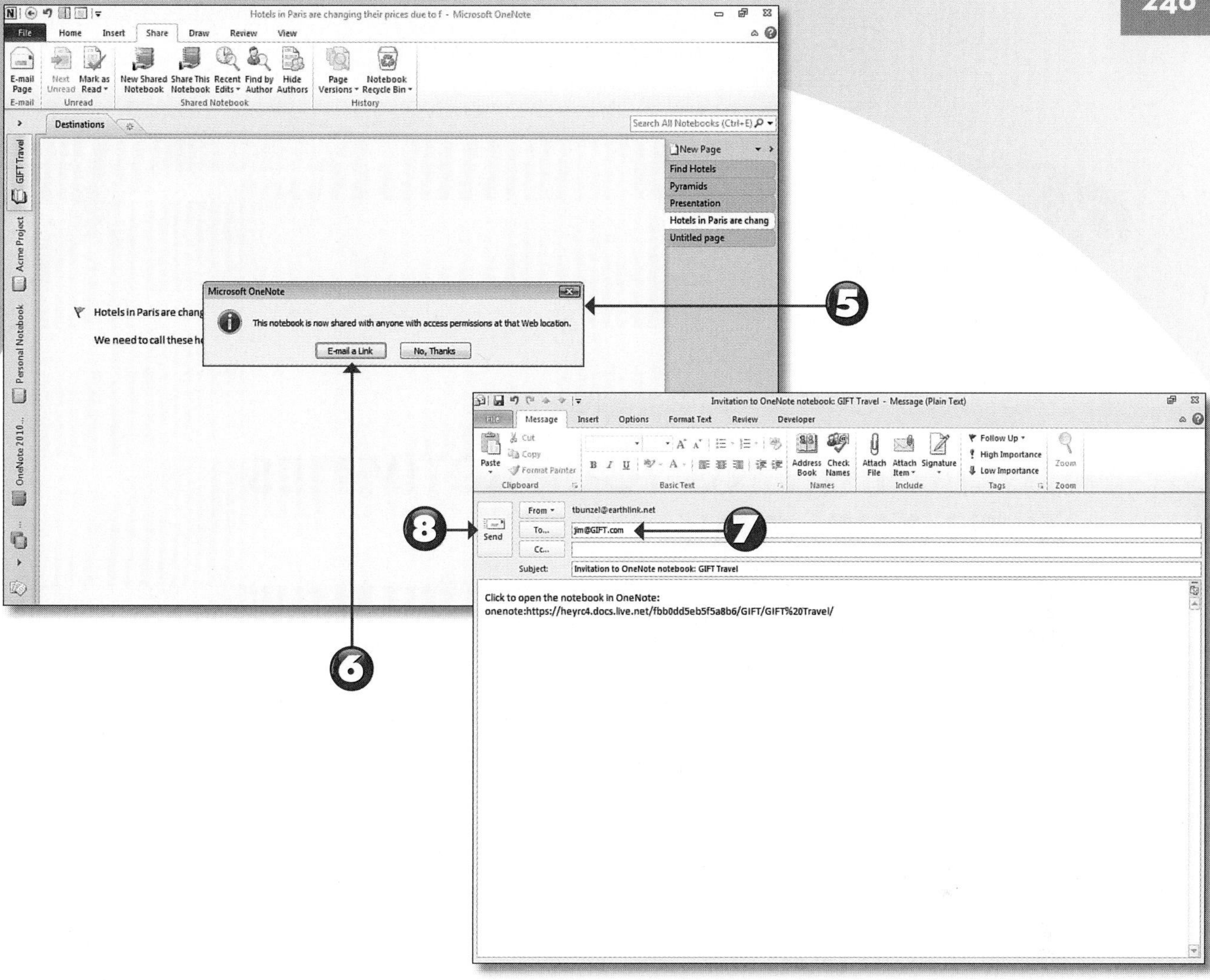

5. OneNote verifies the result.

6. Click **E-mail a Link**.

7. Enter a recipient for the email.

8. Click **Send**.

End

TIP

Contrast to OneNote Web Application A shared notebook is not the same as using the OneNote web application, which is an online program like the other web applications (Word, Excel, and PowerPoint) covered in previous chapters.

COORDINATING YOUR ACTIVITIES WITH OUTLOOK

Outlook is a communications center that serves you like an executive secretary or assistant, sending and receiving email, maintaining your calendar with appointments and events, and managing your contacts with categories and follow-up (flag) reminders.

Each Outlook component has its own folder in the main Personal Folders structure, and you can add your own folders for sorting messages, handling contacts, or creating extra calendars. You can also use a folder for subscriptions to blogs and websites using Really Simple Syndication (RSS).

Like the other Office applications, Outlook 2010 has a Ribbon to provide access to the key features of your mail, contacts lists, calendars, and tasks. A To-Do bar docked at the right of the window provides a quick look at your calendar and imminent tasks.

The key to Outlook is its integration between components and other programs; for example, you can send email from a Contact window and schedule a meeting that will be accessible in OneNote.

Each Outlook component also has various views; for example, you can sort and filter email with rules; review your contacts as business cards or a phone list; or check you calendar by day, week, or month.

THE OUTLOOK EMAIL INBOX

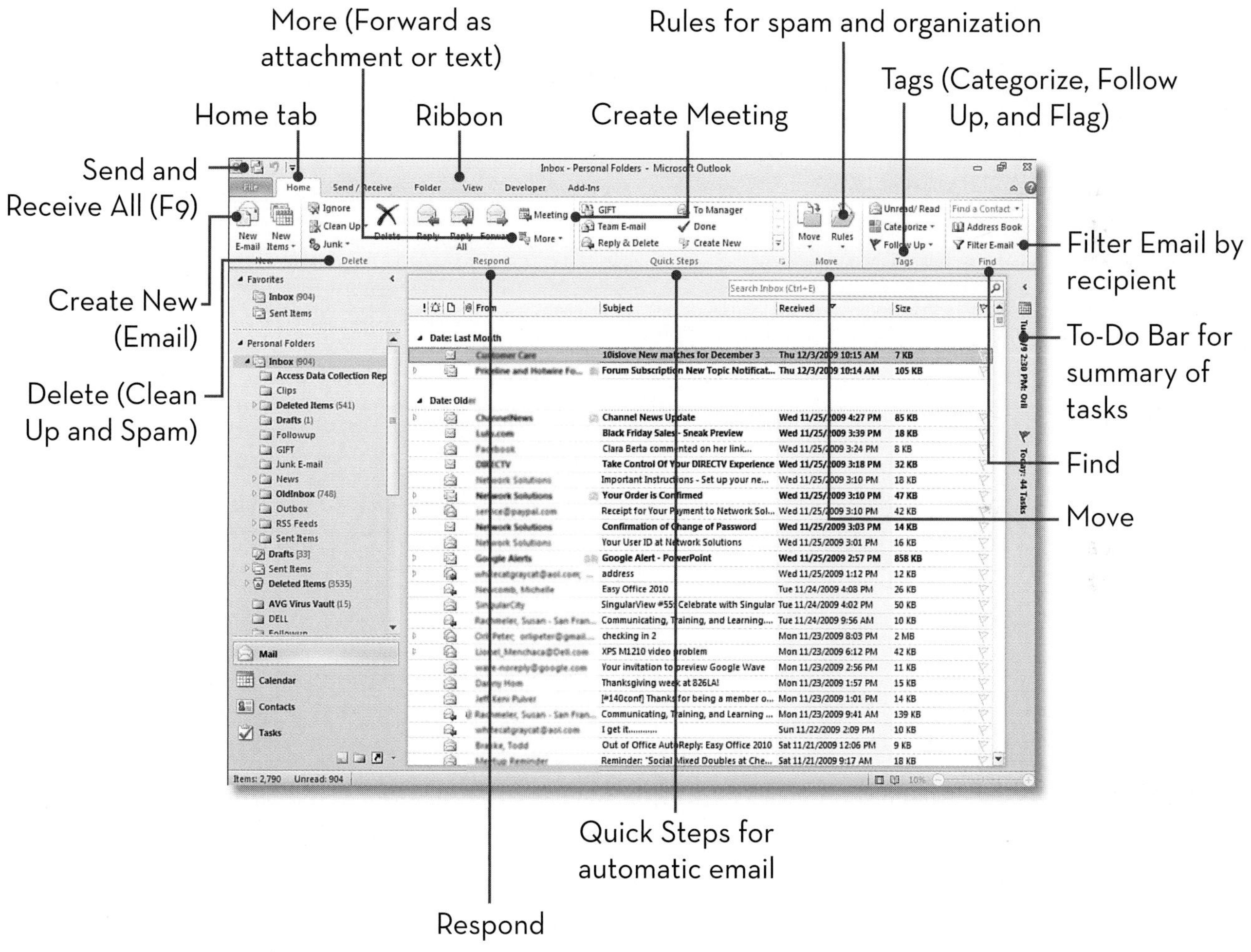
More (Forward as attachment or text)
Rules for spam and organization
Tags (Categorize, Follow Up, and Flag)
Home tab
Ribbon
Create Meeting
Send and Receive All (F9)
Filter Email by recipient
Create New (Email)
To-Do Bar for summary of tasks
Delete (Clean Up and Spam)
Find
Move
Quick Steps for automatic email
Respond

SENDING AN EMAIL MESSAGE WITH AN ATTACHMENT

Handling email is the most basic task you can perform in Outlook, and it is performed mostly in the Home tab on the Ribbon. You can reply to an existing email message, create a new message, and even add attachments to the email before it is sent. When sent, the message goes to your Outbox where, depending on your settings, it is sent at automatic intervals or when you click **Send and Receive** (or press **F9**).

Start

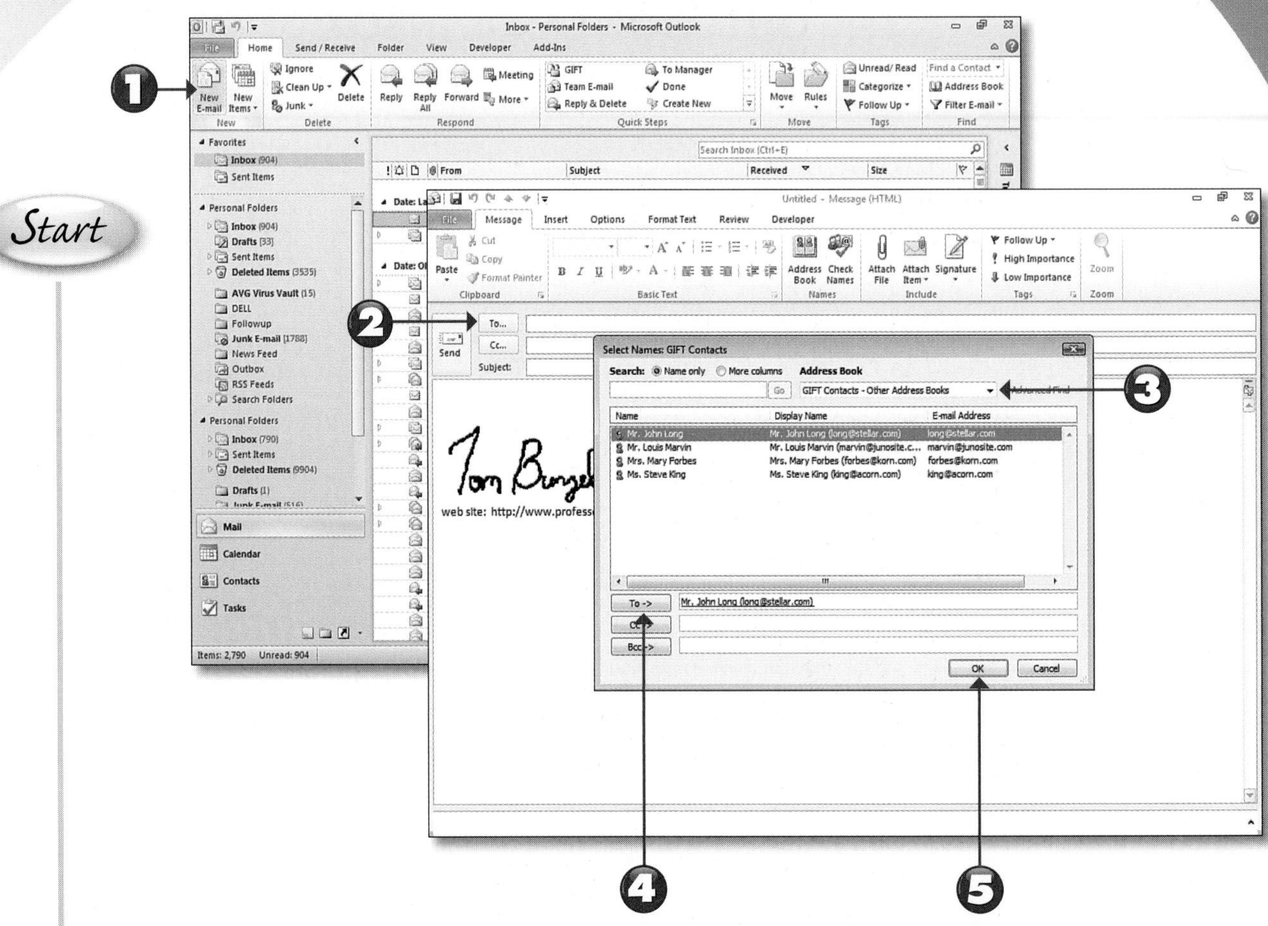

1. On the Ribbon's Home tab, click **New E-mail** to open a new email message.
2. Click **To**. (You can also enter an email address directly if you know it or simply type the name of someone in your Address Book.)
3. Select an Address Book (if you have more than one).
4. Select a recipient and click the **To** button to add that contact to the list of recipients.
5. Click **OK**.

Continued

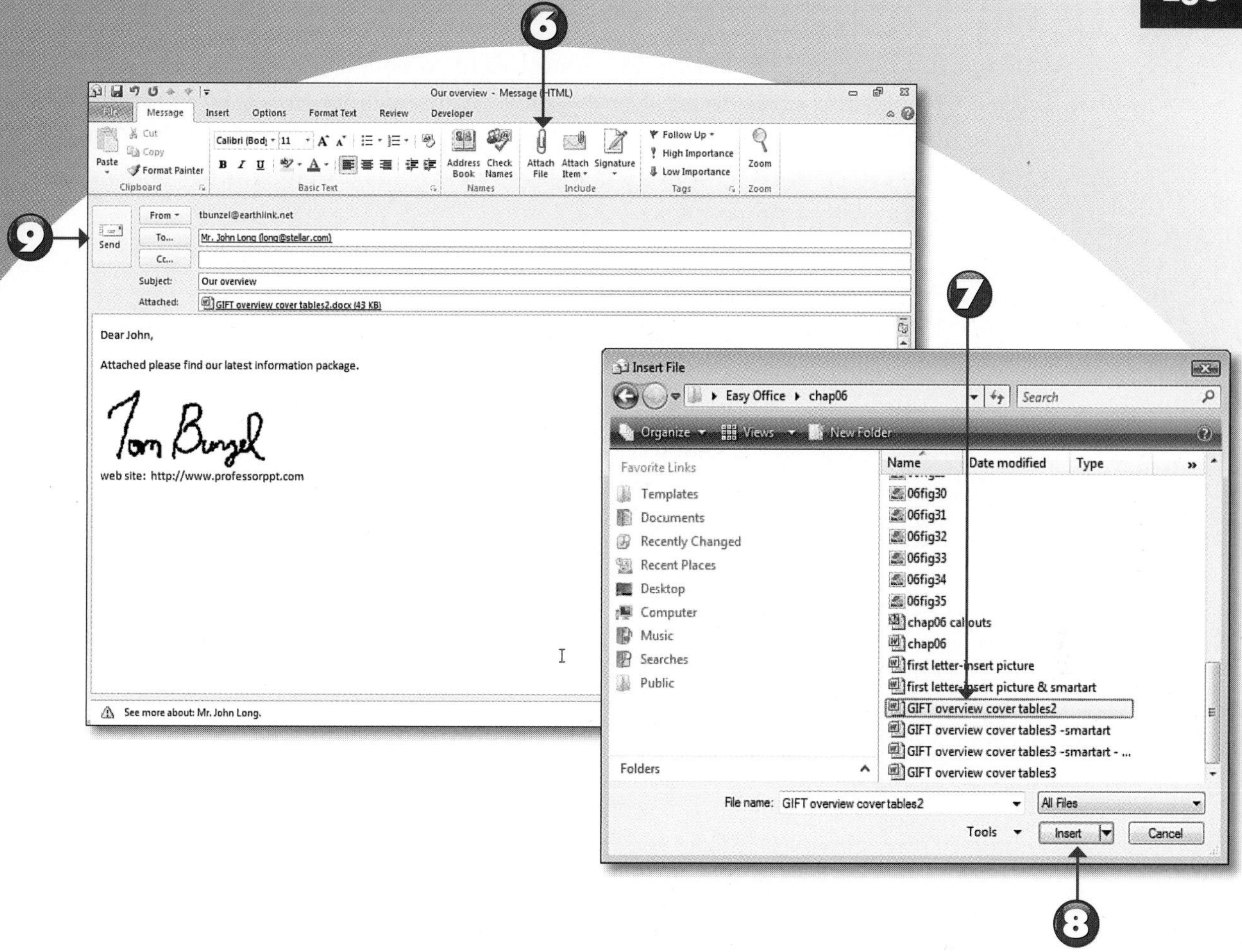

6. Click **Attach File**.

7. Locate and select the file in the Insert File window.

8. Click **Insert**.

9. Complete the email and click **Send**.

End

TIP

Sending from a Contact You can create a new email message directly to a specific contact in your Contacts folder. Just select the contact and click **Email** in the Communicate group of the Ribbon's Home tab.

TIP

Adding an Address Book To make a contacts list into an Address Book for Outlook email, right-click the list in the Folders panel, click **Properties**, and in the Outlook Address tab, select **Show This Folder as an E-mail Address Book**.

USING THE NEW QUICK STEPS

Quick Steps is a gallery in the Ribbon's Home tab for email; it lets you specify key recipients for quick messages and other tasks. Some Quick Steps require an initial setup the first time you use them; for example, to choose a Manager, you can use the New Quick Step option to create your own Quick Step to specify a specific person as a Manager to receive an email that can be begun with a single click.

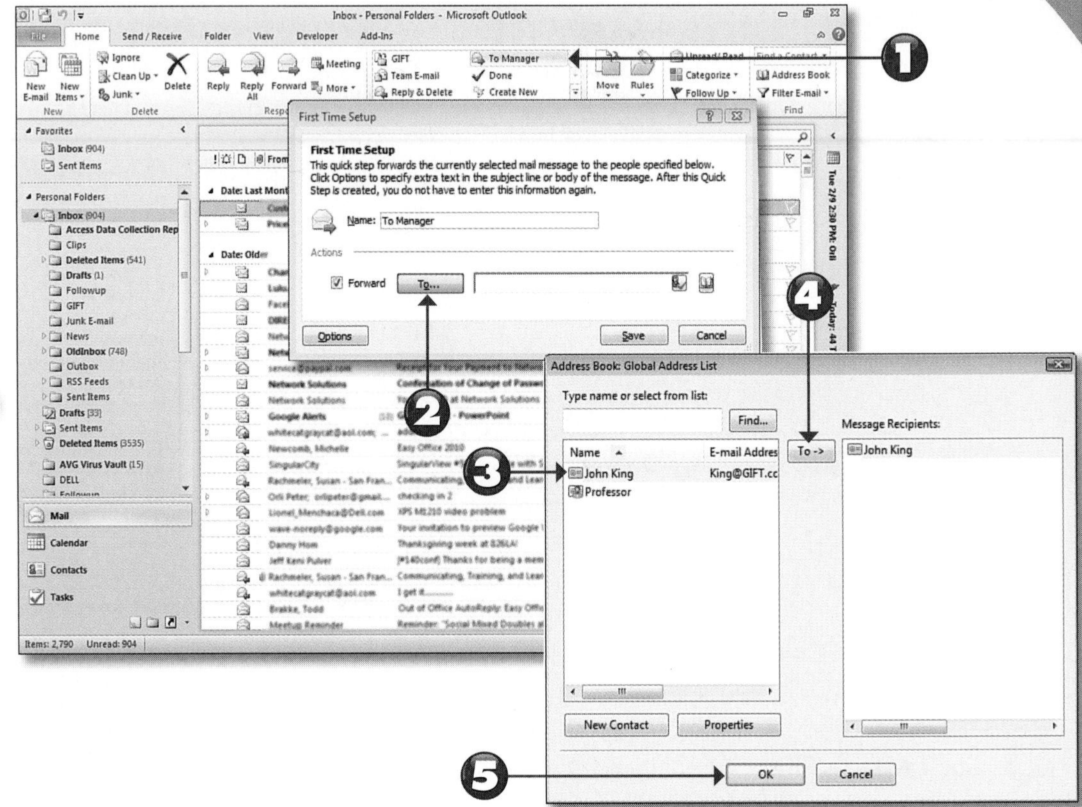

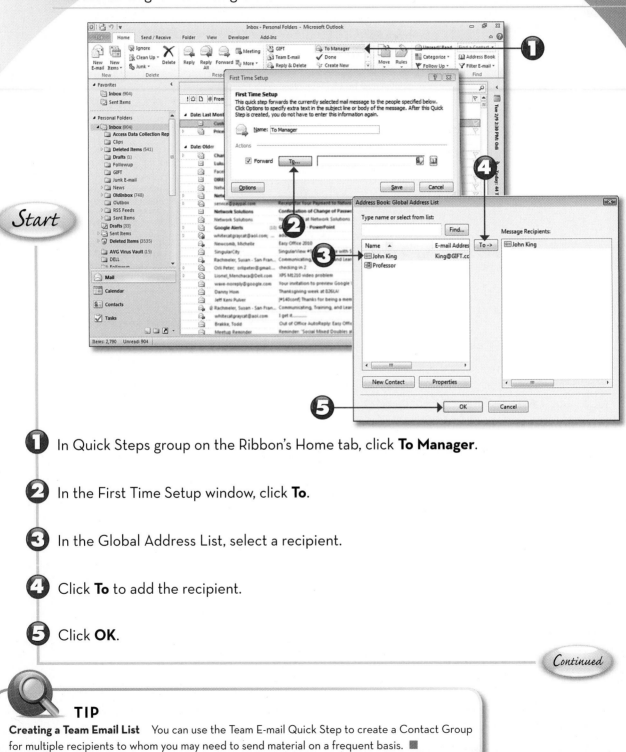

Start

1. In Quick Steps group on the Ribbon's Home tab, click **To Manager**.
2. In the First Time Setup window, click **To**.
3. In the Global Address List, select a recipient.
4. Click **To** to add the recipient.
5. Click **OK**.

Continued

TIP

Creating a Team Email List You can use the Team E-mail Quick Step to create a Contact Group for multiple recipients to whom you may need to send material on a frequent basis. ■

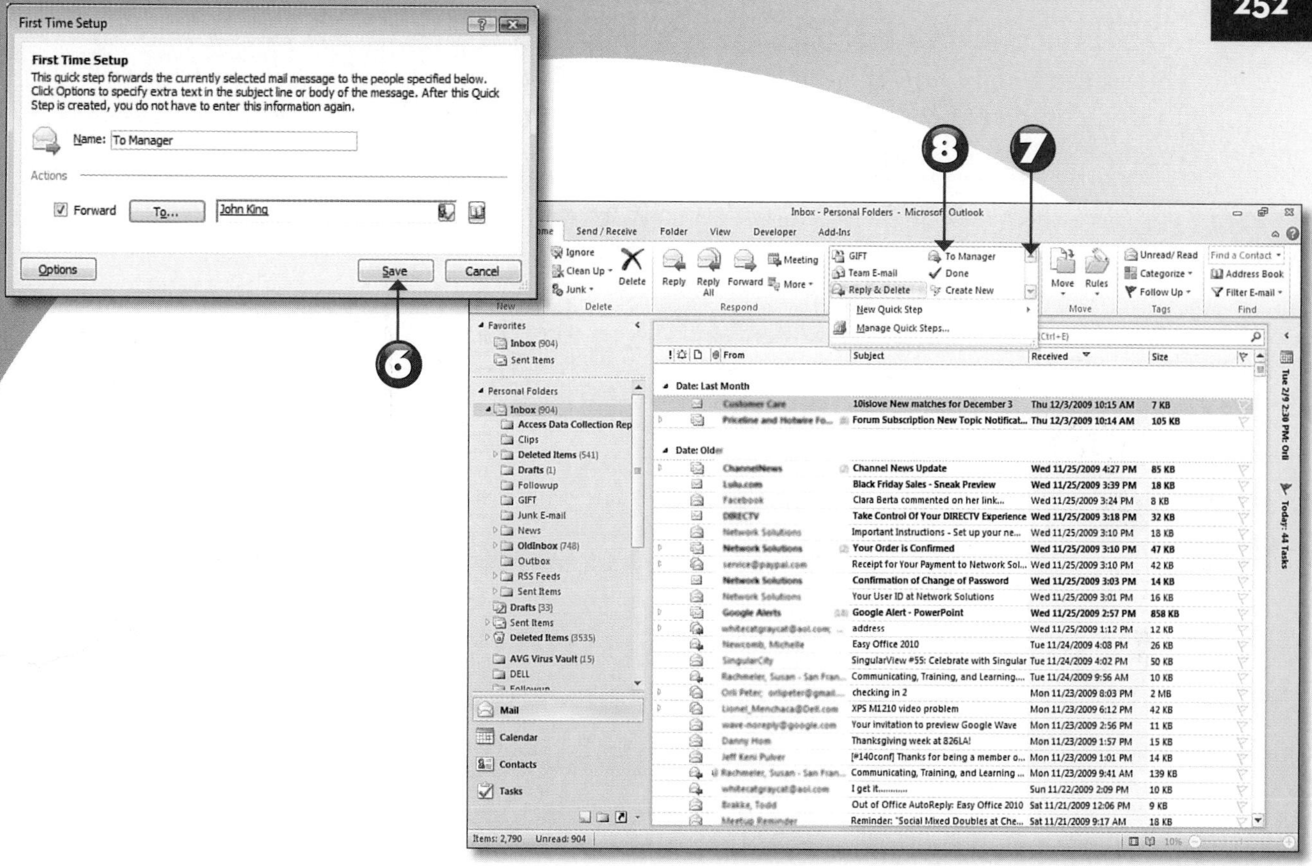

6. In the First Time Setup window, click **Save**.

7. You can click the drop-down arrow in Quick Steps and select **New Quick Step** or **Manage Quick Steps**.

8. Now, when you click **To Manager**, you can send email directly to the recipient designated as Manager in Quick Steps.

End

TIP

Moving Email or Processing Read Email You can create a Quick Step that, when you click it, moves a read and replied-to email to another folder for organization and recordkeeping. ■

TIP

Managing Quick Steps You can click the More arrow for Quick Steps and select Manage Quick Steps to edit or change Quick Steps you've already created. ■

USING CONVERSATION AND READING PANE VIEWS

Messages with a small arrow to their left in your Inbox are part of a *conversation*, or an ongoing thread of correspondence of which they are a part. You can click the arrow successively to expand the conversation to reveal, read, and respond to other emails in the thread.

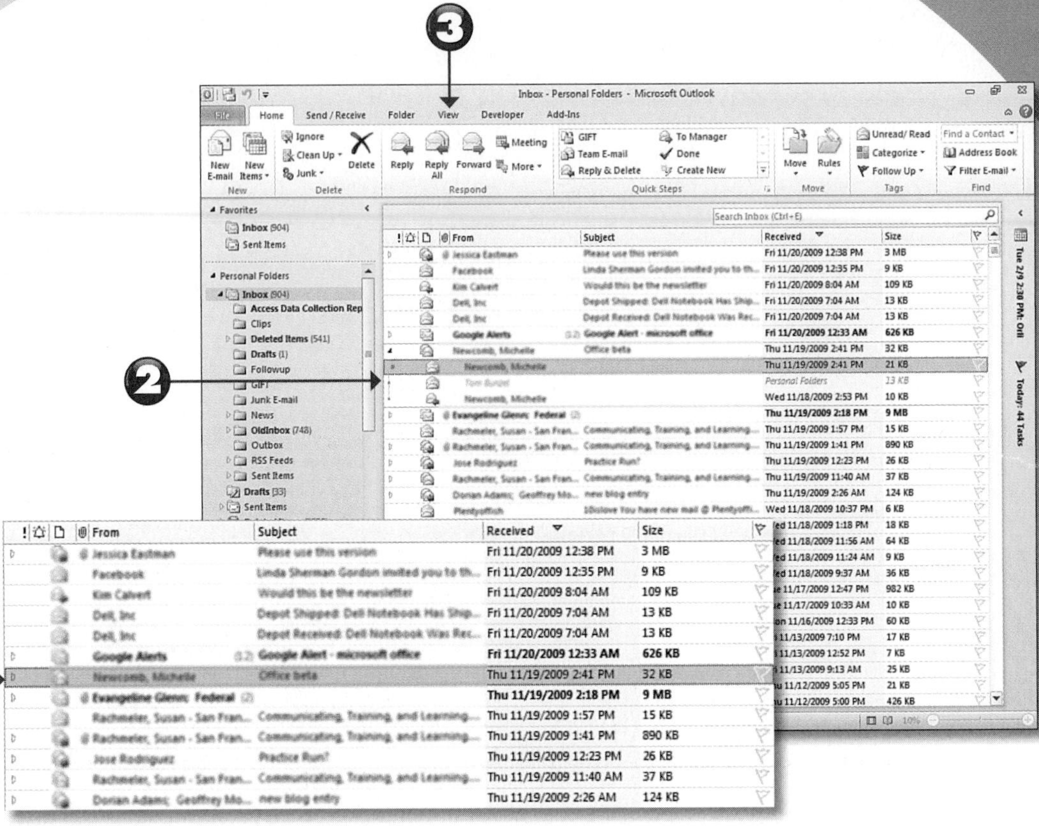

Start

1. Click the **right arrow** next to an email that is part of a conversation.
2. Review the thread of emails between you and the sender.
3. Click to open the **View** tab on the Ribbon.

Continued

NOTE

Conversation Options Clicking **Conversations** in the View tab gives you a list of options as to how conversations should be displayed and arranged. ■

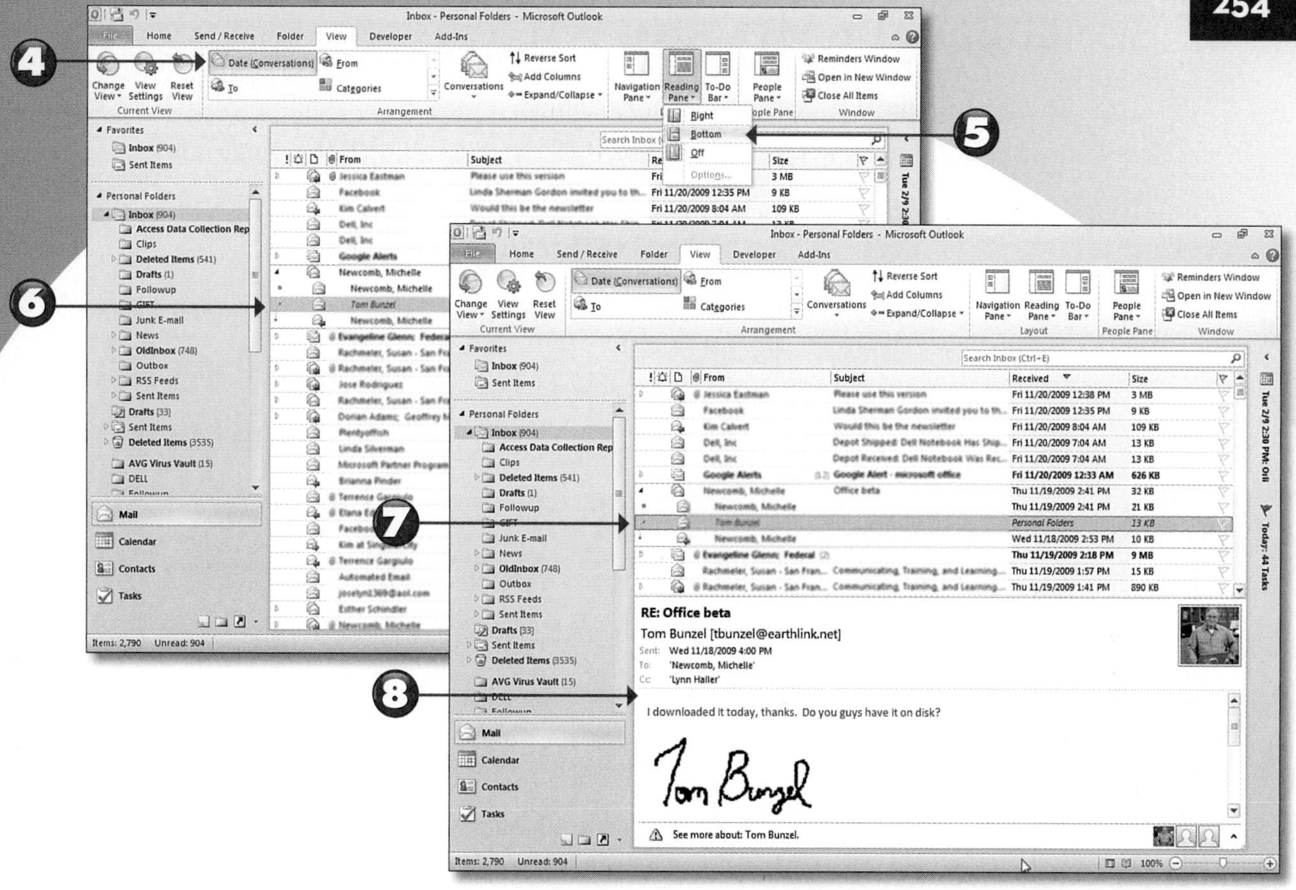

4. The View tab of the Ribbon is active with Date (Conversations) highlighted.

5. Open the **Reading Pane** in the Layout group and click **Bottom**.

6. Click one of the emails in the conversation.

7. You can read the email directly in the Inbox without opening it.

8. You can collapse the conversation by double-clicking the original email message.

End

TIP

Expand/Collapse Clicking **Expand/Collapse** in the Ribbon's View tab lets you expand or collapse the currently selected email conversation or select to expand or collapse all conversations in your Inbox. ■

TIP

Changing Arrangement The Arrangement gallery in the Ribbon's View tab provides different options for sorting, filtering, and viewing your email in the Inbox. ■

SCHEDULING A MEETING WITH EMAIL

You can schedule an appointment or meeting with anyone from whom you've received an email directly from the email message itself. Alternatively, you can locate the person in your contacts list, and the email meeting request will be opened with the email address in the To field.

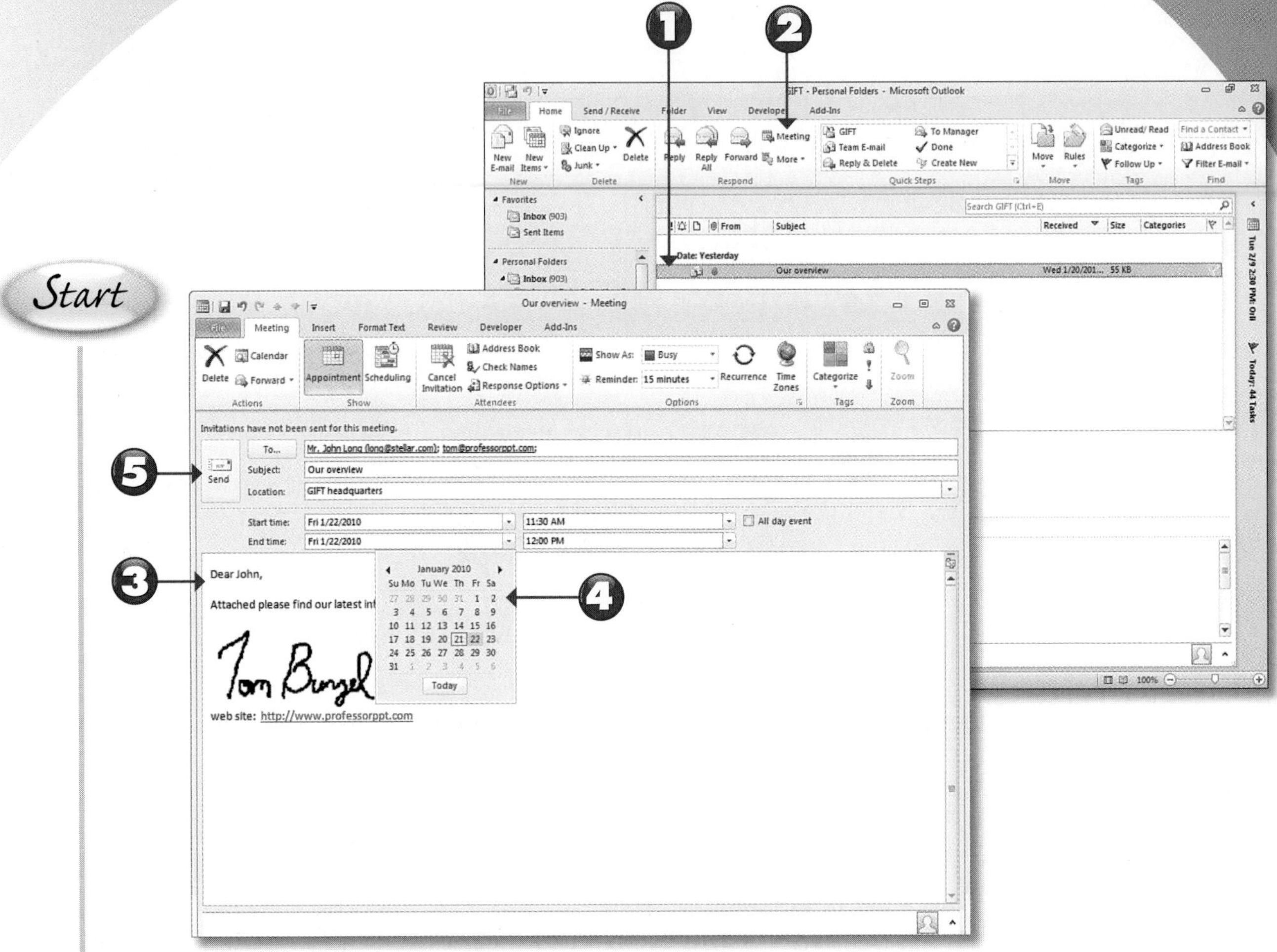

1. Select an email message from the person with whom you want to schedule a meeting.
2. Click **Meeting** to open a Meeting email message. (Note that the Meeting tab on the message is active by default.)
3. Type in a message about the meeting.
4. Fill in the schedule for the date and time.
5. Click **Send**.

Continued

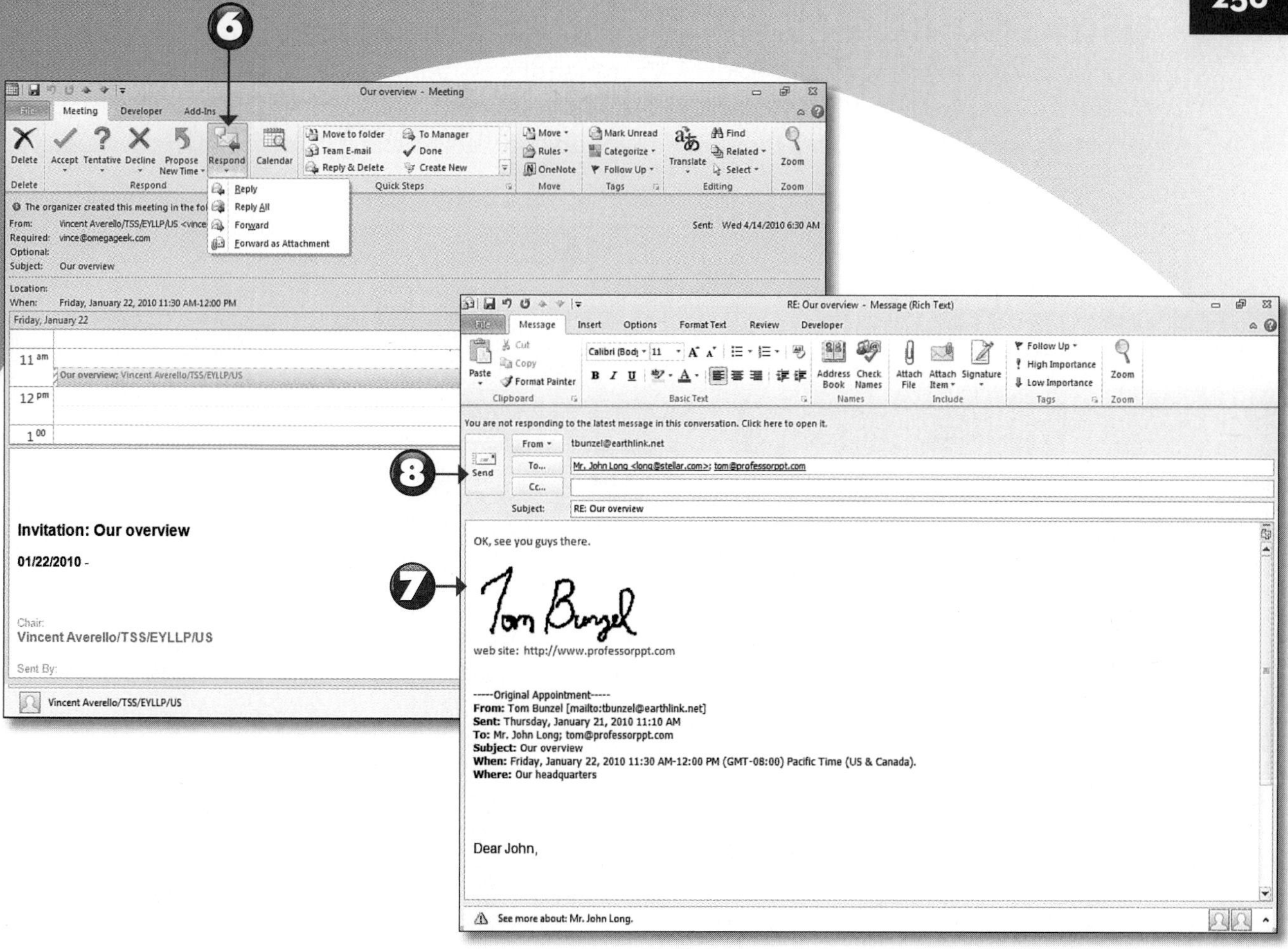

6. The recipient of the meeting request email can click **Respond** and reply to it.

7. The recipient can enter a reply message.

8. After the recipient clicks **Send**, the response is received in your Inbox.

End

TIP

Canceling the Meeting To cancel a meeting, you can click **Cancel Invitation** in the Meeting tab of the Ribbon when you send a meeting request. ■

TIP

Checking Availability You can click **Scheduling** in the Ribbon's Meeting tab to see your schedule for the time period selected to be able to see the best time to schedule a meeting. The recipient can do the same in the reply message. ■

USING SCHEDULE VIEW AND ONENOTE

Schedule View in Outlook lets you see your meetings within a calendar, with a Meeting tab on the Ribbon, so that you can track and revise your meetings. Outlook's integration with OneNote lets you schedule a meeting in Outlook and also have it appear in OneNote's Meeting Details section.

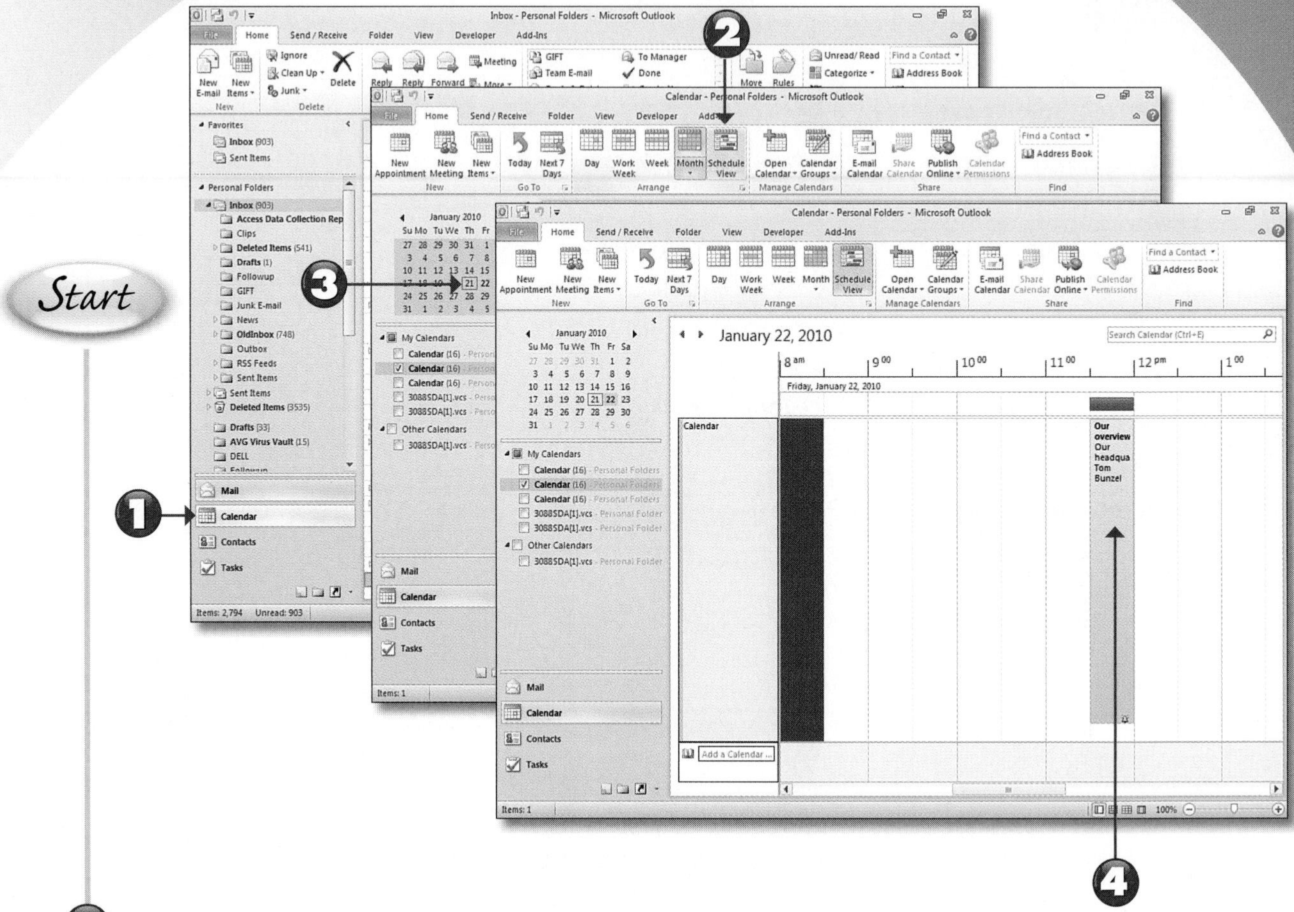

Start

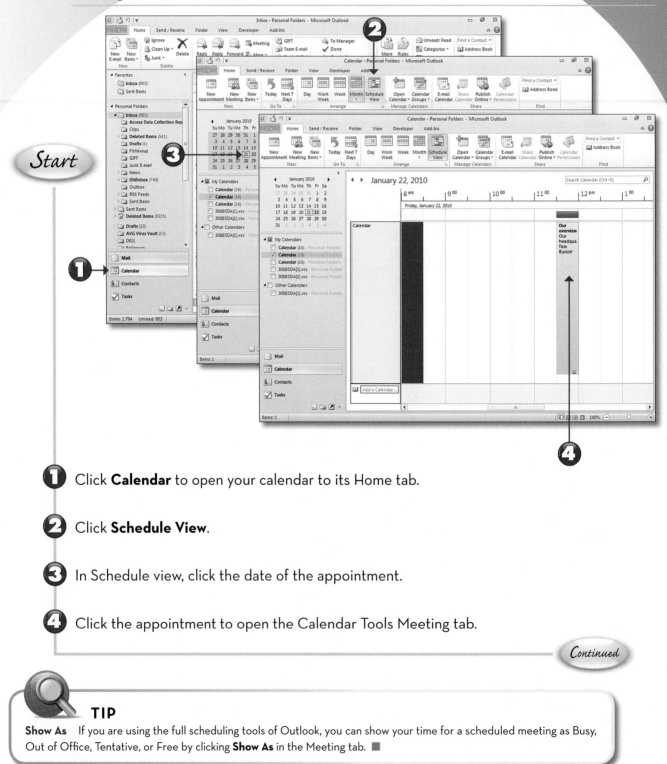

1. Click **Calendar** to open your calendar to its Home tab.
2. Click **Schedule View**.
3. In Schedule view, click the date of the appointment.
4. Click the appointment to open the Calendar Tools Meeting tab.

Continued

TIP

Show As If you are using the full scheduling tools of Outlook, you can show your time for a scheduled meeting as Busy, Out of Office, Tentative, or Free by clicking **Show As** in the Meeting tab. ■

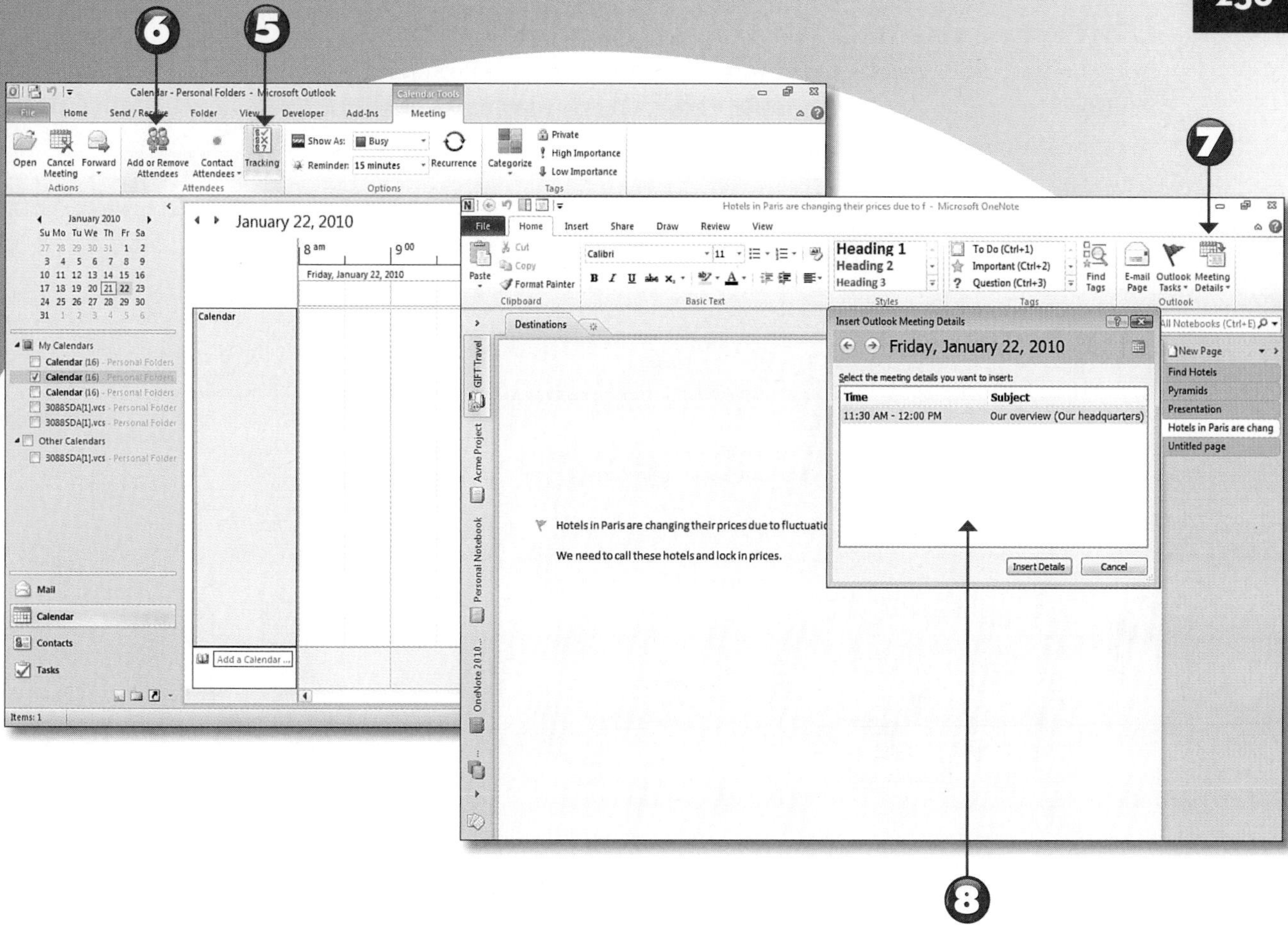

5 You can click **Tracking** to see who has responded to the request.

6 You can also click **Add or Remove Attendees**.

7 To see meeting details in OneNote, open OneNote and click **Meeting Details**.

8 Your meeting information is also available in OneNote.

End

TIP

Tags To organize your meetings, you can apply categories or set importance levels from the Tags group of the Meeting tab.

USING THEMES AND COLORS IN EMAIL

You can use the Options tab on the Ribbon in an email to change the appearance of objects in your message or its background color. You can even use the Ribbon tools to work with specific elements (such as charts).

Start

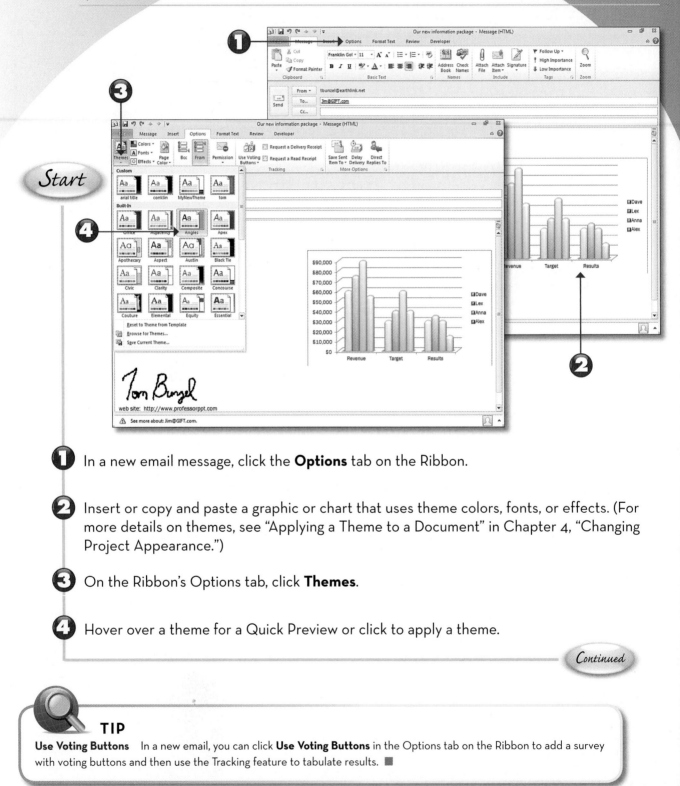

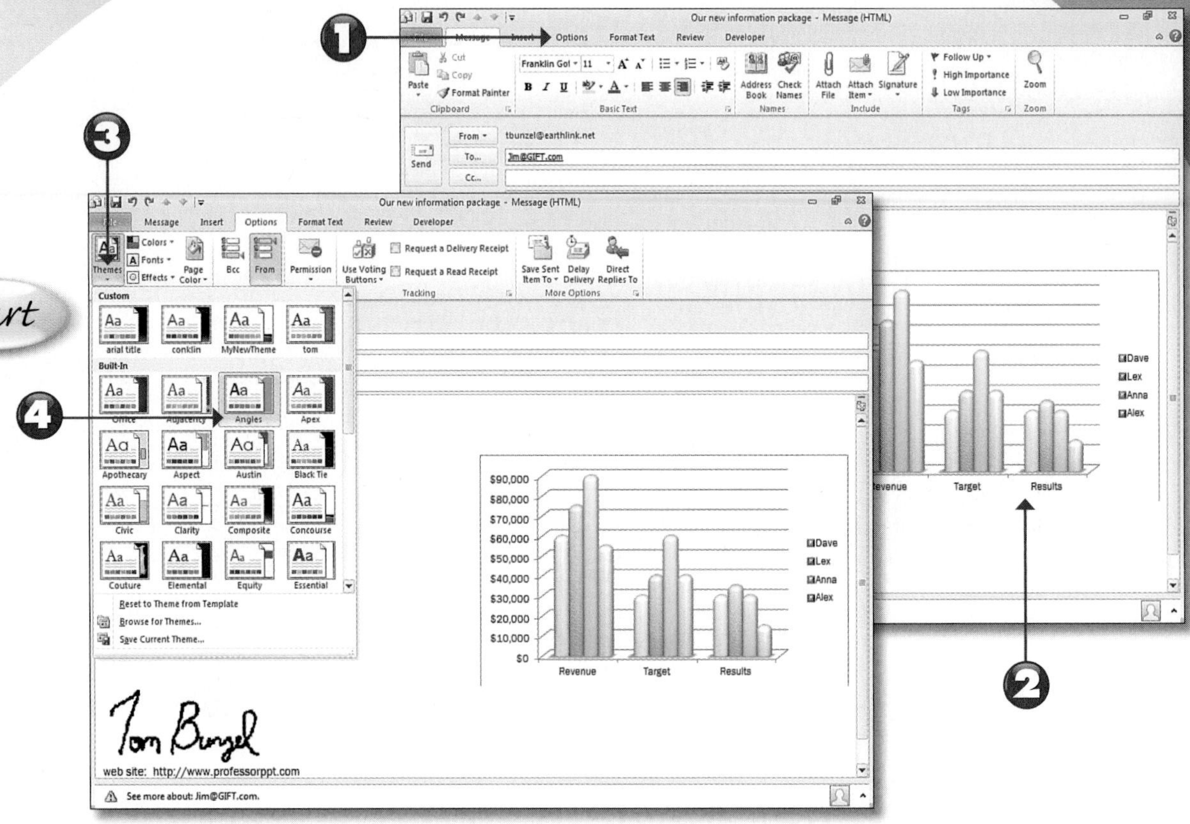

1. In a new email message, click the **Options** tab on the Ribbon.
2. Insert or copy and paste a graphic or chart that uses theme colors, fonts, or effects. (For more details on themes, see “Applying a Theme to a Document” in Chapter 4, “Changing Project Appearance.”)
3. On the Ribbon’s Options tab, click **Themes**.
4. Hover over a theme for a Quick Preview or click to apply a theme.

Continued

TIP

Use Voting Buttons In a new email, you can click **Use Voting Buttons** in the Options tab on the Ribbon to add a survey with voting buttons and then use the Tracking feature to tabulate results. ■

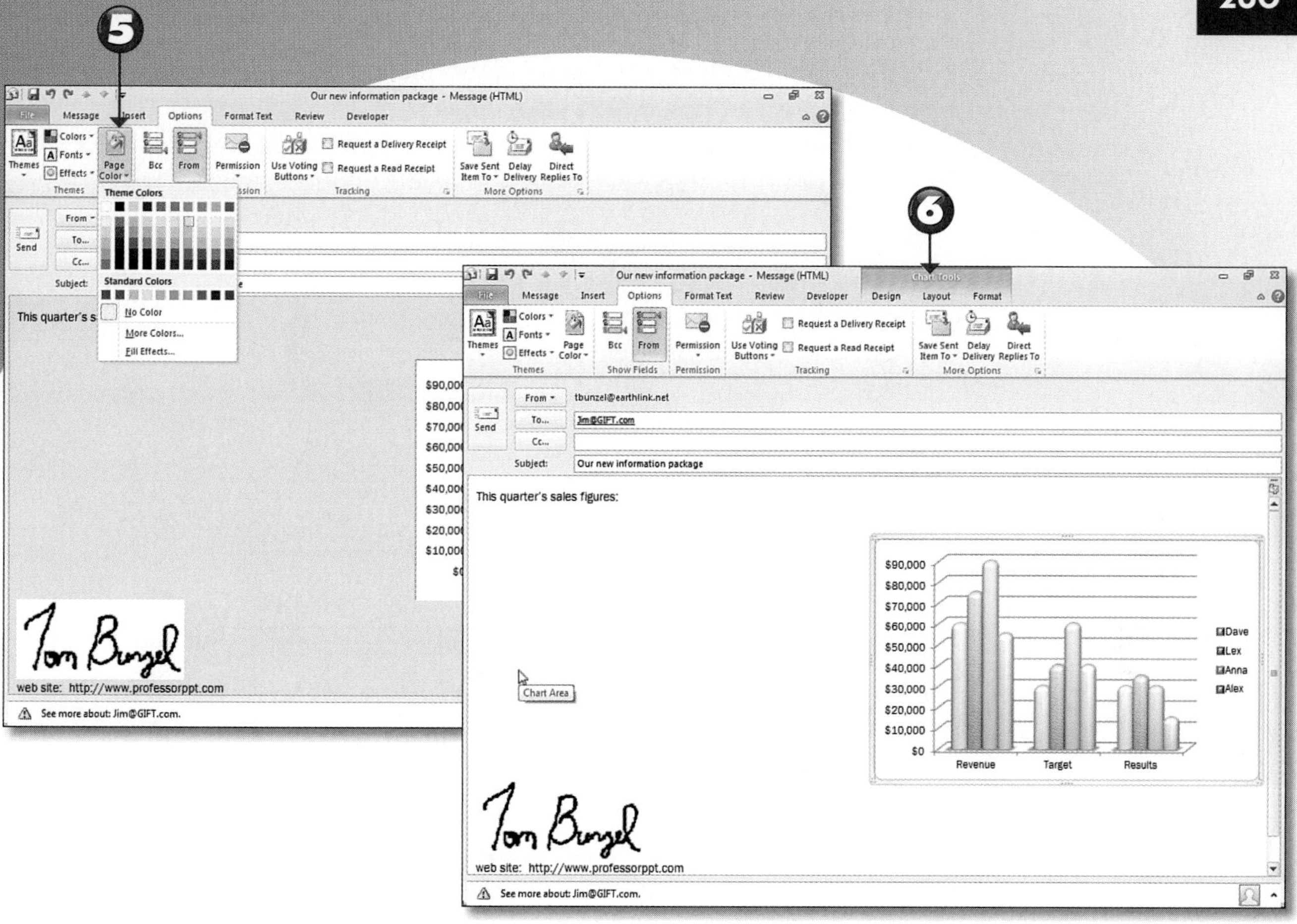

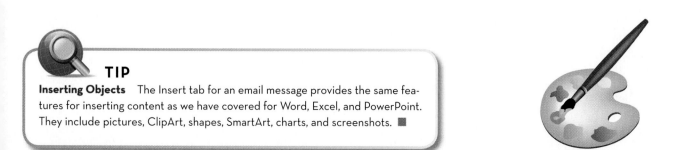

5 Click **Page Color** to apply a color background to the email.

6 If you have inserted a chart or graphic, click it to have the [Chart] Tools become active on the Ribbon. (For more details on working with charts, see Chapter 10, "Creating Charts, Data Tables, and Pivot Tables.")

End

TIP

Inserting Objects The Insert tab for an email message provides the same features for inserting content as we have covered for Word, Excel, and PowerPoint. They include pictures, ClipArt, shapes, SmartArt, charts, and screenshots.

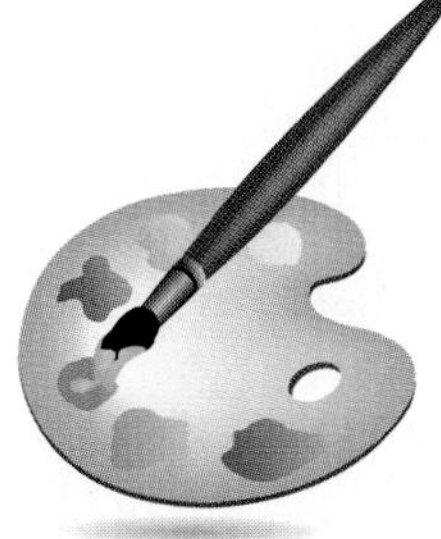

USING RSS FEEDS IN OUTLOOK'S INBOX

Really Simple Syndication (RSS) is an Internet subscription feature that lets you get the latest information from a website that has an RSS feed. Such sites can include news sites, most types of blogs, and much more. You can use Outlook as your RSS Reader by copying and pasting the RSS feed's URL into the RSS Feeds feature in your Outlook Inbox.

Start

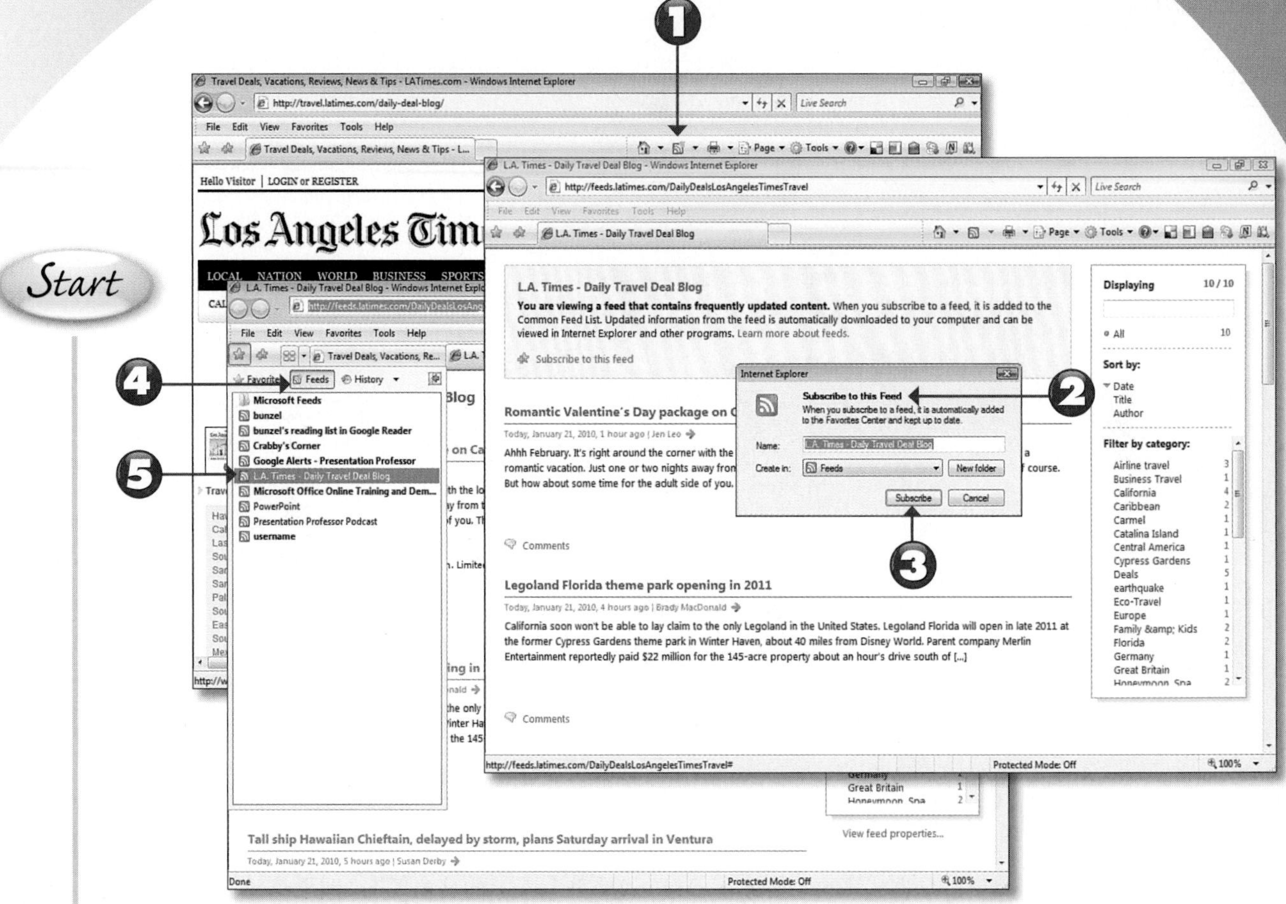

1. Using Internet Explorer as your web browser, locate a site with an RSS feed and click the orange RSS icon on the toolbar.
2. Click **Subscribe to This Feed**.
3. Rename the feed if you prefer and click **Subscribe**.
4. Click **Feeds** in Internet Explorer to go to the Feeds page.
5. Select the URL of the feed page and press **Ctrl+C** to copy it to the Clipboard.

Continued

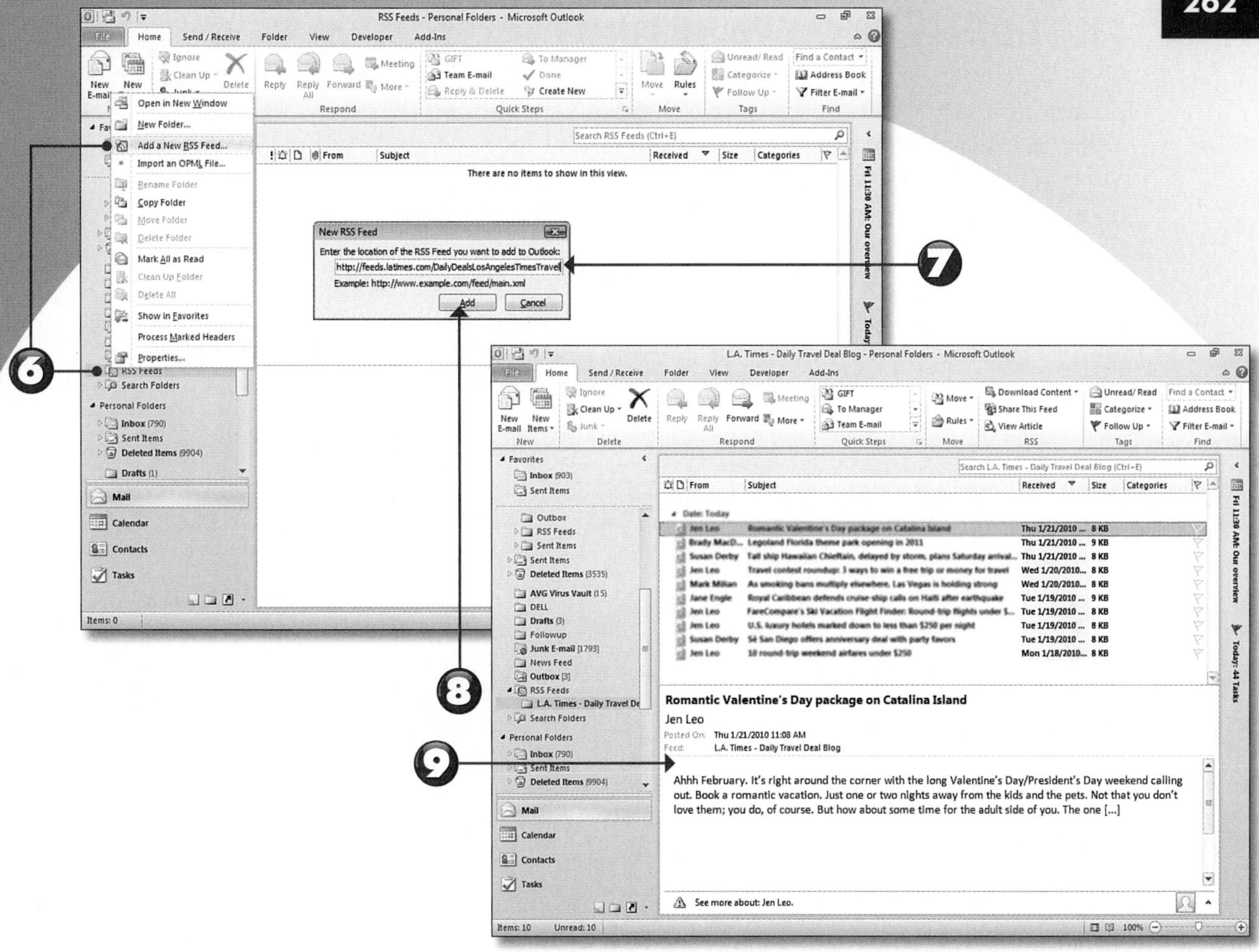

6. Right-click the orange RSS folder in Outlook and click **Add a New RSS Feed**.

7. Press **Ctrl+V** to paste the feed's URL in the New RSS Feed window.

8. Click **Add**.

9. The RSS subscription becomes available for you in Outlook.

End

TIP

Going to the Web Page The main purpose of the RSS reader is to read or at least scan for new site content without having to go to the web page, but most feeds do have links to view the full information back on the website if needed. ■

TIP

What Are Podcasts? Podcasts are RSS feeds that point to audio files that you can listen to, generally in *.MP3 or *.WMA format. If you subscribe to a podcast using Outlook, you can click on the link to the audio file and listen to it using Windows Media Player. ■

FILTERING AND SEARCHING MESSAGES

Outlook 2010 provides a robust filtering capability for email that filters messages by certain preset parameters and opens a Search tab on the Ribbon that provides additional options and functionality. You can use the **Refine Group** on the Search tab to change the parameters of items in the Search panel; for example, click From to search by Sender or Has Attachments to search by attachments.

Start

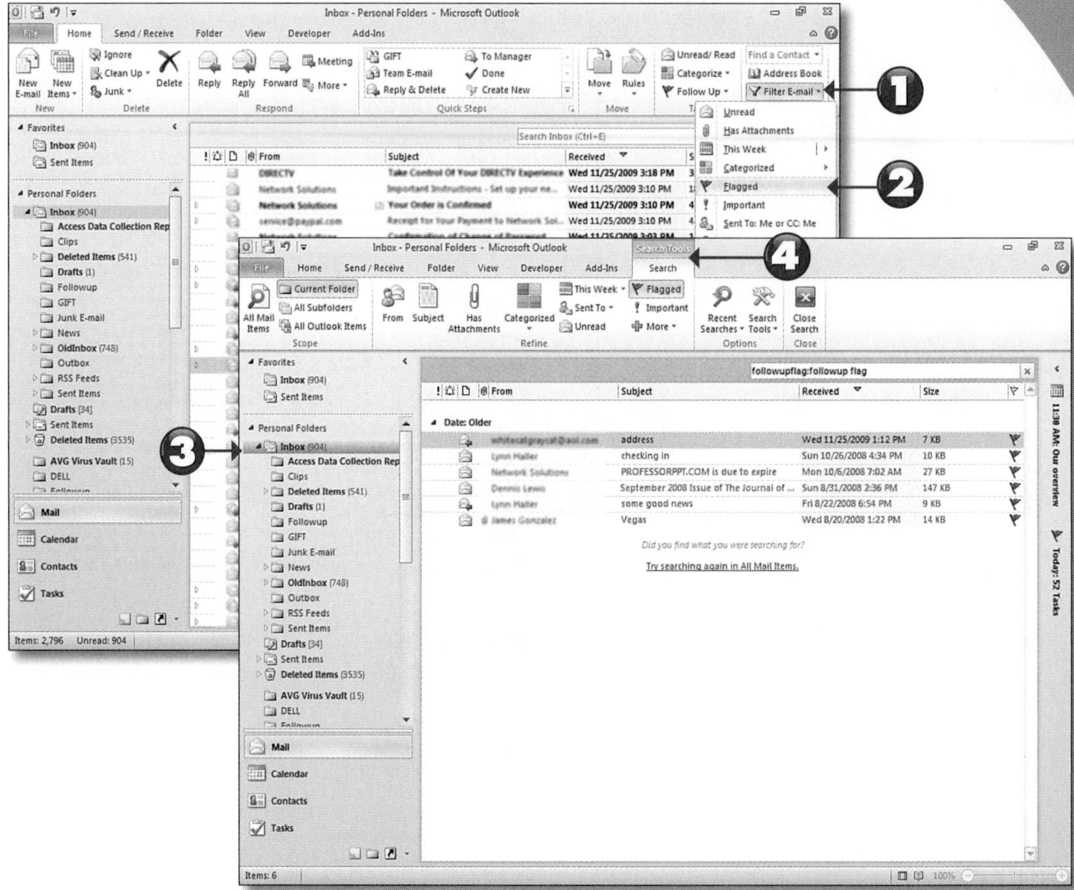

1. Click **Filter E-mail**.
2. Click a filter; for example, click **Flagged**.
3. The Inbox is filtered by the parameter you selected; all flagged messages are shown in this case.
4. The Search tab or the Ribbon is available for additional searches and options**.**

Continued

5 You can click **Recent Searches** to repeat former searches.

6 Click **Close Search** to return to the Inbox.

7 You can click **Categorize** to set categories for selected email.

8 You can click **All Categories** under Categorize to change or create new categories.

End

TIP

Setting Search Scope You can change the scope of a search from the default (Current Folder) to All Subfolders, All Outlook Items, or All Mail Items using the Scope group on the Search tab. ■

TIP

Advanced Find To set more detailed search parameters, you can use the Search Tools in the Search Tab and select **Advanced Find**. ■

USING THE SEARCH TAB

Outlook's Search tab on the Ribbon lets you search extensively throughout your email Inbox. You can search email by Attachments, Sender, Subject, and more. You can refine your search by more than one parameter .

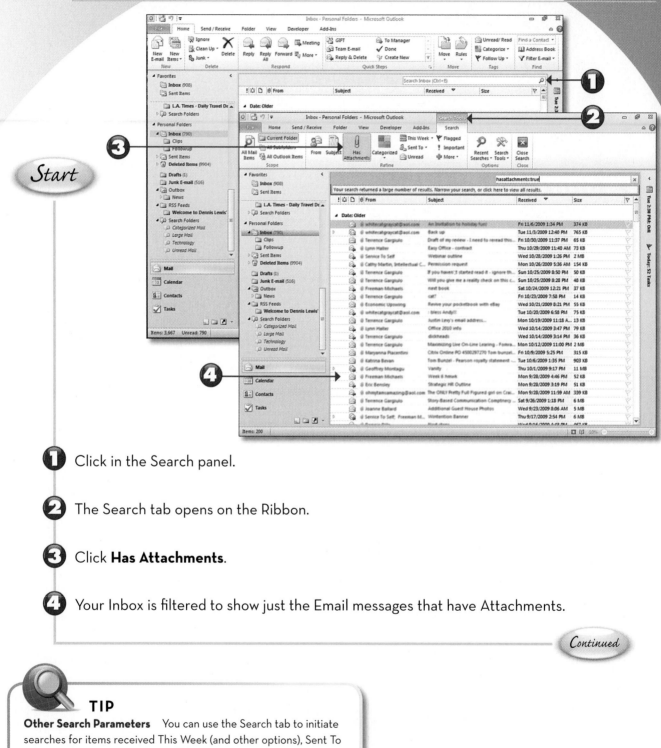

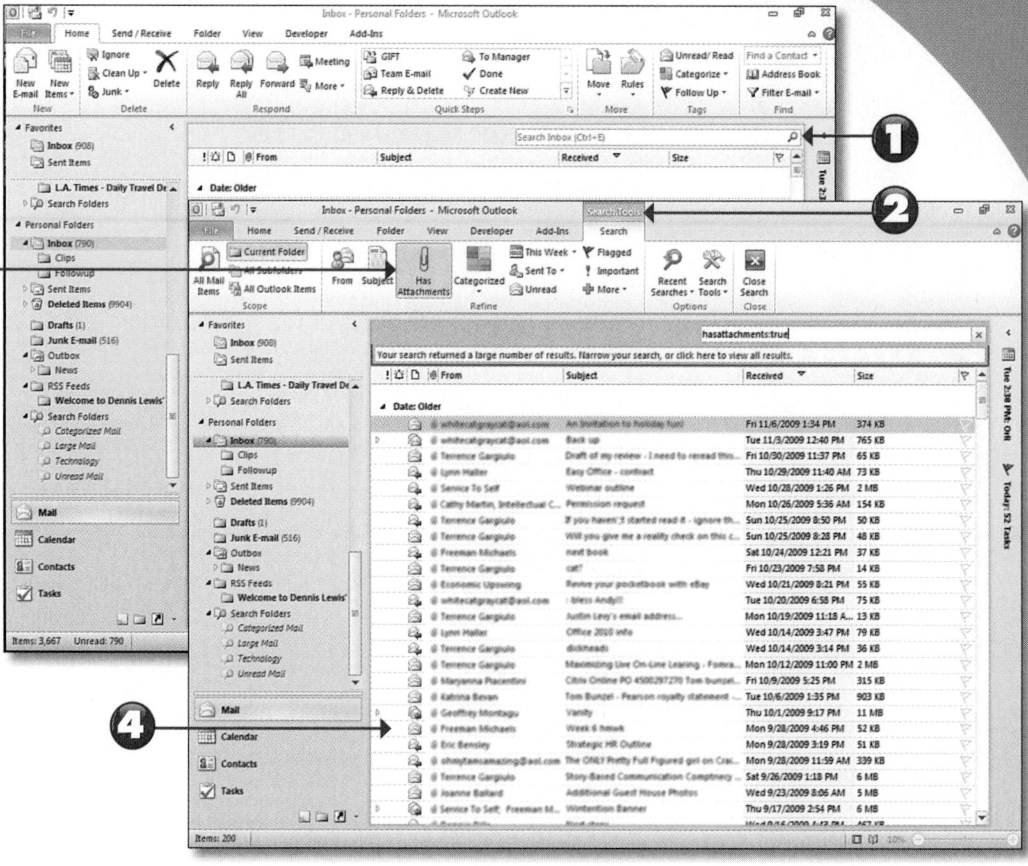

Start

1. Click in the Search panel.
2. The Search tab opens on the Ribbon.
3. Click **Has Attachments**.
4. Your Inbox is filtered to show just the Email messages that have Attachments.

Continued

TIP

Other Search Parameters You can use the Search tab to initiate searches for items received This Week (and other options), Sent To (and other options), and Unread email.

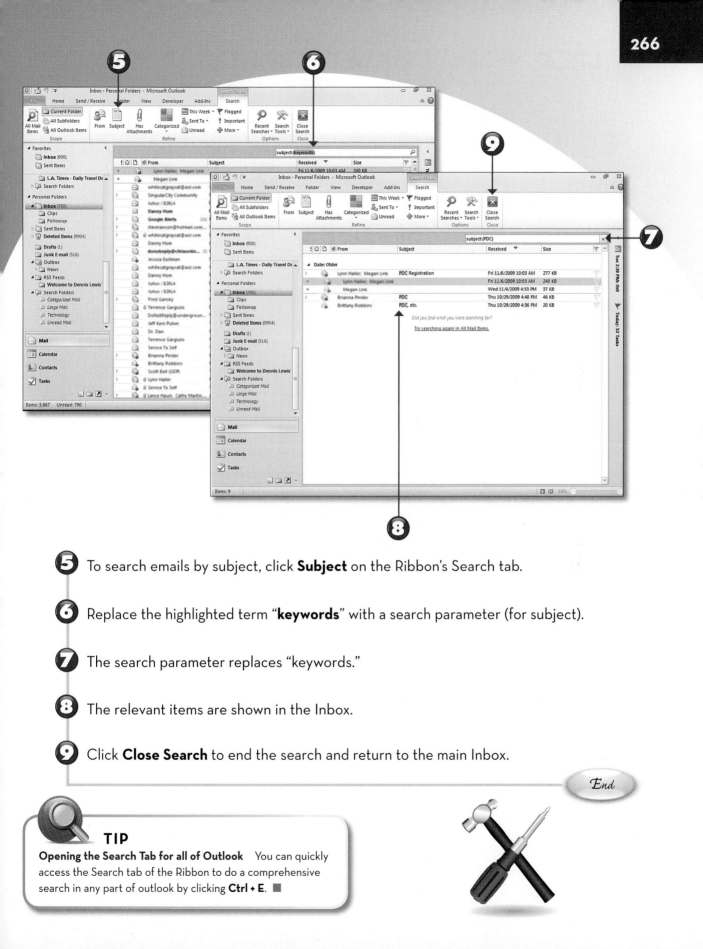

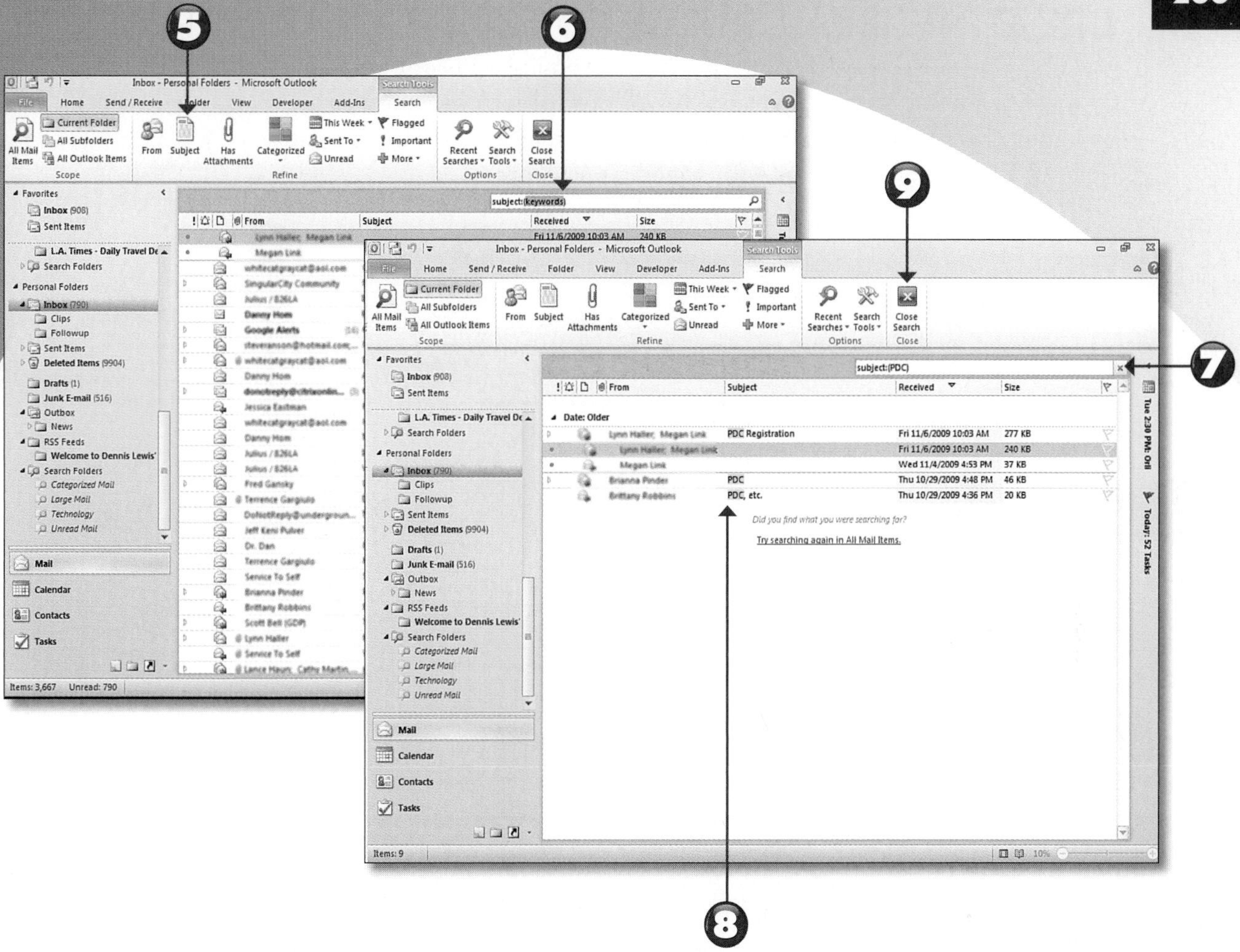

5 To search emails by subject, click **Subject** on the Ribbon's Search tab.

6 Replace the highlighted term "**keywords**" with a search parameter (for subject).

7 The search parameter replaces "keywords."

8 The relevant items are shown in the Inbox.

9 Click **Close Search** to end the search and return to the main Inbox.

End

TIP

Opening the Search Tab for all of Outlook You can quickly access the Search tab of the Ribbon to do a comprehensive search in any part of outlook by clicking **Ctrl + E**. ■

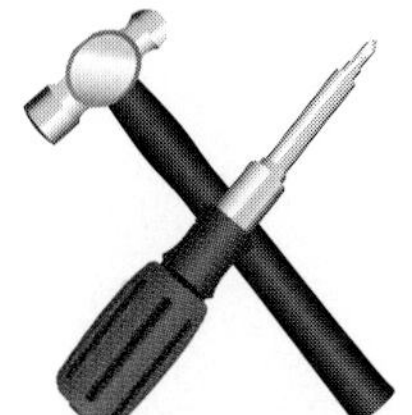

CREATING EMAIL RULES FOR SPAM AND ROUTING

You can create rules that determine how incoming and sent email messages are processed by having individual messages sent to various folders, assigned to a category, and more. You can immediately create a rule for a selected email based on the sender, or you can use the Rules Wizard to create rules with specific parameters.

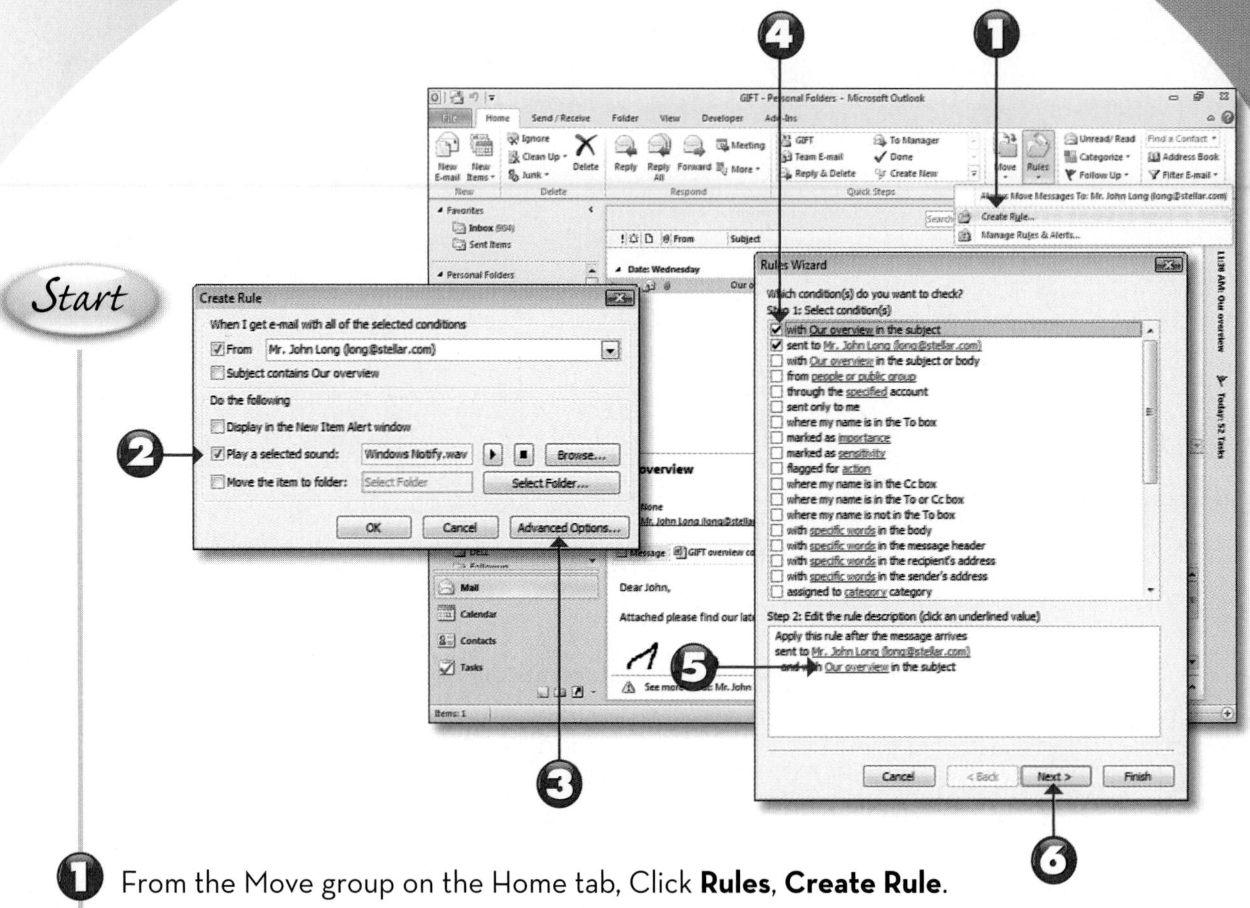

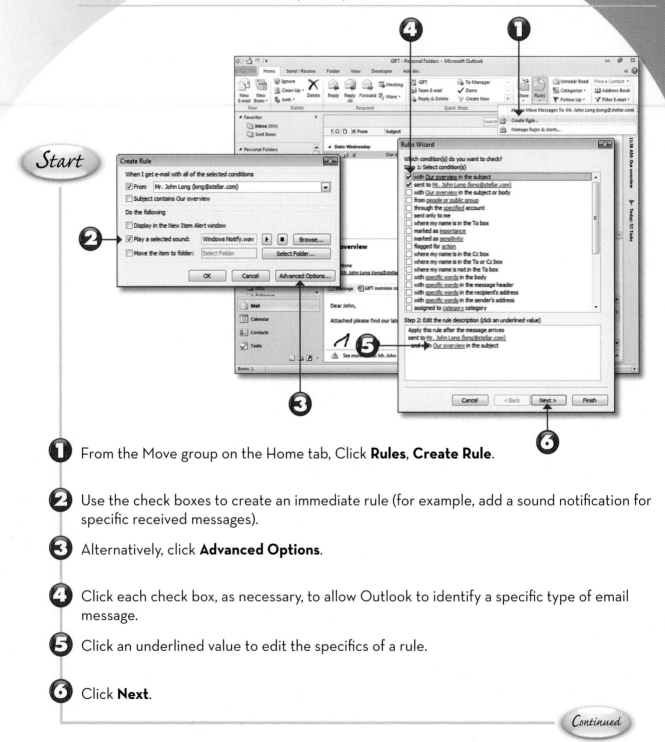

1. From the Move group on the Home tab, Click **Rules**, **Create Rule**.
2. Use the check boxes to create an immediate rule (for example, add a sound notification for specific received messages).
3. Alternatively, click **Advanced Options**.
4. Click each check box, as necessary, to allow Outlook to identify a specific type of email message.
5. Click an underlined value to edit the specifics of a rule.
6. Click **Next**.

Continued

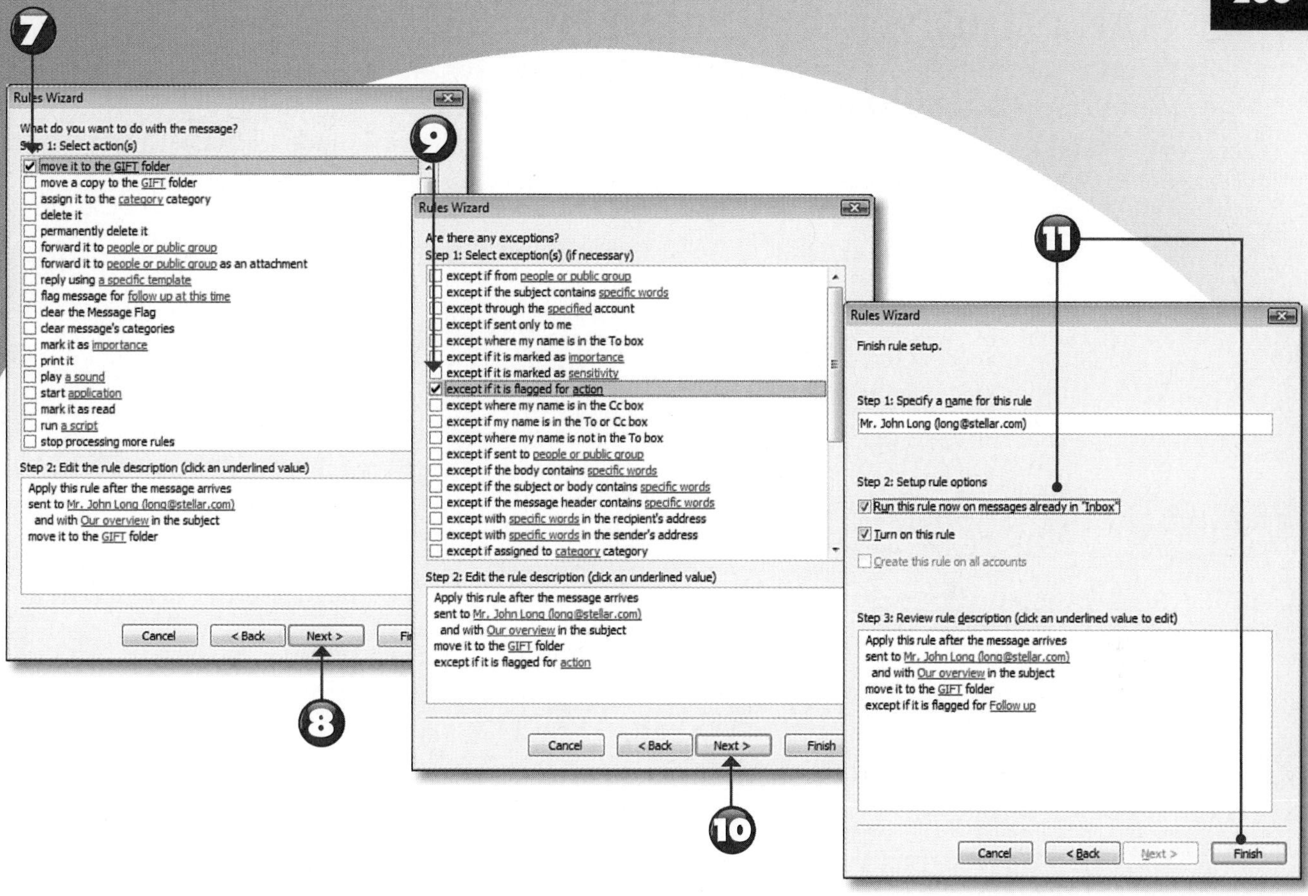

7 Click each check box, as necessary, that tells Outlook what to do with messages that match the rule you've configured. Edit these instructions as needed.

8 Click **Next**.

9 Click each check box, as necessary, to set any exceptions to the rule you've configured. Edit the exceptions as needed.

10 Click **Next**.

11 You can run the rule on your existing messages or merely turn it on for new messages. Then click **Finish**.

End

TIP

Managing Your Rules You can see and modify all your rules when you click **Rules** and select **Manage Rules & Alerts**. ■

TIP

Creating a Move to Folder Rule The easiest rule to create is to select an email and click **Rules** and decide where to send all email from a particular sender. ■

MANAGING YOUR CONTACTS

Contacts are where you maintain your main address book and information about people with whom you want to stay connected in Outlook. You can manage one or more contacts lists to keep track of key colleagues, customers, vendors, or other individuals who are critical to your business or are important personally.

Start

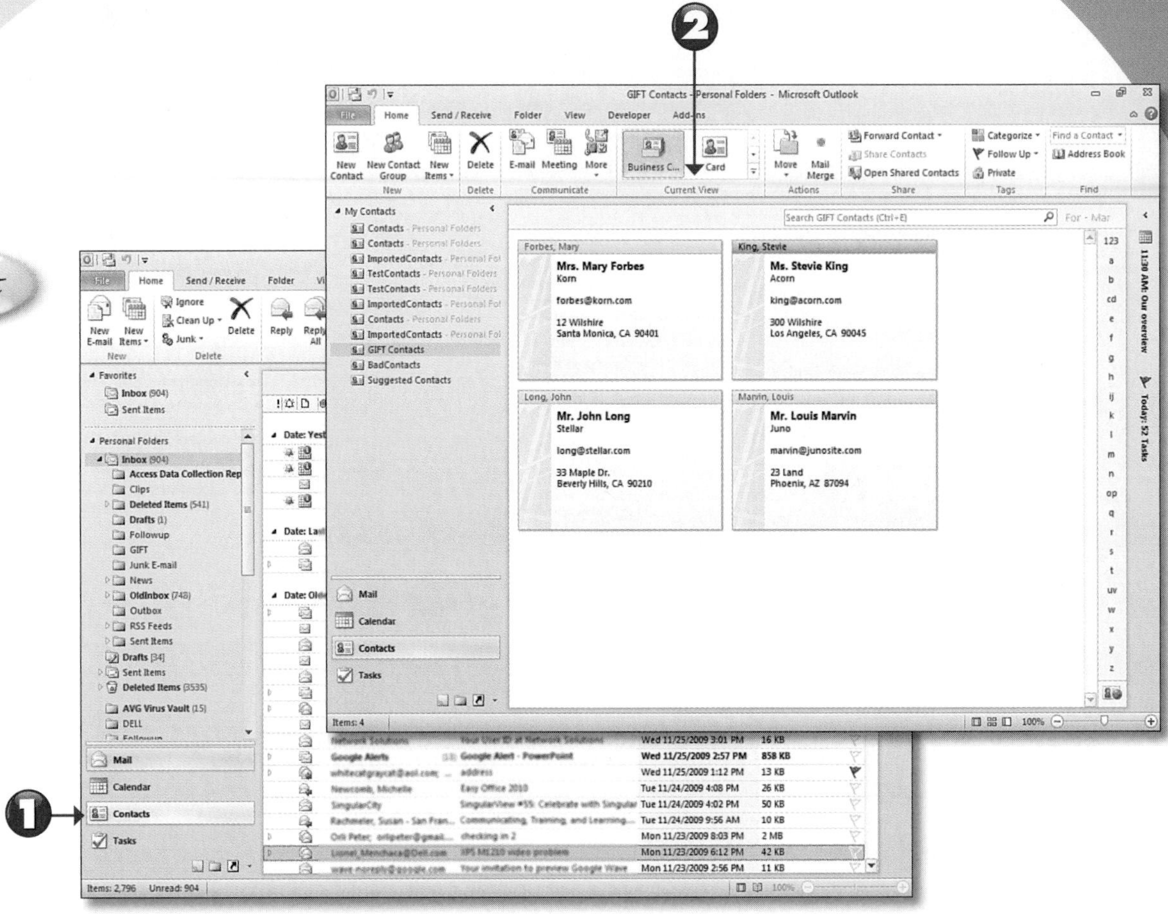

1. Click **Contacts** in the left panel.

2. Your contacts list opens; click **More** from the Current View group on the Home tab.

Continued

TIP

New Contacts List You can create a new contacts list by right-clicking **My Contacts** in the left panel and selecting to create and then name a New Folder Group.

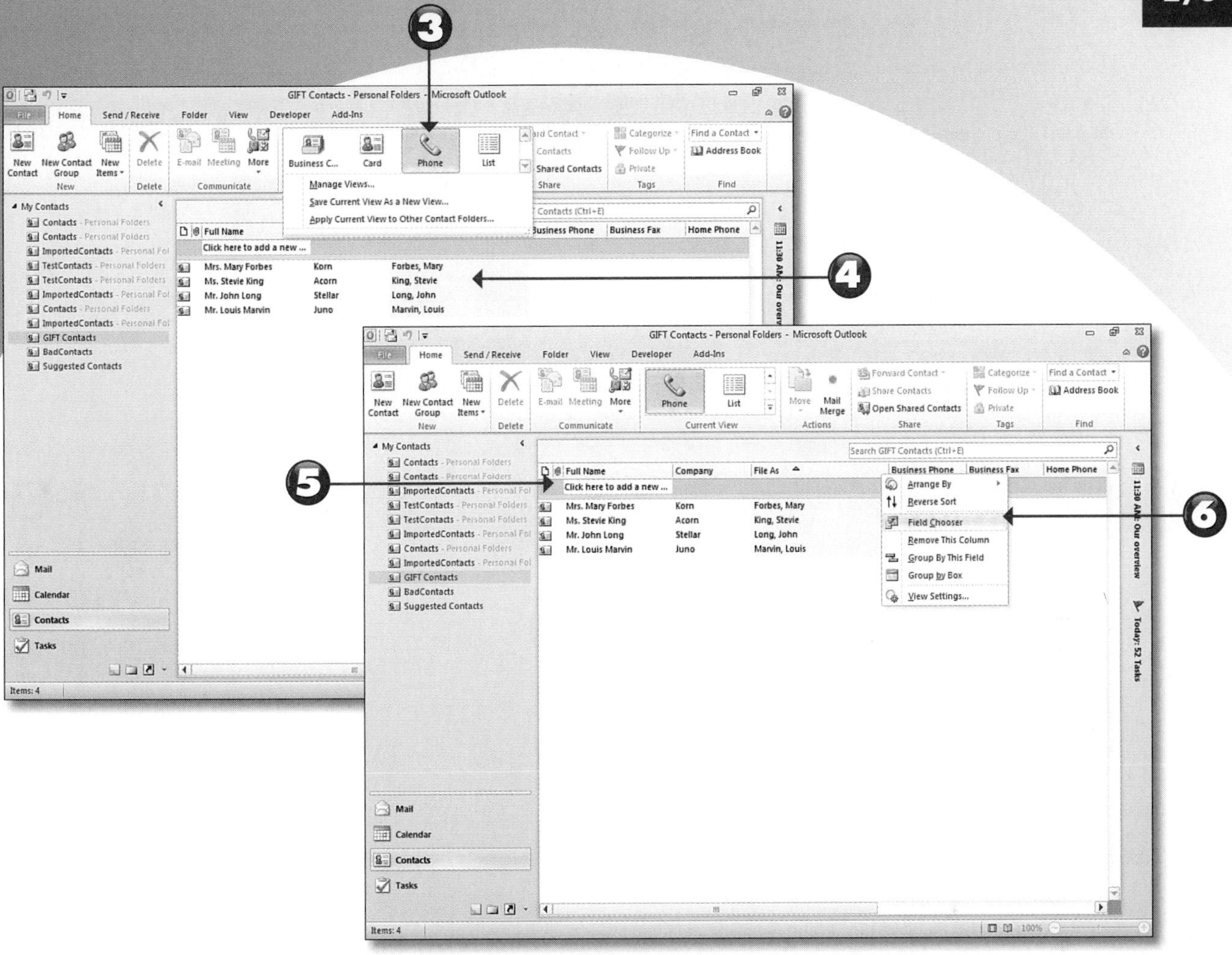

3 Click **Phone**.

4 The list of fields becomes visible.

5 Click the field name to sort ascending or descending; the up or down arrow lets you know how it's sorted.

6 You can right-click the fields to open a **Field Chooser** to add more fields to the Phone List view.

End

TIP

Creating and Editing Contacts For any contact list, you can click **New Contact** to create a new contact, click **Delete** to remove a contact, or double-click a contact to open and revise the contact information and then click **Save and Close**. ■

TIP

New Items When you click **New Items** for a selected contact, you are able to send that person an email, assign a task, set up a meeting, and more. ■

CREATING A NEW CONTACT GROUP

You can collect a set of contacts together and name them as a group to be able to send them all the same email, set up a meeting, create a task, and more. To create a group, click **New Contact Group**, name the group, and add members from your contacts lists.

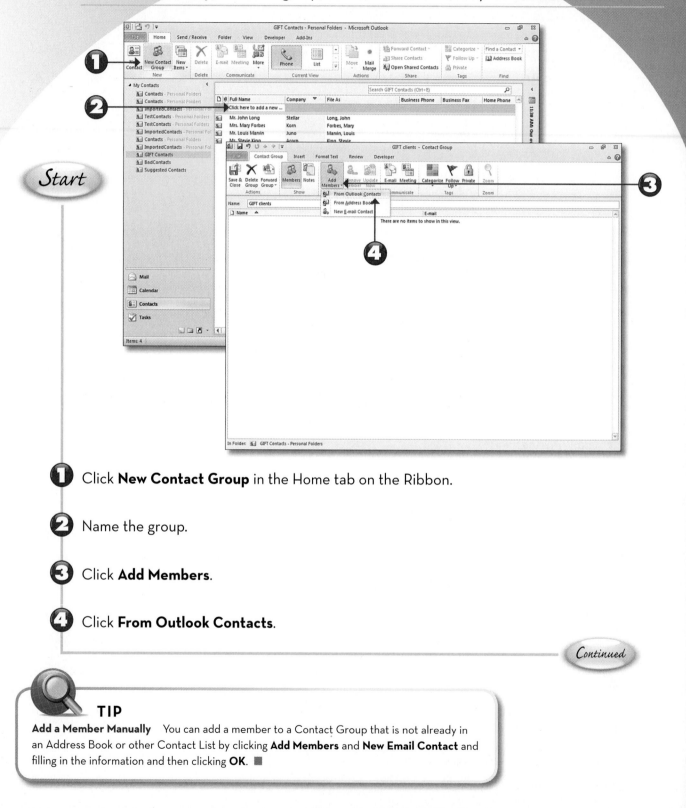

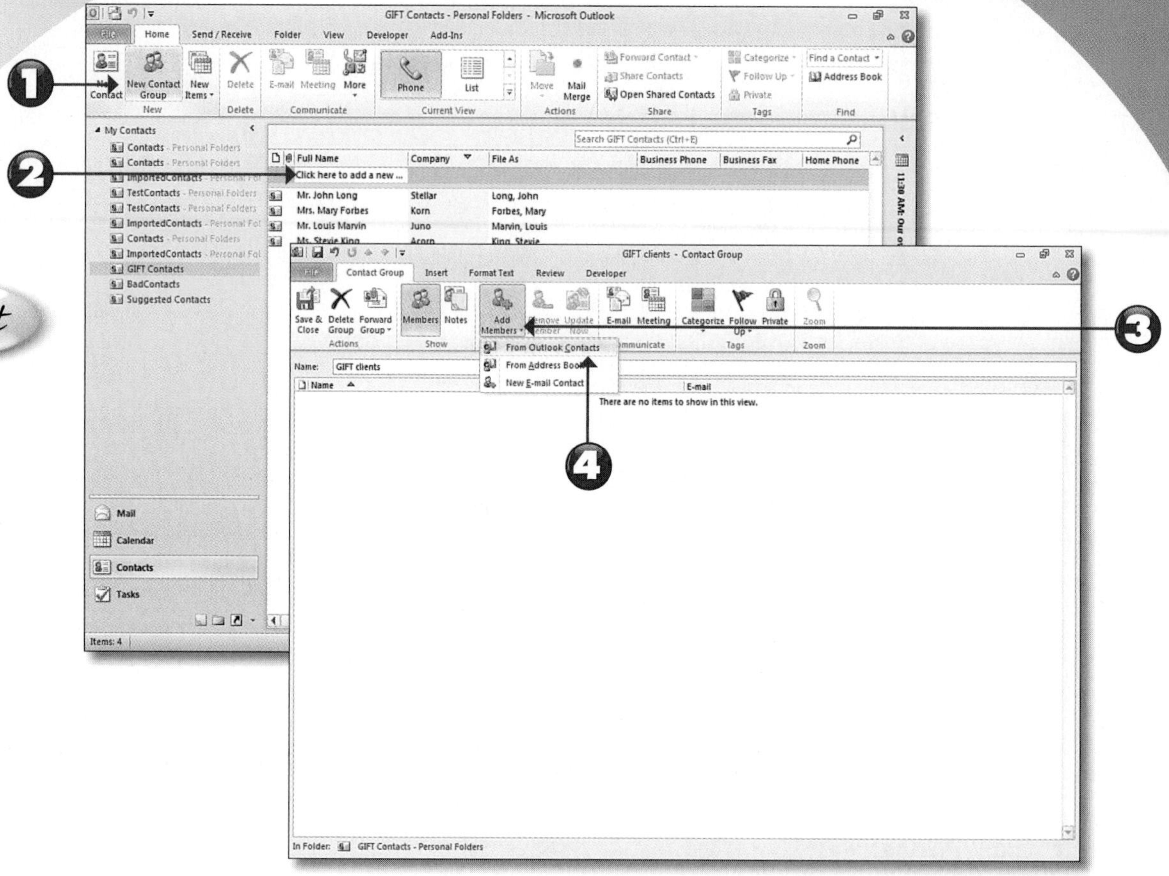

Start

1. Click **New Contact Group** in the Home tab on the Ribbon.
2. Name the group.
3. Click **Add Members**.
4. Click **From Outlook Contacts**.

Continued

TIP

Add a Member Manually You can add a member to a Contact Group that is not already in an Address Book or other Contact List by clicking **Add Members** and **New Email Contact** and filling in the information and then clicking **OK**. ■

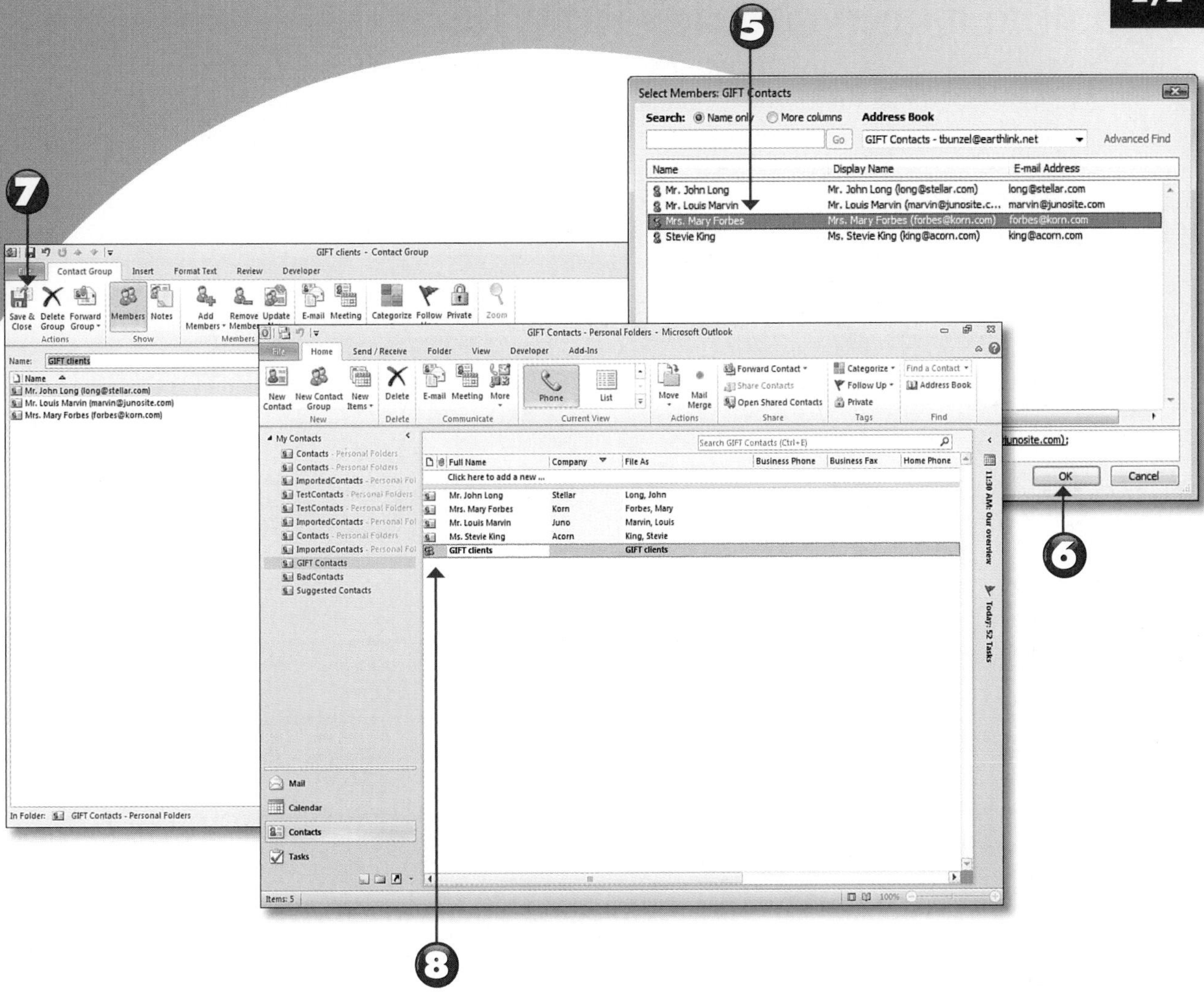

5. Double-click a contact to add that person to the group.

6. Click **OK** after you've added all the contacts you want included in the group.

7. Click **Save & Close**.

8. Your named group is available in your list of contacts.

End

TIP

Moving Recipients to BCC Field When you place the named Contact Group in the To field of an email, the individual recipients can be seen by the other recipients. To avoid this, you can cut and paste the recipients into the BCC field (blind copy); click CC... and then BCC to in the Select Names: Contacts window. ■

PUBLISHING OR SHARING YOUR CALENDAR ONLINE

You can place a calendar online at a Windows Live location and email a message to others to let them subscribe to the calendar and open it in Outlook on their desktop as another calendar.

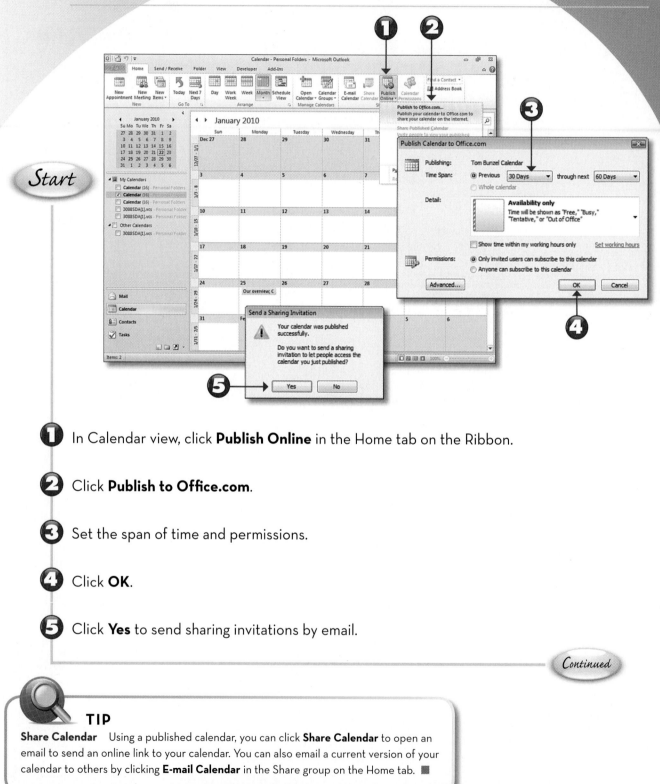

Start

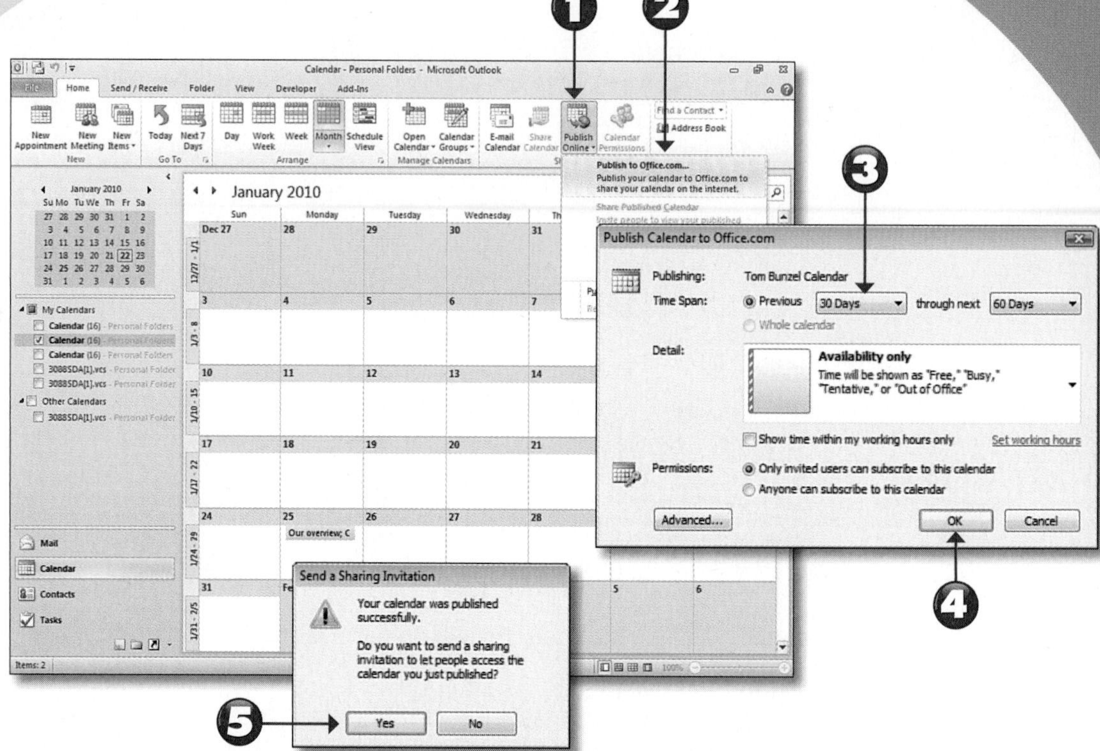

1. In Calendar view, click **Publish Online** in the Home tab on the Ribbon.
2. Click **Publish to Office.com**.
3. Set the span of time and permissions.
4. Click **OK**.
5. Click **Yes** to send sharing invitations by email.

Continued

TIP

Share Calendar Using a published calendar, you can click **Share Calendar** to open an email to send an online link to your calendar. You can also email a current version of your calendar to others by clicking **E-mail Calendar** in the Share group on the Home tab. ■

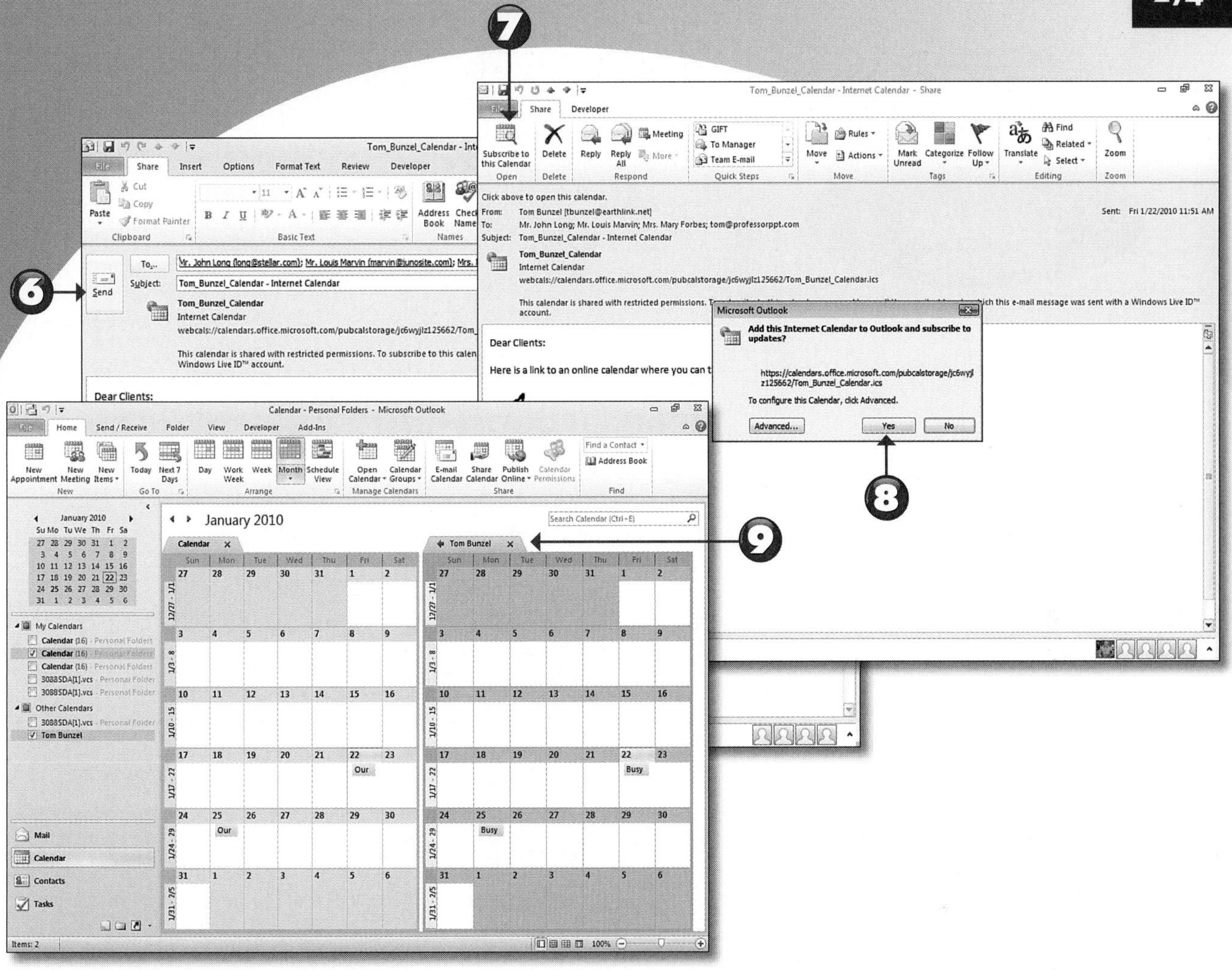

6 Send your email with an invitation to others.

7 Recipients click **Subscribe to this Calendar**.

8 Recipients click **Yes** to Subscribe.

9 Subscribers can see the shared calendar in Outlook under their Other Calendars.

End

TIP

Published Calendar Access This published calendar is shared with restricted permissions. To subscribe to this calendar, recipients need to enroll the email address to which this email message was sent with a Windows Live ID account. ■

TIP

Must Expand Group You cannot email your calendar subscription directly to a named group. Click the + sign in the To field to expand the group and reveal the individual addresses. (To hide them, you can move them to the BCC field.) ■

Index

A

absolute references (cells), 138

accepting/rejecting changes to documents, 101

adding

- animations to slides, 203-204
- attachments to email, 249-250
- charts to presentations, 191-192
- notes
  - *to notebook pages, 229-230*
  - *to slides, 219-220*
- pictures to slides, 195-196
- RSS feeds to Inbox, 261-262
- Sparklines to cells, 153-154
- tables to presentations, 189
- tags to notebooks, 235-236
- themes to email, 259-260
- transitions to Slides, 201-202
- video to slides, 207-210
- web content to notebook pages, 231-232

Advanced Page Setup dialog, Apply To This Point Forward option, 29

aligning

- images, 83
- text
  - *Excel spreadsheets, 113-114*
  - *tables, 68*

Animation Painter tool, 205-206

animations, adding to slides, 203-204

Apply To This Point Forward option (Advanced Page Setup dialog), 29

attachments, adding to email, 249-250

AutoComplete feature, Excel spreadsheets, 131-132

AutoSum function, Excel spreadsheets, 135

Average function, Excel spreadsheets, 136

B

Backstage view (PowerPoint), 1, 175

- Cancel command, 3
- Check for Updates option, 4
- closing, 3
- Exit command, 3
- Info window, 3
- new blank documents, creating, 5-6, 15-16
  - *styling text, 6*
  - *templates, 5, 15-16*

New Document window

new documents, creating, 5-6, 15-16

Recent Templates area, 16

Office templates, 5, 15-16

opening, 3

Options button, 4

printing in, 11

changing orientation, 12

keyboard shortcuts, 11

previewing printouts, 11

Recent button, 4

Recover Unsaved Documents option, 4

videos, creating from presentations, 217-218

blogs, Blog Post template (Backstage view, New Document window), 6

borders, modifying in tables, 71-72

Breaks button (Page Setup group), 29

Building Blocks

Building Blocks Organizer, 61-62

moving, 61

Quick Parts, 59

bulleted lists, 23-24

Define New Bullet option, 24

Define Number Formats option, 24

removing, 23

bulleted text (PowerPoint), converting text to SmartArt diagrams, 92

bullets

adding to slides, 177-178

converting to SmartArt, 197-198

C

Calendar (Outlook)

Schedule view, 257-258

sharing online, 273-274

Cancel command (Backstage view), 3

captioning images, 87

cells (tables)

absolute references, 138

AutoSum function, 135

Average function, 136

Cell Styles gallery, 125-126

copying, 131

deleting, 69

formatting, 114

Insert function, 136

merging, 70

Range Selector, 136

shading, 71

sizing, 67

wrapping text in, 117

centering text, Excel spreadsheets, 118

Change Styles option (Styles group), 47

charts

adding to presentations, 191-192

copying, 150

creating with Ribbon, 143-144

editing in presentations, 193-194

formatting, 147-148

moving, 149-150

pie charts, 146

slices, moving, 149

resizing, 149

type of, changing, 145-146

Chart Tools, 143

Check for Updates option (Backstage view), 4

Clear Formatting button (Fonts group), 20

clip art

adding to documents, 81-82

finding, 81-82

organizing, 82

Clipboard, 41

closing

Backstage view, 3

Navigation pane, 7

collapsing sections, 179

color, changing in SmartArt diagrams, 91

columns

manually adjusting, 43

More Columns options page (Columns option), 44

tables

adding, 69, 119-120

deleting, 69, 120

hiding/showing, 121-122

sizing, 117-118

splitting, 70

comments, adding to documents, 100

comparing documents, 100

conditional formats, 159

contact groups

creating, 271-272

members, adding, 271

contacts, managing in Outlook, 269-270

Content Controls, deleting, 18, 58

conversations, 253-254

converting

bullets to SmartArt, 197-198

documents to other formats, 10

copying

cells (tables), 131

charts, 150

Clipboard, 41

Copy command, 39

formatting, Format Painter, 45, 55-56

Paste command, 40-41

Set Default Paste option, 42

cover pages, 57-58

cropping images, 86

currencies (Excel spreadsheets), adding to, 116

customizing
presentation themes, 184
Quick Styles, 51-52
templates
revising templates, 17
saving, 15
themes, 63
Cut command, 39

D

data recovery, unsaved documents (Backstage view), 4
Data tab, Excel, 111
date/time
adding to documents, 18
Excel spreadsheets, 133-134
Define New Bullet option, 24
Define Number Formats option, 24
deleting
cells from tables, 69
columns
from Excel spreadsheets, 120
from tables, 69
Content Controls, 58
documents, 4
rows
from Excel spreadsheets, 120
from tables, 69
Design tab (Word), Table Styles gallery, 65
Dialog Launch icon (Fonts group), 20
disabling OpenType ligatures, 93
Document Browser, navigating documents, 13
Document Map view. See Navigation pane
documents
Backstage view, creating in, 6
blog posts, 6
New Document window, 5, 15-16
styling text, 6
templates, 5, 15-16
bulleted text, converting PowerPoint bullets to SmartArt diagrams, 92
comparing, 100
converting to other formats, 10
dates, adding to, 18
editing
accepting/rejecting changes, 101
adding comments to, 100
hiding/showing markup, 102
restricting, 99
reverting to original version, 102
tracking changes, 99-100
equations, inserting, 21
formatting
adding styles to Quick Styles gallery, 49
adjusting margins, 52
applying styles, 47-48
Building Blocks Organizer, 61-62
bulleted lists, 23-24
clearing, 20
columns, 43-44
copying formatting, 45, 55-56
cover pages, 57-58
creating styles, 49-50
footnotes/endnotes, 37-38

Format Painter, 45, 55-56
headers/footers, 35-36
Home tab, 19
modifying styles, 51-52
numbered lists, 23-24
page numbering, 33-34
quick formatting, 19
Quick Parts gallery, 45, 59-60
Quick Styles gallery, 45-52
removing styles from Quick Styles gallery, 49
themes, 63-64
updating headings, 51, 54
images
aligning, 83
captioning, 87
clip art, 81-82
cropping, 85-86
documents, adding to, 79-80
effects, adding to, 87-88
moving, 83
Picture Layout, 88
Picture Styles gallery, 87
screenshots, 95-96
sizing, 84
SmartArt diagrams, 89-91
styles, adding to, 87-88
wrapping text around, 83
inspecting, 101
margins, adjusting, 29-30
naming, 17
navigating
Document Browser, 13
Find tool, 13
Navigation pane, 7
Word, 13
orientation, changing, 31
renaming, 17
reviewing
accepting/rejecting changes, 101
adding comments, 100
hiding/showing markup, 102
inspecting, 101
reverting to original version, 102
tracking changes, 99-100
saving, 17
different formats, 9-10
templates, 10
searches, Navigation pane, 8
searching/replacing text, 25
selecting text, quick selection keyboard shortcut, 19
sizing, 31
special characters, inserting, 22
symbols, inserting, 21-22
templates, 15
text
captioning images, 87
OpenType ligatures, 93
viewing multiple pages, 32
doughnut charts, 146
Draw Table option (Word), 67

E

editing

documents

accepting/rejecting changes, 101

adding comments to, 100

hiding/showing markup, 102

restricting, 99

reverting to original version, 102

tracking changes, 99-100

formulas (Excel spreadsheets), 137

presentations

charts, 193-194

texts, 175-176

screenshots, 96

Editing group (Home tab), Find feature, 26

email

attachments, adding, 249-250

conversations, 253-254

filtering in Outlook, 263-264

meetings, scheduling, 255-256

rules, applying, 267-268

searching, 265-266

themes, applying, 259-260

endnotes/footnotes, 37-38

Entrance animations, adding to slides, 203-204

equations, inserting into documents, 21

Excel

Add-ins tab (Ribbon), 111

cells, adding Sparklines, 153-154

charts

creating, 143-144

formatting, 147-148

moving, 149-150

type of, changing, 145-146

conditional formats, 159

Data tab (Ribbon), 111

Excel Function Library, 127

AutoSum function, 135

Average function, 136

Insert function, 136

File tab (Ribbon), 111

formulas

editing, 137

formatting results, 139-140

Formula Bar, 137-138

tracing results, 139-140

Formulas tab (Ribbon), 111-127

function arguments, 136

Home tab (Ribbon), 111

Insert tab (Ribbon), 111

Page Break Preview, 171

Page Layout tab (Ribbon), 111

Pivot Tables, 155-156

fields, selecting, 155

filtering with Slicer, 157-158

Range Selector, 136

Review tab (Ribbon), 111

slides, adding pictures, 195-196

spreadsheets

adding, 123

aligning text, 113-114

AutoComplete feature, 131-132

AutoSum function, 135

Average function, 136

Cell Styles gallery, 125-126

centering text, 118

columns, adding, 119-120

columns, sizing, 117-118

copying cells, 131

currencies in, 116

custom lists, 131

date/time, 133-134

deleting columns, 120

deleting rows, 120

entering data, 117-118

filling series, 131-132

finding data, 129

formatting cells, 125-126

formatting numbers, 115

formatting text, 113-114

hiding/showing worksheets, 122

indenting text, 118

inputting numbers, 115

Insert function, 136

naming, 123

referencing other spreadsheets, 139

replacing data, 130

rows, adding, 119-120

rows, sizing, 117

undoing mistakes, 113

wrapping text in cells, 117

status bar, 135

tables, sorting data, 151-152

View tab (Ribbon), 111

workbooks, referencing other workbooks, 140

worksheets, printing, 171-172

Exit command (Backstage view), 3

exiting Backstage view, 3

expanding sections, 179

F

Favorites folder (Windows Live), 103

fields, selecting in Pivot Tables, 155

files, sending to OneNote, 241-242

File tab (Ribbon), 1

filtering

email in Outlook, 263-264

Pivot Tables with Slicer, 157-158

table data, 151

finding

clip art, 81

data in Excel spreadsheets, 129

Find feature (Home tab, Editing group), 26

headings, 53

images

clip art, 81-82

on computer, 79

search parameters, changing, 26

text, 25

Find tool, navigating documents, 13

folders, Windows Live

changing folder permissions, 104

creating folders in, 103-105

uploading files to, 106-107

Fonts group, 20

footers/headers

Header & Footer tab (Ribbon, Insert tab), 35-36

removing, 36

footnotes/endnotes, 37-38

formatting

charts, 147-148

conditional formats, 159

documents, 20

adding styles to Quick Styles gallery, 49

adjusting margins, 52

applying styles, 47-48

Building Blocks Organizer, 61-62

bulleted lists, 23-24

clearing formatting, 20

columns, 43-44

copying formatting, 45, 55-56

cover pages, 57-58

creating styles, 49-50

footnotes/endnotes, 37-38

Format Painter, 45, 55-56

headers/footers, 35-36

Home tab, 19

modifying styles, 51-52

numbered lists, 23-24

page numbering, 33-34

quick formatting, 19

Quick Parts gallery, 45, 59-60

Quick Styles gallery, 45-52

removing styles from Quick Styles gallery, 49

themes, 63-64

updating headings, 53-54

updating styles, 51

Excel spreadsheets

formula results, 139-140

numbers, 115

texts, 113-114

presentations, charts, 193-194

SmartArt diagrams, 90

Sparklines, 154

tables

creating styles, 74

Quick Tables gallery, 75

saving formatting, 73

Table Styles gallery, 73-74

text

bulleted lists, 23-24

clearing formatting, 20

Home tab, 19

numbered lists, 23-24

quick formatting, 19

formulas (Excel spreadsheets)

editing, 137

formatting results, 139-140

Formula Bar, 137-138

tracing results, 139-140

Formulas tab (Ribbon), Excel, 111, 127

function arguments (Excel spreadsheets), 136

G

graphics

aligning, 83

captioning, 87

clip art

adding to documents, 81-82

finding, 81-82

organizing, 82

cropping, 85-86

effects, adding to, 87-88

file formats, 80

finding on computer, 79

moving, 83

organizing, 80

Picture Layout, 88

Picture Styles gallery, 87

Picture Tools tab (Ribbon), 77

screenshots, 95-96

sizing, 84

SmartArt diagrams, 89-91

styles, adding to, 87-88

Word documents, adding to, 79-80

wrapping text around, 83

H

Header & Footer tab (Ribbon, Insert tab), formatting page numbering, 33-34

headers/footers

inserting, 35-36

removing, 36

headings

finding, 53

updating, 53-54

hiding

columns in Excel spreadsheets, 121-122

document markup, 102

rows in Excel spreadsheets, 121-122

Home tab (Ribbon)

Add-ins, 111

Copy command, 39

Cut command, 39

Editing group, Find feature, 26

formatting text via, 19

Excel, 111

Paragraph group, 23

Paste command, 40-41

Paste Preview menu, 40-42

Styles group

Change Styles option, 47

Manage Styles option, 47

Style Pane Options option, 48

hosting recorded slide shows, 218

I

images

aligning, 83

captioning, 87

clip art

adding to documents, 81-82

finding, 81-82

organizing, 82

cropping, 85-86

effects, adding to, 87-88

file formats, 80

finding on computer, 79

moving, 83

organizing, 80

Picture Layout, 88

Picture Styles gallery, 87
Picture Tools tab (Ribbon), 77
screenshots, 95-96
sizing, 84
SmartArt diagrams, 89-91
styles, adding to, 87-88
Word documents, adding to, 79-80
wrapping text around, 83
Inbox (Outlook)
email
filtering, 263-264
searching, 265-266
RSS feeds, adding, 261-262
indenting text
Excel spreadsheets, 118
tables, 68
Info window (Backstage view), 3
Insert function, Excel spreadsheets, 136
Insert tab (Ribbon), 21
Excel, 111
Header & Footer tab
formatting page numbering, 33-34
inserting headers/footers, 35-36
inspecting documents, 101

J-K-L

keyboard shortcuts
copy command, 39
cut command, 39
Paste command, 39
printing, Backstage view, 11
quick selection, 19
undoing actions, 17

layout of slides, changing, 178
letters
columns in, 43-44
copying/pasting in, 39-42
creating, 15-16
date/time, adding, 18
formatting, 19, 20
Building Blocks Organizer, 61-62
bulleted lists in, 23-24
Clear Formatting button (Fonts group), 20
copying, 55-56
cover pages, 57-58
creating styles, 49-50
equations in, 21
footnotes/endnotes, 37-38
headers/footers, 35-36
margins, 29-30, 52
modifying styles, 51-52
numbered lists in, 23-24
page numbering, 33-34
page orientation, 31
Quick Formatting, 19
Quick Parts gallery, 45, 59-60
Quick Styles gallery, 45-52
searching/replacing text, 25
sizing, 31
special characters in, 22
symbols in, 21-22
themes, 63-64

updating headings, 53-54

updating styles, 51

renaming, 17

saving, 17

viewing multiple pages, 32

ligatures (OpenType), 93

links (Windows Live workspace), sending availability via links, 106

lists, creating in Excel spreadsheets, 131

locked files, 169

M

Manage Styles option (Styles group), 47

managing contacts in Outlook, 269-270

manually adjusting

columns, 43

margins, 29

margins, adjusting, 29-30, 52

markup (documents), hiding/showing, 102

meetings, scheduling with email, 255-256

members, adding to contact groups, 271

merging cells in tables, 70

Microsoft web applications. See web applications

modifying Quick Styles, 51-52

More Columns options page (Columns option), 44

movies

adding to slides, 207-208

online video, adding to slides, 209-210

moving

Building Blocks, 61

charts, 149-150

images, 83

Navigation pane, 7

My Documents folder (Windows Live), 103

N

naming

documents, 17

Excel spreadsheets, 123

navigating

documents

Document Browser, 13

Find tool, 13

Word, 13

footnotes/endnotes, 38

Windows Live workspace, 104

Navigation pane, 1

closing, 7

moving, 7

searching documents via, 8

searching/replacing text, 25

sizing, 7

networks (Window Live), adding people to, 103

New Document window (Backstage view)

new documents, creating

styling text, 6

templates, 5, 15-16

Recent Templates area, 16

newsletters, columns in, 43-44

notebooks

notes, adding to pages, 229-230

saving, 243-244

searches, performing, 233-234

sections, 227

sharing, 245-246

starting in OneNote, 227-228

web content, adding to pages, 231-232

notes. See also OneNote

adding to notebook pages, 229-230

footnotes/endnotes, 37-38

Side Notes, 237-238

Notes Master view (PowerPoint), 219-220

numbered lists, 23-24

numbering document pages, 33-34

numbers (Excel spreadsheets), formatting, 115

numeric keypads, entering numbers into Excel spreadsheets, 116

O

Office 2010, new features of, 1-2

Office.com templates, 15

OneNote

files, sending to, 241-242

notebooks

notes, adding to pages, 229-230

saving, 243-244

sections, 227

sharing, 245-246

starting, 227-228

web content, adding to pages, 231-232

searches, performing, 233-234

Side Notes, 237-238

tags, adding, 235-236

tasks, sending to Outlook, 239-240

online files, opening locally, 169-170

online video, adding to slides, 209-210

opening

Backstage view, 3

online files locally, 169-170

uploaded projects, 163-164

web application files, 110

OpenType ligatures, 93

Options button (Backstage view), 4

organizing images, 80-82

orientation (documents), changing, 12, 31

Outlook

Calendar, sharing online, 273-274

contact groups

creating, 271-272

members, adding, 271

contacts, managing, 269-270

email

attachments, adding, 249-250

conversations, 253-254

filtering, 263-264

Inbox

RSS feeds, 261-262

searching, 265-266

meetings, scheduling, 255-256

Quick Steps, 251-252

rules, applying to email, 267-268

Schedule view, 257-258

tasks, receiving from OneNote, 239-240

themes, adding to email, 259-260

P

Page Break Preview view (Excel), 171

Page Layout tab (Ribbon)

  Columns option, 43

  Excel, 111

  margins, adjusting, 29-30

  orientation, changing, 31

  sizing documents, 31

page numbering documents, 33-34

Page Setup group, Breaks button, 29

Page Setup tab (Ribbon), orientation, changing, 31

Paragraph group (Home tab), 23

paragraphs, indenting in tables, 68

Paste Preview menu (Ribbon, Home tab), 40-42

permissions, changing inWindows Live folders, 104, 107

pictures

  aligning, 83

  captioning, 87

  clip art

    adding to documents, 81-82

    finding, 81, 82

    organizing, 82

  cropping, 85-86

  effects, adding to, 87-88

  file formats, 80

  finding on computer, 79

  moving, 83

  organizing, 80

  Picture Layout, 88

  Picture Styles gallery, 87

  Picture Tools Tab (Ribbon), 77

  screenshots, 95-96

  sizing, 84

  slides, adding to, 195-196

  SmartArt diagrams, 89-91

  styles, adding to, 87-88

  Word documents, adding to, 79-80

  wrapping text around, 83

pie charts, 146, 149

Pivot Tables, 155-156

  fields, selecting, 155

  filtering with Slicer, 157-158

podcasts, 262

posts (blogs), Blog Post template, 6

PowerPoint, 173

  Animation Painter tool, 205-206

  Backstage view, 175

  bulleted text, converting to SmartArt diagrams, 92

  Notes Master view, 219-220

  presentations

    bullets, adding to slides, 177-178

    charts, adding, 191-192

    charts, editing, 193-194

    recording, 215-216

    sections, adding, 179-180

    tables, adding, 189

    text, adding, 175-176

    themes, adding, 183-184

  Presenter view, 221-222

  Slide Masters, 185-186

  slides

    animations, adding, 203-204

    bullets, converting to SmartArt, 197-198

    previewing in Reading view, 213-214

    transitions, adding, 201-202

video, adding, 207-210
Slide Sorter view, 181-182
SmartArt Tools, 188
videos, creating from presentations, 217-218
web application, 223-224
presentations
charts
adding, 191-192
editing, 193-194
hosting on websites, 218
recording, 215-216
sections, adding, 179-180
Slide Masters, 185-186
slides
bullets, adding, 177-178
notes, adding, 219-220
pictures, adding, 195-196
previewing in Reading view, 214
video, adding, 207-210
Slide Sorter view, 181-182
tables, adding, 189
text, adding, 175-176
themes, adding, 183-184
videos, creating from, 217-218
Presenter view (PowerPoint), 221-222
previewing
printing in Backstage view, 11
slides in Reading view, 214
styles in Styles pane, 54
printing
Backstage view, 11
changing orientation, 12
keyboard shortcuts, 11
previewing printouts, 11
Excel worksheets, 171-172
slides, notes, 219-220
projects, opening, 163-164
Public folder (Windows Live), 103
publishing
blog posts, 6
Outlook Calendar online, 273-274

Quick Access Toolbar, 56
quick formatting text, 19
Quick Parts gallery, 45
new entries, creating, 59-60
saving Quick Parts, 60
quick selection keyboard shortcut, 19
Quick Steps (Outlook), 251-252
Quick Styles gallery, 45
adding styles to, 49
applying styles from, 47-48
creating styles in, 49-50
modifying styles in, 51-52
removing styles from, 49
updating styles in, 51

R

Range Selector (Excel spreadsheets), 136
Reading view, previewing slides, 214
Recent button (Backstage view), 4
Recent Folders view (Windows Live), 103
Recent Templates area, 16, 30

recording presentations, 215-216
Record Slide Show feature (PowerPoint), 215
Recover Unsaved Documents option (Backstage view), 4
redirecting spam, 267-268
References tab (Ribbon), footnotes/endnotes, 37-38
rejecting/accepting changes to documents, 101
removing
  bulleted lists, 23
  cells from tables, 69
  columns from tables, 69
  Content Controls (templates), 18
  formatting from text, 20
  headers/footers, 36
  numbered lists, 23
  page numbers, 34
  rows from tables, 69
  styles from Quick Styles gallery, 49
renaming
  documents, 17
  Excel spreadsheets, 123
resetting themes, 64
resizing
  charts, 149
  images, 84
restoring themes, 64
reviewing documents, 99-100
  accepting/rejecting changes, 101
  hiding/showing markup, 102
  inspecting, 101
  reverting to original version, 102
Review tab (Ribbon), 97, 111
revising templates, 17
revising data in web applications, 165-166
Ribbon
  Add-ins tab, 111
  charts
    changing type of, 145-146
    copying, 150
    creating, 143-144
    formatting, 147-148
    moving, 149-150
    pie charts, 146
    resizing, 149
  Data tab, 111
  File tab, 1, 111
  Formulas tab, 111, 127
  Home tab
    Copy command, 39
    Cut command, 39
    Excel, 111
    Paste command, 40-41
    Paste Preview menu, 40-42
    Styles group, Change Styles option, 47
    Styles group, Manage Styles option, 47
    Styles group, Style Pane Options option, 48
  Insert tab, 21
    Excel, 111
    Header & Footer tab, 33-36
    page numbering, 33
  Page Layout tab
    adjusting margins, 29-30
    changing orientation, 31
    Columns option, 43
    Excel, 111
    sizing documents, 31
  Page Setup tab, changing orientation, 31

Picture Tools tab, 77
References tab, footnotes/endnotes, 37-38
Review tab, 97, 111
Table Tools tabs, 65
View tab, 27, 111
routing spam with rules, 267-268
rows (tables)
adding, 69, 119-120
deleting, 69, 120
hiding/showing, 121-122
sizing, 117
splitting, 70
RSS feeds, adding to Outlook Inbox, 261-262
rules, applying to email, 267-268

S

saving
cover pages, 57
documents, 17
different formats, 9-10
templates, 10
notebooks, 243-244
Quick Parts, 60
templates, custom templates, 15
themes, 63
web application files in Windows Live, 109
Schedule view (Outlook), 257-258
scheduling meetings with email, 255-256
screenshots, 95-96
searches
clip art, 81
data in Excel spreadsheets, 129
Find feature (Home tab, Editing group), 26
headings, 53
images
clip art, 81-82
on computer, 79
Navigation pane, 8
parameters, changing, 26
performing in OneNote, 233-234
sections
adding to presentations, 179-180
in notebooks, 227
OneNote, saving, 243-244
selecting, quick selection keyboard shortcut, 19
sending files to OneNote, 241-242
Set Default Paste option, 42
shading, adding to cells, 71
Shape Effects option (SmartArt tools), 89
Shared Favorites folder (Windows Live), 103
sharing
notebooks, 245-246
Outlook Calendar online, 273-274
shortcuts (keyboard)
copy command, 39
cut command, 39
Paste command, 39
printing, Backstage view, 11
quick selection, 19
undoing actions, 17
Side Notes, 237-238
sizing
cells, 67
columns (tables), 117-118
documents, 31

images, 84

Navigation pane, 7

rows (tables), 117

Slicer (PivotTables), filtering, 157-158

Slide Masters (PowerPoint), 185-186

slides

animations, adding, 203-204

bullets, adding, 177-178

layout, changing, 178

notes, adding, 219-220

pictures, adding, 195-196

previewing in Reading view, 213-214

SmartArt, 197-198

themes, adding, 183-184

transitions, adding, 201-202

video

adding, 207-208

online video, adding to slides, 209-210

Slide Sorter view (PowerPoint), 181-182

SmartArt, 89, 188, 197-198

formatting

color, 91

shapes, 90

text, 90

PowerPoint bullets as, 92

text, adding, 198

sorting

contents of Windows Live folders, 108

table data, 151-152

tables, 76, 167-168

spam, redirecting, 267-268

Sparklines

adding to cells, 153-154

formatting, 154

for web applications, 166

special characters, inserting into documents, 22

splitting columns/rows in tables, 70

spreadsheets (Excel)

adding, 123

AutoComplete feature, 131-132

AutoSum function, 135

Average function, 136

cells

Cell Styles gallery, 125-126

copying, 131

columns

adding, 119-120

deleting, 120

hiding/showing, 121-122

sizing, 117-118

currencies in, 116

custom lists, creating, 131

data, entering, 117-118

date/time, 133-134

Excel Function Library, 127, 135

AutoSum function, 135

Average function, 136

Insert function, 136

filling series, 131-132

finding data, 129

formatting cells, 125-126

formulas

editing, 137

formatting results, 139-140

Formula Bar, 137-138

tracing results, 139-140

function arguments, 136
hiding/showing, 122
Insert function, 136
naming, 123
numbers
formatting, 115
inputting, 115
Range Selector, 136
referencing other spreadsheets, 139
replacing data, 130
rows
adding, 119-120
deleting, 120
hiding/showing, 121-122
sizing, 117
status bar, 135
text
aligning, 113-114
centering, 118
formatting, 113-114
indenting, 118
wrapping in cells, 117
undoing mistakes, 113
status bar (Excel), 135
Style Pane Options option (Styles group), 48
Styles group (Ribbon, Home tab)
Change Styles option, 47
Manage Styles option, 47
Style Pane Options option, 48
Styles pane
finding headings, 53
previewing styles in, 54
styling text, New Document window (Backstage view), 6
supported video formats (PowerPoint), 208
symbols, inserting into documents, 21-22

T

tables
adding to presentations, 189
adding to web applications, 167-168
borders, modifying, 71-72
cells
absolute references, 138
adding shading to, 71
AutoSum function, 135
Average function, 136
Cell Styles gallery, 125-126
copying, 131
deleting, 69
formatting, 114
Insert function, 136
merging, 70
Range Selector, 136
sizing, 67
columns
adding, 69, 119-120
deleting, 69, 120
hiding/showing, 121-122
sizing, 117-118
splitting, 70
creating, 67
data
filtering, 151
sorting, 151-152
Draw Table option, 67

formatting

creating styles, 74

Quick Tables gallery, 75

saving, 73

Table Styles gallery, 73-74

Pivot Tables, 155, 156

fields, selecting, 155

filtering with Slicer, 157-158

rows

adding, 69, 119-120

deleting, 69, 120

hiding/showing, 121-122

sizing, 117

splitting, 70

sorting, 76

Table Styles gallery (Word, Design tab), 65

Table Tools tabs (Ribbon), 65

text, aligning, 68

tags, adding to notebooks, 235-236

tasks, sending to Outlook, 239-240

Team Email lists, creating, 251-252

templates

Backstage view Office templates, 15-16

Blog Post template (Backstage view, New Document window), 6

Content Controls, removing, 18

customizing, 17

Office.com templates, 15

Recent Templates area, 16, 30

revising, 17

saving

custom templates, 15

documents as, 10

text

adding

to presentations, 175-176

to SmartArt, 198

bulleted text, converting PowerPoint text to SmartArt diagrams, 92

equations, inserting into documents, 21

Excel spreadsheets

aligning, 113-114

centering text, 118

formatting, 113-114

indenting text, 118

formatting, 20

bulleted lists, 23-24

clearing formatting, 20

Home tab, 19

numbered lists, 23-24

quick formatting, 19

images, captioning, 87

OpenType ligatures, 93

searching/replacing, 25

selecting, quick selection keyboard shortcut, 19

SmartArt diagrams, formatting, 90

special characters, inserting into documents, 22

styling, New Document window (Backstage view), 6

symbols, inserting into documents, 21-22

tables, aligning text in, 68

wrapping

around images, 83

within cells (Excel spreadsheets), 117

themes

adding

to email, 259-260

to presentations, 183-184
applying between programs, 64
changing, 63
customizing, 63, 184
resetting, 64
restoring, 64
saving, 63
time/date
adding to documents, 18
Excel spreadsheets, 133-134
tracking changes to documents, 99-100
transitions, adding to slides, 201-202
triggering animations in PowerPoint, 206
typography, OpenType ligatures, 93

U

Undo command, 17, 113
unsaved documents, recovering in Backstage view, 4
updating
headings, 53-54
Quick Styles, 51
uploaded projects, opening, 163-164
uploading files to Windows Live folders, 106-107

V

videos
adding to slides, 207-208
creating from presentations, 217-218
online video, adding to slides, 209-210
supported formats (PowerPoint), 208
viewing
contents of Windows Live folders, 108
documents, multiple pages, 32
View tab (Ribbon), 27, 111
voting buttons, adding to email, 259

W-Z

web applications, 161-163
data, revising, 165-166
files
locked, 169
online files, opening locally, 169-170
opening, 110
Windows Live, 109
PowerPoint, 223-224
projects, opening, 163-164
Sparklines, 166
tables, adding, 167-168
web content, adding to notebook pages, 231-232
websites, hosting presentations, 218
Windows Live
folders
changing permissions, 104
creating, 103-105
Favorites folder, 103
My Documents folder, 103
Public folder, 103
Recent Folders view, 103
Shared Favorites folder, 103
sorting contents, 108
uploading files to, 106-107
viewing contents of, 108

networks, adding, 103
web application files
creating, 109
opening, 110
saving, 109
workspace, 97
navigating, 104
sending availability notification links, 106
Word
Design tab, Table Styles gallery, 65
documents
accepting/rejecting changes, 101
Building Blocks Organizer, 61-62
bulleted lists in, 23-24
captioning images, 87
clip art, 81-82
columns in, 43-44
comments, adding to, 100
comparing, 100
copying/pasting in, 39-42
cover pages, 57-58
creating, 15-16
date/time, adding to, 18
effects, adding to images, 87-88
equations, 21
footnotes/endnotes, 37-38
formatting, 19-20
headers/footers, 35-36
hiding/showing markup, 102
images, adding to, 79-80
images, aligning, 83
images, cropping, 85-86
images, moving, 83
inspecting, 101
margins, 29-30, 52
navigating, 13
numbered lists in, 23-24
OpenType ligatures, 93
page numbering, 33-34
page orientation, 31
Picture Styles gallery, 87
Quick Parts gallery, 45, 59-60
Quick Styles gallery, 45-52
renaming, 17
reviewing, 99-102
saving, 17
screenshots, 95-96
searching/replacing text, 25
sizing, 31
SmartArt diagrams, 89-91
special characters in, 22
styles, adding to images, 87-88
styles, creating, 49-50
styles, modifying, 51-52
symbols in, 21-22
themes, 63-64
tracking changes, 99-100
viewing multiple pages, 32
wrapping text around images, 83
images
adding to documents, 79-80
captioning, 87
clip art, 81-82
cropping, 85-86
effects, adding to, 87-88
finding on computer, 79

moving, 83

Picture Layout, 88

Picture Styles gallery, 87

Picture Tools tab, 77

sizing, 84

styles, adding to, 87-88

wrapping text around, 83

newsletters, columns in, 43-44

tables

aligning text, 68

borders, 71-72

cells, deleting, 69

cells, merging, 70

cells, sizing, 67

columns, adding, 69

columns, deleting, 69

columns, splitting, 70

creating, 67

Draw Table option, 67

formatting, 73-75

Quick Tables gallery, 75

rows, adding/removing, 69

rows, splitting, 70

saving formatting, 73

shading, adding to cells, 71

sorting, 76

Table Styles gallery, 65, 73-74

Table Tools tabs, 65

templates

Recent Templates area, 16

removing Content Controls, 18

revising, 17

saving, 15

text, wrapping around images, 83

workbooks (Excel), referencing other workbooks, 140

worksheets, printing, 171-172

wrapping text

around images, 83

in cells, 117

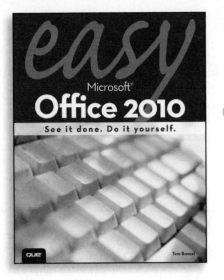